THE BOMB

The bomber campaign against Germany is now the most contentious of the Second World War. Did it help bring the Nazis to their knees? Was the RAF wrong to bomb cities? Did the USAAF attack only military targets? Was anything achieved but the death of German civilians, most of them women and children? If not, are the bombers – and especially Air Chief Marshal Sir Arthur Harris and the aircrew of RAF Bomber Command – not war criminals? Or were all means not justified against the Nazis?

In this controversial book, Robin Neillands examines every detail of the campaign: the strengths and fundamental flaws in doctrine, the technical difficulties and developments from night-time navigation through bomb-aiming to fighter escort, and above all the day-by-day, night-by-night endurance of the crews, flying to the limit in discomfort and danger, facing flak and enemy fighters, and well aware of their likely fate if shot down. Oral history plays a key part in this account; it is illuminated throughout by the personal experiences not only of British but of American, Australian, Canadian and other Allied fliers as well, and also of German aircrew and civilians.

Though the book begins with the pre-war developments that culminated at Guernica, and ends with the destruction of Tokyo, Hiroshima and Nagasaki, it concentrates on Europe, first Warsaw, Rotterdam, London and Coventry, then later Germany: the RAF raids on Cologne, Hamburg, Berlin and the Ruhr, the USAAF missions to Ploesti, Scheinfurt and Regensburg, and the combined RAF-USAAF raid on Dresden – the most controversial of all. Neillands concludes with an analysis of the moral issues, and of the case made against Sir Arthur Harris in particular. This is a timely addition to the history of conflict; the age of freefall bombs has passed, but veterans are still alive to state their case, and to tell a new generation what their war was like.

Robin Neillands is a journalist and writer, a former Royal Marines Commando and 'one of Britain's most readable military historians' (*Birmingham Post*). He has written books on subjects ranging from the Hundred Years War to the myths surrounding the Great War generals. A regular contributor to military magazines and the national press, he also conducts battlefield tours in Europe and the USA, lectures at the National Army Museum in London and to history groups worldwide, and is a member of the British Commission for Military History. He is currently working on a book about the Eighth Army.

The Bomber War

Arthur Harris and the Allied Bomber Offensive 1939–1945

ROBIN NEILLANDS

JOHN MURRAY
Albemarle Street, London

First published in 2001
by John Murray (Publishers) Ltd
50 Albemarle Street, London W1S 4BD

Reprinted 2001 (twice)

Paperback edition 2002

A catalogue record for this book is available from the British Library

ISBN 0-7195-5644-9

Typeset in 10/12½ pt Palatino by Servis Filmsetting Ltd, Manchester

Printed and bound in Great Britain by
St Edmundsbury Press Ltd, Bury St Edmunds, Suffolk

This one is for
Byron Farwell of Hillsboro, Virginia, USA
and
Colin Fox of Reading, Berkshire, England
who taught me a lot about military history

Contents

Illustrations

(between pages 208 and 209)

—————

1. Sir Arthur ('Bomber') Harris
2. Marshal of the Royal Air Force Lord Portal
3. General 'Hap' Arnold, wartime commander of the USAAF
4. General Carl 'Tooey' Spaatz, first commander of the US Eighth Air Force in Britain
5. An RAF Handley Page Heyford of 1936
6. An RAF Handley Page Hampden, 1939/40
7. An RAF Whitley Bomber, 1941
8. Two RAF Wellington Bombers, 1942
9. An Avro Lancaster
10. A young Wellington crew, 1943
11. A Mosquito pilot and his navigator before a night raid on Germany, 1945
12. An RAF Lancaster bomb load
13. A Stirling Bomber crashed in training
14. B-17 Flying Fortresses
15. A group of USAAF B-17s with an escort of P-51 Mustangs
16. The Norden Bombsight
17. Bombs from one USAAF Flying Fortress hit the tailplane of another, December 1944
18. Home safe despite a mid-air collision
19. and 20. Battle damage
21. A B-24 Liberator of the US Fifteenth Air Force destroyed by flak over Germany

The author and publisher would like to thank the following for permission to reproduce illustrations: Plate 1, Hulton Getty; 2, Topham Picturepoint; 3 and 4, USAF; 6, RAF Museum; 12, Mrs Margaret Grant; 15, David A. Mullen; 17, Keystone; 19 and 20, USAF/Boeing; 24, Heiner Wittrock; 25, Richard Braun, from Ludwigshafen Archives; 27 and 28, Richard Braun; 30, Bomber Command Association.

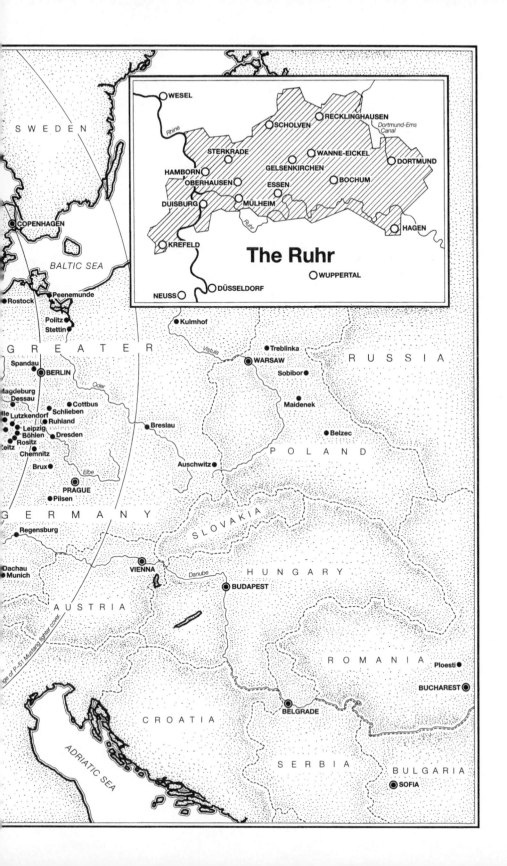

SWEDEN

BALTIC SEA

● Rostock
● Peenemunde
● Politz
● Stettin

COPENHAGEN

The Ruhr

○ WESEL

Rhine

○ SCHOLVEN
● RECKLINGHAUSEN

Dortmund-Ems Canal

○ STERKRADE
○ WANNE-EICKEL
○ GELSENKIRCHEN
● DORTMUND

HAMBORN
○ OBERHAUSEN
○ ESSEN
○ BOCHUM

DUISBURG
○ MÜLHEIM

○ HAGEN

○ KREFELD

● WUPPERTAL

NEUSS ○
○ DÜSSELDORF

G R E A T E R

● Kulmhof

Vistula

● Treblinka
◉ WARSAW

● Sobibor

R U S S I A

Spandau ●
◉ BERLIN

Oder

Magdeburg ●
Dessau ●
● Cottbus
● Schlieben
lle Lutzkendorf
Leipzig ●
● Ruhland
● Böhlen ● Dresden
● Rositz
eitz
● Chemnitz
● Brux

● Maidenek

● Breslau

P O L A N D

● Belzec

Elbe

Auschwitz ●

◉ PRAGUE
● Pilsen

G E R M A N Y

S L O V A K I A

● Regensburg

◉ VIENNA

Danube

H U N G A R Y

Dachau ●
● Munich

A U S T R I A

◉ BUDAPEST

age of P-51 Mustang fighter cover.

R O M A N I A
Ploesti ●

BUCHAREST ◉

C R O A T I A

◉ BELGRADE

ADRIATIC SEA

S E R B I A

B U L G A R I A

◉ SOFIA

War is all cruelty, and there is no use trying to reform it; the crueller it is, the sooner it will be ended. War is Hell.

William Tecumseh Sherman, 1865

It is not the critic who counts, nor the man who points out how the strong man stumbled, or where the doer of the deed could have done better.

The credit belongs to the man who is actually in the arena, whose face is marred by dust and sweat and blood, who strives valiantly, who errs and comes short again and again, because there is no effort without error and shortcoming, who does actually strive to do the deeds, who knows the great enthusiasms and spends himself in a worthy cause, who at best, knows in the end the triumph of high achievement, and at worst, if he fails, at least fails while daring greatly.

His place shall never be with those cold and timid souls who knew neither victory nor defeat.

Theodore Roosevelt, 1898

Introduction

We must make war as we must; not as we would like.

Field Marshal Kitchener, 1915

Why a writer chooses to explore a particular subject is a complex matter, but the origins of this book lie in my previous one. Between 1995 and 1998 I was engaged in researching and writing a book about a much maligned group of men, the British Great War generals, those officers who commanded armies or corps along the Western Front during the First World War and are widely blamed by the general public for all the disasters that took place there. That task completed, I turned my attention to the Second World War and tried to find a man, or group of men, who was being similarly maligned, and before long my attention was attracted to Air Chief Marshal Sir Arthur Harris and the aircrew of RAF Bomber Command. The myths about Bomber Command are – as yet – nowhere near as deeply engrained or damaging as the myths about the Great War generals but the process is well under way and equally unjust. Harris and his men fought a long, costly and ultimately successful war, but largely as a result of one operation, the Dresden raid of 13–14 February 1945, they are increasingly regarded as 'terror bombers' or even as war criminals.

The notion that Air Chief Marshal Harris and his men are little better than mass murderers is clearly being implanted in the public mind and needs to be examined while many of the Bomber Command veterans are still alive and able to refute it. At the end of the twentieth century, 55 years after the end of the Second World War, the Old Comrades associations were finally being wound up, and the attrition of time is thinning the ranks of aircrew veterans more surely than the *Luftwaffe*; if this tale was to be told in full, it must be told soon.

The original concept was therefore to examine the causes and course of the British bomber offensive, to see if the accusations levelled against the participants have any validity. However, during the research phase, I discovered that the actions of RAF Bomber Command and Sir Arthur Harris, Air Officer Commanding-in-Chief (AOC-in-C) of Bomber Command from 1942 to 1945, had already been extensively ventilated by other writers. Since I do not enjoy going over old ground unless I can do it differently, the project seemed to founder – unless I also covered the actions of the United States Army Air Force (USAAF), specifically those of VIII Bomber Command of the Eighth US Army Air Force – the 'Mighty Eighth' – that flew out of Britain from 1942 to 1945.

It had already occurred to me that I must do that anyway, since part of the charge brought against Harris and his crews for the 'area' bombing of German cities rests on the allegation that 'area' bombing by RAF Bomber Command was clearly unnecessary since their comrades in the USAAF were able to carry out accurate 'precision' bombing and only attacked military targets. Or did they? If precision bombing was really that easy, why did Bomber Command not follow the same course?

Two further matters then came to my attention. The first was that no one had yet written a single-volume history of the bomber war, covering the principal actions of all the main participating air forces, using 'oral' history – the accounts of the veterans – to explain in detail how and, more importantly, why the bomber war was fought in the way it was. Histories, both official and more personal, covering the various bomber forces, plus a few thousand aircrew memoirs and squadron accounts, can already be found on the library shelves, but most were written from an individual or national viewpoint, with only passing references to the activities of other air forces engaged in the same struggle. British accounts featured only the British – or rather the British Commonwealth and Empire – contribution, while the USAAF crews seem almost unaware that there were other air forces in the sky – apart from the *Luftwaffe*.

This in itself did not surprise me. I have written a number of military histories, and I know that, during conflict, what was happening to the next platoon, or in the next trench – never mind in another service – was of academic interest to the participant telling the story; at the time in question he was more interested in 'doing his bit' and staying alive – and not necessarily in that order. However, this gave me another angle from which to tell the story. Quite apart from telling the full story of the bomber offensive, introducing the aircrew to each other seemed a worthwhile and long-overdue project. Using individual accounts gave an added dimension in telling a new generation what it was really like in the skies over Germany during the Second World War.

The reason for the absence of a comprehensive single-volume popular history became clear to me as I started to write the book. The topic is huge and the range of subjects that have to be explored to cover it properly is vast: from weather lore to radar, from target-marking to bomb loads and aircraft range, from Air Staff politics and arguments over strategy and tactics to the minutiae of daily life on a bomber squadron. People were soon telling me that the story could not be told in this way, but, to repeat Sir Arthur Harris's terse reply to the suggestion that bombing alone could not win the war, 'My answer is that it has never been tried, and we shall see.'[1]

The second matter came to light when I discovered the surprising fact – surprising to me anyway – that General Henry 'Hap' Arnold, the wartime commander of the USAAF, had been taught to fly by none other than Orville Wright, one of the two men credited with inventing the first viable aeroplane. When this fact was coupled with another fact, that the days of the great, thousand-plus, bomber air fleets ended in August 1945 when bombers in Hap Arnold's USAAF dropped the atom bombs on Hiroshima and Nagasaki, it seemed to me that what we had here was an *era* of warfare, a period of just 30 years that needed to be examined in detail and recorded in full, while those who experienced it were still alive. No bombing operations since that time, even in Indo-China or Kosovo, have employed such numbers of aircraft.

At this point in the process the aims of the book changed somewhat. The subject matter broadened from an examination of the accusations against Harris and Bomber Command, to a study of the Combined Bomber Offensive over Germany in 1939–45; it finished as a critique of strategic bombing as a whole, from its creation during the Great War until the dropping of the atomic bombs on Hiroshima and Nagasaki in August 1945.

That story – the full story of the bomber war – is what this book is about. The emphasis remains on the skies over Germany between 1939 and 1945, where all the theories of strategic bombing were put to the ultimate test. Since then, however, the argument over strategic bombing has changed. Much of the original argument during and after the Second World War was based on technical factors: first on whether the bomber was up to the task it was supposed to carry out, and then on whether the Allied strategic bombing offensive against Germany was a failure. Now, as we leave the twentieth century behind, the nature of the argument has changed yet again. The focus of the debate over the Combined Bomber Offensive today is not simply that it was ineffective, but that it was *immoral*. It is increasingly and popularly alleged that Arthur Harris and Bomber Command should not have bombed the German cities *at all*, and that the attempt to end the war by strategic bombing – which involved massive destruction of the German homeland and the loss of civilian lives – was a war crime, and an inexcusable one. Both allegations are debatable, but, given what happened to the reputation of the Great War generals when the bulk of them were safely dead, one can only wonder what will be done to the reputation of Sir Arthur Harris and Bomber Command in the decades ahead.

As the facts drift from public memory or are distorted by time – and historians – so the moral factor comes to the fore. It is the moral factor in the bomber war that exercises the modern generation, and it is to them that this book is largely addressed. When the great bomber fleets set out from their UK bases two generations ago, it was a very different world. People had different values; the issues of right and wrong were more clear-cut. There was a war on then, and that war had to be won. If Nazi Germany had won the Second World War there would now be no place for moral arguments in modern Europe – what happened in the countries occupied by Nazi Germany is ample proof of that.

But the debate cannot concentrate solely on the moral issue, however convenient it is to do so, for that takes the matter out of context. The bomber war was part of a world war – a struggle waged by a number of democratic nations against a racist, expansionist, militaristic power that had as its purpose the domination of the Western world and the eradication of millions of people it regarded as ethnically undesirable. A moral argument that concentrates on only one aspect of the struggle is fundamentally flawed, not least because it overlooks the fact that war itself, however it is waged, is fundamentally immoral. If man was ruled by reason and settled disputes by discussion and compromise, there would be no wars.

Nor is it possible, as Field Marshal Kitchener shrewdly observed in 1915, to ignore the practical elements of war – those technical snags and tactical difficulties that had to be overcome, whatever the odds or the casualties, if the war against Germany was to be prosecuted at all. These practical difficulties, and how they were overcome, make up a large part of this book.

It therefore quickly became clear that the air war must be studied in some detail, not simply in order to understand what was done, but to see why it was done and whether, as so often alleged by Harris's detractors, there was any other way of doing it *at the time*. When a war is over, we can all be generals – or air marshals – but the generals and air marshals have to fight the war with the men, equipment and knowledge they have at the time.

However, before moving on to debate the questions regarding the effectiveness and morality of strategic bombing, it would be as well to state what this book is *not* about, to define its limits and say why they were set.

First of all, this is not a book about every aspect of Second World War air operations: this book is about the bomber war, not the air war. It will not cover anything other than *bomber* operations, and even those are largely restricted to the operations of RAF Bomber Command and the US Eighth Army Air Force – with some contribution from the Fifteenth Army Air Force – in the skies over Germany, by day and night. The US Eighth Army

Air Force contained a Fighter Command as well as VIII Bomber Command and, since the introduction of the long-range fighter – the P-51D Mustang – was crucial to the development of US bomber tactics from 1944 on, this too will be included. But such diversions will be exceptional: the broad thrust of this book is concerned with the bomber war over Germany from 1939 to 1945 and with nothing else. Bombing campaigns at other times or in other parts of the world are therefore largely excluded. No offence is intended by this omission, but there simply was not the space to do more: to tell the story of bomber operations everywhere would demand a whole library of volumes, not a single book. This concentration is valid, certainly within the stated objectives of this book, for, although bombers ranged all over the world during the Second World War, the skies over Germany were the place where the great bomber fleets were concentrated, where the great air battles took place, and where the theories of the bomber as a *strategic* weapon – one capable of winning the war on its own – were put to the test. However, there are few absolutes in war, or in history, and it is important to put the European bombing campaign in the context of the Second World War, so the final chapters do discuss certain aspects of the USAAF bombing campaign against Japan.

This book is not an 'official' history, though it does draw heavily on official histories and official documents – American, Australian, British, Canadian and German. Much of it is 'oral' history, for, wherever possible, I have fleshed out the dry bones of the official accounts and records with personal memories provided by the men who were there. To meet some of the critics of this method head on, let me admit that many historians are distinctly wary of this kind of history – 'anecdotal history' as they frequently call it – alleging that memories grow dim after a lapse of years and that many of the stories told are confused or relate events that did not actually happen. There is some truth in this allegation, but all oral historians are well aware of the problems and know how to counter it, by checking official sources and comparing one person's account with many others.

Nor are the official histories and records on which the critics of oral history rely always infallible, as Tom Wingham, DFC, a bomb-aimer of No. 102 (Ceylon) Squadron can confirm:

Here are two examples of discrepancies between what was filed and actually what happened. Report on operation of 16 April 1943: target, Pilsen; pilot, Sergeant D. J. Hewlett. Report states: Aircraft attacked primary target at 7,000 ft, on heading 214° magnetic. Ground haze and smoke from flares. Target believed seen in bombsight. Numerous bomb bursts from other aircraft seen. Target difficult to identify owing to glare of fires against ground haze.

Real story: It was a clear dark night and we had flown a long distance using astro-navigation. When we neared our ETA [estimated time of arrival] we were surprised to see the target marked well to the south and subject to heavy bombing. We turned towards it but I notified the skipper that the PFF [Pathfinder Force] had got it wrong; there was no river in the area and the topography was all wrong. We turned north-east to look for the Skoda works and I eventually bombed a spot which had similar river configurations to Pilsen. In the event my photo showed it to be open country, halfway between the real target and the spot marked by PFF. There is no way we could have bombed on a heading on 214° magnetic, as we were heading north by east at the time. In spite of our report and several others that the target had not been hit, the overall intelligence report claimed that this had been a successful raid.

Second story. Report: 23 May 1943. Target Dortmund, attacked at 17,000 ft, Heading 040° true. Six-tenths broken cloud. Yellow TIs [target indicators] seen en route and reds seen at zero minus 2. No greens. Bombed on ETA from yellows. Bombs burst on northern edge of mass of flames. Weather hampered attack, but *Gee* [an electronic position-fixing device] worked close to target and DR [dead-reckoning navigation] run from yellows should result in target being attacked.

Real story. We had come in from the north. To fly in on 040° true would have meant flying up the Ruhr valley – *crazy*. The weather was clear and we were the first to bomb on a primary TI marker. I had a photo showing the whole of the target clear of cloud and with no fires or signs of bombing.

The technical points raised by Tom Wingham will be explained later in this book, but surely the point is clear: even official records have to be treated with caution, and oral history need not be instantly dismissed. Oral history has its dangers, but so does every other kind of history. Official records get doctored, and the memoirs of the commanders or the politicians, on which historians are all too happy to rely, are usually written to prove that the powers that be were right all along.

In the case of flying operations, memories are helped by the fact that all aircrew are obliged to keep logbooks, and all the interviews in this book were conducted with a logbook on the table. When I pointed out to an RAF group captain, the difference between an official account and the logbook entry of a pilot who had flown on one raid, he said that a logbook account, written within hours of the action – and which had to be countersigned by the squadron commander or 'senior bod' – would always be more accurate than any 'official' account.

I also suspect that many of the objections to 'oral' history are based on academic or professional snobbery. Any historian would be happy to record – or even boast – about a chat with Winston Churchill about the Gallipoli landings; I fail to see why the memoirs of a private soldier who actually went ashore in those landings are any less worthy of record or should be automatically suspect. That said, every chapter of this book, draft by draft, has been circulated to other people who served in the relevant theatre, flew with the relevant squadron on the relevant mission or operation, or did the relevant job in the Second World War. The final draft has been read by a number of people, each an expert in his field.

Over 80 people – senior officers, historians and aircrew veterans, Americans, Australians, British, Canadians and Germans – have been over the text, weeding out errors and 'line shooting'. Many have made suggestions for alteration or improvement that I have not hesitated to adopt. The facts are as accurate as we can make them; the opinions expressed, unless attributed to someone else, are mine. Those who seek more enlightenment than these pages can provide are directed to the bibliography.

The concentration is on the period from 1939 to 1945, but to put that period in context there are chapters covering the 'before' and 'after' phases, looking at the Condor Legion activities in the Spanish Civil War and the USAAF bombing offensive against Japan. The book also includes German accounts, from fighter pilots, flak gunners, civil-defence workers and civilians, notably in my chosen 'representative' German cities, Ludwigshafen and Mannheim, which were bombed 124 times during the Second World War.

So, to get some idea of what it was like back then, let us go back over 55 years and pick up the atmosphere in just one bomber squadron, No. 460 Squadron (RAAF), Bomber Command, in the hours before a raid, as recalled by one Bomber Command pilot, Wing Commander Peter Isaacson, AM, DFC, AFC, DFM, at a 460 Squadron reunion in Melbourne, Australia, in 1998:

Fifty-five years ago tonight, 27 March 1943, my aircraft, Lancaster 4892, *Q for Queenie*, is bombing Berlin – my forty-second operation. Crew: pilot, myself; second pilot, Wing Commander Rivett-Carnac, DFC; navigator, Flight Lieutenant Bob Neilsen, DFM; wireless operator, Pilot Officer Copley, DFM; Bomb-aimer, Flight Lieutenant Ritchie DFM; top gunner, Flight Sergeant Hazlewood; flight engineer, Sergeant Delaney; and rear gunner, Sergeant Rust.

Bob Neilsen tells me that the things he remembers are the sights, sounds and smells of that lifetime we spent operating against the enemy, so let us close our eyes for a few moments and recapture some of the things we lived with in those distant days and nights, 55 years ago.

Can you see the briefing room, with the map on the wall, the strands of coloured wool stretching from England, across the Channel or the North Sea, then across Europe to a place on the map deep in enemy territory? Can you see the mess with its operational supper of baked beans and – perhaps – an egg? Can you see the crew room, the truck to dispersal, the last-minute cigarette, the nervous leak against the tailwheel?

Can you hear again the sound of the Merlin engines opening up – port inner, starboard inner, port outer, starboard outer? Can you visualize the trundle round the taxiway, the wait for take-off? Can you feel again the tightening in the stomach as the green light flashes, as the captain opens up the engines? Can you hear the rattle of fire as the gunners test their guns over the Channel? Do you remember the sound of the navigator's voice in the earphones, calling out the changes in course?

Keep your eyes closed and you will hear the cry of the gunners as they spot an enemy aircraft, ahead or above or below. Remember the sight of light flak – those greens and reds and whites, coiling lazily into the air below you? You will see the puff balls from heavy flak off to port or starboard. Remember the smell as the flak got too close and you knew the German gunners were getting your height or position more accurately?

Now remember the sight of the target – the searchlights probing the sky for a victim; the red and green target indicators floating down; the fires on the ground. Can you hear the voice of the bomb-aimer – 'left . . . left . . . right . . . steady . . .' – and then the welcome sound of 'Bombs gone', the silent pause for the photo flash – and then away?

Do you recall the murmur of debriefing, the savour and smell of cigarettes, the anguish on the faces of all as they read the names on the operations board, the ones which did *not* have a 'Landed Time' against them? These were the sights, sounds and smells of life on a squadron all those years ago.

Wing Commander Isaacson and aircrew from a half a dozen nations have contributed their memories to this book. This is their story. This is the way it was in the skies over Germany during their long, hard and victorious war. Their stories – and their sacrifices – deserve to be remembered.

Heinkel He 111H

1

The Advent of the Bomber
1914–1939

Whoever fights monsters should see to it that in the process he does not become a monster; when you look into the abyss, the abyss looks into you.

Friedrich Nietzsche, *Beyond Good and Evil*, 1886

This is the story of a machine. The strategic heavy bomber, a delivery system that took warfare into a new dimension, had a short operational life of about thirty years and we will not see its like again. The day of the great bomber fleets that darkened the skies over Western Europe between 1939 and 1945 is over. Modern inventions – 'smart' bombs, 'cruise' missiles and intercontinental rockets – have seen to that. And yet, in another sense, the story of the bomber is not over, for its use and the effects of its use – especially the moral effect – have still not been fully explored.

The story of the bomber war also describes an era, a period of history complete in itself. General 'Hap' Arnold, wartime Chief of the United States Army Air Force, who had over 60,000 aircraft under his worldwide command when the bomber war ended in August 1945, was taught to fly in 1911 by Orville Wright. It is one of the curious sidelights of history that the man who commanded the greatest aircraft fleets the world has ever seen – or ever will see – was taught how to fly by one of the brothers who invented the aeroplane.

Arnold's force displayed its greatest power on a mission to Germany on 24 December 1944. During the flight, the top gunner in a B-24 Liberator of the 458th Bomb Group came out of his turret and invited his pilot, Robert W. Vincent, to 'go up and have a look'. 'When I got into the turret and looked around,' says Vincent 'there were US bombers all over the sky, as far as the eye could see, all heading for Germany. I learned later that the Eighth Air Force had put up 2,900 aircraft that day, and it certainly looked like it.'

Though accounts vary and the dates are debatable, for bomber aircraft were used by the Italians in Tunisia in 1913 and Royal Naval Air Service (RNAS) aircraft bombed the German Zeppelin sheds at Friedrichshafen in 1914, it is generally accepted that the first recognizable strategic bomber operations – attacking industrial and civilian rather than military targets – took place in 1915. Thus the extent of the Bomber Era is a mere 30 years, from the advent of the bomber in 1915 to the dropping of atomic bombs on Hiroshima and Nagasaki in 1945, acts of massive destruction by a single piece of ordnance that instantly made the great bomber fleets obsolete. This period is easily contained within the working life of one airman, and the story of the bombers and the men who flew in them is that rare piece of history, a period that is over but one in which many of the protagonists are still alive.

These people, the aircrews of the Second World War, are still able to recount, in vivid detail and, with the help of their logbooks, often very accurately, exactly what that era was like when it reached its apogee in the skies over Germany between 1939 and 1945. During those years, 'Bomber Command, initially so weak and ineffective, was to grow into a weapon which, with the United States Strategic Air Forces in Britain, was of decisive importance in the ultimate and total defeat of Nazi Germany.'[1] It seems important to tell the full story of the strategic bomber now, while those who flew or fought it are alive, for the bomber is one of those weapons of war – the submarine is another – which brought with it, at the moment of invention, a number of political and moral problems touching on the way wars are fought, and on the methods and weapons civilized nations might justifiably employ to win them.

It is these problems, especially the moral one, that makes the story of the bomber so relevant and compelling. The story of what happened in the skies over Germany during the Second World War is being transformed into myth, and one of the most persistent myths is the growing public belief that the Combined Bomber Offensive against Hitler's Reich was both ineffective and pursued beyond the point of reason and humanity. As a result, an increasing number of people believe that the Allied aircrews, and especially those of RAF Bomber Command, were little better than war criminals, slaughtering civilians in their hundreds of thousands at the behest of their commander, Air Chief Marshal Sir Arthur Harris.

That this is indeed a widespread opinion is confirmed by Wing Commander John Tipton, once a navigator with No. 109 Squadron:

Post-war generations have the conviction that the bombing campaign was unnecessary, wasteful and evil, and to overturn these impressions in the public mind will be an uphill task. My contemporaries – those that are left from the survivors – have no doubts, but feel they are on the defensive. Harris and, by association, his crews have been branded as war criminals. I am sure we would all have preferred to have flown Spitfires in defence of the white cliffs of Dover to universal approval, but, though the fighter pilots of 1940 saved us from defeat, it was the endurance of the bomber crews that ensured our victory.

The purpose of this book is to examine all the factors affecting the planning and conduct of the bomber offensive over Germany between 1939 and 1945, to see if the popular allegation has any basis in fact. The book will also examine a number of myths regarding the Combined Anglo-American Bomber Offensive that have grown up since the Second World War in Britain, Canada, and the United States, and in particular those surrounding Air Chief Marshal Sir Arthur Harris, chief of RAF Bomber Command from 1942 to 1945.

This is not a book for experts on military strategy or for aircraft buffs, though I hope they will read and enjoy it and recognize its purpose. It is aimed at the general public, and before starting on the main part of the story it is necessary to fill in a little background and make a point about the strategic bomber which is all too often overlooked.

That point is that the strategic bomber was, in many respects, a completely new weapon of war in 1939. The development of military aircraft in the Great War presented the commanders with the possibility of making war in a new dimension, but the main use of aircraft at the start of that war was for reconnaissance – a role previously occupied by the cavalry. Other uses – like artillery spotting, the aerial domination of the battlefield by fighter aircraft, and tactical support for ground operations – developed from this function later. The bomber was recognized as a different kind of weapon, but there was no clear consensus on what sort of weapon the bomber *was* or on what it might achieve. Some held that it was a form of long-range artillery, others that it was of use only for artillery spotting. The general Great War consensus held that the bomber was primarily a *tactical* weapon, best used to support the operations of ground forces, and until 1918 the Royal Flying Corps was part of the British Army.

There was, however, another school of thought – one which developed as aircraft performance improved – which held that the bomber was not just an extension of or addition to the present methods of waging war, but a means by which ground campaigning might become unnecessary. Some went further and felt that, through its potential for carrying destruction to the heart and home of belligerent nations, the bomber was a weapon that might render war itself unthinkable for civilized states.

This is the bomber as a strategic weapon – a role defined by the official history in the following terms: 'The difference between attacking the manifestations of enemy armed strength in the immediate vicinity of the actual fighting and attacking the sources of it, may be conveniently, though not always entirely precisely, be distinguished by the use of the terms "tactical" and "strategic".'[2]

This belief that the bomber could win wars by itself has since become known in military circles as 'the bomber dream'. The skies over Germany between 1939 and 1945 became the place where an attempt was made to turn this dream into a reality.

If there was any truth in 'the bomber dream', then it was a noble dream and that fact has to be remembered. If the bomber, by the very horror implicit in its deployment, could render war impossible except at great cost to the home population, then that was a step to the abolition of war itself. Nor was this dream entirely far-fetched. Nuclear weapons have prevented the outbreak of major world wars for over 50 years, since atomic bombs were dropped on Hiroshima and Nagasaki in 1945. Since that time all nations, however belligerent, have feared that the outcome of a major war involving the use of nuclear weapons would be the extinguishing of life on this planet. Given the moral imperfectability of the human race, such terror is the only means yet invented of keeping man's baser instincts in check – at least up to a point. World wars may have ceased; war itself continues to flourish.

The bomber had been invented – or, more accurately, developed – in the middle of the Great War, but in that war and in a number of other wars between 1918 and 1939, the point at which this story opens, the bomber had been mainly employed as a *tactical* weapon, deployed in support of ground forces. As a tactical weapon the bomber was very successful, and this success obscured the fact that the *strategic* bomber was a failure. That failure arose for a very simple reason. Quite simply, in the first quarter-century of its existence the bomber lacked the navigational aids, the target-marking and bomb-aiming equipment, and the bomb-carrying capacity which would enable it to make a significant contribution to the outcome of any major struggle. As a weapon of war the strategic bomber was totally inadequate, and it would remain so until these deficits were made good.

The first *strategic* bomber raids behind enemy lines were carried out by German Zeppelin airships, which dropped bombs on the east coast of England in January 1915. This first raid killed or injured twenty people, most of them civilians. These Zeppelin raids continued, and two years after they began the Germans deployed a strategic aircraft, the long-range Gotha bomber, which operated from bases in Belgium and first appeared over Britain on 25 May 1917. The Gotha was a formidable machine capable of carrying a 500 kg (1,100 lb) bomb. The first Gotha raid was on Folkestone, a port through which troops were shipped to France; 300 people were killed or injured in this first raid, 116 of them soldiers, but the ferries continued to cross the Channel.

Three weeks later the Gothas attacked London – a daylight raid by fourteen aircraft killed or injured some 600 people. Only eleven of them were servicemen, and among the casualties were 46 children from an infants' school. Such raids continued, and caused considerable public disquiet and not a little panic. Questions about Britain's vulnerability to air attack were asked in the House of Commons, and fighter squadrons were rushed back from France to form a defensive ring around London. As a result the Gothas abandoned daylight raids and began to attack London by night. This led to even more indiscriminate bombing. The Gothas were not able to bomb accurately but they were able to bomb with impunity by night, as the fighters could not find them.

These attacks continued for a year, almost until the end of the war. In that time the Gothas killed or injured some 1,800 people, only a third of whom were connected in any way with military operations. It will be clear from this brief account that any moral restraints on the use of this new weapon, in so far as they ever existed, failed to survive the first contact with the realities of war. By the time the Great War ended in 1918 there had been more than 50 bombing raids on British towns in which around 2,000 people had been killed or injured.

The Royal Air Force was formed from the Royal Flying Corps (RFC) and the Royal Naval Air Service (RNAS), on 1 April 1918. The 'Independent Force' of bombers which then attacked targets in Germany only had time to fly a handful of operations into Germany before the war ended. Most of the belligerent nations now had air forces, and these forces did not disappear with the coming of peace. However, most nations scaled down their military forces and cut off development funds, and it soon became clear that if the Royal Air Force was to survive as an independent force, in the face of budget cuts and the opposition of the two older services, which resented the allocation of funds to this new arm, it must swiftly find a valid, peacetime role.

During the later stages of the Great War, the chief of the RFC, Major General, later Air Marshal, Sir Hugh Trenchard, had regarded the bomber as a tactical weapon, most useful when deployed in support of the British armies on the Western Front. It was only after the war, when he was faced with the prospect of the RAF being broken up and the component parts returned to their original owners, that Trenchard became interested in the bomber as a strategic weapon.

Trenchard found it such a role in the use of obsolescent Great War-vintage aircraft to quell dissident tribes in the far-flung parts of the British Empire – in Iraq and on the North-West Frontier of India. This was 'air control', and in a limited way it proved highly successful, though air operations were continually plagued by inadequate resources. Aircraft dropped leaflets or bombs on rebellious tribesmen during the Third Afghan War in 1919, and against rebellious Kurds in Mesopotamia during the 1920s; writing about the Somalia campaign in 1920, the Colonial Secretary, Leopold Amery, commented that 'air control' had made it 'the cheapest war in history'. Among the officers flying these machines were Wing Commander Arthur Harris and Squadron Leaders Robert Saundby and the Hon. Ralph Cochrane, all veterans of the Great War who would rise to high command in the future struggle.

This 'air control' role justified a modest investment in air power, but the survival of the RAF in the immediate postwar period was largely due to the powerful advocacy of Air Marshal – later Marshal of the Royal Air Force and Viscount – Trenchard, and it is for his work in keeping the RAF a separate service that he has become known as the 'Father of the RAF'.

Trenchard was much more than a senior staff officer. He was a prophet of military aviation, a man who saw what air power might do if it was properly equipped and supported. In particular, Trenchard came to believe that the bomber as a war-winning weapon gained much of its power from its decisive effect on enemy morale: 'The morale effect of bombing', he declared in 1919, 'stands undoubtedly to the material effect in a proportion of twenty to one.'[3] In 1923 he elaborated on this theory, stating that 'It is on the bomber that we must rely for defence. It is on the destruction of enemy industries and above all on the lowering of (enemy) morale caused by bombing that the ultimate victory rests. Army policy was to defeat the enemy army; our policy was to defeat the enemy nation.'[4]

These words present a clear belief in the effectiveness of air power, but there was an unstated, perhaps unrecognized, snag: it all depended on the aircraft being able to deliver this policy in the skies over the enemy nation. Air power required suitable aircraft and well-trained, properly equipped crews, plus a support organization in the form of airfields, training facilities, and servicing and supply depots. Above all, it needed the development of new aircraft types and better navigation and bomb-aiming equipment. In the difficult economic climate of the late 1920s and 1930s there was little money available to expand the RAF and keep it up to date with new machines.

Even in the mid-1930s the RAF – like most other air forces – still depended on biplane bombers: aircraft like the Wapiti and the Heyford that descended directly from the DH-4 and Vickers Vimy bombers of the Great War. Only as the threat from Nazi Germany began to crystallize from 1933 – and especially after the *Luftwaffe* was officially established in 1935 – did the RAF begin to receive an adequate share of the defence vote, by which time it was almost too late to catch up in the Europe-wide arms race.

The prospect of another war concentrated minds wonderfully. New aircraft were quickly ordered and the RAF expanded, but most of the money went on fighters like the Hurricane (first flight 1935) and the Spitfire (first flight 1936) – in other words, for defence. Even here initial orders were small and technical development took time. It would be three more years before these fighters entered squadron service. Meanwhile the bomber force also expanded, but slowly.

New twin-engined monoplane bombers, like the Whitley and Wellington, which were ordered in the mid-1930s, were a long time reaching the squadrons. The Wellington first flew in June 1936 but did not enter squadron service until October 1938, just after the Munich Crisis. Other British bombers, the Fairey Battle and the Blenheim, entered squadron service before war broke out, but proved woefully inadequate or positive death traps when they were actually committed to battle against the *Luftwaffe*. Nor were there enough aircraft of any kind. Bomber Command entered the war with 33 bomber squadrons out of the 55 planned, and only seventeen of these squadrons had the twin-engined Wellingtons, Hampdens or Whitleys – aircraft which then ranked as heavy bombers.

The bombing role – strategic or tactical – and the problems of using bombers in modern war had still not been finally settled, but the general emphasis was on their tactical use. This was understandable for, with the possible exception of the Wellington, the performance of these aircraft was lamentable. The ability of their crews to find and hit their targets was distinctly limited, which naturally restricted their employment as a strategic weapon. Development of such aircraft was also inhibited by the widespread belief in British political circles that 'the bomber will always get through' and that the concentration must therefore be on defence against it, military and civil. Many of the operational and technical snags might have been discovered and dealt with in the pre-war years but, as the British official history states, 'The kind of warfare which Bomber Command embarked on in 1939 was substantially new.'[5]

Despite 25 years of development, countless exercises and a great deal of propaganda, when war broke out in Britain on 3 September 1939 and RAF bombers took off to attack Germany, their commanders made a shocking discovery – as an effective weapon of war the strategic bomber was virtually useless.

Arthur Hoyle, an Australian flyer with the RAF, comments on just one of the problems:

Regarding navigation, to say that it was primitive in 1939–40 is to seriously understate the case. In the years before the war the RAF failed to solve the problem of even navigating around Britain, so that most crews got about by either following the railway lines – known as the *Bradshaw* method, after the railway timetable – or, if absolutely lost, they simply landed at the first airfield and asked where they were. It was not even realized that navigation was a highly skilled profession. Navigators, where they existed, were usually ground staff, taken from their normal duties and paid an extra one shilling [5p] a day flying pay.

That standards of navigation were abysmal was not unknown to many of the senior RAF commanders. Air Chief Marshal Sir Edgar Ludlow-Hewitt, AOC-in-C Bomber Command from 1937 until April 1940 and one of the unsung heroes of the bomber war, had been constantly attempting to alert his superiors to the technical limitations of his Command – in terms of navigation, operational range and bombing accuracy – in the pre-war period. Ludlow-Hewitt was also doubtful if his aircraft could defend themselves against enemy fighters. 'Experience in China and Spain has shown that fighter escorts are considered essential for the protection of bomber aircraft . . . but as far as I am aware, this policy is contrary to the views held by the Air Staff.' It was certainly contrary to the views of Air Marshal Sir Charles Portal, who was to be Chief of the Air Staff (CAS) for much of the war and set his face firmly against the development of a long-range escort fighter.

Ludlow-Hewitt advocated the development of a long-range fighter, but his comments were not listened to. Nor were most of the necessary improvements and developments to bombers and bombing equipment made or put in train before war broke out in September 1939. The price of this failure was paid by the aircrews who flew on operations in the first months of the war. One of these crew members was Jack Whorton:

I joined the RAF as a tradesman in 1936. I was a corporal in the Armoury Section when war broke out, and on aircrew as a gunner and bomb-aimer in No. 149 Squadron, which by 1939 had Wellingtons – the famous 'Wimpy'. When I started flying in 1938 we had the Harrow, a twin-engined monoplane bomber, but had only just converted from the Vickers Virginia, which was a biplane bomber. Not all who joined the RAF wanted to fly, and those who did were often considered to be eccentric, but in my case my weekly wage as a tradesman was £2 12s 6d – about £2.65 – a week and the extra flying pay of ten shillings a week [50p], was very welcome. It may not sound much today, but in 1940 £3 a week was a fair wage for a family man.

We were technicians first and bomber crews second, and it was all quite primitive. Never during my service did I take off from a concrete runway – all the airfields were grass. There was a white circle – the landing circle – in the middle of the airfield, which we used for bombing practice, and we did a lot of practice bombing raids by day and night. The landing strips were marked out at night with paraffin lamps, and electric lamps came later. It all seems a bit primitive now, but that was how it was in 1939 on most of the stations.

Another early flyer was Flight Sergeant Graham Hall of No. 102 (Ceylon) Squadron:

I joined up in 1930 as a Halton apprentice, aged sixteen. It was good technical training and quite well paid: a second-class tradesman earned 24 shillings a week – about £1.20. When Hitler came to power in 1933, a lot of tradesmen were asked if they wanted to do aircrew duties as well for extra pay, and some of us were able to go on a flying course. Well, I did that – went solo after three hours' dual at the flying school in Montrose (the aircraft were simpler then) – and eventually became a sergeant pilot on Handley Page Heyfords in 1938.

It was all a bit hit-and-miss, even in peacetime; I remember we had six aircraft crossing from Aldergrove in Northern Ireland to Driffield in Yorkshire and five of them crashed in the Pennines. I was on No. 102 Squadron at Driffield when war broke out, when we transferred to Whitleys – marvellous aircraft after the Heyfords.

I cannot say we were well trained. We had aircraft landing all over the place on exercises, and I remember one pilot who got lost every time he took off. The crews consisted of two pilots (one of whom did the navigation), a wireless operator and two gunners. We went on ops the first night of the war, dropping leaflets somewhere east of the Ruhr – my log says we were up five hours – and we did a lot of leaflet raids after that. There was no formation flying. We plotted our own course and flew individually.

I was eventually shot down over Norway in May 1940. I was pretty experienced by this time and had to fly with a new crew, none of whom I knew, who had just arrived on the station. Anyway, off we went and we did three runs over the target and the bomb-aimer still said he couldn't see it, so I told the second pilot to jink about a bit while I went and pointed out the target to the bomb-aimer. That was when the flak hit us and set us on fire, and although we made it back to the Dutch border it was no go and we had to bale out. I went out through the front hatch, landed all right, and had stopped at a farm for a drink when a gun was poked in my back. It was a man from a German flak unit, and they were so convinced we were all starving in Britain that the first thing they did was give me a meal. And so I went to Dulag Luft and stayed a prisoner until the end of the war.

One of Graham Hall's comrades on No. 102 Squadron was Bill Jacobs:

I had trained as a wireless operator at Cranwell after I joined in 1934 and was later selected for flying duties as an air gunner. When I joined 102 in November 1938 the squadron had just started converting from the Heyford, the last of the biplane bombers, to the Whitley. No. 4 Group had six squadrons equipped with Whitleys or in the process of conversion, and No. 102 was only fully converted in February 1939 – seven months before war broke out. On 3 September 1939 I was a leading aircraftsman wireless operator aircrew, the full title for what became a wireless operator/air gunner or WOP/AG; my daily pay was five shillings [25p], and there was an additional one shilling [5p] as flying pay, plus sixpence [2½p] for my gunnery qualification – at just over 30p a day, I was quite a big earner in those days.

Our first op was on the following day, Monday 4 September, a leaflet raid to Germany, and you will understand our emotions at not being allowed to deliver anything more lethal than paper and rubber bands. It was a chilly flight and it took some time to discharge all the leaflets, which left the fuselage full of brown paper. At dawn, 0640 hrs, we found ourselves over French territory and landed to refuel at a small airfield near Dieppe, having been airborne for 6 hours and 55 minutes – our longest flight so far. The first squadron losses came a few days later when we lost two aircraft of 'A' Flight, one over Kassel; the crew survived and remained POWs for the next six years.

Gilbert Haworth, DFC, DFM, joined the RAF in 1931 and went to his first bomber station, RAF Abingdon, in 1937:

> After four years' training and two years' practical experience, I was given a Hawker Hind bomber to look after. Also about that time it was proposed that some ground crew could be trained in air navigation, air gunnery and bombing, the reward on completion being promotion to the rank of corporal. I volunteered and joined a course with 22 other aspirants in January 1938. It is sobering to consider that by the end of 1941 I was the only member of that course left alive.
>
> Anyway, I passed the course and was sent back to Abingdon for officialdom to decide where to send me in my elevated role as air observer. I was finally sent to Waddington, to replace an observer who had been killed. Having dumped my kit, which included my bicycle, outside the squadron office, I went in to report and returned after about twenty minutes to find my bike being looked after by two service policemen, who put me on a charge for 'Negligently leaning a bicycle against the side of a hangar'. For this grievous crime I was marched up before the CO, who told me grimly that 'For some mysterious reason you appear hell-bent on ruining your career before it has really started.'

Up to 1939 the focus of official attention, even in the bomber squadrons, was on the pilot. The pilot was seen as the key man, the one on whom it all depended. This had been so from the first days of flying, and it had not yet dawned on the authorities that, while a fighter aircraft demanded one man – the pilot – or at most two, in a night fighter, the bomber aircraft demanded a *crew* – and a crew that worked as a trained and disciplined team. It took the war to reveal that too much was being left to the pilot and that many tasks – navigation, bomb-aiming, gunnery, wireless communications – were specialized functions requiring careful training and could not be left to ground-crew volunteers who were often regarded by the pilot as little more than passengers.

In 1934, for example, the pilot was also responsible for navigation. By 1937 it had been appreciated that flying a modern bomber aircraft was a full-time job, especially at night, and a second pilot was introduced to take over the navigation role and assist the pilot on long-range operations. This led to a demand for yet more pilots and for a further emphasis on pilot training; it was not until 1941 – two years into the war – that the role of the navigator was fully appreciated and crew duties were organized on a specialized basis. That such a specialization was long overdue is borne out by the fact that, between 1936 and 1938, 478 RAF bomber aircraft made forced landings as a result of the pilot getting lost.

Navigation was to remain a problem for much of the war. In May 1939 the commander of 3 Group, Bomber Command, Air Vice-Marshal Thomas, told Bomber Command HQ bluntly that dead-reckoning (DR) navigation – using a compass for direction and a chronometer and the air-speed indicator to fly at so many knots for so many hours or minutes – on a cloudy day could only bring an aircraft to within about 50 miles of its target. What could be achieved by DR at night can be judged from this assessment, which was not disputed – and this in peacetime. The pilots and their crews tended to rely on a form of navigation popularly referred to as 'By guess and by God'.

The group commanders were fully aware of these problems, and were also aware of the problems of bomb-aiming, of actually hitting the target after finding it. At the first meeting of the Sub-Committee on Bombing Policy in 1938, Ludlow-Hewitt was quite blunt about this situation as well: 'The result achieved at Training Camps', he told the Committee, 'bore no relation to bombing under war conditions and a definite effort should be made to try to get data as to war probabilities of bombing.'[6]

Operational limitations are not usually revealed in peacetime exercises. It is a fact of military life that peacetime exercises and training, however realistic, are no substitute for actual warfare. If the weather is foul, an exercise can be cancelled. If the bombs fail to hit the target on the bombing range at 15,000 ft, the obvious answer is to bomb from 12,000 or 10,000 ft. If fighters appear and 'attack' the bombers, the fighter pilots may claim to have shot the bombers down; the bomber crews reply that they beat the fighters off. It is all theory.

Even commanders who have seen combat are often guided more by the evidence of peacetime exercises than by cold estimates of what might happen in combat with the enemy. Then all theories disappear: whatever the weather, the target must be attacked. If the bombs fail to hit the target the bombing height will be reduced; but, while the target may then be hit, ground fire will be accurately deployed against the bombers. There will be no argument now over who won the aerial battle: whether the fighters won or the bombers got through is demonstrated by the casualty and loss figures. War destroys all the theories assembled in the years of peace; it is only in war that soldiers, or airmen, really learn to fight and discover the limitations of their training and equipment.

From the middle of the 1930s, when it became clear that war with Germany was probable and the RAF started to expand, there was a lot of ground to make up. More aircraft meant more crews, and a fresh source of pilots and navigators was established with the setting up of the part-time Royal Auxiliary Air Force and the RAF Volunteer Reserve. One of the first to join the RAFVR was Douglas Mourton:

I joined in 1937, after a friend suggested it. I had an interview and a medical in London and reported to Woodley airfield, near Reading, at 6 p.m. one evening for an aptitude test. This consisted of 30 minutes' worth of spins, loops, rolls and the whole range of aerobatics, and when it was over the instructor asked me if I had been scared and I answered truthfully that I had not. So he told me to report the following weekend and my pilot training would commence.

We had to report every other weekend, from 2 p.m. to about 5 p.m. on Saturday and from 9 a.m. to 5 p.m. on Sundays. The beauty was that it was not only interesting, it was well paid. We got 1s 6d [7½p] an hour for all the time we were at the airfield, and travelling expenses and an annual bounty of £25 a year. To put that in perspective, in 1937 you could buy a car for £25, and £25 was more than enough for a deposit on a house.

We flew two types, the Tiger Moth and the Hawk trainer, and I went solo after twelve hours. Then came cross-country flying – plenty of it – plus a blind flying test under a hood, and in no time I had notched up 80 hours. This weekend training was matched by two weeks' annual training when we flew for three or four hours daily.

In May 1936 the RAF was reorganized into functional 'Commands': Training Command, Fighter Command, Coastal Command and Bomber Command, to which Maintenance Command and Balloon Command were soon added. New aircraft were brought into service, more airfields were built, a host of eager volunteers were taught to fly and fight, and by 1938 the RAF share of the Defence budget had risen to 40 per cent, most of the money being spent on bombers, with the intention of forming 41 bomber squadrons and 28 fighter squadrons. As a result of these measures, by 1939 the RAF was ready – just – to shoulder the burdens of another war and Bomber Command went to war in September 1939 with just over 200 front-line aircraft – Wellingtons, Whitleys, Hampdens and Blenheims – organized in four groups.[7]

The comments so far have been devoted to RAF Bomber Command, but they apply to a greater or less degree to the other national air forces, all of which were confronted with the fact that public and political fear of the bomber was not matched by the potential of the machine itself. Across the Atlantic the United States Army Air Force – or the US Army Air Corps as it then was – the RAF's future ally in the Second World War, while keeping a watchful eye on European activities, was in no better condition in terms of manpower or equipment and was working on a very different kind of solution to the basic problems of navigation and bombing accuracy.

The United States Army Air Force (USAAF) of the Second World War was born in 1907 as the Aeronautical Division of the US Army Signal Corps. In 1914 this developed into the US Army Signal Corps Aviation Section, and in June 1918 the Aviation Section became the Air Service. The Air Service was a part of the US Army, and had the primary task of supporting the Army in the field. Much of it was on active service with the American Expeditionary Force (AEF) in France when the Great War ended. The USA had entered the Great War in April 1917 with just two aerodromes on which, according to General John Pershing, commander of the AEF, there were '55 trainers, of which 51 were obsolete and the other four obsolecent'.[8] By the time the Great War ended, nineteen months later, in November 1918, the USA had around 16,000 military aircraft and an aircraft industry capable of producing about 13,500 aircraft a year. Most of these, however, were based on European designs.

The Air Service contained officers like Carl 'Tooey' Spaatz, Henry 'Hap' Arnold, Billy Mitchell and Ira Eaker, all of whom had seen service with the American Expeditionary Force in France and were to make their mark on the history of air warfare. In the Great War the Air Service had not managed to achieve much as a bomber force, dropping only 138 tons of bombs and penetrating no more than 160 miles behind the front line before the war ended, but it had taken part in a major war and had learned the potential of aerial interdiction. After the War ended, however, the Air Service, like the RAF, was swiftly reduced. The casualties of the Great War had produced a worldwide revulsion against all forms of military activity, and the idea of expanding into a new kind of warfare was simply not acceptable to civilized nations – at least in theory. That apart, the US Army 'brass' resisted all attempts by Air Service officers to have their branch hived off from the Army and re-created as a separate service, like the RAF. And so the battle for air power was joined.

The great apostle of air power in the United States was Brigadier-General Billy Mitchell, Assistant Chief of the Air Service from 1919 to 1925. Mitchell had met Trenchard in France, and the two men shared a common opinion on the future importance of strategic air power. Mitchell saw air power as the vital element in the defence of the United States, a nation which had no obvious land enemies but was vulnerable to attack from the oceans on the east and west. He then antagonized both the Army and the Navy by suggesting that the bomber could – and eventually would – make land operations a subsidiary function, and that long-range bombers could sink enemy warships hundreds or thousands of miles off the US coast, thereby making the Navy obsolete.

The role of bombers for maritime defence – however vehemently rejected by the Navy Staff – had a long-term effect on the development of US bombers. Hitting a moving ship on the heaving ocean required great accuracy against small targets rather than a widespread plastering of the waves, and this led to the development of daylight precision bombing as the prime task of the USAAF bombardment squadrons in the Second World War.

In 1921 Mitchell arranged two demonstrations in Chesapeake Bay in which his First Air Provisional Brigade bombed and sank some captured

German ships, including the cruiser *Frankfurt* and the battleship *Ostfriesland*. Further demonstrations followed up to 1923, during which three obsolescent US battleships – the *Alabama*, the *Virginia* and the *New Jersey* – were sent to the bottom. But the Navy, the Army and Congress remained firmly against any expansion or technical development of the US bomber fleet.

In an effort to shut Mitchell up, the Army High Command then transferred him to Texas, as Air Officer on the Staff of the 8th Army Corps. While there, in September 1925, he issued a statement to the press accusing the US military commanders and politicians of neglecting the air arm and therefore the vital cause of national defence. Mitchell was court-martialled and suspended from duty for five years – a sentence which led to his resignation.

Mitchell had gone, but his influence was kept alive by a series of articles and books which he produced throughout the next decade. These included *Our Air Force: The Keystone of National Defense*, published in 1921, and *Winged Defense*, published in 1925. In these books, Mitchell foresaw and described a new kind of war in which the airplane would 'strike directly at centers of production, means of transportation, agricultural areas, ports and shipping . . . they will destroy the means of making war'. This was 'strategic bombing', a strategy which offered an entrancing prospect to a technologically advanced nation like the USA, and in proposing this development Billy Mitchell was pushing at a gradually opening door.

During the late 1920s and the 1930s, US air power gradually expanded. This process was aided by the rapid growth of civil air transport, a new and necessary way of shrinking the vast distances of the continental USA. Developing technical aids and techniques for civil aviation also aided bomber development, but otherwise the similarities with the RAF situation continued. The main US warplanes brought into service in the 1920s – the Martin bomber of 1921 and the Barling bomber of 1923 – were biplanes or triplanes, clear descendants of Great War machines; not until the mid-1930s did a new generation of single-wing, multi-engined, aluminium bombers come into service.

However, the exploits of people like Charles Lindbergh and Amelia Earhart kept public interest in air power alive. The Air Service became the Army Air Corps in 1926, and in 1929 two Air Corps officers, Major Carl Spaatz and Captain Ira Eaker, set up a flight endurance record by keeping a high-wing monoplane, *Question Mark*, in the air over California for 151 hours using a primitive form of in-flight refuelling. Two years later, in October 1931, the US bomber crews received a useful aid when C. L. Norden, a Dutch civilian inventor, produced the latest of his bombsights, the Mark XV, a piece of equipment which proved highly accurate and was soon in service with some of the Army bombardment squadrons, though the Mark XV was largely appropriated by the US Navy for its carrier aircraft and the US Army Air Force was very short of Norden bombsights in the first years of the war.

The snag with the Norden – and with all other bombsights – was that to bomb accurately the bomb-aimer had to see the target. This was not difficult from 10,000 ft in the cloudless, peaceful skies over bombing ranges in Texas or Florida. When the bomber had to operate in the cloudy, dangerous, flak- and fighter-infested European skies and bomb from high altitude it would be a different matter.

Another issue now being tackled in the USA was the creation of the self-defending bomber. By 1933 US scientists calculated that an aircraft could in theory fly up to 5,000 miles at a speed of 200 m.p.h. carrying a 2,000 lb bomb load. This theory led to Project 'A', a scheme to develop a machine with just such a potential. The task was given to the Martin and Boeing aircraft companies, and led to the development during the late 1930s of the Boeing B-17 Flying Fortress, the B-24 Consolidated Liberator, and later the B-29 Super-Fortress – three aircraft which, in various Marks, were to provide the heavy bomber element of the USAAF in the Second World War. The first of the B-17s was delivered in January 1937. By that time the war clouds were gathering over Europe and *Luftwaffe* pilots were gaining useful experience while serving in the Condor Legion, bombing Republican cities in support of General Franco's Nationalist forces during the Spanish Civil War.

The long-range bomber was seen as the answer to America's potential defence problems. Here was a machine capable of attacking ships far out at sea, and rapidly reinforcing distant US territories like the Philippines or the Hawaiian Islands, but there was no body of opinion in the USA supporting the view that the bomber could win wars on its own or make war impossible for an industrial nation. The US government saw the bomber as a means of national defence, and developed a basic bombing philosophy based on *daylight precision bombing*, using the Norden bombsight. Another strand in the US bombing philosophy was that close formations of heavily armed bombers could penetrate enemy defences in daylight and make their way to the target *without the need for fighter escorts*.

One major difference between the British and US bombing philosophies should be noted at this point. Lord Trenchard, whose influence was total in RAF circles during the inter-war years, believed that attacking enemy morale – which effectively meant the civilian population – was a way of winning wars, and that air attacks would have to be concentrated on the industrial towns. The US Army Air Corps believed in precision bombing of military and industrial targets vital to the enemy's war industry and declared that it would never attack population targets. In practice the difference was small, but the difference in the underlying philosophy was considerable.

Both air forces believed that the bomber was essentially a strategic weapon, and neither believed that the long-range bomber should be escorted by a long-range fighter. Quite apart from the fact that no long-range fighter existed, the RAF believed that such a fighter, weighted down with fuel, could not fight effectively against a light, agile, short-range fighter. RAF bombing philosophy held that the bombers could reach the target anyway, even if that meant flying at night. However, night bombing would be less accurate, so day bombing was the official doctrine, even though RAF bombers were inadequately armed for daylight operations. The USAAF, being totally wedded to daylight precision bombing, crammed machine-guns on to its aircraft and believed that heavily armed bombers, flying in tight formations, could beat an attacking fighter off even in daylight. It took some years and some very hard times to disprove both these philosophies.

In Nazi Germany a different philosophy prevailed in military aviation circles, one stressing the tactical rather than the strategic use of bombers. The Versailles Treaty of 1919 prohibited Germany from having an air force, but the Germans soon found ways to get round this restriction. By the early 1920s great number of young German males were learning all about flight in a nationwide network of glider schools, and engine-aircraft pilots were being trained secretly at airfields in Soviet Russia. German aircraft factories were building civilian passenger aircraft by 1920, and many of these early types could be quickly modified into bombers. The air-transport-company training schools also produced a considerable number of pilots and navigators, far in excess of commercial requirements. In 1922 and again in 1924 the Versailles Treaty members attempted to limit the number of civilian aircraft Germany could produce, but the main manufacturers – Heinkel, Junkers and Dornier – simply established subsidiary companies in friendly states like Russia, Sweden or Turkey and carried on building aircraft there.

All limitations on the size of the German aircraft industry were removed by the Paris Air Agreement of 1926, though bans on the development of military aircraft continued – and were duly ignored – and in that year the separate German airlines were consolidated into the national airline, Lufthansa. By 1931, two years before Hitler came to power, the German Air Force, the *Luftwaffe* – which did not officially exist – had four fighter squadrons, three bomber squadrons and eight light-reconnaissance squadrons. The German Air Sport Association had already trained some 1,500 engine-pilots and had another 3,000 engine-pilots and some 15,000 glider pilots under training.

This expansion escalated after Adolf Hitler came to power in 1933. Hitler promptly abrogated the Versailles Treaty, the *Luftwaffe* came into official existence in 1935, a German Air Ministry was established with Hermann Goering as Air Minister and Commander-in-Chief of the *Luftwaffe*, and the German Air Force rapidly expanded. The *Luftwaffe*, like the *Heer* (the

Army), was part of the *Wehrmacht*, the German armed forces, under the overall command of General Werner von Blomberg, Minister of Defence and Head of the *Wehrmacht*.

Blomberg was totally opposed to the idea of an independent air force, and this led to a now familiar argument. In 1938–9, Goering and his senior commanders, Erhard Milch, Ernst Udet and Hugo Sperrle – officers with recent experience of bombing in the Spanish Civil War – wanted a balanced air force with a strong element of strategic bombers. Blomberg, a senior Army general, wanted the *Luftwaffe* to be a tactical force devoted to helping the Army in its ground campaigns, and his arguments convinced Hitler that a strategic force was unnecessary. This fact is sometimes disputed, but Field Marshal Albert Kesselring, one of the *Luftwaffe*'s Second World War commanders, said in 1954 that 'Even if the role of the *Luftwaffe* had been seen as a strategic one and a well-thought-out production programme devised to cover it, by 1939 there would still have been no strategic *Luftwaffe* of any significance.'[9]

German military philosophy for the coming war was based on the experiences of all the armies on the Western Front in the Great War, when attack after attack had ground to a halt because, although the Great War armies could attack with great *force*, they lacked *momentum*: a marching and horse-drawn army could not develop a 'breach' in the line into a 'breakthrough' before the defending forces could bring up reserves and seal it off. By 1939, now equipped with fast tanks and lorried infantry, a mobile force backed up with tactical aircraft – especially the Junkers Ju 87 Stuka dive-bomber – the German armies aimed to overcome their opponents with a rapid and overwhelmingly powerful attack, a lighting war – or *Blitzkrieg*.

The final argument went Blomberg's way and the *Luftwaffe* became essentially a tactical airforce composed of fighters and twin-engined medium bombers like the Heinkel He III and the Dornier Do 17. These were soon joined by the Junkers Ju 88, which entered service in 1940 as a twin-engined bomber and later did good service as a night fighter. As well as the Stuka dive-bomber, there were also a number of reconnaissance machines. The bombers were protected by two main fighter types: the twin-engined Messerschmitt Bf 110 (later Me 110) and the single-engined Messerschmitt Bf 109 (later Me 109).[10] This last aircraft was to be one of the most successful fighter aircraft of the war. These types were joined later in the war by the Focke-Wulf FW 190 and then by early jet aircraft.

These aircraft underline the fact that the *Luftwaffe* was mainly designed for army support – which is not to say that in 1939 the *Luftwaffe* lacked strategic bombing potential or advanced target-finding equipment. Indeed, by late 1940 the *Luftwaffe* was well ahead of the British and Americans in developing navigation and target-finding aids and had an efficient ground-to-air control-signals network. As we shall see, the *Luftwaffe* was therefore able to undertake a strategic bombing campaign against Britain from August 1940 to March 1941 – the period of the Battle of Britain and the Blitz – with the aim of driving Britain out of the war, hopefully without the need for a seaborne invasion – the Teutonic version of the bomber dream.

It has to be remembered, however, that in this campaign in 1940–1 the *Luftwaffe* could fight at very close range from airfields in France, Belgium and the Low Countries, which lessened its navigation problems and ensured a quantity of fighter cover. When Bomber Command and the USAAF struck back at Germany later, their aircraft had much further to travel, with all the problems this extra distance involved.

Blomberg retired in 1938, when Hitler assumed direct command of all the German armed forces; the *Luftwaffe*, along with the German Army and the Navy, then gained the right of direct access to the Führer. Hitler used the *Luftwaffe* in March 1938 when he took over Austria at the *Anschluss*, sending in 2,000 SS troops by air to seize vital points in Vienna, and he used it again in September 1938 when 500 bombers were deployed to overawe the Czechs and help the German seizure of the Sudetenland. By the time war broke out in 1939 the *Luftwaffe* had around 4,000 aircraft, of which 1,800 were bombers, and was organized into four air fleets – *Luftflotten* – each composed of a number of air divisions equipped with first-rate aircraft and manned by skilled aircrews, many of them veterans of the Condor Legion.

The *Regia Aeronautica*, the Italian Air Force, declined rapidly after the Great War, in which Italy had fought on the side of France and Great Britain. By 1922 the Italians had only about 100 obsolescent aircraft, but in that year the dictator Benito Mussolini came to power and ordered a rapid expansion and improvement in the Italian Air Force, following the ideas advanced by the air-force commander General Giulio Douhet, who laid them out in a widely read and highly influential book, *The Command of the Air*, first published in 1921.

Like Hugh Trenchard and Billy Mitchell, Douhet believed that the advent of the bomber had changed the nature of war at a fundamental level. Warfare need no longer be confined to land or sea, and victory would not depend on the unpredictable fortunes of fleets or armies. Now, said Douhet, it would depend on the outcome of air battles. Achieve command of the air and the enemy was at your mercy. In total war the entire population were belligerents, so a nation's entire resources must be thrown at once into the fray, with victory going to the side which first overcame the enemy's resources in morale, industrial capacity and military might.

Douhet's strategy depended on first defeating the enemy air force and then smashing the enemy industry. All of this must be done quickly, allowing no time for industrial recovery or a revival of civilian morale. To this end Douhet advised the formation of a separate air force, but one controlled through a combined headquarters – a Department of National

Defence. Douhet was advocating total war with a vengeance, and arguing that victory went to the side which, having obtained mastery in the air, used that mastery to shatter the enemy nation, city by city and street by street, until surrender.

The Italian Air Force was to be tested in actions against tribesmen in Ethiopia in 1935–9 when it was used as a tactical force, aiding the Army in its attempts to crush the forces of the Emperor Haile Selassie and, with greater relevance to the coming worldwide struggle, in the Spanish Civil War of 1936–9, when Italian bombers based on Mallorca carried out strategic air attacks against Barcelona and other Republican strongholds. The *Regia Aeronautica* entered the Second World War with about 2,500 aircraft, but what little reputation it had was soon lost in combat with the Greeks and the British. Douhet's theories may have had considerable influence, but the *Regia Aeronautica*'s attempts to carry them into practice were little short of lamentable.

The above is only a broad picture, a brief look at the advent of the bomber, at developments between the two world wars and at the state of affairs among the main air forces on the outbreak of the Second World War in 1939. Although there are exceptions in every case, it is still a useful outline and the main point which arises is that in 1939 the bomber was mainly regarded as a tactical weapon – certainly by the then all-powerful *Luftwaffe* – and, let it be admitted, it was initially a successful one. The bomber's success as a tactical weapon tended to obscure the fact that as a strategic weapon it was simply not up to the task.

The RAF certainly saw the bomber as a strategic weapon but, as we shall see, when the bomber was used in war, employed independently against the enemy homeland, it rapidly became apparent that a great many lessons had to be learned and a great deal of equipment to be invented and developed before the bomber force could be employed efficiently.

This point has to be noted and remembered now, because it was either totally ignored or rejected in the inter-war years, when the bomber was regarded as a terrible weapon, a destroyer of cities and civilian lives. The destruction of Guernica by the German Condor Legion during the Spanish Civil War and the use of bombers by the Japanese in China and Manchuria seemed to add weight to this conclusion, while public apprehension was heightened by films like *Things to Come*, in 1936, in which terrified civilians were depicted cowering in the streets while fleets of bombers droned overhead, dealing out death and destruction. This fear was not unreasonable, but in Spain and China the bomber was used against undefended cities, in daylight, and at short range. Using bombers on long-range operations against a well-armed enemy would be a different matter entirely.

Between 1918 and 1939 the bomber came to be regarded as an unstoppable weapon, the ultimate deterrent, a threat to civilization. This belief was held by many politicians, who believed that 'the bomber will always get through'. This being so, its use could not be contemplated and attempts were made to get bombing banned at the Washington Conference in 1922 and by the Hague Rules of 1922–3: rules which never got beyond the draft stage. In 1936 the British Joint Planning Committee, reviewing the prospects for an aerial war, estimated that civilian casualties in Britain might exceed 150,000 a week if a bombing campaign was launched against British cities. This belief in the power of the bomber, however persuasive and strongly held, was a complete delusion; as a war-winning weapon the strategic bomber of 1939 was a failure.

This fact was not entirely due to obsolescent aircraft and inadequate navigation and bomb-aiming equipment: the problem went rather deeper than that. Part of the problem was due to a failure to define exactly what sort of weapon a bomber *was*. Was it really long-range artillery, or an army-support weapon, or was it something entirely new – something that completely changed the face of war?

These points are not academic. Depending on the point of view taken, so the bomber would be designed and equipped, men would be trained to use it, and a doctrine for its use would be developed. If the bomber had been seen as a delivery system, a means to an end rather than an end in itself, steps might have been taken much earlier to ensure that the crews it carried could find and hit their targets and to make the bombs it carried more effective. Jack Livesey of the Imperial War Museum at Duxford expands on this last point:

> At the start of the War the RAF found that the damage from their bombs was not as good as they had expected. The high-explosive (HE) filling was not very great, and a 500 lb bomb might have only 300 lb of high explosive in it – and the 500-pounder was the largest bomb we had. Then came the 1,000-pounder and then, but only in March 1941, came the 2,000 lb high-capacity bomb, first used on the night of 31 March/1 April. It took until July 1942 to develop the 4,000-pounder, the 'Cookie' or 'Blockbuster', a bomb that could make whole houses jump into the air. On the night of 15/16 September 1943 the 12,000 lb general-purpose 'factory-buster' made its debut, made by bolting three 4,000-pounders together.
>
> At first these high-capacity bombs were not too popular with the crews, who felt that flak or machine-gun fire could set them off, but the results were far too good to give these new types of bomb up. Incidentally, the US bombers had a much smaller bomb load. The B-17 could only carry about 4,000 lb to Berlin, the equivalent of one 'Cookie', the same as a Mosquito, and the 'Cookie' contained more explosives than the similar weight of US bombs, the largest of which was a 2,000-pounder. US aircraft usually carried the 500 lb general-purpose bomb that only had a 50 per cent HE filling. At the start of the war neither the bomber nor the bombs were up to much.

To examine these points in detail it will be necessary to take a closer look at how the bomber developed as a weapon of war and how the air forces eventually found the scientific means to deliver the sort of strategic blows the apostles of the bomber had always said were possible. This process took time, and we will come to it later, but before we move on to the tactics and technology it is necessary to discuss how the political and moral objections to strategic bombing were gradually eroded.

Aircraft made a large number of technical advances during the Great War, steadily improving in speed, ceiling and range, but the bomber did not develop as quickly as the fighter. The bomber – in the shape of the Zeppelin – did not make a serious debut until 1915, and it was not until 1918, at the end of the war, that the bomber became a strategic weapon, capable of attacking targets far away from the battlefields – and so the moral problem arose.

At first sight, the invention of the bomb-carrying strategic aircraft was a boon to military commanders. Here was a weapon of great range and power, capable of crossing defence lines and attacking enemy installations – artillery parks, barracks, munitions dumps, arms factories, railway lines, army camps, military and economic targets of all kinds – in places far beyond the range of artillery. But there was a snag. The inventors and commanders of this new weapon were unable to guarantee that the explosives – bombs – dropped by these aircraft would always fall on strictly military targets. They might hit schools, hospitals and private homes, and kill civilians – even women and children – as well as soldiers. And here was a moral problem: Were civilians a legitimate target in war?

When it became clear that the bomber was a painfully inaccurate weapon, very apt to kill women and children, the wartime leaders, both military and political, were faced with a number of options. One option was to say that the inventors should take this weapon away and bring it back when it had been so refined that its weapons – those 'bombs' – would fall only on military targets. It took another 80 years before 'cruise' missiles and 'smart' bombs offered military commanders even a glimpse of that facility – and the Kosovo air campaign in 1999 produced many examples of bombs being dropped on civilian buses, foreign embassies and even neutral capitals.

Another option was to restrict the bombers to attacks on purely military targets – armies in the field and warships at sea, where there would be no civilians in the vicinity – in other words, to use the bomber as a *tactical* weapon, in support of armies or navies. This option was exercised by the RAF at the start of the Second World War, but, as we shall see, this restraint did not last.

A third option was to fudge the issue and offer counter-arguments. If it was legitimate to bomb arms factories, why was it unethical to bomb the homes of those who worked in them? What was the difference between bombing the people who *made* the weapons and bombing the soldiers who *used* them. Were they not all part of the same military machine? After all, wars were no longer fought by medieval warlords, but by modern nations, who put all their military and economic muscle, including their productive manpower, into the struggle. In an era of total war, could the civilian expect to be excluded? Perhaps bringing the war home to the civilian population and showing them exactly what war was like was long overdue. Writing of his experiences in the Spanish Civil War, George Orwell wrote, 'Sometimes it is a comfort to me to think that the aeroplane is altering the conditions of war. Perhaps when the next great war comes we may see a sight unprecedented in all history, a jingo with a bullet hole in him.'[11]

This point raises a further consideration. Twentieth-century wars are fought by people at the command and direction of their governments and leaders, those politicians to whom the people have given their votes and/or their support. If these people could be so cowed by aerial bombing that they would rise up and compel their leaders to *stop* fighting, would that not be a legitimate use of the bomber? Could the bomber be a way of bringing the harsh realities of war home to the civilian population, far from the battlefield, and, by destroying their morale, force them to rise against those leading the struggle?

These arguments for and against strategic bombing were voiced quite early on in the bombing era and have continued, but, though sincere, they do contain an element of cant. Every bombing campaign ever launched has had an attack on civilian morale as one of its aims. The aim of such campaigns is to cause a collapse of that morale, and that can be achieved only by terror bombing – the bomber, when deployed strategically, is fundamentally a *terror* weapon, and that fact has to be faced and not fudged.

The major aim of strategic bombing – to force the enemy nation to surrender without a ground campaign but by depressing popular morale – has never been achieved. Bombing has *never* destroyed civilian morale in any meaningful way: not in Spain in the 1930s during the Civil War, not in London during the 1940–41 Blitz, not in Germany from 1943 to 1945, not in Vietnam in the 1960s and '70s, not in Iraq in 1991 or in Serbia in 1999. Yes, there were panics during the actual air raids, and seeing their cities and homes destroyed was depressing to the people at home and worrying to the men at the front, but there is no evidence that bombing has ever caused a nation to sue for peace.

If anything, the effect of bombing is to enhance the morale of those bombed, to arouse the population against the enemy and strengthen the government through a sense that the government and the people are 'all in this together'. The 1999 air campaign against Serbia may have produced a victory for NATO but it did not destroy Serb morale and, unlike the Germans of 1939–45, the Serbs of 1999 lacked adequate defences against air attack. Had they been able to shoot down the attacking aircraft in any quantity, the NATO air campaign might well have been abandoned.

The moral arguments against the bombing of civilian targets have always been undermined by events, or by the fact that the enemy *did it first*, or by the understandable – if morally deplorable – desire for retaliation. The restraints against the use of the bomber were largely eroded in the course of using it, and the moral arguments against bombing cities first took a severe knock in the Spanish Civil War, when area bombing – 'carpet bombing' as it was then called – was used by the German Condor Legion against the Basque city of Guernica.

The Condor Legion consisted of about 100 aircraft – four bomber and four fighter squadrons – commanded by Major-General Hugo Sperrle, a senior *Luftwaffe* officer, with Colonel Wolfgang von Richtofen, cousin of the Great War 'Red Baron', as his Chief of Staff. The Legion also contained a tank force, commanded by Colonel Wilhelm von Thoma, commander of the German Afrika Korps during the Second World War. Many other officers of the Second World War learned their trade in Spain, including the fighter ace Adolf Galland, and to give their commanders and aircrews experience of wartime flying the Germans rotated their crews, sending out fresh contingents to Spain every few months. The Germans used the Spanish population to try out their air-war and *Blitzkrieg* theories, and a foretaste of things to come came on 26 April 1937, at Guernica.

Guernica was a small town of 7,000 people in the Basque country of north-west Spain, 20 miles from Bilbao. The town lay ten miles from the front line and, as it was crowded with refugees and retreating soldiers, the attack can be regarded as small edition of the Dresden raids of 1945, when a similar situation existed. After some preliminary bombing, the main attack developed in the late afternoon and went on for some hours during which 43 aircraft dropped about 40 tons of bombs on the town. After the bombing stopped, fighter aircraft swooped down to machine-gun the streets and when the aircraft flew away perhaps a thousand people lay dead in the ruins; 70 per cent of the town was totally destroyed, and the rest of it was badly damaged.[12] The town fell to Franco's forces two days later, so it could be argued that this was tactical bombing in support of a ground offensive; nevertheless, the outcry over the bombing of Guernica was already spreading and continues to this day. Picasso's most famous painting represents the bombing of Guernica. The Condor Legion never again carried out an area attack on a city, and the outrage against this brutal attack on an undefended target made a great impression on the Western world. Although Franco's apologists declared that the Republican aircraft had destroyed the town to cast blame on the Nationalists and that anyway Guernica was a military target, the odium of this atrocity clung to him till the day he died. The outcry also demonstrated to the current generation of politicians and military leaders that the bombing of civilians was regarded by the public as a deplorable act.

Guernica arguably was a military target, and it was certainly bombed as part of a tactical plan, but that is only part of it. Guernica was a *town*, and with the destruction of a town another prop holding shut the door against attacks on civilians was knocked away. A town had been bombed, and further city bombings of Barcelona and Madrid were made that much more acceptable because a rule of war had already been broken. Guernica is a landmark in the history of the bombing war, a milestone on the trail that leads to Nanking, Warsaw, Rotterdam, London, Coventry, Berlin, Dresden, Tokyo, Hiroshima and Nagasaki – each a step on the road to total destruction.

The truth is that the notion that bombing could be controlled, or restricted to purely military targets, never stood a chance of success in the circumstances of total war. War is not the sort of activity where ethics can thrive; war is an activity so abhorrent that the only thing to do is to end it as quickly as possible, by any means possible. Those who talk of ethics in the context of total war are entertaining the notion that some types of war or some methods of waging it are 'all right' and acceptable in human affairs – which is self-evident nonsense.

That said, there are actions which are clearly beyond the pale, even in the context of war. For example, a submarine might sink a passenger vessel without warning, drowning women and children; that would be a tragedy. If the submarine then surfaced and cruised about, ramming the lifeboats while the crew machine-gunned the survivors in the water, that would be a war crime. Others might allege that the use of submarines is itself immoral – if not actually criminal. In 1901 Admiral Sir Arthur Wilson, Controller of the Royal Navy, wrote to the First Sea Lord proposing that 'the crews of all submarines captured should be treated as pirates, and hanged'.

In the case of bombing operations, the situation is more complex. The passengers in that hypothetical vessel were to some extent placing themselves and their children at risk by sailing in a ship that entered a war zone. People living in a city, even an industrial city engaged in war production, are simply civilian workers going about their daily affairs. On the other hand they are producing war matériel, and if the factories are bombed and they are killed at their machines then that is the fortune of war. The same argument might hold good if bombs missed the factory but fell on the nearby factory estate and killed workers resting between shifts. But what if those bombs were deliberately aimed at those housing estates, with no other object than killing those workers?

The position at once becomes blurred, and can be resolved only by taking the action as part of a wider conflict and placing it in the context of all-out war. *The object of fighting a war is to win it.* Only after the Second World War did the notion arise that, quite apart from the obvious atrocities, some *methods* of fighting wars, some operational tactics, might amount to criminality – a charge increasingly directed since the war at RAF Bomber Command.

It is curious, for example, that no such charge was laid against the Royal Navy after the First World War, during which tens of thousands of German civilians, including women and children, died of malnutrition and starvation because of the British naval blockade. It is estimated that between half a million and a million people died of hunger in Germany between 1914 and 1918,[13] yet there has been no public condemnation of the First World War admirals as there has been of Sir Arthur Harris and the aircrews of Bomber Command.

War erodes humanity. When Britain went to war in 1939 it was accepted that, if the RAF could not attack a target without putting civilian lives at risk, that target should not be attacked at all. That policy was introduced partly from humanitarian motives, partly to impress neutral nations, partly to attract the approval of Franklin D. Roosevelt, the President of the United States, who had asked the belligerents to refrain from attacking cities, and partly for fear of retaliation. Nazi Germany followed the same course, but could not maintain it. Other countries, like Japan, did not even try to do so – the Japanese had already sent in squadrons of bombers to pound the helpless civilian populations of Shanghai and Nanking before the war spread to the West.

So we have come to the outbreak of war in 1939. To understand what happened after that, to explain how – and why – the bombing campaign moved from a purely military purpose to ravaging the cities of Western Europe, is the purpose of this book. Some of the reasons have already been aired; now they have to be explained in detail. This chapter has provided a broad background to the bomber war that broke out in September 1939 and will have provided the reader with a grasp of the overall situation and the development of the bomber and bombing theories in the decades between the two world wars, and illustrated some of the problems affecting the bomber's use.

All of this will be expanded on in the forthcoming chapters, but this is the way it was on 1 September 1939 when the Second World War began and Hitler launched his *Blitzkrieg* against Poland. The attack was spearheaded by the *Luftwaffe*, which sent 1,000 bombers and 1,050 fighters across Germany's eastern frontier, bombing and strafing the Polish Army and Polish centres of resistance. With their aid the *Wehrmacht* forced Poland to surrender in just twenty days. A major element in compelling this surrender was the *Luftwaffe*'s destruction of the Polish capital, Warsaw.

Junkers Ju 87D

2

Blitzkrieg and the Blitz
1939–1941

Tactics and Strategy are two activities mutually permeating each other in time and space, but at the same time are essentially different activities . . . which cannot be intelligible to the mind until a clear conception of each activity is established.

Karl von Clausewitz, *On War*, 1820

The first two years of the Second World War represented the learning curve in strategic bomber operations. Those years also provided confirmation that the bomber– or at any rate the fighter-bomber and the light bomber: *tactical* bombers – had a significant role to play in ground operations, a fact clearly demonstrated by the *Luftwaffe* during the German invasion of Poland.

When Great Britain and her Empire entered the Second World War on Sunday 3 September 1939, the *Luftwaffe* had already been in action for two days, with the primary task of aiding the rapid advance of German ground forces. With the Ju 87 Stuka dive-bomber making a particular contribution, the *Wehrmacht* rapidly swept across Poland to meet up with invading forces from Germany's then ally, Soviet Russia, by the end of September. The Germans sent some 2,000 aircraft into Poland on 1 September, of which 897 were bombers or dive-bombers. Apart from their ground-support role, as 'flying artillery', and the rapid destruction of the 300-strong Polish fighter force, in the air or on the ground, the *Luftwaffe* was also used to attack Polish cities.

The first of these was the town of Działoszyn, which was bombed and dived-bombed to support ground operations launched by the German IX Corps, which 'took the city without loss'.[1] Polish civilian losses are not recorded. The *Luftwaffe* then moved to attack railways, trains and stations, paralysing the movement of Polish troops before the *Wehrmacht* reached the Polish capital, Warsaw, which came within artillery range on 6 September. The Germans seemed to have the notion that Warsaw was an 'open city' that the Poles should not defend but should allow the Germans to occupy without resistance; however, when Polish artillery beyond the Vistula fired on German forces entering the western suburbs of the city on 7 September, this was taken by the German commanders as carte blanche for a series of devastating air raids.

On 8 September, 140 Stukas attacked the part of the city on the east bank of the Vistula, while other aircraft, the 'battle planes', bombed the western suburbs, ahead of the German ground advance. When this advance was stemmed by the defenders, the *Luftwaffe* was again called in to shatter the Polish positions. This may be regarded as legitimate tactical bombing, but that view overlooks the fact that the Germans had no business being in Poland, let alone bombing a city from which the Poles had not yet had time to evacuate their women and children. The lofty resolutions of the Hague Rules and the pleas of President Roosevelt had not outlasted the first week of total war.

On 13 September the *Luftwaffe* intensified its attacks on Warsaw, using level-flight aircraft as well as dive-bombers, creating 'a sea of flame, so that accurate assessment of results was impossible'.[2] When the Poles continued to resist, the Germans then tried leaflet drops, urging the defenders to capitulate. The Poles still declined to surrender their city, and on 25 September the full might of the *Luftwaffe* was unleashed against Warsaw. This attack began at 0800 hrs and went on for hours, until a great pall of smoke hung over the city – 'not an open city', intones the *Luftwaffe War Diaries*, 'but a beleaguered fortress; [the bombs falling] not on the dwellings of civilians but on a deeply staggered defence system, manned by 100,000 soldiers'. The *Luftwaffe* claims that *only* 400 bombers were deployed over Warsaw, dropping 500 tons of bombs and 72 tons of incendiaries; other accounts double that number of bombers. Whatever their number, each aircraft made three or four sorties, and by nightfall the centre of Warsaw was little more than burning rubble. On the following day the garrison offered to surrender, and city fell to the Germans on 27 September. The bomber war had claimed its first victory.

Over on the Western Front the Royal Air Force was still exercising restraint, though after the British declaration of war, at 1100 hrs on Sunday 3 September, the RAF wasted no time taking to the air. The first operational RAF sortie of the war took place at noon that day, when a Blenheim bomber of No. 139 Squadron took off to fly a reconnaissance mission to Wilhelmshaven, seeking German warships. A further operation, by Hampden and Wellington bombers, also searched for naval targets, but without success. Some naval vessels were detected by the reconnaissance

Blenheim, but when the wireless operator attempted to send this information back to base he discovered that his radio had frozen and he was unable to transmit.

By the time the Blemheim got back it was too late to launch another strike and the next operational sortie was made by ten Whitleys which went out that night to drop leaflets over the Ruhr. On the following day, 4 September, ten aircraft – Wellingtons and Blenheims, five each from No. 107 and No. 110 Squadrons – found shipping in the Schillig Roads and Wilhelmshaven harbour, including the battleship *Admiral Scheer* and the cruiser *Emden*. The bombers did no damage to the warships, but five aircraft were shot down by anti-aircraft fire (flak) one of them crashing on the *Emden*. Another two Wellingtons were shot down by fighters. Five Blenheims from No. 139 Squadron failed to find the Roads and turned back, as did most of the Wellingtons, and at least one aircraft dropped two bombs on the Danish town of Esbjerg, more than 100 miles from the target area; those who actually managed to bomb the German warships saw their bombs bounce off the enemy decks without exploding. And so, with no damage done to the enemy and seven aircraft shot down, the RAF began a bombing campaign that was to last for the next five and a half years.

Most of the problems that were to plague Bomber Command for the next few years made their appearance on 4 September. Since this was a daylight raid, those aircraft which found the target did manage to bomb it; but many bombs failed to explode. Bomber Command flew 30 sorties, and seven aircraft – 23 per cent of those committed – were lost. If this loss rate had been suffered by Bomber Command as a whole, the entire Command would have been destroyed in five operations.

The RAF started the bombing war by imposing certain rules on the aircrews. First, the government ordered that Bomber Command should not attack any land targets, partly because it was difficult to define a purely military target and partly to avoid the risk of killing civilians; this restricted the bombers to naval targets actually at sea, as ships in harbour were deemed too close to civilians to risk attack. An account of these early operations comes from Jack Whorton, a bomb-aimer with No. 149 Squadron of 3 Group:

> After the first raid of the war, on 4 September 1939, offensive action was confined to shipping, in our case in the North Sea, and the order was that in no circumstances were we to drop our bombs on enemy land. Sorties were made in daylight, flying in V-shaped 'vics' of three, which enabled the rear gunners to shoot at attackers coming down on the formation from above and behind, the most common form of fighter attack.
>
> These sorties were soul-destroying. We flew for hours over the North Sea, a bleak place at any time, and never saw an enemy ship. Near Heligoland it could get quite exciting as there were a large number of enemy fighter stations in the German Bight. Intelligence had informed us that the enemy were

'not up to much' when compared, say, with the Hurricanes with which we had practised fighter tactics, but that was not my experience. When we met up with the Me 109 it was quite a shock, and the Me 110 was, in my opinion, absolutely deadly. They could fly in formation with us but stay out of range of our .303 machine-guns and shoot at us at will with their cannon – it was as if we were targets in a shooting gallery. The other bad thing about these 'sweeps', as we called them, was the extremely bad weather forecasts we were given at briefings.

Target-marking had not even been thought of at this time. The crews were given a target and a secondary target, in case the first one was cloud-covered or whatever, and it was pretty much up to the individual crews how they made the attack. The basic procedure for an op was set course at medium height and check wind speed and direction by dropping a flame float over the sea and by noting any geographical feature over the land – enemy flak guns or known searchlight batteries could be useful in this context. It was rare for the target to be sighted visually, so that when we were reasonably sure we were over the target we released a parachute flare and, we hoped, illuminated the target. The route, altitude and so on were left to each crew, and you made up your own strategy for the attack in the light of what you found out when you got there – cloud cover, opposition, whatever.

This account reveals more of the problems and constraints affecting British bomber operations at this time. Weather forecasts were poor, target-marking unknown, formation bombing non-existent. Pressing an attack home came down to the skill and dedication of the individual aircrews and, although the 'Press on' spirit of Bomber Command was already appearing, this was not in itself enough to mount an effective bombing campaign against Germany, even had the crews been permitted to do so.

Worse was to follow. Operations over Germany continued throughout the winter of 1939–40, but on most of them the aircraft carried nothing more lethal than leaflets. These leaflet drops – code-named *Nickel* operations – were made by Whitley aircraft and continued throughout the long winter months of the 'Phoney War', the period between the outbreak of war in 1939 and the German attack on France and the Low Countries in May 1940. Although *Nickel* raids achieved very little and caused a number of losses, they were allowed to continue because they gave the crews operational experience.

Bombing operations were fairly primitive at this time, certainly in relation to what came later, as Robert 'Topper' Brown of No. 61 Squadron describes:

In early 1940 there were two pilots per aircraft in Hampdens – one acting as navigator – plus a wireless operator/air gunner and a rear gunner. Helmswell was one of three stations in 5 Group under the command of Arthur Harris. I never met him, but I do remember he had the reputation at that early stage of being forceful and aggressive as far as the enemy were concerned. We flew on operations independently, not in formation, and there would probably be only six crews from the squadron out at any one time. There was no such thing as mass bombing, as we simply did not have the number of aircraft. As far as briefing before the raids was concerned, the crews were called together in the early evening and simply given details of the target, the weather forecast and the wind directions. Normally it was not difficult to find the target area but almost impossible to be anywhere near a specific target, so we just dropped the bombs at an estimated position and hoped for the best. I very much doubt if we ever hit a specific target.

Pointing out this inability to hit specific targets is not to imply that a strategic role for Bomber Command was not being considered. An Air Targets Sub-Committee had been set up and was busy putting forward suggestions for attacks on Germany's power supplies – particularly oil refineries, coking plants and power stations – as well as transportation links like marshalling yards and canals. These plans were held in abeyance to avoid causing civilian casualties which would provoke the *Luftwaffe* into reprisals. It was also appreciated that to find and hit these targets would call for a higher standard of training and more sophisticated equipment than the RAF squadrons currently possessed.

More serious operations were attempted, including an early attack on shipping near Heligoland – an operation mounted on 29 September by eleven Hampden bombers from No. 144 Squadron, 5 Group. Two German warships were found and bombed without results – and then the Me 109s appeared, shooting down five aircraft including that of the squadron commander; 45 per cent of the aircraft taking part were lost and eighteen aircrew were killed.

By now, almost a month into the war, it was beginning to dawn on the RAF that finding the target, never mind hitting it, was not the easiest of tasks. Daylight operations were discontinued but leaflet operations went ahead until December, when the *Luftwaffe* again demonstrated that the cost of daylight operations could be unacceptably high. On 14 December twelve Wellingtons from No. 99 Squadron took off to hunt for the German cruisers *Leipzig* and *Nürnberg*. The weather was foul, but the aircraft found the target and attacked at low level, being greeted by a storm of flak as they went in. Then German Me 109s arrived and rapidly shot down five Wellingtons and damaged a sixth, which crashed on arriving back in Britain. This was a loss rate of 50 per cent and, although one Me 109 had been shot down, no bombs had hit either of the German cruisers.

Four days later, on 18 December, in perfect weather, 24 Wellingtons of Nos. 9, 37 and 149 Squadrons, were dispatched to Wilhelmshaven and ordered to fly about and attack 'targets of opportunity' – any shipping they happened to find – but on no account to fly below 10,000 ft, to avoid the worst of the flak. These aircraft were intercepted by Me 109s, which shot down twelve of the Wellingtons – 50 per cent of the attacking force – for the loss of two German fighters. This rate of attrition could not continue, and Air Chief Marshal Ludlow-Hewitt, AOC-in-C of Bomber Command, was ordered to consider a switch to night bombing.[3] The complete failure to develop the heavy bomber as a strategic weapon was suddenly revealed, as were the pre-war failures to make the bomber viable in the face of fighter attacks.

Dereck French, an Australian pilot, confirms this point:

> The first rule in war is 'Be prepared', and frankly we weren't. In the pre-war RAF we thought we were well trained and equipped, but when we began our operational flying we discovered that we were undertrained and our aircraft were not as good as we had been led to believe. We could not defend ourselves. We had .303 machine-guns when we should have had larger calibre or even cannon. We did not have armour plating or self-sealing fuel tanks, and we did not get them until after 1940. Why? As for the training, when I commenced bombing operations I had as much experience as any other squadron pilot, yet I had flown only 3 hours and 30 minutes at night, in twin-engined aircraft. It is no wonder we had such high casualties.

Daylight operations continued, but on a much-reduced scale. For a time at least the main focus of Bomber Command operations was on anti-shipping patrols in the North Sea, on mine-laying – code-named *Gardening* – which was to prove highly successful against German shipping and submarines, and on those night leafleting sorties to Germany – a task which, said Air Vice-Marshal Arthur Harris, then commanding 5 Group, 'served to supply the Continent's requirement for toilet paper for the five long years of war'.

Night bombing might have been safer, but it had an inherent snag. Even in daylight the bombers had difficulty finding their targets; at night this task was virtually impossible, and it would remain so until some means had been evolved to help the RAF navigators. The only method then in use was dead reckoning (DR), supplemented at night by astro-navigation, taking a star 'fix' to establish the position of the aircraft. Both were tried-and-tested peacetime methods, and both proved woefully inadequate in war. Dead reckoning is simple in theory but far less so in practice. The navigator – though this was a task for the pilot or second pilot at this time – plots a course between his base and the target and, having calculated the speed of the aircraft and the effect of wind, lays off a course that will take the aircraft from one to the other in a given number of hours.

The pilot then flies this course – hopefully accurately – and on the way the 'navigator' or observer checks progress by visual observation of points on the ground that should appear below if the course set is correct, the effect of wind has been accurately calculated, and the pilot has kept to the correct compass heading. Clearly, this method is more useful in daylight than at night, but even in daylight it has its limitations. European weather is often poor, especially in winter, and cloud or mist can obscure reference points on the ground in any season. The scope for error is obvious even in daylight, and navigation errors on DR were almost inevitable at night.

Astro-navigation, fixing the position of the aircraft on the track flown by reference to the stars, is even more tricky and requires clear skies and a navigator skilled in the use of a sextant. Few RAF navigators had such skills, and there was also the matter of aircraft speed. Celestial navigation is all right on ships, which move relatively slowly. However, aircraft flying at speeds around 200 m.p.h. will have moved on a considerable distance before the navigator can finish his calculations and give the pilot an accurate position and the necessary course corrections. In an attempt to improve standards of navigation, a special ten-week course had been introduced in 1938; although this must have raised standards, during exercises in August 1939 it was discovered that more than 40 per cent of RAF crews were unable to find a British city *even in broad daylight – and in peacetime*.

Even so, since these daylight losses could not be sustained, a switch to night bombing, where losses on *Nickel* operations were running at around 2 per cent, was clearly advisable. These began on 19/20 March 1940, when 50 aircraft – Whitleys and Hampdens – were sent to attack the seaplane base on the German island of Sylt. It was a bright, moonlit night, and 41 aircraft found the target and accurately bombed it – or so the crews claimed at the subsequent debriefing. This sounded good, until a photoreconnaissance mission brought back pictures of the seaplane base which failed to reveal any sign of bomb damage at all.

Dereck French, of No. 50 Squadron, recalls this operation:

> From the outbreak of war until about the end of the Battle of Britain, great emphasis was placed on the limitations to targets: for months we were not allowed to fly over German territory or attack any land targets. The idea behind this was to avoid German civilian casualties and a possible escalation of the war. This limitation was lifted on 20 March 1940, when we attacked the naval base on the island of Sylt. Twenty Hampdens and a number of Whitleys from 5 Group went on this raid, and on return to Waddington we were told that a DFC had been awarded to J. J. Bennett of No. 50 Squadron, the most senior pilot on the trip. This system of decorating the most senior surviving member of an operation was the norm in those days, and even extended to VCs, as after the Dortmund–Ems canal raid in June 1940. However, a few days later, after our navigation logs had been checked, it was discovered that Bennett had bombed Esbjerg in Denmark – for which error the British government paid compensation. Bennett retained his DFC and earned it many times over in subsequent operations.
>
> Our bombing accuracy in those days was poor, and this could have been a factor in the evolution of – so-called – precision bombing into area bombing. The fear of bombing civilians was certainly to the fore during the Norway campaign, when a squadron of Hampdens from Waddington were

sent out to find and attack German shipping but were recalled after doubts were expressed that they might cause Norwegian casualties. There was definitely an awareness about this. I can remember that when it was proposed that we should bomb Heidelberg in Germany there was argument about this among the intelligence officers, though I cannot recall the outcome. This would have been in the first year of the war, when I cannot recall any briefings specifying 'open city' targets – our targets were definitely of a strategic, military, nature.

The pattern of indifferent results and heavy losses continued into the spring and summer of 1940, during the Norwegian campaign and the German surge into the Low Countries and France, which culminated in the evacuation of the British Expeditionary Force from Dunkirk in June 1940. One event in this second German *Blitzkrieg* was another city raid, the bombing of the Dutch port of Rotterdam, although, as with Warsaw, this attack took place after the garrison had declined to surrender to the encircling Germans.

The Dutch defenders were advised to capitulate on 13 May, and that evening the general commanding the German 39th Panzer Korps told the Dutch that, unless resistance was brought to a close at once, the city would suffer 'complete destruction'. Negotiations broke down and a storm of high-explosive bombs devastated the old heart of the city on the afternoon of 14 May 1940.[4] A fire storm then swept through the streets, and at 2030 hrs that night the German Army entered the city. It later transpired that the Dutch garrison had surrendered before the air raid but, although the German commander had attempted to recall the bombers, the message had not got through.

Bill Jacobs of No. 102 Squadron flew over Rotterdam on 16 May:

We were able to see for ourselves the dreadful effects of the German bombing of Rotterdam. Our bombing effort was now directed against the Ruhr industry and railways, and I believe our attack on the night of 16 May was the first strategic attack of the war. At the briefing for this raid the intelligence chap told us that Rotterdam would be our landfall but not to worry as we would be at about 10,000 ft and the Germans did not have anything in the area to affect us. We took off at 2157 hrs and soon saw before us the raging inferno that was Rotterdam, with smoke rising densely to well above our height. Most of the smoke seemed to be coming from the port area and the seaward side of the city. We were looking at the scene below when there was a flash and the loudest detonation we had yet experienced – a flak burst. So much for the idea that nothing could touch us at 10,000 ft!

During the period of the Battle of France – 10 May to 29 June 1940 – I flew on sixteen operations and logged a total of 104 hours and 50 minutes operational night flying. Four of these operations were between 14 and 24 June, including one to the oil refinery at Gelsenkirchen and one to Mannheim on the 24th. This was a rough trip, with dense cloud over the target area, lightning,

searchlights and intense flak. We had to stooge about a bit too and get down
dangerously low over the target, where we got a large dose of concentrated
light flak which was bloody fearsome to say the least, but our minds were occupied with the task in hand. After 7 hours and 15 minutes we landed back at
Stradishall, gasping for fuel ... and so it went on, to Duisburg (another hot spot)
on the 27th, and the ammunition factory at Hochst on the 29th and so on ... we
had now lost a number of aircraft and crews and the rate of loss was to increase.

With the bombing of Rotterdam another prop against city bombing was
knocked away, and within a month the Germans had succeeded in
pushing the British Expeditionary Force off the Continent. With the fall of
France, and Britain's refusal to surrender, the German Army now had to
invade England. To do that, however, the *Luftwaffe* had first to defeat the
RAF fighter force in what was to become the Battle of Britain.

RAF Bomber Command had already moved on to strategic bombing.
The official history dates this move from 15 May 1940, when 99 bombers
were sent to attack oil and railway targets in the Ruhr – and 'Thus began
the Bomber Command strategic air offensive against Germany.'[5] During
the period leading up to the collapse of France and the Dunkirk evacuation, the RAF concentrated its efforts against German oil targets, refusing
French demands for army tactical support other than by the obsolescent
Fairey Battles of the Advanced Air Striking Force (AASF) which was
already in France, and declining to weaken the air defences of Britain by
sending more fighter squadrons – especially Spitfire squadrons – across the
Channel.

Whether, given such assistance, the French and British armies in France
could have withstood the German onslaught is debatable. The Anglo-
French armies were so ill-equipped for mobile warfare and so stunned by
the speed of the German advance that the available air power would have
probably been inadequate to tilt the balance and stave off defeat.

After Dunkirk came the Battle of Britain. This lasted from the end of June
until October 1940, and ended in victory for Fighter Command. Bomber
Command was also active in this period, bombing the invasion barges the
Germans were assembling in the Channel ports and attacking German
troop concentrations and airfields. The Battle of Britain also provided some
useful lessons in bomber operations, not least a second example, provided
this time by the *Luftwaffe*, that bombers, even when escorted by fighters,
were very vulnerable to defending fighters in daylight. The air assault on
Britain was launched from close range and the German fighters were able
to escort the bombers from bases in France and the Low Countries as far
as London, but they could not stay around long after reaching that point.

The RAF fighters also had the advantage of radar control from the
ground, which directed them on to the German formations, and were able
to take off and gain height before the German squadrons crossed the coast
of Kent or Essex. As a result, though the *Luftwaffe* losses claimed by the

RAF pilots were exaggerated, the *Luftwaffe* suffered a decisive defeat in daylight and was forced to turn its attention to night bombing – the Blitz. This night bombing, even if aimed at legitimate military and economic targets, like the London docks and railway stations or naval bases like Portsmouth and Plymouth, inevitably caused severe casualties among the civilian population.

The strategic lesson leading to the Blitz of 1940–41 was that yet another air force, the *Luftwaffe*, having sustained severe losses in daylight operations – as had Bomber Command – was forced to switch to night operations – as had Bomber Command – even though the *Luftwaffe* did have a reasonable degree of fighter cover. Granted, *Luftwaffe* daylight losses were smaller than Bomber Command's in percentage terms, but they were still unacceptable and could not be sustained. The conclusion drawn from this was that no air force could keep up a daylight bombing campaign once the losses got too high, and night bombing was therefore the only possible alternative – though that would not be effective without the use of radio or radar aids.

British histories of the Battle of Britain rightly praise the use of radar as a vital element in the air defence of Great Britain. Without the use of radar as part of a fully integrated fighter-control system, it is arguable that the Battle of Britain could not have been won. This well-known fact tends to conceal another fact: that the *Luftwaffe* had the use of several equally useful navigation and bombing aids to aid its night bombing campaign against Britain, the first of which became generally known as the *Knickebein*.

Evidence of this particular bombing and navigation aid first came to light in March 1940, in a scrap of paper found in a shot-down German bomber referring to 'Radio Beacon *Knickebein*, from 0600 hrs on [bearing] 315 degrees'.[6] All shot-down bombers were routinely examined by scientists, British or German, for signs of new inventions, and the RAF scientists were already aware that the Germans had a radio navigation device, though no one was sure what this was or how it worked. The hope was that this *Knickebein* was something similar and, by interrogating captured German aircrew and by scanning the airwaves electronically, steps were taken to find out more about it.

The full story of the 'Battle of the Beams' and how it was won has been told elsewhere,[7] but, put simply, the *Knickebein* consisted of two radio beams laid over Britain from stations in Germany or, after the fall of France, from stations in Western Europe. One station would lay a beam directly across Britain, running through a target city such as Coventry. Another beam, from another station, would 'cut' this first beam over Coventry. All the bomber pilot had to do was to fly down the first beam, kept on course by a series of Morse code 'dots' on one side and 'dashes' on the other, until the sound of the 'cutting' beam told the bomb-aimer that the plane was over the target and the bombs could be dropped.

This system had been developed from the *Lorenz* blind-landing system which was widely used by the civil aircraft of many nations before the war broke out. It had been believed that the *Lorenz* system could not be used over long distances, since the beam would be blocked by the curvature of the earth. Clearly, the Germans had got round this problem and were now ahead of the British in some aspects of radio communications. While the British were trying to combat this new development – and not letting on that they knew about it – the Germans began the night bombing of British cities, culminating in November 1940 with a devastating night attack on the city of Coventry, the most notorious in the winter-long Blitz.

The Blitz began on 7 September 1940, when German bombers attacked London in daylight and returned that night to 'stoke up' the fires left burning below. By dawn, 306 Londoners had been killed and over 1,300 had been wounded. This German night attack was not made simply because daylight bombing operations were becoming too expensive: there was also an element of retaliation – even of pique. On the night of 25/26 August 1940, following daylight attacks on London, the British government had authorized an attack on Berlin. Only about 50 bombers managed to find Berlin, though the city covers an area of several hundred square miles, and bombs were dropped through heavy cloud to damage a summer house and injure two people; other bombs fell harmlessly in open country south of the city.

Although this attack achieved very little – a euphemism for absolutely nothing – it embarrassed Reichmarshal Hermann Goering, who had promised the citizens that if any bombs fell on Berlin 'you can call me Maier'.[8] Goering talked to Hitler and a reprisal raid was ordered on London, where the results were far more damaging. From then on, London and a number of other British cities – Manchester, Birmingham, Liverpool, Bristol and many more – were raided night after night for months, right through the winter and early spring of 1940–1, before the bulk of the *Luftwaffe* was drawn off for the invasion of Russia, Operation BARBAROSSA, in June 1941.

Although most of the children were evacuated to the countryside – over a million of these 'evacuees' left London alone – their parents and elder siblings stayed on in the cities to work. In the first three weeks of the Blitz some 7,000 British civilians were killed. A single raid on Glasgow killed or injured 1,200 people, and by the summer of 1941 the British civilian death toll had reached over 40,000, with another 60,000 being seriously injured. Almost a quarter of a million homes were destroyed, and more than three-quarters of a million people were made homeless. Nor was Britain spared firestorms: on the night of 29 December 1940, hundreds of incendiaries fell in a two-mile area around St Paul's Cathedral in the City of London; high winds fanned the flames and before long 1,500 separate fires were raging in London, many of them out of control, the two largest covering an area of nearly two square miles. On that night Germany 'sowed the wind' for the whirlwind that would engulf Hamburg and other German cities in the years to come.

But the raids had little effect on civilian morale – and civilian spirits perked up considerably after anti-aircraft guns were brought into London and positioned in the parks to blaze away into the night sky at the droning bombers. However, the generally phlegmatic British reaction to German bombing does not mean that there were no instances of panic. John Scott, later an air gunner with Coastal Command, remembers one evening in London during the Blitz:

> In those days, early in the war, when the air-raid siren sounded a notice to that effect would appear on cinema screens, asking those who wanted to go to the shelters to leave quietly. On this occasion we were in a cinema near Victoria station when the manager appeared on the stage and told us that bombs were dropping. A few minutes later we could hear them; everyone rose and headed for the exits. In the streets outside there was chaos – people charging about, shouting, searchlights flashing, guns going off, bombs dropping, and already the glow from fires in the sky over the river. It was very frightening, and there was sometimes a lot of panic before people got used to these nightly raids.

When the Blitz began, those who could get away left the cities to find refuge in the countryside. The heavily bombed working class of East London came to resent the shelter facilities enjoyed by the inhabitants of the West End, and on one occasion a mob invaded some of the smarter London hotels. There were similar instances in other bombed cities, so there was some reason for the British government to believe that bombing could affect civilian morale, unless the civil defence was adequate and the anti-aircraft guns and defending fighters were seen to be hitting back. However, the general attitude in Britain was one of dogged determination to endure – a view typified by the action of Lady Rachel MacRobert.

By 1941 Lady MacRobert had lost her three sons in this war, all while flying with the RAF. One was killed in training, another was shot down while strafing a German aerodrome, and the last – Ian MacRobert, aged 24 – was lost over the North Sea in 1941 while searching for the crew of a shot-down bomber. These successive blows might have shattered any mother, but Lady MacRobert was made of sterner stuff. She responded to her loss by sending a cheque for £25,000 to the Secretary of State for Air, Sir Archibald Sinclair, ordering him to buy a Stirling bomber for No. XV Squadron and send it against the enemy; this aircraft was to be called *MacRobert's Reply.* 'If I had ten sons', wrote Lady MacRobert, 'I know they would all have followed that path of duty . . . and may the blows you strike with her bring us nearer to Victory.'

Stan Smith was one of the ground crew servicing the first *MacRobert's Reply*:

> On 28 January 1942, ten aircraft left Alconbury for Lossiemouth, each carrying a 2,000 lb bomb and two ground crew. I was flying in Stirling No. 6086, *F for Freddie* – *MacRobert's Reply* – and the pilot was Flight Officer 'Red' King. From Lossiemouth we flew some abortive sorties against the battleship *Tirpitz*, and on 8 February we flew back to Wyton – or we tried to. Just before becoming airborne we lost power on both port engines and, slewing off the runway at about 70 knots, crashed through a Spitfire dispersal, finishing up with our nose in the mud, the port undercarriage bent, and a Spitfire we had collected on the way jammed under our tail.
>
> Luckily no one was hurt, and I was left behind with a bent aircraft and instructions to remove the MacRobert crest, the bombsight and the clock, and an aircraft would come and collect me in a few days. Unfortunately, though I removed the crest, I did not paint out the words *MacRobert's Reply* and ten days after I got back to the squadron I was sent for by the CO, who put a flea in my ear. Apparently the 'Queen Mary' transporter, carrying the fuselage, had passed through Stirling and Aberdeen and word of what had happened had got back to Lady MacRobert, who was not best pleased. The aircraft was repaired in Cambridge and went to No 1651 Conversion Unit and the crest went to another aircraft, which was lost in a minelaying sortie later in the war, when the name was transferred to a Lancaster bomber.

Since that time No. XV Squadron has always had an aircraft called *MacRobert's Reply*; the MacRobert crest is currently – 2000 – being carried by a Tornado GR1.

The nightly fusillade from the guns of London achieved very little against the *Luftwaffe* and littered the streets with jagged shell fragments – shrapnel – but it did wonders for the morale of the people in the shelters and the Underground stations, who now felt that they were not just sitting there and taking it: in some way they were also hitting back. In the morning, these people emerged from their shelters and went back to work, stepping carefully round craters and shattered buildings. 'Britain can take it' was the national watchword, and the endurance of the Londoners under the bombing attracted the admiration of the world. The German attack on Coventry, on the night of 14/15 November 1940, attracted only horror, although, as an industrial town, Coventry was a legitimate target.

The first intimation of the Coventry attack came from deciphered intercepts of German radio messages encrypted by the *Enigma* coding machine. On Sunday 11 November 1940, the *Enigma* decoders at Bletchley Park reported that a major German air operation was being planned and would shortly be launched against one of three targets in England. By the evening of 14 November it was known that the target was in the Midlands, but the detailed *Enigma* intercept was not broken until the morning of 15 November.[9] There is therefore no truth in the story that the British Prime

Minister Winston Churchill knew that Coventry was the target but chose to let the city be destroyed in order to preserve the secret that *Enigma* had been cracked.

The scientists had equipped RAF aircraft from a new formation, No. 80 Wing, with the means to jam the *Knickebein* – if they knew where it was laid. Lacking that information, they had to roam the skies and try to pick it up. This proved inadequate in the circumstances and over 500 bombers, led by pathfinders of the *Luftwaffe's* KG 100 (Kampfgeschwader or Battle Wing 100) were on their way to Coventry soon after dark on the evening of 14 November. The first flares lit the skies over Coventry by 1915 hrs and the *Luftwaffe* stayed over Coventry for the rest of the night, bombing the fires below, stoking them up with fresh showers of incendiaries. The destruction of this city gave such destruction a new word – to *coventrate*.

Five hundred tons of bombs fell on Coventry that night, and 60,000 buildings were destroyed, including more than half the private houses in the city centre and the cathedral. More than 500 people were killed, over 1,200 were injured, and Coventry joined Warsaw, Rotterdam and Guernica in the growing list of European towns shattered by bombing – 'coventrated'.

The destruction of Coventry shocked the British people and led to an immediate call for reprisals. The high ideals with which the RAF and the British government had entered the war were being rapidly eroded by the realities of the conflict; enemy morale was now a prime target, and the way to attack it was by bombing the enemy out of house and home, factory and warehouse, by attacks on cities, which were the only strategic targets the bombers could bomb – always supposing they could find them. Attacks on Coventry and Southampton had shown how a city might be attacked and, although the RAF had no navigation aid like the *Knickebein*, greater bombing accuracy could be obtained with the use of flares. A month after the destruction of Coventry, on the night of 16/17 December 1940, the RAF launched a reprisal raid – code-named *Abigail Rachel* – by 134 bombers against the Rhineland city of Mannheim.

The Mannheim force consisted of the full variety of Bomber Command aircraft: 61 Wellingtons, 35 Whitleys, 29 Hampdens and nine Blenheims. Mannheim had plenty of military and industrial targets, including the I.G. Farben chemical factory, a river port and marshalling yards, but the target on this night was the city itself – a departure from the motives and targeting of all previous RAF raids. This, the first RAF 'area' operation of the war, was a reprisal for Coventry – and one specifically ordered by the War Cabinet. It was a clear, moonlit night and the city defences had not yet been developed, so there was very little flak. The first wave of eight Wellingtons attempted to illuminate the target by dropping flares and incendiaries over the centre of the city. The incendiaries certainly started fires, but the rest of the bombing was wildly inaccurate.

The Mannheim City Archives reveal that some 500 buildings were destroyed or damaged by fire or high explosives; 115 people were killed or injured, and over 1,000 people lost their homes. About 200 of these lived in the town of Ludwigshafen on the far side of the river. Most of the bombs that landed on Mannheim fell in residential areas and, although the railway station and some river barges were hit, so were a hospital and a school. Three aircraft were lost: two Hampdens and a Blenheim.

The raid was considered a highly successful operation until a week later, when an RAF reconnaissance Spitfire brought back some aerial photographs revealing to the new AOC-in-C, Bomber Command, Air Marshal Sir Richard Peirse, that 'the operation had failed in its primary objective . . . although considerable damage had been done, the photographs showed a wide dispersal of the attack'. Nevertheless, with the raid on Mannheim, another plank was laid on the platform of the bomber war. City bombing was now an accepted policy, carried out by both sides without any attempt to disguise the fact by naming military targets within the urban conurbation.

Air Marshal Peirse had taken over as chief of Bomber Command in October 1940. That month saw a number of other changes in the RAF command structure, not least in the appointment of Air Chief Marshal Sir Charles Portal, KCB, DSO, MC, the previous head of Bomber Command, to the post of Chief of the Air Staff, Portal having taken over Bomber Command from Sir Edgar Ludlow-Hewitt in April 1940. Portal was to remain the head of the RAF for the rest of the war, and his career and character should be examined now.

Charles Frederick Algernon Portal – known to friends and family as Peter – was born in June 1893, a scion of an English county family from Hungerford in Berkshire, a family that contained six other boys. He was educated at Winchester and Christ Church, Oxford, where he intended to study law, although his main interests at this time were hawking, sport and riding a fast motorcycle. When war broke out in 1914 this last interest took him into the Motor-Cycle Section of the Royal Engineers with the rank of corporal. He was immediately sent to France, and for his work during the BEF retreat from Mons to the Marne he was awarded both a commission and a mention in dispatches. In July 1915 he transferred to the Royal Flying Corps as an observer for the artillery, flying in Morane Parasols from which he occasionally engaged German fighters with fire from a Winchester rifle.

In January 1916 Portal started training as a pilot, graduating in April 1916 as a temporary lieutenant (flying officer, observer) RFC, with a total of 29 hours in the air, dual and solo. He was posted to France to join No. 60 Squadron, and survived the Battle of the Somme and numerous other engagements to become CO of No. 16 Squadron in June 1917. When the Great War ended in November 1918 Portal was a Lieutenant Colonel, with two DSOs, the Military Cross and two mentions in dispatches – all by the age of 25. Portal then decided to make the newly formed RAF his career, and he was granted a permanent commission in August 1919 with the rank of squadron leader.

Portal was already seen as a rising star, and he rose steadily during the inter-war years, which he spent in both staff and operational duties. He spent two and a half years as chief flying instructor at the RAF College, Cranwell, where his 'rockets' to careless or reckless cadets, if rarely delivered, were never forgotten. He was a strict disciplinarian: according to his biographer, Denis Richards, 'when he gave an order he was always sure in his own mind that it could be executed and ensured that it was and if the execution proved difficult he expected his subordinates to use their ingenuity. If the subordinate failed too frequently, Portal got another subordinate.'[10]

In 1922 Portal attended the first course held at the new RAF Staff College, where his fellow students included such people as Sholto Douglas, later chief of Fighter Command, Richard Peirse, who was to succeed Portal at Bomber Command, and New Zealander Keith Park, who was to command 11 Group, Fighter Command, in the Battle of Britain. The RAF staff course lasted a year, and in 1923 Portal went to the Directorate of Operations at the Air Ministry, where he stayed for three years and took part in the ongoing struggle waged by Trenchard to keep the RAF in being. In 1925 he was promoted to wing commander, and in March 1927 he took command of No. 7 Squadron, a unit equipped with Vickers Virginia bombers and based at RAF Worthy Down, near Winchester.

There were three other heavy-bomber squadrons at Worthy Down, and one of them, No. 58, was commanded by Wing Commander Arthur Harris. One of the plum jobs in the RAF of the time was the chance to participate in the annual Hendon Air Display, and the way to get that job was by success in a bombing and navigation competition. No. 58 Squadron had won in 1924, and it was anticipated, not least by Harris, that they would win again in 1926, but in fact Portal's squadron won with a score of 763 marks out of a possible 800. In 1927 and 1928 Portal acted as bomb-aimer for his squadron's entry in the Lawrence Minot Memorial Trophy and scored the highest number of hits on each occasion.

In 1928 he attended a course at the Imperial Defence College in London, which was followed by a tour of RAF bases in India before he returned to the Air Ministry, where he stayed for three years. In 1934 he took command of the RAF base at Aden, where the forces under his command took on 'air control' of the Radfan tribes on the Yemen frontier.

By now, in the mid-1930s, Hitler had already come to power in Germany and the RAF was gradually expanding to meet a growing threat. In 1936 Portal returned to the UK to join the staff of the Imperial Defence College, where he stayed until the middle of 1937, leaving on promotion to air vice-marshal to become Director of Organization at the Air Ministry. Here he was responsible for the provision of equipment and stores and the control of transportation and works – a job which, in this period of expansion, kept him extremely busy. He later became responsible for the balloon barrage – and the formation of Balloon Command – and the supply of aviation fuel and camouflage.

These duties, time-consuming and important though they were, took second place to his main task of organizing personnel – especially the vital matter of reserves, notably with the Royal Auxiliary Air Force and the Royal Air Force Volunteer Reserve, which had been founded in 1936. Portal was also involved in the establishing of what were then called 'group pools' within the various operational Commands, including Bomber Command – units in which trainees could be brought up to full operational standards. These 'pools' later became known as operational training units (OTUs).

In February 1939 Portal became a member of the Air Council as Air Member for Personnel, and was now directly responsible for many of the training schemes that prepared RAF volunteers for imminent war. One function was the establishing of flying training schools in Canada, where, in the clear skies and open plains of Alberta, British aircrews, especially pilots, could quickly get in the required number of flying hours. The idea was that the Royal Canadian Air Force (RCAF) would undertake this training task, and in April 1939 the RCAF agreed to train 50 RAF pilots a year. On the outbreak of war this scheme was rapidly expanded into the Empire Air Training Scheme (EATS). Bob Smith, an Australian navigator in No. XV Squadron, 3 Group, was one of thousands of airmen who took part in this scheme:

I would say that the Empire Air Training Scheme was regarded as the greatest experience ever by those who took part in it. It brought together members from all parts of the Empire, for six months or more, in another Commonwealth country where we made friends and met people with a common language. I trained as a navigator at No. 2 Air Observer School in Edmonton, Canada. Our aircraft were Avro Ansons, and our instructors were bush pilots who knew the country like the backs of their hands.

It was probably not the best introduction to the problems of flying over Europe. With clear skies and visibility to the horizon over the prairies, your destination on any leg of an exercise was always visible and the bush pilot always seemed to be on track, no matter what heading you gave him. Theory and practical training was intense, as you had to qualify for your 'wings' after four months, following about 75–80 hours of daylight flying and 35–40 hours of night flying. Training comprised navigation, maps and charts, magnetism and compasses, wireless, meteorology, photography, signals, armament and aircraft recognition, plus a few more. By the end of the war it was apparent that the EATS had developed into a highly efficient system for training aircrew of all categories, and by the end of 1944 the scheme was strengthened by operationally experienced instructors.

The EATS eventually consisted of 80 separate flying schools – in Canada, Rhodesia, Australia and New Zealand, and also in the USA, which, under what became known as the 'Arnold Scheme', was training aircrew for the RAF in Florida, Arizona and Texas in 1940–1, long before the United States entered the war. These EATS schools covered the main aspects of aircrew training, from elementary flying training to bombing, navigation and air-observation. The prime task was to produce pilots and navigators, and by mid-1942 the EATS schools were capable of producing 11,000 pilots a year and up to 17,000 other aircrew, mainly navigators and bomb-aimers; the other bomber crew members – gunners, flight engineers and radio operators – were usually trained in Britain.

Portal stayed on the Air Council until 13 April 1940, when, having been promoted Air Marshal, he replaced Air Chief Marshal Sir Edgar Ludlow-Hewitt as AOC-in-C, Bomber Command. Ludlow-Hewitt was a highly-efficient officer who did great service for the RAF, but he did not trouble to conceal the deficiencies in his Command from the powers that be in Whitehall. Ludlow-Hewitt had not believed that the light bomber squadrons containing the obsolescent, single-engined Battles should be sent to France in 1939 to form a bombing element in the Advanced Air Striking Force, and, as he rightly predicted, they proved useless and were shot down in quantity. That was bad enough, but when Ludlow-Hewitt insisted that he could not attack Germany by day without hazarding the majority of the force committed, and demanded not only a longer and more rigorous training for bomber crews but also the assigning of scarce new aircraft types to the operational training units – and was entirely right to do so – his days were numbered. A 'more optimistic' commander was called for, and Portal took over Bomber Command on 4 April 1940.

The force Portal took over consisted of just 24 operational squadrons, containing a mixture of Wellingtons, Blenheims, Whitleys and Hampdens. Fifteen of these squadrons – a total of 240 aircraft – were available for strategic bombing, with perhaps two-thirds of their aircraft being serviceable and ready for operations at any one time. Portal stayed at Bomber Command for only six months, until October 1940, through the Norwegian campaign, the fall of France and the Battle of Britain. During this time, bomber operations largely consisted of *Nickel* operations over Germany and mining operations in the North Sea. Mining, mostly by Arthur Harris's 5 Group, was proving fairly successful, but the campaign in Norway and operations of the AASF in France, from the opening of the German attack in May up to the evacuation at Dunkirk in June, cost the RAF a great many good crews for no visible gain.

By the autumn of 1940 Britain had survived the Battle of Britain and the immediate threat of invasion, but the future looked bleak and the pros- pects of carrying the war to the enemy by strategic bombing seemed extremely remote. Daylight bombing was impossible, night bombing was inaccurate, navigation and target-marking were a matter of luck rather than judgement. At this juncture the thoughts of those charged with the bomber offensive turned inevitably to area bombing – an attack on German cities. This thought was certainly in Portal's mind when in October 1940 he took up the post of Chief of the Air Staff (CAS), which made him the most powerful RAF officer in Britain. He was to remain in this post for the rest of the war, and his actions and decisions in that post – and his relationship with Arthur Harris – form the main core of his rele- vance to this book.

'Peter' Portal was a man of fixed views, and once his mind was made up he was not eager to change it. For example, he did not believe in the need to provide the bomber formations with long-range fighter escorts, largely on the grounds that a short-range fighter was inherently more manoeuv- rable: 'Increased range can only be provided at the expense of performance and manoeuvrability . . . The long-range fighter, whether built as such or whether given increased range by fitting extra fuel tanks, will be at a dis- advantage compared with the short-range, high-performance fighter.'[11] Portal was wrong in this assessment, but he stuck to this view for some time to come.

There is some evidence that he was a firm supporter of city bombing. This evidence has to be sought carefully in the records but the picture that emerges is that he was an advocate of area bombing and attacks on morale. During his time as AOC-in-C, Bomber Command, Portal was dubious about the targets proposed in the Air Staff Directives of 13 July, revised and reissued on 24 July 1940. (Such Directives were orders which gave Harris and his predecessors a strategic direction for the forces under command, although the detail of the actual implementation of the Directives was left to the AOC-in-C, who therefore had some room for manoeuvre.) These particular directives called for attacks on precision targets ranging from oil refineries to aircraft factories and aluminium smelters, which Portal objected to largely on the ground that these targets were 'too small to be found with any certainty on moonlit nights by average crews'.

By September 1940 Portal had moved further and suggested that a great effect on German morale could be achieved if twenty German towns were told they were to be targeted – this dire news being passed on by the BBC – and were then attacked by upwards of 150 aircraft which would drop about 130 tons of bombs on each operation. These attacks were to be made on towns like Essen, the home of the Krupps armament factory, or on other towns with known military objectives – but the focus of attack would be the town, not the factories.

Portal continued to press for attacks on German morale until he left

Bomber Command on promotion to CAS. This promotion put him in a position to order a policy he had previously been able only to suggest, and he was not long in doing so. On 25 October a draft Directive was sent to Portal's successor at Bomber Command, Air Marshal Sir Richard Peirse, stating that, now the immediate threat of invasion was over, the time was 'particularly opportune to make a definite attempt with our offensive to attack the morale of the German people'.[12] The way to do this, the Directive suggested, was to pick 20 or 30 German cities and attack them with 50 or 100 bombers every few nights. This could be done during the dark periods, with attacks on the smaller oil targets being made on moonlit nights.

Peirse had inherited a force which had suffered a great deal and was, if not disheartened or demoralized, at least somewhat disillusioned with the way it had been used in recent months. Nothing had been achieved, many friends had been lost, and it was clear to all that unless and until some aids to navigation and bomb-aiming were produced by the scientists – the 'boffins' – nothing much could be achieved, certainly in the coming winter, while the Blitz on London and other British cities continued unabated.

There was another change at this time when Air Vice-Marshal Arthur Harris left 5 Group and went to Washington as part of the British Military Mission, the body charged with buying equipment and supplies for the British armed forces. Harris was replaced at 5 Group by Air Vice-Marshal Norman Bottomley.

On 30 October 1940 Peirse received a revised Directive from the Air Ministry, advising him that Germany's oil supplies were to be his *primary* target and must be attacked whenever conditions permitted, but he was also directed to attack industrial targets, railway yards and ports, to lay mines and to attack airfields. This Directive merely emphasized the original draft, for, whatever the specific targets chosen, other than oil, the main objective was to undermine German morale. To that end, the attacks were to be opened with incendiaries, then 'successive sorties [i.e. aircraft] should focus their attacks on the fires, with a view to preventing the fire fighting services dealing with them and giving the fires every opportunity to spread'.

The official history points out that 'Thus the fiction that the bombers were attacking military objectives in the towns was officially abandoned. This was the technique which was to become known as area bombing.'[13] It would therefore appear that the introduction of area bombing, the charge so often laid against Sir Arthur Harris, can be traced directly to Sir Charles Portal, the Chief of the Air Staff. However, the official history's comment is slightly contentious: Bomber Command certainly went over to attacking cities, but these were industrial cities, containing military or industrial targets.

Peirse pointed out that if he were to do all this – attacking oil and other vital targets, and mounting area raids every few nights – finding the aircraft to carry out the primary task would be impossible. The Directive was duly amended, ordering him to concentrate on 'oil . . . and other targets as opportunities arise'. In view of the attention devoted to oil in 1944–5 and the arguments over the oil offensive at that time (see Chapter 15), it is worth pointing out that the British were always well aware of potential German difficulties over oil and were attacking the German oil industry from the first days of the war.

Peirse would have been hard-pressed to carry out these various instructions effectively for a number of reasons. Bomber Command was getting weaker rather than stronger, not simply in overall strength, but because some of the types still in service were obviously useless – like the Fairey Battle, of which there were still 85 with the squadrons. The Blenheim was also on its way out, but Bomber Command still had 150 of them on strength. When the useless or obsolescent aircraft had been whittled away or discounted, Bomber Command's true strength stood at around 230 aircraft – Whitleys, Wellingtons and Hampdens – of which about 150 were available for operations at any one time. Thus equipped, Bomber Command entered 1941.

On 15 January 1941 Peirse received another Directive. This stated that, since the oil position in Germany would become critical in the next six months, he was to concentrate his efforts on oil and specifically on the synthetic-oil plants, seventeen of which were named in the Directive, of which the nine most important were at Bolen, Gelsenkirchen, Leuna, Lutzkendorf, Magdeburg, Politz, Rhuland, Scholven and Zeitz. If these nine could be destroyed, the Directive continued, 80 per cent of Germany's internal oil production capacity would be lost.

Peirse accepted this Directive without demur and in the next moon period, in February, sent his aircraft against oil targets – with mixed results. On the night of 14/15 February, 44 Wellingtons were sent to bomb Gelsenkirchen and 44 aircraft (Wellingtons and Hampdens) were sent to bomb the synthetic-oil plant at Homburg. Only nine of the Gelsenkirchen bombers found the target and only sixteen of the Homburg aircraft claimed to have bombed it accurately. No aircraft were lost but no worthwhile results were achieved, and the same was true for operations against the Holton oil plant at Sterkrade on the next night, when Homburg was attacked again.

Before the attack on oil could be fully developed, Bomber Command suffered the first of what was to become a chronic series of drains on its strength – a diversion from its strategic purpose. Prime Minister Winston Churchill decreed that the submarine menace was growing and must be combated and for the next four months all Bomber Command aircraft were to concentrate their attacks on submarine bases and construction yards. This decree was confirmed to Peirse in a Directive dated 9 March 1941 – though he was also directed to devote a part of his strength to oil. Peirse took up this task with a will, and it was still being implemented vigorously when, in June 1941, Germany invaded Russia.

This 9 March Directive remained in place until 9 July 1941, when another Directive from Portal landed on Peirse's desk. This referred yet again to the subject of German morale, asserting that

> the weakest points in the enemy armour lie in the morale of the civilian population and in his inland transportation system. The wide extension of his military activities is placing an ever-increasing strain on the German transport system and there are many signs that our recent attacks on industrial towns are having great effect on the morale of the civil population.
>
> I am to request that you will direct the main effort of the bomber force until further instructions, towards the dislocation of the German transport system and to destroying the morale of the civil population as a whole and of the industrial workers in particular.[14]

This is the first major indication that the Air Staff had finally come to see that the RAF bombers simply did not have the navigation equipment and bombing aids to hit small targets like refineries and factories – certainly not at night. Therefore, since one could not hit what one wanted, one would hit what one could: the industrial cities and those suburbs where the factory workers – and their families – lived. On the matter of transportation, the Directive went on to list the vital targets: places with railway marshalling yards, like Hamm, Cologne and Duisburg, feeder junctions for the great industrial area of the Ruhr.

Peirse, ever willing, was prepared to implement this Directive in full, but he lacked the means to do so. Aircraft numbers remained low and, although the Battle and Blenheim had been transferred from the Bomber Command inventory to other Commands, the new types coming into service – the Manchester, the Halifax and the Stirling – were not available in quantity and all were beset by teething troubles. Moreover the RAF was still unable to hit its targets accurately, even when it could find them.

Lord Sandhurst – then Flight Lieutenant the Hon. Terence Mansfield – was a navigator/bomb-aimer flying Wellingtons with No. 149 Squadron at this time:

> I trained on Ansons for navigation, on Fairey Battles for bombing and gunnery, and then at the Wellington OTU, reaching Lossiemouth and No. 149 in mid-April 1941, having joined up in September 1939. Do not assume from this lapse of time that I was a well-trained navigator. Such was the lack of facilities that I did not start training until March 1940, and in the next twelve months I amassed a total of just 160 hours flying, of which only fifteen hours were at night. My fourth night flight in a Wellington was also my first operational trip, and the combination of inexperience and appalling weather nearly made it my last.

I have read most of what has been written since the war about Bomber Command and have often been puzzled by the surprise at the errors made in 1941. My logbook only records six occasions when I positively claimed to have identified the aiming point. My logbook for June/July 1941 records what happened. 13 June: Brest, smoke and low cloud, no target identification. 16th: Düsseldorf. This time I got a visual and claimed to have seen Düsseldorf, 6,800 ft. 18th: circled Brest for 55 minutes before giving up hope of seeing the battleships; went to Cherbourg and attacked at 4,000 ft. This proved stupidly low as we were caught in a lot of light flak and I had to let the bombs go hurriedly. 22nd: Bremen. Another cock-up, bombs brought back. 25th: Bremen. A night of severe electrical storms; navigation affected by a considerable change in compass variation; fewer than 10 of the original 55 dispatched got through to Bremen. 1 July: Another effort to see the graving docks at Brest, but as usual the smoke pots got there first. 14th: Bremen. This was *Old Faithful's* last flight. As we attacked in clear weather at 8,000 ft, we were caught in a large and determined cone of searchlights. The flak seemed to have us all to themselves and after a long attempt to get clear we eventually got away to the north, almost at zero altitude and riddled with holes. We were last back by an hour, no one hurt, just frightened.

Our skipper on these ops, Sergeant Tony Gee, was a good steady pilot who got us out of some hairy situations. He went to OTU and was killed in 1942 when his aircraft lost an engine on take-off and was unable to climb over the hill in front. All his crew were lost as well, and I looked after his family at the funeral – something I wanted never to have to do again.

The squadron strength was sixteen aircraft. We lost four in April, one in May, two in June, four in July, three in August, none in September, one in October and none in November, when we started to convert to Stirlings. I think that by the end of 1941 I had stopped making friends. Of course I had friends, but they just did not seem to stay around very long. When you live in close proximity with death, perhaps friendship ceases to have the same meaning it would ordinarily have and friendship becomes a casual acquaintanceship instead.

After completing 24 ops with No. 149 Squadron I went on a bombing leaders course at Manby, which I finished in November 1941, before transferring to a new Canadian squadron then being formed, No. 419, which had 'Moose' Fulton as CO. The expansion of the Command and the splitting of the navigator/bomb-aimer jobs meant a restraint on qualified officers, and Moose told me that I would only fly on ops when no other navigator was available.

I see from my logbook that I flew once or twice a month until the end of May, when Moose set me free to finish my tour; coincidentally, I began with him on the Cologne Thousand Raid. Incidentally, on 12 June 1942 we arrived back at Mildenhall to find the place in uproar as the King and Queen were about to make a visit. The squadron were lined up in a hangar, and when the Queen got to me she asked the rather tricky question 'How do you like being one of the few Englishmen on a Canadian squadron?' In fact I was rather proud of it and I remained with the squadron, flying with Moose, until I had completed my first 30-op tour. Moose was a remarkable man and leader of men, and had been a wonderful inspiration to a brand-new squadron. I was then, and remain, proud not only to have served with him, but to have flown with him too.

All the RAF bombing achieved in this period was to prepare the German cities for the onslaught to come and persuade the *Luftwaffe* to devote such resources as it could spare from Russia to the development of flak and night-fighter forces for the defence of the Reich. This effort became a priority in July 1940 when, in the face of mounting RAF attacks, General Josef Kammhuber was appointed to take charge of the air defence of Germany. Later that year Kammhuber began to create an integrated system of flak, searchlights and night fighters in a belt around western Germany and, as a result, bomber losses began to climb steadily, from 2.2 per cent of night sorties in the period March to July 1941, to 3.5 per cent in the period July to November. Alex Kerr, an Australian flyer, was shot down in one of these attacks:

It was a clear night, activity over the target had been particularly brisk, and we were on our way home when Andy, the rear gunner, said, 'Night fighter on our tail!' There it was, a dark shape, hovering expectantly and moving into position off our starboard quarter. As we turned away, I saw the fighter straighten up and could imagine the pilot lining up the bulk of the Wellington for a sitting shot. As I watched, he squeezed the trigger.

Fire spat from the fighter's wings, and I saw tracer shells coming like fiery pinpoints towards me. Before I could move I felt a heavy blow, as though someone had punched me simultaneously all over my body. The shells which ripped through the fabric knocked me over on to the canvas bed. For a few seconds I was conscious; I had no idea I had been shot, although I knew I had been hit and hit hard. Then I lost consciousness.

I came to my senses some way down the aircraft, by the escape hatch. Flames were lighting up the interior to the accompaniment of a loud crackling and hissing and the acrid smell of petrol and oil. Dave, another crew member, was standing over me, parachute in hand, and my own chute had been clipped to my chest. I saw Bill, the navigator, half-lying across the astro hatch, evidently hit by the same burst that had got me, but he stirred and evidently was not dead. Dave smiled and beckoned me to jump – the flames were roaring now and I must jump – and I felt Dave kicking me into space.

Alex Kerr was found by a party of German soldiers and taken to hospital. 'My tally was ten wounds altogether, on the arm, chest and leg. Added to this was an incision on my leg, two bullets in the liver, and a six-inch incision in my stomach.'

November 1941 brought with it the Butt Report, objective, irrefutable proof of what most people in Bomber Command had known for the past two years: that the strategic bombing offensive was a failure, largely because the bombers were not finding or hitting their targets.

While it is obvious from aircrew reports that many of the crews were well aware that they were not finding and hitting the targets, the impression put about by the Air Ministry was that the bombing campaign on Germany *was* effective and achieving at least some of its objectives. In some ways creating this impression was necessary, not least to divert attention from the demands of the other services that Bomber Command be devoted to attacks on submarines, or used tactically in support of the Army. It was essential to keep the other services at bay until the RAF obtained the right aircraft in sufficient numbers, and with the right equipment, to do a proper job.

However, the carefully fostered impression that Germany was being reduced to rubble by the RAF was rudely shattered after Winston Churchill's scientific adviser Lord Cherwell (the former Sir Frederick Lindemann) directed a civil servant in the War Cabinet Secretariat, Mr D. M. B. Butt, to make a careful study of photographs showing the results of bombing operations on Germany. Starting in August 1941, Mr Butt examined over 700 photos taken on 100 raids on some 28 different targets and came up with some disturbing conclusions.

First, only about one aircraft in three dropped its bombs *within five miles* of the target – and only about a third of those aircraft claiming to reach the target actually did so. Since the inquiry defined the target area as having a radius of five miles, this meant that bombs were being dropped anywhere in an *area of 75 square miles around the target*. If the attacking aircraft were met with intense anti-aircraft fire, the number of aircraft bombing within five miles of the target fell still further. Operations were also inhibited by industrial haze, which was constantly present over the Ruhr. The Butt Report went into considerable detail and parts of it were strongly contested, but the broad picture it presented was generally accepted: that even at the most basic level of finding and hitting the target the bombing offensive of 1939–41 had been a failure.

The admission of this fact, if long overdue, was still a step forward. The first step in solving any problem is to admit that it exists, and with this bad news accepted steps could – and had to – be taken to remedy the situation. The remedies – new aircraft and radar aids to navigation and target-finding – were already in hand, though they would take some time to bring into service.

When Mr Butt delivered his damning report the RAF had been at war for almost exactly two years. During that time the bombers had achieved very little against Germany's military-industrial complex but the aircrews had at least learned what not to do, which is always something. They had also gained an immense amount of operational experience, developed their operational techniques and seen the development of new types of aircraft, and their commanders had set up a long and intensive training programme that would provide a steady supply of first-class aircrew in the years ahead. If only the technical side could come up with some good equipment, there was plenty of hope for the future.

One hoped-for aim of strategic bombing – the avoidance of war and the abolition of land campaigns – had proved impossible, or at least unrealizable. In 1939 neither the RAF nor the *Luftwaffe* was able to defeat the opposing nations with air power alone. Successes had been obtained in brief campaigns, in Poland, France and the Low Countries and the Battle of Britain, but none of these victories had stopped the war.

The question now was whether air power could provide vital strategic help in the coming years. This was still possible, but the learning curve of 1939–41 had given the German opponents of Bomber Command a chance to build up their defences and learn techniques that would make the task of strategic bombing a good deal harder in the future – far harder than it might have been had the problems of strategic bombing been thought through and solved before the outbreak of war. Recognizing this fact, the RAF settled in for a long haul. Meanwhile, as a hard year drew to its end there was one good piece of news, at least for the British. On Sunday 7 December 1941 the Japanese attacked the US Pacific Fleet at Pearl Harbor and the United States of America entered the war.

Messerschmitt Bf 109E

3

The Scientific Air War
1939–1942

<hr>

I foresee a never-ending struggle to circumvent the law that one cannot see in the dark.

Air Commodore Alan Coningham, AOC 4 Group, Bomber Command, 1940

At this point in the story – with the failure of strategic bombing fully exposed by the Butt Report, the Germans rapidly developing an integrated air defence system, and the United States in the war – it is time to take a look at the history of those scientific and technological aids developed by both sides in the first years of the war, either in an effort to make bombing operations more effective or to counter the measures to that end taken by the other side.

By now it will be obvious that pre-war notions of how accurate and decisive strategic bombing operations might be had proved invalid. In spite of the havoc wreaked on Warsaw, Rotterdam, Coventry and London, the strategic bomber stood revealed as an ineffective weapon, largely because the crews were unable to find their target, let alone hit it. This situation could not be allowed to continue, and the scientific aids described in this chapter are by no means the end of the story. The scientific air war went on for as long as the war itself, and to the aids developed by the scientists must be added the tactical changes introduced by the bomber commanders. This battle was a see-saw struggle – every move produced a counter-move, every innovation produced a snag – but the aims remained clear: either to turn the strategic bomber into an effective, war-winning weapon, or to render it totally ineffective.

War is a catalyst of change – a process produced by a combination of necessity and adequate resources – and from 1939 a great deal of time and effort was devoted to improving the bomber weapon. Obvious steps included improving the meteorological forecasts – for weather was, and would remain, a limiting factor affecting day and night bomber operations – as well as extending and improving instruction in navigation and bomb-aiming at the training schools. All this helped to a degree, but the most effective work was carried out by scientists – the 'back-room boys' or the 'boffins', as they were called – working in the field of radar and electronics to develop reliable navigation and target-finding aids. Whole books have been devoted to the efforts of the back-room boys, and this chapter will only present an outline of the technological side of the air war. This outline will be expanded in later chapters as new devices were introduced, but a grasp of the technical problems will be useful now, especially in understanding the fundamental problems of navigation, target-finding, and bomb-aiming.

The first in the field with an effective night navigation aid was the *Luftwaffe*. This is curious, because the *Luftwaffe* did not have heavy, four-engined bombers – other than the Focke-Wulf Condor used for maritime operations – or any kind of strategic bombing force. Even so, German bombers and transport aircraft had a need for *Lorenz* landing equipment, and that need led to the development of those radio target-finding aids used in bombing London and Coventry. These German aids, codenamed *Knickebein, X-gerät* and *Y-gerät*, were quickly employed when the Luftwaffe took up the night bombing of Britain in the autumn and winter of 1940. The *Knickebein* has already been described, and was believed to be similar to the *X-gerät*, which the RAF Intelligence officers already knew about from prisoners. This was believed to be a 'a bombing apparatus, using a system of interlocking radio beams',[1] and information on these devices was collated by Dr – later Professor – R. V. Jones of the Air Scientific Intelligence Branch. Having examined all the evidence, Dr Jones came to the conclusion that the *Luftwaffe* had an interlocking-radio-beam navigation system capable of being used over Britain and offering a position accuracy of up to one mile – which, if true, was much better than anything Britain could manage, and very worrying indeed.

At first Dr Jones's theory was dismissed on the grounds that no radio beam could stretch more than about 250 miles before it was blocked by the curvature of the earth, but evidence from shot-down German aircraft showed that they carried something resembling a *Lorenz* blind-landing set, of a type familiar from pre-war passenger transport aircraft, but far more sensitive.

The *Lorenz* system was basically quite simple. It consisted of two radio beams, one transmitting Morse 'dots', the other 'dashes'. Where these beams joined, they formed a continuous note, known as the 'equi-signal', and this signal marked the centre of the runway. When about twenty miles from the airfield, the pilot would tune the on-board *Lorenz* set to the correct frequency and follow the beam to the runway, staying on course between the dots and dashes, keeping close to the 'equi-signal'. The speed of descent was controlled by watching the altimeter, and the two together provided an effective landing system, though it could only be used at short range. Clearly with the *Knickebein*, the *X-gerät* and the *Y-gerät* the Germans had developed a system of extending the range of the beam; the task of Dr Jones and his team was to jam it.

By July 1940, the Telecommunications Research Establishment (TRE), near Swanage in Dorset, had developed a counter-measure to the *Knickebein*, codenamed *Aspirin*. This superimposed a UK-produced beam over the German-produced one, rendering the latter useless or inaccurate. This process has been incorrectly known as 'bending the beam', but the beams were never 'bent' (which it is sometimes alleged would have inadvertently led the *Luftwaffe* bombers to other targets). Eventually there were 28 *Aspirin* sites in the UK, some of them mobile, and they made the *Knickebein* virtually useless. Meanwhile, however, the Germans had introduced another aid, the *X-gerät*, a more sophisticated method of direction-finding employed by a special Luftwaffe unit, Kgr 100, a force specifically charged with target-marking for the *Luftwaffe* bombers.

Information on Kgr 100 aircraft using *X-gerät* first came from *Enigma* signals intercepted at Bletchley Park in September 1940, which referred to test flights of Kgr 100 using *X-gerät*, which appeared to be a fully automatic system of blind bombing. This information was added to Dr Jones's *X-gerät* file, and he came to the disturbing conclusion that the *Luftwaffe* was now testing a bombing or marking device accurate at distances of up to 100 miles – roughly from the German-occupied French coast to London.

The *X-gerät* employed four beams: an 'approach beam', which was followed by the pilot, and three 'cross-beams', which were monitored by the navigator, who also controlled a visual indicator and a bomb-release computer, pre-set to calculate the wind speed and altitude. The pilot flew along the approach beam and was warned of the target by the first, or 'coarse', cross-beam. On cutting the second, 'fine', beam, which was laid exactly 30 km from the target, the observer started the computer, which went into operation when it crossed the third, 'fine', beam, exactly 15 km from the target and dropped the bombs directly over the target by closing an electrical circuit. The usual accuracy of this system was 100 yards at 200 miles.

This was a wonderful achievement in 1940 – an aid accurate enough to hit any fairly large industrial plant. It did require specially-trained crews, and the *Luftwaffe* did not want the British to get their hands on it, so the *X-gerät* was used by Kgr 100 only as a target-marking device for dropping flares and incendiary bombs to light up targets for the following waves of bombers. Yet again, the British problem was how to jam it.

The 'coarse' beams could be jammed by stronger radio signals, codenamed *Bromide*, but the 'fine' beams proved more resistant and could not be quelled before twelve *X-gerät*-equipped bombers of Kgr 100 led the *Luftwaffe* to Coventry in November 1940. Attempts were made to jam the 'coarse' beam on this occasion, but the *Bromide* signals were transmitted on the wrong frequency, *X-gerät* functioned perfectly, and Coventry was wrecked. Fortunately, a week before the Coventry raid the RAF scientists obtained an *X-gerät* machine from a shot-down bomber of Kgr 100, which revealed the correct frequencies to jam, and the new, highly secret, magnetron valves produced by the British then proved capable of producing a strong jamming signal.

X-gerät remained useful to the *Luftwaffe*, but it soon had another bombing and navigation aid in service, codenamed *Y-gerät* or *Wotan*. This latter name gave Dr Jones and his team some idea what *Wotan* was, for Wotan is a one-eyed god in German mythology, which suggested that, unlike the *Knickebein* and *X-gerät*, the *Y-gerät* employed only one beam. And so it proved.

Information on these German devices was coming in from a number of sources: from the interrogation of captured aircrew, who often forgot to stick to name, rank and number and gave away more than they should; from scientific examination of shot-down aircraft; from *Enigma* intercepts; and from the monitoring of radio and radar signals by ground stations in the UK and airborne units of the 80 Wing search unit – a force that was later to develop a full-blown role in RCM – radio counter-measures – as 100 Group, RAF Bomber Command. All this information, however gathered, found its way to Dr Jones and the boffins at TRE, which for the sake of security was soon moved from its position on the exposed south coast to the spa town of Malvern by the Welsh border.

Wotan made its first appearance in December 1940. Although it was the most sophisticated of all the German beams, with an accuracy of 100 yards at 250 miles, it proved relatively easy to jam. *Wotan* was a *Lorenz*-type beam, with the usual system of dots, dashes and 'equi-signal'; the bomber picked these up and re-radiated them back to the ground station, which could then fix the aircraft's exact position while the beam guided the bomber over the target. The aircraft was then put on automatic pilot, flying by itself up to the target, where the bombs were dropped by a signal from the ground station. The system was jammed by picking up the re-radiated signal sent out by the aircraft and re-radiating it yet again; this caused confusion between the aircrew and ground control, with each accusing the other of making mistakes or using faulty equipment.

Although the information obtained from shot-down bombers and captured aircrew proved useful in jamming the German equipment, it was of little help to the British in developing their own navigation and target-finding aids. Simply copying the *Knickebein*, *X-gerät* or *Y-gerät* would be useless, since the Germans would know how to jam it. Nor were the operational circumstances similar. The *Luftwaffe* could attack Britain from bases just across the Channel; the RAF had to fly hundreds of miles to reach the industrial heart of Germany. Clearly, whatever aids were needed must be developed by the British themselves.

By January 1941 all three German systems had been effectively jammed, and with the coming of shorter nights in March 1941 the London Blitz gradually petered out. Had the German beams remained undetected or unjammed, the Blitz would have been far more effective and the Germans more inclined to continue it; as it was, the British learned a lot about blind navigation systems and were to put this to good use when they started, rather late in the day, to develop their own. This brief account of the 'Battle of the Beams' also reveals the basic pattern of the scientific air war, which would last until victory in 1945 – a pattern of measure followed by counter-measure, with neither side enjoying the advantage for long.

Before a problem can be solved it must be recognized and accepted as real, rather than seen as an excuse for failure. There is plenty of evidence that the crews and the chiefs of Bomber Command, quite early on in the war and long before the Butt Report, were well aware that they were not seriously damaging German industry. Indeed, one of the points raised by Sir Richard Peirse, when he replied to Portal's Directive of 25 October 1940 – a year before Butt – was that 'on long range attacks only one out of every five aircraft despatched actually reaches the target'.[2] This figure was revised by a conference of the Bomber Command group navigation officers at High Wycombe, the Bomber Command HQ, three weeks later, when they reached the conclusion that *at best* only about 35 per cent of bombers dispatched actually reached their primary targets.

This was gloomy news, and encouraging both to the Germans and to those in Britain who felt that the bombers would be better employed on anti-submarine operations in the Atlantic or in army co-operation in North Africa, or that the resources devoted to bomber development and production should be switched to some other purpose entirely.

Nor did the situation improve. In May 1941 it was generally accepted that about half the bombs dropped fell harmlessly on open country – but the actual percentage was far higher. This information, while generally known, was not generally admitted. At squadron level there was a general feeling that 'we are hitting the targets frequently but that lot in the squadron over there are 'line-shooting'. At the higher level the failure to find and hit targets became obscured by the greater need to get more national resources devoted to expanding the bomber arm, in terms both of numbers and of technical performance with the introduction of new types. The failure of the bomber therefore had to be concealed or at least explained, for the RAF would not get a larger share of scant resources if it became accepted that the entire bomber campaign was a failure. Besides, the failures were technical and technological: the bomber itself was fundamentally a war-winning weapon, *if it could only be made to work.*

The elements necessary to remedy this situation can be broken into four sections: weather forecasting, especially in the accurate assessment of winds, the vital element in aerial navigation; navigation aids, so that the bombers could find their targets; some form of illumination, so that the pilots and bomb-aimers could see their targets; and an improved bomb-sight, so that the bomb-aimers could hit their targets. The most fundamental problem was 'wind-finding'.

An aircraft floats in the air as a ship floats in the sea, and an aircraft is affected by winds as a ship is by tides; passengers flying across the Atlantic will be aware that the Europe-to-USA flight is always longer than the one coming the other way, because the prevailing winds over the Atlantic are westerlies and add considerably to the speed of a Europe-bound aircraft – or slow down an aircraft heading for the USA or Canada. Quite apart from affecting speed, lateral winds can also carry an aircraft off course.

Accurate assessment of wind force and direction is clearly essential to navigation, but was extremely hard to achieve, especially in wartime and at night. The task was not helped by the fact that with the outbreak of war the weather forecasts provided by various governmental weather bureaux promptly ceased. From September 1939 the weather forecast became classified intelligence information. There was also a reduction in the number of weather ships stationed in the Atlantic and a fall-off in information coming from neutral stations in Iceland, Spitzbergen and the Azores. RAF weather forecasters therefore had less and less information on which to base forecasts that were ever more vital to the success of bomber operations. It is hardly surprising that when the met officer got to his feet at a squadron briefing he was greeted with an ironic cheer from the assembled aircrews.

The winds given to the navigators at this briefing were known as 'forecast winds'. They were based on the information available at the time but were subject to change not only over time but also depending on the aircraft's position. As the aircraft flew to its target some hours later it was necessary to check the winds constantly. This could be done by dead reckoning, plotting the aircraft's position relative to the ground by identifying some fixed feature and knowing that, apart from pilot error in not maintaining a steady course, any major variation was probably due to wind. Wind speed and direction, if correctly assessed at that point, could be factored into the navigator's flight plan for the next leg of the flight. However, dead reckoning was not always possible, especially at night or in thick cloud, so another method was to drop a flare and let the rear gunner see what happened to it. If it was blown off to the flank, relative to the course of the aircraft, that was a good indication of what the wind was doing. Another method was for the wireless operator to pick up radio signals from ground stations in the UK and give their bearings to the navigator. Here again, fixing where the aircraft actually was, as opposed to where it was on the navigator's plot, helped the aircraft pick its way across Europe to the target area.

The problem with all these methods was that they worked only on an individual-aircraft basis; since navigator skill varied, the aircraft became scattered. In 1940–1 this was acceptable, but as the German air defences improved and thickened it became necessary to form the bombers into a 'stream', in order to swamp the *Luftwaffe* flak and fighter defences at one point and let the bulk of the bombers get through. This meant a degree of co-ordination, co-operation and accurate course-keeping. One method adopted to achieve this end was by appointing 'wind-finders', experienced navigators who assessed the winds during the flight and then radioed their findings back to the UK. Their estimates were averaged out and the result was broadcast back to the aircraft in the bomber stream. Every navigator was then expected to use these 'broadcast winds' in his plot so that any error was a common one and the stream stayed together. This technique may seem crude, but it worked after a fashion and proved a vital element in navigational accuracy and concentrating the aircraft over the target.

How some of this worked is explained by Freddy Fish, a navigator with No. 153 Squadron:

> The most critical factor in navigation was wind-finding. One had to work out what course was required to make a good fixed track despite a wind speed and direction that tended to push you to one side or the other. You also had to find your ground speed, i.e. the actual speed over the ground, as opposed to the airspeed – the speed registered in the aircraft, which was the ground speed plus or minus the wind speed, bearing in mind that height and temperature also affected the speedometer reading. Before each flight the navigator had to work out the course for each leg of the flight, using a forecast wind and a Dalton hand-held computer – actually a form of calculator – which could work all this out. In practice, the actual wind would be different from the forecast wind, and this would throw all your calculations out. We were then supplied with 'broadcast winds' calculated from flight reports and averaged out at base. We then had *Gee* [a position-fixing device], from which we had to obtain fixes every six minutes until we were out of *Gee* range or the Germans jammed it. Equipment was not always the answer, though, and to give some idea of the problems there is the time we went to Nuremberg, later in the war.
>
> Soon after take-off the *Gee* set caught fire, and though we put the fire out it was completely useless. Rather than turn back and risk being accused of cowardice – LMF or Lack of Moral Fibre – we pressed on and I told my pilot to simply follow the bomber stream until it got dark. This we did while I ran a DR plot, getting estimated winds from the wireless operator and hoping that I could get help from my H_2S [airborne ground-search radar] set when I switched it on. When that time came H_2S worked for a few minutes – and then failed. So back I went to DR and we managed to arrive at Nuremberg just four minutes from our allotted time and bombed. Then we had to get

back again, which involved one leg of 253 miles, or about 90 minutes, to the French coast. We had no idea where we were and could have been 100 miles off course. Luckily my DR paid off, because just before the French coast we felt the buffeting of other aircraft and found that we were right in the middle of the bomber stream.

We crossed the English coast at Orford Ness, about four miles off track. We still had 130 miles back to base, so I got the crew looking for *Occults* and *Pundits*, which were flashing beacons dotted about the countryside, the location of which I knew. I was able to take a bearing on some of these by eye and get an approximate position, and with all eyes on board straining we finally found our own airfield beacon and landed safely. At debriefing, after reporting the failure of all our navigation equipment, I was asked, 'When did you first know exactly where you were?' and I replied, quite truthfully, 'When I was over Nuremberg and they were bloody well shooting at us.'

The navigation aids referred to in the above account will be explained shortly, but at the start of the war the RAF relied on one method of navigation, dead reckoning – DR – aided by celestial or 'astro' navigation. DR was of limited use at night and in poor weather, and celestial navigation was too slow. What was needed was some form of electronic aid for rapid position fixing, and the first such aid arrived at the end of 1941 – *Gee*.

Gee was developed at the TRE after a meeting in June 1940 when one of the Air Staff, Air Marshal Sir Philip Joubart de la Ferté, complained about the poor bombing results caused by navigational difficulties. Sir Robert Watson-Watt, the pioneer of radar, was present and suggested that something useful might be developed out of those blind-landing aids, like *Lorenz*, that already existed. The development work was entrusted to a Mr Robert Dippy, *Gee* was worked on over the winter of 1940–1, test flights began in the spring, and in August 1941 operational flights began over Germany. Information on the performance of *Gee* on operations, and on German counter-measures and aircraft equipment, was gleaned from the aircrew, especially those who had been shot down on operations over enemy-occupied Europe and made their way back to Britain. One of these was Sergeant J. T. Bennett, a flight engineer of 4 Group, whose account notes that the crew were careful to destroy the *Gee* set before abandoning the aircraft:

The aircraft took off from Linton-on-Ouse at 23.35 hrs, 27 July 1942, target Duisburg. About 40/50 miles from the target a considerable volume of flak, accurate in height, was encountered. It burst in salvos of three, close behind the aircraft. Almost immediately the navigator said that the TR 1335 [i.e. the *Gee* set] was flickering, so the Germans were getting a radar fix on us. This phenomenon had been noticed on previous trips but was more pronounced on this occasion and ceased after the flak belt had been passed, when we saw very accurate flak bursting just below two following aircraft which were seen to be lifted by the bursts.

The aircraft was one of the first over the target. The TR 1335 functioned perfectly and visibility was also good enough for the objective, the centre of the town, to be seen. Two 4,000 lb bombs and leaflets were released from 18,500 ft and bombs were seen to burst among houses. On the way home a bank of cloud was seen and the pilot made towards it. Just before reaching it the aircraft was attacked on the port side by cannon fire which hit and set the fuselage on fire, wounding the rear gunner in the shoulder, leg and stomach. The captain ordered the flight engineer and the wireless operator to put the fires out but the extinguishers were quite inadequate for this purpose. The engineer also tried to rotate the rear turret to rescue the gunner but it had jammed and nothing could be done. Soon afterwards the ammunition inside the aircraft began to explode, making attempts to extinguish the fire even more difficult. Another fighter attack then set the port wing on fire and flames set the dinghy on fire.

The captain then gave the order to bale out. The engineer believes the navigator, wireless operator and, though he fears improbably, the front gunner may have escaped through the escape hatch. He himself escaped by diving head first through the fuselage exit door. He was later told by the Dutch that two other men, probably the wireless operator and the navigator, had been rescued. He also heard that the Germans had sent three coffins to the wrecked aircraft. The engineer praised the courage of the pilot, who remained at the control to give the remainder of his crew the chance to escape and thereby lost his life. Before baling out the wireless operator detonated the IFF [Identification, Friend or Foe] device and verified that the TR 1335 detonating switches were wired.[3]

Sergeant J. T. Bennett escaped from German hands soon after capture, was aided by the Dutch and Belgian resistance, picked up a useful amount of intelligence information, and was back in Britain by September.

Basically, *Gee* used a 'master' station and two 'slave' stations to create a web-like system of radio beams over Germany. These beams were picked up on cathode-ray tubes carried in the aircraft, and the result was a kind of grid, hence the name *Gee*, from the initial G. By plotting the signals from each station, the navigator could work out where he was to a high degree of accuracy. The other great attraction of *Gee* was that the aircraft played an entirely passive role: it picked up signals but did not send any, and therefore did not provide any information to the enemy night fighters regarding its position. Without the *Gee* equipment the radio pulses meant nothing, and it was hoped that the Germans would simply take them for radar signals – at least for a while. *Gee* was not the complete solution, but it was a great leap forward in navigation aids, for the navigators could use it not only to plot their positions over western Germany but also to guide them back to the UK – a feature which was greatly appreciated by the bomber crews.

It was accepted that sooner or later – probably sooner – a *Gee*-equipped aircraft would be shot down over Germany. Although shot-down crews were instructed to destroy the sets if possible, it was inevitable that the Germans would soon get hold of one and work out a counter-measure – and in spite of orders to keep their mouths *shut* on capture, giving only name, rank and number, it was clear from British intelligence work with captured German aircrew that some British airmen would say too much during interrogation and the secret would inadvertently leak out. The time this might take was estimated at about six months from the start of *Gee* operations, so there was gloom when a *Gee*-equipped aircraft was shot down on a flight over Germany in August 1941, shortly after the system was put on trial. That made it likely that *Gee* would be jammed within weeks, but in fact the Germans did not find out about *Gee* until well into 1942 and they did not realize what it was, and jam it, until the spring of 1943. *Gee* therefore remained a useful operational aid for a full year, and the *Gee*-box was a useful piece of kit until the end of the war in both RAF and US Eighth Air Force planes.

The first *Gee*-led operation took place on the night of 8/9 March 1942, when 211 RAF bombers attacked Essen. *Gee* only enabled the aircraft to get in the target area – it was not a pinpoint system – and as industrial haze obscured the town the raid was a disappointment. The Krupps armaments factory was untouched; the only damage was to houses and a restaurant, and eight aircraft were lost.

This raid was repeated on the following two nights, to no great effect: industrial haze always cloaked Essen and the other Ruhr towns, which were also heavily defended. Something else was needed, for while *Gee* was clearly useful in getting the aircraft to the general area of the target – and home again – the boffins had to think about marking the precise target – and bomb-aiming.

Thinking began at once, and the next navigation aid developed was *Oboe*. The brief for *Oboe* was to find a system that would enable the bombers not just to find a city – *Gee* could do that if the city was big enough – but to find a precise spot in that city, a factory, airfield, barracks or mar-shalling yard, even at night or when cloaked by haze or ten-tenths cloud. That meant a device that could measure the precise range from the oper-ating set to the target.

Oboe was developed at the TRE during 1941–2 by two scientists, Dr A. H. Reeves and Dr F. E. Jones. In simple terms, it consisted of two beams, not unlike the *Knickebein*, a system identified aurally by dots and dashes sent out from two UK stations, one in Norfolk and one in Kent. The first station, codenamed the 'Cat', and the second, codenamed the 'Mouse', sent out synchronized signals. The 'Cat' signals kept the aircraft flying on a track that would take it over the target; the 'Mouse' plotted the aircraft's position, height and ground speed (i.e. airspeed, plus or minus wind speed) and therefore the distance the aircraft was from the target. Knowing the ballistic properties of the bomb load, the *Oboe* operators in Britain could transmit a 'release' signal to the aircrew at the appropriate spot and the bombs would be dropped.

The range of *Oboe* was around 250 miles – good enough to attack targets in the Ruhr – and the accuracy at that range was around 100 yards off the aiming point. *Oboe* was first used on a Mosquito-led operation in December 1942, when one bomb dropped from 30,000 ft scored a direct hit on the target factory and the rest of the bombs fell within 150 yards.

Wing Commander John Tipton, of No. 109 Squadron, flew on *Oboe* operations:

> I did my first tour on Wellingtons, flying ops to Germany from the UK before the squadron went to Malta. When I was 'tour-expired' I returned to the UK and spent a year instructing at Pershore. There I met an Australian from 109 who said the squadron were looking for second-tour navigators, and since I knew I had to go back on ops soon I put my name forward and duly joined 109 at Wyton. I did not know about *Oboe* at this time – June 1943 – though it had been in use with the Pathfinder Force for about six months. *Oboe* was only used for Pathfinder operations, mainly by No. 109 Squadron, although we were later joined by No. 105 Squadron, another Mosquito unit.
>
> The *Oboe* apparatus looked like a number of grey metal boxes with a few knobs on, stuck in the front of the Mosquito aircraft. *Oboe* provided ground control of the aircraft by means of a radar beam, but it called for very careful flying. The width of the beam was inside the wingspan of the Mosquito, and it was not really a 'beam', for beams tend to spread out over long distances and the *Oboe* signal was extremely narrow all the way, but the word will serve. *Oboe* was really a way of measuring range. The pilots flew on this narrow 'beam' while the navigator picked up signals on the *Oboe* set to monitor the aircraft's position down the beam. As you approached the target along the beam, *Oboe* provided four check signals and finally a bomb-release signal when you were actually over the target. As a result, pinpoint targets like the Krupps works in Essen, which were always hidden by haze, could be attacked with great accuracy.

In *Oboe* the RAF had a precision bombing tool, but there were inevitably a few snags. The main one was that the 'Cat' and 'Mouse' system could handle only one aircraft per frequency at a time; it was therefore decided that *Oboe* should be used as a marking aid rather than for precision bombing, and it was mainly used, as described above, by the RAF Pathfinder Force (PFF), which was set up in 1942 to improve navigation and bombing accuracy. The other snag was that *Oboe* range was limited and restricted to targets in western Germany, mainly the Ruhr. Although attempts were made to increase the range by using 'repeater' aircraft, which picked up the ground signals and relayed them to the marker aircraft ahead, these experiments were not fully developed before the Allied landings in June 1944 enabled the RAF to establish *Oboe* ground stations on the Continent.

According to some estimates, before the advent of *Gee* and *Oboe* only about 23 per cent of bombs were dropped on the actual target; after the introduction of *Oboe* the figure rose to 70 per cent, thus allegedly increasing the effectiveness of bomber operations by 300 per cent. Inevitably, the Germans got to hear of it and *Oboe* was jammed by October 1943, although counter-measures against the jamming enabled *Gee* and *Oboe* to contribute to bombing accuracy until the end of the war.

Useful as *Gee* and *Oboe* were, they had an intrinsic limitation: the beams transmitted from the ground stations were eventually blocked by the curvature of the earth. *Gee* had a range of some 450 miles, *Oboe* around 250 miles, though it could be picked up at greater ranges by No. 109 and No. 105 Squadrons' high-flying PFF Mosquitoes. What was needed was a device that could be carried in the Main Force aircraft and be operated by the Main Force crews, without the need to rely on ground signals. The answer here was an airborne radar, codenamed H_2S.

H_2S was developed almost accidentally from the air-interception (AI) sets introduced into night fighters during 1942. These AI sets proved very useful in tracking and shooting down German bombers flying intruder operations over the UK – so much so that, to conceal the existence of this new aid, RAF Intelligence put it about that the night-fighter pilots' vision had been marvellously improved by a diet of carrots, which, it was alleged, did wonders for the eyesight. Since Britain's civilians were having to cope with the blackout at this time, the national consumption of carrots increased enormously, but it is doubtful if the enemy were fooled by this tale for long, if at all.

The real story begins one day in November 1941, when a Blenheim navigator noticed that when the radar on his AI set was pointed down it gave a very good outline picture of the ground below, showing not only built-up areas but outlines from the coast and features such as woods, lakes and towns in open country. A note was made of this interesting fact, and eventually found its way to TRE. There the possibilities were explored, and the outcome, after a great deal of work, was H_2S, a ground-search radar which operated from an aerial rotating in a small dome positioned outside the belly of the aircraft. This aerial sent out a narrow beam which swept the ground below, creating a picture which was shown on a cathode-ray tube in the navigation compartment.

There were the usual problems, the first of which was that H_2S was much less effective at altitude. A stronger signal was needed, and that meant using the new and secret magnetron valve, which the Air Staff decreed was far too secret and valuable to risk using over enemy territory. In May 1942, the Air Staff relented somewhat and said this rule could be relaxed if TRE could demonstrate that H_2S enabled an aircraft to home in on a target from fifteen miles' range at 15,000 ft,[4] but disaster followed in June when the H_2S test-bed Halifax aircraft crashed in the UK, killing all on board, including five of the scientists working on the project.

Their work and sacrifice was recognized a few weeks later when Winston Churchill overrode the objections of the Air Staff and ordered that two Bomber Command squadrons were to be equipped with H_2S forthwith, and in any event not later than October 1942. As had happened with the *X-gerät*, H_2S was first installed in pathfinder aircraft – two squadrons of 8 (PFF) Group, Bomber Command, which had the Halifaxes of No. 38 Squadron and the Stirlings of No. 7 Squadron ready for the first H_2S operation, leading the Main Force to Hamburg on the night of 30/31 January 1943. Hamburg was chosen as it seemed to be the ideal H_2S target: a large built-up area with a distinctive coastline – the kind of target that would show up well on a radar screen. Although 135 Lancasters attacked Hamburg, led by seven H_2S-equipped Stirlings and six H_2S Halifaxes, the raid was not a success. The bombs were scattered over a wide area and little damage was done, although many fires were seen and about 230 people were killed or injured. Five Lancasters were lost to flak or fighters.

Other raids followed – to Cologne, to Turin, back to Hamburg, and to the Ruhr. H_2S was soon accepted by Bomber Command as a useful aid, but then a new difficulty appeared: the *Lichtenstein* airborne radar on the German night fighters was able to home in on the emissions of H_2S sets, find the bombers, and shoot them down. The boffins now had to find some means of jamming the *Lichtenstein* sets . . . and so the scientific battle went on, the advantage swinging to and fro in the dark and dangerous skies over Germany.

H_2S was also adopted by the USAAF Eighth Air Force for use in ten-tenths cloud conditions, when the ground was totally concealed and the B-17s or B-24s had to bomb blind. The USAAF called their version H_2X, and it remained in use with their squadrons from 1944 until the end of the war. H_2X is often referred to in US accounts as '*Mickey*', a 'pathfinder' or 'blind-bombing' aid.

Finding the target was only the first task: it then had to be illuminated, marked and hit. The marking problem will be discussed in a later chapter, covering the redevelopment of the RAF Pathfinder Force, which was charged with marking targets for the Main Force bombers. The final task was to hit the target, and problems with that remained acute until the war ended and have not been completely solved to this day. To hit the target the bomb-aimers needed a reliable bombsight – one that could swiftly calculate the various factors affecting the progress of a bomb between the aircraft and the target.

Apart from the basic difficulty that the target was often invisible, even in daylight, bombsight calculations had to include the aerodynamic characteristics of the bomb. Even heavy bombs did not drop vertically from the aircraft on to the target; the aircraft – and the bombs within them – were travelling at horizontal speeds approaching 200 m.p.h., and the bombs therefore had to be dropped some distance from the target. After leaving the bomb bay the bombs 'flew' towards the ground: they were 'lobbed' into the target area, rather than dropped directly into it. Factors that had to be taken account of were the speed and drift of the aircraft and the force and direction of the wind – all these could affect the bomb in flight and therefore the accuracy of the drop. Even air temperature was a factor – and all this in a sky torn by flak and other distractions. Accurate bomb-aiming could never be easy. These factors could not be eliminated by using some simple device like a rifle sight. A bombsight had to offer some way of handling complicated calculations, and yet be used by unscientific people, in considerable danger and under great stress.

The RAF went into the war with the Mark IX Course Setting Bomb Sight (CSBS). Jim Brookbank, a bomb-aimer with No. 9 Squadron, 5 Group, describes this as 'a Heath Robinson lash-up with a graticule sight that you laid on the target and dropped the bombs when the time seemed right. It took a lot of practice, but it could be done.' With the CSBS, as the official history points out, 'small deviations in the air produced large variations on the ground'.[5] Various improvements to the CSBS were made until 1942, culminating in the CSBS Mk IX A. This sight was then replaced by the Mark XIV Stabilized Vector Sight, a much better device, and then in 1942, an RAF officer, Squadron Leader Richard Richardson, came up with the Mk II Stabilizing Automatic Bomb Sight (SABS), which incorporated a gyro and a primitive computer.

Primitive the computer may have been, but in skilled hands the SABS was capable of dropping a stick of bombs with an *average* error of less than 100 yards from 20,000 ft, and many bomb-aimers could do much better than than. Attaining such accuracy was far from easy, however: attacking from that height, the bombs had to leave the aircraft two miles short of the target and fall for almost a minute before they hit the ground.

When the Mark XIV came into service in the summer of 1942 the first people to get it were the target-marking Pathfinders and it was another eighteen months before the Main Force crews enjoyed this equipment – not least because using the Mark XIV required special training. Bob Knights of No. 619 and No. 617 Squadrons, comments on this bombsight:

> By 1943 most heavy bombers in the Command had the Mk XIV sight. This was a stabilized sight, and once the bombing data had been put in – e.g. the wind strength and direction etc. – the bomb-aimer could not correct it on the bomb run. He simply gave corrections to the pilot in an endeavour to get the graticule back on the target. This was considered a good enough sight by the C-in-C, at least for area bombing, and Main Force squadrons were equipped with it.
>
> The SABS was a precision sight and, although one or two squadrons had it for a while, eventually the only squadron in the Command fitted with it was No. 617, which had the Mark II A. This was also a stabilizing sight, but the data put in could be adjusted all the way to the target. The drift had to be

adjusted with great care, as every movement of drift correction registered on an indicator on the pilot's instrument panel which was marked off in one-degree segments. This meant that the pilot could fly a course to an accuracy of one degree! 617 was taught to use this sight by Squadron Leader Dickie Richardson – known to us all as 'Talking Bomb' – who regarded it as his very own.

Using the SABS required teamwork. The gunners took wind drifts, to help the navigator work out precise wind speeds and direction, while the navigator and bomb-aimer calculated instrument corrections. The aircraft's instruments were not designed for such fine work, and a small error in calculation could throw a bomb well away from the target. The pilot had to fly at precisely the right track, height and speed on the run-up to the target, and when the bomb-aimer had a precise fix on the target he flicked a switch and the bombsight took over, tracking the aircraft to the target, passing corrections to the pilot and, when the right moment arrived, even dropping the bombs. The SABS first went into service with No. 617 Squadron, which from the end of 1943 was charged with high-level precision bombing operations and was soon using it to drop the new *Tallboy* bombs accurately on to small targets.

The USAAF, dedicated from the start to precision bombing, went to war with the highly accurate – and highly secret – Norden bombsight, a device considered so vital to the USAAF's success that the bombsight was fitted with an explosive self-destruct device powerful enough to blow the nose off the aircraft. US bomb-aimers – bombardiers – had to remove the bombsight from their aircraft between missions, and the sights were kept under armed guard at all times – at least to begin with.

The Norden bombsight was a complicated precision instrument; when USAAF bombardier Major Albert E. Hill of the 386th Bomb Group responded to this author's request for a *simple* explanation of how he used the Norden bombsight, the steps involved between lining up the sight and pressing the bomb release took up four pages and involved the use of gyroscopes, bubble levels, tachometers, course knobs, rate knobs, arming triggers and an 'intervalometer' to vary the spacing of the bombs on the target. All this while requiring 'an accurate forecast of wind direction and velocity, accurate ground speed, perfect aircraft trim, perfect pre-set of bombsight data, and the cross-hairs should stay on the aiming point once the bombardier gets the aircraft flying straight and level with the Pilot Direction Indicator on centre'.

The other snag with the Norden – and with all precision bombing instruments – was that for the bombsight to work accurately the bombardier had to see the target. He also needed enough visual checks to get accurate information on the winds and aircraft drift. This information and much more, like the speed and height of the aircraft and the aerodynamics of the bomb load, were then fed into the bombsight computer. As the war went on and the Eighth Air Force bomb groups got used to European conditions, other aids were added – various kinds of marker, the operations of Scouting Force reconnaissance aircraft to assess the weather and target visibility, and a range of electronic devices – but for the Norden bombsight to work at its designed best at any time the bombardier had to see the ground.

The Norden bombsight was originally developed for the US Navy and, since each one had to be made individually and hand-finished, Norden sights were in very short supply when the United States entered the war at the end of 1941. Nor was every bombardier capable of using the Norden effectively, and in the end the USAAF went over to a system whereby the best bombardier in each group was the one who made the sight calculations and dropped the first bomb load. In all the other aircraft of that group, an airman known as a 'toggelier' pulled a toggle to salvo the aircraft's bombs on to the target. This depended on adequate visibility – the toggelier had to see the lead aircraft's bombs fall, so this method could not be used at night – and the inevitable delay in catching sight of the 'lead ship's' drop led to a further scattering of the bomb load – though if the first drop was accurate the target, and much of the area around it, was thoroughly drenched in bombs.

Many other radar and other electronic devices came into use as the war went on, but *Gee, Oboe* and *H₂S* were the main ones used for navigation. Jamming devices – code-named *Window, Monica*, the *Mandrel Screen, Airborne Cigar* and so on – together with the tactics used to employ them or restrict their use, will be described later as they were developed and came into service.

The German air and ground radar systems will also be covered in detail in future chapters, but before leaving these technical developments it might be as well to look briefly at the two basic elements of the German radar defences: *Freya* and *Würzburg*. *Lichtenstein*, an integrated ground-to-air detection and fighter-control system – a flying radar set for use in night fighters – would come into service later.

The object of radar defence was to give the defending fighters and anti-aircraft gunners adequate warning of a coming aerial attack, so that preparations could be made to resist it. These precautions took time, and the first element in the German defences was a long-range radar system code-named *Freya*. *Freya* was first reported on an *Enigma* decrypt in July 1940. Since this was scientific intelligence, it found its way to Dr R. V. Jones, who correctly identified *Freya* as an aid to interception and aircraft detection.

In fact *Freya* was rather more than this. A few days later the destroyer HMS *Delight* was attacked by Stukas and sunk off Portland Bill and a German *Enigma* message reporting this success added that it had been made possible 'with the aid of *Freya* reports'. Once again the German love of mythological names hinted at what *Freya* could do, for the goddess

Freya was guarded by Heimdall, the Watchman to the Gods, 'who could see a hundred miles by night or day'.

Photographic reconnaissance of the French coast eventually revealed the existence of a radar station at the village of Auderville on the Cap de la Hague, east of Cherbourg – a large station, with two radar dishes. Radar pulses from this station were picked up on the south coast at a distance of some 80 miles from Auderville, and the first *Freya* station was noted on the map. It was obvious that the Germans would have other *Freya* stations and that they must form part of an even large network, probably involving other forms of radar. *Enigma* transcripts were scanned for information and agents in Occupied France were directed to look out for other radar installations, and before long word arrived of yet another form of installation – code-named *Würzburg*.

The supposition was that, while *Freya* was an early-warning system, *Würzburg* would be more localized and therefore more precise: *Freya* would detect the coming bomber formation; *Würzburg* would detect the height and track of the individual bomber. This was only a supposition, and more information was being sought when aerial reconnaissance of a *Freya* site on the coast of France near Bruneval revealed a smaller, parabolic, radar aerial nearby. This might well be a *Würzburg* set, and when low-level photoreconnaissance revealed the existence of a 10-ft-wide radar dish the decision was made to send in a force to raid the Bruneval station, examine the equipment there carefully, and if possible bring the *Würzburg* radar home.

This operation – the Bruneval raid: Operation BITING – was launched on the night of 27/28 March 1942 by men of 'C' Company, 2nd Battalion, The Parachute Regiment, led by Major John Frost (who, two and a half years later, commanded the 2nd Battalion of the Parachute Regiment in the battle for the bridge at Arnhem). Frost's men were to protect a party of Parachute Engineers and an RAF radar expert, Flight Sergeant Cox, who had never parachuted before. Cox was to examine the *Würzburg* and makes notes, the Engineers were to dismantle as much of it as possible and above all get the radar aerial from the centre of the dish, while Frost and his men held off the German garrison. Once Cox had what he wanted, the party would withdraw to the nearby beach, where they would be picked up by landing craft and brought back to Britain.

The Bruneval raid went off as planned and vital parts of the *Würzburg* were delivered to TRE, where it was noticed that the Germans were once again in the lead in this form of radar – though means could now be devised for catching up. However, this sort of scientific work is never static, and before long word came through of another form of *Würzburg* – *Reise Würzburg* or 'Giant Würzburg' – with a 20-ft-diameter dish. One of these dishes was identified by an Allied agent in Berlin, and another was spotted by aerial reconnaissance on the island of Walcheren in the Schelde, west of Antwerp. With this information, Jones was able to work out the basics of German radar defence: the *Freya* was to provide early warning, the *Würzburg* to give the height and speed of the bombers for the search-lights and flak guns, and the *Reise Würzburg* to track individual bombers and guide the night fighters on to them, close enough for the fighters' air-borne radar to pick the bomber up and for the pilot to close in for the kill. This last device, code-named *Emil-Emil* by the Germans, was finally iden-tified by the somewhat desperate measure of despatching a Wellington from No. 1473 Wireless Investigation Flight to fly over Germany and invite attack.

This aircraft, packed with monitoring equipment, took off on the night of 3 December 1942 and flew into Germany with the Main Force bomber stream. Once over Germany the aircraft left the bomber stream and flew on as 'flying bait' for the German night fighters and radar. Eventually the aircraft, piloted by Pilot Officer Paulton, with Pilot-Officer Jordan as his special radio operator, picked up the *Emil-Emil* tracking signals and the crew waited as the night fighter got close and the tracking signals grew stronger.

When there was no doubt that they had been tracked accurately by a night fighter using radar on a particular frequency, the information was passed by radio to Britain – just as the fighter, a Ju 88, swept out of the night and laced the Wellington with cannon fire. The rear gunner fired back until his turret was hit and he was wounded, as was the radio operator. Fortunately, the night fighter broke off the attack and Pilot Officer Paulton was able to fly his badly damaged aircraft back to Britain, where it crash-landed in the sea just off the coast of Kent. The crew brought with them the final piece in the jigsaw of the German defensive radar system, and all members of the crew were later decorated for their part in this hazardous mission.

Put together, these radar systems provided the German flak and fighter forces with a formidable amount of information and formed a major part of their anti-aircraft defences, which were now being integrated into a defence line which would eventually stretch across the west of Germany from Alsace to Norway. The British needed a name for this system, a network put together by the general in charge of Germany's night-fighter forces, so they named it after him – the Kammhuber Line.

The story of General Josef Kammhuber and the defences of Germany will be continued in Chapter 6, but this broad outline of the scientific side of the bomber war will make a lot of what follows more understandable. Most of the technology that now makes air travel so safe and simple did not exist in the early 1940s and the necessary aids had to be developed in daunting conditions, in the course of continuing operations and in the face of enemy opposition, much of it equally technical. This story will track the development of other devices with curious code names: *Window, Naxos,*

Lichtenstein, Monica, Schrage Musik and others besides – each one a scientific tool in the prosecution of the bomber war. The bomber war was never easy, but the first years of the war, before science came to the aid of the aircrews, were very difficult indeed. It is to those aircrews that this story now returns.

Bristol Blenheim Mk IV

4

The Aircrews
1940–1943

More than any other British service, the RAF represented the British Empire at war.

Martin Middlebrook, *The Battle of Hamburg*, 1980

According to the Bomber Command memorial that stands on Plymouth Hoe in Devon, men from seventeen nations served with the Command during the Second World War. They came from all over the Empire and Commonwealth: from Canada, Australia, New Zealand and South Africa, from the islands of the Caribbean and the colonies of Africa. Nine squadrons were manned by aircrew from the countries of Occupied Europe: four Polish (Nos. 300, 301, 302, and 303), one Czech (No. 311), one Dutch (No. 320) and three French (No. 342 (Lorraine), No. 346 (Guyenne) and No. 347 (Tunisie), French Air Force). Bomber Command was actually the free world in arms, flying against Nazi Germany.

A number of RAF crews contained members from Norway and Denmark and volunteers with British roots in the expatriate communities of South America. A surprising number of Bomber Command aircrew came from the United States of America, having travelled up to Canada to join the RCAF, enlisting to fight Hitler long before the United States entered the war in December 1941. Up to 25 squadrons came from the Empire, including No. 44 (Rhodesia), No. 102 (Ceylon), eight Australian (RAAF) squadrons, two New Zealand (RNZAF) squadrons and fifteen Canadian (RCAF) squadrons, but in spite of these titles the squadron crews were mixed: British aircrew flew with Australians, Canadians with Scots, South African with New Zealanders – the crews seemed to like it that way.

Geoff Whitten of No. 35 Squadron says:

When I was at Linton-on-Ouse in 1942–3, the two squadrons on the base had
aircrew from the UK, Canada, USA (usually with RCAF badges), Australia,
South Africa, Rhodesia, Jamaica, Norway and Argentina. Off-duty fliers seen
in the nearby city of York included Poles and Free French. I am unaware of
any friction between us, either on or off the base, even though it was known
that there were some anomalies, in terms of pay for instance.

No doubt other differences, e.g. disciplinary codes, dress etc., were partly
concealed by the existence of squadrons overtly Canadian, Free French or
Australian. There was a widespread feeling that the Air Ministry bent over
much too far to favour our Commonwealth cousins, a view strengthened
later when the North Riding's sixth and last pre-war bomber base, one with
all the comforts, had to be vacated to accommodate two Australian bomber
squadrons.

Peter O'Connor, of No. 467 (RAAF) and No. 83 (PFF) Squadrons,
comments:

Mixed crews? An interesting question. I had two crews. The first, formed at
27 OTU in 1943, consisted of five Australians and two Englishmen, average
age twenty, all NCOs. We went to Waddington and did one op together
before I was withdrawn; sadly, they were all killed in May 1944. I joined
another crew in February 1944; this consisted of two Australians, one
Canadian, an Irishman, and three Englishmen – from Newcastle, Warwick
and Dorset. We got along like a house on fire, with never a cross word. We
socialized on the squadron, though on leaves we 'Colonials' tended to go to
London while the others went to their homes.

This comradeship has never waned. We kept in touch after the war, and
visited to and fro in the UK, Canada, Australia and the USA. Sadly, only three
of us are still alive. I don't think background mattered; we were all very
young, with a common cause, and in combat our lives depended on teamwork. We started as sergeants, and although three of us became officers the
relationship never changed.

Bob Westell, a Canadian navigator with No. 428 Squadron, RCAF, confirms this point: 'We had mixed crews in our squadron at Dalton:
Australian, New Zealand and British, it did not matter. Our crew contained an English mid-upper gunner and an English flight engineer.
English aircrew got less pay than we Canadians, and we got less than the
Americans, but this was not a problem. Crew loyalty was all that mattered,
and it was total.'

In the United States it was the same story. USAAF aircrew came from
every state of the Union and from every occupation, from Wall Street
bankers to Arkansas farmers, from Alaskan fishermen to Texan cowboys.
The US Army Air Corps started expanding in 1939, when recruits poured

in, and many Americans soon found themselves at flying schools in Florida and other Southern states, sharing flying and navigation courses with aircrew trainees from Great Britain and the Empire. Among these was David 'Taffy' Bellis:

> I joined the RAF as a trainee navigator in 1940, but it was not until 1941 that the training actually started. In May 1941 several hundred of us were shipped to Toronto, as part of the Empire Air Training Scheme, but about 100 of us were then sent on to Miami in Florida for navigation training. The USA was not yet in the war, which meant we had to be converted into 'civilians' beforehand. As can be imagined, this was a wonderful experience for youngsters, most of whom had never been abroad before. There was no service discipline, the locals overwhelmed us with kindness, and we soaked up the sunshine and the swimming and we all had girlfriends with cars and sailing boats.
>
> The course was run by Pan-American Airways at their School of Navigation in the University of Miami; it was very intensive, and air exercises were carried out in PAA civilian Commodore or Sikorski flying boats, trundling over the Caribbean at 70 knots. At the end of the course we were qualified navigators, able to plot courses and work out fixes using DR, astro sights and the radio links.

David Bellis went on to win the DFC and bar, flying with No. 239 and No. 141 Squadrons.

Bill Bullen, a Pathfinder navigator, recalls his call-up, and the fate of his friends:

> I joined the RAAF in 1941 after being conscripted into the Army, and flew 57 sorties against the enemy. In the initial flight course at Bradfield Park in Sydney we had a roller-skating speed champion, a Sheffield Shield cricketer, a ballroom-dancing champion and many youths of great talent. Norman Craig, the ballroom dancer, was killed flying Spitfires in Italy. The cricketer, D. K. Carmody, was shot down into the English Channel and became a POW. My first flying partner, Curly Burnham, an Englishman, was killed in Canada during training. My next training partner, Roy McLean, a Canadian, was killed early on, in an operation to Berlin. I know a lot about the life and times of Norman Craig, as his fiancée has never ceased to mourn his death since he was killed in 1943. War not only takes its toll of the participants, it decimates the lives of those who are left to grieve.

A number of RAF aircrew were American volunteers; among them was Nick Knilans, who was later to fly with No. 619 and No. 617 Squadrons of 5 Group:

> I come from Delavan, Wisconsin, and in October 1941 I drove up to Canada to join the war. I didn't want to wait and I wanted to be a pilot, and the Canadian immigration officer at the border directed me to the nearest

RCAF office. They passed me on to a recruiting base in Toronto, where we were divided into flights; my flight had 28 Americans and four Canadians in it.

We started training, and when the Japs bombed Pearl Harbor in December some of the Americans requested permission to transfer back to the USAAF. I asked to be transferred from the one-year RAF pilot course to the six-week air-gunnery course, but they told me to stay on the pilot course. This I did, and so I went to the war and No. 619 Squadron.

Nick Knilans went on to have a distinguished flying career, winning the DSO and DFC while serving with RAF Bomber Command, and we shall meet him again.

All the aircrew on both sides, Allied and Axis, were volunteers; no one was forced to fly. They were fighting in the air because they chose to do so, and for a wide variety of reasons. Like Nick Knilans, many simply wanted to fly, and especially to become a pilot – even in a crew-dependent bomber, the pilot was the role everyone wanted to fill. Others flew because they did not fancy spending their war in the infantry. Many of the Empire and US airmen joined the air force and came to Britain because it offered a chance to travel and see the world. Some came because the war sounded exciting. Others came because their friends were coming, and they did not want to be left behind. There was, however, a deeper reason, harder to dig out two generations later, but a reason that underpins all the rest: most of them came to the war in Europe because they thought it was the right thing to do.

Howie Steen sums up the attitude of many Dominion aircrew: 'You ask me why I volunteered for the RCAF? My prime reason was that I wanted to be a pilot. I must also admit that I enjoyed my four and a half years in England and look back on them as some of the best years of my life. I not only made some lasting friends in the service, I also met some wonderful civilian Brits – people I will never forget. However, there was another reason: in the 1930s and 1940s there was a thing called patriotism, and most of us were patriotic.'

Some of these volunteers continued to fly when they had no reason to. Lee Fegette came to England with the USAAF 303rd Bomb Group in 1942 and was shot down over France on his third mission – 'and as we went down our tail gunner was still firing his .50s at the *Luftwaffe*'. Lee Fegette was captured, escaped, linked up with the French resistance, got back to England and, as was the practice with formerly captured crews, was returned to the USA and given a training post.' Well, then I thought it over and I decided that I had to go back to the war. It took a lot of time, since there was no routine for it, but I got back to England and the 303rd. In fact I flew on the first 303rd mission in 1942 and their last one in 1945 – 33 missions in all. Some people thought I was crazy, but if I had not gone back I could not have looked myself in the face.'

All aircrew joined up eager to fly, but reaching a bomber squadron took time. Up to two years from joining the RAF to arriving at an operational squadron was not unusual, certainly for pilots, navigators and bomb-aimers, who were usually trained abroad under the Empire Air Training Scheme. The process began when the volunteer attended a three-day selection interview for a series of tests to decide whether he was suited for flying duties at all. Those accepted were then graded as potential pilots, navigators or bomb-aimers. Many navigators and flight engineers began as trainee pilots but, having been 'washed out' at some point in training, were switched – or 'remustered' – to other roles, though their flying training was often useful to back up the pilot on operations.

Those not selected for one of these three roles went directly on to a shorter wireless-operator, flight-engineer or air-gunner course. There were exceptions, but these crew members were usually trained in the UK, while the pilots and navigators did their flying training abroad, in Canada, the USA, South Africa or Rhodesia – places where the better weather allowed longer hours in the air and so reduced the training time.

One of the British aircrew volunteers was Freddy Fish, who makes the point that no one joined the Air Force and was dispatched to bomb Germany in a matter of weeks:

I was an air-raid warden until I was called up in 1942, and then I had to decide where to go. I didn't fancy the Army – where you might end up peeling spuds – or the Navy – with all that horrible water under one's feet – so I considered the RAF. I was a very fit young man with a reasonably good education, and at that time, after the Battle of Britain, every boy wanted to be a pilot. So I volunteered for the RAF and was accepted as aircrew, aged nineteen and a half. After initial training I was sent to Canada on the liner SS *Andes*, packed in like sardines, well below the waterline, sleeping in hammocks set eighteen inches apart. I ended up at No. 3 EATS, at Bowden, Alberta, roughly halfway between Calgary and Edmonton, where I started training as a pilot. This was in early 1943, after the RAF had decided to dispense with second pilots; this increased the supply of pilots, all of whom needed crews. At the same time the old observer job of navigator plus bomb-aimer was split in two and, since my piloting was not quite good enough, I volunteered as a navigator. I think I made a far better navigator than I would a pilot, which was proved when we went on ops, and I graduated with my navigator's wings in November 1943.

Then came more training back in Britain, at OTU (operational training unit) and HCU (heavy conversion unit – flying four-engined types), including 'Bull's-eyes' – simulated raids on British cities like Bristol. Accidents in training were very common; I believe we were the only course to get through our HCU without a fatal accident, but I can remember a crashed Halifax on fire a few fields away – we could hear the cries of the trapped crew, plus the sound of exploding ammunition. I did my first op on 14 October 1944 – a daylight raid on Duisburg with No. 166 Squadron, the first RAF 1,000-bomber daylight raid – before we transferred to No. 153 Squadron for the remainder of our 30 ops. As can be seen, it took over two years after joining to actually going on ops, but this was largely due to bottlenecks and hanging about in holding stations waiting for the next course to start. My feeling was that our training was very long but thorough. We went through each stage with as much realism as possible before starting on the real thing. I found it all stood us in good stead in coping with difficult situations later on.

This extensive RAF training at OTUs gave the crews plenty of experience before they went on operations. Their operational training was in the UK, where they got used to the uncertain weather and the wartime atmosphere and, in many cases, took part in short-range sorties dropping leaflets, before joining their squadrons. The US crews, on the other hand, did all their training in the USA, joined their squadrons on arrival in the European Theatre of Operations (ETO) and were pitched directly into combat. This was not wise, and before long a period of extra training in the ETO was introduced, in order to acquaint the new crews with the wartime situation and flying conditions in Europe.

Derek Jackson joined the RAF as an air gunner:

Like everyone else I wanted to be a pilot, but most of all I wanted to fly and when they told me that they had enough pilots and navigators and needed gunners – this was in 1943 – that was enough for me. It still took time. I volunteered for RAF aircrew in June 1943, aged eighteen, and didn't get called up for another six months. I then went through the usual training for recruits and air gunners and got my AG brevet in May 1944, after six months in the RAF and just twenty hours' flying.

We then crewed-up at Lossiemouth OTU, went to HCU flying Halifaxes, and then to a Lancaster finishing school for just one week before being sent to our operational squadron, No. 149, 3 Group, at Methwold, arriving there on 10 December 1944, a year after joining up. There were four squadrons on the station, Nos. 90, 218, 62 and 149, each with about 30 aircraft and 40 crews, so with WAAFs and ground crews there were about 1,500 people there. It was very mixed: Aussies, New Zealanders, Canadians and South Africans as well as British – quite a little world for a lad of nineteen.

There are few absolutes in war, and a number of aircrew seem to have slipped swiftly through the training net as James Berry, also of No. 149 Squadron, confirms: 'Our flight engineer had had a very brief training, just the usual square-bashing that all recruits endure then a six-week course at St Athan's on flight engineering and then to our crew on Stirlings. He was a good sort, and we are still in touch.'

Kenneth McDonald of No. 78 Squadron also states that flight engineers were rapidly sent to their squadrons:

I was lucky, for I was posted to Canada in August 1939 as an instructor, and by the time I flew a Ventura back I had 1,300 hours in my logbook. Flying experience has much to do with survival, and I still marvel at the majority of Bomber Command pilots, taking off into the 'clag' with only 250 hours' flying time or even less. In our branch of the Air Crew Association we had Nick Carter, a flight engineer who flew in Stirlings, and I once asked him how much flying time he had before his first op. He said, 'Let's see. I had a couple of air test flights in a Hampden and a training flight in a Stirling – at a guess about eight or nine hours all told.' Eight or nine hours and off went Nick Carter in a Stirling bomber to Germany! However, survival is still luck. Of the 47 RAF pilots who gathered at Netheravon for training in September 1937 I know of only eight – including me – who survived the war.

US bomb groups suffered losses on a similar scale. Frederick J. Gerritz Sr gives an example from his unit, the 466th Bomb Group: 'We lost a total of 94 B-24 Liberators from my group alone. The number of flyers killed in action was 333, with 171 captured as prisoners of war and 27 interned after landing in neutral countries. Of the 540 crew members of the 466th who failed to return from combat missions, only 180 survived when their aircraft were destroyed.'

Many aircrew were lost in training, as John Musgrove of No. 567 Squadron recalls:

I was in an all-Australian crew, except for our flight engineer, Bert Roberts, who came from Newcastle upon Tyne in the UK. At the OTU we trained on Wellingtons. We returned early from one flight because of engine trouble to find ten-tenths cloud at base. Our pilot saw a chink in the cloud and landed off the runway, breaking an airscrew. Phil Vallender, in the next plane down, came in too low looking for base, pranged, and all the crew were killed. The mid-upper gunner belonging to that crew, Roy Vesperman, had not flown that night – being replaced by his best friend – so he replaced one of our crew who refused to fly and went LMF [Lack of Moral Fibre]. Roy is a close friend of mine in Sydney; he recently had a leg amputated due to damage done to it by burns during one of the wartime ops.

The majority of the Bomber Command aircrew – about 70 per cent – came from the UK. Canada – which had no conscription during the Second World War – provided the next highest total of Bomber Command aircrew volunteers: some 20 per cent. In 1943, after strong pressure from the Canadian government, the Canadians formed their own group, 6 (RCAF) Group, based in Yorkshire and with all its costs paid by Canada, though many Canadians continued to fly with RAF crews and many RAF men served in 6 (RCAF) Group, especially as flight engineers. Australians were always a force in Bomber Command, while tiny New Zealand, whose air force had only been in existence for two years before the war broke out, agreed to train sixty aircrew up to OTU level every month, before sending them to the UK, where crews were formed by an unusual process that took place at an operational training unit.

One day at the start of the three-month OTU course, all the trainees – pilots, navigators, wireless operators, bomb-aimers and rear gunners – would be assembled in a hangar and told to form themselves into crews. There was no pressure from the instructors: it was left entirely to the trainees to decide whom they flew with; no one was 'detailed off'. Those who already knew each other got together and went about seeking others who needed their particular skills; a gunner and wireless operator would chat to a pilot and, if all went well, the three of them would pick out a likely navigator and then this four would find a another gunner or a bomb-aimer. Other crew members, like flight engineers, were picked up later, at the heavy conversion unit.

Leonard Thompson, a flight engineer with No. 550 Squadron, remembers this final process:

> RAF Lindholme in Yorkshire was a heavy conversion unit (HCU) where those who had flown twin-engined types were introduced to the four-engine kind. As I recall there were about 24 of us in the room – all pilots and navigators – and we sorted ourselves into crews. Mine had a Canadian bomb-aimer, an Australian mid-upper gunner and an American serving in the RAF as a rear gunner. The wireless operator decided he could not fly on ops so we lost him, but we got a good replacement when we arrived at RAF Waltham for operational duties . . . but on 23 December 1943 I awoke with the flu. My pilot took me to the sick bay and they kept me there while our pilot, Flight Sergeant John Woods, went back to the billet and got my kit.
>
> That was the last time I saw him, or any of my crew. On their next op, while climbing to gain height over the base before setting course for Berlin, they collided with a Lancaster. All John Wood's crew were killed, as were the pilot and flight engineer of the other aircraft. This crash occurred on Christmas Eve 1943 – a terrible Christmas present for the families of the men involved.

These men were to fly, fight and – all too often, as here – die together. It therefore seemed logical to the powers that be that they should have a major say in who they 'crewed up' with. It may seem a strange system – the USAAF aircrew veterans think it was very strange indeed – but it worked. As a result, crew loyalty was total at the time and remains so half a century later.

The other strange thing about RAF crews was that even if the pilot was a sergeant, as most RAF pilots were, at least to begin with, he became the captain of the crew – the 'skipper'. Even if some other members of the crew were officers, the sergeant pilot was the captain of the aircraft.

'By the time we crewed up, I was a flying officer,' writes Jack Furner, then a navigator with No. 214 Squadron and later an air vice-marshal. 'My skipper was John Verrall, a tall, laconic New Zealander, at that time a sergeant, and Army visitors could never understand this. An officer calling a sergeant 'Skipper' – very infra dig! But in the air it worked. We all had our separate jobs and we worked as a team; woe betide those crews that could not work together.'

Supplied with a mid-upper gunner and a flight engineer, these volunteers went on as a full crew to an HCU, where they learn to fly and operate in four-engined bombers – the Stirling, Halifax or Lancaster – before being posted to their operational squadrons.

William I. Jefferies was an RCAF officer instructing at an HCU:

My unit was the heavy conversion unit at Topcliffe, near Thirsk. The main function of an HCU at this time was to bring aircrew personnel together and train them to become operational in a Lancaster aircraft. We gave lectures on defences, fighters, anti-aircraft belts, escape, weather, radar – just about anything that seemed applicable to getting them there and back safely. As the crews became more and more familiar with flying the Lancaster they often flew at the same time as genuine bombing raids, but on different routes, to act as a diversion or 'spoof' to confuse the defenders, dropping *Window*, a tinfoil-covered strip which affected enemy radar.

Before these 'dummy' raids there would be a full-scale briefing and afterwards a full-scale interrogation, just like the real thing and equally necessary. We wanted as much information as possible on searchlights, anti-aircraft fire, fighter attacks, aircraft crashes seen on the ground, sightings of survivors and exact location, because it would be useful later.

On arrival at their squadron, it was usual for the new crew to have more training as part of their integration into the operational routine, and the pilot would go on one or two operations with an experienced crew as a second pilot – or 'Second Dicky', as he was usually called. A number of new pilots were lost when flying as 'Second Dicky', and when this happened his colleagues, now a 'headless crew', had to return to the OTU, pick up another pilot, and start all over again. Bomber Command training was not without risk: some 8,300 men were killed in training accidents, and a considerable number were seriously injured, the combined total of losses in training coming to around 12 per cent of Bomber Command's strength by the end of the war.

This personal approach to crew selection and the non-commissioned status of the pilots has amazed USAAF aircrew, who, while allegedly more egalitarian, had their crew members appointed by direct order. In the USAAF the 'senior' members of the crew – the pilots, navigators and bomb-aimers – were always officers and usually college graduates; only the gunners were NCOs, and there was a fairly rigid demarcation between the crew members during the off-duty hours.

The basic unit of Bomber Command was the squadron. A squadron was a fairly flexible structure in terms of numbers, was led by a wing commander, and usually consisted of either a three-flight squadron of 30 aircraft or a two-flight squadron of 20 bombers, each flight being led by a squadron leader. All Bomber Command operations were 'Maximum Efforts', when every serviceable squadron aircraft that had a crew was put into the air. Once again, there are no absolutes: few squadrons could ever operate at full strength for long, mainly because of servicing difficulties. The number of aircraft 'put up' largely depended on the skill and hard work of the ground crews – the unsung heroes of Bomber Command – who often worked at night and in all weathers out at 'dispersal' to keep 'their' aircraft in flying trim.

Bomber Command HQ was at High Wycombe in Buckinghamshire. By 1944 the Command had 54 operational airfields spread around the country, mainly in the east, from Middlesborough to Cambridge. The usual arrangement was two squadrons to an airfield, each airfield being equipped with a full range of operational facilities, from hangar repair shops and bomb dumps, to barracks, messes and briefing rooms. The pre-war RAF stations, which had brick accommodation and all the proper facilities, were greatly preferred to the more recent wartime creations, which had draughty prefabricated Nissen huts and temporary accommodation and became seas of mud in winter.

The facilities, flight offices and aircraft 'dispersals' were spread out round the station, and all the aircrew, in RAF Bomber Command or the US Eighth Air Force, record that the most useful piece of kit on any airfield was a bicycle. RAF bomber squadrons formed part of a 'group', commanded by an air vice-marshal, each group consisting of ten or more squadrons: 1 Group had fourteen, 3 Group eleven, 8 Group twelve, and so on, a typical squadron having around fifteen aircraft at the start of the war, increasing to twenty or more by 1944. By May 1945 Bomber Command had 98 squadrons and could put up about 1,600 aircraft every day or night. The USAAF, though employing similar names – squadron, wing and group – used them for different functions, and the USAAF organization will be introduced later.

By the end of 1943, Bomber Command – having lost 2 Group, which operated medium bombers and Mosquitoes and was detached to provide the basis for the Second Tactical Air Force (2nd TAF) – had seven operational groups. Five of these belonged to the 'Main Force': numbers 1, 3, 4, 5 and 6 (RCAF). To these can be added two training groups; these did not figure in Main Force calculations, though, as noted above, crews in training were often sent on leaflet raids and 'spoof' operations as part of the training process. Then there was 8 (PFF) Group, of which more anon – a group charged with target-finding and marking. To this can be added 100 (Bomber Support) Group, which handled everything from radar-jamming and 'spoof' operations to operating Mosquito night fighters hunting German night fighters attacking the bomber stream.

The Main Force squadrons were equipped with a variety of bomber aircraft. Indeed, one of the problems affecting Bomber Command during the war was the wide range of aircraft types it had under command at various times. Bomber Command's first aircraft included the Battle and the Blenheim, both of which left the inventory early on, though the Blenheim was still with the Command in 1942. Then came the Hampden, Whitley and Wellington, all of which were twin-engined types. These also gradually faded away or were transferred to other Commands; the Whitley, for example, was later used by Transport Command to tow gliders or drop paratroops. The Vickers Wellington – the 'Wimpy' – was a robust aircraft, very popular with the crews, and stayed in the front line until 1943 and in RAF service until the 1950s. Some squadrons were briefly equipped with the Avro Manchester, which had a short and unhappy life, being unreliable mechanically with an unfortunate tendency to catch fire in the air.

By mid-1942 the Manchester had been transformed into the Lancaster, the best all-round bomber of the war and highly popular with the crews, who now had three four-engine types – the Short Stirling, the Handley Page Halifax and the Avro Lancaster, of which only the last two were really capable of standing up to the demands of bomber operations over Germany. The Stirling, though cherished by its crews, did not have a sufficiently high operational ceiling to make it fully viable and was gradually phased out and replaced by the Halifax III and the Lancaster, which, in various Marks, stayed in service until the end of the war. None of these aircraft were pressurized: like their comrades in the USAAF B-17 Fortresses and B-24 Liberators, RAF aircrews had to go on oxygen when their aircraft got above 10,000 ft.

By March 1942 an RAF heavy-bomber crew consisted of eight men, each with a specialized role: two pilots, a navigator, a flight engineer, a bomb-aimer, a wireless operator/air gunner, and two gunners for the mid-upper and rear turrets. A shortage of pilots in 1942 forced a change in this set-up: it was decided that a second pilot was unnecessary, though it then became the practice for the flight engineer to learn how to fly the aircraft, if not how to land it – if anything happened to the pilot, the crew had to bale out. Pilot training was the most rigorous, and the safety of the crew, while the responsibility of all the crew members, depended most of all on the skill and leadership of the skipper. If the aircraft got into trouble it was the pilot who stayed at the controls while the rest baled out, and if a large share of decorations and public attention went to the pilots, no other crew member resented this.

Next came the navigator, the man who gave the pilot the course to fly and used the various navigation aids that came in over time to keep the aircraft on track. Navigation was the crux of Bomber Command operations, and a squadron's navigators tended to be clannish, jealous of their reputation as skilled members of the crew, and ruthless at correcting any navigator who fell short of the required standard – the 'Navigators' Union' is frequently mentioned in RAF aircrew accounts. On operations, the navigator maintained the plot, recording all course changes, made adjustments for wind, and directed the pilot on the course to the target and home again. Navigators needed a light and a table to do this work, and had a screened-off section just behind the cockpit, where many navigators spent the entire flight, declining invitations from the pilot to come and look at what was going on over Germany during the actual raid.

Each squadron had a senior man – a leader – in overall charge of each of the various crew functions: a 'bombing leader' to check bomb loads and rule on maximum 'all-up' bombing weights, a 'navigation leader' to advise on routes and oversee the work of the squadron navigators, and so on. Navigation leaders were well known for conducting squadron inquests if the navigation on a particular operation had failed to meet the expected standards of the Navigators' Union.

Bomb-aimers appeared in 1942. Before that, in the earlier, smaller and simpler aircraft, bomb-aiming was the second duty of the navigator. In a heavy bomber the bomb aimer also manned the front turret and helped out in the more mundane in-flight tasks, like scanning the H_2S set, before coming into his own when the aircraft began its straight and level run-up to the target.

The wireless operator was responsible for communications. He had to maintain a listening watch on the set, picking up messages from base – especially the 'broadcast winds' for the navigators – and sending out replies. Radio transmissions had to be as short and infrequent as possible, because of the guidance they gave to the German fighter-control stations. The crew could talk to each other on the aircraft 'intercom', another vital piece of equipment. If the intercom failed the crew could not communicate and were obliged to abort the operation and turn for home. Until 1943 the aircraft had no means of communicating with each other, though VHF radios, first used by No. 617 Squadron on the Dams Raid in May, were then introduced throughout the Command and enabled the designated 'master bomber' to control the attacks.

By 1942, German radio-interception sets were so sensitive that they could detect the RAF and USAAF radio operators warming up their sets on the bomber bases back in Britain and thus accurately estimate the strength of that night's operations, so radio traffic was always kept to the minimum even on the ground. Later in the war, as radar aids became more sophisticated, the wireless operator had a role supporting the gunners, watching the *Fishpond* radar screen which gave indications of approaching fighters or listening to the *Monica* set, which had the same purpose but covered the vulnerable rear of the aircraft. The wireless operator also acted as a spare gunner if necessary, but for most of the flight he was glued to the radio set listening for messages – the vital link between the aircraft and the home base. He was also responsible for sending out SOS messages when the aircraft was hit and going down – an especially vital task if the aircraft was ditching in the sea.

The flight engineer assisted the pilot. He took the former second-pilot seat in the cockpit, helped the pilot with the throttles on take-off and landings, and was usually capable of taking over the controls if need be. A large number of flight engineers were 'washed-out' pilots who had learned enough about flying to do this, but others had been taught the elements of flying on 'link trainers' back at base or were instructed by their pilots and encouraged to take over the controls and stay in practice on training flights. Flight engineers were also responsible for keeping an eye on the mechanical side of the aircraft's performance in flight and making fuel calculations, switching tanks as necessary. They could also act as a reserve bomb-aimer and could move about the aircraft, checking on other members of the crew.

Finally there were two air gunners – at least on British aircraft: the Americans had many more. RAF gunners – the rear gunner and mid-upper gunner – were responsible for the defence of the aircraft, not only by engaging enemy fighters with their .303-calibre machine-guns, but by maintaining a constant lookout during the flight. Being a gunner was a cold and lonely job. Though the rest of the crew had to keep their attention fixed on the task in hand – the navigation charts, the radio or the instruments – they were close to the others and shared a sense of community. Not so the gunners. In spite of various aids, most of which came in late in the war, the survival of the crew throughout the tour largely depended on the alertness of the gunners, who, shut in their turrets throughout the flight, had somehow to stay alert, straining their eyes out into the night sky for hour after hour, looking for a brief patch of extra darkness that might be an enemy fighter. A sudden cry of 'Fighter, corkscrew right!' from a gunner was often the first and only warning the pilot would receive. Unless he acted on it promptly, the aircraft could be lost.

Both gunners had important and dangerous jobs, but in a Bomber Command aircraft the rear gunner may have had the worst and loneliest job of all. Stuck on his own at the far end of a vibrating fuselage, sucking on the oxygen line and often deprived of heat, the rear gunner was particularly vulnerable to the first strike of an enemy fighter coming up from astern – a fighter that was equipped with machine-guns and cannon which outmatched the bomber's guns in both range and firepower. The awards given to air gunners were well earned, not just for particular actions, but for keeping their guard up, night after night, when nothing much happened at all.

This short listing of their separate responsibilities should not obscure the fact that a crew could only survive *as a crew*. The most brilliant pilot, the most astute navigator, the most accurate and alert air gunner was *useless* without the total support of his crewmates. Crews were reckoned to be particularly vulnerable during their first five or six operations, while they were getting the hang of the job, and again at the end of their tour, when they were becoming tired, overconfident and perhaps careless. Keeping the crew up to the mark was another task for the skipper.

Bomber Command aircrews were all mixed-nationality crews, drawn from every corner of the Empire. Even 6 (RCAF) Group had some proportion of non-Canadian personnel, with most of the flight engineers and many other crew members coming from the UK or other parts of the Empire. Similarly, many Royal Canadian Air Force aircrew continued to serve in other squadrons or aircraft of Bomber Command after the formation of 6 (RCAF) Group. The Royal Australian Air Force had several squadrons in Bomber Command, but their crews, though predominantly Australian, always contained members from other nations. Nationality did not count at 25,000 ft over Germany: crew loyalty was the thing that mattered, the vital element that kept the men alive.

Group Captain Peter Bird, who flew with 5 Group, recalls another aspect of the bomber war:

> It was a curious war. You could go into battle within perhaps only an hour from the warmth and comfort of an officers' mess, where you got a good meal served by a pretty girl before the operation. Then you went out to wait in your aircraft, bombed-up and ready to go, waiting for the signal to start your engines, looking out the open side window of your Lancaster, over the perimeter hedge of the airfield, to see a young man and a girl, about your age, walking hand in hand to the pub through the peaceful English countryside. You were going to Germany, and before they walked home again you might be in the throes of battle – or dead.

Although it varied, and was calculated differently at the start of the war, the standard Bomber Command first 'tour' during the Second World War, was 30 operations over enemy-held territory. Other operations, on 'easy' targets in France, counted for less – perhaps half an op – so more such ops had to be flown until the total of 30 was reached – and 'early returns' or aborted ops did not count at all. Depending on the weather and the operations flown, completing a tour could take anything from a couple of months to the best part of a year, and only about 35 per cent of the aircrews survived their first tour. After completing their tour, the men went on leave and were then sent to train other crews at OTUs or HCUs for at least six months, before returning for a further tour of twenty ops, after which they could not be asked to fly on operations again – unless they wanted to.

A surprising number did, for plenty of aircrew enjoyed the excitement of operational flying and the comradeship of an operational station. When transferred to training or staff duties they hankered to be back with a front-line squadron and pleaded for a return to ops. These people – the 'old lags', as Arthur Harris called them fondly – continued flying until they had amassed a considerable number of ops – 70, 80, 90 or more – and went on until they had finally had enough, were shot down, or the war ended.

There were others who could not take operational flying at all. Station and squadron commanders were always on the lookout for men who were showing signs of nerves, or failing in one way or another to complete their tasks on operations. A pilot who aborted the flight and came home early was sure to face an interview with his commanding officer, and aircraft that seemed to develop a chronic series of faults, leading to the crew making an 'early return' after jettisoning the bombs in the North Sea, would be gone over carefully by the ground crew for evidence that the faults were genuine. The squadron and station commanders were well aware that operational flying was a dangerous and stressful business – all of them had done their share of it, and many flew ops themselves from time to time – but the war had to be won, and it did not do to be too considerate with those who consistently failed to make the grade.

Those who were unable to continue or had done more than their share or had a particularly distressing experience, or simply did not have the temperament for this sort of work, were usually treated with sympathy and posted to other work. In most cases a spot of leave, a chat – pleasant or direct – from the group captain or, in extreme cases, a short spell at the Air Crew Correction Centre at Sheffield for a dose of discipline put an end to the problem or at least enabled the man to finish his tour. Crews were given a week's leave every six weeks, and were encouraged to get off the station at other times when no operations were actually being planned.

Some men, however, flatly refused to fly, in which case their treatment was harsh. These men were graded 'LMF' – Lack of Moral Fibre – or, put simply, regarded as cowards. They were stripped of their flying brevets, removed from the flying station immediately, and either posted to menial ground duties or dismissed from the RAF and promptly called up for service in the infantry. Even today this is not a matter that the aircrew veterans wish to dwell on.

Leonard Thompson of No. 550 Squadron expresses a point made by many other aircrew on this matter:

> I did not suffer from fatigue during my tour of 32 operations but when it was over I knew I needed a rest. How the PFF boys managed with 45-op tours I just can't imagine! This fatigue must have led to losses, but that is hindsight. On LMF, I just felt that many of our lads had really given their all and the top brass, of whom only a few had personal experience of operations from mid-1943, just did not have a clue about how an individual felt. They looked on it as cowardice in the face of the enemy. They should have tried it themselves, night after night, and maybe they would have changed their tune. Sorry, but that is how I feel, and have felt since my operational days.

Air Gunner Derek Jackson agrees with this:

> I think grading a man 'LMF' was a scandal. These men were all volunteers
> and if they lost their nerve, well, it could have happened to any of us. I think
> they should have simply been taken off ops and posted away, not disgraced
> and sent to do menial jobs, or kicked out. Perhaps some of the people who
> judged these men should have tried it out themselves. Halfway through our
> tour the navigator told our pilot that he could not go on, but the pilot had a
> word with him and he stayed with us. He was as sick as a dog before every
> op, but he kept going and finished the tour – and that took real guts.

Those of a later generation, who have not endured what the aircrew
endured, cannot judge this issue. Many may feel, with Derek Jackson, that
to grade any man as 'LMF' and brand him as a coward is a monstrous act,
but many station commanders and even famous squadron commanders
like Leonard Cheshire felt that fear was an infection which could spread
through a squadron like a virus and had therefore to be rooted out. Their
reasoning was that if one man could decline to fly and get away with it
unpunished, what sort of example did that set to the rest?

Nor is it right to assume that the aircrew were composed of a majority
of heroes and a few frightened men. Everyone who flew on ops was afraid,
and rightly so: there was a great deal to be afraid of, and anyone who says
he was never afraid is a liar. So, while regretting the branding of some men
as 'LMF', some thought should be spared for the tens of thousands of other
young men, like Derek Jackson's navigator, who, though equally frightened, continued to fly and do their duty, rather than let their crew and their
country down.

A good description of what stress the aircrews were under comes from
Howard Jackson, a bombardier with the USAAF 454th Bomb Group,
Fifteenth Air Force:

> The Operations Board listed me as a bombardier, and my first task on mis-
> sions was arming the bombs. Each bomb had a front and a rear fuse secured
> by arming wires; when the bomb was released the arming wire would leave
> the fuses and the bomb would be alive. That could only happen when the
> bombardier first removed the safety pins. This required the bombardier to
> leave his position in the nose, strap on a portable oxygen tank, and crawl
> back to the bomb bay. None of the aircraft were pressurized, and we went
> on oxygen at around 10,000 ft. The passage to the bomb bay was tight, so
> your parachute had to be left behind and that could cause some anxious
> moments.
>
> The bomb bay was divided by a nine-inch-wide catwalk above the bombs,
> and you went out on that to arm the bombs, taking off the heavy gloves and
> wearing a light pair – at temperatures of minus twenty degrees human skin
> would adhere to the metal. It was usually easy to remove the pins with a pair
> of pliers – at least if the aircraft was steady, but that was rarely the case. On

the larger bombs the process took some fifteen minutes; however, when we were arming fragmentation bombs, cluster on cluster, it took a lot longer. On occasion a bomb would fall from an aircraft up above and crash through the fuselage; then only the action of an alert member, who had to grab it and throw it overboard, prevented a major problem. So it was not easy. The only requirement for a flying officer was to be ready to fly and die upon command.

The terror starts on the night before the mission. This should not be confused with fear. Fear is when you have to ask a girl to dance who might say no, or when waiting in class to be asked a question you don't know how to answer. Terror is anxiety, dreams, rationalization of excuses not to fly, headaches, loose bowels, shaking and silence. No one ever discussed these conditions, so they were not acknowledged – the Air Force said they did not exist. Dr Death, our flight surgeon, was kind enough to supply sleeping pills and early-morning wake-up pills. It was during this pre-flight experience that most self-inflicted wounds and deaths occurred. I always remember wondering with admiration and respect how the silent, strong, flying men were able to sustain a combat tour. Aged nineteen, a flying officer and a poor risk, I had little experience to share with my manly associates.

Second Lieutenant Howard F. Jackson completed his tour of missions and was awarded the Purple Heart for wounds sustained in action.

Like Howard Jackson, most of these men were young. Flying was as a game for young men, and even those in their mid-twenties were often called 'Grandad' by the rest of the crew. The average age was somewhere between 19 and 22 and to give just one example, David Shannon, an Australian pilot with No. 617 Squadron, flew his Lancaster bomber at 50 ft against the Ruhr dams three weeks before his twenty-first birthday – and by that time Dave Shannon was a very experienced bomber pilot indeed.

The same holds true in the US bomb groups. Ben Love, a pilot with the 351st Bomb Group, records in his memoirs that 'On October 10, 1944, orders arrived from Eighth Air Force HQ promoting me to 1st Lieutenant. I had then been flying missions for two months and was still six weeks away from my 20th birthday.'

However, not all the crews were composed of very young men, as Canadian bomber pilot Jim Brown of No. 429 (Bison) Squadron, RCAF, can confirm:

My flight engineer was English, an ex-policeman who had spent six years at Scotland Yard, and my navigator was an expatriate Brit who had grown up in the USA. The bomb-aimer was a Canadian from Moose Jaw, and the gunners were both in their forties, which was unusual. In fact we were not a typical crew. The flight engineer was 38, the navigator 22, the bomb aimer 41, and the gunners 41 and 44; between us we had a total of four wives and seven children. I was 27, so we were known as the 'Old Mans' crew', but that did not hurt us one bit.

This, in outline, describes the men who flew with Bomber Command and some of their comrades in the Eighth Air Force. The mission routine for the American aircrews is described in another chapter, and much of what applies to these Allied flyers also applies to the *Luftwaffe* aircrews. Like their bomber opponents, they were mostly young and all volunteers – a fact that created a bond that seemed to unite all the flyers once the fighting was over; the research for this book revealed that many bomber crew members have since made friends among the *Luftwaffe* veterans.

The organization of the USAAF bomb groups and the *Luftwaffe* fighter squadrons differs from that of the RAF and for the sake of clarity is covered in future chapters, but the recruitment and training of USAAF and *Luftwaffe* crews can also be covered here. The men were not unlike their British, Australian, Canadian, New Zealand or Continental counterparts: they were young and willing and eager to fly. And, like the British, the Americans had a score to settle.

When the Japanese shocked America by the treacherous bombing of Pearl Harbor, young Americans flocked into the Army – and so into the Army Air Force – in vast numbers. Some were recalled reservists, some were volunteers, many were simply drafted. Those who wanted to be aircrew had to volunteer, and a typical example of what happened after that comes from William Chapin, a newspaper reporter from Vermont:

I graduated from Dartmouth College in New Hampshire in June 1940. I didn't pay much attention to the war then; I knew that France had surrendered and Great Britain was fighting for its life and that the USA might get involved, but I was busy being a cub reporter. I guess my main reaction to the war was that I didn't particularly want to be in it.

Then came Pearl Harbor, and on a Sunday evening in early 1942 my draft notice arrived. I knew one thing: I didn't want to be a foot soldier. I considered submarines, but then I heard that there was a university course going on meteorology for the Army Air Force, so I applied, got accepted, and spent nine months learning all about synoptic charts and isobars and cold fronts. I completed the course in November 1942 and was commissioned as a second lieutenant in the Army Air Force and assigned to duty as met officer at Pope Field, North Carolina. Then, having got married, I applied to be a flying weather officer and went through flight training.

First stop was Nashville, Tennessee, where we 'aviation cadets' were put through a medical exam and a battery of tests to see how we could stand stress. I passed that and went to Maxwell Field in Alabama for pre-flight training. We took things like basic math and airplane recognition and hung around the Officers' Club, where we played the slot machines and drank a lot of beer. Not once at Maxwell did we climb into an airplane.

After that we went to Camden, North Carolina, for primary flight training. Camden was a grass field, and the whole place was low-key. We flew PT-17s, Stearman biplanes, which were very forgiving and terrific for aerobatics. My instructor was Mr Poe, a civilian and a sadistic tyrant, who ranted and raved at me. I felt sure I was going to be washed out, but I soloed after eight hours, which was slightly better than average, and after two months' training I was one of the three top pilots who flew in the Graduation Day fly-past.

That night Mr Poe invited us home for a party. He was the soul of Southern hospitality, so I asked him why he had been so rough on us and he said, 'Ah reckon yo'all gonna have it much worser than that when you ovahseas, fightin'.' I didn't tell him that as a flying weather officer I didn't expect to see much fighting – unlike one of my good friends, Ben Benitez, a West Point-trained officer from Puerto Rico; Ben went to England to fly fighters and was killed on his first mission.

Basic training was at Shaw Field, South Carolina, where we flew BT-13s – single-engined monoplanes, whose propellers gave off a distinctive whine when you changed the angle at which they bit through the air. It was also very hard to get them out of a spin, and I made sure I had plenty of height before I spun it. Advanced twin-engine training took place at Lawrenceville, Illinois, on A-10s, but it was no longer much fun. The weather was terrible, training seemed to go in fits and starts, and the A-10s were not very good aircraft. By now we were flying cross-country missions by day and night, and more than once I got lost. By night, from 5,000 ft, Terre Haute looks like any other small city.

During the last week of training, Captain Harry Arp, a fellow weather officer, flew his A-10 into a fog-shrouded house a hundred yards or so from the end of the runway. My wife, accompanied by the base commanding officer, had to call on Evelyn Arp and tell her that her husband was dead. That's a hard thing to do.

Soon after that we got our wings. We also got word that we were to become bomber pilots. Now that *was* a surprise, after that 'flying weather officer' bulletin, but American bomber losses in Europe were much too heavy and replacement crews were needed desperately. My reaction to the prospect of combat wasn't fear, rather it was curiosity: what would it be like to get shot at? So bombers it would be, and we were given a choice: twin-engine or four-engine. I chose four-engine – it might, I surmised, turn out to be a handy civilian skill, maybe as a commercial airline pilot.

With my new wings pinned to my tunic – and I was really proud of them – I was sent to Maxwell Field, where I learned to fly B-24 Liberators. The B-24 was known as the 'Flying Boxcar', and for good reason. It was a graceless machine, built for business, and in repose it was squat and sullen. But it was rugged, and its four Pratt & Whitney engines could take a lot of battle damage and still turn over. It was a heavy airplane, and it took muscle and sweat to jerk it off the ground when it was full of people, fuel and bombs. I flew it for 514 hours, in training and in combat; it won my respect but never my affection.

The B-24, in combat, was a paradox. It had a long wing, 110 ft long, and this persuaded the B-24 to fly higher and faster than comparable aircraft – a factor that made people who are paid to think about these matters conclude that the B-24 could fly higher and faster than German fighters; thus it would need fewer guns and less armour; thus it could carry more bombs for greater distances than the B-17.

It didn't work out that way. German fighters could fly as high and fast as a B-24. Consequently, when B-24s and B-17s went on a mission, the German fighters pounced gleefully on the B-24s. So the only answer was to put the armour and the guns back. But then the B-24 could no longer fly so high or so fast – not even as high as the B-17. In essence, the B-24 screwed itself. On bombing missions I regularly saw the B-17s flying 2,000 ft above me, their pilots presumably laughing. This made me mad as hell, but nothing could be done about it.

I wasn't very good at instrument-flying the B-24. I recall seeing a member of my class take off in his B-24, lose an engine, stall out at 1,000 ft, and spin into the ground. Big explosion and then – nothingness. That sticks in my memory. But I made it through all right, and in March 1944 I was transferred to Westover Field, Massachusetts, where I was assigned a crew, and we went to Charleston Field, South Carolina, for the final bit of training, which was called 'Staging'.

'Staging' consisted of formation flying, simulated bombing missions, target practice for the air gunners, night flights, the occasional cross-country trip. We were assigned an instructor, but we often flew on our own and we began to come together as a *crew*. Ten men: pilot, co-pilot, bombardier, navigator, flight engineer, radio operator, nose gunner, tail gunner, ball-turret gunner, top-turret gunner. The flight engineer and the radio operator also served as gunners.

All of us got along with each other good-naturedly. On the ground, officers and enlisted men alike, we called each other by our first names. In the air, on the interphone, it was 'pilot to navigator' or 'nose gunner to pilot' and so forth. Later, in combat, there was no question who was in command: I was. I was also, at 25, the oldest member of the crew.

Staging at Charleston concluded in early July 1944; I had been training for a year and a half, and in mid-July we got our orders: we were assigned to the 746th Squadron, 456th Bomb Group, 304th Bombardment Wing, Fifteenth Air Force. We were given a shiny new B-24 – so new that it should have had a price tag attached to the propellers. It had been built at Willow Run outside Detroit by the Ford Motor Company, and we were to fly it to Italy and join the war.

William Chapin joined his squadron in Italy, and we shall hear from him again.

The German fighter pilots mustering to oppose the American and British bombers over Germany had followed a slightly different path to operational flying. Since the prime purpose of the *Luftwaffe* at the start of the war was army co-operation, its bomber aircraft were – with the exception of the Focke-Wulf Condor – the smaller, twin-engined types and a large number of bomber pilots were eventually switched to fighter operations, especially night-fighter operations in the twin-engined Me 110.

A German fighter pilot did not fly a tour: unless he was lucky and posted to a training station as an instructor, he simply went on flying until he was killed. If he was shot down and survived, he was given another aircraft and sent straight up again. By the end of the war only the U-boat crews had suffered more casualties than the German fighter arm.

As with the Allied aircrews, becoming a flyer took time, as *Luftwaffe* ace Paul Zorner relates:

I was born in 1920 at Roben, a village in what is now Polish Oberschliesen. From 1930 I attended the Carolinum Grammar School, one of the monastic schools founded in the seventeenth century in Austria and Prussia. I passed the university examination there in 1938 and then did six months' National Socialist Labour Duty.

In October 1938 I began service in the Air Force Airmen Replacement Department, and in March 1939 I was, as officer cadet, posted for officer and pilot training to the Aerial Warfare School at Gatow, Berlin. I left there at the end of 1939 as a sergeant with the Air Force Pilots' certificate. In November 1939 I want on other courses learning to fly all types of aircraft and stayed on at the school as a flying instructor. In April 1940 I was promoted to second lieutenant. The rest of 1940 was spent on flying courses, including a blind-flying course, and in March 1941 I was deployed to KG ZBV 104, a transport group flying Junkers 52s between Sicily and North Africa – in aircraft carrying Iraqi markings – and then went to Russia to fly missions in the Ukraine and south Russia.

In October 1941 I requested transfer to night-fighter training in Munich. There was already a lack of fuel and the usual four-month course lasted nine months, but at the end of it I was promoted first lieutenant and posted in July 1942 to *NJG 2* [*Nachtjäger* or Nightfighter 2nd *Staffel*] flying Ju 88s. I made my first attack on the night of 17 August 1942, over Holland. By the end of September I had made six more attacks with the Ju 88 and then changed to the Dornier 217 and went to Grove at Jutland. I made a further six attacks with the Do 217 but it was too clumsy for a night fighter, though it could stay in the air for five hours.

So far no 'shot-downs', but on 17 January 1943 I shot down a Halifax over the Friesian Islands. I was now a squadron leader with II/NJG 3 at Wittemundenhafen. In March 1943 I went as a squadron captain to Vechta, where we made attacks on American bombers; on one attack I was shot up and had to make an emergency landing. We then went back to night fighting, and in July 1943 after 38 attacks I shot down another Halifax, though I was hit by return fire and had to bail out.

In August 1943 the English started to use *Dupple* (*Window*), aluminium strips by which the radar was made ineffective, and in September I was posted to III/NJG 3 at Lüneburg, near Hamburg, where we re-equipped with the new Me 110, with the new radio navigation apparatus SN2 (*Lichtenstein*). With this a promising free night-fighter operation, independent from guidance, was possible. In the next four months I shot down 29 British bombers.

Paul Zorner finished the war with the Knight's Cross of the Iron Cross with Oak Leaves, having shot down 59 Allied bombers. We shall also hear from him again.

When considering the composition of the *Luftwaffe* in the Second World War it is important to remember that large parts of it consisted of anti-aircraft – flak – units, that the *Luftwaffe* also contained parachute units, and that the strategic bomber element was very small. Indeed, until the late summer of 1940 hardly any night bombing operations were carried out, and the introduction of night operations arose from the fact that day bombing operations over Britain were proving exceptionally costly. However, the *Luftwaffe* could afford heavy losses, for there were plenty of aircrew and their quality was exceptionally high. Goering had always been determined to make the *Luftwaffe* the *corps d'élite* of the *Wehrmacht* and attracted into the ranks of the Air Force the cream of the *Hitlerjugend*, the Hitler Youth, which all German youngsters were obliged to join.

Peter Spoden was a night-fighter pilot:

> Before the war you had a choice at fifteen or sixteen to join any sports group, and I decided to go with the glider group and became a glider pilot by the age of seventeen. I was called up in 1940, aged nineteen, and my father, who had fought at Verdun in the first war, advised me to join the *Luftwaffe*. They gave us tests and asked us what we wanted to become, and I said a night-fighter pilot, because the English were already bombing Essen, where my family had a house, and nothing but a night fighter would do me. The training was very long, and it was not until 1943 that it was finished and I joined a nightfighter squadron flying Me 110s at Pachim.

Luftwaffe volunteers were accepted from the age of seventeen, by which time many, like Peter Spoden, had had glider training and not a few had already learned how to fly in one of the National Socialist Flying Corps schools. The *Luftwaffe* was a wholly professional force, requiring officers to serve for up to twelve years, and when an officer had finished his flying service Goering promised to arrange for further lucrative employment in Lufthansa, the state airline, or in one of the *Luftwaffe* ground units. Since the Nazi 'Thousand Year Reich' only lasted twelve years, very few *Luftwaffe* aircrew were able to take up Goering's offer, though Peter Spoden joined Lufthansa after the war and became a Boeing 747 pilot.

Initial training in peace time could last up to twelve months, though this period, when such basics as drill, discipline, map reading and physical training were covered, was reduced in wartime to around three months. After recruit training, those selected for flying duties spent two months studying aeronautical subjects, before going on to the Elementary Flying School for about 100–150 hours of instruction, going solo after about five hours. Then followed hours of 'circuits and bumps' around the airfield, leading on to longer cross-country flights. During this time the trainee was assessed for his suitability as a fighter, bomber, dive-bomber or transport pilot, and at the end of this course he was awarded his wings and a certificate. From that point on all training was related to one of the four roles outlined above.

Those selected for training as fighter pilots went on for a further three months' training, either on the single-engined Me 109 day fighter or the twin-engined Me 110, which, as Paul Zorner has related, later became a popular and successful night fighter. As new types and marks were introduced later in the war, further training was supplied, often at squadron or group level, but in the early days a pilot might get about 50 hours' training on fighters before being posted to his *Gruppe*. Once there he would receive further training and be appointed to a *Staffel*. Though the number of aircraft employed are not the same, it is convenient to regard a *Staffel* of nine aircraft as similar to an RAF flight, a *Gruppe* of 30 aircraft as similar to a squadron, and a *Geschwader* as similar to an RAF fighter wing, with a total of some 124 aircraft, of which four belonged to the *Geschwader* staff.

By September 1939 the *Luftwaffe* was turning out some 12,000 fighter pilots a year, a number far in excess of estimated requirements, so some of these pilots were remustered into other specializations. One difference between the *Luftwaffe* and the Allied air forces, at least in the early days, was that in twin-engined fighters and bombers the observer was the captain of the aircraft if his rank was senior to that of the pilot; this practice died away in the first years of the war. *Luftwaffe* observers were highly trained. All of them had received up to 60 hours' pilot training as well as specialized instruction on map reading, navigation, gunnery and radio work, though this last task was later taken over by a trained radio operator – the *Funker* – who also operated the radar aids in night-fighter aircraft.

German bombers had a crew of three – pilot, observer and radio operator. German twin-engined night fighters had a crew of two – the pilot and his radar operator, the *Funker* – and pilot and *Funker* had to work closely together in the night sky if they hoped to find a bomber and shoot it down. In 1939 the *Luftwaffe* could muster some 4,000 aircraft of all types, all manned by skilled crews, many of them veterans of the Condor Legion in the Spanish Civil War. As the surviving bomber crews of the RAF and the USAAF willingly attest, these men were to prove formidable foes in the skies over Germany as the bomber war began to hot up in 1942.

When Germany went to war the *Luftwaffe* did not possess a specialized night-fighter arm or a specially designed night fighter, or a night-fighter training programme – the leading Nazis, and especially Herman Goering, could not visualize enemy bombers flying over the Reich by day or night. Although they achieved very little in terms of damage, the early RAF night bombing raids did give the German commanders pause for thought. They also gave them time to think and to develop a night-fighter arm, at least in outline, before the heavy raids began in 1942. In June 1940, before the opening of the Battle of Britain, Goering ordered the creation of a *Nachtjagd* or 'Night-Fighting Arm', tasked to shield the industrial cities of Germany from night attack. The first element in this new force, the 1st *Nachtjagd* Division was established in July 1940 at Zeist in Holland, and placed under the command of General Josef Kammhuber, a former bomber pilot during the recently completed Battle of France – an officer who was to become one of the leading night-fighter commanders of the war.

Kammhuber did not see the night fighter in a purely defensive role, operating only over the cities of the Reich. Such activity would employ only part of his force. Another part, the *Fernnachtjagd*, or 'Long-Range Night Force', would act in what the British would later come to call the 'intruder' role, hunting out the Allied bombers at their UK bases. 'A wasp's nest is best eliminated when the wasps are in it, or by blocking the hole through which they fly in and out,' wrote Kammhuber, 'otherwise there is nothing one can do but chase after every individual wasp.' Unfortunately for General Kammhuber and luckily for the Allied aircrews, interference from Hitler prevented the full development of the *Fernnachtjagd*. Hitler wanted Allied bombers shot down in quantity over the Reich's territory, where their destruction would be obvious and provide a boost to civilian morale, though the *Luftwaffe* did continue to mount intruder operations and attack Bomber Command airfields.

The *Luftwaffe* entered the war with a number of advantages – a large number of modern aircraft, a quantity of well-trained aircrew, many of them battle-hardened by the war in Spain, a constant supply of reinforcements from well-established training schools, and a workable doctrine which concentrated on the tactical role. All this gave it an immediate edge over the British – and later over the Americans – who, on the outbreak of war, found that almost every aspect of their pre-war experience, from aircraft and training to navigation, bomb-aiming and doctrine, was unsuitable for the realities of war. While this lesson was being learned, the *Luftwaffe* and the German defenders of the Reich were not slow to exploit their superiority.

In 1942–3, when the RAF – and later the USAAF – was at last able to attack Germany with large numbers of aircraft and a quantity of hard-won experience, it found that the task of defeating the *Luftwaffe* was much harder than it might have been had the equipment and ideas been got right before the outbreak of war. Peacetime training generally proved inadequate for wartime conditions. It was not until the war was more that two years old that the training the aircrew were getting began to bear some relation to the conditions they were meeting in action.

For the Americans, the skies of Europe offered many challenges – the constant clouds and frequent bad weather as well as flak and fighters. For the Germans, with the switch of British attacks from day to night, much peacetime training was no longer applicable – fresh techniques, equipment and skills had to be developed and mastered. As for the British, after two years of groping their way towards a proper offensive, by the middle of

1942 Bomber Command was finally getting the aircraft, the equipment, and the adequate supply of trained, skilled men its offensive needed. The Command had also got a new leader – one who would stay with it until victory and stamp his imprint on the bomber war – Air Chief Marshal Sir Arthur Harris.

Vickers Wellington B. Mk III

5

Harris Takes Command
1942

*There are a lot of people who say that bombing cannot win the war. My reply to that is
that it has never been tried . . . and we shall see.*

Air Chief Marshal Sir Arthur Harris, AOC-in-C,
RAF Bomber Command, 1942

Air Chief Marshal Sir Arthur Harris was Air Officer Commanding-in-
Chief of RAF Bomber Command from February 1942 until the end of the
European war in 1945. In that role he became the focus for all the arguments that raged about strategic bombing at the time, and most of the subsequent contention surrounding the strategic bombing offensive has
centred on Harris – not least on his persistence in attacking the industrial
cities of Germany.

Those arguments will be ventilated again in this book, but Arthur Harris
was far more than a man with a one-track mind. Harris was the living
embodiment of the 'bomber dream', the theory that bombing could win
wars without the need for land offensives and perhaps, by taking wars off
the battlefield and into the homes of the civilian population, make war
itself impossible. That was, and remained, Harris's aim. The bombing of
cities was a means to that end, which he shared with many other senior air
force commanders, including Carl Spaatz and 'Peter' Portal.

Arthur Harris – 'Bomber' Harris to Prime Minister Winston Churchill
and the general public, 'Butch' to his aircrews, and 'Bert' to his friends – is
the enigmatic figure of the strategic bombing offensive. He took over
Bomber Command on 23 February 1942 and entered into his new responsibilities at a fortunate hour, when many of the problems that had dogged

the Command since 1939 were at last being solved. Better aircraft were coming into service, navigation aids were improving, plenty of aircrew were coming forward from the training schools, and the hard-won experience of the last two years was starting to pay off in operational efficiency. Equally important, the United States had now entered the war and would eventually add its weight to the effort.

What Bomber Command needed now was a forceful, resolute officer who would both prosecute the air war over Germany with vigour and fight Bomber Command's other on-going battle – with the Admiralty, the Staff at the Air Ministry and the Ministry of Aircraft Production. Harris, being naturally combative, took up all these challenges with relish, and a fresh air of optimism swept through the squadrons of Bomber Command. Harris was known throughout the RAF as a man who did not suffer fools at all, never mind gladly, a man with a reputation for getting things done, a leader.

Arthur Harris is a hard man to understand. His character was complex, and opinions on his abilities varied. He was aggressive – a condition aggravated by a chronic stomach ulcer he took with him to his new appointment – usually blunt in speech and sometimes extremely rude. He made few friends, but those he did make stayed loyal, and he in turn was always loyal to them. His leading subordinates – men like Robert Saundby, Ralph Cochrane and Donald Bennett – and his direct superior, 'Peter' Portal, had been his friends for years.

It is also worth noting that, more than half a century after the war, the surviving members of Bomber Command remain fiercely loyal to their old commander, though he never went out of his way to court popularity and rarely visited a bomber station. This was not an indication of indifference; since Harris had to plan an operation almost every day and give the target order at 0900 hrs every morning, his absence from the bomber stations is hardly surprising.

Besides, high command is not a popularity contest. Harris was a commander-in-chief, and that role kept him fully employed. The bomber crews knew that Harris had their interests at heart, however rarely they saw him on their stations. They also knew that, while they took on the flak and the fighters, he was fighting another war on their behalf: to obtain the aircraft and the equipment they needed, to get them the appropriate amount of pay and leave, and a fair share of medals and public recognition. He fought to get Bomber Command sufficient productive and scientific resources from industry, and he fought to fend off the attempts of the commanders of the Army and the Royal Navy to reduce his bomber strength or to turn Bomber Command's efforts to other purposes, like submarine interdiction or army co-operation in the Middle East. The bomber crews were, and remain, Harris's men, and the judgement of his subordinates and contemporaries – that he was a fine man and an inspiring leader – should not be lightly dismissed by a later generation.

'He was a leader,' said Charles Carrington, an army liaison officer at Bomber Command HQ:

> His sheer force of personality held his team together, and he inspired the whole Command with devotion to the task of defeating Germany by industrial bombing. No one doubted that he was a master of his trade and had been so since the first years of the RAF's existence. With his power of concentration on the aim, while excluding the irrelevant, he retained a rugged common-sense which was displayed in flat statements about unpalatable facts; he enjoyed shocking the pedants. As I came to know him better I realized that he was not unco-operative, not hostile to the interests I represented. When committed to a combined operation with the Army or the Navy he gave his full support; he never shirked; he never compromised with half-measures.[1]

Whatever is said about him now, it has to be admitted that Harris was the right man for the job in 1942.

Arthur Travers Harris, though claiming in his memoirs to be a Rhodesian, was born in Cheltenham, England, in 1892, and was just 50 when he took up his appointment at Bomber Command. He had emigrated to Rhodesia (now Zimbabwe) in 1910, and he went to war in 1914 with a cavalry regiment, taking part in the South-West Africa campaign until 1915. He then returned to the UK, entered the Royal Flying Corps, and spent the rest of the war in France, flying in operations over the Western Front and in night fighters over London, ending the war with the rank of major. He then elected to stay on in the newly formed RAF and was sent to the Middle East to command a bomber squadron, where his two flight commanders were Robert Saundby and the Hon. Ralph Cochrane, both of whom became close friends and stout supporters of Harris during the Second World War.

Harris then went to Cairo as SASO (Senior Air Staff Officer) Egypt, and on his return to Britain in 1933 he took command of No. 210 Squadron, a flying-boat unit based at Pembroke in South Wales. There he met a brilliant young Australian officer, Donald Bennett, an expert pilot and navigator and another staunch supporter of Harris in the coming war. Harris did not stay long with No. 210 Squadron, being promoted to the rank of group captain in 1933 when he went to the Air Ministry as Deputy Director of Operations and Intelligence. In 1934 he became Deputy Director of Plans (DDP), and he spent three years in this post at a time when Britain finally got to grips with the menace of Germany and began to expand and equip its forces for the coming struggle. As DDP, Harris was directly involved in drawing up the various contingency plans prepared at the Air Ministry for use on the outbreak of war, until in 1937 he was posted to the newly formed 4 Group, Bomber Command, with the rank of air commodore.

The squadrons of 4 Group were re-equipping with the Whitley, and

Harris oversaw the introduction of this aircraft to squadron service – Whitley first flew with No. 10 Squadron, 4 Group, in 1937 – insisting that the group training programme laid a heavy emphasis on navigation and night flying. This appointment did not last long, for in 1938 Harris was sent to the United States to purchase Hudson bombers and Harvard trainers. He was then posted to the Middle East as Air Officer Commanding (AOC), Palestine, returning to Britain to take command of 5 Group, Bomber Command, on 14 September 1939, eleven days after the outbreak of war.

Harris's command in 5 Group consisted of eight squadrons of Hampdens, and the operations of some of these squadrons have been briefly described in earlier chapters. Harris did not like the Hampden: he considered it underpowered and poorly armed, and since it did not have self-sealing fuel tanks it was terribly inclined to catch fire when attacked and therefore a menace to his crews. The Group played a leading part in all the early operations and made a particular mark in mining the inshore waters around the Reich and off the German submarine bases on the French coast.

Harris remained in command of 5 Group until November 1940, right through the first, hard year of the war, during the losses of the daylight bombing campaign and the shift to night operations. His work was recognized by his being made a Commander of the Order of the Bath in July 1940, but his appointment to the Air Ministry as Deputy Chief of the Air Staff was not one he welcomed, though he got on well with the new Chief of the Air Staff, Air Chief Marshal Portal.

In mid-June 1941 Harris left this post to head the RAF delegation to Washington DC, where, apart from arranging for the supply of US aircraft under the Lend-Lease Agreement, he entered into discussions with the US military, and especially with the commanders of the United States Army Air Force, on what might be arranged for mutual support and co-operation if and when the United States entered the war. Two results of Harris's activities in Washington were the purchase of twenty of the latest American bomber, the B-17C – the Flying Fortress – and a growing friendship with Generals Arnold, Spaatz and Eaker – men who would soon become his colleagues in the bomber war over Germany. Harris was still in the USA in February 1942 when he was appointed to replace Air Chief Marshal Peirse at Bomber Command.

When Harris took up his post at Bomber Command, his first task was to get more and better aircraft – a task that brought him into conflict with the politicians, the Air Staff and the Admiralty. In his memoirs, Harris records that he had just 378 bombers under his command, of which only 69 were heavy four-engined types and 50 were the light bombers of 2 Group.[2] He actually had more aircraft on strength than this, but he was not far wrong when he put the effective size of his force at 250 medium and 50 heavy bombers – a force totally inadequate for the task he had been set. Harris was also unhappy with the navigation and bomb-aiming equipment then in service – 'the average crew in average weather could not find its way to the target by visual means alone' – and with the shortage of trained crews. These problems were about to be dealt with, but before that could happen Bomber Command came under attack in the House of Commons and in Whitehall.

On 25 February 1942 the Lord Privy Seal, Sir Stafford Cripps, got up in the House of Commons and made a speech that seemed to put the whole future of strategic bombing in doubt:

> A number of Honourable Members [said Cripps] have questioned whether in the existing circumstances, the continued devotion of a considerable part of our efforts to building up this Bomber Force is the best use we can make of our resources . . . I would remind the House that this policy was initiated at a time when we were fighting alone against the combined forces of Germany and Italy and it seemed that it was the most effective way in which we . . . could take the initiative against the enemy. Since that time we have had enormous support from the Russian Armies . . . and also from the great potential strength of the United States. Naturally, in such circumstances the original policy has come under review. I can assure the House that the Government are fully aware of other uses to which our resources could be put and the moment they arrive at a decision that the circumstances warrant a change, a change in policy will be made.[3]

This speech had some dire effects, not least in Washington, where the 'Germany first' policy of concentrating Allied might against Hitler was already under attack from people like Admiral Ernest J. King, a vocal Anglophobe who believed that the main enemy of the USA was Imperial Japan. Cripps's speech was received gloomily in the upper reaches of Bomber Command, still reeling from the Butt Report, but caused glee at the Admiralty, where it was felt that the current bomber force should be diverted to anti-submarine operations and new aircraft types be supplied in quantity to Coastal Command.

These supplementary attacks were stoutly opposed by Harris, but they do illustrate a point about war at the higher command level which ought to be borne in mind. The overall conduct of war – where to place the weight of always scarce national resources in men and equipment, as well as pro-duction and research capacity – is always a matter of debate. Wars are not fought by commanders who are totally in agreement with each other: more frequently the service chiefs are at each other's throats, each convinced that his arm of the service is the key to victory and must have a major share of the available assets. The final decision on who gets what has to be taken at an even higher level, usually by politicians, and calls for a high level of objective judgement. This is understood by all concerned, but the working out of the argument is complicated.

A commander given a task has also to be given the tools to carry it out; it he cannot do the job he must say so. The problem is that these tools are never adequate in themselves, and there is usually great scope for argument in the way they are used. Bomber Command is a good example of a service that claimed to be the war-winning arm but had so far failed to produce much evidence to support that assertion. Harris and Portal felt – rightly in the circumstances – that this was because it had never received the necessary level of resources. Other senior officers – notably Admiral Sir Dudley Pound, Chief of the Naval Staff, and General Sir John Dill at the War Office – felt that Bomber Command would never contribute anything substantial to the war effort and that the manpower and productive capacity committed to the strategic bombing of Germany should be *entirely* devoted to supporting naval or military operations: in short, that the RAF should abandon its attempt at making a strategic impact on the war and revert to being a tactical force.

The soldiers and the sailors had a case, and Harris knew it. However, he could not admit it. If he did, his cause was lost and Bomber Command would *never* get the resources it needed. There was also another issue: the very survival of the RAF as a separate service. If it failed to make a separate, individual, contribution to the defeat of the Axis, perhaps it would be better re-formed as the Royal Flying Corps or as an extension of the Fleet Air Arm. This was, after all, the position of the US Army Air Force, which, in spite of enjoying a large degree of operational autonomy, was not a separate service in 1942 and did not become one until after the war. Harris needed to demonstrate that Bomber Command could mount crushing attacks on Germany, and he needed to do it soon.

Bomber Command HQ was set in an underground bunker near High Wycombe in Buckinghamshire, a small town thirty miles west of London, famous in peacetime as a centre for the furniture industry. All plans for bombing operations were drawn up at High Wycombe, and orders for attacks on targets on the Continent were issued directly by Harris after his morning conference. Unless the weather was quite remarkably foul, Bomber Command operated every night, the actual bombing being the final outcome of a routine process that started at Harris's 'Morning Prayers', his daily 0900 hrs conference. This was attended by the entire staff and began with a briefing on weather conditions by the meteorological officer, Group Captain Magnus Spense. After this had revealed the limits of action that night, the navigation and intelligence officers would advise on routes, targets and likely enemy opposition.

Harris would personally select the target or targets for that night's operations, and his Senior Air Staff Officer, Air Vice-Marshal Robert Saundby, and his team would do the detailed planning and draw up an operation order which would be sent to the groups by teleprinter. Before starting this work they would already have sent a warning order to the groups, for relaying to the airfields and squadrons, listing the target and the bomb loads. With this preliminary information, work at the bomber stations to prepare the crews and aircraft for action could begin. Every station and squadron was expected to 'put up' every serviceable aircraft and every crew member fit to fly, every night if need be, though the variable European weather made continuous operations unusual. By early afternoon the detailed orders were going out, and the crews would then be briefed for that night's operation. Take-off would follow at dusk, and on the following day the routine would begin all over again. That was how it was in 1939, and that was how it went on for the remaining 1,300-plus nights of the war.

The need to be at the centre of operations and personally select the 'Target for Tonight' each morning kept Harris close to his HQ for most of the war. He was unable to get about and visit the bomber stations, and yet, by some mysterious process, he knew the crews and they knew him – a curious example of the link that a strong commander can forge with his subordinates.

Harris began his task by reviewing the state of his Command, and he was less than happy with what he found. In May 1942 Bomber Command had 407 bombers on strength with crews, of which just over half – 214 – were twin-engined Wellingtons. Only 29 of the new Lancaster bombers were so far in service, and the force still contained 27 Hampdens and fifteen Whitleys – both types which were clearly obsolescent. Most of the rest were Stirlings (45), which were slow and had a low ceiling, and Halifaxes (62). The Halifax was to become one of the more reliable bombers in due course, but was then enduring teething problems. The Lancaster, Stirling and Halifax were four-engined bombers, and the force needed more of them. Finally, there were fifteen of the lamentable Manchester.

Harris was slightly better off when it came to crews, with a steady supply of trained men now coming forward from the OTUs and HCUs, but the Command strength was steadily eroded by losses on operations – currently running at around 3 per cent – by crews leached away to fly with Coastal Command on anti-submarine operations, and by the demands for bomber aircraft and crews in other theatres of war, especially the Middle East.

Harris therefore had three immediate priorities. First, he had to increase the size of his striking force by getting more aircraft – and these aircraft must be the new types, the Lancaster and the Halifax, not the obsolescent Wellington, Hampden or Whitley or the disastrous Manchester, though for the moment the Stirling would do. Second, he had to get more crews and hang on to them, resisting poaching from the Middle East and by Coastal Command. Finally, he had to bring the new radar and electronic aids, notably *Gee*, into service with the Main Force and so improve the navigation and effectiveness of Bomber Command operations.

Harris had nine squadrons equipped with *Gee*, deployed in 3, 4 and 5 Groups, and he also had a new set of instructions, Air Ministry Directive 23, dated 5 May 1942. Directive 23 urged Harris to begin operations against primary industrial targets, including Cologne, Duisburg, Düsseldorf, Essen and the north-German ports, using *Gee*. Bomber Command was only likely to enjoy the unrestricted use of *Gee* for six months before the Germans found some way of jamming it. Targets beyond *Gee* range were to be attacked on clear nights, concentrating on the ports of Hamburg, Lübeck and Rostock, with Berlin as a possibility.

Harris was also directed to use incendiaries and to employ his efforts 'without restriction' until further notice, but – the Directive continued – his primary task was to be focused on 'the morale of the enemy civilian population and in particular on the workers in industrial areas vital to the enemy's war effort'.[4] Directive 23 relates to a letter sent by the Air Staff in February to Air Marshal J. E. A. Baldwin, the officer who had filled the chair at Bomber Command until Harris returned from the USA. Harris had no hand in framing this Directive and was not consulted about its contents – a point worth making to those who allege that bombing attacks on German civilians were always and entirely Harris's idea.

However, before Harris had time to warm his chair at Bomber Command HQ, the whole question of strategic bombing came up in the House of Commons, following the outcry caused by the 'Channel Dash' – the escape back to Germany of the German warships *Scharnhorst* and *Gneisenau* – when several MPs questioned whether the nation was putting too many resources into bombing with very little to show for it. This point was reinforced by the MP for Cambridge University, Professor Bull, who stated that, since the Blitz had not damaged public morale in London, there was no reason to suppose that British bombing would do any better in Germany. The debate concluded with the statement from Sir Stafford Cripps quoted above.

Harris was more than ready to fight his case with the politicians, but the most obvious answer to these parliamentary charges was some effective operations. On the night of 3/4 March he sent 235 aircraft to attack the Renault factory at Billancourt near Paris, a plant manufacturing trucks for the German Army. The attack was made by three waves of bombers, all flying at 6,000 ft. After the target had been identified, marked with flares and bombed by the first wave, the other two waves came in and attacked with 1,000 lb and 4,000 lb bombs – the new 'Cookies' – while the first wave circled about and kept up a steady illumination with flares.

Gee was not used on this raid, as it was still in the final testing stage, but the bombing was deliberately concentrated, with 121 aircraft passing over the target in an hour. Only one aircraft was lost, and photoreconnaissance the next day revealed that considerable damage had been done, though more than 300 French people were killed. The 4000 lb 'Cookies' were to become one of the main weapons of Bomber Command and were especially effective when used in combination with incendiaries: the high-explosive 'Cookies' would blow off roofs and do structural damage, enabling the incendiaries to penetrate the buildings and start fires.

Targets in France did not rate as highly as targets in Germany, and on the night of 8/9 March, just five days later, Harris used *Gee* when 211 bombers attacked the town of Essen in the Ruhr. The *Gee*-equipped aircraft went in first, to illuminate the target with flares but without identifying it visually first – a tactical process known as the 'Shaker' technique. All did not go entirely to plan: only eleven of the twenty *Gee*-equipped aircraft dropped their flares blind – the rest attempted to identify the target visually and failed to do so, since it was obscured by smoke and industrial haze and the German defenders were quick to use dummy flares and light distracting fires.

The attack on the following night was also a failure, when, although Essen was the target, the bombers got lost and dropped their bombs on Duisburg and Hamborn. Both were industrial targets and some useful damage was done, but clearly the crews needed to have more faith in *Gee* if it was to be used successfully for target-finding as well as navigation.

More attacks followed, on Cologne and again on Essen, implementing the tasks laid down in Directive 23, as well as the ongoing mining campaign which was to prove a highly effective way of reducing Germany's maritime capability. Then, at the end of March, Harris made the first of his city attacks, sending 234 bombers against the Baltic port of Lübeck on the night of 28/29 March.

Lübeck was an old and very beautiful town, largely composed of wooden buildings. It lay beyond *Gee* range, but *Gee* came in useful in the early stages of the flight and on this moonlit night most of the bombers – 191 of them – found the target and attacked in three waves, some flying as low as 2,000 ft over the town centre. The aiming point was the centre of the old town, the *Altstadt*, and the combination of blast bombs and incendiaries soon had the port in flames. Once again the bombers were concentrated, most of them passing over the target inside two hours. Photographs and subsequent reports from Germany indicated that over 60 per cent of the buildings had been destroyed, including the Dragerwerk factory, which made oxygen equipment for U-boats. About 1,000 people were killed or injured – the highest toll so far for any raid on a German city – and twelve aircraft were lost, almost 5 per cent of the force.

This raid was regarded as a considerable success and, while continuing his attacks against the Ruhr cities and Cologne, Harris followed it up in April with two more experimental area attacks: one by day on Augsburg, one by night against the port of Rostock. The Augsburg operation, on 17 April, was a deep-penetration raid, very dangerous in daylight. Augsburg lay 500 miles from the Channel coast, but Harris thought that a low-level flight by a small force of the new Lancasters could get the job done. The specific target was the MAN diesel-engine factory, which made submarine engines, and the force consisted of twelve Lancasters, six each from No. 44 and No. 97 Squadrons, which spent a week on low-flying training before the operation.

Diversion sorties were made to northern France in an attempt to draw off the German fighters, but these distractions did not mislead the *Luftwaffe*. Four Lancasters were shot down on the outward flight and three more near the target. Those aircraft which reached Augsburg did bomb the target accurately, but the loss of seven out of twelve – 58 per cent of the force – was another proof that daylight bombing without fighter escort was simply not possible – a fact that the USAAF bomb groups which were now assembling in the UK might have noted with advantage.

The attack on Rostock, on the night of 23/24 April, achieved mixed results. The attack followed the pattern of the Lübeck operation in that the aiming point for the Main Force was the city centre, though a small force of bombers from 5 Group attempted a precision attack on the Heinkel aircraft factory in the suburbs. Neither attack was accurate: the Main Force bombed well away from the *Aldstadt*, and the Heinkel factory was untouched. This became apparent on the following day, so on the next night, 24/25 April, Harris sent his bombers back to Rostock again. This time the bombing was more accurate and the city centre was destroyed, but the Heinkel factory still remained untouched. The bombers therefore returned on the following two nights – 128 bombers on the third night, 106 on the fourth and final night – though servicing and flak-damage problems were steadily reducing the number of aircraft available for these continuous operations.

When the smoke cleared away on the morning of the fifth day, it was seen that most of Rostock – the estimate is 60 per cent of the city centre – and the Heinkel factory had finally been destroyed. About 300 people were killed or injured – a total that would have been much higher had the city not been evacuated after the first and second raids. The aircraft defences, slight on the first night, were becoming significant during the last raid, and eight bombers were lost over the four nights. The fact that if a raid failed Harris would order it again and again until it succeeded was not lost on the bomber crews.

The Germans were also impressed; the Propaganda Minister, Josef Goebbels, recorded in his diary that daily life in Rostock had come to an end and that this RAF operation was a *Terrorangriff* – a terror raid – a phrase that would be used increasingly by the Propaganda Ministry as the bomber war continued.

From these raids on Lübeck, Augsburg and Rostock it is easy to see what Harris was attempting. The first was an area raid by night, and was highly successful. The second was a daylight precision attack and, though the results were good, the losses were prohibitive. The third was a night pre-cision and area attack and, although good results were finally achieved, it took four attempts to get them and the area attack was far more destruc-tive than the precision bombing night attacks on the Heinkel factory, where many of the townspeople worked. Production would have been further disrupted since the workers and their families fled into the surrounding countryside and came back to find their homes destroyed. Area bombing, in short, was the only feasible method of attack – and a highly effective one.

As Bomber Command settled down to mount operations night after night, the strain on the crews began to tell – particularly on the pilots. For some months a debate had been going on in Bomber Command about whether an aircraft actually needed two pilots, and on 29 March 1942, it was decided that one pilot per crew would be sufficient. It was now that Harris also decided that a limit should be set to the number of operations flown in any one tour of duty: 30 in the first tour, 20 in the second.

Besides facing questions in Parliament and snags in the use of *Gee*, mounting operations, and setting a limit to operational tours, Harris was also having continual trouble with the Admiralty. This was partly over the Navy's insistence that Bomber Command should devote more time to attacking submarine bases and naval targets like the *Tirpitz*, and partly over the Admiralty demand that more Bomber Command squadrons should be transferred to Coastal Command. Coastal Command, under Admiralty control, was committed to the Battle of the Atlantic, through attacking U-boat bases and sinking submarines at sea. Even the presence of patrolling aircraft greatly reduced submarine operations. Harris was not unaware of the importance of attacking U-boats and U-boat production and, as the above accounts illustrate, many Bomber Command operations were mounted against places which produced U-boat equipment. In addi-tion, *Gardening* – mining – operations were flown almost every night. None of this did much to placate the sailors.

Gardening operations continued throughout the war, took a heavy toll of German ships and submarines – and were distinctly dangerous. Aircraft on *Gardening* operations flew in small groups, were easily detected on radar, and were quickly tracked by German fighters. John A. Johns, of No. 153 Squadron, gives an overview of a typical *Gardening* operation:

> Every *Gardening* operation required the squadron to provide five aircraft –
> never more, never less – each carrying six airborne magnetic/acoustic mines.
> Each mine was ten feet in length, with a diameter of eighteen inches and
> weighed around 1,500 lb, of which the explosive charge amounted to 740 lb.
> Take-off was usually at dusk, and the return flight times were between six
> and six and a half hours. To avoid detection by enemy radar, the outward
> route was over Scarborough and, at under 1,000 ft, out over the North Sea;
> dropping height was about 11,000 ft. In the Kattegat or the Baltic Sea there
> are very few deep-water channels suited to large vessels and, since both sides

knew this, the Germans knew where to vector their night fighters. Sweden was neutral and well lit up, so German fighters used to fly out from Denmark and try to catch us silhouetted against the lights of the Swedish towns. H_2S emissions could be picked up on night-fighter radar, and the crew felt themselves cruelly exposed to any enemy action. And if you were shot down into the sea the chances of survival or launching a dinghy into the northern seas, where survival times were unlikely to exceed ten minutes, did not bear thinking about.

Freddy Fish, also of No. 153 Squadron, recalls one *Gardening* operation:

We carried six parachute mines, and as soon as these had been dropped a German fighter appeared, obviously vectored on to us by ground control. We fired and corkscrewed and vanished into the cloud, but in the next 30 minutes we saw three aircraft shot down; our squadron lost one aircraft that night and had another badly damaged. Owing to heavy losses on *Gardening* ops, the Wing Commander sensed a drop in morale and offered to go on the next op. His aircraft, plus another from 153, were shot down that night, and all the crews were lost. If you went down in the sea at night, you did not have much of a chance.

Many aircraft – damaged by flak or fighters, low on fuel, and slowed by the westerly winds – did fail to make it to the English coast and were forced to ditch in the English Channel or the North Sea. One survivor of a 'ditching' in a Whitley aircraft was a New Zealand pilot, Hugh James Miller:

The op was to Turin on 5 November, and the start of the problem was icing, which often occurred in cloud, especially in the winter. Soon after we took off, the windscreens frosted over and as we gained height chunks of ice began to fly off the propellers and were hitting the fuselage with resounding crashes. The starboard engine cut out, but revived when 'warm air' was selected; de-icers were turned on, and we kept climbing as well as we could, broke out into brilliant starlight at 14,000 ft, and pressed on to bomb Turin.

With the bomb load gone and half our fuel used, we turned for home and all went well until we ran into thick cloud and the icing began again. The controls grew soggy and we could not maintain height, so down and down we went, while the cloud remained solid and unrelenting. We needed to see the ground and get some kind of fix or we might head out into the Atlantic until we ran out of fuel, and eventually we dropped a flare from 500 ft and glimpsed land, though I was then very worried we might run into a hill.

At 0530 hrs we dropped another flare and saw water – long rollers and white horses on the waves, no land in sight – and we knew all too well what our fate was likely to be if we came down in a sea like that. It was now 0600 hrs and our petrol would give out at 0630 hrs. We threw out everything we could – machine-guns, ammunition, oxygen cylinders and so on – and ran through our ditching drill, while we purred on north-west, straining for a sight of England.

At 0700 hrs one motor coughed. With the remark 'Well we might as well get as close as we can to old England before we go down', I banked the plane and we began to turn – and then the gunner shouted, 'A ship, a ship!' I continued the turn and saw, a couple of miles away, a tiny vessel – a trawler. It took less than two seconds to decide what to do: 'Stand by to ditch!'

The engines had picked up and were purring again as I went down, hoping to ditch as close to the ship as possible. We were soon skimming the waves – big rollers eight or ten feet high – holding her off and keeping the nose up. What if our engines cut out now and we dived in? Fatal! Stick back, close throttles gently, a shudder as the tail clips the top of a wave, and then crash – a green wall of water overwhelms us.

Fortunately the hatch over my head was shut, otherwise I would have drowned as that wave swept over us. Slowly the water subsided, the green mass grew lighter, and suddenly I could see the surface of the sea. I whipped out the pin of my safety belt, burst open the hatch, and was out on top of the fuselage. By the time I was down to the rear door the dingy was out and inflated and the crew were climbing into it. The plane was going down, and I stepped from the top of the fuselage straight into the dinghy, without even getting my feet wet. We seized paddles and moved clear, in case we should be taken down with the aircraft, and, although the waves were a little alarming at first, we moved about and trimmed ship and she rode remarkably well.

We then looked around for the trawler, and, as we reached the crest of a wave, there she was, just weighing anchor and moving towards us. She eventually came up, hove to, and drifted down on us. The sea was so rough that one minute we were looking up ten feet at the hull and the next were level with the ship's rail. Each time she rolled, one of us was grabbed by strong hands and hauled on board, and at last we were all on board – including the dingy – and heading for port. Never has a skipper's hand been shaken so fervently; we could hardly express our thanks we were so overwrought.

And where were we? Four miles off the north-east coast of England. The trawler was in fact a minefield patrol boat, and had we landed a couple of hundred yards nearer the coast we would almost certainly have landed in the field and blown ourselves up.

There was merit on both sides of the argument raging between Harris and the Admiralty. In the long run, the war would be won only by destroying Nazi Germany and, whatever Harris believed, that task would require the united efforts of all three services. In 1942–3, however, the German U-boats looked likely to win the Battle of the Atlantic. At worst this would sever Britain's lifeline and give Germany the victory; at best this would inhibit the build-up of US forces in the United Kingdom – the essential prelude to an invasion of the Continent. In the long run, Harris was right: battering Germany was to be Bomber Command's major contribution to victory. In the short term the Admiralty was right: the next step towards winning the war – or avoiding defeat – was beating the U-boat menace in the North Atlantic.

Harris felt that, given adequate resources, he could smash Germany from the air – which would make a seaborne invasion unnecessary – and he wanted to get started on that task with the greatest force and the least possible delay. Having his resources eroded by the demands of Coastal Command or diverted to attacking targets like U-boat pens in La Pallice or Saint-Nazaire, where the reinforced concrete was impervious to any bomb then in service, simply struck him as a waste of time and effort. Far better to go out and hit the Hun where he lived, in the cities.

Aids to this end, in the form of better aircraft and target-finding equipment, were becoming available, but it would take more than new equipment and fresh allies to beat the devil out of Germany. Crushing Germany also required a new frame of mind: a degree of ruthlessness that it took the realities of war to create. The war had to be carried to the enemy, and the only way to reach the home and heart of the enemy in 1942 was by strategic bombing. Therefore, before looking at further developments in the bomber war, it is necessary to look behind the operational problems and examine some of the thinking on the way in which this new kind of war should be fought and what it might achieve.

At the end of March 1942, Professor Frederick Lindemann, now Lord Cherwell, one of the Cabinet's scientific advisers, sent a note to Prime Minister Winston Churchill – a message supporting some estimates Cherwell had made about the possible effects of area bombing on the industrial cities of Germany. Lacking precise information from Germany, Cherwell had taken as his basic data the measurable effects of German bombing on Britain and had come to the conclusion that 'one ton of bombs destroyed between 20 and 40 houses and therefore made some 100–200 people homeless'. Extrapolating these figures in the belief that the RAF would have some 10,000 bombers delivered in the coming year, that each bomber could make at least thirteen operation flights before being shot down, and that on each sortie flown it could carry a three-ton load (6,720 lb) of bombs to Germany, he reckoned it should be possible to destroy the homes of – 'de-house' was the term employed – the civilian population of some 60 German industrial cities.

Apart from the fact that most of these civilians – or at least the men – would be working in the war industry, this should lead to a fall in morale both within Germany and in the German forces fighting in Russia, where the soldiers' concern for their families at home would clearly be a factor. It should be pointed out that, at this stage in the war, German industry did not employ women in factories. Sending women to work on factory benches flew in the face of the Nazi doctrine by which women were supposed to keep to their traditional tasks of *Kinde, Kirche, Küche* – children, church and kitchen. To make up the labour shortfall caused by the calling-up of younger men for the armed forces, German industry increasingly relied on forced labour, using imported workers from France, Holland and the other occupied countries of Western Europe, and on slave labour by half-starved Russian POWs and prisoners from the concentration camps which stood near many German industrial cities.

This was war by slide rule and estimate, but as a policy it met with a certain amount of approval from Churchill and Sir Archibald Sinclair, the Secretary of State for Air. It met with rather less approval from Portal, mainly on the grounds that, though the new aircraft, the Halifax and the Lancaster, could carry twice Cherwell's estimated bomb load, the RAF did *not* have 10,000 heavy bombers, or any likelihood of getting them. Also, to achieve Cherwell's estimates, target-finding and bombing accuracy would have to be improved well beyond present standards. A more comprehensive rubbishing of Cherwell's theory came from his fellow scientist and great rival Sir Henry Tizard, currently the Scientific Member on the Air Council, representing the Ministry of Aircraft Production. Tizard had a wide brief, extending well beyond the confines and interests of Bomber Command, and he simply did not believe that Cherwell's thesis was either valid or worthwhile.

Tizard felt that the main weight of bomber operations should be directed at the submarine menace. While agreeing that the bombing of Germany forced the enemy to divert resources to home defence that might otherwise have been sent to the fighting fronts in Russia and North Africa, he felt that such a result could be achieved only by a policy of steady, continuous bombing throughout Germany, rather than any massive – and in his view ineffective – campaign aimed at the civilian populations in a small number of designated cities. In short, if Cherwell's plan was to work at all, it must be on an even larger scale of bomber commitment and with even greater accuracy. Since neither seemed possible for the moment, Tizard proposed that a more useful Bomber Command contribution at this time would come from a concentration of attacks on submarine bases and construction yards and on vessels of the German Navy – a point that was seized on rapidly by the Admiralty.

This fundamental disagreement between two of its top scientific advisers put the government in a dilemma, so in April 1942 it was decided to set up an independent inquiry under a High Court judge, Mr Justice Singleton. Singleton was given complete access to RAF records and technical developments and was charged to examine the current state of bomber operations and to judge 'what results we are likely to achieve from continuing our air attacks on Germany in the greatest possible strength during the next six, twelve and eighteen months respectively'.[5]

Singleton went at this task with enthusiasm, and reported back on 20 May. His report was clearly coloured by the results obtained by Bomber Command in the Augsburg, Rostock and Lübeck raids described above. Regarding the 'de-housing' plan, he did not believe that German morale would be a factor worth targeting and suggested that better results could be achieved by concentrating attacks on the factory centres of the industrial cities, for, if these last operations were anything to go by, RAF bombers could now hit these cities accurately. Singleton added that improving bombing accuracy was a paramount task and that *Gee*, while most useful, was an area-finding method that would probably not yield much more in terms of accuracy and would soon be jammed. He therefore urged the speeding up of work on H_2S, the airborne target-finding system, which was then being developed.

In short, Singleton did not see anything vital being achieved in the next six months. He believed that this should therefore be regarded as a development period in terms of bombing strength and accuracy. This must be followed up by a period of sustained, ever increasing effort, which, if linked to successes on the ground, in Russia and North Africa, should – or at least might – lead to a decline in German morale. His report concluded, 'if this was coupled with the knowledge . . . that this bombing would now be on an increasing scale until the end, and the realization that the German Air Force could not again achieve equality, I think this might well prove to be the turning point – provided always that greater accuracy could be achieved'.[6]

With hindsight, Singleton's report can be seen as a model of accuracy, a breath of fresh air in a gale of biased opinions and a fair estimation of what would happen in the months ahead; but that was not how the report was received at the time. And had its suggestion of concentrating on the *factory centres* of the industrial cities, rather than on the city centres, been followed, the subsequent moral arguments might never have arisen. The problem with Singleton's report was that everyone read into it what they wanted to find. Portal said it came to no clear conclusion. Sir Dudley Pound, the First Sea Lord, said it supported his demand for more bomber commitment at sea. Tizard thought it added weight to his conclusions, and Norman Bottomley, the Director of Bomber Operations at the Air Ministry, thought it supported the notion that bombing would be the deciding factor in winning the war.

As a result, the Singleton Report faded from view and no action was taken on any part of it; everyone continued to argue as before. It had, however, confirmed Harris in his belief that, if his Command was to get the attention and resources it needed, he must do more to demonstrate the effectiveness of the force already under his command. If the small but effective raids on the Baltic ports could influence Singleton's conclusions, how much more could be achieved by a major strike against a single German city? This conclusion led to the Cologne raid on the night of 30/31 May 1942 – the Thousand Plan.

The Thousand Plan was not simply a very large bomber operation. It was a propaganda exercise designed to catch headlines and see off Bomber Command's critics in Parliament and at the Admiralty. It was also a means of testing a new method of attack: the 'bomber stream' – a way of swamping the flak and the civil defence (especially the fire services), countering

German radar and fighter activity, and demonstrating to the Germans and to the British and their American allies just what Bomber Command might do when it had the right amount of aircraft. It was, in short, a demonstration of the prime element in the bomber dream – overwhelming air power, the sort of power that should have been available for deployment on the first day of the war.

Bombing – or at least the kind of bombing envisaged by Douhet, Trenchard, Mitchell and the other bomber prophets – depended on the rapid application of overwhelming force to vulnerable targets. To the physical effects of this power could be added the impact of that force on the morale of the civilian population – and their political leaders – in the first days of a war. If the civilian population could be dragged into the front line as soon as war was declared, the results – the effect on morale – must be considerable. The problem was that – as already described – when the Second World War opened that force was not available and what force was on hand was totally unable to achieve the results promised. The result of that failure was that bomber strength and German military and civil-defence resistance rose in parallel: a force that might have achieved a great deal in 1939 was totally inadequate to surprise and dismay the enemy in 1942. On the other hand, putting 1,000 bombers over a single city on one night might do the trick. Such a force had never been deployed before, and the result might be dramatic – if it could be done.

The idea for mounting a 1,000-bomber raid was floated by Harris in April 1942. Having obtained the approval of Churchill and Portal, he gave the task of putting the force together to Air Vice-Marshal Saundby, whose first task was to find 1,000 bombers. In fact Saundby needed a few more than that, as there was a difference between the number of aircraft 'on strength' and the number actually 'put up' each night. Bomber Command now had four operational groups – Nos. 1, 3, 4, and 5 – and two training groups – Nos. 91 and 92. Their aircraft were under Harris's direct command: 485 in the operational groups and 330 in the training groups – a total of 815. Coastal Command responded by offering a further 250 aircraft, and Flying Training Command chipped in with a 'clapped-out' collection of 21 Hampdens and Wellington IAs which would be flown by experienced aircrew currently serving as instructors. This gave Harris 1,086 aircraft – enough to mount the operation and still allow for a shortfall on take-off.

The operation order was prepared and went out to the groups on 23 May, though the date of the raid would depend on the weather. This not only had to be a big raid, it had to be a highly successful raid, and Harris wanted to give his crews every opportunity to find and hit the target. The target city at this time was either Hamburg or Cologne – Harris preferred Hamburg – and weather flights flew out over the Atlantic every day, checking on approaching fronts. The big blow, however, came not from the weather but from the Admiralty. On 25 May, the naval chiefs ordered Coastal Command to withdraw its 250 aircraft from the Thousand Plan force.

Other than sheer spite, there seems to be no reason for this action. The documents at the Public Record Office reveal no official reason, but this decision cut Harris's force back to an uninspiring 836 bombers – a force which, if massive, did not have the same ring to it at all. Another man might have taken the matter to higher authority, but Harris was not the type to go cap in hand to anyone. If the Admiralty would not help, to hell with them. Harris would raise the number from his own resources, even if this meant – as it certainly would – using aircraft currently at OTUs and HCUs, with crews not fully trained for operations.

Crews in training did make operational flights, normally 'Nickeling' leaflet flights over France or to the Dutch coast, so there was some precedent for using them as part of the Thousand Plan, but if losses were heavy Harris would be destroying the seedcorn of his force and jeopardizing the expansion of his Command. This proposal was also very risky because it was an accepted statistical fact that even fully trained crews were at greatest risk during their first five operations. Finally, this operation was not a normal one, for Harris intended to swamp the city defences by packing the aircraft into a tight stream, giving each aircraft a height and time over the target to minimize the risk of collision. The aim was to pass 1,000 aircraft over the target *in just 90 minutes*, an as yet unheard of concentration of force, though the introduction of *Gee* made it easier to keep the aircraft together.

With the aircraft assembled and the plan laid, everything now depended on the weather. This remained uncertain until the morning of 30 May when Group Captain Spence offered Harris the possibility of cloud over Hamburg but clearing skies over the Rhine. That spared the citizens of Hamburg for another year. The order to attack went out to the groups: the Thousand Plan was on, and the 'Target for Tonight' was Cologne.

One of the men taking part in the Thousand Plan was Douglas Mourton, a wireless operator:

> I was still at OTU, flying Wellingtons, when we heard that we were all confined to camp and the rumour had it that something really big was planned. Then we heard that all OTU crews were going on a bombing operation, which was unusual, and this was the 1,000-bomber raid on Cologne. The city was to be attacked in waves at three-minute intervals, with radar-equipped aircraft leading, and the raid was to be over in 90 minutes. At briefing they told us that only two aircraft would be lost to collisions, and some wag shouted out, 'Yes, but which two?'
>
> We took off at 2340 hrs and flew across the North Sea to the vicinity of Cologne. I plugged in the intercom and, although I could hear shrapnel hitting the side of the aircraft, there was no conversation among the crew, so

as the rear gunner was not telling the pilot about any night fighters I decided to go up to the astrodome, the plastic bubble on the top of the fuselage, and see what was going on. We were flying along straight and level with flak bursting on our port side; I told the pilot to corkscrew to starboard, and as we did so there was a near miss on the port side, where we would have been. I shouted to the pilot and bomb-aimer to drop the bombs quickly and get us out of there, as we were over the town and there was no point in hanging about – especially straight and level, which was a sure recipe for disaster. Also there were Lancasters and Halifaxes about, and to hear a big rumble and be rocked by a passing four-engined bomber or take the risk of being hit by bombs falling from above was very stressful. I went back to my radio, but it was completely dead and I only hoped that the navigator was sufficiently proficient to get us back. Actually things went very well and we landed at five in the morning and went to the mess for the usual bacon and eggs, a couple of cigarettes and the feeling that you had completed another trip and survived.

Bomber Command put up 1,047 aircraft that night – more than 600 of them Wellingtons – of which about 890 reached Cologne, dropping 1,455 tons of bombs. Two-thirds of these were incendiaries, but there was no fire-storm. Unlike the wooden cities of Lübeck and Rostock, Cologne was fairly modern – a city of wide streets lined with shops and flats, certainly outside the older parts along the Rhine and around the great cathedral. As a result, the many fires tended to stay within the block or street or individual building. Even so, the damage was immense: more than 15,000 buildings were destroyed or damaged to some extent, and the city archives covering this attack, including a 119-page report by the Police President – the local Chief of Police – make interesting reading:

> The weight of this attack is most significant because for the first time in air war history more than 1,000 aircraft took part. This is not an estimate but a concrete number and on the German side one could not imagine such striking power. The attack was carried out by successive waves of aircraft, dropping of high-explosive bombs lasted one and a half hours and incendiary bombs were dropped during the whole attack. From the beginning bombs fell regularly in the city centre and the focal point of the attack could not be recognized. Areas affected were the living areas, the city centre and the suburbs of Raderthal, Zollstock, Nippes, Deutz, Poll, etc. etc. Over 13,000 houses were destroyed or damaged.
>
> The number of homeless is put at 45,132. For the first time, after this attack there was a drastic fall in population numbers. During the beginning of May, 684,995 inhabitants were counted, but some weeks later it had fallen to 620,995. This difference of around 64,000 does not give the actual number, because many Cologne citizens were now living in the surrounding countryside as evacuees.
>
> As for the factories and business premises, 1,505 were totally destroyed, 630 badly damaged and 420 lightly damaged. Air-defence-system factories

suffered as follows: 36 with total production loss; 70 with 50–80 per cent production loss; 222 with under 50 per cent loss. Water mains, light cables, telephone cables and gas mains were broken. Tramcar traffic in the city was still stationary one week after the attack, and the traffic out of the railway station did not resume for some days. On the number of dead (469), 248 were not in air-raid shelters. Of the 5,027 wounded, the majority were not in air-raid shelters.[7]

The list of damaged installations goes on for pages, and the Thousand Raid clearly did great harm to local industry, if only for a short period of time. It also achieved its other objectives: it brought the focus of public attention in Britain back to Bomber Command, the only force then capable of striking back at Germany. Losses were within the acceptable range of 4 per cent; 41 aircraft were lost, half of them from flak or night fighters over the target, the rest from night-fighter activity on the way out or back – and, curiously enough, the losses in the training crews, 3.3 per cent, were lower than the 4.1 per cent loss sustained by the operational crews. The overall loss came out at 3.9 per cent.

Elated by the success of the Thousand Plan, Harris decided to repeat the process with another 1,000-bomber raid, this time on Essen on the night of 1/2 June, before the force dispersed. In fact only 956 bombers were dispatched, and attempts were made to see through the low cloud and the chronic Essen haze with the aid of a heavy concentration of flares dropped by the leading aircraft from 3 Group. This did not help much; the bombing was very scattered, the Krupps works were untouched, and some bombs also fell on Duisburg and Oberhausen. Clearly, when it came to actually hitting the right target, Bomber Command still had a long way to go.

Smaller forces continued to chip away at Essen and the other Ruhr towns, but the next Thousand Raid – the last of the series – took place at the end of June, when the force was reassembled and 960 aircraft were sent against Bremen – a fact that must have pleased the Admiralty, for Bremen was a major base for the German Navy and a shipbuilding centre. This time the Admiralty even permitted Coastal Command to participate, though the 105 aircraft it dispatched are classified as a separate Coastal Command operation. The results were mixed – better than the Essen 1,000-bomber operation but not as good as the Cologne raid. The target was located with *Gee*, but, contrary to the weather forecast given at briefing, the city was found to be under heavy cloud. The leading aircraft bombed on *Gee* and managed to start a number of fires which served as aiming points for the rest of the force, and about 700 aircraft claim to have found Bremen and bombed it. Many houses were destroyed or damaged, and some military installations were hit, including a Focke-Wulf fighter factory, where a workshop was destroyed by a single 4,000 lb 'Cookie'; several shipyards were also damaged. It is fair to say, however, that the damage done to the city centre and private houses was far more extensive than the damage done to the shipyards and factories. Nearly 500 people were killed or injured, and over 2,300 lost their homes. The RAF lost 48 aircraft – 4.9 per cent of the force committed.

These summer operations, and the advent of the USAAF, which made its first contribution to the air war in Europe on 4 July 1942 – Independence Day – with a raid on airfields in Holland, tended to focus higher minds on the aims and methods of the bomber war. By the autumn of 1942, though matters were going more or less as envisaged earlier in the year, it could not be said that anything decisive was being achieved. The bomber war was continuing, but where was it going?

Clearly, according to Portal and the Air Staff, it was going in the right direction, but it needed to get there quicker. This meant a larger force, greater accuracy and a revised strategic plan. On accuracy, the widespread introduction of H_2S and the appearance of *Oboe* would be a great advantage, but something more was needed – some means of coping with the weather conditions common over Germany, some means of directing, even controlling the Main Force attack over the target – and here the newly formed Pathfinder squadrons were the focus of many hopes for the immediate future.

The idea for what became the Pathfinder Force – PFF – arose in March 1942 in a note to Harris from Group Captain S. O. (Sid) Bufton, Deputy Director of Bomber Operations at the Air Ministry. Bufton proposed the creation of a 'Target Finding Force', and suggested that Harris should pick six squadrons from the operational groups and set them the task of developing precise target-finding and marking techniques. Bufton was an experienced bomber officer who had commanded Whitley and Halifax squadrons on operations in 1940–1 and had kept up his contacts with the bomber squadrons after his move to a Staff job at the Air Ministry. The thinking behind his proposal was that equipment alone was not enough. In March 1942 some of the squadrons had *Gee*, but this device, while useful, was only effective in the hands of well-trained, experienced crews. However, such was the attrition in operations that such crews did not last long. What was needed, according to Bufton, was a large force of well-trained crews, capable of finding the targets and leading the less experienced or less able crews to them.

Harris did not welcome Bufton's suggestion, but he discussed it with his group commanders at their weekly conference. They came up with an alternative proposal: for a monthly competition among the squadrons, in which the one which produced the best crop of on-target photographs in one month would be responsible for target-finding in the following month. Such a competition would, they averred, create a healthy rivalry among the squadrons and lead to a rise in target-finding skills across the Command. Harris was also completely against the creation of what he referred to as a 'corps d'élite', which, he felt, would lead to 'a serious loss of morale and efficiency among the other squadrons'.[8] This latter point may have had merit: after the creation of PFF it is apparent that some Main Force crews paid less attention to navigation and target-finding than they might otherwise have done, being content to bomb target-markers whether or not these were actually in the right place.

Harris's rejection of Bufton's proposals was checked by the fact that, in spite of *Gee*, target-hitting did not improve to any marked degree – a fact brought out by the target photos and photoreconnaissance. This being so, Bufton's proposals did not go away, but were revived regularly at the group commanders' weekly meetings. Harris was therefore being nudged into accepting the idea when, on 11 June 1942, he received a letter from Portal, suggesting that it was no longer logical for Harris to reject 'the final and essential step of welding the selected crews into one closely-knit organisation, which, as I see it, is the only way to make their leadership and direction [i.e. to the Main Force squadrons] effective.

'What we need . . .' Portal continued, 'is an effective degree of illumination and incendiarism in the right place and only in the right place.' This last point was extremely valid, for the bomb-aimers were tending to concentrate on fires already burning on the ground when they arrived in the target area, whether these fires were on target or not. The Germans were also lighting dummy fires, outside the target area, to attract the bomb-aimers' attention. Better to have no fires at all than fires in the wrong place, and it was therefore essential to have a force which could find the right target and mark it accurately. But, said Portal 'this admittedly difficult task can only be done by a force which concentrates upon it as a specialized role and which excludes those less-expert crews whose less discriminating use of flares or incendiaries in the vicinity of the target have recently led so many of our attacks astray'.[9]

There was more discussion, but Harris eventually agreed to the setting-up of what he called a Pathfinder Force. This would consist of two squadrons transferred from each of the existing groups, and the group commanders were advised that the squadrons selected were to be composed of first-class, experienced crews who had done at least fifteen operations – this was *not* to be seen as a chance to get rid of their least effective crews or squadrons.

Bill Grierson was one of the early members of the Pathfinder Force:

> The PFF was set up as a kind of mythical 'force', not as a group. Each group in Bomber Command contributed its best squadron, and each squadron was then stripped down to its most reliable crews, then we all named individuals to be invited to join our respective squadrons. The bait was promotion of one rank – e.g. as squadron navigation officer I went from flight lieutenant to squadron leader. Originally the PFF was a group of experienced crews, all of whom had survived a few ops of 'on-the-job' training – the majority of losses came in the first five ops – but thereafter the top three students, or

student crews, from each OTU class were also invited to volunteer for PFF; after a few ops, if they were deemed capable, they were awarded the PFF badge.

At PFF Navigation Training Unit we gave each crew three days of intensive lectures and three days of screened flights; as long as we got battle-hardened crews or first-class pupils from the OTUs, this worked amazingly well. As you know, we had to fly 45 ops on a PFF tour, but that was a problem as some of the crew had done a different number so you might have to do more to finish as a crew. Peter Cribb took over Cheshire vc's crew, all of whom had flown varying numbers of ops, and he tried to see them all through until he was caught rigging his own number – I think he was caught flying his third 'sixtieth' op – and by the end of the war Peter had flown 95 ops. For much the same reason I did 49.

Syd Johnson, an Australian flying with No. 156 Squadron, was another PFF recruit:

The great PFF recruiter was Wing Commander Hamish Mahaddie, known as the 'horse thief', who went roaming the Bomber Command airfields, sniffing out good crews and hijacking them for the PFF. Hamish was a firm believer in having crews of mixed nationalities and, although the Canadian and Australian governments were keen on having their own squadrons, the aircrew were generally not bothered: as one bloke said, it was a case of 'Here today and gone tonight' and the aim was to strive for maximum efficiency, getting the job done and surviving. I was one of five Australians who were interviewed at Brighton and offered a berth at PFF after training, but I think this was pretty unusual. Most PFF crews were taken from the Main Force, but in our case after three months at AFU – Advanced Flying Training Unit – we went straight to the PFF Night Training Unit for three weeks, and then on to ops.

Harris was not alone in his initial opposition to the Pathfinder Force. Most of his group commanders – and especially Air Vice-Marshal Sir Ralph Cochrane of 5 Group – were dubious about the PFF and saw its creation as a reflection on the ability of their own crews and squadrons – which it undoubtedly was. However, having decided to accept the concept, Harris was determined that everyone, including himself, should give it every chance of success.

Volunteers were preferred, for Pathfinder work would be even more dangerous than normal bomber operations, where all the crews were volunteers anyway. That apart, they must be skilled in air operations *as crews*, and to maintain that essential level of expertise a Pathfinder tour would consist of 45 operations. Operations made with the Main Force, before transfer to Pathfinders, would count towards this total, but those who transferred to Pathfinders at the end of their first tour had to sign up for the full PFF tour and might do 75 operations without a break.

As inducements, Pathfinder crews would receive extra pay or an increase in rank and would be allowed to wear a special PFF badge, of the RAF eagle, below their medal ribbons. It took time to persuade the entrenched powers that be at the Air Ministry that these inducements were necessary, but Harris eventually won the argument. This is typical of Harris: he was opposed to the PFF concept, but once it was a *fait accompli* he made every effort to ensure its success – not least in the appointment of the commander of this new force.

An exceptional unit would need an exceptional commander, and for this role Harris selected Group Captain D. C. T. Bennett, an Australian officer who was the finest navigator in the RAF – and probably one of the finest in the world – and an exceptional pilot. He also had recent operational experience of the most practical kind, having been shot down over Norway when attacking the battleship *Tirpitz*. Bennett had escaped via Sweden and had only recently returned to the UK, where he was now awaiting reassignment.

Although he refers to himself as British in the second line of his auto-biography,[10] Don Bennett – later Air Vice-Marshal D. C. T. Bennett, CB, CBE, DSO, was born in Toowoomba, Australia, in 1910, the youngest of four boys. His father ran a cattle station, and when Bennett was four he took the boys to Toowoomba airfield to watch a flying display. This early experience made a deep impression on the young Don Bennett, and in 1930 he applied for a commission in the RAAF, went solo after eight hours, came out top of his class, and was duly transferred to the RAF in Britain in 1932, where he began as a fighter pilot with No. 29 Squadron, flying Siskin biplanes.

He then transferred to flying boats, joining No. 210 Squadron, which was then commanded by Arthur Harris, with whom Bennett struck up a firm and enduring friendship. Serving with Harris was, says Bennett, 'a privilege and a pleasure', and it was during this period that Bennett developed an interest in navigation. At this time pilots were responsible for navigation, but Bennett was not interested simply in being a competent navigator, or a skilled instructor in navigation. Though he became both, he wanted to be one of the best, and in 1934, after months of intensive study, he became only the seventh person in the world to hold a First Class Navigators' Licence – a very rare qualification indeed. He also obtained a first-class rating in wireless operation, and was one of the best-trained pilots in the RAF by the time he finished his engagement in 1935 and left to join Imperial Airways (later BOAC and now British Airways).

Bennett stayed with Imperial Airways as a senior pilot until well after the outbreak of war. After war broke out in September 1939, he was given the task of organizing the transfer of Liberator bombers from the USA to Britain, but he went back to the RAF in 1941 and was given the command of No. 77 Squadron in Bomber Command with the rank of wing commander. Here Bennett displayed those qualities of leadership that were to mark him out from the pack. He flew with a different crew every night of operations, watching their performance and giving practical on-the-job advice on navigation and flying skills. He was especially keen to improve the navigation standards of his crews, and devoted long hours of training to this purpose.

Bennett stayed with No. 77 Squadron, flying Whitleys, from December 1941 to April 1942, when he was sent to command No. 10 Squadron, flying Halifaxes, and was promptly shot down over Trondheim. Having escaped capture, he was now back with a wealth of recent, practical experience and just the man Harris wanted for the PFF.

Bennett was steadfastly loyal to Harris, while in his memoirs Harris describes Bennett as a man 'who was, and still is, the most efficient airman I have ever met . . . his courage, both moral and physical, is outstanding and as a technician he is unrivalled'. Harris goes on to add that 'he will forgive me if I say that his consciousness of his own intellectual powers made him impatient with slower or differently-constituted minds so that some people found him difficult to work with. He could not suffer fools gladly and by his own high standards there were many fools.'

Harris was being charitable. Don Bennett was another of those officers who did not suffer fools at all – never mind gladly – and his brusque manner made him many enemies, though his abilities were freely admitted. On the other hand, his crews, while admitting that he could be demanding, are still Bennett disciples to a man – and with good reason. Bennett was an outstanding pilot, who knew all about operational flying, and a superb leader, who led from the front.

Bennett established the PFF on 17 August 1942, starting with just five squadrons: No. 7, affiliated to 3 Group, flew Stirlings; No. 35, affiliated to 4 Group, flew Halifaxes; No. 83, affiliated to 5 Group, flew Lancasters; and No. 156, affiliated to 1 Group, flew Wellingtons – as did No. 109 Squadron, which was not affiliated to any particular group but filled in as required and later flew Mosquitoes. The idea was that, by flying different aircraft, these squadrons could be attached for marking operations to groups flying that type of aircraft. Harris ordered that the PFF was to fly its first target-marking mission on the day the PFF was formed. Bad weather intervened and it was not until the following night, 18/19 August 1942, that the PFF led the Main Force into action for the first time with an unsuccessful raid on Flensburg.

Bennett had more to do than find good crews and drill them to a high standard of navigation and target-marking, but that was where his task began. For the former he set up a navigation school and descended on any crew or squadron that failed, on the basis of photographic evidence, to live up to his own high standards in navigation and bomb-aiming. The main PFF requirement, as with the Main Force squadrons, was to find a reliable target-finding aid. *Gee*, on which so many hopes rested, was jammed by the

Germans for the first time in August 1942, just as PFF operations started, and *Oboe* and H_2S were not yet available, though one of Bennett's first actions was to visit the TRE and urge the boffins to press on with the work and let the PFF have *Oboe* and H_2S as soon as possible. For a time, however, good navigation depended largely on navigator skill and training.

For target-marking only the most basic illumination flares existed, and the early PFF technique consisted of marking the target with a primitive marker bomb stuffed with flares and therefore known as a 'Pink Pansy' and then bombing it accurately with incendiaries, in the hope that the Main Force bomb aimers would aim at any fires and drop their bombs accurately.

This concentration on navigation and bomb-aiming paid off, and the accuracy of RAF night raids gradually improved. But progress was nullified to some extent by a chronic problem: 'creep-back', a tendency for the bombing to move away from the target and back down the line of approach.

Creep-back occurred when the bombers of the Main Force started their bomb run and ground fires appeared in the graticule of the bombsight at the edge of the target area. The more resolute bomb-aimers kept on, chanting instructions to the pilot – 'Steady, Steady . . . Left . . . right . . . Steady . . .' – until the bomber was well over the aiming point. Only then did they press the bomb release and say 'Bombs gone', to pilot and the anxious crew. However, less resolute bomb-aimers tended to drop their bombs as soon as the ground fires appeared in their sights. Others then did likewise, and the fires created by these 'fringe-merchants' – as Don Bennett called them – gradually created the 'creep-back' effect as they moved back down the incoming flight path. Creep-back was already well known – and greatly deplored – and in an effort to do something about it, or even employ it to useful effect, it became common practice for PFF markers to place the aiming point some way *beyond* the actual target, so that bombs still fell across the target area as they 'crept back' from the aiming point.

Bennett also needed some way to direct the fall of bombs on to the target, and to move the bombing around the target area if need be. The method selected was a series of different-coloured target indicators – TIs – which could be used to mark the target precisely and provide the Main Force bomb-aimers with more to aim at than a random collection of fires. Moreover, these coloured TIs could be replenished as the raid continued and other TIs be used to mark the target area with 'sky-markers' even when the ground itself was obscured by smoke or cloud.

Alan Vial, DFC, tells how the system worked:

> I only flew on ops with the PFF and only with No. 35 Squadron, and my knowledge is contained within a twelve-month period from May 1944 to the end of the war. We used mainly yellow, red and green TIs; other markers were

used to cancel out markers laid inaccurately. Yellows were mainly used in daylight. A prime colour would be selected for primary marking and a second colour would be the back-up marker, when the primaries were extinguished. Backers-up also dropped loads of incendiaries on to the primary markers.

These markers could be used in several combinations, which were identified on PFF orders by code names. Visual groundmarking was known as *Newhaven*. If it was necessary to ground-mark blindly this was called *Paramatta*, and if the target was totally obscured and the bombs had to be aimed at sky-markers this was known as *Wanganui*. Various combinations of these marking techniques were also employed, and as new navigation devices came into service so they were used to improve marking accuracy or to give the PFF crews another option; for example, blind ground-marking using *Oboe* was known, appropriately, as *Musical Paramatta*, and could be very accurate. I recall one night when drifting fog was covering the target and two of us decided to drop using H_2S. Our markers fell exactly on the aiming point – confirmed by the flight engineer, who was in the nose – and the visual markers fell exactly on them a few minutes later. The target – a military rest camp in Austria – was then bombed with 4,000 lb 'Cookies', and our 'Cookie' fell right in between two of the buildings.

At night time the flare-droppers – called illuminators – went in first to light the place up, about three to five minutes ahead of the Main Force and just before the primary markers. Using the light from the flares, the primary visual marker would mark the target and the Main Force would bomb. Most often the illuminators would then have to come round again for a second run in order to drop their own bombs – not many crews appreciated that.

However, the real essence of PFF was the navigation teams. PFF aircrews had two navigators – Nav I and Nav II – one for the plot and one for the radar set. With the pilot they made up the Nav team, and this team had to live up to Don Bennett's exacting standards.

Syd Johnson again:

The normal routine was that the radar-set operator did the *visual* bomb-aiming or marking, if and when he was able to do it accurately, but started marking using the H_2S – that is *blind* marking, dropping green TIs – when targets were obscured. If he could mark blind with consistent accuracy he graduated to become a primary blind marker, dropping the initial markers for the other PFF markers to back up visually. When weather conditions permitted a visual attack, the master bomber [of which more later] would carry a 'primary visual marker'. I was qualified as both, but that was unusual: I only know of one other in 7 Squadron.

One of the side effects of this PFF marking was to add great colour to the air war: many of the aircrew mention that a PFF-led night bombing attack was amazingly colourful, a mixture of cascading markers, flares and illuminators, tracer, white bomb explosions and the red glare of fires reflected up on to the underside of clouds.

Modern wars are not won by men alone or by the simple application of technology: it takes a combination of the two to achieve any worthwhile result. When Bennett took over the infant PFF he had a great deal to do in order to equip his force properly and train it to his own high standards in flying, navigation and bomb-aiming. Everything he needed had to be fought for: *Oboe* and H_2S, a range of target-markers and better aircraft – particularly the Lancaster and the fast and adaptable Mosquito.

Frank Beswick, a New Zealand pilot, flew *Oboe* sorties with a Mosquito Squadron, No. 109:

> 109 was a Pathfinder Squadron and we flew *Oboe* blind bombing sorties and target-marking following a synthetic beam. The pilot had to fly a steady course at very high altitudes along an arc-shaped radar beam. The navigator was responsible for plotting the course from base to the start of the beam. The great advantage of the Mosquito for this type of work was its height, and by the end of the war this kind of activity took place at 32,000 ft, carrying four 500 lb target-markers.

Desirable items like Mosquito aircraft were sought by other group commanders, and Bennett's insistence that PFF must have priority did not endear him to his peers. Air Vice-Marshal C. R. Carr of 3 Group was a supporter of Bennett and the PFF, but others were at best lukewarm. There is some evidence that Bennett did not get on well with Air Vice-Marshal Cochrane of 5 Group, another outstanding bomber commander, who felt that 5 Group contained the best bomber squadrons in the RAF – and had some grounds for that belief. Bennett's memoirs refer to the opposition of 'a certain Group Captain and his Independent Bomber Force' – which everyone knew meant Cochrane – and relations between the two are still a matter for debate among Bomber Command veterans.

'Let me tell you first of all that I was and am a 5 Group man,' says Wing Commander Ernest Millington, DFC:

> I served in five squadrons in 5 Group and ended up commanding one, and the first point I want to refute is the notion that 5 Group airfields were awash with PR men, creating publicity, as some 8 Group people allege. I never saw a PR man, or heard of one on a station. If 5 Group did well and got noticed it was because the crews earned it, and while there may have been a number of factors one of them was leadership. Bennett was a driver; Cochrane was a leader. We also had great pilots in 5 Group – people like Micky Martin, Leonard Cheshire and Guy Gibson – and such men set the standard . . . and in time we developed our own methods of marking, better than anything 8 Group could manage.

By the end of 1942, Bomber Command was becoming the sort of striking force it should have been on the outbreak of war, three years before. It had new aircraft and new navigation equipment – the Lancaster entered squadron service in March 1942, and *Oboe* came into service on 20 December. The PFF gradually obtained its target indicators, and the strength of the Main Force squadrons increased in terms of better aircraft – the Lancaster and the Halifax – if not in terms of overall aircraft numbers. In November 1941 Bomber Command had 506 aircraft with crews. By January 1943 this total had risen to only 515, but 178 of these were Lancasters (nil in November 1941) and 104 were Halifaxes (seventeen in November 1941), while the Whitleys, Hampdens, Blenheims and Manchesters – totalling 322 aircraft in 1941 – had been removed from the inventory entirely. Only the old reliable Wellington would soldier on into 1943, as Bomber Command turned its full and growing might against the industrial heart of Germany.

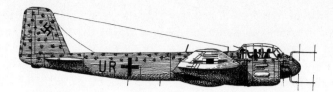

Junkers Ju 88G

6

The Defences of Germany
1939–1942

In descriptions of the bombing war, one important point is often missed . . . the real contest was between the Allied bomber forces and the German cities themselves.

Martin Middlebrook, *The Battle of Hamburg*, 1980

By the time Arthur Harris flung his power against Germany, the defences of the Reich had begun to reach a high level of efficiency, both military and civilian. This last element was important, for in an air war there is one vital difference between the attacker and defender. Unlike in a land battle or a naval engagement, where the combatants on both sides are servicemen, in an air war, while the attacking force will be entirely composed of aircrew – though backed up by ground crew in their distant bases – the defenders must make use of civilians as part of the defending force.

A strategic bomber war is largely a contest between the attacking aircrew and the 'civil defence' – the fire and rescue services and the organ-ization of shelters, food, transportation, power supplies and hospitals. The role of the flak and fighters is to extract a heavy price from the attacking force, but it is on the civilian population – on their courage and resolution in the face of adversity, on their ability to maintain some semblance of normal life under air attack, on their willingness to return to work and go on producing the weapons of war – that a nation's ability to withstand attack will chiefly depend.

On the military side, there is a need to develop suitable defensive tactics. Even in an air war these conform to standard military norms, in that the only effective defence is *defence in depth*. A single defence line, however strong, is rarely sufficient to halt an attack. The attackers can usually carry a single line of defences, if only by surprise, and the aim of defence in depth is to enable the defender to slow down the attacker, reduce the impact of the assault, cause casualties, bring the attack to a halt, and then repulse it by a counter-attack. These well-established military tactics can be applied with very little variation to an attack by air. The aim is to 'write down' the attacking force, to break up the formations, disrupt the bombing, and cause sufficient losses to make the attackers break off their offensive entirely.

A bombing offensive contains another significant difference from a ground offensive. An army attack is followed by 'consolidation' – digging in to hold the ground gained against counter-attack. Not so an air attack; once the bombers have fought their way in and delivered their bombs, the bombers have to fight their way out again. The defending flak and fighters can hack away at them both coming and going.

The pre-war belief that 'the bomber will always get through' was true only up to a point: the bombers might get through only at the price of unacceptable losses, large enough to wipe the attacking force out in the course of a few weeks. Some bombers will indeed get through, but the aim of the defenders is to knock down enough to make the continuation of the offensive impossible. For the British bombers, this meant consistent losses in excess of 4 per cent – they key word being 'consistent', for the RAF frequently lost a higher percentage of aircraft on particular operations. If the *Luftwaffe* could achieve that 4 per cent loss rate on a regular basis, few crews would complete a tour of 30 operations and the offensive would have to be halted or switched to easier targets until some solution could be found. That was the case with the RAF daylight attacks in 1939–40, which resulted in the switch to night bombing.

The Americans, having larger resources, could accept a higher loss level – certainly towards the end of the war, when they had a more than adequate supply of men and machines – but, here too, steady attrition, losses of 7 to 10 per cent per mission, could cause unacceptable losses in a 25-mission tour and, as we shall see, losses in excess of this figure curtailed the range and actions of the Eighth Air Force over Europe in 1942–3.

To inflict these loss rates and so deter attack, the German defenders needed to create an *integrated* defence system, in depth, from the coast to the heart of Germany – a system that employed radar, fighter control, searchlights, flak, and day and night fighters, all working together to break up the bomber offensive.

Just as the British bomber force should have been able to deliver a crushing blow to German industry in 1939, so Germany should have been ready to resist it. In the event, neither side was ready, but the advantage, the benefit of time, went to the Germans; the delay in building up the RAF bomber force and developing the means to make it effective gave the Germans ample warning of what was coming and a chance to develop counter-measures.

Every nation has its wartime philosophy, and those in command of Germany – the leaders of the Nazi Party – were firmly convinced that the war they were about to launch in 1939 would be fought on the territory of other nations and do no real harm to the people or industrial fabric of the Reich. This had been the pattern of Prussia and Germany's previous wars in the decades since the 1860s: before and after German unification, against Denmark and Austria in the 1860s, against France in 1870–1, and against France and Britain in 1914–18. During these wars great damage had been done to the fabric of other nations while Germany remained virtually untouched, and the German leaders saw no reason why this war should be any different.

This philosophy extended to the *Luftwaffe* as much as to the land forces, but British bombs started to fall on the Reich within a few weeks of the outbreak of war and, until the defeat of Germany five years later, bombs continued to fall with increasing effect and weight especially after the USAAF took up the struggle in 1942. Some cities were attacked repeatedly because they contained vital industrial targets – like the Krupps armaments factories in Essen, a town almost totally devoted to arms production for the *Wehrmacht*, or the ball-bearing works at Schweinfurt – but, as example of what happened to German cities as a whole, I have selected two towns astride the Rhine: Mannheim and Ludwigshafen.

'Mannheim and Ludwigshafen were probably not typical of the whole of urban Germany in the 1930s, but certainly of the West,' writes Dr Stefan Morz, the city archivist of Ludwigshafen:

> They were religiously mixed, half-Protestant, half-Catholic, with a strong working class and consequently had a strong Communist–SPD socialist movement before 1933. They were not classic NSDAP [Nazi Party] voting areas – and the massive bombing after 1943 effectively eroded any support the Nazis might have enjoyed before, due to full employment and the victory over France in 1940. This part of Germany was in the French Zone of Occupation after 1918 and the French were therefore extremely unpopular. The feature that made these cities a prime target for Allied bombers was the Ludwigshafen branch of I.G. Farben [nowadays BASF] and the importance of Mannheim–Ludwigshafen to the German rail and river transport system. In Ludwigshafen there were – and are – quite a few more pretty big chemical plants, while Mannheim was famous for its metalworking industry.

These two cities were certainly industrial targets, containing major railway marshalling yards, a river port and the I.G. Farben chemical works, which manufactured, among other products, Zyklon-B for the gas chambers of Auschwitz and petrochemicals for the *Luftwaffe*; I.G. Farben also ran a factory inside Auschwitz, and paid out large sums in reparations to the surviving slave workers after the war. The I.G. Farben works in Ludwigshafen were the major employer in the area, with a workforce running into tens of thousands, but these two cities were – and are – typical German cities, of moderate size, containing normal, hard-working, German people. They were attacked over 100 times, by day and night, during the Second World War, and what happened to these towns was repeated again and again in other towns and cities across the Third Reich.

Because of the basic military philosophy and Goering's assurances, Germany made few military preparations to repel or resist air attacks before the outbreak of war; if all went well, they would not be needed. Civil defence was considered, however, and some plans and preparations were made and implemented on the outbreak of war, as Richard Braun of Ludwigshafen points out:

> It is common knowledge that the Second World War began on Friday, 1 September 1939, when Germany attacked Poland; the British came in two days later. On the following morning, 2 September, official leaflets were found in every house of the town. They said that, with immediate effect, a total blackout had to be observed during darkness, the windows of the cellars had to be protected by means of sandbags, one of the rooms in the cellars adjacent to a neighbouring house had to be converted into a shelter, and a small passage had to be broken into the wall between such a room and the neighbour's cellar, so that people could move about and escape if need be, etc., etc.
>
> One of the orders required all grown-ups to gather at a certain time on a certain date at a certain place (mostly the yards of nearby schools) to collect gas masks for their families and small water pumps for their houses, and for practical training on the use of these and other facilities, for being familiarized with the signals from the air-raid warning sirens and the expected different kinds of enemy bombs, as well as for organizing the civil defence among the population.
>
> To obey the blackout order, those people who had shutters at their windows simply lowered or closed them. The others, having windows without shutters, used thick curtains, heavy woollen blankets or wooden frames of the size and shape of the windows, to which some suitable fabric was nailed. In accordance with the orders given in the leaflet, the initial protection of the windows of our cellars consisted of sandbags. As the war progressed, many house-owners replaced the bags by wooden crates into which they put the bags, or they replaced the bags altogether by large wooden boxes filled with loose sand. Others had brick parapets built instead, but these brickworks made the cellars behind them real traps when the house above had collapsed. The shelters in houses with cellar windows protected in this way had to be marked on the outside walls with an arrow.
>
> The gas masks we were given turned out to be of green rubber covering all of the head, with a very tight fit. In front of one's mouth, there was a flat aluminium filter of about 20 cm diameter. Generally, they were much disliked, because the tight fit, together with the reduced breathing possibility and restricted sight, produced rather an uncomfortable feeling. Our family never used them. The water pumps were for manual operation. Together with buckets of water, buckets of sand and a shovel, they had to be placed, ready

for use against incendiaries, on every storey in the staircase of the house. During the first large-scale air raid on our town, on the night of 9/10 August 1943, when we tried to halt the fire that would destroy half of our three-storey house, we discovered that these pumps were too weak, so we threw them away after only a few minutes of using them. Throughout the rest of the war we never touched them again, simply pouring water on the fires directly from buckets.

To warn the population of air raids, two signals were sounded before and two after such a threat or a raid. Before it, the first signal consisted of three sustained tones of equal pitch and duration, separated from each other by two brief intervals; this signal indicated that enemy aircraft had penetrated into our territory, heading for our town. When this *'Voralarm'* (pre-warning) was heard, people used to get ready for going to the shelters. The second signal was a continuous wailing tone, sounding for about a minute. At this point, the enemy aircraft were only a few minutes' flying time away and on their run-up to the target. Now everybody started hurrying to the shelters.

After the raid, or when the enemy aircraft had passed by without attacking us, the sirens again sounded their three-part signal to let the people know that the raid or the danger of a raid was over for the time being. We called it the *'Vorentwarnung'*. When this signal was heard, a large number of people used to start leaving the shelters for home. As soon as the enemy was again beyond our frontiers, the all-clear (*'Entwarnung'*) was sounded, consisting of a long sustained tone of uniform pitch.

Later in the war, a certain frequency on our radio (wireless) was installed to keep the population informed about the constantly changing situation in the air above Germany, thus preparing the people for air-raid warnings. We boys soon found out that the flak broadcasts could be picked up on our wireless sets, so from mid-1941 we only listened to this station, transferring the news to a map carrying co-ordinates and letters of the alphabet which somebody had stolen from the flak people and from which copies had been made by a friend of ours. I still possess my copy. As for the sirens, I do not know when they were installed but I am sure that they must have already been in place before the war started.

Wardens for each house (*'Hauswarte'*) and for each street (*'Blockwarte'*) were appointed – a measure of which I am at a loss to remember any practical significance. For instance, the warden for our house was my grandfather: a clandestine Social Democrat and opponent to the Hitler regime.

Not all our prescribed civil-defence measures proved to be really useful but one of the exceptions was undoubtedly our public air-raid shelters. These huge buildings, in reinforced concrete, were responsible for the surprisingly low casualty count in our town, and it is to the foresight and courage of the then mayor that these shelters were constructed in great number as early in the war as 1941, when large-scale air raids had not yet started.[1]

Beside a lesser number of large, public underground shelters, Ludwigshafen had (and still has) 28 of these enormous, tower-like shelters built above the ground. Inside they had lifts (elevators) and supplies of water – all that was necessary to support a large number of people for long hours of air attack. During the opening two and a half years of war these public shelters were not popular, but after the first all-out attack on our town, on 9/10 August 1943, the majority of the people never stayed at home when the sirens sounded but rushed into the shelters as quickly as possible.[2]

A large proportion of the citizens – mainly elderly and sick persons, as well as mothers and children – gradually made the public shelters their second home, leaving them very seldom and only for very brief whiles, withdrawing into them even without any air-raid warning. Our family began going to the nearest public shelter after the second heavy attack on Ludwigshafen had taken place on 5/6 September 1943.[3] However, this does not mean that we youngsters entered the shelter right away. In fact my friends and myself used to stand outside until the very last moment, until the coloured sky-markers – '*Christbäume*', 'Christmas trees', in our slang of the time – appeared in the darkness above us or until the smoke markers started indicating us from a clear or overcast sky. It was only then that we retreated into the shelter. In this way we had the advantage of being unable to get any further into the room behind the second door (called the '*Gas-Schleuse*'), so we could leave again when the raid was dying away.

Although a public shelter meant safety against the bombs, it was no pleasure spending a raid in it. All the rooms, staircases and corridors were packed with people. Sometimes they were standing so tightly that, when somebody lost consciousness for some reason, this person could not collapse but was kept upright by the sheer pressure of the other persons around. To add to the uncomfortable situation the electricity supply was cut by our power plants each time a raid started, so the ventilators and the illumination failed – the first causing a gradually increasing lack of fresh air, the latter having a very serious depressive effect.

The culminating point was reached when the bombs were heard approaching – this was particularly frightening when the American bombers salvoed their loads, which sounded like express trains coming up to us – and when they were exploding. At this point the shelter was trembling, shaking, lurching like mad, the children crying, the women shrieking, and the men cursing loudly. Hell cannot be worse. . . .

There were house-owners who built their own shelters, mostly in their gardens, either single-handed or with the help of neighbours who were also allowed to use these shelters in return for the work and/or material they had contributed to the construction. This private initiative was mainly found at places far away from public shelters. Naturally, the private ones would not have withstood direct hits by high-explosive bombs, but they were better than nothing.

The large public shelters were generally reserved for Germans. Foreigners were not admitted, with a few exceptions for foreign forced labour who did not have any means of protection in their camps. We could not allow them to be killed or injured in raids, because our industry needed them, therefore a few of our public shelters were open both to Germans and to foreigners. In our area of the town, such an exception to the rule was a hexagonal shelter. If a foreigner was detected in the other shelters, he or she was thrown out – even if a raid was in full swing; even if the Germans themselves got into danger by opening the doors.

You may wonder what part our fire brigade was playing during those 124 air raids sustained by Ludwigshafen between 1939 and 1945. I myself had no personal experience with this organization. There was no help from it when our house was on fire during the 9/10 August 1943 raid by Bomber Command: we had to help ourselves, together with a few neighbours and Ukrainian auxiliaries from a nearby flak battery. Our town certainly had a well-organized, relatively modern fire brigade at that time, but it is also certain that, as in many other German towns, our firefighting force was too weak for such catastrophes as fires started by the thousands of incendiaries dropped during a raid. Furthermore, large parts of the firefighting organisation were wiped out by the bombardments. Besides what can a fire brigade do, even if it is left intact, when there is no water because the supply lines have been cut by bombs?

The only one occasion on which I witnessed our fire-fighters in action was on 8 September 1944, when I came across the smouldering wreckage of an American B-17, on to which a few of our firemen were hosing water to prevent the ammunition from going off.

Many Allied aircraft were brought down by anti-aircraft fire – flak – and many of the guns producing that flak were eventually manned, at least in part, by teenage children from the Hitler Youth called *Flakhelfer* – 'flak helpers'. An outline of flak defence preparations comes from the City Archives of Cologne, in a report that dates from after the 1,000-bomber raid of 1942. This covers the recruitment of young men and schoolboys to service the anti-aircraft guns:

In the latter half of 1943, due to the manpower shortage in the German Army the Defence Ministry decided to enlist schoolboys born in 1926/7, then aged fifteen or sixteen, as 'helpers' (*Flakhelfer or Luftwaffenhelfer*) on the anti-aircraft batteries defending Cologne. Officially they were members of the *Hitlerjugend* – the Hitler Youth – and their dress uniform was that of the *Flieger-Hitlerjugend*, and part of that uniform was the swastika armband, which they did not wear on duty or in action. Because the boys did not feel they were part of the *Hitlerjugend*, they removed the armband when they left the *Flakstellung* – the battery sites. They were recruited with the full co-oper-ation of their parents, and it was decreed that they would be located as close to home and school as possible, in order that they could continue their edu-cation, either via the local school or by a teacher attached to the battery in which they served. Maximum distances from home, both in distance and in time for travelling, were laid down, and frequent leave was promised. These high-minded intentions were of course not adhered to, due to the logistic and redeployment problems involving the boys. Conditions on some of the bat-teries in terms of accommodation and food were very poor. Uniforms, being servicemen's issue, were nondescript, and poorly fitting. Many of the boys contracted diphtheria and other diseases when working in the flak bunkers.

The batteries varied from light to medium batteries of 20–30 mm calibre, to entrenched heavy batteries of 88 mm guns, all manned by soldiers aided by these boys and commanded by a non-commissioned or junior commissioned officer. Later, in 1944–5, when the Allied armies were advancing on several fronts towards Germany, the High Command became anxious about the boys in the event of their capture. They issued them with a purpose-made insignia armband, and a note which stated that if taken prisoner they were to be regarded as enlisted men in the German Army and not considered as 'partisans'. In the pattern bombing of the cities by the Allies which preceded the collapse of the German Army and subsequent occupation by the Allies, many of these boys were killed. Some were more fortunate in being posted to airfields to do salvage work, or became couriers at the disposal of the local Nazi district supervisors (*Gauleiters*). It is worth noting that in June 1944 some of these boys removed the swastika armband.

As the Allies entered Germany in the spring of 1945, the anti-aircraft batteries became more concentrated, heavily fortified and part of the ground defence system; the *Helfer* dug trenches around the battery sites, and anti-tank armour was fitted to guns etc. The heavier guns were adapted to fire horizontally over the protecting walls, and machine-gun emplacements were installed close to them. The 88 mm guns were equally useful in the anti-tank role when supplied with armour-piercing ammunition, but only when operated by experienced crews. These flak guns could put up a tremendous volume of fire, and the crews became very expert in working in conjunction with radar and searchlight batteries, as well as using the illuminations that arose during a raid, from fires or flares, to detect and open fire on Allied bombers.[4]

In cities under regular air attack, the flak gunners and searchlight crews soon began to develop skills and techniques to detect and shoot down the attacking bombers. In the city of Cologne for example, the city archivist's summary of the city defences continues:

The surrounding factories emitted smoke which hindered the range of the searchlights, so a further strategy was evolved which used this smoke and that from the fires. The searchlights were coupled with the reflection from the fires, and with searchlight beams playing on the smoke base it acted as an illuminated screen against which the bombers could be clearly seen from the ground – 'like flies on opaque glass'. At such times it appears that radar control from the ground was ignored and the height and range of the anti-aircraft fire were predetermined when these strategies were employed.

As the war intensified, one of the problems for the defence arose from the reliance on radar-controlled apparatus, both for early-warning systems to the night-fighter commands and for ranging the anti-aircraft batteries. The flak- and fighter-control networks depended entirely on such radar apparatus, and when it was upset – by jamming of the same frequency or the dropping of aluminium strips (*Dupple* – *Window* to the British) by the bomber aircraft – this upset the use of the radar systems. This, however, was only a temporary problem. More serious was that, as the demands upon the German ground forces increased, many of the guns, especially the 88 mm, were withdrawn to support the Army in the anti-tank role. They were, however, replaced by other guns, and indeed some areas increased in strength: the flak defences of Cologne reached their high point in October 1944.

The Germans defended their cities under Allied air attack in much the same way that the British had done during the Blitz of 1940–1, and with equal courage and tenacity. The British government's long-held belief that the Germans would be less resolute and that their morale would crumble under continual air attack proved quite unfounded. Certainly the bombing depressed the civilian population and worried their menfolk at the front, but there is little evidence that it ever seriously damaged the German will to fight on.

Richard Braun again:

> According to my experience, the general morale in our country was not weakened by the repeated air raids. On the contrary, it appeared to become stronger as they continued at a constantly intensified strength, in that the German opponents of the Hitler regime who originally regarded the Allies as their political friends were gradually driven into hatred against them by the ongoing merciless bombing and the continuous destruction of lives, homes and cultural goods. For personal reasons, those political dissidents opposed to Hitler were made his associates by the Allied air-war strategy. For instance, I still clearly remember my father – always a passionate Social Democrat – saying one day after another raid, 'If I come across one of them [bomber crew] I shall beat him to death.'
>
> It seems that quite a number of Allied aircrew were lynched by German civilians. A surprising aspect of this fact is that the greater part of these incidents was created by villagers in rural areas, away from the air-raid targets in the towns. Strangely, very little is known of such violence within target areas – those towns and cities where the citizens certainly had more reason to take revenge. Besides outraged civilians, it was Nazi officials that were responsible for murdering Allied aircrew. I know of a case where a shot-down member of a Halifax was shot dead in cold blood by the mayor of a village and the local *Voltsturm* (Home Guard) leader.
>
> However, it would be only half the truth not to mention that there were also many Germans who treated shot-down aircrew in a humane manner, although this was strictly forbidden. If I am not mistaken, it was Goebbels in late 1943 who issued a directive that every Allied airman found at large was to be killed. For all these reasons it can be said that if an Allied airman was captured it was best to be captured by the police or, better, by soldiers of the armed forces – the *Wehrmacht* or the *Luftwaffe* – not by Nazi Party people.

This seems to be correct. Peter Menges of Ludwigshafen reports the case of two German soldiers who, on the night of 21/22 February 1945, shot dead a British pilot, Sergeant Cyril Sibley of No. 158 Squadron. Sergeant

Sibley had been shot down during a raid on Würms and parachuted into a garden in Dirnstein, where he was found by a woman who treated his wounds. Then Adolf Wilfert, a soldier and a Nazi Party member, appeared, abused the woman for helping the pilot and, with another man, Georg Hartleb, a member of the *Volksturm*, took the prisoner away. The woman later heard three shots and on the following morning found the dead airman lying on a handcart.

Wilfert and Hartleb were tried for this crime at Hamelin in 1946 and found guilty – the woman who helped Sergeant Sibley gave evidence against them – and they were hanged at Hamelin on 11 October 1946, just two of the 196 people hanged in Hamelin prison for war crimes between 1945 and 1949.

A number of contributors to this book who were shot down over Germany can confirm that some elements in the German population were kind to them while others were actively hostile. Malcolm Hinshaw of the 392nd Bomb Group reports that 'when passing through Frankfurt I saw several British airmen, hung by their necks from lamp-posts'. Nor was this action restricted to British *'Terrorflieger'*. Corbin Willis, a US pilot shot down in 1944, records that 'Five of us survived the crash and four of our crew members were killed on the ground by German civilians; the radio operator that was wounded in the plane was killed on his stretcher, by civilians, when on his way to hospital.'

Irv Pliskin of the 95th Bomb Group parachuted into Germany from his striken B-17 in January 1945 and was generally treated well and guarded from a hostile crowd by soldiers.

> Nobody tried very hard to do us harm . . . they just seemed to stare at us and we at them. The strangest odyssey began next morning, when we began to walk out of Gravensberg down the main street. We walked down the middle of the street, and the civilians on the sidewalk hurled epithets and threats at us, *'Kaput machen!'*, again and again – a frightening litany. We passed a group of nuns, and even they spat at us. We learned later that they really hated the fighter pilots because they came down and shot up anything that moved on the roads and even farm animals in the fields. Our fighter pilots generated a lot of anger and distress, and if they were shot down they were in great jeopardy – the civilians would gang up and beat them mercilessly.

Many other accounts mention attacks or beatings by civilians as POWs were being taken through German cities en route to the Dulag Luft interrogation centre and then to the POW camps, but Corbin Willis adds that 'The people who attacked us were mostly incensed by the RAF bombing of Cologne the last six nights, so you wouldn't expect them to greet you with cheers. I'm sure my own family would be out there hitting and swinging in the circumstances.' It is also fair to record that a large number of accounts detail individual Germans or German families defending aircrew from enraged mobs or Nazi Party killers, treating their wounds, or giving them food.

Archie McIntosh, whose tale of being shot down over Mannheim is given elsewhere in this book was also well treated on capture:

> On landing I was taken to a house and soon joined by two crew members, Harrison and Nicolas. We were kindly treated. An older lady brought me a basin of water to get the blood from my face, which had been scraped, and a younger man, of about our age, came in when I was attending to my arm and neck. He looked concerned and asked if he should fetch a doctor, but I said I was OK. Then – and I did not dream this – he asked, 'Is it true that Louis Armstrong is dead?' and was clearly relieved to hear that Satchmo was still alive and blowing. He told me he was taking a day off from his anti-aircraft battery in Mannheim, but then a small truck arrived to take us off to prison. Before leaving he came round to my side of the truck and said, 'Good luck. I am on your side.' I did not hear from him again until February 1999. His name is Heinz Bentz, and he wrote me a letter – in fluent English – recalling our meeting in that cellar in 1943 and I enclose it for you to see.

You were the first Englishman I met in my life,' writes Heinz Bentz:

> I did not know that you were Scottish. Before that I had only heard of the English from my father, who had had a leg torn off by an English hand grenade in France in 1915. He was only nineteen at the time and always spoke with great respect of the brave English soldiers. I learned English in grammar school, but in 1943 (Russia!) soldiers became scarce and so schoolboys, sixteen/seventeen at that time, were taken to a flak battery, 88 mm or 105 mm.
>
> Our teachers came and gave lessons at the battery, and we were allowed home one day a week – which is how I came to be at home on that night in September 1943. Why did I ask about Louis Armstrong? American jazz and 'swing' was not allowed in Germany – it was 'nigger music', 'music of an inferior race' or 'decadent' American music – but of course we boys were enthusiastic about it and had records via Holland and by listening to the BBC's *Germany Calling*. So that is why I asked you.
>
> When the truck arrived to take you to Würms I was annoyed at the unfriendly way the guards were talking to you. So I wanted to shake hands and wish you good luck. On that night your raid had intended to destroy the northern part of Mannheim, but through some mistake or misunderstanding the bombing crept back across the Rhine and so the small town there was completely burnt out. My flak battery was there and we had some casualties, among them a friend of mine, aged sixteen, who was hit in the chest by an incendiary bomb.
>
> My home town of Würms was bombed at the end of the war and 70 per cent destroyed, two days before the Americans arrived. They threw us out of our house and took my father's Iron Cross, First Class, and my mother's gold watch but left us chocolate and some food.

I first went to England in 1950 and have been back many times since, to Würms' twin town, St Albans in Hertfordshire, and my wife and I like England very much – its towns, villages, cathedrals and scenery. After the war I became a teacher, finishing as headmaster of a local school, and am now retired. That is the outline of my life since we met in that cellar so many years ago. Thank God we have overcome the past and can enjoy life, and we wish that you can do so for many years to come.

An American bombardier, Quinton V. Brown, also mentions the kindness of some Germans:

We were shot down near Berlin on 18 April 1944; I was over the bombsight when the fighters came in, and in two passes they knocked down ten B-17s out of the eighteen in our group, in what I later estimated to be about 45 seconds. I went out the escape hatch in the nose, but the right leg strap of my parachute caught on something and I hung there long enough to count the rivets under the fuselage on the bottom of that dying silver B-17. I ended up at the Hermann Goering Hospital in the Rhenickendorf area north of Berlin, and stayed there for two and a half months.

Let me tell you about Sister Maria Lorenzen of Hallig Langeness on the North Sea. Maria was the dedicated, bouncing, upbeat German nurse of that place. She would not let you get a down on yourself, and attended daily to fifteen or twenty Allied wounded aircrew and many more *Luftwaffe* aircrew. I have about 75 pages of accolades written to that 'Florence Nightingale' of Hitler's Germany by grateful and healing young American and British flyers. My wife and I have been back to visit her at least six times, and she still lives on her bleak island on the North Sea coast, now aged 88.

Whatever the extent of *civilian* air-raid precautions and preparations undertaken from 1940 to 1942, Germany went to war in 1939 without making any adequate *military* preparations for the air defence of the Reich. The root of this failure is very simple: hubris.

Hitler's strategy was based on *Blitzkrieg* campaigns of great speed and weight, fought entirely on the defenders' soil and delivering victory in a matter of weeks. To set up defensive arrangements in Germany was therefore not only unnecessary but a diversion of strength from the battlefield – and a denial of the Führer's military genius. In 1939 and 1940 this belief in Hitler's prowess seemed well founded. The *Wehrmacht* swept through Poland, Holland, Beligum and France, drove the British into the sea at Dunkirk, took Denmark and Norway, and ended the war in the West in a matter of weeks. Then came June 1941 and Operation BARBAROSSA, the invasion of Russia. Before long, it became apparent that matters there did not seem to be going with the now familiar speed – and by early 1941 the RAF was scattering bombs, with no great accuracy but with apparent impunity, across the sacred soil of the Reich.

The man ultimately responsible for the air defence of the Reich was the head of the *Luftwaffe*, Hermann Goering, who commanded both the flak and the fighters. Goering had been a fighter pilot in the First World War, a member of the famous Richthofen squadron, a friend of the famous 'Red Baron'. After that war he drifted into politics, becoming an early member of the Nazi Party and the founder of the Gestapo. After Germany created a new air force in the 1930s, Goering became Reichmarshal of the *Luftwaffe* and a stout defender of *Luftwaffe* interests.

The *Luftwaffe* also contained the flak element of the German armed forces, and by 1943 these flak units had become the largest element in the *Luftwaffe*, mustering almost a million men, all deployed in the defence of Germany – men who might otherwise have been fighting in Russia or the Western Desert. The Allied air forces were, in effect, creating a 'Second Front' over Germany, and supplies of men, artillery and aircraft had to be diverted from land campaigns abroad for the air defence of the Reich's territory.

When British raids began to reach Germany in 1940–1, Goering at first believed that the flak guns – light and heavy – would be more than enough to defend the cities of the Reich. As time passed and the RAF attacks grew in numbers, bomb load and frequency – if not in accuracy – and especially following the first raid on Berlin on the night of 25/26 August 1940, more elements were added: radar, searchlights and day and night fighters. In the early days of the bomber war this was an ad hoc arrangement, designed to cope with a temporary situation, but such arrangements are rarely effective and are not in line with the German military method, which prefers system and order. Besides, as the months passed it became apparent that the RAF attacks would continue and could only grow in strength and effectiveness.

General Josef Kammhuber was appointed General of Fighters in July 1940 and charged by Goering with the creation of a night-fighter force. The first night-fighter *Gruppe*, – *I/NJG 1* – with a strength of twenty Ju88s was created in the same month, and was to be commanded by Major Falk, 'The father of the night-fighter force'. Falk's force had a lot to learn, and it was not until a year later – and two years into the war – that a full night-fighter division, *Fliegerkorps XII*, was formed.

From then on matters speeded up. By the middle of 1941 Kammhuber had created not just a night-fighter force but an *integrated* system of searchlights, flak guns, radar and night-fighter stations running from the shores of the Baltic Sea through Holland and France to Switzerland. By the autumn of 1942 this system extended from the south of Norway to south of Paris, gradually extending as the British found ways to fly round it. The main defensive line lay along the Channel and North Sea coast and employed an integrated system covering the early detection of incoming bombers and the vectoring of fighters on to them using *Würzburg Riese* radar, fighter-control stations, and the deployment of fighters in *Räume* –

or 'boxes'. This system was known to the Germans as the *Himmelbett* – 'the four-poster bed' – though, as already related, the British called it the Kammhuber Line.

This line was not fully operational until September 1942, but, to avoid the spreading defences and varied dangers of the Kammhuber Line and still reach Germany, the RAF bombers would now have to fly either north of Denmark or south of Paris. If the bombers were reduced to using just these two approaches, the Germans would line the routes with flak and fighters and turn flying to Germany into a form of running the gauntlet. As a long-term course of action this was impossible; the Kammhuber Line could not be avoided, so clearly it would have to be forced.

The slow build-up of the British air offensive and the reasons for that delay have already been explained. What has to be appreciated is that the build-up of Britain's offensive capability was matched by a similar increase in Germany's defensive capability; in effect, the two sides learned the bomber-war business together, and overall they remained evenly matched for much of the war, with the advantage resting only briefly with whichever side enjoyed some temporary technological advantage.

Even without the wide range of existing technical aids, Germany enjoyed some fundamental advantages in maintaining the Kammhuber Line. The defender usually gains the advantage of odds – three attackers to one defender is the normal military rule – and here the fighters were over their own territory and close to their bases. This factor was a 'force-enhancer' in various ways. First, the German fighters could refuel and rearm quickly and return to the attack within a short space of time. Second, any German pilot shot down unharmed was safe – and was promptly given a new aircraft and sent up again; any Allied crew member who parachuted to the ground became a prisoner of war. The fighters could be controlled and vectored on to the bombers by radar, from nearby installations. As for the German gunners and radar and searchlight operators, they were able to train and work as teams in fixed positions and had access to unlimited supplies of ammunition; when the raid was over, they could relax for a while.

The Allied bombers had no such advantages. They had to fight their way to the target and then fight their way home again, facing bad weather, the prevailing westerly winds and night fighters as they did so. A high number of Allied bombers got home safely but crashed on landing, their crews tired out or their aircraft crippled by battle damage. When all the factors are taken into account, the German defenders held the edge of advantage for much of the war and swamping the defences of Germany came down to a matter of numbers – and organization.

The core of the Kammhuber Line was the series of fighter *Räume* or 'boxes', each the province of a single night fighter flown by an experienced pilot, but the first line of defence was radar. Radar – and radio interception – gave the Germans early warning of impending attacks and the likely strength and target of the approaching bombers. This information came in as the attack built up, starting with information from *Freya*.

German *Freya* radar sets could pick up Allied bombers at considerable distances – even the sound of radios being tested on UK airfields before an attack could be picked up and give advance warnings of that night's operations. Allied bombers – American as well as British – were therefore eventually obliged to take off to a pre-timed plan, without radio contact with the control tower. *Freya* – the first line of the German defence system – tracked the bombers as they crossed the North Sea and then handed the tracking over to the *Würzburg* radars, the radar control element of the night-fighter *Räume* as the bombers reached the coast of Continental Europe.

The control of the fighters in the night-fighter boxes was based on two *Riese Würzburg* radars: one to pick up the approaching bomber entering the box, the other to mark and control the night fighter defending it. These radar sets, both *Freya* and *Würzburg*, fed their information into a fighter control room where the controllers – Jägerleitoffiziere or JLOs – plotted the courses of the bomber and the intercepting fighter on a glass table, the *Seeburg* table. The JLO guided the fighter until it was in visual sight of the bomber and able to put in an attack or, later on, when the night fighters had been fitted with air-interception (AI) radar, until the bomber was within range of the fighter's *Lichtensteingerät* radar set, which was effective at a range of two miles. This system was similar to that employed by the RAF controllers during the Battle of Britain, but the German system was more sophisticated. Given accurate information, skilled control and good flying, the *Himmelbett* system could quickly put the Allied bomber in the night fighter's gun sights, as Claud Michel Becker describes:

> The Reich was speckled with radar stations – *Würzburg Reisen* – each with a range of 50 km and this in turn to a night-fighter control – *Nachtjägdleitstelle* – which led the fighter to the bomber. For example, there is this attack on a Halifax II of No. 51 Squadron, pilot Sergeant E. W. Cox. This bomber was picked up by radar close to Frankfurt at 0256 local time, and attacked at Limburg at 0311 hrs and crashed two minutes later; total time from initial contact to crash, seventeen minutes.

This 'box' method of fighter control was highly effective, but limited: the radar could track only one bomber and fighter at a time and, although the Kammhuber Line was long, it was thin. While one bomber was being tracked, others were getting through. To confuse the fighters in the *Räume*, the RAF developed the bomber stream, bunching the aircraft together – a tactic first used on the Cologne Thousand Raid in 1942. The RAF was willing to accept a higher risk of collisions in a bid to improve navigation and bomb-aiming accuracy, but the bomber stream proved equally useful in swamping the night-fighter boxes.

In using the bomber stream the RAF was, in effect, rushing the German defences, hoping to swamp the defending radar and fighters and so get most of the bombers past. The crews soon came to realize that safely lay in staying with the stream: aircraft which strayed out of it were quickly picked up by the *Würzburg* sets and fighters were soon hunting them across the night sky; after that, survival became a matter of skill, experience and luck.

To avoid being attacked, or to beat off fighter attacks, called for a great deal of co-operation and concentration among the individual bomber crews. The more experienced pilots never flew a level flight except in the few minutes of 'run-up' to the target; the rest of the time they were constantly 'banking' and rolling the aircraft, partly to allow the tail and front gunner a view of the blind spot underneath the aircraft, partly to deny any stalking enemy night fighter a steady target.

A banking and weaving bomber was rarely attacked, but, when it was, a cry of 'Fighter – corkscrew!' from one of the gunners would alert the pilot, who would instantly corkscrew the aircraft, attempting to distract the enemy's aim and, with any luck, lose him in the darkness. Later in the war – as we shall see – the German twin-engined night fighters carried their own on-board radar set, the *Lichtenstein SN2*, which was manned by the radio operator, the *Funker*.

The *Luftwaffe* fought for much of the war with aircraft available when the war started, the later Marks, or variants, of these aircraft – the single-engined Me 109, the twin-engine Me 110, and two converted bombers, the Ju 88 and the Dornier 217 – being improved models of the 1939–40 machines. A later arrival, the radial-engined Focke-Wulf 190 (FW 190), was a very fine aircraft. The Me 110 and the Ju 88 were the backbone of the night-fighter force. These aircraft were slow, but speed is not all that important in a night fighter, provided it is fast enough to catch the bombers; far more important is the need to provide a steady gun platform for the cannon, and crew space for the *Funker*. The Me 109 and the FW 190 were day fighters, at least until the *Wilde Sau* tactic, employing single-engined day fighters on night operations, was introduced following the Hamburg firestorm raid of 1943 (see Chapter 10).

These German aircraft, with the exception of the unreliable Dornier 217, remained in service throughout the war. One of the many side benefits of the Allied bomber war was that the need to maintain a constant supply of fighter aircraft for the defence of the Reich prevented Germany developing a four-engined strategic bomber to attack Great Britain, though it did not prevent work on the V1 and V2 rockets or the first operational jet aircraft, the Me 262 and the Arado 234, which entered service in the autumn of 1944.

Luftwaffe officer Alfons Altmeier gives an overview of the German fighters deployed in the air defence of the Reich:

Let's start with day fighters. The main German fighter aircraft during the whole war was the Bf/Me 109, in various variants. From the technical stand-point, this aircraft had reached its peak in 1942, and all the later versions could not overcome the main handicap of this type: a lack of range. The reason for continued production after that time was the relatively cheap and simple building process. The Me 109 was basically a low-wing sports plane, and this was the main reason for the less than useful range, because the wing space for greater fuel tank capacity was not available – a problem that plagued your Spitfire variants also. A much more versatile and sturdy fighter was Professor Tank's Focke-Wulf 190. This plane in all its variants was very modern and had great development potential.

The night-fighter story is more complicated, because night fighting is a completely different environment. It is no secret that the *Luftwaffe* preferred heavy armament for both day and night fighters – cannon as well as machine-guns. Speed was not at first the main requirement for night fight-ers, though this changed as the war progressed. At first the night fighters were bomber-type aircraft like the Dornier Do 17, and later the more advanced Do 217 played a main role against the Allied – British – bombers. Apart from their respectable armament, their six hours' flight endurance was the main reason for their use.

By 1942 more speed was necessary and so the above types were phased out and specially equipped Ju 88 and Me 110s appeared on the scene and gave night fighting another quality. The most versatile German night fighter was the Ju 88 in its various variants, followed by the Heinkel 219, which was available in small numbers only – not to forget the old but very successful Me 110 G-4. Of course we must not forget the later use of the jet fighter, the Me 262. A night-fighter version was flown by First Lieutenant Welter and proved very successful due to its heavy armament, but by then the time was over and the war came to an end.

There is also the matter of radar and electronic measures by both sides. The use of brand-new electronic devices like *Lichtenstein* radar and the *Spanner* infra-red target designator forced the RAF to develop some counter-mea-sures as soon as possible, but until it did the German night fighters enjoyed a really short but very effective time and destroyed a lot of RAF aircraft. The introduction of *Chaff – Window* – changed the situation, for this worked against the night fighters – and then were was the matter of different tactics necessary to shoot down different types of bombers.

Paul Zorner, the night-fighter pilot, was still building up his score against the Allied bombers, and his career in 1943–4 gives some idea of what a skilled night-fighter pilot could achieve:

In February 1943 I made seven attacks and shot down four aircraft: a Halifax, Lancaster, a Boston and a Stirling. In March I made five attacks and shot down two aircraft, both Wellingtons. I did not shoot down another bomber until June, when I shot down another Wellington. But in July I shot down three British bombers, and in August two Lancasters in one night over Peenemunde. From then on shooting down two or three bombers a night was

not unusual, and by the end of 1943 I had nineteen air victories. In the following months until March 1944, in attacks over Germany, France and
Holland another 22 aircraft were shot down.

On the night of 24/25 February 1944 I shot down five Lancasters around
Stuttgart,[5] and on 26/27 March three more Lancasters over Belgium. In this
month I was promoted as group commander to III/ NG 5 at Mainz and later
to Laon-Athies in France and stayed with this unit until the end of July 1944,
by which time I had 58 air victories, including four in one night – two
Lancasters and two Halifaxes over Chartres and Dreux in France. I was then
awarded the Knight's Cross and posted to Lübeck. My final air victory was
south-west of Graz in Austria, on the night of 5/6th March 1945, when I shot
down a B-24 Liberator.

This restriction of fighter development to a few basic types paid off in
terms of reliability and the ability to disperse factories and increase production; one of the arguments used to support the claim that the bomber
offensive was ineffective is that German fighter production actually
increased while the bomber offensive was at its height. Between
November 1942 and July 1943, German fighter production increased from
400 to over 800 aircraft per month, including repaired machines. This
increase in production during the bomber offensive is largely accounted
for by the fact that until 1943 most German factories only worked one shift
a day; to increase production by 100 per cent it was only necessary to run
a second shift.

By 1943 the *Luftwaffe* had about 1,000 aircraft coming into front-line
service each month, and between January and June 1943 average fighter
strength for the defence of the Reich's territory rose from 1,250 to 1,800.[6]
This, however, was only barely enough to keep up with the growing
number of losses after the P-51 Mustang came into service with the Allies
at the start of 1944. The *Luftwaffe* was finally defeated by superior
machines, a shortage of fuel – which inhibited training as well as operations – overwhelming numbers, and the steady loss of its best pilots.

Those bombers who got through the Kammhuber Line were the responsibility of the searchlights and flak guns, the third element in Germany's
defensive system. Flak batteries were established in thick belts around the
principal German cities, and by the end of 1942 industrial centres like the
Ruhr valley – 'Happy Valley' to the bomber crews – were surrounded by
more than 200 88 mm flak batteries. Each battery contained six or eight
guns, many radar-controlled and some mounted on railway cars which
were able to follow the bomber stream and keep it under attack. Claud
Michel Becker again:

The most important cities were protected by flak and searchlights, but these
were concentrated in the industrial areas which the British attacked, like the
Ruhr and the Rhein/Main area around Frankfurt. Between these areas was

a hole of over 100 km with absolutely no heavy defence: this was the *Kölner Loch* – or, as you say, the Cologne Hole or the Gateway – and was the area where I lived. The German leaders saw this and decided to station several night-fighter groups in this Hole, for example NJG 6, which was based in Mainz-Finthen. They also built trains carrying flak guns – some 20 mm, 50 mm or 105 mm guns which ran on the tracks between Cologne and Frankfurt; one of these trains stayed in the marshalling yards at Dillenburg for over two weeks.

Fighters and heavy flak were supported by large amounts of light and medium flak, and some cities – Hamm, Essen and Berlin, for example – became notorious 'Flak Cities', feared by the crews for the amount of anti-aircraft fire the defending guns could produce. And so, gradually, the defences of the Reich thickened and became harder to beat.

The details above refer generally to the RAF night bombing offensive, but some of the problems the RAF encountered were shared by the USAAF. Eighth Air Force missions were also detected and tracked by the *Freya* and *Würzburg* radars, but, since these were daylight missions, the fighter pilots' problems in finding and then attacking the bombers were somewhat easier. The main aim of the flak was to break up the US defensive formations – the 'lead', 'high' and 'low' groups with their interlocking fields of fire from .50-calibre machine-guns – to cause damaged aircraft to fall out of formation and let the fighters in. If this could be done, the B-17s and B-24s could be picked off one by one.

Flak was the best way to break-up the US bomber formations. Following their first mission to Germany on 27 January 1943, when 91 bombers of the 1st and 2nd Bombardment Wings attacked Wilhelmshaven, the US aircrew soon developed a healthy respect for the German gunners, and especially for the radar-guided 88 mm gun which fired 'predicted' flak, which could pick off individual bombers at considerable heights. In the period from July 1943 until March 1944, USAAF missions into Germany were un-escorted by fighters for most of the way and the US bomb groups suffered severe losses from the combined efforts of the flak and fighters.

By the spring of 1943, many of the flak batteries were radar-directed and at night were closely tied in to searchlight batteries which aimed to catch and 'cone' the RAF bombers, holding them in their beams until the guns could concentrate and blow them out of the sky. The 'blue beam' of the 'master searchlight' was particularly feared and appears in many RAF aircrew accounts.

The air defenders of the Reich suffered from a problem that the British and USAAF bomber commanders would have found familiar: their attempts to build up a viable force were constantly interrupted by demands for support from other theatres. Even as the RAF bombers were diverted into Coastal Command and the Eighth Air Force lost whole bomb groups to the North African campaign, so the *Luftwaffe* fighter controllers, charged with the defence of the Reich, lost many *Geschwader* to the Russian Front and the war in Italy. Flak batteries lost guns and crews to the Russian front, for the 88 mm was the main army artillery piece and was deadly against tanks when fed with armour-piercing ammunition.

The German aircrews also needed more help to find the bombers. The *Würzburg* could put them into close contact, but that was not always enough in the dark and cloudy skies. It took time for good airborne radar – the *Lichtenstein* – to come into service, and for the first few years the night-fighter pilots had to find the bombers by roving about the sky, largely relying on their eyesight and luck.

Operationally, the main difference between day and night fighters was in their methods of attack. Night fighters – Ju 88s or Me 110s – operated alone, stalking their prey in the night sky using radar, either ground-based *Würzburg* or the later *Liechtenstein* airborne device. Day fighters – the single-seat Me 109s and FW 190s – were directed on to the bomber forma-tions in *Staffel*- or *Gruppe*-sized formations and attacked in large numbers, in groups of four or in pairs, putting in constant attacks until their fuel and ammunition were exhausted.

On posting to their *Staffeln*, the German fighter pilots simply got on with attacking the enemy, by day and night, and continued to do so until they were killed. There were no 'tours' for *Luftwaffe* pilots. Many of these pilots were shot down, some several times, but those who survived became aces – *Experten* – with a large score of shot-down Allied bombers, a claim on the best *Raum* along the Kammhuber Line and a chestful of highly valued decorations.

Backing up the fighters was the flak. The most feared anti-aircraft gun was the dual-purpose 88 mm, which could hurl a powerful shell five miles into the sky with great accuracy. The Germans eventually deployed thou-sands of these 88 mm guns around the German cities – weapons that could have made a great difference to anti-tank defences on the Eastern Front. Two other heavy guns were the 105 mm and the 128 mm, but the German 88 mm was the finest artillery piece of the war. High-flying bombers had less to fear from the light flak – 37 mm and 20 mm cannon – which could throw up a great deal of fire but only to around 15,000 ft.

Flak was detested by the US daylight bombing crews, not least because if the flak guns could knock a few aircraft down or even force them out of formation, this weakened the 'defensive integrity' of the attacking forma-tion as a whole. Straggling bombers became a magnet for German fighters and were quickly shot down, and, if the process continued, the entire for-mation could be prised apart and destroyed piecemeal.

Other methods and equipment came in as the bomber offensive grew in intensity. The *Wilde Sau* system, using day fighters against the bomber stream, and the introduction of the *Schrage Musik* cannon will be covered later, but it is important to realize that General Kammhuber's defensive line was a complete, integrated system, embracing every form of technology from radio surveillance to small-calibre cannon. As such, it took a heavy toll of Allied bombers. But, in spite of all the efforts of the German defenders, a high percentage of bombers still got through. In fact, the aim of the defences was not to stop all the bombers getting through – that was soon seen as an impossible task – but to cause such heavy losses that the attacks would be called off by the Allied air-force commanders.

This was the aim during the first years of war and, although the Kammhuber system failed to stop the attacks, it did force the RAF to give up daylight bombing and switch to night attacks on area targets. That apart, night bombing was a difficult task that required a large amount of technical help in the shape of radar and electronic aids if it was to be carried out accurately and effectively.

Until those aids were in service, night bombing achieved very little and Germany had little to fear from Bomber Command. By the early summer of 1942; this technical help – first *Gee*, then *H₂S*, and later *Oboe* – was starting to arrive or was under development. These aids would eventually have a profound effect on Bomber Command operations, and on the defenders of the Reich. The technological war was not over by the end of 1942; it would go on until the end of the war, and both sides had many more scientific shots left in their locker as the bomber war hotted up in 1943.

At the same time a new element of the bomber war arrived in the European skies. In the summer of 1942 the first formations of the United States Army Air Force appeared over Occupied Europe – a force that had no intention of attacking area targets, or of attacking at night. The USAAF had a different philosophy for the bomber war – one that clashed with that of their RAF ally – and a tactic for the conduct of bomber operations that was to bring it into head-on collision with the *Luftwaffe* airmen defending Germany.

B-17F Flying Fortress

7

Enter the Mighty Eighth
1942

We won't do more talking until we have done more fighting.

Brigadier-General Ira C. Eaker, Eighth Air Force,
USAAF, speech in High Wycombe, England, 1942

Although the US government had been openly aiding Britain's war effort almost since the outbreak of war in 1939, the United States finally entered the Second World War only on Sunday 7 December 1941, after a Japanese air attack crippled the US Pacific Fleet at Pearl Harbor in Hawaii – a sudden, savage introduction for the American people to what air power could do in war. The natural reaction of all Americans was to turn on Japan and retaliate for this unprovoked attack, but at the 'Arcadia' Conference between the US President, Franklin D. Roosevelt, and the British Prime Minister, Winston Churchill, in Washington on 20 December 1941 it was agreed that the main weight of Allied arms should first be directed against Germany.

This decision followed the well-established principle of strategic doctrine which dictates that, when a nation is faced with an array of enemies, the strongest enemy should be defeated first. Even so, the US President's decision to go for Germany was controversial, was subject to certain conditions, and had several long-term aims. Many people in the higher echelons of US military and political life felt that the principal target for American arms should be Japan. Chief of these was Admiral Ernest J. King, Commander-in-Chief of the US Navy and a member of the new Anglo-American body set up to run the war, the Combined Chiefs of Staff. Admiral King's service had suffered a major blow at Pearl Harbor, and his men wanted revenge. The war in the Pacific would necessarily be a naval and amphibious war, where the US Navy would play a leading role, and King had no objection to that. Like many US citizens, King felt that the war in Europe was of marginal concern to the USA and that Germany posed no immediate threat to his country. Finally, he was an Anglophobe. Admiral King's fingerprints can be found on many of the decisions adversely affecting the European war – the allocation of landing craft for D-Day being a particular example.

The 'Germany First' decision was made on the understanding that the Allies should invade the Continent of Europe and defeat Nazi Germany with the least possible delay, and the two Allies were soon disputing just how short that delay might be. Three weeks into their war, many American politicians and commanders thought that this cross-Channel invasion – code-named Operation SLEDGEHAMMER, a landing on the Cherbourg penin-sula – could be carried out in the summer of 1942, about six months after the USA entered the war. The British, with a little more experience in these matters – and considerable experience in fighting the Germans – were rather less sanguine, and the impossibility of a rapid landing in Europe was bloodily underlined by the slaughter of Canadian troops in the Dieppe raid of August 1942.

President Roosevelt had known for years that the USA would eventu-ally either have to enter the war or see half the world lost to the totalitar-ian powers, but he had to cater for the varied military and political opinions at home and he also had a few aims of his own. One of these was the eventual destruction of the colonial empires of Britain, France and Holland. These countries now needed US assistance, and they could have it – at a price. The price was the post-war loss of their colonial possessions – partly because Roosevelt, like many Americans, felt that colonialism was wrong, partly because it would open up large areas of the post-war world to American trade and reduce the risk of a post-war recession on the scale of the 1930s. Roosevelt was taking the long view, but in the meantime he had to sell the European war to the US public.

This was not hard to do, for Germany declared war on the USA a few days after Pearl Harbor and this, plus the aftershock of the Japanese attack, was enough to unite the American people behind their President. The European War was regarded – and presented – as a moral issue. The stamping-out of German aggression and the restoration of peace, justice, and common decency to a war-torn and currently enslaved Europe was a valid reason to commit American arms to battle, the right thing for decent folks to do. Not for nothing were General Dwight D. Eisenhower's subse-quent war memoirs entitled *Crusade in Europe*.

In the event, the Allies were not able to cross the Channel and invade France until the summer of 1944, some two and a half years after Pearl Harbor. The intervening period was spent beating the U-boat menace in the North Atlantic, building up invasion forces in the United Kingdom, driving the Germans out of North Africa – where the US Army suffered a considerable shock when it met the German Army for the first time at the Kasserine Pass – and, after the surrender of Italy in September 1943, forcing a passage up the Italian mainland to the gates of Rome; the city fell on 5 June 1944, the day before D-Day. Meanwhile, the direct attack on German economic and industrial power had been delegated to the combined air forces of the British Empire and the USA – specifically RAF Bomber Command and the Eighth and Fifteenth US Army Air Forces. The main US component here was the bomber element based in the United Kingdom, VIII Bomber Command of the Eighth Air Force.

Unlike the RAF, the USAAF was not an independent force when it entered the war in 1941; indeed, until June 1941 it had been the Army Air *Corps*. Although the Air Force enjoyed a great deal of autonomy, it was still an integral part of the United States Army – and would remain so until 1947. Nor was it very large: in 1939 the US Army Air Corps ranked seventh in size – behind Romania – among the world's air forces. In many other respects the USAAF had several problems in common with the RAF. Like the RAF, the Air Corps had had to fight for such autonomy as it had and was still under constant attack from the other services. The US Navy was jealously guarding its strategic defensive role, while the higher echelons of the US Army still saw the Army Air Force in terms of tactical battlefield co-operation and not as a strategic force. In the inter-war years the Air Corps had been starved of resources, and when the Second World War began in 1939 it was woefully short of aircraft and lacked a reliable supply of trained crews.

After the USA entered the war, the USAAF – and especially the Eighth Air Force based in Britain – had, again like Bomber Command, to endure the constant erosion of its strength by demands for more aircraft in the Pacific or the diversion of aircraft and crews for army co-operation tasks in North Africa and Italy, or for anti-submarine duty off the Atlantic coast. One benefit of this, however, was that, through sharing common problems, the RAF and USAAF commanders – Portal, Harris, Saundby, Arnold, Spaatz, Eaker and the rest – had a common enemy – the Higher Command – and generally got on well together.

However, in some respects the USAAF was well equipped to enter the struggle in Europe. The Air Corps had expanded steadily since 1939 and had two outstanding bomber aircraft, the B-17 and the B-24, and the famous Norden bombsight. It also had plenty of American get-up-and-go and the backing of the vast scientific, industrial and training resources of the United States – a combination that within a few years would provide all the USAAF needed to wage a decisive war on a worldwide front. The USAAF also came to the European war – the ETO, the European Theatre of Operations – with both a strategic doctrine and a bombing philosophy. All in all, it was not a bad start.

The bombing philosophy of the USAAF had two strands: the practical and the moral. The moral issue was simple: the USA did not believe that war should be waged against civilians, and especially not against women and children. This is a decent, clear and eminently sane position, and at the start of the war the British people and their leaders had felt exactly the same way. It will be recalled that in 1939 the RAF was forbidden to attack targets in Germany, even warships in German ports, if the attack was likely to cause civilian casualties.

Nor was this restriction only on the Allied side. In 1936, before the opening of the Spanish Civil War, the *Luftwaffe* training manual stated clearly that 'attacks on cities for the purpose of terrorizing the civilian population are absolutely forbidden' – which did not prevent the Condor Legion from attacking Guernica in April 1937. The point is, however, that at the start of their war *all* the air forces declared their objection to attacking civilian targets: in 1939 President Roosevelt had asked the belligerents to refrain from attacking civilian targets from the air, and both sides had agreed to do so. The first to break this agreement, within days of the outbreak of war, was Germany, outside Warsaw. After that, as we have seen, the moral objections to the area bombing of cities had been gradually been eroded, even by the British, largely on technical grounds: the choice was bombing German cities or not bombing Germany at all.

There are few absolutes in war, especially over moral issues, but it is fair to say that the USAAF commanders' objections to area bombing were on professional and tactical grounds rather than on moral ones. It is possible to quote statements both for and against 'moral bombing' – attacks on civilian targets – from most of the USAAF commanders, but a few examples will serve for the moment.

The practical side is exemplified by General Curtis LeMay – a man who, twenty-five years after the Second World War, declared his willingness to 'bomb North Vietnam into the Stone Age'. Speaking after the Second World War about the bomber offensive in Europe LeMay said, 'To worry about the morality of what we were doing? Nuts! A soldier has to fight. We fought. If we accomplished the job in any given battle without losing too many of our own folks that was a pretty good day.' However, LeMay also said, 'If you are cursed with any imagination at all, you have at least one horrid glimpse of a child in bed with a ton of masonry tumbling down on top of him, or a three-year-old girl crying *'Mutter, mutter'*, because she has been burned. You have to turn away from that picture if you intend to retain your sanity and do the work your nation expects of you.'[1]

A different, pro-morality, point of view comes from General Laurence Kuter, the USAAF Assistant Chief of Air Plans. Kuter rejected the idea of area attacks on German cities partly because it would divert the USAAF from more productive attacks on military and economic targets and partly because, as he stated in 1944, 'it was contrary to our national ideals to make war on civilians'.

However, General Kuter must have meant *European* civilians, for six months later, on 9/10 March 1945, the USAAF fire-bombed Tokyo and, according to the US Strategic Bombing Survey, killed or injured some 120,000 Japanese civilians. Tens of thousands more Japanese died when atomic bombs were dropped on Hiroshima and Nagasaki. This point is made not to question General Kuter's sincerity but to point out the difference between the US attitudes to bombing cities in Europe and to bombing those in Japan, and to suggest a reason for it. The difference is that the USA had been attacked directly by the Japanese at Pearl Harbor. Attacking the Japanese homeland was therefore different from attacking the German homeland: for the Americans, the Japanese 'had it coming to them' in a way the Germans did not. The element of retaliation in the bombing war was common to both sides and all nations.

The beliefs of the other leading US commanders, Spaatz and Eaker, are less clear-cut or at least more ambivalent. Fundamentally, it is fair to say that their basic objection to area bombing was again technical rather than moral. After the war, General Spaatz stated that 'It was not for religious or moral reasons I did not go along with urban area bombing . . . but because attacks on strategic targets would be more effective.' General Eaker agreed with this, stating that he 'never felt there was any moral sentiment among the leaders of the AAF'. As the war went on and losses mounted, the early reluctance to bomb German cities tended to fade: the USAAF was losing a lot of good men over Germany on every mission, and the way to stop that loss was to end the war as soon as possible, by any means available. In March 1944, for example, commenting on USAAF 'blind bombing' using instruments like *Oboe* and H_2S to attack cloud-covered cities, General Frederick Anderson, head of VIII Bomber Command in 1943, said that 'If it comes up here, where we can get one of those damn cities that we can see and have our force on, there won't be a damn house left.'[2]

On the practical side, the USAAF did not believe that area bombing, or night bombing of any kind, was effective: at best it knocked down a lot of buildings, but it did nothing to reduce the enemy's capacity for effective war – or so it was thought. The USAAF strategists certainly thought so, and they had some evidence to back up this belief. As a neutral nation, the USA had maintained an embassy in Berlin and consulates in other German cities after 1939, and the attachés sent reports back to Washington stating that the claims of the RAF regarding the effectiveness of area attacks were mostly hogwash. The RAF was quite well aware of this, but, as already described, it had its own reasons for exaggerating what the RAF bombers were doing. The USAAF commanders were not interested in helping the RAF commanders maintain a fiction; the evidence they had was that night area bombing was a waste of time and effort – and the fact that this was so helped to reinforce their own belief in the current USAAF strategic bombing doctrine.

That strategic doctrine was *daylight precision bombing*. The background to the development of that doctrine has already been covered: to briefly recapitulate, it stemmed from a belief that the US Army Air Corps bombers could rapidly reinforce America's far-flung possessions in Hawaii and the Philippines and attack and destroy the ships of any seaborne invader far from the shores of these possessions or the US mainland. It is worth pointing out that this aspect of the doctrine failed: Japanese aircraft, launched from carriers of the Japanese Navy, bombed the US Fleet at Pearl Harbor and the Japanese Army rapidly overran the Philippines without a great deal of interference from the Army Air Force. Nevertheless, daylight precision bombing of small targets – like ships – is what the US Army Air Force had been trained to do, and it was very good at it. With the aid of the Norden bombsight, it was claimed that US bomb-aimers – bombardiers – could 'drop a bomb in a pickle barrel from 30,000 ft'.

This ability underpinned the belief that the enemy's ability to fight could be destroyed or severely curtailed by the destruction of certain key industries, especially where these were concentrated in certain specific factories – or 'choke points', in the jargon of the time. These would include factories producing aircraft and submarine engines, oil refineries, aluminium and steel plants, ball-bearing factories, and other places of strategic importance.

In mid-July 1941 the USAAF set up an Air War Plans Division, A-WPD/1. This consisted of a small committee dedicated to the idea of precision bombing, and one of its first tasks was to recruit two former Wall Street business analysts, Captains Richard D. Hughes and Malcolm Moss, whose task was to identify those German and Japanese industries and plants which, if destroyed, would render the Axis powers incapable of waging war.[3] These two officers eventually came up with a list of 154 German factories, including about twenty aircraft factories and a selected number of oil refineries, ball-bearing works, aluminium smelters and so on. This done, the A-WPD/1 Committee then calculated the possibilities of hitting these plants, in daylight, using the Norden bombsight, balancing a number of factors to produce an 'accuracy probability'. Their first calculations indicated that to hit a target 100 ft square from 20,000 ft would take a mission by 220 bombers, and when all the other elements were factored in – flak, fighters, weather, whatever – the resources required to achieve a 95 per cent chance of destroying such a precision target amounted to either 30 bomb-group missions or a single mission by 1,100 aircraft – which hardly sounds like precision bombing at all.

On this basis, applying adequate force to the 154 targets which the USAAF needed to destroy in order to knock Germany out of the war was clearly not going to be easy. The A-WPD/1 Committee mulled over this problem for some months, and then delivered its judgement. Based on probability theory, its conclusion was that a force of 98 bomb groups or some 6,800 US heavy bombers, plus suitable reserves – enough to supply 1,245 replacement bombers every month – could knock Germany out of the war in six months.

Hindsight enables us to see this projection as more 'pie in the sky' than bombers in the air, but, in the absence of any more precise information at the time, slide-rule calculations, if totally valueless in practice, were perhaps inevitable; as we shall see, the British also had their share of slide-rule fanatics. It is also fair to say that if a miracle had happened and the USAAF *had* been able to put up some 7,000 bombers over Germany soon after it arrived in the European Theatre of Operations, the effect on the war could have been dramatic. Even so, as Richard D. Hughes, by now a colonel and the target-selection officer for the Eighth in Britain, was to say later, 'In retrospect it seems fantastic that the air power program for the USA in World War II should have been based on the arbitrary and hurried opinions of two junior reserve captains'.[4]

Colonel Hughes was an interesting man, not least because, although a USAAF officer, he was British-born and had served with distinction in the British Army. Hughes had been commissioned into the British Army before the Great War, in which he served in the 5th Royal Gurkha Rifles, which he later commanded on the North-West Frontier of India in the Third Afghan War. Coming home via the USA in 1926 he met and married an American girl, and in 1929 he left the British Army, emigrated to the USA, and became an American citizen. Sensing the coming of war, in June 1941 he joined the US Army and was swiftly sent to the Army Air Corps as an intelligence officer. When the Eighth Air Force came to Britain in 1942, Hughes came with them, tasked to select the German targets for the attention of the US bombers. For this duty he eventually set up his own group, the Enemy Objectives Unit.

Hughes was totally committed to precision bombing. On both moral and practical grounds he regarded area attacks as anathema – an attitude that eventually brought him into conflict with another USAAF colonel, the Deputy Director of USAAF Intelligence, Lowell P. Weicker. Colonel Weicker was an advocate of 'morale bombing' – area attacks – and the dispute between these two influential officers was to go on until the end of the war. It will be seen, therefore, that the arguments about the ways and means of conducting an air war by the US Army Air Force ranged far beyond the matter of putting up an adequate number of aircraft: one fundamental question was what these aircraft should attack – vital industries and particular factories, or cities and civilian morale?

Attacking vital industries was a sound project in theory, but there was always the small matter of the Germans, who were well aware that certain industries were vital to their war effort and vulnerable to air attack. By 1942 these factories had been moved east (out of bomber range) or duplicated, or were well hidden or heavily defended, or their products had been matched by supplies from neutral countries. The American list of 'choke points' is not unlike what Arthur Harris came to despise as 'panacea' targets: important though they were, their destruction was peripheral to the overall strategy for knocking Germany out of the war.

There was a subsidiary problem with the US precision-bombing doctrine which no pre-war thinking or air exercise had revealed: the matter of ensuring that a US bomber could even get to the target in daylight in the face of enemy fighter opposition – a task that had already depleted the resources of the *Luftwaffe* and the RAF. In 1941 no fighter then in service with any of the world's air forces had the range to escort a bomber over long distances, all the way to the target and back – and defending fighters were hardly likely to allow the bombers an unimpeded passage in either direction. This problem had confronted the *Luftwaffe* and the RAF, and in both cases they had been forced to switch to night bombing, with all that meant in terms of navigation errors and a loss of bombing accuracy.

The USAAF commanders had an answer to that. According to the USAAF doctrine, the solution to fighter attack was to arm the long-range bombers – the B-17E and F, and later the G models of the Flying Fortress, and the B-24J and H Liberator – with a large number of machine-guns and send the aircraft out in quantity and in closely knit formations. This had not yet been tried in combat, but the theory was that, if at least 300 aircraft were dispatched, the massive amount of firepower produced by up to ten .50-calibre machine-guns on each aircraft would be more than adequate to beat off enemy fighters. This was far greater than the defensive firepower produced by any British or German bomber, and the theory seemed logical – or at least feasible. The USAAF firepower certainly bothered the *Luftwaffe* at least for a while, as Alfons Altmeier relates:

> Attacking and shooting down Allied bombers was a difficult game, and to attack the heavily armed US bombers – the B-17 and the B-24 – was an extremely dangerous business because their defence armament remained strong in all directions, and later on if the very effective fighter cover was present nearly any attempt to attack was some kind of '*kamikaze*' – suicide. There was no 'best method' of attacking bombers. It depended on the type, and many pilots told me that many factors had to be observed, like visibility, altitude, sky conditions, the co-ordination of the bomb group or bomber stream, and the tactics of the escorting fighters. In case the defensive cover of the bombers could be broken, attacks from the rear, or out of the sun, or from directly above, below or head-on, proved very effective at times.

Sam Ross, a ball-turret gunner with the 384th Bomb Group, gives another view of the US formations:

> The big planes, B-17s or 24s, looked like they were flying through smooth air, cruising at 165 m.p.h. Actually they bounced about in very unstable air, not

least because of the 'prop wash' from planes ahead and all around. We lost quite a few airplanes due to mid-air collisions from tight formation flying; we lost our two wingmen that way, and I was watching them from my ball turret as they hit. One started straight down; the wings on the other one folded over the fuselage like on a paper airplane and I did not see any parachutes come out.

One reason for such tight flying was for tight pattern bombing: the experienced lead bombardier would zero in on the target with his bombsight and when he let go the rest of us just hit the salvo switch. The other reason was for protection: when a German fighter attacked a US squadron he had 76 machine-guns aimed at him from 38 turrets.

My ball turret was actually a steel ball with some small windows on the side and between your legs; it was suspended from inside the fuselage, half in, half out, and you did not stay in it for take-off or landings. After take-off you climbed down into it and closed the door. There was no room for a parachute, and you actually had to curl up in the ball, the two .50-calibre machine-guns parallel along the sides of your legs, capable of about 800 rounds per minute. Electrical motors powered the turret in a 360° circle and 90° up and down – what a view!

Risky though it was, the tighter the formation the better, as Captain Ben Love of the 351st Bomb Group points out:

Our best defence was to fly close together so that our wings almost touched those of the nearest B-17. Tight formations stopped the German fighter planes picking off any B-17s flying in a loose formation, where they could be picked off without the German fighter pilot risking the concentrated fire from a squadron in tight formation. The second advantage of a tight group was a tight bomb pattern. Each bombardier dropped his bombs when he saw the lead plane's bombs drop. The tighter the bomb pattern, the greater the damage inflicted on the target.

When the USAAF entered the war in 1941, it did so in the belief that these heavily armed bombers, packed in tight formations, could fight their way to the target and back without fighter escort and hit industrial and military targets precisely, without what is now called 'collateral damage' – the destruction of civilian property and the loss of innocent lives. The USAAF believed totally in both the daylight-precision-bombing doctrine and the defensive capability of their strategic bombers, and it arrived in Europe determined to 'put up' those bombers in great numbers and make that doctrine succeed. Thus determined, the USAAF Eighth Air Force crossed the Atlantic in early 1942, set up bases in Britain, and flew off to engage the *Luftwaffe*. Only then did it discover the snag with both these doctrines: they didn't work.

There is an element of culpability, hubris, or wishful thinking here. Many US Air Corps officers – including Arnold, Spaatz and Eaker – had spent time as observers on RAF stations in the two opening years of the war and had seen at first hand just what difficulties the RAF was encountering in action, but the problems facing the RAF had clearly made no impression on the USAAF commanders – and these problems were essentially the same problems the *Luftwaffe* had encountered when it attempted the aerial destruction of Britain in 1940–1.

None of this experience had been taken on board by the American commanders. They had come into the war armed with a doctrine and the belief that they knew better, so the hard-learned lesson that the bomber could not operate on its own in daylight over German-occupied territory had to be learned all over again – at a considerable cost in young American lives. This fact was not accepted at the time, and a number of US veterans still cannot accept it, claiming that daylight precision bombing and the self-defending bomber were a success from the moment they were first employed in the ETO in the summer of 1942. The fact is that both were virtually useless until the spring of 1944, when radar aids and the Mustang P-51 fighter came to the rescue of the bomb groups.

The underlying facts that limited the success of the USAAF bombing campaign until 1944 were that continental Europe was not the continental USA and that peacetime training has very little bearing on actual operations in time of war. These will be brought out time and again in the accounts that follow, but the broad picture can be outlined now.

The first problem was navigation. The British Isles and the continent of Europe lie on the eastern side of the Atlantic, in the path of the Atlantic weather systems. Cloudy skies, unreliable weather, ice and variable wind speeds and direction all inhibited navigators who were used to flying over the peaceful plains of the USA in good, or at least reliable, weather. Flying in Europe was *different*, and a large number of USAAF navigators simply could not cope with it. In an attempt to improve performance, each bomb group eventually appointed a 'lead navigator', an especially skilled exponent of the art, and the rest of the group followed the 'lead aircraft' to the target – though, in case they had to abort the mission and make their own way back to base, the other navigators were expected to maintain a plot.

Then there was the enemy. The *Luftwaffe* pilots were very experienced and outstandingly brave, and it did not take them too long to work out that, for all their firepower the B-17 Flying Fortress and the B-24 Liberator had a blind spot. Both aircraft had a rear turret, a top (mid-upper) turret, two waist guns and a ball turret under the fuselage. These guns had been positioned to cover attacks from the 'traditional' angle, above and to the rear, from where an attacking fighter pilot could put in a sustained burst of accurate fire without having to worry too much about the need to 'aim off', firing ahead of the aircraft under attack so that the bullets would arrive at the right spot as the bomber flew into the cone of fire. The USAAF had assumed that the enemy would always attack from this angle, and the majority of the machine-guns therefore covered the rear of the bomber, with the two waist guns covering the flanks and the ball turret covering the space below. Only two guns were in the nose, for use against frontal attacks, and the *Luftwaffe* pilots soon began to concentrate on this area.

Milton Hamill arrived in Britain in November 1942, to fly with the 303rd Bomb Group:

> I was a radio gunner. When I was not on the set I was manning a .50-calibre machine-gun. We did not have many aircraft at that time. There were about three bomb groups in the ETO, and on a maximum effort we could put up anything from 90 to 120 planes. When we went out we met the Me 109s and the FW 190s, and they had fantastic pilots who came right in to attack. On our 25-mission tour we lost most of our crews, and the bombs we dropped on places like the sub pens at Saint-Nazaire just bounced off the roofs, which were twelve foot of reinforced concrete.
>
> We had the flak and the fighters to contend with, and to begin with the B-17F had no nose guns, no forward defence; but eventually we fixed up a 20 mm gun in the nose. We tested that gun over the Wash, and when it let go the recoil nearly stopped the aircraft dead in the air. But at that time we never got enough aircraft or enough replacement crews, so our effort got less and less.
>
> It was just a bunch of crazy guys. We were all scared, and one or two were not willing to go on, but for most of us we were willing to go and glad to get back. I guess we looked on it as an adventure. We did not have the things that came in later. We had no body armour, no helmets, the heated suits did not work – the waist gunners used to come back with their faces and oxygen masks thick with ice and they nearly froze . . . but we kept on flying.

George Pederson, of the 306th Bomb Group, describes his first encounter with the *Luftwaffe*:

> My first experience with enemy fighter attacks came on 20 December 1942, soon after we entered the enemy air space over France. I could see the fighters climbing up to our altitude and had an almost overwhelming feeling of fear. They got into position ahead of our formation, but because their attacks were head-on I only had a fleeting glimpse of them as they flew through. On most of our missions the fighters were waiting for us as we emerged from the flak. Their favourite targets were planes that had been damaged by flak and were straggling behind the rest of the formation.

This flak was aided by visual sightings as well as by radar. It is fair to say that the US crews *hated* flak, not least because they could see it. Flying into a 'box barrage' put up by the German gunners was a terrifying experience, and there was further terror in the fact that there was nothing the crews could do about flak but put up with it: the 'integrity' of the bomb group was essential to its survival against fighter attack, so the flak had to be endured, without weaving or any kind of evasive action. The flak also forced the bombers to fly and bomb from a far greater height than they were used to. Training missions on bombing ranges in the USA were flown at around 16,000 ft, and if the bombardier could not hit the target from that altitude the aircraft could fly lower. In combat over Germany, flying lower brought the bombers within the effective range of light flak – and even at height they were vulnerable to the fearsome 88 mms.

The effects of flak were recorded by Top Sergeant Walter Crane Fifer:

> Captain Booth was flying as command pilot when he was hit by a piece of flak. I was standing right behind him and he leapt about a foot off the seat as if he had had an electric shock. The flak took off the tips of his finger, the top of his right knee and then lodged in the back of his left leg. We were at 25,000 ft, where the air temperature was minus 40, so the wounds did not bleed much. I called Lieutenant Moore up from the waist, and we did what we could for the Captain while Moore took the co-pilot seat. The Captain took it like a man and would not let me give him any morphine, so we went on in and bombed; I got a glance at the factory and it was in ruins. I was pretty busy but it seemed like we would never get home, and when we landed we had some bombs hung up. We had about ten holes in the aircraft, the life-raft was ruined, and two of our ships were missing. The Eighth lost about 35 aircraft that day.[5]

In spite of the doctrinal problems and the subsequent losses, the USAAF continued to put up aircraft over Europe, and the next two accounts relate how the Eighth Air Force went to war. First a B-24 pilot, Charles C. Russell:

> The operation order for a mission came by telex from Wing HQ and gave all the information needed for the initial preparations: the target, bomb load, number of planes, take-off time, assembly beacon and altitude, plus the position of the group in the bomber stream. Group Operations then started the ball rolling by notifying the engineering, armament and navigation sections and getting the mess hall and motor pool ready to feed the men and take them to the aircraft. Hundreds of ground crew worked all night to load bombs and ammo into the aircraft, gassing up the planes, checking out the engines and the other systems.
>
> Operations then made up the briefing material for the crews, with a special briefing for the 'lead' crew, navigators and bombardiers and a gunner briefing. The main briefing came in the morning after a very early call, say 0330 hrs. Sometimes I never even got my shoes off, coming back from the pub to be told about a mission that I did not know about when I went out – it all made for a long day. The general briefing covered the target, route, expected fighter opposition, flak areas and formation. Then we got dressed in our flight clothes and went out to the aircraft.
>
> At the aircraft there was usually a few minutes for the crew to talk, but I do not recall that we ever discussed the mission. At each hardstand – concreted areas where the aircraft stood – there was a box where the flak suits

were kept. These were pretty heavy and designed to cover the torso, and I remember that some crew-members would swipe suits from nearby hard-stands and use them to provide more protection around their positions. I made them put them back, as our load was heavy enough.

Take-offs were usually 30 seconds apart and the take-off order had been given at the briefing – so we did not need to use our radios – and we taxied out in order, around the perimeter track. The lead ship then lined up on the runway and waited for the green light from the tower. Each ship had a flare pistol ready to fire a red flare for an aborted take-off if that was necessary, but you had to have a good reason, as all the Brass would descend on you to find out what the trouble was.

So we took off and climbed away, usually through cloud, and then we had to get in formation. The assembly of hundreds of bombers into a bomber stream was scary as hell to a new pilot. The lead ship used to circle a ground radio beacon and he would be firing flares of various colours to gather his group. Most groups eventually had a stripped-down B-24 painted all kinds of colours that flew with the lead ship to help the group come together; this 'assembly ship', as it was called, left the formation after it was formed and flew back to base. This was a dangerous time, and I did once see a B-17 and a B-24 collide during assembly, probably because they were engrossed in finding their position in their formation and did not see each other; they both lost a wing, and how many of the crews got out I do not know.

The main tactical unit in the USAAF was the group, not the squadron, as Ted Homdrom, a B-17 navigator, explains:

Our 381st Bomb Group had four squadrons. The 381st Group navigator chose the four squadron navigators, as well as handling a lot of administration and paperwork. When someone who had been a squadron navigator finished his tour of combat he could be promoted to group navigator if there was a vacancy. We squadron navigators also had a hand in the training of replacement crew navigators and in aids that came in to cope with the European weather, like the *Gee*-box. Squadron navigators usually flew when their squadron led the 'combat wing' of 54 bombers. So that is how the navigation worked.

On a mission, though the number varied later, in 1942 a squadron put up six aircraft and a group put up three of its four squadrons, resting one. Therefore, at three groups to a wing, a 'combat wing' had 54 aircraft, while a 'division' could consist of two or more wings. That is a lot of aircraft and a lot of guns – over 500 big .50s per wing alone. As you can see, a 'wing' could provide a lot of firepower against enemy fighters.

However, within weeks – days – the *Luftwaffe* fighter pilots had worked out that the safest and most effective way to attack a US bomber formation was from the front, where the machine-gun defence relied on just two fixed machine-guns firing through the nose – guns fired by two of the officers when not otherwise engaged, rather than by trained gunners. These head-on attacks, when the aircraft were closing on each other at combined speeds approaching 600 knots, certainly took a steady nerve, but *Luftwaffe* pilots were not short of nerve. They came barrelling in against the US bombers from above and ahead, swooping down from the 'twelve o'clock high' position to blast fire into the front cockpits, kill the pilots – US bombers had two pilots – break up the bomber formations, and provide a number of crippled bombers for their future attention.

The USAAF aircrew soon developed a healthy respect for the *Luftwaffe* pilots. US bombardier Charles Hudson tells of a wartime poster put up in his crewroom which showed a smiling bomber pilot over the question 'Who's afraid of the new Focke-Wulf?' Minutes after this poster went up on the bulletin board, a piece of paper was pinned to it with a note saying 'Sign here'. Every flyer in the group signed that paper – including the group commander.

So, swiftly, every member of the US bomber crew – pilots, navigator, bombardier and gunners – came to realize that combat in the ETO was different. It says a great deal about the courage and tenacity of the US crews that, facing these problems and saddled with an unworkable doctrine, they continued to press home their attacks.

Some idea of what they endured from flak comes from this account by Bill Blaylock, a ball-turret gunner with the 446th Bomb Group, flying B-24s from Flixton air base in Britain, of a mission to Ludwigshafen in August 1944:

> Having checked the ball turret, cleaned the Plexiglass and checked the ammunition state and turret operation, I was ready for take-off. We lifted off at 0800 hrs, reached the required altitude, and headed for our destination. We met some flak over Holland but it wasn't accurate, and flying at 23,500 ft with a P-51 fighter escort we passed over Ludwigshafen and had dropped our bombs as did the other ships in our formation when flak burst fearfully close. As the bombardier yelled 'Bombs away!' a hailstorm of shrapnel hit with fierce intensity and shells rocked our plane, riddling the aircraft from front to rear, cutting some of the oxygen hoses. Algee, the nose gunner, lost his oxygen mask and had to breath from the end of the hose – you cannot stay conscious without oxygen at that altitude – but our pilot, Dean Peppmeier, was not fazed and told the engineer gunner to get Algee a spare mask.
>
> I stayed in my turret, parachute outside in the ready area. Flak had come through my turret, striking the armour plate of my seat, radiating outward to hit my legs, but apart from bruises I had no other injuries. Then it became apparent that we were in more trouble, losing fuel, with oil leaking from our No. 1 engine and a steady loss of oxygen pressure. We ploughed on but then 43 minutes from England there was a terrible explosion and the pilot's bell rang: *Bale out!*
>
> When the explosion occurred, Fred O'Dell was struck by the force of the left waist window being blasted into the plane. As I climbed out of my turret I could see him on the floor by the window, pain and shock mirrored in his

face. My feeling was instant terror, driving me to escape. Novak, the other waist gunner, already had his chute on and I had mine on a split-second later. He pulled up the escape hatch, but before he could lock it open the plane lurched, throwing us to the floor – Novak across the hatch opening, the door on top of him, me on top of the door. All this time smoke was pouring in the window, filling the body of the ship. It was a long moment. Then the plane righted itself and we were able to lock the door open. Novak dropped through the hatch, and I plunged after him; Anderson and Fred O'Dell I saw no more.

Up on the flight deck, Peevley, top-turret gunner, went for the front hatch. Reaching the bomb bays, Jack Strain, the radio gunner, burned his hands and the hair on his head, plunged across the bomb-bay walkway –the bomb doors were shut – and made his way to the rear; then he found he had somehow pulled the ripcord on his chute and it was spilling out. Then the plane lurched again, throwing him against the open hatch, and his parachute went out and pulled him after it; it caught the tailplane but pulled loose, and Jack got down OK.

My first feeling, having left the plane, was one of immense relief. Having been told to delay pulling the ripcord I did so, but my body started to spin, faster and faster, and when I could not see the ground I pulled the cord and felt the shock as the chute opened. I looked up and saw the plane coming down at a steep angle. Further to the right and above me was another parachute, and below, watching us come down, were people, all watching us. The plane crashed into a field, and the wings, burning fiercely, were right below me. This was my first jump and the descent was fast, the ground coming up, and I landed with a thump, getting out of my harness to go over to the plane and see if I could help anyone remaining in it.

By later report of Lieutenant Peppmeier, a near direct hit of anti-aircraft fire took out the lower front of the plane and killed our nose gunner and the bombardier. It also critically damaged the plane and set it on fire. Four of the crew stayed with the plane and were in it when it crashed. Lieutenant Peppmeier, after giving the 'Bale out' signal, baled out and survived. Three of the crew were captured by the Germans, and Sergeant Novak was reported to have been shot. I was helped by the Dutch and later by the French resistance, and they got me back to the Allied lines, where we were welcomed by the Canadians. As of this writing, years later, all of my crew are lost to me now – some killed in battle, some died at home. I think of them often and of the comradeship we shared, and feel proud that I belonged with those brave men. I am left with a great sense of loss.

In spite of the flak and the fighters, a large number of US aircraft did survive and reach the target. Then bomb-aiming difficulties appeared. The Norden bombsight was a magnificent piece of kit, but it had two snags. The first was that to *hit* a target, the bombardier had to be able to *see* the target – again, no real problem over a peaceful bombing range in Texas, or Florida, but a vastly different proposition when rocking in the prop wash of other aircraft in close formation, or under flak and fighter attack, bombing through the haze, smoke and cloud shrouding a typical European target. Visibility was the advantage of daylight bombing over night bombing – at least in theory – but, over Europe in general and Germany in particular, visibility was often restricted.

The second snag was that the Norden bombsight was complicated. It was virtually an airborne computer into which the bombardier had to feed a great deal of information to get the right result, and the usual problem of all computers – that what goes in affects what comes out – applied equally to the Norden bombsight. Using it took skill, as Lieutenant-Colonel Charles 'Combat' Hudson, who flew as lead bombardier with the Eighth Air Force, describes:

> Bombardiers are usually the sharpest, smartest, best-trained member of any bomber crew – and often the best-looking too. They had to fly the aircraft under the most harrowing conditions, straight and level over the target, for the pilot who flies the aircraft to and from the target never drops the bombs. The Norden bombsight was the most sophisticated bombsight in the world. This bombsight, through manipulations by the bombardier, takes into consideration several factors, including air density, wind force and direction, air and ground speed of the aircraft, drift, bomb configuration and other readings. Then it gradually centres two cross-hairs on the target, which might be miles ahead, telling the bombardier, who by now has taken charge and is actually *flying* the aircraft, how to get into the exact position and altitude and precisely when to drop the bombs. The Norden bombsight was a marvellous device.
>
> In combat, usually only the planes of the commander and the deputy commander of each squadron had a Norden bombsight. In the early days these sights were removed and kept under guard when the aircraft landed. We were told to destroy the sights at all costs if we were shot down, maybe by shooting it – though that would only lead to bullets bouncing around the cockpit – they were *tough* little instruments. Later still, if the lead ship was shot down or had to turn back, the second in command took over and sighted on the target and when he dropped his bombs all the other aircraft in the group could see it and they dropped their bombs. These were not always real bombardiers – some were just 'toggeliers', who dropped the bombs by pulling on a toggle rope.

The use of the Norden bombsight to actually fly the aircraft – called Automatic Flight Control Equipment, or AFCE – was introduced in March 1943. Though very unpopular with the pilots, who thereby lost control of their aircraft on the run-up to the target, the AFCE meant that adjustments to the bombsight were automatically taken into account by the aircraft controls and the aircraft tracked inexorably to the target. The problem with this – and there was always some snag in every development – was that it resulted in the individual bombers veering about the sky as they approached the target, with a high risk of collision. Spreading out was not the answer, for the integrity of the bomb group and the production of a great quantity of defensive fire was the main security against fighters.

The AFCE device was eventually used only in the lead aircraft. All the rest 'formatted', or stayed in formation, on the lead 'ship', and when the lead bombardier dropped his bombs the toggeliers in the other aircraft pulled their releases. This caused the bombs to drop over a wider area, creating the pattern of the formation on the ground below, and various techniques and devices were brought into service to overcome this – including the aptly-named 'intervalometer', which could delay the bomb release until the follow-up aircraft were in the bombing position or in line with the bombing position of the lead aircraft. Even so, 'dropping a bomb in a pickle barrel' was found to be unattainable in combat, and would remain so until the fighters and the flak had been crushed in the final months of the war.

That fact established, it has to be added that, whatever their bombs hit, the US bombers were always – or at least in the majority of cases – tasked to attack specific military or industrial targets. At least as far as their operational orders were concerned, *daylight precision bombing* remained the doctrine of the USAAF bomber crews. This fact underpins much of the USAAF's certainty about its moral position in the controversy over the bombing of Germany: it was the RAF who bombed civilian targets, not the USAAF. The USAAF might have – must have – hit civilian targets, but that was not the intention.

Richard Braun of Ludwigshafen finds this claim convincing:

> We, the plain German people during the war, did not know anything of the official Allied bombing philosophies, but we soon realized the difference between the RAF night attacks and the American daylight raids. When the English attacked us, it seemed that they mainly concentrated their efforts on the built-up, residential areas of our town. When we were the target of the Americans, we had the impression that their interest was mainly directed to such places as factories, marshalling yards, port areas, etc, while such damage and destruction caused to the houses of civilians on such occasions appeared to be unavoidable side effects, which were not part of the attackers' plan.

In this, Richard Braun is quite correct. In the vast majority of cases, dropping bombs on civilian areas was not part of the USAAF plan – but it did happen, and US bomber tactics ensured that it happened. Archivist Gebhard Aders-Albert of Cologne points this out:

> Area bombing by the USAAF . . . make yourself a drawing of a combat 'box', scores of aircraft flying in formation. Work out the length and breadth of that formation, make some calculations of the speed and sequence of dropping the 250 lb and 500 lb bombs and remember that all the aircraft dropped their

bombs at the same time and you will have some idea of the area which was covered by bombs – and consider that a lot of combat wings did it at the same time. 'Blind bombing' was a pure euphemism for 'area bombing' and had a more devastating effect success than the RAF area bombing. And for what reason did the Eighth USAAF drop about 30 per cent incendiaries on the marshalling yards, bridges and railways of Cologne in autumn 1944? Not necessary to destroy a station or interrupt a railway line, but very 'useful' to devastate a built-up area.

With these problems and disputes in the open and USAAF doctrine and philosophy understood, it is time to return to the United Kingdom in early 1942, as the first elements of the US Eighth Air Force started to arrive. The United States' intention was to send a full air force to Britain, the Eighth Army Air Force – 'the Mighty Eighth' – and it is with the operations of the Eight Air Force, and especially with its bomber element, VIII Bomber Command, that this book is chiefly concerned. However, some actions of the Fifteenth Air Force, based in Italy, and the Ninth Tactical Airforce, which was formed in North Africa and later based in the UK, will also be included.

It should be remembered that the Eighth Air Force was a full air force and contained a fighter command and various transport and maintenance commands to back up and support bomber operations. Bomber Command, on the other hand, was simply one element in the RAF, and therefore much smaller than the Eighth.

The overall commander of the USAAF was Lieutenant-General Henry 'Hap' Arnold, the son of a Pennsylvania doctor. Arnold's father disciplined his children so rigorously that when the young Arnold entered West Point as an army cadet he is said to have found the harsh atmosphere almost benign. Arnold wanted to become a cavalry officer, but in 1911 he transferred to the Signal Corps's fledgling Aeronautical Division. In 1912 he established a world altitude record, taking his biplane to 6,540 ft – a great feat at the time – and during the First World War he ran the Army Aviation Schools, rising steadily in rank throughout the 1920s and 1930s to become head of the Army Air Corps and a general by 1938.

Arnold was not an easy man to serve under. He admitted that he was 'personally never satisfied' and drove his subordinates relentlessly, being always impatient, eager for results and unwilling to accept any reasons for failure or delay, even when the reasons were perfectly valid. It is said that his criticism of one subordinate was so severe that, in the middle of hearing it, the officer pitched over on to Arnold's desk, dead of a heart attack. Difficult though he may have been, Arnold was widely respected both in the Army and in political circles, and had many friends in the USAAF. His impact was softened by his appointment to command of a number of rising officers – 'Hap Arnold's Wonder Boys', as they were called – officers like Brigadier-General Ira C. Eaker, Colonel Frederick L. Anderson Jr and

Major-General Carl 'Tooey' Spaatz, all of whom would rise to high command in the air war over Europe.

Carl Spaatz was of German descent. His grandfather came from Eberfeld in Prussia and in 1865 emigrated to Philadelphia, where he started a German-language newspaper. Spaatz graduated from West Point in 1914, was taught to fly at the Signal Corps school in 1915, and in 1916 was flying over Mexico seeking the bandit Pancho Villa during Pershing's campaign across the border. In 1917, when the United States entered the Great War, Spaatz went to France, serving first in Billy Mitchell's head-quarters and then with the Second Pursuit Group. In combat over the Western Front in 1918 Spaatz shot down three German fighters.

During the inter-war years Spaatz commanded fighter squadrons in the USA and gave strong support to Billy Mitchell in his troubles with the US High Command. Between 1939 and 1941 he served in the War Plans Division and alongside Hap Arnold in Washington. Then, in May 1940, Arnold sent him to Europe. He arrived just in time for the Dunkirk evacu-ation and spent the next four months in Britain, visiting RAF stations, flying British aircraft, watching the Battle of Britain and the start of the Blitz. As a result of all this, Spaatz reported to Arnold and the US Chiefs of Staff that in his opinion Britain would not be defeated – a report which contradicted those being sent to Washington by the US ambassador Joseph Kennedy, the father of the future President John F. Kennedy, who was pre-dicting Britain's defeat.

Spaatz returned to Washington in October 1940. In the summer of 1941 he became Chief of the Air Staff when the Army Air Corps became the Army Air Force, and the A-WPD/1 Committee worked under his direc-tion. He was still Chief of the Air Staff, reporting to Hap Arnold, who was now Deputy Chief of the Army for Air, when the Japanese attacked Pearl Harbor and the USA entered the war.

In February 1942, Spaatz, now a major-general, took command of the Army Air Force Combat Command – a force which would shortly become the Eighth Air Force – with the task of preparing it for rapid deployment in the ETO. Spaatz's first task was to select his subordinates, and his main appointment was the choice of Brigadier-General Ira C. Eaker to command VIII Bomber Command, the bomber element in the Eighth Air Force.

Brigadier-General Eaker, a Texan, joined the US Army before the Great War, in which he served as an infantry officer before switching to the Air Service. In the inter-war years he filled a number of Staff and Command appointments, rose steadily in rank, and became an expert in public rela-tions – maintaining a high profile for the Air Corps was vital to its survi-val, especially during the constant budget cuts of the late 1920s and 1930s. Eaker also spent a lot of his spare time in furthering his education. While serving in Washington he took courses at Georgetown University, a posting to Long Island enabled him to attend Columbia University in New

York, and in 1934 he received a degree from the University of Southern California. As a result of all this Eaker became head of the Air Corps Information Division and wrote three books on military aviation, all co-authored with Hap Arnold. Well connected and likeable, Eaker was a good choice for this post as US bomber commander in the ETO – and it did not go unnoticed that he was also a good friend of Arthur Harris, who had just been appointed head of RAF Bomber Command.

Eaker and Harris were two of a kind. Neither was typical of the popular image one nation held of the other: Eaker was a sophisticated, well-educated and experienced commander; Harris a blunt, no-nonsense, get-on-with-the-job leader; it is no wonder that they hit it off. Eaker lived in Harris's house for the first three months of his stay in Britain in 1942, and regularly brought gifts and toys from the USA for Harris's young daughter. He also attended the 0900 hrs briefings at Bomber Command HQ, when Harris and his staff chose their 'Target for Tonight'. At the command level, Bomber Command and VIII Bomber Command were practically one force, and the USAAF records contain full appreciation of the help the RAF gave to the USAAF when it first arrived in Britain.

The Eighth Air Force command structure had Carl Spaatz at the head, with Brigadier-General Ira Eaker as head of VIII Bomber Command and Colonel Fred Anderson as head of the 4th Bombardment Wing, the first of the two original elements in VIII Bomber Command. The Eighth Air Force command structure sounds like that of the RAF, but it was actually somewhat different and needs to be explained here.

The basic structure of the Eighth Air Force is shown below.

Eighth Air Force
(equivalent to the RAF)
|
VIII Bomber Command and VIII Fighter Command
(equivalent to Bomber Command and Fighter Command)
|
Bombardment Wings – later called Air Divisions – three per air force
(no real equivalent, but similar to RAF groups)
|
Bombardment Groups – five per wing or division
(similar to RAF bomber squadrons)
|
Bombardment Squadrons – four per bomb group
(similar to RAF bomber flights)

The 'similarities' listed largely relate to the number of aircraft put up by each element, at least to begin with. A USAAF squadron had nine aircraft – plus a few spares and those of the squadron commander – but at the start of the war put up only six of these, to allow time for maintenance and to rest the crews. A US group therefore put up eighteen aircraft, six each from three of its four squadrons, and this can be compared to an RAF squadron, which put up something between sixteen and twenty aircraft, depending on crews and availability. As the war progressed US elements at every level had more aircraft and more crews to fly them, as did the RAF.

The two main elements in this USAAF structure were the bomb groups and the bombardment wings – sometimes called combat wings or, as they soon became, air divisions. Mort Fega of the 305th Bomb Group explains how this organization worked:

> Briefly, at the top were the Air Force Headquarters for the Eighth and Ninth Air Forces – the Ninth being the tactical force. An air force was made up of divisions, which were made up of wings, which were made up of groups, which were composed of squadrons. For example, I was stationed at Chelveston in Northamptonshire with the 305th Bomb Group (Heavy). The 305th BG was composed of the 364, 365, 366 and 422 Squadrons. A group's combat formation consisted of three squadrons. As you know, each squadron would 'put up' six planes, though sometimes the lead squadron would put up seven. The extra plane was called 'Tail-End Charlie', so named because it was lonely for that plane, with no others flying alongside.
>
> So, there was the 'lead' squadron, with six or seven planes. The 'high' squadron flew above and off the right wing of the leader, and the 'low' squadron below and off the left wing of the leader. All eighteen or nineteen planes flew at elevations that allowed the gunners firing the thirteen .50-calibre machine-guns in each aircraft to clear those flying with it in the group. This meant that a *Luftwaffe* pilot attacking a group of B-17s from the front (twelve o'clock), would be looking at eighteen or nineteen bombers, all at different altitudes and all firing big .50-calibre weapons, all of which could be brought to bear. A Jerry fighter pilot attacking a group of American bombers needed a big pair of balls.

B-17 and B-24 crews consisted of ten men. Four of them were trained gunners who operated the ball turret, the tail turret and the two waist guns and were all enlisted men – 'other ranks' – often Pfcs (private, first class) or corporals on volunteering for aircrew, though they became sergents or staff sergeants when they joined their operational squadrons in the UK. Two other members of the crew – the wireless operator and the engineer – were also enlisted men, the engineer doubling as the top-turret gunner. The pilot, co-pilot, navigator and bombardier were officers, and usually college graduates. The bombardier and navigator could also man guns in times of stress or when not carrying out their other duties. All crew members – officers or enlisted men – were volunteers. USAAF crews initially flew a single 25-mission tour, after which they rotated back to the USA, but this tour was later extended to 35 missions and, as in the RAF, many crews flew far more than this and racked up a considerable number of missions before they were rotated back to the USA – or shot down.

These men flew heavy four-engined bombers, either the B-17 or the B-24, the Liberator. The B-17 – the Flying Fortress to the British, the Boeing to the *Luftwaffe* pilots – went through various Marks but the B-17G, the last Mark of the B-17 to enter war service and the most notable US bomber of the war, had a theoretical ceiling of 35,000 ft, a range of 4,400 miles and a maximum speed of 300 m.p.h. – though a B-17G with a normal bomb and fuel load travelled at about 160 m.p.h. on most bombing missions. Many B-17s were equipped with extra, internal, wing tanks, known as 'Tokyo Tanks'. The B-17G was fitted with a 'chin' turret under the nose, armed with two .30-calibre forward-firing machine-guns – a response to the *Luftwaffe* frontal assaults – as well as the standard armament described above.

The B-17 carried a bomb load of between 2,600 and 8,000 lb, depending on the types of bomb and the amount of fuel carried. The 'fuel-to-bomb-load' ratio was always a trade-off; long flights meant more petrol, so the bomb load had to be reduced to keep the all-up weight of the aircraft within technical limits or the bomber would not get off the ground, and a normal B-17 bomb load would be around 6,000 lb. This was, at best, less than half the bomb load carried by the RAF Lancaster, and even the twin-engined RAF Mosquito could carry a 4,000 lb 'Cookie' all the way to Berlin. As a result, a gentle, 60-year long argument has existed between RAF and USAAF bomber crews as to which aircraft did the most effective work during the war. The RAF claim they dropped the greater load of bombs; the USAAF point out that their bombs hit more important targets – both sides admit that, whatever the bomb load, the other side did a lot of good work in the air war over Europe.

The Consolidated B-24 was visually a less attractive aircraft and had a tendency to catch fire when attacked. The most common Mark, the B-24D, could fly at a theoretical 260 m.p.h., carried a greater bomb load than the B-17, and was favoured for long-range missions and maritime operations. The main disadvantage of the B-24 was the narrow wings, which made it unstable at higher altitudes and hard to hold in formation. It had a lower operational ceiling than the B-17 and was therefore more vulnerable to flak and fighter attack than its high-flying cousin. Richard Atkins of the Scouting Force comments that 'When used in the 3rd Air Division, Curtis LeMay had the B-24s and B-17s at the same altitude, but it just didn't work. The B-24s were eventually transferred to the all-B-24 2nd Air Division'.

Tom Parry of the 93rd Bomb Group puts in a word for the B-24:

> Most B-24 flyers are still upset because the B-17 is always featured in any account of the war while the B-24 is often ignored. More B-24s were built than any other aircraft, and it was first flown in 1939 so it was newer, faster and carried a bigger bomb load than the B-17. With a full bomb load it took off at 130 m.p.h. – if you were lucky – and cruised at 180–185 m.p.h. After it went

into mass production, the Ford Motor Company turned out thousands. In the ETO it normally carried a crew of nine – four officers and five airmen – and was armed with eight machine-guns, though the lower ball turret was removed from some aircraft because we reckoned that the extra weight did not offer enough firepower in compensation.

I was offered a choice of aircraft when I finished training and I chose the B-24, as from a pilot's viewpoint the tricyle undercarriage made it easier to land, though the B-17 was safer in combat since the B-24 had a 'wet' wing, full of fuel, which tended to explode when hit. I often watched B-17s spinning all the way to the ground, but the B-24s usually exploded after about three turns. If the aircraft did not explode the trapped crew had three or four minutes to think about things before impact.

Dick Atkins of the Striking Force also speaks up for the B-24:

The Consolidated B-24 Liberator was the 'other' heavy bomber of the fleet. When discussed in the same breath with the B-17, there is a tendency to downgrade the B-24 because of the 'it got me home in spite of being shot full of holes' image acquired by the B-17 early in the conflict. The B-17 was a very sturdy, easy-to-fly airplane that would take lots of damage and get you home, and if you had to ditch it was a nice boat to be in. It was an effective weapon, and attained legendary status early in the war.

The B-24 was faster and carried a larger bomb load, but was not quite as sturdy as the B-17 and was not as easy to fly. It could still take lots of combat damage, but was not a good airplane for ditching, due to its high-wing configuration. It was faster than the B-17 because of its long narrow wing, and was as good a bombing platform as the B-17 when operated at its best design altitude of 20,000 to 23,000 ft.

Quantities of the B-24 were not available to the Eighth Air Force until late 1943 and early 1944. This was due to the demand for its long-range capabilities, high speed and heavy bomb load for American and British Atlantic anti-submarine warfare and the US Air Force Pacific campaign. Though initially misused by attempting to place it in the same formations with the B-17, which was designed to bomb from higher altitudes at slower speeds, the Liberator eventually gave a good account of itself when properly applied. In terms of bombs on the target, it was equal to all and better than most Eighth Air Force bombers, and, contrary to anecdotes and published stories, it had a loss rate considerably better than any of its contemporaries.

The USAAF had been committed to join the RAF in the air assault on Germany at the Washington Conference of January 1942, when it was clear that the bulk of the offensive carried out against Germany until the opening of the Second Front – the invasion – would fall on the two Bomber Commands of the RAF and the Eighth Air Force and that the commanders of these two forces must act as a team.

Like Eaker, Spaatz was a close friend of Harris, but neither Spaatz or Eaker had any intention of allowing the USAAF to become an extension of

Bomber Command – a fate which the USAAF commanders appear to have constantly feared. Even had they been willing to subordinate their forces to the more experienced British commanders in 1942, Hap Arnold would not have allowed it. In any case, there is no evidence that either Portal or Harris ever entertained such an intention, though both thought the USAAF would find daylight operations difficult and suggested that the USAAF join the RAF in night attacks on Germany. This suggestion was firmly declined, and it was clearly understood on both sides that the USAAF was, and would remain, an independent force, though a number of American historians have alleged otherwise, perhaps confusing well-meant advice with attempted coercion.

Even after the Eighth Air Force arrived in Britain in early 1942, a great deal of work still had to be done to get it ready for combat in the ETO, and this was carried out with the willing co-operation of the RAF. RAF airfields were handed over to the USAAF or new ones were swiftly constructed; British radar and communications systems were integrated with the USAAF operations centres, and weather and intelligence information was shared – the vital weather and photoreconnaissance flights before and after missions were undertaken by RAF high-altitude Spitfires on behalf of the USAAF for much of the war.

The popular history of the Eighth[6] is full of references to RAF co-operation and help, ranging from the supply of petrol bowsers – 'fuel trucks' to the USAAF – to places at RAF training schools and the provision of bombing ranges and fighter escorts. Whatever the Eighth wanted, the RAF was happy to provide. Although the two air forces never became close at the group and squadron level – the level of ignorance among the aircrew veterans about the other air forces' operational procedures constantly amazed this author – at the higher level co-operation was total, and relations were friendly. Pete Henry, a B-24 pilot, records his first impressions of life in the UK:

> We sailed in up the river Forth, past sunken ships, and when we boarded the train the English Red Cross were on hand with tea, coffee and doughnuts. They were all middle-aged women in very long dresses that reminded me of pictures I had seen of them in the last war. We left Glasgow at 12 a.m. and headed for Stone in the English Midlands. The engines looked funny compared to ours, but they seemed to make just as good time. As we passed along the boys leaned out of the train and tossed out the small packages of cigarettes that came in our K-rations, as well as candy, cheese and crackers and American money. Another impression was that we never seemed to really get into the country – we were always coming to a station or another small town.
>
> At about five o'clock we passed through Manchester, and there we saw the first signs of a city hit by air raids – much of the factory district had been hit, there were many new rail tracks, and barges were sunk in the canals; heaps of bricks could be seen everywhere. When we got to Stone it was very dark

– not a light could be seen anywhere – but while we were there another train pulled in full of girls, factory workers, and we talked to them for a few minutes. We learned that the girls here were all drafted into war work; every one was sent to a factory.

At the camp we had an orientation lecture and they showed us a film, *Welcome to England*, starring Burgess Meredith. Five days later Lee and I got a pass and went into Hanley, to the Golden Lion, a popular pub, where Lee and Al started downing some of that warm English beer. I was quite interested in the pub because it was my first visit. After Lee had downed a couple of beers he went looking for a girl, and soon found one. Apart from all the soldiers and the pick-ups, there were a number of townspeople. I could not see what pleasure they got, sitting round a sticky table, but that seemed to be the custom here. There was a lot of noise, with groups of people singing different songs, and the girls could not believe that I did not drink or smoke, so I was soon the object of much kidding, but it was all in fun and we all enjoyed ourselves.

Many friendships were forged between the men of the Eighth and their British hosts and these friendships have endured, as James H. Lorenz, an American B-24 pilot who flew from Attlebridge, near Norwich, can confirm:

We crowded their pubs and trains, and yet they held a dance every Friday in Norwich and invited us into their homes, sharing their rationed food with us. We enjoyed the company of the children, and often held parties for them at the base. At the time I thought many of them were orphans, but they were 'evacuees', disbursed to the country from their homes in the large cities. These relations led to the founding of our 2nd Air Division Memorial Room at the library in Norwich. We count many good friends from our former neighbours in the Weston–Longville area, and have a reunion every time we go over. I didn't join the war to be a 'hero', and I don't believe I am one, but I'm mighty proud that I did contribute in a small way to preserving our country and the Allied countries. We all hope it was not in vain.

The VIII Bomber Command HQ was based at the former Wycombe Abbey Girls School at High Wycombe in Buckinghamshire, a few miles from Bomber Command's underground HQ in the Chiltern Hills, and it became usual for the USAAF commander to attend Harris's 0900 hrs briefings, where the decision was taken on the coming night's target.

This co-operation did not extend to doctrine. Daylight precision bombing was still the paramount US bomber doctrine, and the USAAF was anxious to start flying missions and show the RAF, and the folks back home, just what the Air Force could do. The Eighth Air Force was formally established in the UK on 18 June 1942, but it was not yet the mighty force it would eventually become. When Major-General Spaatz set up his headquarters he had only some 200 assorted aircraft and about 2,000 men – but it was a start.

The Eighth Air Force first went into action in the ETO on Independence

Day, 4 July 1942, when six Boston bombers of the 15th Bombardment Squadron supported Bostons of No. 226 Squadron, 2 Group, RAF, on a daylight strike against German airfields in Holland. From this operation, two USAAF Bostons and one RAF bomber failed to return.

Six weeks later, on 17 August 1942, the Eighth mounted its first independent mission, when General Eaker led twelve B-17Es to attack the marshalling yards at Sotteville-les-Rouen, on the Seine west of Paris. Flying as co-pilot in the lead aircraft was Major Paul Tibbets, who, three years later almost to the day, was to drop the first atomic bomb on Hiroshima. This was a short-range mission, heavily escorted by RAF Spitfires. All the US aircraft returned safely, and air reconnaissance revealed a gratifying amount of damage to the Rouen marshalling yards. This seemed to bode well for daylight operations in other parts of the ETO, but there was, as ever in this war, a snag.

The US doctrine held that unescorted bomber missions required a large force of bombers, enough to create the required amount of interlocking fire against fighter attack, if they were to be successful. The Eighth Air Force commanders calculated that this meant a minimum of 300 bombers on any one mission. This slightly exceeded the number of USAAF bombers currently in the UK, and this force would have to be almost doubled before any 300-bomber missions could be launched. This was partly because of servicing and maintenance difficulties and the growing amount of combat damage; not every aircraft would be available for every mission, and plenty of reserve aircraft would be needed to put up 300 on any particular day. There was also the fact that USAAF doctrine dictated that only three out of four squadrons in a US bomb group were employed on any one mission. This rested the crews and enabled a bombing campaign to be kept up day after day, but it meant that the minimum number of US bombers that must be assembled in Britain before 300 could be sent to Germany would be at least 500 – with an even larger number of crews.

This number of bombers was simply not available, and would not become available for another year. As Harris constantly lost bombers and crews to the Middle East and Coastal Command, so Eaker also found his aircraft and crews taken from VIII Bomber Command – or diverted away before they even reached him. Some were sent to North Africa to support the upcoming invasion, Operation TORCH; others were to provide anti-submarine cover for the convoys now bringing troops across for TORCH and the US build-up in Britain. A large number were sent to the Pacific, where the long-range B-24s were much in demand. Eaker protested, but to no avail: the USAAF was the *Army* Air Force, and the Army wanted some of it supporting the troops fighting in North Africa. The strategic bombing of Germany would have to wait.

As a result, Eaker had to manage with what he had, which at the end of August 1942 amounted to just three bomb groups – the 97th, the 301st and the newly arrived 92nd Bomb Group – and four fighter groups. This meant confining his activities to targets in France or on the German coast, within range of fighter cover. This had the benefit of giving his crews operational experience, but before long some disquieting news began to percolate back to VIII HQ and Bomber Command. The first was that the Norden bomb-sight, while highly accurate in good conditions, was proving much less effective in the cloudy, fighter- and flak-infested skies over European targets. The second was that the claims coming back from the bomb groups appeared to indicate that the US air gunners were shooting the *Luftwaffe* out of the sky, but the *Luftwaffe* fighters kept coming back for more on sub-sequent days, and the *Luftwaffe* losses seemed very high given that only two fighter *Geschwader* – JG 2 and JG 26 – were covering the Channel coast with about 200 aircraft. On one mission to Lille in October 1942, for example, the USAAF put in claims for 48 fighters shot down and another 38 damaged – on a day when only 60 *Luftwaffe* fighter aircraft took to the air in the West at all; subsequent German records show that only two fight-ers were lost and none were damaged that day.

All claims regarding shot-down enemy aircraft were liable to error and exaggeration, regardless of which side or air force made them. For example, on 18 August 1940, during the Battle of Britain, RAF Fighter Command claimed to have shot down 155 German aircraft when the actual *Luftwaffe* losses that day amounted to 71. But the claims of the US gunners swiftly reached a different order of magnitude. If ten gunners fired on a *Luftwaffe* fighter and it was seen to go down, all ten would claim it, and in many cases each gunner would be credited with the kill. In itself this did no harm, and it might even have done some good: it certainly increased the confidence of the crews in the ability of the B-17 and B-24 to withstand attack and in the value of the close-group formation and the .50-calibre machine-gun as a defensive combination. Unfortunately, even if they pri-vately discounted many of these claims, it also gave the US commanders the belief that the US doctrine of unescorted long-range bombing missions to Germany was perfectly feasible – a belief for which the Eighth Air Force was shortly to pay a heavy price in aircraft and lives.

In spite of the diversion of bomb groups to North Africa to support the TORCH landings due in November, the build-up of the USAAF in the UK continued. The 93rd and 306th Bomb Groups arrived and were flying mis-sions by October, but not all of them were successful. Bad weather caused eleven missions to be cancelled in the first three weeks of October, and when the 97th, 301st, 306th and 93rd Bomb Groups sent 66 B-17Es and 24 Liberators to bomb the submarine pens at Saint-Nazaire on the 21st, only the 97th Bomb Group found the target and attacked; all the rest turned back in the face of the low, thick cloud which obscured the target. The 97th Bomb Group found a gap and bombed, but was then set upon by a force of Focke-Wulfs which rapidly shot down three aircraft and damaged another six – the heaviest USAAF losses to date, and an ominous forecast of things to come. Then Eaker's force was further depleted when the 97th and 301st BG were taken away and sent to North Africa.

However, other bomb groups continued to arrive. By December 1942 there were six bomb groups in the UK, either in training or operational: the 91st, 303rd, 305th and 306th B-17 groups and the 93rd and 44th Liberator groups. Among the aircrew arriving was Brigadier-General James H. McPartlin, then a lieutenant, a pilot in the 401st Squadron of the 91st Bomb Group:

> I had trained as a fighter pilot, but the urgent need for bomber pilots saw me transferred to fly B-17s. I started as a co-pilot, but checked out as a first pilot after about 100 hours. Our training in the USA for the task of daylight bombing in the ETO was totally inadequate, especially in formation flying and bombing tactics, but I was excited at going to the UK and I still am; I love that country. The people are fighters and made of the right stuff, but the climate was not my cup of tea and hell to fly in.
>
> My first mission was on 11 September 1942, to the submarine pens at Saint-Nazaire in France. I was 'ranked out' of my cockpit by Colonel Stan Wray, who was leading the 91st Bomb Group, so I was flying as a waist gunner, firing a .50-calibre. We went in at 10,000 ft and the flak was just awful at that altitude – it sounded like rain on a tin roof. Shortly after the target we were attacked by Me 109s and Focke-Wulfs; we lost three B-17s from my squadron and I can't recall the total for the group. We also did very little damage to the sub pens, as they had reinforced-concrete roofs.
>
> German fighter tactics at the time were to attack from the tail. They would position in the sun and dive down and fire at close range before doing a half-roll away. They had armour plate on the underside for protection, but they soon realized that this tactic led to losses and in the spring of 1943 we began to see the 'head-on' attacks, which aimed to knock out the formation leaders and scatter the formations so they could pick off individual bombers.
>
> The weather story I can sum up a word – lousy. We lost a lot of aircraft and crews to the European weather. As for the flak, it was always a threat in the target area and frightening because you never knew what burst would hit you. The German 88 mm was a remarkable gun, and I always give credit to the German gunners for their accuracy – especially over cities like Hamburg, Bremen, Brest, Saint-Nazaire or Lorient.

So, slowly, the Eighth built up its strength. But winter – a season which came as a shock to many of the US aircrew – was now gripping Europe, adding more hazards to operational flying. In North Africa the TORCH operation was going well, and in January 1943 the Combined Chiefs of Staff of the USA and Great Britain, together with Winston Churchill and President Roosevelt, met at Casablanca in Morocco to discuss the next phase of the war – and in particular the opening of what eventually came to be called the Combined Bomber Offensive.

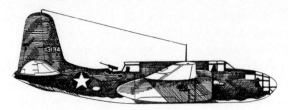

Boston Medium Bomber

8

Towards a Combined Offensive
August 1942–January 1943

Germany is a fortress, but a fortress without a roof.

Franklin D. Roosevelt, President of the United States, 1944

The Calvary of the German people under the Allied bombers began in the spring of 1943, a year which marked the third phase of the bomber war. In the first phase, from 1939 to the end of 1941, the RAF learned its business in the hard circumstances of total war. The second phase, which took up most of 1942, was a development period, with the arrival of the Americans, new aircraft coming into squadron service in adequate numbers, the gradual introduction of electronic and radar aids, new tactics like the bomber stream, and the creation of the Pathfinder Force. There was still a great deal to be done, but finally, by the end of 1942, the Allied air forces were ready to take the war to Germany. From now on the Germans would come to realize what strategic air power really meant.

The spring of 1943 saw the start of the great raids: increasingly powerful daylight missions up to and beyond the frontiers of Germany by the USAAF, and the beginning of Arthur Harris's 'Main Offensive', a series of 'battles' against the German cities, with continuous attacks against major centres like Hamburg, Berlin and the Ruhr. This 'Combined Bomber Offensive', first agreed at the Casablanca Conference in January 1943, would continue with growing strength and accuracy for another two and a half years and leave Germany in ruins from the Rhine to the Oder, but to describe the opening moves it is necessary to go back to the summer of 1942, when both air forces were in the field in varying strength, and about to turn their united force against the Third Reich.

On arrival in Britain, the first task of the USAAF was to get organized, and this took time. Eaker arrived in February 1942, but it was not until 18 June that Spaatz assumed command of the Eighth Air Force and was able to order the first missions. 'Organization is a dry topic', wrote Arnold and Eaker in a book published in 1941. 'It is likely for that reason that it will receive less attention than it merits. Actually, organization is the most important of all the military functions.'[1] This point was well made, and very welcome to their British allies. Following American pressure for SLEDGEHAMMER, a cross-Channel invasion in 1942, the British had gained the impression that the Americans intended to arrive in Britain, invade France inside a few weeks, and win the war by the end of the year. A little time at the sharp end soon curbed US enthusiasm, and by the middle of 1942 the USAAF knew it was in for a long haul.

Following its first independent mission to the marshalling yards at Sotteville-les-Rouen in August, the Eighth mounted ten more missions in the following weeks, all short-range daylight missions to France. Bombing accuracy seemed acceptable, and losses were slight: just two aircraft were lost in the first ten missions. So what evidence there was seemed to confirm that daylight precision bombing was possible in the ETO – or at least on the western fringes.

To go further afield and attack Germany more aircraft were needed, but any spare bomb groups were being sent to support TORCH and the build-up of the Eighth Air Force in the UK continued to be painfully slow. The total number of RAF and USAAF aircraft sent to support TORCH – and therefore lost to the strategic air forces in this period – exceeded 800 planes of various types. It was not until 27 July 1942 that the Eighth Air Force had a full heavy bomber group, complete with air and ground echelons. The first mission to Germany, on 27 January 1943, was made by only 91 aircraft – less than a third of the force the US doctrine decreed necessary for such a mission. Until the Eighth had more groups, the bomber offensive against Germany could not expand. It was also discovered, as the USAAF official history tactfully points out, that 'the new units were found to need more training in the theatre than had originally been planned'.[2]

During 1942, arguments had continued among the British Chiefs of Staff about the need to prosecute the bomber offensive at all – an argument fuelled by demands from the Admiralty for more support in the Battle of the Atlantic against the submarines. Compared with the need to defeat the U-boats at a time when Britain's Atlantic lifeline was being worn to a thread, the bomber offensive against the German homeland was seen by the sailors as a diversion. Admiral Sir John Tovey, Commander of the Home Fleet, described the bombing of Germany as 'a luxury'. This sort of comment did not go down well with either Churchill or Portal – let alone Air Chief Marshal Harris – but Admiral Tovey had a point. Before the war could be won, it was important not to lose it.

With the United States now in the war, the next decisive step would be reached when the build-up of US forces in the UK permitted an Allied invasion of the Continent. There was no argument on this point: rapid progress towards the invasion of enemy-occupied Europe had been agreed at the 'Arcadia' Conference in 1941 and underpinned the policy of 'Germany first'. The factor inhibiting the implementation of this policy was the U-boat, and the best means of curbing the U-boat was by aerial interdiction – attacking U-boats at sea or in their bases, bombing construction yards, mining the routes by which they reached their patrol areas. There was no disagreement about that point either.

The figures for vessels sunk by U-boats provided irrefutable evidence of the extent of the submarine menace. A total of 1,594,489 tons of Allied shipping was sunk in the North Atlantic in the last three months of 1942. In June 1942 alone the Atlantic swallowed 834,195 tons of Allied shipping, and a great quantity of lives; as the year passed, many other months' 'shipping lost' figures edged towards that grim total. The Atlantic was becoming a graveyard and until the shipping losses were stopped or stemmed, the progress towards an invasion was virtually at a standstill. If the prime aim of the war was to defeat Germany, the first task now – in the coming months of 1943 – was to defeat the German U-boat, and to that end all resources, including those of the RAF, should be devoted.

On this point Tovey was clearly right. But there were, as ever, problems. Bomber Command had already attacked German U-boat construction yards and the submarine pens at Saint-Nazaire, La Pallice and the other U-boat havens, but the yards were heavily defended and hard to hit at night, and the submarine pens, built of reinforced concrete many feet thick, were quite impervious to any bombs yet in service – bombs simply bounced off the roofs of the pens or exploded harmlessly, barely chipping the concrete. The other way to sink U-boats was at sea, but Harris was not far wrong when he described this as 'looking for a needle in a haystack' – and it would remain so until the boffins developed a better air-to-sea radar. Anyway, for this there was RAF Coastal Command, under Admiralty control and flying Short Sunderland flying boats and B-24 Liberators. There was also the need to halt or damage U-boat construction in the German shipyards, and the Admiralty wanted Bomber Command to be more active in this task, but this brought on a clash with Harris, who maintained that his force was already doing all it could.

Mining operations – *Gardening* – were already a major feature of Bomber Command's activities and, as Harris was not slow to point out, a highly effective one – by mining the RAF was already sinking more U-boats than the Royal Navy, and would continue to do so. All in all, he felt that Bomber Command was doing its share of fighting in the Battle of the Atlantic and should be free to concentrate the bulk of its energies on its main purpose: the strategic attack on Germany.

In this, Harris was right, and his struggle to put across his point illustrates his basic abilities as a great commander. The first task of a military commander, the first principle of war, is *the selection and maintenance of the aim*. The commander has to consider a large number of factors and a great deal of advice from other quarters but *selecting the aim* is crucial. Without a clear aim, a commander has no idea where he and his forces are going, and even less idea of what is needed to get there in terms of resources in men and matériel.

That, however, is almost the easy part. The next task, a linked and ongoing one, is *maintenance of the aim* – stepping up the pressure, remembering the objective, 'keeping the eye on the ball'. This is harder, because over time there will be constant pressure to divert from the main aim and carry out any number of other tasks, urged on the commander by his superiors, or his political masters, or the other services. To this can be added the difficulties of maintaining the aim anyway, through a lack of suitable kit, or the weather, or for a hundred other reasons. Yet a commander who cannot select and maintain the aim is no commander at all.

Harris had selected his aim: 'the defeat of Nazi Germany by the use of strategic air power'. That done, he had worked out the resources and tactics he needed to achieve that aim: more aircraft and men, better aids to navigation and bomb-aiming, and so on. Getting those resources was his current task. But he also needed time – and a free hand – to get on with the job of shattering Germany without the constant, nagging diversions of strength and concentration.

Harris was not the most tactful of men, and his insistence that bombing Germany was his chief priority clearly irritated many people, including some of his colleagues in the RAF. But he was quite right. The whole purpose of Bomber Command – the only reason it was equipped with long-range, four-engined bombers, capable of delivering heavy bomb loads over long distances – was to carry the war to the enemy. If Harris never succeeded in his aim of shattering German resistance, many other people, not least in Parliament and on the Chiefs of Staff Committee, must bear a large part of the blame.

The argument at Chief of Staff level came down, yet again, to the point about the perceived effectiveness of the strategic bomber as a *war-winning* weapon. Harris, and to a lesser extent Portal and the USAAF commanders, believed that bombing alone could force Germany to surrender – if applied in sufficient force. If they were right, there would be no need for a cross-Channel invasion at all: the Allied armies could cross over after the German surrender and enter Germany as a police force. Harris said as much, though adding that the success of his theory depended on the application of overwhelming and currently unavailable force: 'If I could send 20,000 bombers over Germany tonight, Germany would not be in the war tomorrow. If I could send 1,000 bombers over Germany every night, it would end the war by the autumn.' Harris backed up this statement with a call for a force of 3,000 strategic bombers,[3] and the Air Staff – effectively Portal – called for the Allied bomber force to be expanded rapidly.

The Air Staff maintained that an Allied Strategic Bomber Force – the USAAF VIII Bomber Command and RAF Bomber Command – a combined, if separately commanded, force – might muster between 4,000 and 6,000 bomber aircraft sometime in 1944. If so, it would then be possible to drop some 95,000 tons of high explosive on Germany *every month*. This would surely have some effect on Germany's willingness to fight on, and with this in mind on 3 November 1942 Portal sent a note to the Chiefs of Staff Committee concluding that at the present rate of progress in bombing capability about one and half million tons of bombs would be dropped on Germany by the end of 1944: 'an attack on this scale would lead to the destruction of some eight million German homes. Civilian casualties are estimated at about 900,000 killed and about 1,000,000 seriously injured. These estimates make no allowance for the fact that the number of persons per house would tend to increase as the destruction of dwellings progressed'.[4]

'Peter' Portal was a decent man. His proposal to launch attacks that would kill or maim some 2 million civilians – a kind of aerial Auschwitz – simply indicates how the war had eroded, and would continue to erode, the morality with which Britian had entered the war three years before. Portal knew this. His note admits that he was proposing 'a scale of bombardment which would far transcend anything within human experience. But I have no doubt that against a background of growing casualties, increasing privations and dying hopes, it would be profound indeed.'

Much of the post-war odium attracted by area bombing has been directed at Harris, but many of the ideas and proposals on which area bombing was based emanated from Portal. There is no question of blame here: Portal was simply pointing out the results of continued Anglo-American bombing, if that bombing was directed against the industrial cities of Germany. The Allied commanders were reluctant to face this, or at least to admit publicly that their attacks killed civilians – civilians working in German industry, but civilians nevertheless. The Anglo-American Bombing Policy document drawn up at a Combined Chiefs of Staff Conference in Washington in the summer of 1942 had stressed the useful effects on morale of bombing German centres of population, but the Air Ministry had played down this aspect of the Policy Document, admitting that the wilful bombing of civilians was 'contrary to the principles of international law'.

To admit that such bombing was official Allied policy would contradict previous public statements that British bombing policy was not designed to terrorize the civilian population, even in retaliation. There was some dichotomy in the Air Staff thinking on this point, because, three weeks before this paper was circulated, the Assistant Chief of the Air Staff

(Policy), Air Vice-Marshal John Slessor, had sent a letter to Harris and the bomber groups reminding them that 'bombing should be confined to military objectives', that 'the intentional bombing of civilian populations was forbidden' and that 'reasonable care must be taken to avoid civilian casualties'. This letter then added, however, that 'attacks on enemy morale were authorised'. How Harris and his Command could make the latter, given the former, was not explained.

Anyway, that policy had now come apart, and in 1943 the growing strength of the Allied air forces would now be flung directly, by day and night, by precision or area attacks, against the industrial cities of Germany – and their populations.

The proposal to raise a force of between 4,000 and 6,000 Allied bombers in 1944 was dropped and replaced by a more modest aim of 3,000 Allied bombers by the end of 1943. It was also pointed out by Churchill that an improvement in the bomb-aimers' accuracy would itself be the equivalent of a major increase in bomber strength. Having more bombers scattering more bombs across the German countryside would not damage German industry in any significant way – a fact illustrated by a raid on Mannheim on the night of 19/20 May 1942, when, although the aircraft used *Gee*, the results produced a harsh note from Harris to his group commanders:

> It is apparent from the night photographs and from the reports of crews that almost the whole effort of this raid was wasted on bombing large fires in the local forests, and possibly decoy fires. Nevertheless, in spite of the now incontrovertible evidence that this is what in fact occurred, the reports of the crews on their return from the raids were most definite in very many cases that they reached the town and bombed it. Many spoke of recognising features in the town and the river, and of fires definitely being located in the town . . . the results on this occasion show that few if any of the crews took the trouble, or came low enough to make certain of the nature of these fires . . . Apart from impressing on the crews the necessity to avoid being sold dummies, they must be made to realise that within the short compass of their operational career, if they do not on every flight make some worthwhile contribution to the aim of destroying valuable objectives, then the whole of the effort that has been put into training them is being thrown away and the conclusion of the war indefinitely postponed.

Harris added that crews were to be told that if such failures continued they would be sent back again and again until they did do the job.

In 1942 the German cities were learning how to defend themselves and divert the bombers, and the lighting of dummy fires on their outskirts, to distract and confuse the night bombers, was only one of many techniques. General Kammhuber was getting more aircraft, and the crews and ground controllers were becoming more skilled in finding the bombers and shooting them down. The air-interception *Lichtenstein* radar, introduced in 1941, had also improved, and the first *Lichtenstein* victory took place in June 1942.

Apart from this aid, German night-fighter strength was increasing. In January 1942 General Kammhuber had 152 aircraft in service in the West; by December this total had more than doubled to 362, and the number of crews had increased from 386 to 441 – which meant that Kammhuber's night fighters could roam the skies all night and every night, occupying the 'boxes' across the Kammhuber Line, or circling the radio beacons, waiting for instructions and guidance from their ground controllers.

Attempts to jam *Freya* and the *Würzburg* led to the development of two new British devices. *Shiver* – a modification of the IFF (Identification, Friend or Foe) device carried by Allied aircraft to prevent them firing on each other – would, it was hoped, disrupt *Freya* signals, while the *Mandrel Screen* was introduced in an attempt to block *Würzburg* emissions. Another device was *Tinsel*, which attempted, with some success, to drown out the voice messages passed to German night-fighter pilots by their ground controllers. German-speaking intelligence officers also took to the airwaves, broadcasting false instructions to the night-fighter pilots and when the *Luftwaffe* brought in female controllers in an attempt to disrupt this practice the RAF was prepared for this move and brought in German-speaking WAAFS of the 'Y' Service. All these moves and devices were in service, with varying amounts of success, by the end of 1942, and would improve gradually throughout 1943.

Peter Weston flew some of these *Tinsel* jamming missions:

> On the way to a target in Germany, one of the jobs I had to do was to jam the German night-fighter radio frequencies. During the pre-flight briefing I would be given the different frequencies of the *Luftwaffe* ground stations, and once in the air I would search around and find one. There was a microphone in the port inner engine and, having tuned in to the station, I would switch on the microphone as soon as they spoke. The engine noise would blot out any chance of the pilots picking up their instructions. Now and again I would use the internal mike and get the whole crew in on the act, singing popular English songs; certain members of the crew would sing obscene songs, and the German fighter controllers, some of whom could speak English, would cuss us to hell. One popular song that I remember was entitled 'Who dat down there saying who dat up there?', which went down very well – having fun in a dangerous situation.

Navigation aids like *Gee* were a help – though *Gee* was being jammed by the late summer of 1942 – and the new aids about to come into service, *Oboe* and H_2S, would doubtless be invaluable, but they were aids, instruments, nothing more. Some improvement was needed from the bomber force itself, some application of expertise to the matter of developing tactics for finding and marking targets. The answer to this need was the Pathfinder

Force, which had flown its first sortie in August 1942 and was still developing its navigation and target-making techniques as the year ended.

William Davies of No. 103 Squadron and No. 156 PFF Squadron gives a picture of operational flying at this time:

> When an operation was being planned, the station was closed; even incoming telephone calls were not allowed, for security reasons, though I doubt if anyone could have told an outsider where we were going until after the main briefing. Only the petrol load was an indication: a full load – 1,954 gallons, as I recall – indicated a long flight, deep into Germany or beyond. When we went out to the aircraft in 1,500 cwt trucks, I recall there was always a faint odour of vomit in the back, which I assumed came from someone being sick; I later learned that this was the smell of fear, released by a gland in the back of the neck. People did throw up though: I recall on three occasions seeing men of 103 Squadron leaning against a wall and vomiting before an op – but they still went.
>
> We frequently took off in ten-tenths cloud up to 500 or 1,000 ft and broke through suddenly into brilliant sunshine. During these long ascents we would be climbing utterly blind, with the windscreen wipers going at maximum. On three occasions during such ascents we became aware of a pink explosion higher up and at a distance; seconds later we were drenched in a liquid which some of the crew claimed was engine glycol from a collision between two aircraft during the climb. I vividly recall taking off on one typically English winter's day at about 3–4 p.m. and on breaking through the cloud finding ourselves among hundreds of aircraft, all heading east – a fabulous sight.
>
> There were the flak and the fighters, but the searchlights were a real bind. One of the most frightening experiences was being coned by enemy searchlights. The regular searchlights were white, but there was one which had a blue or purple hue and many aircrew believed that this was the master searchlight, which would lock on to a bomber and attract all the rest. Once caught, a bomber rarely escaped and all the guns got on to it and shot it down. We were caught just once, and the experience of trying to escape was frightening – we only managed it by getting into cloud.

A PFF attack on Frankfurt by 226 aircraft on 24/25 August 1942 was another disappointment, as the PFF had great difficulty finding the town, only a few bombs hit the target, and sixteen aircraft were shot down – a third of them from the PFF. A raid on Kassel three nights later was rather more successful. There was only slight cloud cover over the target, so the PFF was able to mark the target clearly, but many bombs fell well outside the city area and 31 aircraft – 10 per cent of the attacking force – were shot down. On the next night, 28/29 August, 159 aircraft attacked Nuremberg at low level, after the town had been marked with primitive PFF indicators. The Main Force crews claimed a good attack, but subsequent photos failed to confirm this: only about a third of the Main Force bombers actually bombed the town, and 23 aircraft – 14.5 per cent of those dispatched – were shot down.

Three nights later it was the turn of Saarbrücken, and another shambles. Instead of marking Saarbrücken, the PFF marked Saarlouis, a small town some miles away. The irony is that Saarlouis, which was not an industrial town, was then hit hard by over 200 aircraft, and severely damaged. Only four aircraft were lost, but no bombs fell on Saarbrücken. If it went on like this, the PFF would be broken up and the squadrons returned to their groups.

Bennett used these early PFF operations to find out what his force needed and seek ways to provide it. Clearly, the first task was to find the target and illuminate the target area. A heavy concentration on navigation training – essential now that *Gee* was less reliable – helped in this. Then came the introduction of new aids. *Oboe* had been tried out by No. 7 and No. XV Squadrons in a strike against German warships in Brest in December 1941, but it was still not accurate, though work on it had continued throughout 1942. The best forecast was that it would perhaps be ready for employment in 1943, when it would be installed in high-flying PFF Mosquito aircraft.

As for H_2S, that device was still embargoed by the Admiralty, who needed it for Coastal Command submarine-hunting. Fearing the Germans might obtain some of the H_2S magnetron valves from shot-down aircraft, Coastal Command had not allowed it to be used over enemy territory, but it was eagerly awaited by the PFF as an aid to target-finding. Meanwhile, in the autumn of 1942, a collection of flares and makeshift 250 lb and 4,000 lb marker bombs stuffed with chemicals – 'Pink Pansies' – were tried out by the PFF in an attempt to concentrate the bombing on the target itself.

The point being grasped was that, even if the bomb-aimers could not see the *target*, at least they could see the *markers*. If the target was obscured by cloud, then their bombs could be aimed at sky-markers, flares floating over the target area. Main Force crews were still ordered to find the aiming point (AP) given at the pre-raid briefing for themselves, and it was clear that some time would pass before the PFF could make any significant contribution to either navigation or target-marking. Nevertheless, the PFF was making progress; Bennett had a clear aim and was concentrating on steps towards achieving that aim – and fending off criticism in the meantime.

This failure of the PFF to produce instant results caused a certain amount of ill-concealed glee in certain quarters, but by the New Year of 1943 target indicators specially designed for the PFF were starting to appear, and Bennett had evolved a series of standard marking techniques that the PFF would employ, with ever more refinements, until the end of the war. Bennett had more energy than most men, but all this took time and the history of the Pathfinder Force[5] concedes that the first six months were very much a learning period. This fact was reflected in the loss figures: in its first six months the PFF lost 4.6 per cent of its aircraft per operation – a rate which, if it continued, would wipe the Force out long before the crews completed their 45 PFF operations.

The autumn and winter months of 1942–3, from the formation of the Pathfinder Force in August 1942 to the opening of the Battle of the Ruhr in March 1943, was a difficult one for Bomber Command. Winter weather added to the problems of the bombers, *Gee* was jammed, *Oboe* and H_2S were not yet available – though two PFF squadrons, No. 35 and No. 7, would have H_2S by mid-January 1943 – the the German night-fighter force was growing ever stronger and more expert. Nick Knilans, the American volunteer from Wisconsin, was a pilot with No. 619 Squadron at this time:

I was at Woodhall Spa, and remained there for eighteen months of operations. Forty-two aircraft, with 294 men aboard, were lost, mostly killed, in that time. In the first six months, no crew was able to complete its first tour. One Canadian pilot's hair turned from brown to grey before he was shot down. My friend Mac went down on his first trip, with all his crew. We still had training to do before I could be sent off as captain with my own aircraft and crew.

Some idea of what the aircrews endured on operations can be gauged from the following two accounts, the first from Nick Knilans on an operation to Kassel on the night of 3/4 October 1943:

At 2121 hrs *Monica*, the fighter-detection device, indicated an aircraft within 300 yards, which we believed to be another Lancaster – until tracer started streaming past under the port wing. Roy, the mid-upper gunner, noticed tracer entering the rear turret and causing an explosion, and he was temporarily blinded by Perspex which hit him in the eyes. We had to feather the port inner engine, but we went on to bomb and stayed with the stream.

We kept checking on Jerry, the rear gunner, who was slumped over his guns, and when we landed I told the crew they need not stay on to see Jerry taken from his turret. The ground crew were unable to open the turret doors, as the force of the cannon shells had driven Jerry against them, and I had to use a screwdriver to prise them apart. Then I got hold of Jerry's collar and pulled him backwards, free of the turret. I carried him out and laid him on the grass. The middle of his flying suit was badly torn and bloodstained, and, after examining him, one of the ambulance helpers suddenly became ill and had to walk away. The cannon shells had cut Jerry in half.

Archie McIntosh was a navigator with No. 57 Squadron:

On 23 September 1943 we took off for Mannheim. Take-off was at 1900 hrs, and by 1830 hrs we were in the aircraft checking it over, especially the main compass, which had been giving trouble. But it seemed OK, so off we went. It was a fine, clear night, and as we climbed we could see other aircraft rising from bombers stations all over East Anglia. We climbed to 21,000 ft and had just set course when Greg, our Canadian pilot, said, 'Look at the compass.' The main compass was all over the place, but we had another one and pressed on. Then we discovered that the oxygen was not flowing well and, a final straw, the power to the mid-upper turret had failed. Things were not looking good: oxygen sporadic, mid-upper turret u/s, main compass u/s. We had heard that if the rear turret went u/s you could 'boomerang' back to base, but that seemed to be OK so we again decided to press on.

We were on the last short leg to the target when I heard the stutter of machine-gun fire. At first I thought it was our guns, but then I looked out of my den and saw the fuselage was full of smoke, the oil lines were blazing, and the port inner engine was on fire. Over the intercom I heard Greg say, 'Prepare to abandon aircraft.' We got rid of the bombs and I had clipped on my parachute when Greg said, 'Let's go' – followed by the voice of our rear gunner, Pete Mann, saying, 'I can't get out!'

With the oil lines severed there was no hydraulic power to rotate his turret, so it had to be done manually, from inside the aircraft. I reckoned that I could go back, let him out, and go out the rear hatch, but when I got hold of the oxygen bottle I found the fitting on my mask was not compatible with the fitting on the bottle . . . and that's all.

The next thing I remember – and the only thing I can still remember, years since – is walking on the ground between two Germans, soldiers. They took me into a room and Johnny Harrison, our flight engineer, was there and someone said, 'Two kamerads safe', but it was all strangely dreamlike and stayed that way for some time. I have no idea how I got out of the aircraft. Later that night we met up with Nick, our bomb-aimer, and Harold Hill, our mid-upper gunner. That was four out of seven. But Greg Bourdon, our pilot, Pete Mann, the rear gunner, trapped in his turret, and Raymond Diggle, our wireless operator, they died I'm afraid, and the feeling of guilt is still with me.

This was a follow-up raid on Mannheim, after a major attack on the night of 5/6 September. Thirty-two aircraft were lost, but large parts of the city and the I.G. Farben works were severely damaged.

Training accidents also took their toll, as this account from Norman McHolme indicates:

We were on the last part of our training at No. 1666 HCU in Yorkshire, flying Halifax Mark IIs. The weather was foul, but when we let down through cloud we were in the clear, so we landed at another airfield and then asked permission to take off again and try for home. We had just about reached flying speed when the aircraft swung to the left; the port outer had failed, and though I tried to control the swing with throttle changes it had no effect. We went through a stone wall, down a slope into a small river, and burst into flames.

From that point on, I don't remember what happened. The next thing is waking up in an ambulance, unable to breathe. I was the only one hurt in the crash, and my crew got me out, in spite of the flames, taking their lives in their hands to rescue me. Apart from burns I had crushed vertebrae in my spine and torn ligaments, and will always be grateful to my nursing sister, Kathleen Robb, from Ayr. I was then sent to the burns unit at the Queen Elizabeth Hospital, East Grinstead, where Dr McIndoe and Dr Ross were in charge.

This hospital was set up to repair aircrew who had suffered burns or disfigurement in crashes, and there were people there who looked as if they could never be repaired. I wrote a letter to my mother at the time, and part of it is worth quoting:

> When I see the others here and the state they are in, it almost makes me ashamed to be here. There are chaps here so badly burned they are almost not human looking but there is a whole village, a whole community, devoting their time to convince these chaps that they are not that bad to look at and some day they will be able to take their place in life again. There were chaps getting new faces, noses, eyelids, lips, new fingers and toes, all through the miracle of plastic surgery.

I can't but rave about this hospital, but I must tell you about East Grinstead. The doctors discovered that men who were terribly disfigured had no psychological problems *when they were with other burned aircrew*. The problem was that few of them wanted to move outside the grounds and face other people. So Dr McIndoe and Dr Ross and Dr Tillay took pictures of these badly burned men around East Grinstead, into the shops and the pubs, and they showed these pictures to the townsfolk, telling them the problem and that they would be sending these men into town twice a week. It took a bit of pressure, but finally two or three brave chaps thought they should walk into town and give it a try – and they found that no one paid any attention to their injuries.

You see, in July 1943, during a German air raid, a bomb fell on the Whitehall Cinema in East Grinstead when many of the town's schoolchildren were in there; 108 were killed and 235 injured. East Grinstead was a town with a broken heart, and hardly a family escaped loss. So when these chaps went into town, with their shapeless, raw faces, trying not to see themselves in the shop windows, fingerless hands deep in their pockets, some without ears or eyes or noses, what do you do? The first time you see one of these men, well, your stomach rocks. You curse yourself, but you can't help it. But what did the townsfolk do? They talked to these chaps, chatted to them in the street, invited them home for tea, or for a meal. The girls asked them out on dates and to dances, *and nobody stared*. Not even the children stared. From their own grief, they understood the problems, and everyone in East Grinstead, the whole town, did their part.

So I became a member of the Guinea Pig Club – so called because in those early days of plastic surgery the doctors were learning as they went along, and we were the guinea pigs. We had a president who could not talk because his jaw was wired shut, a secretary who could not write because his fingers were in bandages, and a treasurer who could not make off with the money as his feet were in plaster. I was treasurer of our Toronto Branch for eighteen years; at the end of the war there were 148 Guinea Pigs in Canada but there are not many left today.

Aircraft were also lost landing at base after operations, as Frank Tasker, a rear gunner with No. 90 Squadron, remembers:

> It was our eleventh sortie and I don't recall that anything remarkable happened. We arrived back at base and our pilot called up our return and we heard that we were Turn 4 – three other aircraft had beaten us back. We also heard that the weather had closed in – the cloud almost down to ground level – and when our turn came we started descending, trying to find the runway approach. We had just started doing so when we hit something.
>
> I thought we had crashed into another aircraft, then realized that we were far too low and there would be no time to bail out. I thought I was going to die, and wondered how it would happen. I must have been knocked out, for when I came to our aircraft was on the ground, in pieces. Sitting in my turret, I realized that the rear part of the plane had snapped off from the rest of it and my turret had broken off from that. I was looking down between my four machine-guns, pointing straight at the ground. In a panic to get out, I tried falling forward but I could not do so; in my thick flying gear I was stuck, and I called out for help – a call heard by our mid-upper gunner, Robbie Roberts, who had come to find himself lying on the ground outside the aircraft, with no idea how he got there. He came along and opened my turret doors and out I popped, in spite of a broken arm.
>
> We then staggered around looking for the rest of the crew. The front of the aircraft had been smashed and we only saw two of them, and there was nothing we could do for them. There were several fires burning and live ammunition scattered about, and some people came running up from a nearby farmhouse and took us in and made us comfortable. Robbie and I were the only survivors.
>
> I ended up with No. 622 Squadron, flying Lancasters, and finished my full tour with them.

'Press on regardless' was the unofficial motto of Bomber Command – an attitude typified by this account from Squadron Leader Ted Hicks, an English pilot flying Wellington Xs with No. 466 Squadron, RAAF:

> It was our seventh op, target Stuttgart, on the night of 14/15 April 1943. We took off from our base at Leconfield and were somewhere near Mannheim when we were attacked by a fighter . . . the first thing I knew the cockpit was full of cordite fumes. I flung the aircraft into a steep dive and corkscrewed, but he caught up with us and I had to do it again. That time I lost him, but we had been hit hard.
>
> The aircraft and crew were in a bad way, but I decided to stay with the bomber stream if I could, as it was safer that way – on your own you could get picked off quickly by a fighter. So we pressed on and tried to find out what the damage was. The bomb-aimer and the navigator had been hit, and the rear gunner had been mortally wounded. We got him out of his turret and gave him morphine, but he died. As for the aircraft, we had lost our hydraulics. The bomb doors were down and I could not close them. The flaps were

down and I could not get them up . . . and the wheels were down. Not good. However, we went on and we bombed the target.

We then had five hours' flying time back to the UK – plenty of time to decide what we would do when we got there. But we could not make base and made for Ford on the south coast of Sussex. As we got close I put all our lights on and got the wireless op to send a message asking for an ambulance and telling the control tower we had to come straight in. There was not a lot of control without the flaps, but we made the runway. I could not hold her straight, and as we ran off a wheel collapsed and we ground-looped, but everyone got out without further injury. And that was that.

Well, not quite. Following this operation, Ted Hicks was awarded the Conspicuous Gallantry Medal, and gallantry awards went to other members of his crew. Twenty-three aircraft were shot down that night over Stuttgart.

Losses of aircraft and crews continued to mount, but in spite of this Bomber Command strength was gradually increasing, in both numbers and performance. Harris had 31 front-line squadrons on 1 January 1943, and had been able to up-grade his force, completely phasing out the Manchester, Hampden and Blenheim. The sturdy Wellingtons remained, but more squadrons were being equipped with Lancasters, Halifaxes and Stirlings. As for bombing aids, the PFF was now getting the Mk XIV Stabilized Vector Sight, which was also fitted to Main Force aircraft as more became available, and by February 1943 a number of PFF aircraft were getting the Mark II Stabilized Automatic Bomb Sight (SABS), though this would later be withdrawn from PFF and sent to No. 617 Squadron, the precision-bombing force in 5 Group.

Heretofore, Bomber Command aircrews had usually been of mixed nationality, not least because the crews themselves wanted it that way. As already described, trainees formed their own crews, milling around in the hangar at the OTUs, and by all accounts they greatly enjoyed the extra dimension brought on by sharing their lives with people from other countries. It may be this aspect of Bomber Command's ethos that has prevented any post-war historian creating the myth that one nation fought harder or did more than any other nation in the air war over Europe or – as has been frequently alleged about the Great War – that the Second World War was largely fought and won by the Australians and Canadians, while the British stayed in safety, drinking tea. The mixed aircrews of RAF Bomber Command would know the falsity of that kind of allegation and swiftly reject it. However, the Canadian government now wanted Canadian servicemen to serve together, and the RAF agreed. The result was the creation of 6 (RCAF) Group, Bomber Command.

When the war broke out in 1939, the Royal Canadian Air Force had one bomber squadron, No. 10 Squadron, equipped with Westland Wapiti biplanes. This force was rapidly expanded until the RCAF had fifteen bomber squadrons, and one of these, No. 405, flying Wellingtons, was established in the UK by April 1941 – by which time Canadians were serving in all the squadrons of Bomber Command as well as in Fighter Command and other branches of the RAF.

Four RCAF squadrons – all numbered in the 400s like the Australian squadrons – were in service with Bomber Command by the end of 1941, and one of them, No. 405, was selected to provide the Canadian element in the PFF in 8 Group, transferring from 6 Group in April 1943. Though the RCAF squadron COs were usually Canadian, they were often officers seconded from the RAF and not from the RCAF. If an RCAF crew finished training at OTU or HCU and a Canadian squadron needed a crew, they would go to it, but a 'Canadian' crew usually meant only that the majority of the crew – or the pilot and the navigator – were Canadian. The rest could come from anywhere, and a great many Canadians continued to serve, by their own choice, in the aircraft of 'British' or 'RAF' squadrons. One of the best-known was Wing Commander Johnny Fauquier, DSO, DFC, one of the commanders of No. 617 Squadron, the 'Dam Busters', in 5 Group.

The number of Canadian (RCAF) squadrons gradually increased from 1940, and as early as July 1941 the Canadian Air Minister had requested that an RCAF group be formed when sufficient RCAF squadrons were established in the UK and the necessary ground and maintenance back-up was in place. This situation was reached in May 1942, when Air Vice-Marshal G. E. Brookes was appointed to form an all-Canadian group. 6 (RCAF) Group was established on bases in Yorkshire and became operational on New Year's Day 1943. The strength of the group eventually reached thirteen four-engined bomber squadrons – plus two more PFF squadrons, most of them flying Halifaxes – but it was never to be an entirely Canadian formation. According to Air Vice-Marshal Brookes, 'In the two years I was with 6 Group, we never achieved that. We did not have flight engineers, for example, as someone in Canada forgot to include them in our training programme, so we started the group with some 15,000 all ranks, of which maybe 1,500 to 2,000 were Canadians, and when I left in March 1944, and A.V-M. McEwen took over, we had about 12 or 13,000 Canadians with about 2,500 RAF.'[6]

Not all the aircrews wanted this move to an entirely Canadian group, and some people at home agreed with them. An editorial in the Toronto *Globe and Mail*, Canada's leading newspaper, commented:

> Setting up a separate Canadian bombing command is working against the whole trend that has been reaching fruition – that of unity of command. The RAF has experienced officers who have gone through three years of the sternest fighting and proved their ability time and again. Canadians will without doubt rise to their places in operational command but to have a separate bombing command simply for nationalistic purposes interferes with the effective fighting of the war in the air.

In saying this the *Globe and Mail* was a trifle confused. There was no intention of creating a Canadian Bomber Command to match the RAF's or the USAAF's VIII Bomber Command: 6 (RCAF) Group remained an integral part of RAF Bomber Command throughout the war, though it was entirely financed by the government of Canada. There was no cataclysmic change: RAF aircrew, particularly flight engineers, continued to serve in RCAF crews, and Canadians continued to fly with RAF squadrons. The only real difference is that Canadians were now encouraged to crew up with other Canadians, and individual Canadian replacements went to the Canadian squadrons.

The results of all these various changes in the bomber war would be seen in 1943, but at the end of 1942 only Russia and the Middle East could demonstrate improvements in the Allied strategic position. The German summer offensive had been checked before Moscow, and the British Eighth Army had defeated Rommel's Afrika Korps at Alamein in October and was now driving the enemy west across the desert. The tide was turning, but was still at slack water. Everyone was waiting for the coming year and better times.

As for the Eighth Air Force crews and their commanders, they too were having difficulties. Between November 1942 and May 1943 their contribution to the air war over Europe was limited to the work of six bomb groups: the 91st, the 97th, the 303rd and the 306th, all flying B-17Fs, and two B-24D Liberator groups, the 44th and the 93rd. Each of the four squadrons in each group had about nine aircraft, so the total came to 140 B-17 aircraft at full strength, plus the two Liberator groups, which could barely muster twenty aircraft. With battle damage and the usual servicing difficulties, the Eighth could not put up more than 80 aircraft for any mission. The rest of the promised bomb groups had either not yet arrived or been sent on to the war in North Africa, so when General Eaker described his Command as 'a piddling little force' in a letter to General Arnold he was speaking no more than the truth.

The history of VIII Bomber Command of the Eighth Air Force in 1942 closely mirrors that of the RAF bomber squadrons in 1939. The American bomb groups were usually employed on missions against German U-boat bases, but even these were proving difficult in the face of German flak and increasingly active fighter opposition. On a low-level mission to Saint-Nazaire by the 91st and 306th Bomb Groups in November 1942, every one of the 91st's aircraft returned with flak damage and three aircraft from the 306th Bomb Group were shot down over the target. That put an end to low-level missions, and now winter was coming on, when the weather and navigation performance deteriorated together.

On 17 November 1942, sixteen B-17Fs of the 303rd Bomb Group set out for a strike at Saint-Nazaire; they returned with full bomb bays some hours later, having failed to locate the target under the clouds. Next day the 303rd tried again, sending nineteen aircraft against the submarine pens at La Pallice. This time they bombed, but it later turned out that they had bombed Saint-Nazaire which, though another submarine base, was 100 miles from La Pallice. Nor did these raids achieve much except the further destruction of French homes: the U-boat pens were quite impervious to the 250 lb and 500 lb bombs the USAAF then had in service. The attacks continued, but with no better luck: on 21 November the Eighth sent 76 aircraft to attack Lorient on the south coast of Brittany, but only eleven aircraft from the 303rd Bomb Group found the target and bombed – all the rest were defeated by relentless cloud cover.

If the weather was proving a chronic problem, affecting navigation and the working of the Norden bombsight, worse was to follow, for the German fighter force was getting the measure of US bomber tactics. The defence of the German U-boat bases in France was entrusted to III/JG 2, commanded by Oberstleutnant (Lieutenant-Colonel) Egon Mayer. Mayer, a very experienced fighter pilot, had trained his crews to mount head-on attacks against the Boeing '*Pulks*' – the *Luftwaffe* term for B-17 and B-24 formations. His first chance to try out this approach came on 23 November 1942, when the 91st and 303rd Bomb Groups put in a high-level mission against Saint-Nazaire. The weather was again vile, the formations broke up in the clouds, and many aircraft turned back, but Mayer and his men fell on the nine Boeings from the 91st Bomb Group that were still coming on. The *Luftwaffe* pilots put in head-on attacks, shooting two of the 91st's aircraft out of the sky and badly damaging a third, which crashed while returning to Bassingbourne. Many of the aircraft that made it back had dead or wounded crewmen on board, and these terrifying head-on attacks were to continue.

H. B. Howard, of the 100th Bomb Group, recalls this time:

We did more training when we arrived in England – practice missions in formation flying and dropping bombs in the Wash. My first mission was a 'milk run' to bomb submarine pens on the French coast, during which we saw plenty of flak but no enemy fighters. Enemy fighters would make head-on attacks to break us up and cause damage and then concentrate on shooting down any B-17s that were out of formation. We concentrated on the LeMay tactic during frontal attacks, the lead squadron turning fifteen to twenty degrees to one side while the high and low came alongside, and this permitted more of the gunners to fire at the attackers as they came in.

The flak would sometimes cripple a bomber. Every little town had some war-making matériel and would have flak batteries nearby, so a bomber could not fly more than ten or fifteen minutes in any direction without being fired on. An 88 mm shell came right through my B-17 fuselage, just in front of the bomb bay, but it did not explode until it was about 80 ft above us; other than punching holes through the aircraft, it did no damage. Incendiary bullets from fighters caused a couple of engine fires, but I feathered the props quickly and they did not spread. Fighter escorts were nil until the spring of 1944, when the P-51s appeared and could escort us to the target, and that made a real difference.

The story of the missions of the Eighth Air Force in 1942 and 1943 is a tale of gallantry in the face of adversity. The same tale could be told every day: of missions aborted by heavy cloud and aircraft hacked down by flak or enemy fighters, of targets missed or other places bombed, and of a steady waste of lives. The plain fact was that the USAAF doctrine did not work in the cloudy, flak- and fighter-filled skies of Western Europe. But the Eighth kept at it – buoyed up by the belief that the system *must* work or must be made to work, and by the scores of *Luftwaffe* aircraft it thought it was shooting down.

The US bombers did have fighter cover from RAF Spitfires, or Spitfires flown by the Eighth's fighter groups, but the Spitfire was a short-range fighter, built for defending the UK, and did not have the range to go all the way to Saint-Nazaire or La Pallice. The *Luftwaffe* pilots simply waited until the Allied fighters turned for home and then came swarming to the attack. In theory, the USAAF bomber formations did not need fighter protection – and anyway a long-range fighter was not yet available – but the reality was a relentless attrition of US bombers and crews.

The Eighth Air Force mission of 20 December 1942 is typical of the time. The Eighth mustered 101 bombers for a raid on Romilly-sur-Seine, a *Luftwaffe* servicing and repair base close to Paris, and for part of the flight out this force was escorted by no fewer than twelve squadrons – over 100 aircraft – of RAF or USAAF Spitfires. The last of these had to turn back near Rouen, and then the *Luftwaffe* came barrelling in. Two B-17s of the 91st Bomb Group went down in the first pass. Then another 50 *Luftwaffe* fighters came in to harry the bombers as they plugged on towards Romilly, bombed, and turned for home. The US gunners kept up a furious fire, but four more B-17s went down, two more crashed on crossing the English coast on the way home, and several of the 29 aircraft shot up were written off with excessive battle damage. A dozen B-17s were destroyed on this mission. Although the gunners claimed to have shot down 53 German aircraft, this claim was eventually reduced to 21, plus 31 'probables'. The *Luftwaffe* actually lost five aircraft that day.

The bomb groups were naturally anxious to do something about this situation, none more so than the 305th Bomb Group at Chelveston – a group commanded by the stern and dauntless Colonel Curtis LeMay. LeMay would make a great career in the USAAF after the war and a considerable reputation as an air commander during it, in both the ETO and the Pacific Theatre. LeMay realized that the twin problems of maintaining a defence against fighter attack and accurately bombing the target could both be helped if the aircraft maintained a tight formation and dropped their bombs on a signal from the leading aircraft, instead of the current system where every bombardier took over the controls of his aircraft, via the Norden bombsight, and in effect flew the aircraft in the run-up to the target. This inevitably led to a loosening of the formation as the bombers weaved about the sky, seeking a gap in the cloud cover.

LeMay therefore selected the best bombardier to fly in the 'lead' aircraft, and when that bombardier dropped his bombs all the other aircraft did the same. This was the start of the 'toggelier' system, which was soon widely adopted in the Eighth and greatly improved the accuracy of USAAF bombing. Not much could be done about the weather, though, and in the winter of 1942–3 the tally of missions dropped. In October only three missions were possible and eleven were cancelled; in November and December over half the bombers brought their bombs back since they could not find the target. And losses were mounting: in December 1942 the Eight's losses rose to 8.9 per cent of the aircraft dispatched.

So it went on until the end of 1942, by which time the Eighth Air Force bombers had flown a total of 30 missions to targets in France or the Low Countries. With the New Year, these targets would change: the Eighth was to join the RAF in the strategic bombing of Germany and, with the prospect of more bomb groups and the approach of spring, the now battle-hardened USAAF aircrew began to look ahead to the time when they could play a more decisive part in the bomber war.

However, the future of strategic bombing still looked uncertain, as neither air force had yet solved some fundamental problems. The RAF had still not found a reliable way to bomb accurately at night, and the Eighth had been unable to demonstrate that daylight precision bombing was a feasible proposition in a war zone. Clearly, it was time for a general reappraisal of the bomber war and the way it was being fought, and that reappraisal could not be restricted to the practical problems of strategic bombing. Now that the United States had been in the war for a full year, it was time for a fresh look at Allied policy as a whole, and this was the purpose of the Casablanca Conference in Morocco in January 1943.

At the Casablanca Conference, President Roosevelt, Prime Minister Winston Churchill and their political advisers and military commanders met to discuss and co-ordinate plans for the conduct of the war against the Axis powers in the coming year. The Conference began with a restatement of the 'Germany first' policy. In the immediate future, after the defeat of Rommel's forces in North Africa, the war would be carried into Sicily and Italy. This decision represented an admission by the Americans that their proposals for a cross-Channel invasion in 1943 – Operation ROUNDUP – would have to be abandoned. It was also admitted that, until the U-boat menace had been defeated, the build-up of an American army in Britain would be delayed, and until that task had been successfully completed, hopefully sometime in 1943, no invasion of the Continent was possible.

Plans would now be laid for a cross-Channel attack – Operation OVER-LORD – sometime in the spring or summer of 1944; meanwhile the Allied air forces in Britain would mount a joint operation – the Combined Bomber Offensive – against targets in Occupied Europe and Germany. This offensive had already been outlined by the British Chiefs of Staff in December 1942, and their proposals were adopted without much discussion for the Allied air forces as a whole, though Portal pointed out that it would still be necessary to mount land campaigns, as 'air bombardment alone was not sufficient'.[7]

At Casablanca the air forces – both US and British – were told that 'Your primary object will be the progressive destruction and dislocation of the German military, industrial and economic system and the undermining of morale of the German people to the point where their capacity for armed resistance is fatally weakened.'[8] Even now, three and a half years into the war, the belief that aerial interdiction could affect enemy morale was still an article of faith among Allied commanders and here at Casablanca it became a stated aim of Allied policy. The Combined Chiefs of Staff entrusted the responsibility for directing this UK-originated policy to Portal, but his responsibility did not include the authority to control tactics or techniques. Decisions on these matters were left to Eaker and Harris, who, as we shall see, thereby gained scope to interpret what the subsequent Directive really meant.

The Casablanca Directive – which replaced Bomber Command Directive No. 23 of the previous year – was issued to Harris in February 1943 and also contained instructions that, within the framework of the 'primary object' given above, attacks were also to be made on other 'primary objectives' – specifically, submarine yards, the aircraft industry, transportation targets, oil refineries, storage tanks and German industrial targets. The Directive also stated that other important targets such as submarine bases and Berlin might also be attacked, and that the Allied air forces would also be required to aid Allied forces landing in Sicily and Italy sometime in the coming year.

It is clear from this that if Harris had hoped for a clear run at the German industrial cities in 1943, he was not going to get it. If the powers that be decreed that other targets took precedence, the assault on the industrial cities of Germany would again be put back. Harris brooded over the Casablanca Directive for some weeks and then came back with comments which modified his instructions and the part he proposed that Bomber Command might play, rewording the Directive slightly to say that 'the primary objective of Bomber Command will be the progressive destruction and dislocation of the German military, industrial and economic system aimed at undermining the morale of the German people to the point where their capacity for armed resistance is fatally weakened'. This version implies that Bomber Command was to concentrate on undermining

German morale *by attacking industry*; meanwhile the USAAF would concentrate on specific targets – which, as everyone knew, was the USAAF's intention anyway.

Whatever Portal or the Air Staff felt about this subtle rewording of their instructions, no one corrected or amended Harris's interpretation and it is clear that, when it came to actually carrying out the Casablanca Directive, both air forces – Bomber Command and the Eighth – would go their own way. The commanders – Spaatz, Eaker and Harris – always had scope to do this: they were the ones who chose the targets, day by day, and they decided what attacks were feasible. The Directives laid down the policy, but how that policy was implemented was left to the commanders, who therefore had plenty of scope for manoeuvre. When referring to the Casablanca Directive in his post-war memoirs, Harris states – incorrectly – that 'the subject of morale had been dropped . . . and giving priority to certain aspects of it [German industry], U-boat building, aircraft works, oil production . . . and so forth, allowed me to attack pretty well any German industrial city with 100,000 inhabitants and above',[9] which is not what the Casablanca Directive had said at all.

At this point it is useful to consider the context of the decisions arrived at in Casablanca. The aim was to carry the fight on to the European mainland via landings in Sicily and Italy, to support Russia, and to take all possible steps to build up US strength in Britain for the forthcoming Allied landing in Normandy. The most important of these aims was to build up US forces in Britain for OVERLORD, the invasion of France. To achieve that end it was clearly necessary to defeat the U-boats which were currently ravaging the North Atlantic convoys. This being so, attacks on submarine construction yards in Germany and U-boat bases on the Atlantic coast were of primary importance, as the Casablanca Directive stated. Harris chose to assume that these targets, being precision targets, could be left the USAAF, while his Command returned to the job of shattering German cities.

However, while accurate, this rather overstates the case. Harris was perfectly willing to attack U-boat construction yards, and if he felt (with good reason) that attacking the reinforced-concrete U-boat pens along the French Atlantic coast was a waste of time, he could point out with equal truth that RAF mining operations – *Gardening* – were a constant Bomber Command task and were already sinking a number of U-boats. As for the U-boat construction yards, these provided the principal employment for the industrial workers of the city he chose for the second major Bomber Command campaign of 1943: Operation GOMORRAH – the Battle of Hamburg. Before that, however, Harris launched another major onslaught on German industry: the Battle of the Ruhr, which took place between March and July 1943.

The coming year was to prove a hard one for both the RAF and the

USAAF aircrews, with many reverses for the bombing commanders – reverses inflicted not only by the enemy but by the competing demands for their services made by the Allied commanders. These demands, especially for support in the lead-up to Operation OVERLORD in June 1944, meant that the balance of advantage would swing to and fro many times before the Allied victory in the air was finally achieved. OVERLORD, however, still lay a long way ahead in January 1943. For the next year at least the Allied air forces attacking Germany had time to prove their point and show what they could do – and a lot of hard lessons to learn along the way.

Focke-Wulf Fw 190A

9

Bombing Round the Clock
1943

Modern warfare resembles a spider's web; everything connects; there are no 'independent strategies', no watertight compartments, nor can there be.

John Terraine, *The Right of the Line*, 1985

From the moment he went to Bomber Command in 1942, Arthur Harris's principal aim was to devastate Germany by relentless bombing until the Nazis were forced to surrender. Harris believed that, if air power could be fully brought to bear, this aim could be achieved before the Allied armies invaded the Continent, making a land campaign in Western Europe completely unnecessary. The shadows of the Great War, the losses of the Somme and Passchendaele, hung heavily over British military thinking, even as late as 1943.

History tells us that one aspect of war, one campaign, one arm of service, is rarely decisive on its own: it takes a national effort, a combination of strength and will, political, military and civilian, to bring a war to a conclusion. In this struggle every arm contributes what it can, and the idea that one service has the ultimate solution is a pipe dream; as Churchill said, *'all we can do is persevere'*.

Until 1999 history does not record an example of a war won by air power. Then the ending of the Kosovo conflict in the Balkans after a campaign against Serbia by NATO air power seemed to indicate that that air forces could indeed win wars – and win them decisively – thus tending to support the arguments on air power advanced decades ago by Douhet, Mitchell and Trenchard and put into effect by Harris, Eaker and Spaatz during the Second World War.

Air Marshal Sir Ivor Broom believes that the collapse of Serb resistance in Kosovo undermined the long-held belief that air forces cannot win wars:

As far as I am aware this was the first time air power has won a war without the use of ground forces. There is no doubt that most media commentators – and accredited historians – deeply underestimated the significance of bombing with *precision* weapons of extraordinary accuracy. These brought the war to an end without involving ground forces in the fighting. I think it would be correct to say that the day of the large bomber fleets with huge numbers of free-falling unguided bombs is over and the success of the air war in Serbia will have worldwide repercussions.[1]

Since that letter was written, in the spring of 1999, more information has come in about the effect of the NATO bombing of Kosovo and Serbia. Some 40,000 missions were flown, mostly by well-equipped, state-of-the-art US aircraft, but, although a great deal of damage was done to Serbia's infrastructure, the number of military targets hit was far fewer than the original NATO reports had alleged. Only thirteen Serb tanks were hit during the campaign – not the tens and twenties reported destroyed each day. Losses in Serb personnel, estimated at 10,000, appear on closer investigation to have been about 400. Serbian morale did not collapse, and the Serbian government of President Milošević remained in power for a further eighteen months.

The view that air power was not totally effective over Kosovo is supported by a Ministry of Defence document, *Airpower 2000*, published in September 1999, outlining the lessons of Kosovo and making points that seem all too familiar to a student of air power in the Second World War. Comprehensive bombing of strategic targets, like bridges over the Danube or civilian power stations, to destroy a country's national will 'may not be the most effective way of achieving an objective'. Air power should not, or should only rarely 'be used in isolation'. The document admits that air power can cause panic and destroy the morale of those targeted, but continues that 'over time, target populations become inured to attack'. Regarding the outcome of such panic or fall-offs in morale, the document adds, 'If the enemy government or group is inherently authoritarian it is likely that the leadership will take little notice of public opinion.' The report concludes that the withdrawal of political support by Russia was more crucial to the Serbs' decision to submit than any amount of NATO bombing.[2]

A similar political cause may be the truth behind another claim for strategic bombing: that the LINEBACKER II campaign during the Vietnam War – eleven days of heavy US bombing of Hanoi and the port of Haiphong in December 1972 – brought the North Vietnamese to the conference table. Henry Kissinger later stated that this campaign 'speeded the end of the war', which may be true, but the Vietnam War was won by the North

Vietnamese, not by the United States. A suspicion of realpolitik hangs over this allegation – a suspicion that LINEBACKER II simply provided the excuse for a conference that got the US out of South Vietnam so that the North could move in.

It is also debatable if a campaign fought under the conditions encountered in Serbia, where the defenders had no means of resistance to the air war waged aganst them by NATO, can really be compared with the sort of air campaign fought over Germany in 1939–45. Had the Serbs been able to cause even moderate losses to the attacking aircraft, the outcome might have been very different. Today's technology may be more advanced, but it was notable that the laser-guided bombs failed to hit their targets in Serbia or Kosovo if cloud intervened, and many missions had to be called off because the weather was unfavourable; five decades after the ending of the Second World War, one can only wonder when weapons scientists are going to notice that European skies are frequently cloudy.

Lessons drawn from the Kosovo conflict are probably peculiar to that conflict alone and not a reliable guide to other situations. As for the point that the dropping of two atomic bombs forced Japan to surrender in 1945, that argument supports the use of atomic weapons, rather than the strategic use of air power. It was 'The Bomb', not the bomber, that forced Japan to capitulate.

Air forces have won *battles*. The destruction of the German Seventh Army in the Falaise Pocket in 1944 is a particular example of what air power can do, and in the Gulf War of 1991 the air forces made victory certain well before the ground forces advanced – but the ground forces still had to advance and overrun the enemy's positions before the Iraqis surrendered. In many Second World War campaigns, air power – especially *tactical* air power – was essential to military success, but wars are won when the infantry take and hold the enemy's territory. That is what infantry are for: the task of most other arms – tanks, artillery and air support, both strategic and tactical – is to make the infantry's task easier. The Second World War in Europe was won in May 1945 after American and British ground forces had crossed the Rhine into Germany and Russian infantry had entered the Berlin Reichstag. Those were the decisive moments: everything else was subordinate or peripheral or a contribution to bringing them about.

The debate on whether the 'bomber dream' was ever truly feasible has gone on for decades, and it will be continued in the final chapter of this book, but during 1943 Harris had a fairly free hand to prove his point, aided by more and better aircraft, some effective navigation aids, the growing skill of the Pathfinder Force, and the daylight activities of the Eighth Army Air Force. The Allied invasion of Europe, Operation OVERLORD, which Harris and Spaatz, with varying degrees of conviction, hoped to render unnecessary, was still a full year and a half away. In the meantime Harris devoted his Command to what he came to call the 'Main Offensive', a series of all-out assaults on German industrial targets.

When OVERLORD moved to the head of the Allied calendar, the support of all the air forces, strategic and tactical, would be demanded by the Supreme Allied Commander, but that time was not yet. In the meantime, the task of 'writing down' the strength of Germany, carrying the war to the enemy and assisting the Russians, depended on the Allied armies in Italy and on the air forces, specifically Bomber Command and the US Eighth Air Force, battering Germany from the air.

The Casablanca Directive required the RAF and USAAF to step up their attacks on German industry, on morale, and on certain specific targets. Harris began his share in this task in March 1943 with the first of what came to be called 'battles' – the Battle of the Ruhr – a series of devastating raids which began on the night of 5/6 March and went on for four months, until the night of 9/10 July 1943.

For this battle Harris had the advantage of the latest navigation and target-finding aids, *Oboe* and H_2S, which Bomber Command had finally obtained and had been experimenting with throughout the winter, trying them out on targets like Essen in the Ruhr, which was usually obscured by cloud or industrial haze. A raid to Essen on 3/4 January 1943 was one of a series of experiments in using *Oboe* by PFF Mosquitoes, and on this occasion three of them were marking for nineteen Lancasters of 5 Group. Three Lancasters were lost on this operation, and the fate of one of them is recalled by John Banfield, a bomb-aimer with No. 207 Squadron:

> That night we were briefed to take part in an experimental blind-bombing raid on Essen. Flying above 18,000 ft, my task was to aim at a flare laid at that height by an *Oboe*-marking Pathfinder Mosquito, at a given time and a given course over the target. We overshot the first flare by 30 seconds and circled round to line up on the second flare. As we did so we were harassed by searchlights, but we were eventually successful in aiming at the second flare.
>
> Setting course for home we had been told to lose height by at least 5,000 fet a minute, in order to slide off the screens of the German ground-control radar, which would have to be reset in order to catch us – this was the *Würzburg* radar, used to vector a night fighter on to a bomber. We were flying through the night-fighter belt between Roermond and Venlo, and I had no sooner suggested to my pilot, Barry Chaster, that we should start descending than we were attacked by a night fighter from astern and below.
>
> The first attack set the starboard-engine petrol tank alight, and fire also went through the main batteries aft of the main spar, causing the intercom to go dead. The order to bale out was by word of mouth. We could not escape by the front hatch as it would not open, probably having been hit by a cannon shell. I followed the navigator aft and saw him go out through a shell hole where the starboard blister had been. Fortunately the starboard engine had been feathered and he escaped successfully, though he hit the tail unit and suffered deep cuts in his left leg. I followed him the same way.

After I baled out, my last recollection is of seeing our Lancaster a mass of flames and I lost consciousness. I came to hanging in a tree, so knocked out that I could not release my parachute harness. I don't know if I hit the tail, but I had a badly wrenched shoulder and concussion and both the navigator and I ended up in the *Luftwaffe* hospital in Amsterdam, where we received good medical treatment. Our pilot evaded capture, made contact with the *Comet* escape line, and was back in the UK within three months. After the war he told me that the aircraft was attacked twice more after I baled out – attacks in which the night fighter raked the length of the fuselage with cannon fire, killing the two gunners, the wireless operator and the flight engineer. They are all buried in the Jonkerbos War Cemetery at Nijmegen in Holland.

This attack was made by Oberleutnant Manfred Meurer, flying an Me 110. Meurer was CO of his squadron and based at Venlo. He rose to the rank of Hauptman (captain) and command of I/NJG1, and had racked up 65 'air victories' when he was killed in January 1944, after his aircraft collided with an RAF bomber east of Magdeburg.

These experimental *Oboe* flights were necessary because there is often a difference between the designed performance of any item of equipment, with trials over home territory, and the use of that equipment in a war situation. Like *Gee*, *Oboe* had a limited range and the *Oboe* stations on the ground could handle only one aircraft at a time. It therefore made good sense to fit the first *Oboe* sets in PFF Mosquito aircraft, which could climb to 30,000 ft and so extend *Oboe* range – which was otherwise blocked by the curvature of the earth – well into Germany, where *Oboe* would be a useful aid to accurate PFF marking.

The Eighth Air Force had started its offensive against Germany before the winter was over, buoyed up by the fact that losses had not been severe on the 30 short-range and escorted missions to France the Eighth had launched between August 1942 and the end of the year. This confidence was supported by the belief that the American air gunners were shooting down vast numbers of German fighters. It has to be said that by no means all the USAAF people believed these claims of enemy aircraft destroyed or failed to realize that unescorted bombing missions deep into Germany would be a very different proposition to the first missions to France. However, the last four months of operations did seem to indicate that unescorted bombing of Germany by daylight *was* possible, contrary to what the RAF commanders had constantly maintained.

When two organizations disagree over a course of action, the only solution is try it out. This the Eighth set out to do on 27 January 1943, when 91 B-17s set off to bomb a target in Germany, Vegesack on the river Weser. Poor weather obscured the target and caused the force to divert to the 'secondary target', the naval base of Wilhelmshaven; 58 aircraft claim to have bombed accurately, and both flak and fighter response was mild. Three US aircraft were shot down and the gunners claimed 22 German fighters;

1. Air Chief Marshal – later Marshal of the RAF – Sir Arthur ('Bomber') Harris, AOC-in-C, Bomber Command, from February 1942 until the end of the war in 1945

2. Marshal of the Royal Air Force Lord Portal, head of Bomber Command from April to October 1940, the Chief of the Air Staff

3. General 'Hap' Arnold, wartime commander of the USAAF

4. General Carl 'Tooey' Spaatz, first commander of the US Eighth Air Force in Britain

5. An RAF Handley Page Heyford of 1936

6. An RAF Handley Page Hampden, 1939/40

7. An RAF Whitley Bomber of 1941

8. Two RAF Wellington Bombers in 1942

9. An Avro Lancaster: this aircraft was the backbone of RAF Bomber Command between 1942 and 1945

10. A young Wellington crew in 1943

11. A Mosquito pilot and his navigator sitting on a 4,000lb 'cookie'
before a night raid on Germany in 1945

12. An RAF Lancaster bomb bay containing one 4,000lb Cookie and 10/12 cases of incendiaries. Note the H_2S dome behind the bomb bay

13. A Stirling Bomber from RAF Ridgewell in Essex crashed in training at nearby St Margaret's, Tilbury

14. B-17 Flying Fortresses of the Third Air Division, US Eighth Air Force, over
Chemnitz

15. A group of USAAF B-17s with an escort of P-51 Mustangs

16. The Norden Bombsight

17. Bombs from a B-17 hit the stabilizer of a B-17 of the 94th Bomb Group on 19 May 1944 which went into an uncontrollable spin and lost a wing. There were no survivors

18. Home safe despite a mid-air collision. The bombardier and engineer baled out before the pilot rescinded his bale-out order

19. and 20. Battle damage: one USAAF B-17 flies on, though almost cut in half. Even this B-17G got back to base, despite terrible damage

21. A B-24 Liberator of the US Fifteenth Air Force destroyed by flak over Germany

22. Over Toulon in August 1944, this B-26 Marauder has an engine sheered off by flak

23. Messerschmitt cannon fire has chopped off the wing of this B-17, as it turned for home

24. All that was left on 19 May 1940 of a Whitley N1408 (MH-K) from RAF 51 Squadron. All crew members became POWs

25. The front section of a USAAF B-17 in Ludwigshafen on 8 September 1944

26. The rear gun-turret was a prime target for German nightfighters.
This Stirling had been flown by RNZAF Pilot Officer Buck, aged 19.
It was his last 'op'

27. and 28. Concrete shelters designed to withstand Allied bombing (and so
effectively beyond demolition). These two are in Ludwigshafen

29. Remnants of Cologne in 1945, taken from a Mitchell Medium Bomber of 226 Squadron, RAF

30. The centre of Wesel, on the Rhine, in March 1945

though actual German losses amounted to seven aircraft, this was still a good ratio.

On 4 February 1943, 86 American bombers set off for Hamm in the Ruhr. Bad weather caused the mission to be abandoned, though a number of bombers attacked Emden instead. German fighters were more active and aggressive this time, shooting down five B-17s; many more returned with flak damage.

These daylight raids continued, but the results were inconclusive – mainly because of poor weather and thick cloud cover over the primary target. German fighter activity also grew stronger, and fighter attacks became more persistent. The *Luftwaffe* day-fighter *Geschwader* were now getting used to attacking the US formations, probing for weak spots in their defensive armament.

Reggie Robinson was a B-17 pilot with the 306th Bomb Group:

I arrived in May 1943, and by that time the B-17F had two .50-calibre machine-guns in the nose, at least in our group. This was done on the base, and the bombardier manned these guns. Later there was a single .50 firing forward as well, manned by the navigator. The B-17Gs came in when I was there, but I never got one: all my missions were in the B-17F, and we did have trouble with fighters.

In August 1943 we went to Wilhelmshaven, flying 'Tail-End Charlie' in the low group. We were diverted to Heligoland and the fighters hit us good, knocking out the right outboard engine, where the propeller ran away and could not be feathered. The group then flew away from us and then the port inner seized up – we had taken shots in the oil cooler. We had five fighters on us at this time, and my gunners shot down three of them. They shot out our interphone in mid-message, and tail gunner misheard and baled out. He landed in the sea, but it was July and warmer and the Germans picked him up, chilled but living. So I dived the aircraft down to 300 ft and into cloud and the fighters did not follow us, though it was real hard to pull out of that dive. I saw a B-17 ditch in the sea and a British bomber come up and drop the crew a life-raft, but we decided to make it back on two engines and so we threw out everything – guns, ammo, whatever. The crew did not like throwing out their parachutes, but I asked them what good a parachute was at 300 ft?

Then the third engine started to run rough and we began to worry. My co-pilot was in shock at this time – he eventually got a medical discharge – so I was pretty busy just keeping the ship in the air. After we were waved away from the first landing strip, we eventually came in on the second one, just as all the engines quit. We landed in a field full of buttercups, and I told the guys that the next aircraft we had would be called *Buttercup*, and so it was.

Eaker was not receiving enough aircraft or crews to make up these losses, but the missions continued and on 4 March 1943 the 91st Bomb Group made a strike against the Hamm marshalling yards in Germany, a regular target for both Bomber Commands. Four bomb groups set off for the target, but two were forced back by the weather and bombed Rotterdam, the secondary target, and one group brought its bombs back. However, fifteen B-17s of the 91st Bomb Group, flying well above cloud cover, kept on for the target and dropped an accurate pattern of bombs across the railway lines – an example of the 'Press-on regardless' spirit that any RAF Bomber Command aircrew would have appreciated. The cost was high, though: *Luftwaffe* fighters appeared in strength, four bombers of the 91st Bomb Group were shot down – 26 per cent of the force – one was damaged beyond repair, and all the rest had battle damage.

These missions continued. Another successful strike against the submarine yards at Vegesack did great damage, and the fact that only two bombers were lost out of the 99 B-17s and B-24s dispatched did seem to show that daylight precision bombing of Germany was possible. Spirits naturally soared. Later in March the Eighth concentrated on targets in France, and the raids included a mission against the Renault truck factory near Paris, where the plant suffered considerable damage, although many bombs landed off the target and a number of French civilians were killed. Then came 5 April 1943, a memorable day in the history of the Eighth Air Force, when the first US airman to complete a 25-mission tour, Top Sergeant Michael Roscovich, landed back in England. Roscovich stayed on in England for a while as a gunnery officer, training newly arrived crews, and was killed when the aircraft taking him back to the USA crashed in the Scottish hills.

During this time, from early January to the first week of March 1943, the RAF was pounding Germany and German submarine bases along the Atlantic coast. Lorient was attacked nine times in as many weeks, and attacks were made against the dockyards of Wilhelmshaven and Bremen; other raids went in against Berlin, Cologne, Düsseldorf, Essen and Hamburg. Bomber Command went out on 58 nights out of 78 in this period, and lost a total of 251 aircraft on night operations.

As the spring of 1943 arrived, two balancing factors affecting daylight missions began to emerge. First, the Eighth's bomber force was getting stronger. Second, so too were the *Luftwaffe* day-fighter *Geschwader*. A major clash between the two opposing forces was clearly coming. On 17 April, 115 US bombers set off for the Focke-Wulf factory at Bremen. Two combat wings set out, making six 'boxes', led by the veteran 91st Bomb Group. This large formation was detected by radar over the North Sea, but the *Luftwaffe* did not appear in strength until the bomb run to the target had started. Then two *Gruppen* of JG 1, flying Focke-Wulf 190s, came storming in to make head-on attacks on the US formation, demonstrating that the *Luftwaffe* had now worked out how to attack American bombers and avoid the worst of their defensive fire.

The US gunners put up a storm of fire against these fighters as they swept in, but with little effect: the *Luftwaffe* kept knocking the US bombers out of the sky. Fifteen B-17s were shot down over the target area from the first wing alone, all but one by fighters and including the entire contingent of six bombers from the 401st Squadron of the 91st Bomb Group; the overall loss rate in this wing was 12 per cent. The second wing came through intact, but the loss of fifteen bombers from one wing was a shock – and every aircraft on the mission came back with battle damage.

Bruce Kilmer arrived in the ETO about this time with the 384th Bomb Group:

> Our first mission was to Antwerp in May 1943, to attack the Ford plant. Our group put up a total of eighteen B-17s, and the USAAF had no fighter planes available at this time and we would be escorted by British Spitfires – little did we know that they barely had the range to cross the water. Nor were we mentally prepared for the number of yellow-nosed FW 190s and checkerboard Me 109s that seemed to be everywhere. The German pilots were very good and very daring, and at that time we thought the flak over the target was very bad – we had not yet been to Germany. Suddenly, when the bad guys started shooting at us flying was no longer fun. We lost two planes and twenty men that day – our first mission; 24 to go.

The *Luftwaffe* pilots had already worked out that the B-24s were more vulnerable than the B-17s as Allison C. Brooks of the 1st Scouting Force and the 401st Bomb Group recalls:

> I flew both the B-17 and the B-24, the latter in training only, in the USA. Two points I well remember are that, over about 12–15,000 ft, the B-24 was hard to handle and keep in tight formation and the usual altitude for missions to Germany was 25,000 ft so the B-24 crews had their work cut out. I have a vivid memory of returning from a mission in June 1943 when we were attacked from about two o'clock, that's the right front, by a formation of Me 109s. Before a shot was fired, the German leader saw a B-24 formation straggling along parallel to our course and about one to two miles away. He pulled up and led his men directly over us to attack the B-24s, shooting down five or six of them in about two minutes.

A vivid picture of what happened during one of these fighter attacks is given by Bill Campbell, a bombardier and front-turret gunner with the 94th Bomb Group:

> We formed up in the usual manner as dawn was still approaching and we used flares to find our formation. We crossed the Channel in daylight – sunny, with scarcely a cloud in the sky – but as we neared the IP – where we turned for the target – I could see there was cloud cover over Paris.
>
> A few minutes before 1000 hrs, Angie – Angelo Revers, our navigator – tapped me on the shoulder and pointed to the rear, off our left side, where contrails were coming up fast where ships were overtaking us. He gave the

OK sign, because at briefing we had been told that RAF Spitfires would give us some fighter cover. There was not much fighter support at this time, due to the lack of fighter range. Then, just short of the IP, we experienced some flak, and then we were attacked by fighters. Those contrails had been FW 190s and possibly some Me 109s.

In a few seconds, the ship piloted by John Ples of the 410th Squadron was hit head-on by an FW 190 and exploded above us, on the right front. How many were hit on that first pass I will never know, but more fighters were coming in, head-on. I saw one and I opened fire, but we were hit hard. Our radio had gone dead, so I don't know if we were being attacked from other directions or not. Our No. 2 and 3 engines were on fire, and the smoke in the nose was very dense – more so than from the firing of the guns – so we had some fire in this vicinity. Angie had been firing the fixed-flexible machine-gun on the right side of the nose while I was firing the chin turret, and he was standing to the rear of me, just off my right shoulder. He was hit and mortally wounded on this fighter pass, though I did not realize this right away as I was trying to get in contact with the other crew members.

It was then that the remaining nineteen planes in our formation executed a manoeuvre that had me questioning my sanity for a moment: all of the formation had been on our right and higher than us, but now they were on our left and climbing steeply. I then realized that they were turning on the IP and we were in a steep dive. Our air speed was increasing rapidly, along with a fast loss of altitude. It was then that I left my seat and saw Angie on his back and quickly checked the extent of his wound. I cannot describe what his physical condition looked like – it is too painful to recall.

Our air speed kept increasing and the altimeter was unwinding very fast. Also, unknown to me at that moment, our bomb bay was on fire. I was trying to reach the hatch behind and below the flight deck when we suddenly levelled off in some cloud cover. I was able to continue back more easily, opened the hatch, and poked my head up to see what was happening – it was a most confusing time.

I yelled at Bill Porter, our pilot, and Hank Pohl, our second pilot, but got no answer and noticed that they were both slumped in their seats, Bill to the right and Hank to the left, with no movement at all. The windscreen was completely shattered, and I am sure they were both mortally wounded. Before I could get to them, away we went in another steep dive and I fell back into the nose section. I realized now that our situation was desperate. I don't recall seeing Frank at this time, but I found out later that he checked Bill and Hank and they were both dead.

Snapping my chute on, a last look at the air-speed indicator showed the speed hand right around the nine o'clock, which indicated a real high speed. I made my way to the escape hatch and Frank was right behind me. Frank said later that I seemed to be opening the hatch rationally but very hurriedly. I had trouble opening the hatch and – this I know to be my imagination – I thought I saw a picture of the girl I eventually married and, for the only time ever, I popped her on the chin. The door flew open and out I went, rolling over several times to slow my descent before I opened up, so my time in the air would be relatively short. I clearly remember the pilot chute coming out, the folds of the regular chute itself lazily unfolding, rigging lines and all, and then – *Karump!* – I was jerked back to reality. Frank and I later estimated that we were at under 5,000 ft when we left the aircraft, and how high we were when we opened I don't know, but we were pretty darned low.

Bill Campbell and Frank Moast evaded captivity and eventually returned to the UK. Five of Bill Porter's crew were killed; the other three were wounded and taken prisoner.

This is the sort of frontal attack that devastated the 17 April mission and, though the US gunners claimed to have shot down 63 German fighters that day, the actual *Luftwaffe* losses were about ten. The *Luftwaffe* had worked out a tactic that broke up the US bomber formations, and from now on USAAF losses would start to mount alarmingly.

These head-on attacks needed good weather, for the *Luftwaffe* pilots had to see what they were doing and to calculate precisely when to break off the attack and dive away, under the approaching bomb groups. Therefore the days when the US bombers were most likely to appear – clear days, with good visibility – were just the days most suited to the *Luftwaffe*'s frontal tactics.

Fortunately, help was on hand. During April 1943, six new bomb groups arrived, adding their strength to the four veteran units – the 91st, 303rd, 305th and 306th – still in action in the UK, other veteran groups having been moved on to the Middle East or diverted to a training role. Thus reinforced, the Mighty Eighth returned to the fray, but losses continued to mount. One of the men arriving was Lieutenant Mort Fega, a pilot with the 305th Bomb Group:

I can describe a typical mission at this time – maybe the one to Bremen, which was my first and so remains engraved on my memory. Our training had been adequate, but there was nothing in it to tell you how to react when your oxygen system is shot out at 28,000 ft or how to compensate when four feet of the tail has been shot away. In such situations you learn on the job.

So, Bremen. On the eve of a mission all you are told is the gas load. If it was maximum, you knew it was a deep penetration. On the night of 15 December 1943 I was advised that my crew would be flying the next day. All ten of us were anxious and nervous, but it was the policy of the 305th that a crew flew its maiden mission with the benefit of a first pilot who had some combat experience. So my crew, minus the co-pilot, flew to Bremen on the next day: Frank Hunter was the pilot, and I flew as co-pilot. Frank came from New York. Wake up was at 0300 hrs, briefing at 0400 hrs, and take-off at 0800 hrs.

Briefing was very businesslike. The first to speak was the group commander, who started by saying, 'Today the target will be Bremen.' He told us about the strategic importance of the target and why it was important to get good results. Then came the operations officer, who described how the formations would be constituted, who would fly lead and so on, the route to take, radio frequencies etc. Then came the intelligence officer, who showed us pictures of the target area and talked about the defences. Bremen in 1943 was a 'Flak City' where 'only 450 guns can be brought to bear at any time'. Then came the met officer – 'Cloudy Joe' – who told us about the weather. When the briefing ended we were all issued with a Mars Bar and directed to the chaplain of our choice.

So, take-off time. On the flare from the control tower the group leader started to roll. As he did, the next aircraft moved out on to the runway and began rolling, and so it went on until the entire force was airborne. To reduce the risk of collisions, each group had a prescribed heading after take-off and a set rate of climb. We were directed on to a 'Splasher', a radio beacon whose signal went straight up, and on this signal all the aircraft in your group would focus. From the co-pilot's seat I did whatever Frank told me, though in fact he said very little. We crossed the coast by the Wash, and headed over the North Sea to hit the enemy coast due north of Wilhelmshaven, where we began a slow turn to the right – the south. As we did so I saw a lot of black objects in the sky ahead. 'More B-17s?' I asked Hunter. He shook his head, slowly from side to side. It was the flak over Bremen, which now lay dead ahead.

Presently we hit the IP, opened our bomb-bay doors and commenced to fly straight and level up to the target, right into the heaviest concentration of flak. If I live to be a hundred I shall never forget the sight of Hunter's face over Bremen. His eyes were like diamonds, framed between his flying helmet and his oxygen mask. I was kind of hypnotized by all that was going on – the flak, the fighters, the release of the bombs, the fact that I had survived the bomb run – I wasn't that stupid – and the remarkably heavy flak. Nothing of the flight back remains in my memory. We landed, went to debriefing, drew our allotment of Scotch, and went back to our quarters to clean up for dinner.

Four days later, our group went back to Bremen. This time my crew flew intact, the first of the 27 times I'd fly as first pilot. Sad to say, on that mission Lieutenant Frank Hunter and his crew were shot down. I never learned if they survived or perished.

While the Eighth was assembling its strength, RAF Bomber Command had been pressing on with its war and was well into the Battle of the Ruhr, its four-month-long assault on one important industrial area. The Ruhr – 'Happy Valley' – had been under attack since the early days of the war. It was a military-industrial target, the home of the Krupp armaments complex, an area where the towns and factories were all concentrated into one long, shallow valley. Unfortunately, the Germans were well aware of both the importance and vulnerability of the Ruhr and had taken steps to defend it with a thick flak belt, a forest of searchlights and an adequate supply of fighters.

Essen was a notorious 'Flak City', as Jim Weaver, a Canadian pilot with No. 102 Squadron, remembers:

On every trip there would be variable amounts of flak and some fighters about, depending on the target. The large German cities were the most heavily defended, and any trip to Essen – or indeed anywhere in the Ruhr –

was like going into 'the Valley of the Shadow of Death'. The favourite crew expression when asked about flak on one of these trips was 'You could get out and walk on it.'

The Ruhr was almost equally well protected by the constant industrial haze created by the factory chimneys, which obscured many targets from direct observation and proved a sore trial to Allied bomb aimers, American and British.

The bombing certainly damaged a large number of Ruhr factories, but in the years since 1939 it had become clear that an industrial target needed constant bombing if it was to be kept out of production. Even the most accurate raid rarely achieved the total destruction of the target and, unless the raid was repeated, the damage would quickly be made good, the machines and jigs be replaced, and production be resumed. It was also possible to move the plant to some safer location, but it was less easy to move and rehouse the hundreds or thousands of skilled industrial workers. It was the workers, rather than the factories or the plant, that kept German industry immobile. And, since German industry was working far below its possible production level, all it needed to do to maintain or even increase production was put on more shifts. The only answer to that was to shatter the factories and keep them out of action with regular bombing.

Two further points should be remembered about the Battle of the Ruhr. First, only the Ruhr and the North Rhine cities were within *Oboe* range: targets further south or east had to be attacked using *Gee*, or DR, or whatever skills the navigators possessed to find the target. The second point is that Harris could not concentrate all his attacks on the Ruhr during this period. He had to attack other targets, as widely dispersed as possible, to prevent the Germans concentrating all their fighters, guns and searchlights in the Ruhr area. So on moonless nights, when long-distance raids were possible, Bomber Command went deep into Germany to attack other cities and keep the defences busy and widely deployed.

The problem was that this gave the Ruhr defenders – servicemen, civil defence and civilians – a chance to rest, clear up the damage, and prepare more 'spoof' targets in the shape of dummy fires in the surrounding countryside. Thus the need to vary the targets diverted Harris from the strategic aim of his battle: to shatter the industrial cities of the Ruhr in one short, intensive period, and so strike a major blow at German industry – and the workers' morale. The problem was one of numbers. Harris simply did not have a sufficient force to keep up heavy attacks on the Ruhr cities *and* send bombers elsewhere in adequate numbers to distract the defenders. So even here, in just one battle of the overall campaign, a lack of adequate resources cut deeply into his aim.

As the first target in his campaign against the Ruhr, Harris had naturally selected Essen, home of Krupps, a town heavily defended by guns and searchlights, and a regular target for both the RAF and the Eighth Air Force. On the night of 5/6 March, PFF aircraft opened the attack by dropping yellow navigation markers at a point fifteen miles short of the target, where the Main Force aircraft were to begin their run-up. This attack, by 442 Main Force bombers was led by eight *Oboe*-equipped Mosquitos from No. 109 Squadron of 8 Group, PFF, and it was not a great tactical success.

The first blow came when no fewer than 56 aircraft – more than 10 per cent of the force – turned back because of various mechanical defects. The chosen aiming point was the centre of the Krupp works, and the attack opened at 2100 hrs, when the Mosquitoes used *Oboe* to drop red TIs on the main factory buildings. This was 'blind ground-marking with *Oboe*' – *Musical Paramatta* – as the usual Ruhr haze obscured the ground. These TIs were backed up by PFF aircraft constantly dropping green TIs during the 38 minutes it took the three waves of the Main Force bomber stream to pass over Essen. As a result of all this PFF activity it was not necessary for the Main Force crews to identify Essen or the Krupps works *visually*: all they had to do was drop their bombs accurately on the *markers* – if they could get into the target area.

Many aircraft still failed to find the Ruhr valley, let alone the Krupps works in Essen. Fourteen aircraft were shot down and, in addition to those who had turned back, another 44 failed, for one reason or another, to bomb the target. When all the evidence had been gathered in, Bomber Command calculated that only 153 aircraft – some 40 per cent of the attacking force – had dropped their bombs within three miles of the target. However, those bombs which did hit the city did good work. The Krupps works was well hit, and reconnaissance photos showed that more than 50 factory buildings had some kind of damage and a large part Essen had been destroyed. It is an indication of how 'hit or miss' night bombing could be that this was regarded as a 'good show'. It was certainly a better result than any of the previous raids on Essen had achieved and justified the use of *Oboe* as a target-finder and an aid to blind marking.

The next major effort came three nights later, when 335 aircraft, including 170 Lancasters, attacked the city of Nuremberg. Nuremberg was outside *Oboe* range, so the target-locator employed on this occasion was H_2S, carried in 36 PFF aircraft, fourteen of which were to use H_2S to drop illuminating flares over the target; the aiming point would then be marked by the rest dropping green TIs. This was to be followed by the PFF 'backers-up' marking the aiming point with red TIs, and the Main Force would then come in to bomb in three waves, concentrated into no more than 30 minutes. This was the classic form of Bomber Command attack – one that would be repeated time and again until the end of the war.

Here again, though, the results were disappointing. Cloud cover obscured the city, H_2S did not provide adequate target definition – a number of sets did not work at all – and a number of the Pathfinder TIs were dropped blindly or using inaccurate visual identification. The Main Force bombing was well scattered, and a subsequent study of the photos suggested that only 142 aircraft had dropped their bombs within three miles of the aiming point. Another feature of this raid was a pronounced 'creep-back', stretching for more than ten miles down the approach path taken by the bomber stream. However, in spite of the creep-back, photo-reconnaissance also revealed that a gratifying amount of damage had been done to factories in the Nuremberg area, including the Siemens electrical works and the MAN plant that manufactured diesel engines for U-boats – and only seven aircraft had been shot down.

It appeared from these two raids that *Oboe* was a more useful target-locator than H_2S, but range remained the problem and *Oboe* attacks were therefore mainly concentrated on the Ruhr. Essen was attacked again, successfully, on 12/13 March, as was Duisburg on 26/27 March, and the month ended with a major raid by 396 aircraft on Berlin. Berlin was beyond *Oboe* range and this raid was a failure, most of the bombs falling anywhere between five and seventeen miles from the aiming point.

Berlin – the 'Big City' or the 'Big B' to the bomber crews – was always a difficult target. It lay a long way into Germany, close to the eastern frontier, and was a very big and very flat city, with few physical features, other than lakes and the river Spree, as a guide to the vital points. The lakes should have been visible on H_2S screens, but the Germans were soon covering the lakes or floating large wooden screens on them to confuse the bomber crews. Geoff Whitten, a navigator with No. 35 Squadron of the Pathfinder Force, describes some of the problems that the PFF encountered at this time:

> Our bomb-aimer was Tim Green. When we learned we were to be introduced to the mysteries of H_2S we decided that I would do the plotting and Tim would become the set operator, apart from the time when we were over the target and he was dropping bombs visually. Using H_2S we had, in effect, two navigators. Like most Pathfinder crews we pretended to be 'Press-on' types, but I will not pretend that we were star performers or ever inclined to reckless bravery. For example, on a raid to Cologne in June 1943 we took such a pounding from the flak that none of us dissented from the only decision we ever made to dump the bomb load and get the hell out of it. Yet three nights later, when we lost an engine before reaching enemy territory, we all cheerfully agreed to fly all the way to the target and back on three. We survived twenty PFF ops and all came through as officers, with a gong apiece, so we must have had some skill as well as luck.
>
> Having survived two months we found ourselves promoted to primary markers for a raid on Pilsen, a very long trip across Germany to Czechoslovakia on 13 May 1943. To help the Main Force, PFF aircraft were to drop markers at the last turning point. At the appointed time we were flying in Stygian darkness and, as far as we could see, there was not another aircraft within 50 miles of us. After orbiting for a few more minutes, hoping

someone older and wiser would take the lead, we dropped our marker and headed for the target, hoping we had not led the rest of the force astray. In the event the raid was a failure, as the aiming point was the Skoda works on the edge of the town and, though almost all the bombs fell within three miles of the target, most of them landed in open fields.

Another incident I recall at this time involved a couple of remarkably gallant Canadian officers, Julian Sale and Gordon Carter, pilot and navigator respectively. Gordon had already been shot down once and walked back to England; after the war he married the French girl who helped him evade capture. Julian, having also been shot down, also evaded and returned to the squadron, and in December 1943 his aircraft arrived over the circuit with a fire in the bomb bay, where a fused target indicator had detonated.

Julian ordered the crew to bale out and was about to do the same himself when his mid-upper gunner, Bob Lamb, appeared in the cockpit, holding his charred parachute pack. Julian dropped back into his seat, stuck his head out the port window as the cockpit filled with smoke, and calmly took the aircraft in for a normal landing. Roaring off the end of the runway, the Halifax slid to a halt in a ball of fire, but Julian and his gunner got out safely before the final eruption. Julian got a bar to his DSO for this effort, but two months later he and Gordon and Bob Lamb were shot down again over Germany and Julian died of his wounds in a German hospital.

Harris's first major battle was not getting off to a good start. In March, Bomber Command attacked the Ruhr just three times – no more than they might have done in any month of the war. Although these raids were heavy and fairly accurate, they did not add up to a major blow against a vital section of German industry, or something dramatic to startle the German workers and the Nazi leaders, on the lines of the Cologne Thousand Plan raid of 1942.

Clearly these attacks had to be stepped up, and in April Essen was attacked twice and Duisburg three times. In May the pressure on the Ruhr was stepped up yet again, with no fewer than eight attacks on various centres in 'Happy Valley', including a massive 826-bomber raid on Dortmund – the largest raid since the Thousand Plan attack on Cologne, and a very successful one. The PFF markers went down in the right place and the north and east of Dortmund were almost totally destroyed, with the Hoesch steelworks put out of production and many other factories damaged or set on fire; 1,700 people were killed or injured, and many houses were demolished. This was the sort of devastating raid Harris had in mind, and it should have been followed up with another raid within a few weeks, but Bomber command had to move on to other targets and Dortmund was not attacked again until 1944.

The Dortmund raid was followed by a 719-bomber raid on Wuppertal on the night of 29/30 May, a successful operation in which some 475 of the 644 bombers which claimed to have attacked actually dropped their bombs within three miles of the aiming point. Large areas of Wuppertal were destroyed and over 100,000 people were rendered homeless; 33 British bombers failed to return. Bad weather and the shorter summer nights now began to restrict operations, but on 11/12 June another major raid, by 783 bombers, was launched against Düsseldorf. This was the follow-up to a raid by 759 aircraft on 25/26 May which had had only a marginal effect, most of the bombers failing to find the target. The June raid was far more successful, although part of the force was led astray by a misplaced target indicator.

RAF bombers were now using a tactic of dropping high-explosive blast bombs to blow off roofs and expose the interiors, followed by showers of incendiaries to set the contents on fire. The effect on Düsseldorf was dramatic: a fire was raised that covered an area of some 40 square kilometres. Over 8,000 separate fires were started, many of them serious; over 1,200 people were killed, and about 140,000 were rendered homeless. This was an 'area' attack but, like the other towns in the area, Düsseldorf was an industrial centre: many factories were damaged, 77 companies reporting either a complete stoppage of production or structural damage. Twenty military installations – either army barracks or vehicle parks – were also hit.

The Düsseldorf operation was an accurate, worthwhile raid which did great damage to an industrial city, but again it was not followed up: the Ruhr was simply too big and too full of good targets to justify pounding one city to pieces. On the following night 503 aircraft attacked Bochum, and on 13/14 June 203 aircraft from 1 and 5 Groups attacked Oberhausen. Two nights after that, 212 aircraft from 5 and 8 (PFF) Groups attacked Cologne, which, though not a Ruhr town, is no great distance away and an important river port and transport centre. And so it continued, night after night, for months – attacks on the Ruhr towns mixed in with attacks on other targets in Germany or France or as far away as Italy.

Bomber Command could not devote all its attention to the air assault on Germany: *Gardening* operations continued, and during the moon period, when long-distance raids were not advisable, Bomber Command flew supply sorties to the French resistance, the Maquis, as James Berry of No. 149 Squadron recalls:

> No. 149 Squadron was equipped with Stirlings in 1943. My first sortie was a mine-laying trip to the Gironde estuary. We made our approach over the sea and went up an estuary to see where we were – not a good idea as we were greeted with AA fire, did a smart 180° turn, dropped down to the wave tops, and went back out to sea before finding our heading and dropping the mines. Five days later we went *Gardening* again near the Friesian islands – fortunately very quiet – and then, to get some experience of Main Force operations, I did two 'Second Dicky' flights to Germany: one to Frankfurt, which was aborted because the oxygen supply to the rear turret failed, and the other to Berlin, which went like a charm apart from a little trouble at the Dutch

coast. We then did three strikes against installations on the French coast near Abbeville and a special high-level mining job to the Heligoland Bight.

In early February, during the moon period, we were told we had to take supplies to the Maquis. This would be low-level work, across the Channel at 12,000 ft and then down to 2,500 ft, map-reading our way to the dropping point, where we would receive a Morse signal with a torch from the ground. We tried, but it was not to be: nothing was seen, and we brought all the stores back. The rest of the month saw more mining operations, and then in the next moon period we tried again. This time we went at low level all the way, crossing the French coast near Deauville at 2500 ft, our gunners exchanging fire with light batteries as we did so, and we found the drop zone and left the goodies.

We had a large crate to drop out the rear hatch, and this was a bit hairy. It took three people to manoeuvre the sling into position by the open hatch, and there was little room between the aircraft sides and the crate but two of the crew had to stand there – toes in space and no parachutes on – and be ready to shove it out when the bomb-aimer released the packages held in the bomb bay. By now we would be at about 300 ft, and I usually did a trial run over the laid-out lights to see what the get-out was like, as quite often the run took us towards a hillside. This one went well, and we did two more on 5 and 10 March. Then came more ops to France and Germany, and shortly afterwards – when we had done 24 sorties – we were told we were being transferred to Pathfinders, on Lancaster IIIs.

In spite of these diversions, Bomber Command's concentration remained on the Ruhr. By the time the 'battle' was concluded, at the end of July, Bomber Command had flown over 23,000 sorties, the majority against the Ruhr, and had lost 1,000 aircraft – some 4 per cent of the force committed, the majority shot down by fighters. Ignoring the smaller raids, mainly carried out by Mosquitoes, which were now starting to make a significant and growing contribution to the bomber war, Bomber Command carried out 22 major raids against the industrial cities of the Ruhr, and the principal centres – Essen, Duisburg, Wuppertal, Dortmund, Bochum, Oberhausen, Mülheim, Krefeld and Düsseldorf – had all felt the weight of Harris's Command.

Some cities and some plants were severely damaged. The Essen raids did great damage to the Krupps works, especially the one on the night of 12/13 March. It took four raids to do any significant damage to Duisburg, but the Thyssen steel works and the river port were also severely damaged that night. It took just two raids to destroy Wuppertal: the damage in the first raid, on 29/30 May, destroyed five of the six major factories in the town and more than a square mile of the city centre was devastated by fire; in the second raid, on the night of 24/25 June, more than 90 per cent of the Eberfeld part of Wuppertal was destroyed, according to the British Bombing Survey, putting this town out of action as an industrial centre. On the previous night, 22/23 June, Mülheim had been attacked by 557 aircraft

and severely damaged, much of the damage extending into the neighbour-
ing town of Oberhausen. The British Bombing Survey's post-war estimate
is that this single raid destroyed more than 60 per cent of Mülheim, though
at a price: 35 aircraft were lost – 6.3 per cent of the force committed – and
over 500 people were killed. Krefeld, a Rhine town which lies just outside
the Ruhr valley, was devastated by a firestorm on the night of 21/22 June,
when almost half the city was destroyed and some 70,000 people lost their
homes. Gelsenkirchen, being both a Ruhr town and an oil target – it contained a large synthetic-oil plant at Scholven – was attacked twice, but
neither raid achieved a great deal and the refinery was back in production
within a few weeks.

Although the Battle of the Ruhr did a great deal of damage to certain
cities, it did not destroy the Ruhr as an industrial centre or greatly reduce
its contribution to the German war effort – or at least not for long. Once
again it came down to the application of adequate and sustained force. To
be effective, a raid had to be in overwhelming force and totally destructive;
that done, the effort had to be kept up with further raids to prevent the
damage being repaired. To achieve that it would have been necessary to
keep the bombing up every few weeks until the end of the war. As it was,
much of the damage was cleared up within days, fresh equipment was
brought in, and most of the factories resumed production in a matter of
weeks. The big effect was on the workers, who lost their homes and all
their possessions – and the loss of life among skilled workers was not insig-
nificant. Nearly 600 people were killed and 1,275 injured in the Dortmund
raid of 23/24 May, around 3,400 people were killed in Wuppertal on the
night of 29/30 May, and another 4,000 people were killed or injured in the
second raid on the city on 24/25 June.

These raids cost Bomber Command a large number of aircraft and a
quantity of valuable lives. Although the overall RAF loss rate in this period
was a just acceptable 4.3 per cent, the losses on many of the Ruhr raids
exceeded this figure. The Ruhr was heavily defended, and the average
figure is reduced by lower losses on raids outside the Ruhr and by including Mosquito sorties. Remove those and the rate of heavy-bomber losses
in the Battle of the Ruhr climbs steeply. The Essen raid of 12/13 March cost
5 per cent; the Essen raid of 3/4 April 6 per cent, the Bochum operation of
13/14 May 5.4 per cent, the Duisberg raid of 12/13 May 5.9 per cent. Many
other operations cost over the 'acceptable' 4 per cent aircraft figure – plus
a large number of trained crews, many of whom died in their aircraft.

'Something on which I have seen no comment is the relative ease with
which one could get out of a Halifax as opposed to a Lancaster,' writes Bill
Grierson of No. 35 PFF Squadron:

Tommy Lane, one of the 35-ers, compared the survival rates for PFF crews,
Halifaxes *v*. Lancasters. Of 538 Lancaster crewmen shot down, 90 survived –

i.e. 1 in 6 lived. Of 35 Halifax crewmen shot down, 34 survived – i.e. only 1 in 35 died. I note that everyone seemed to denigrate the Halifax, except those of us who entrusted our lives to this lovely aircraft. Obviously the Lanc could not be redesigned to the Halifax's roomy configuration, but I know of no reason why its escape hatch could not have been enlarged to be as big as that of the Halifax, just two inches bigger each way.

Since 1,000 aircraft were lost during the Battle of the Ruhr, it follows that some 7,000 trained aircrew were lost with them – heavy losses in just four months. Not all the lost aircraft were taking part in operations over the Ruhr, but the majority were and losses of that kind were hard to sustain over a long period.

The snag was that the bomber war was, and remained, a long game. When all the factors are taken into account, the Battle of the Ruhr was a draw: the cities had suffered, but the Ruhr was still functioning though the bombers would continue to plough the debris of those cities until the very end of the war.

Bomber Command was, however, attacking these targets more effectively, thanks to the greater accuracy provided by PFF marking. James Berry, having transferred to Pathfinders in April, was now flying PFF sorties to Germany:

We were with No. 7 Squadron at Oakington and did 'Second Dicky' trips from there to get the feel of the new job. We had H_2S, which picked up features on the ground, and the navigator and bomb-aimer worked to relate the H_2S features to points on the topographical chart, in order to provide the navigator with the all-important pin-points, bearings, etc.

As a new crew we had to do at least six operations as 'supporters', going in half a minute ahead of the 'illuminators', the idea being that the 'supporters' attacked the flak while the 'illuminators' did their work, lighting up the target for the master bomber and his deputy. We qualified as markers on 4 July, and could then wear the coveted eagle badge underneath our flying brevet. We qualified as blind markers and had to demonstrate that we could get to within 400 yards of the target, at night or in cloud, using the H_2S set.

Still more might have been achieved during the Ruhr campaign if the Eighth had been able to come in and add its daylight 'precision' attacks to the 'area' devastation wrought by the RAF at night. This indeed was the intention of the Combined Bomber Offensive, but the *Luftwaffe* had other ideas and had succeeded in stopping the Eighth's contribution virtually in its tracks within a few weeks of the start. Eaker and Spaatz were not daunted, for it was believed that in return the Eighth had taken a heavy toll of enemy fighters – accepted claims in early 1943 added up to 450 German fighters shot down for the loss of 99 bombers, an acceptable arithmetic. The actual score of German fighters shot down was around 50.

Pitting fighters against bombers was always a chancy business, and as the air war over Germany intensified it rapidly became clear that a major gap in the Allied air forces' armaments was a long-range fighter – one able to escort the bombers all the way to the target and back, over distances of 1,000 miles or more. No such fighter was then available, but the problem had been recognized and a new fighter, the P-51 Mustang, was to appear in 1944 and change the face of the air war over Germany – certainly in daylight. Nevertheless, this failure to develop a long-range escort is another outstanding example of military myopia.

Fighters are built for defence against bombers. Therefore they can be heavily armed and based close to the potential targets, rising from their bases as required to attack the incoming bomber formation and break up its attacks; fighters, almost by definition, are short-range machines. When the RAF attacked Germany in the early days of the war, the bombers flew alone because it was thought they could defend themselves – and anyway no fighter had the range to go with them. During the Battle of Britain the *Luftwaffe* bombers had fighter escorts because they were operating from airfields in northern France and had only 100 miles to fly before they dropped their bombs on London.

German fighters could cover this distance, but they were still short-range machines which could not hang around for prolonged 'dogfights' over Britain, so the RAF harried the bombers after their escorts turned back. Fighter Command soon worked out a useful tactic to cope with the German attacks by dividing up the defending role, the sturdy Hurricane attacking the bombers, the more agile Spitfire taking on the Me 109s and Me 110 escorts. Fighter activity forced the *Luftwaffe* to switch to night bombing, but when the USAAF arrived, with its doctrine of daylight precision bombing, the whole subject of long-range escorts came into the open again.

In this area there was no help or advice available from the RAF. Portal had set his face firmly against the development of a long-range fighter for technical reasons. He believed that a long-range fighter must inevitably be totally outmatched by a lighter, short-range, fighter. It will be recalled that in 1941 he had told Churchill that 'Increased range can only be provided at the expense of performance and manoeuvrability,' adding that 'The long-range fighter, whether built specifically as such or whether given increased range by fitting extra tanks, will be at a disadvantage compared with the short-range, high-performance fighter.'[3] There is some truth in this, not least in combat time: at extreme range, an escort fighter from the UK could stay over the nearby reaches of enemy-occupied Europe for just a few minutes; a German fighter from a local airfield inside the Reich, could stay in the air for an hour and a half.

However, technical developments were already outpacing Portal's views – the versatile, twin-engined Mosquito was already faster than the early marks of Spitfire and would become one of the best night fighters of the war and no mean performer as a day fighter – but while Portal maintained that attitude the RAF bombers were not going to get a long-range escort.

Besides, where was the range to come from? Longer range meant more fuel. Bombers carried their fuel in capacious wing tanks, but the wings of fighters were full of machine-gun and cannon mechanisms and thousands of rounds of ammunition. This meant that a fighter pilot already had to share the fuselage with the fuel tanks, and when an incendiary bullet hit a fuel tank the pilot had to get out quickly or be barbecued. Going into action in a flying fuel tank was not something Portal cared to contemplate.

The eventual answer to the range problem was 'drop tanks', external fuel tanks which were jettisoned when the enemy fighters appeared, but drop tanks were not in service with the Allies in the first years of the war, though the *Luftwaffe* had used them in a small way during the Battle of Britain and was to make great use of them in the airy wastes of Russia. Anyway, the British had their answer to the short-range fighter by operating at night. The Americans, committed to flying by day, had no such option.

The US doctrine of self-defending bomber formations had already been put to the test and found wanting by the spring of 1943, but recognizing the problem did not solve it. In 1942 the USAAF bombers were first escorted by Spitfire Vbs; these had a range of 335 miles without refuelling, out and back, but this was reduced by the fuel consumed in warming up the engines, taxiing out, waiting for take off, climbing to altitude, the effects of head winds and the need to keep a reserve of fuel for emergencies – and the increased consumption when the engine was boosted for combat. All this taken into account, the Spitfire Vb could not go much more than 100 miles from the UK coast.

These limitations also affected the other potential escorts. The B-17 and the B-24 had fully bombed-up ranges of around 2,000 miles, which could be increased by reducing the bomb load and increasing the amount of petrol carried. Their escorts, P-38 Lightnings had a range of 450 miles, the P-47D Thunderbolts a range of 475 miles (the 'P' stood for 'Pursuit'). Both could fly to the Rhine – just – but they could not operate inside Germany without drop tanks. In 1942–3 the fighter escorts took the bombers out and met them on the way home, but, especially during a mission to Germany, that left a long period when the bombers were on their own. The range limitation of the US escorts was soon noticed by the *Luftwaffe*, who simply waited until the escorts reached the limit of their endurance and had to turn back; then the Me 109s and FW 190s came swooping in and the slaughter began.

Fighter range gradually extended and performance improved as new Marks came into service, but it was not until the introduction of the P-51

Mustang in the spring of 1944 that the US bombers finally had the fighter they needed. The P-51D, the most common version of the Mustang, had a range of 950 miles and could fly to Berlin and back. The Mustang was one of the great fighter aircraft of the war; had it been developed earlier, the history of the air war in 1943 would have been very different.[4]

The need for fighter escort on daylight missions was underlined by the losses on the Bremen mission of 17 April 1943, and when the Eighth set off for the Continent again, on 4 May, the 79 B-17s were accompanied by twelve squadrons of fighters, six composed of recently arrived US P-47 Thunderbolts; as a result, the *Luftwaffe* held off and the B-17s returned without loss, demonstrating the deterrent effect of fighter escorts. The P-47s were unable to escort the bombers into Germany, however, so there remained plenty of opportunities for the *Luftwaffe* to strike on missions beyond the Rhine.

May 1943 began on a high note for the Mighty Eighth. Six new bomb groups were added to its strength – five from the USA, plus the rejuvenated 92nd Bomb Group that had spent the winter on training duties. Five of these groups had B-17Fs, and a refinement was the presence in the 92nd Bomb Group of a squadron of YB-40 Fortresses. The YB-40 B-17s had plenty of armour and extra turrets, mounting a total of fourteen .50-calibre machine-guns. The idea was that these planes were to act as flying gunships, charged with beating-off and shooting-down enemy fighters; however, the YB-40 was another good idea that simply did not work. Weighed down with ammunition and armour plate, it was tail-heavy in the air and could not keep up with the regular formations. After a few months of unspectacular service it was withdrawn from operational missions.

This additional strength gave Eaker the means to form a second combat wing – later called an air division – and the 4th Wing, consisting initially of the 94th, 95th and 96th Bomb Groups, with Brigadier-General Frederick L. Anderson in command, flew its first mission on 13 May 1943 and on the following day the Eighth put up 200 bombers for the first time. Missions were still concentrated on French targets and the coast of Germany, Wilhelmshaven being attacked again on 15 May, when five B-17s were shot down from the 59 that reached the target.

Further missions followed throughout the month, losses being moderate but steady and cumulative, nudging towards the prohibitive 10 per cent limit, until on 11 June another major raid was mounted against Bremen. Bremen was cloud-covered, so the force turned to the secondary target, Wilhemshaven, and promptly ran into flak which scattered the leading groups. Then the fighters arrived, putting in head-on attacks notably against the 379th Bomb Group, flying in the 'high group' position. Eight B-17s went down, six of them from the Kimbolton group, which thereby lost a complete squadron in just two missions. When the losses were totted up at the end of June, the 4th Wing had lost twenty bombers – and 200 men – in just eight missions. Worse was to follow.

On 14 June, B-17s of the 1st and 4th Wings took off for Kiel. They had just crossed the enemy coast and were starting their bomb run from the IP when the fighters came in. The first aircraft to go down was from the 95th Bomb Group of the 4th Wing – an aircraft carrying Brigadier-General Nathan Bedford Forrest. Bedford Forrest was on this mission as an observer, and he became the first US general to be killed in action in the ETO. His aircraft was shot down on the first pass; then the *Luftwaffe* came swarming in again, hacking at the 95th, shooting down another seven B-17s, one of which fell out of formation and smashed into another bomber. Only six of the sixteen 95BG aircraft that crossed the German coast made it back to Britain, all of them full of holes. The rest of the bombers had been well hosed with fire; only sixteen actually bombed the target, and the survivors were on their way home when the *Luftwaffe* came chasing after them again, catching the bombers off the Norfolk coast and swifly shooting nine more B-17s into the sea.

When the score was added up at the end of the day, 26 B-17s had been lost – 22 of them from Anderson's 4th Wing. The 95th Bomb Group had lost nearly half its strength in aircraft and crews in just nine missions – and those surviving still had sixteen missions to go. The weather was hardly like summer in US terms, targets were not being decisively hit, and the *Luftwaffe* seemed to have an endless supply of fighters, flown by skilled and aggressive pilots. The gunners claimed over 40 German fighters destroyed or damaged on 13 June but only eight German fighters were actually shot down.

In spite of these losses, the Combined Bomber Offensive was having one definite effect: it was forcing the Germans to divert more *Luftwaffe* and artillery resources to the defence of the Reich and to recall fighter squadrons from Russia and Italy. The night-fighter strength and deployment will be covered later, but the *Luftwaffe* day-fighter strength on the Western Front in Germany and Holland rose from 207 in April 1943 to over 600 in August, most of the increase being in Me 109s. All of this was due to increased USAAF activity. Five German fighter *Gruppen* were moved home from Russia or the Mediterranean, and a new *Geschwader*, JG 11, had been formed by splitting the veteran JG 1 in two and adding some of these returned *Gruppen*. These new formations were full of experienced pilots, eager to play their part in defending the Reich, and, as they began to fly and fight, the Eighth's losses mounted yet again.

The attrition continued on 22 June, when 235 Fortresses from both combat wings set out to attack the synthetic-rubber works at Huls in the Ruhr. This raid was successful; the bombing was accurate and, although some production was resumed within a few weeks, it was six months before Huls was back at full capacity. The cost, however, was high: sixteen

B-17s failed to return from Huls, and a further four were lost on the diversion mission to Antwerp. Three days later, eighteen aircraft were lost on a mission to Hamburg – and to no avail, for low cloud obscured the target and the mission had to be abandoned. The Eighth was being roughly handled, but even so the missions went on, and the losses mounted.

This was the situation in July 1943. The RAF had achieved some results in the Battle of the Ruhr and the Eighth was making its presence felt over Germany, though at considerable cost. One history of the USAAF concludes that at this point in the war, apart from the Huls mission, the Mighty Eighth's contribution to the offensive was 'not very inspiring, particularly in view of the effort expended'.[5] This may well be so, but the truth is that the basic resources necessary to fight a daylight bombing offensive had not been provided – not least because of that prior peacetime belief that US bombers could fight their way through to the target unescorted and hit it when they got there. As everyone has to discover, war is different. The enemy defences – both flak and fighters – were getting stronger and taking an increasing toll of Allied bombers, and some way had to be found to reduce these losses.

As for the Combined Bomber Offensive proposed by the Casablanca Directive, there was little sign of it bearing fruit or even being actively implemented. The two Bomber Commands had enough to do in fighting their own corners of the bomber war and, although they co-operated closely at the Command level, there was little unity over the selection of targets or in combining to mount mixed area and precision attacks on specific targets.

However, a combined attack was coming. Each Bomber Command was still going its own way in midsummer; then Harris opened the second of his 1943 battles – Operation GOMORRAH, the Hamburg raids at the end of July 1943, a sustained assault on a major German city and a combined Anglo-American battle, with the Eighth adding its weight and precision to Bomber Command's all-out attack.

B-24J Liberator

10

The Great Raids: The Dams to Ploesti
August 1943

Hello, all Cooler aircraft, I am going in to attack.

Wing Commander Guy Gibson, DSO*, DFC*,
over the Möhne Dam, 16 May 1943

The next two chapters cover some of the major raids mounted by the two Bomber Commands in the summer and autumn of 1943. By the spring of 1943, Bomber Command and the Eighth Air Force were attacking the German military-industrial machine by day and night, within the Reich and in the occupied countries, with ever increasing force and precision. The 'missions' or 'operations' mounted varied from individual sorties by a single bomber, dropping supplies to the French resistance, all the way up to massive attacks by large formations numbering hundreds of aircraft.

Among all these raids, some have to be singled out as especially interesting not necessarily because of what they achieved, but because they were, in their various ways, pivotal to the conduct of the bomber war as a whole. Both Bomber Commands mounted such raids, which taken together present a picture of Allied bomber operations at the very tip of the learning curve, before the lessons on how to conduct a strategic bombing campaign were finally implemented. It is this aspect, viewing these raids as progressive steps in the bomber war, rather than offering a detailed account of each operation, that forms the subject of this chapter. The accounts may also serve to point out that, behind all the statistics and the paperwork, the arguments over policy and the struggles for resources, young men were fighting a hard and bitter war in the skies over Germany.

The first of these raids is Operation CHASTISE, the RAF attack on the Ruhr dams. This took place on the night of 16/17 May 1943, and was a raid by a single squadron of Lancaster bombers under the command of Wing Commander Guy Gibson, one of the crack pilots of Bomber Command. Gibson raised this squadron especially for the raid and, although No. 617 Squadron of 5 Group was to become a highly specialized *precision* bombing unit, that first operation gave it the name by which it is still known – 'the Dam Busters'. The dams raid is especially interesting, for not only was it a great feat of arms, the story also illustrates that scientific aids alone were not the answer: they had to be allied to training, aircrew expertise and courage. Finally, the Dams Raid displays the close liaison that often existed between the aircrews and the boffins and a further development in bomber tactics.

The Dams Raid had its genesis in the mind of a scientist, Dr Barnes Wallis. Wallis was 53 when the Second World War broke out, and had established a sound reputation as an aeronautical designer in the 1930s, being part of the team that designed the R100 airship and the main designer of the Wellington bomber – the mainstay of Bomber Command until the middle years of the war, and an aircraft that was still in service in 1952. When the war broke out, Wallis switched part of his mind away from aircraft design and began to think about bombs.

The RAF started the war with a great shortage of bombs, and those it had were too small. The mainstays were the 500 lb and 250 lb bombs, and it was not until early 1939 that the Air Staff commissioned a new bomb design and not until March 1940 that an order was placed for a 1,000-pounder. Like other air forces of the time, the RAF preferred to drop large quantities of small bombs rather than one big 'blockbuster', though evidence accumulated about the German bombs during the London Blitz revealed that small bombs were less effective. One account relates how a workshop was hit by a stick of seven 250 lb German bombs; only 24 out of 500 machines were damaged, all except two were repairable, and the workshop was back in full production in a couple of days.[1]

Wallis quickly came round to the idea of big bombs – even very big bombs, capable of knocking down large targets like city blocks – and, since bombs and targets go together, he eventually set about designing a 10,000 lb bomb that would be capable of destroying the large dams that supplied water to the population and armaments factories of the Ruhr valley. And so, early in 1940, three years before the raid took place, the idea of attacking the Ruhr dams was born, not at the Air Ministry, but in the mind of a scientist.

The first dam-busting bomb envisaged by Wallis was too big for any aircraft then in service or on the drawing board, but Wallis made the discovery that if a bomb could be placed right against the dam wall, instead of dropped in the water close by, the pressure of the water would tamp the bomb against the dam and multiply the effect of the charge. Wallis knew that destroying the dams would not be easy: the Möhne Dam was 112 ft thick at the base and 130 ft high, and the 25 ft wide top supported a road. The Eder Dam was even bigger. However, after a great deal of calculation and experiment, Wallis estimated that a 6,000 lb bomb – or two – if correctly placed, should be enough to blow these dams apart and let a tidal wave of water out to swamp the surrounding countryside – and the Lancaster bomber could carry a 6,000 lb bomb with ease. The big problem – and there was *always* a problem – was to get the bomb in the right place, hard against the dam wall.

This requirement led Wallis to design a 'bouncing' bomb, a round missile – technically a mine – that would skip across the water like a stone, strike the dam wall, and then roll down to the appropriate depth, where a hydrostatic pistol would set off the charge. Months of work followed in order to calculate the exact point – at the right height and distance from the dam wall – and speed at which the attacking bomber must drop the bomb to achieve this end. This was eventually calculated at 60 ft above the water, at a speed of 240 m.p.h. and at an exact spot some distance off the wall. This was a tall order for any aircrew, but by now – early 1943 – Harris was behind the project and he decided to put a special squadron together from 5 Group and give Wallis's bouncing bomb a try.

It should be noted that the bouncing bomb was for use against the concrete walls of the Möhne and similar structures, certainly not against the earthen dam of the Sorpe. Many detractors of Wallis and Bomber Command have cited the failure to breach the Sorpe Dam with the bouncing bomb – code-named *Upkeep* – and have suggested that the *Tallboy* bomb – also designed by Wallis – should have been used instead. This argument ignores the fact that the *Tallboy* had not been invented in May 1943 – it was not available for another year – and even when the Sorpe was attacked with *Tallboys* the dam was not breached, though direct hits were scored on the wall.

Harris was about to start his 'Main Offensive' and was therefore reluctant to take a squadron out of the line for one special operation. He therefore elected to call on his much admired 'old lags', those aircrew who were reluctant to leave operational flying at the end of their tour and would surely be willing to fly just one more mission. This new squadron would be open to tour-expired volunteers, and as their leader he chose the commander of No. 106 Squadron, a man who had already carried out over 100 operational flights in bombers or night fighters and was just coming to the end of his third bomber tour. He was a 25-year-old RAF wing commander, Guy Gibson, DSO*, DFC*.

Gibson formed No. 617 Squadron at Scampton at the end of March 1943. The twenty-one crews that assembled there on the evening of 21 March, six weeks before the raid, were the cream of 5 Group. All had done at least one tour, and some had done two; DFCs adorned most of their chests, and their names were well known among the squadrons of Bomber Command. No. 617 Squadron was a quasi-international force, typical of Bomber

Command squadrons in 1943, and the crews contained men from the UK and other parts of the Empire. Among the pilots were the Australians Micky Martin and Dave Shannon, the Canadians Sergeant-Pilot K. W. Brown and Burpee, the old Etonian Englishman Henry Maudslay, the New Zealander Les Munro, and an American, Joe McCarthy. 'Dinghy' Young, a pilot who had been shot down into the sea twice in this war and had paddled back to fly again, had a mixed background – raised in California, educated at Cambridge. Like the other 'Yank', Joe McCarthy, Young had joined the RCAF in Canada and had then transferred to the RAF before the United States entered the war. McCarthy was still clinging on in Bomber Command, resisting transfer to the USAAF. Of the 133 aircrew who flew on CHASTISE, 29 were Canadians and twelve were Australians; 56 men were to be lost on this single operation, only two of those shot down surviving to become POWs.

They were not told their target, but low-flying exercises began at once and over the next few weeks the problems of flying no higher than 60 ft over water at night and dropping a bomb at precisely the right spot were gradually overcome. A crudely constructed Y-shaped sight which would align on the towers at the end of the dams solved the distance problem; when the sight arms were in line with the towers, that was the moment to press the bomb release, at between 400 and 450 yards from the wall of the dam. The height problem was solved by having two spotlights fixed under the aircraft, angled together so that the beams came together on the water at exactly 60 ft. Nothing was said about the fact that the aircraft would now be attacking a heavily defended target, at night, over water, at very low level and with lights on.

Attacking the dams was a team effort, as the operational order confirms: 'Aircraft are to use the method of attack already practised. The pilot being responsible for line, the Navigator for height, the Air Bomber for range and the Flight Engineer for speed.'[2] When all was ready and the dams were full of water, the attack was ordered.[3]

At 2110 hrs on the evening of 16 May 1943, nineteen aircraft – 'special Lancasters' – of No. 617 Squadron took off for the Ruhr dams. Nine were tasked for the Möhne, Target X. After that had been destroyed, those aircraft which still had bombs were to go on to the Eder, Target Y, while the Sorpe, Target Z, would be attacked by five aircraft detailed for that dam alone. The last five aircraft were to form a 'flying reserve', either to back up the first aircraft or to attack other dams.

All went well until the first aircraft were crossing the Dutch coast. There Les Munro's aircraft was hit by light flak and lost the intercom. Without intercom Munro could not speak to his crew, so, cursing, he turned for home. Then Geoff Rice, trying out his spotlights, found they were badly adjusted and flew his aircraft into the sea. By some miracle Rice was able to drag the aircraft into the air again, but the *Upkeep* bomb had been torn off and the tail gunner nearly drowned as a flood of sea water poured into his turret. Rice flew his crippled aircraft back to Scampton and the rest flew on. Then Barlow and Byers were shot down by flak or fighters and never seen again. All these aircraft were part of the Sorpe contingent. Of that force only Joe McCarthy was left, flying on alone against the dam.

The Möhne force lost one aircraft on the way to the target, that of Bill Astell, who was shot down en route, so fourteen aircraft were airborne there when Gibson arrived over the Möhne. Gibson circled the dam for half an hour, waiting for the other aircraft to appear, and then took his air-craft, *G for George*, into the attack. By now the defences were fully alert and ten anti-aircraft guns and cannon opened fire on Gibson's aircraft as it came in low across the water, made clearly visible by the spotlights shining down on the water and the streams of tracer pouring back at the German guns from the front and upper turret. Gibson dropped his weapon accu-rately, the bomb skipped across the water and as he hauled the aircraft up into the sky it exploded against the dam . . . but when the water subsided the dam was still there.

Hopgood then attacked. His aircraft was hit by flak on the run across the lake, caught fire, and crashed into the hills beyond the dam, while the bomb skipped over the wall and destroyed the pumping station. Micky Martin then attacked. To draw the enemy fire, Gibson came in with him, both aircraft flying low across the water, every gun on board firing at the German defences. Martin's drop was accurate . . . but the dam held.

Dinghy Young then attacked. This time both Martin and Gibson came in with him, one flying on each wing-tip of Young's aircraft, their guns going to draw the enemy fire. Again an accurate drop, but the dam was still there as Young soared over it and climbed away into the night sky. Now David Maltby came in, Gibson and Martin again flying alongside, now with their aircraft lights and spotlights on, 60 ft above the water. Maltby dropped his bomb in the right place, the three aircraft just clearing the dam wall as the bomb went off. These three aircraft then began to circle the valley, waiting for the water to calm down before David Shannon attacked. All seemed as before and Shannon was just starting his run across the lake when – quite suddenly – the dam wall collapsed.

A wall of water twenty feet high surged over the masonry and swept off into the night, drowning houses and factories – and people – as those bombers which had yet to drop their bombs followed Gibson east to the Eder.

The Eder dam was, if anything, a tougher proposition than the Möhne. Although there were no guns, the dam was in a narrow, steep-sided valley which was now gradually filling with mist. The first to attack was Dave Shannon – and it is worth noting that this Australian pilot, now flying a heavy bomber at night against the great Ruhr dams, had not yet reached his twenty-first birthday. At first Shannon was confused by the hills and the mist, and overshot the dam several times before deciding to hang about and get the feel of things before he tried again. Henry Maudslay then went in, overshot like Shannon, went round, tried again, overshot again, and on his third try dropped his bomb – but too close. The bomb hit the top of the dam and went off just as Maudslay's aircraft passed overhead, and the bomber crashed into the hills. Shannon then came back and made a good run, dropping his bomb accurately, and when Les Knight swept across the water and dropped the last bomb it did the job. The Eder dam collapsed and another tidal wave swept away down the valley. That done, the surviving aircraft turned for home.

Elsewhere over the Ruhr, McCarthy was making his lone attack on the Sorpe, which he hit successfully; though the dam held, most of the crest was destroyed. Two of the reserve aircraft – those of Brown and Anderson – also went to the Sorpe, where Brown was able to bomb and hit the dam, but Anderson was driven back by the rising fog and took his bomb home. Of the last two aircraft to attack, Ottley was shot down and Townsend, diverted to the Ennerpe dam, hit it accurately. The other reserve aircraft could not find its target and returned to England.

Nineteen aircraft had set out to attack the Ruhr dams. They had attacked five of them, destroying two and damaging two. Eight aircraft were lost – 42 per cent of those committed. Great damage was done – the subsequent German report referred to the attack as 'a dark picture of destruction'. The floods spilled out across the Ruhr valley for over 50 miles, extinguishing blast furnaces, flooding coal mines, and swamping homes and over 100 factories. Over 1,200 people drowned.

On the other hand, the damage was quickly repaired, and within a few months the dams were filling up again. Post-war reports indicate that the damage done was not as severe as the post-operational photos seemed to indicate, but, whatever the material results might have been, the Dams Raid was a stepping stone to a brighter future for Bomber Command. This had been a precision raid at night and at very low level – something new in the history of air warfare. Another new feature was the use of VHF radios that Gibson had had fitted to all the aircraft, enabling him to communicate with his crews and act as a flying commander throughout the raid. This idea was taken up, and soon all Bomber Command aircraft had VHF and the Pathfinder Force was using a 'master of ceremonies', or 'master bomber', to direct the activities of Main Force bombers over the target, as Gibson had done over the Möhne, with a resulting improvement in accuracy and a definite reduction in 'creep-back'. These factors alone – the introduction of night precision attacks at low level and the control of the bombers over the target using voice radio – marked the Dams Raid as a step forward in the development of night bomber tactics.

Harris was delighted and told Air Vice-Marshal the Hon. Ralph

Cochrane, the commander of 5 Group, that No. 617 Squadron should be kept for special operations, filled with experienced crews, and trained in the precision dropping of Barnes Wallis's expanding range of bombs. In future years No. 617 Squadron, later joined by No. 9 Squadron, attacked difficult precision targets like the Antheor viaduct in Italy, the Michelin tyre factory in Clermont-Ferrand, the Saumur railway tunnel, the Bielefeld viaduct and the battleship *Tirpitz*. These targets could only be destroyed by direct hits, and using the SABS bombsight the *average* 617 error was reduced to less than 100 yards. Under Group Captain Leonard Cheshire, No. 617 Squadron also developed a very successful, low-level marking technique for 5 Group, though one unlooked-for and unwelcome result of this development was a growing and profound disagreement between Cochrane and Bennett of the Pathfinder Force.

As for Gibson, he was awarded the Victoria Cross for his courage and leadership over the Möhne Dam and was taken off operations. Away from the front-line squadrons, however, Gibson pined. In early 1944 he persuaded Harris to let him go back on operations, and Wing Commander Guy Gibson, vc, dso*, dfc*, was shot down and killed flying a Mosquito over Holland in September 1944; he was just 26 years old.

'Gibson was a born warrior, but he should never have been allowed to go on as long as he did and what happened was inevitable, I suppose,' writes Peter O'Connor of No. 467 (RAAF) Squadron, who flew on Gibson's last operation.

> The target that night was Munchen-Gladbach and the weather was bad, with minor enemy opposition. We iced up over the target and attacked at 15,000 ft. It was a successful attack, controlled by Gibson as master bomber in his usual professional fashion. I vaguely remembered his last words over the radio: 'Good show chaps, you've got the bugger . . . now you can piss off home', but I cannot guarantee this. We had a routine trip back, and we couldn't believe it when we heard that Gibson had got the chop.

Having suffered by water, the Germans were now about to suffer by fire. In late July, RAF Bomber Command launched Operation GOMORRAH, the start of a short series of raids on a north-German port – the Battle of Hamburg. If the Dams Raid was an unparalleled example of a 'precision' raid, the Hamburg attack was an 'area' attack par excellence: one which involved the USAAF as well as Bomber Command, saw the introduction of *'Window* – *'Chaff'* to the Americans and *'Dupple'* to the Germans – led the Germans to introduce *Wilde Sau* – 'Wild Boar' – tactics into their fighter operations, and produced results which were to be as dramatic and as horrific as those of any bombing operation of the Second World War, not excepting the later area raids by the RAF and/or USAAF on Berlin, Dresden, Tokyo, Hiroshima and Nagasaki.

Harris states in his memoirs that he had 'long wanted to have a crack at

Hamburg', the second city of Germany, a major port and a production centre for submarines and aircraft; in fact the city had already been attacked 98 times since 1939. Harris was now well into his 'Main Offensive', the crux of the bomber dream, an attempt to force a German surrender before the Western Allies landed an army in Normandy. The Battle of the Ruhr had just ended, and Harris regarded the results of that campaign as satisfactory. Now he intended to shatter a large but more concentrated target – one ideal for Bomber Command tactics and equipment. Hamburg was especially suitable because a coastal target like this would show up well on H_2S. Harris also had the promise of support from the Eighth Air Force and a new invention, '*Window*', that the scientists believed would baffle the German fighter controllers and flak gunners.

Harris did not intend to make just one attack on Hamburg: the first attack would be a major strike, but he intended to repeat it, night after night, until Hamburg had been completely destroyed. The battle opened on the night of 24/25 July 1943, when 791 British bombers attacked the city and dealt it a shattering blow; only twelve aircraft – 1.5 per cent of the attacking force – were lost.

This low loss rate was largely due to *Window*, strips of paper-backed aluminium foil which the bomber crews hurled out by the million from the flare chutes of their aircraft to create a blizzard of false echoes on the German *Würzburg* and *Lichtenstein* radar sets. The result of this first *Window* operation was a total paralysis of the German defences: the guns could not be accurately ranged and sighted; the fighter controllers and night-fighter pilots and observers had no idea which of the blizzard of 'blips' on their radar screens was an Allied bomber and which a floating piece of foil. *Window* is another excellent example of science coming to the aid of the aircrews, and it gave the bombers over Hamburg a brief unrestricted opportunity to hit the city hard. The German fighter tactics, restricting the fighters to their 'boxes', also contributed to the result, as night-fighter pilot Peter Spoden relates:

> I was at the Hamburg raid and I remember the terrible fires, but at that time we had tactics that were completely wrong. We were given boxes, areas of sky 150 km by say 200 km, and there we had to stay. I was over Greichswald and I could see because the fires were so terrible the silhouettes of the four-engined aircraft over Hamburg, but I was not allowed to leave my box. We were shouting, 'We must go to Hamburg, we can see them, we can see them!' but we were not allowed.

As a result, the bombers gave Harris his 'crack' at Hamburg. The RAF bombers dropped 2,290 tons of bombs that night and did a great deal of damage to the city centre. They might have done more but for a vast creep-back from the aiming point, which did not, alas, extend across the city dockyards and submarine shipyards.

On the following day, Sunday 25 July, the Americans arrived in the shape of the Eighth's 1st Combat Wing – 127 aircraft in all – tasked to drop 350 tons of bombs on two specific targets: the Blohm & Voss shipyards, which would be attacked by the 303rd, 379th and 384th Bomb Groups, and the Klockner aero-engine factory, which would be attacked by the 91st, 351st and 381st Bomb Groups. All these groups were flying B-17Fs. Other bomb groups from the 4th Combat Wing were also in action that day, either attacking other targets or on diversionary raids, but this account will cover only the Hamburg mission – part of a series of missions flown by the Eighth at this time, a period known to USAAF history as 'Blitz Week'.

The groups took off from fifteen airfields in East Anglia at 1300 hrs on a fine sunny afternoon and were close to their target when the first fighters came in. Thirteen aircraft had already aborted the mission for one reason or another, reducing the force to 114 aircraft, but diversion missions flown by the 4th Combat Wing to Kiel had distracted German attention and the Hamburg groups started their bomb run without interruption. The IP was ten miles from the target, which was largely hidden under a pall of smoke that rose to around 15,000 ft. Flak rose to greet them but no aircraft were shot down, though four were damaged and fell out of formation – a mark for the German fighters, which were starting to make head-on attacks. Two more B-17s were damaged, but two German fighters had been shot down and the wing was still fairly intact when the Hamburg flak got it in range and sent up a storm of shells.

Smoke over Hamburg was another problem, for unless the bombardiers could see the target the Norden sight was virtually useless. The bombardiers found that the great pall of smoke rising from the fires started by the RAF on the previous night, plus the smokescreen laid by the defenders, was obscuring their targets. So another lesson was learned the hard way: in future, when the two Bomber Commands attacked together, the Americans must go in first. On this day only a few bombs fell on the Blohm & Voss shipyard, and the Klockner aero-engine plant could not be seen at all; subsequent reports show that only a few bombs hit the shipyard and none at all hit the aero-engine factory. Many bombs fell harmlessly in the water, but some struck and sank two ships, and another stick hit and set fire to a vegetable-oil factory. The final total of bombs dropped came to 186 tons, a large number of bombers had been damaged by flak – and now they had to get home.

Flak and fighters made a formidable combination. Flak broke up the tight formations, and the aircraft damaged by flak and unable to keep formation or maintain height were sitting ducks for *Luftwaffe* fighters. In the flight back from Hamburg nineteen B-17Fs were shot down – seven from the 384th Bomb Group alone – slightly less than 12 per cent of those who attacked; almost all the rest sustained battle damage. The gunners claimed to have shot down 41 fighters and damaged 27 more, but the actual total, according to *Luftwaffe* records, was six fighters destroyed and six damaged.

Two raids in twenty-four hours, and the ordeal of Hamburg had hardly begun. That night the RAF was preparing to attack again, but was deterred by the smoke pall over the target and elected to bomb Essen instead. Next day, Monday 26 July, the Eighth went back to Hamburg – the same six bomb groups of the previous day tasked to attack the same targets, though the order was reversed: those who had attacked the shipyards on Sunday now attacked the engine plant, and vice versa.

Matters did not go too well, even at the start, for the 379th Bomb Group, tasked for the Klockner works, fell well behind the rest and decided not to continue. The two remaining groups for the Klockner works, the 303rd and the 384th, attached themselves to other groups. There was then further loss when Captain William Gilmore, leading the 384th Bomb Group, was unable to identify the group he had joined. Suspecting that they might have long-range 'Tokyo tanks', which were not fitted to the aircraft in his group, Captain Gilmore reluctantly but wisely decided to turn back, rather than risk following them and running out of fuel. This reduced the attacking force to just 88 aircraft, and this number fell still further as a number of aircraft aborted and turned back. A further 25 aircraft had dropped out before reaching the IP, where the remaining 63 aircraft turned to attack.

On the run-in, the pilots and bombardiers could see that a heavy smoke pall was already spreading over the city – the defenders were lighting smoke pots before the bombers reached the bombing point. This left the lead bombardiers with two choices: either to bomb on a timed run from the IP or to seek an uncovered secondary target. This last was the course adopted, part of the force bombing the Howaldswerke U-boat yard and the rest attacking the Neuhof power station. All the aircraft bombed in the space of a minute, dropping 118 tons of bombs. The bombing only slightly damaged the Howaldswerke shipyard, but the Neuhof power station was well hit and the city was deprived of half its electric power. Other bombs were widely scattered over the city and did no great harm. American losses were slight: of the aircraft that attacked, only two were lost – one shot down by fighters with the loss of four men, the other crashing into the sea from battle damage, all the crew being recovered by RAF Air–Sea Rescue.

The other USAAF missions flown that day – to Hanover and the North Sea ports – were not so fortunate. Sixteen B-17s were shot down from the Hanover mission, and a further six from the force that attacked Wilhelmshaven and Bremen – 11.5 per cent of the force committed. The gunners claim to have shot down 60 German fighters; actual German losses that day were four shot down and three damaged.

That night it was quiet over Hamburg. The RAF Main Force had been out for two nights in a row, putting up every aircraft that had a crew, and now the men were tired and needed a break. One night's sleep and then on Tuesday 27/28 June 787 bombers were tasked for another strike at Hamburg. By now the Battle of Hamburg was attracting a certain amount of attention from high-ranking officers, and among the senior officers flying to Hamburg with the RAF that night would be Brigadier-General Frederick L. Anderson, the new commander of the USAAF VIII Bomber Command.

Since the end of 1942 there had been some changes in the USAAF command structure. Spaatz had gone to North Africa to command the Allied air forces – the North-West African Air Force – in the final stages of the desert war and, although remaining the leading USAAF officer in the ETO, would not return to England until December 1943. Eaker had now been promoted to command the Eighth Air Force, and Anderson had taken over Eaker's post at the Eighth's Bomber Command. Anderson flew to Hamburg as 'Second Dicky' in a Lancaster of No. 83 Squadron.

For the British aircrews this night started like so many nights, right up to the moment when the Pathfinders opened the attack by dropping target indicators over the city. The effect of *Window* on the previous raid had delighted the RAF crews, but the German radar operators were already starting to get to grips with the problem of distinguishing a bomber 'blip' in the snowstorm on their screens. Moreover, a *Luftwaffe* officer, Major Hajo Herrmann, a former bomber pilot, had already come up with a new tactic which was to cause an increased level of losses over Hamburg and lead to a relaxation in the *Luftwaffe*'s current tactic of containing each night fighter inside its own box.

Up to now, the German defences, both flak and fighters, had depended on radar. Radar was the core of a fully integrated system in which night fighters, flak, searchlights and ground controllers, as well as the *Würzburg* and *Lichtenstein* operators, were combined into a highly effective whole, controlling the fighters in their boxes. The advent of *Window* had made all that ineffective. The RAF had been prevented from using *Window* before this operation because of a fear that the Germans would learn how to use it and bring it to bear against Britain's defences in a new Blitz; the irony is that the Germans already had their own version of *Window* – called *Dupple* – and had refrained from using it over the UK for exactly the same reason.

As with most of these Second World War inventions, the scientists did not believe that *Window* would be effective for long; within months the Germans would find a way to overcome it. In fact the process of fighting back against *Window* had already begun when the RAF returned to Hamburg on 27/28 July. The *Luftwaffe* radar operators were very experienced and were already able to identify some of the bombers on the plot, but the big defence breakthrough came from Hajo Herrmann.

The Germans left the local defence of cities to the flak while, as already described by Peter Spoden, the night fighters were deployed in *Räume* ('boxes') in the path of the bombers and directed on to them by radar. A major problem with the *Räume* was that they restricted the operational range of the fighters; the fighter controllers could direct only one fighter at a time in each *Raum*, and while they were doing that other bombers would slip past. It was to partly to counter the boxes that Harris had introduced the bomber stream, to swamp the defences. Major Herrmann had now thought of a way to get round that tactic and, thanks to the confusion caused by *Window* and the protests from Peter Spoden and other *Luftwaffe* pilots, he found a ready ear among the *Luftwaffe* controllers. He already had the support of many competent pilots, who wanted to have a crack at the bombers but were held back while a score of aces occupied the best boxes and built up large scores – 'air victories', as the *Luftwaffe* called them.

When he came up with his new tactic, *Wilde Sau*, in 1943, Hajo Herrmann had not yet flown a fighter. He had been a bomber pilot with a long string of operations over Britain to his credit. His idea was to use single-engined day fighters, usually Me 109s, directly over the cities under attack but operating above the level of the flak, say over 20,000 ft. The bombers would be illuminated from below by the fires, searchlights and target indicators, and could be easily picked out and, he alleged, be shot down in quantity. Herrmann was allowed to try this out over Cologne on the night of 3/4 July 1943 and although the results were not conclusive, he was allowed to form a special *Gruppe* of 30 modified Me 109s and try again.

Eventually, Hajo Herrmann's idea led to three *Wilde Sau Geschwader* – JGs 300, 301 and 302 – which were based at day-fighter airfields and used the same Me 109 aircraft; other pilots flew these aircraft during the day against the USAAF, and Herrmann's pilots took them over and flew them against the RAF at night. These single-seat fighters had no radar, but in the skies over Hamburg they shot down seven RAF bombers in the three nights of the raid, which was a good start and a justification of Herrmann's faith in *Wilde Sau* tactics. From now on RAF bombers would have to cope with Herrmann's fighters operating over the target on every raid, as well as their usual opponents – the flak, the searchlights, fighters in the *Räume* – and, before long, roving twin-engined night fighters flying in the bomber stream.

All that lay ahead at 00.55 hrs on 28 July, when the first bombs fell on the city. By 0100 hrs the raid was in full flood and going well, at least from the point of view of the aircrews. The TIs had been accurately laid, there was a minimum of creep-back, and the centre of Hamburg was starting to erupt in flame. The raid on Hamburg by 735 bombers lasted just 1 hour and 12 minutes, and 2,326 tons of bombs were dropped in that time; the last bombs fell at 0147 hrs. Seventeen bombers were lost, and ten minutes after the last bomber left the city was ablaze. The raid was over, but the ordeal of Hamburg by firestorm had just begun.

Flight Lieutenant Jimmy Davidson of No. 35 Squadron, PFF, flew on the Hamburg raids:

On 24 July I had not been on ops since 11 July. With 39 ops behind me, the leave had felt like a reprieve. The announcement that the target would be Hamburg was not the sort of thrill I would have chosen, for I had been there twice with No. 78 Squadron; the defences were excellent, with heavy flak and many searchlights, not to mention night fighters. There was nothing to indicate that this briefing introduced a week of hell for the German port, and anyway we had our own problems since we were to lead the raid.

The first attack on 24 July was rough. We made our run at 15,500 ft, and the bomb-bay doors were open when predicted flak began to burst all around us and we could hear the shrapnel hitting home. To continue flying straight and level was to invite disaster, so I took the necessary avoiding action, though this meant that Tim, the bomb-aimer, could not drop his TIs. PFF marking rules were precise: if markers could not be dropped within two minutes of the ETA on target, they had to be retained; anything else brought down the wrath of A.V-M. Bennett, which was allegedly worse than anything the Germans could devise.

The next raid, on 27/28 July, was again undistinguished. We had been briefed as blind markers, but our H_2S became unserviceable. We bombed from 16,000 ft on a city still blazing from our previous raid and the USAAF raid that had followed it. There was then considerable astonishment when the briefing for 29/30 July disclosed yet another Hamburg raid. This must have been the most intensive bombing of a single target any of us had experienced. The weather over England had become oppressively hot with high humidity, but over Hamburg the skies were clear. Only the fires below flicked under drifting banks of smoke.

We bombed from 14,000 ft, this time as re-centerers, to get the bombing back on to the main target. After marking we were coned by searchlights for two minutes – an energetic time, with Geoff hanging on to his equipment like grim death while the others either lost their stomachs or were squashed into their corners by *g* forces. We returned to base unscathed, with a photograph north of the AP.

We were then briefed for the last attack on this unfortunate city, when we flew off on the most hair-raising op of my experience. A storm hung over Hamburg, and it proved impossible to get the Halifax over the clouds. We therefore plunged into them, ice crackling on the wings. Lightning struck not once but half a dozen times, the starboard outer packed up, and as we came out of the clouds at 11,000 ft the flak picked us up. *G for George* picked up a few more holes before Tim located the target area near the Zoo and we marked at zero minus two and a half minutes, apparently first on target.

That was the end of Hamburg for us, and indeed almost the end of Hamburg, although it was bombed again more than once before the end of the war. I saw the city again in July 1945, when on a tour of the Baltic ports. The desolation appeared complete – acre upon acre of lifeless ruins – and I was more than glad that no one could point the finger and say where my bombs had fallen. It was one thing to bomb in the heat of battle and another to see one's contribution against the background of a defeated enemy. There are those who contend that the unusual weather conditions whipped up the fires into an all-consuming firestorm that was a moral retribution on the Germans. Perhaps, but I can only reflect that it was activated by man.

A number of factors contributed to the Hamburg firestorm. The weather had been hot and humid for days, and a strong wind was blowing to fan the flames. The blast bombs and incendiaries had set many of the buildings alight, and the updraught caused by the wind swept the flames and sparks over other buildings. Where the roofs had gone, the walls still stood and acted like a chimney for the fires within. The city's fire crews had been on the go constantly for four days, putting out the fires raised in previous raids, and as a result were scattered all over the city and in no position to attack the firestorm when it began – and it began quickly. The effect of heat and wind created a tremendous updraught that swept the flames right across the city, causing even undamaged buildings to burst into fire. There was no escape; people died as the hot air sucked the very breath from their lungs, and within half an hour of the firestorm starting, 4 square miles of the city centre, home to tens of thousands of people, most of them now crouching in shelters, was fully ablaze. Within an hour the firestorm had swept across the city.

Books have been written about the Hamburg firestorm, and there is no space here for more than an outline. From the point of view of effect, the 27/28 July raid was a triumph. Large areas of the city were destroyed, hundreds of factories and offices were damaged, and the bulk of the population had to flee the city, with a devastating effect on industrial production. All this has been overshadowed by the human cost – the number of people killed.

The exact number of people who died in the Hamburg firestorm has never been accurately computed, but is estimated at around 46,000. According to local records, around 22,000 of these were women and 5,000 were children. It was, by any standard, a horrific event – hard to justify, terrible to contemplate in later, peaceful, years. And yet, at the time, in the context of total war, it may almost have achieved its purpose. The reports filed by the city officials were so terrible that the general public in other parts of Germany were not informed of what had happened to Hamburg; Hitler ordered a news blackout and refused to visit the city. Goering went instead and was greeted by sarcastic shouts of 'Hello, Maier' from the surviving citizens, before SS troops arrived and made their presence felt among the population. Rather more to the point is the comment made by Albert Speer, one of Hitler's inner circle and the German Minister of Production, who wrote: 'Hamburg put the fear of God into me. At the meeting of Central Planning on July 29, I pointed out: If the air raids continue on the present scale, within three months we shall be relieved on a number of questions we are at present discussing. We shall be coasting downhill, smoothly and relatively quickly.'[4]

So the question arises: What if Harris had been able to carry out another devastating raid on the scale of Hamburg, swiftly destroying another German city and then another? Could even the German people, resolute as they were, have stood that? We cannot know, but it is hard to believe that any country, or any people, even the German people, could have withstood more Hamburgs. The problem is that there were no more Hamburgs – terrible though such a thing is to contemplate. The next raid to match the devastation of Hamburg was the Dresden raid nearly two years later, when the war was almost over.

Other German cities were smashed, and by the time the war ended most of them were in ruins, but the process took time. It was the *shock* of Hamburg, the speed and scale of the disaster, that frightened Hitler and his clique; the destruction of other cities over time lacked the same impact. Besides, Harris now had another target for destruction in his sights – Berlin, a city far too large to shatter as Hamburg had been shattered. It would have taken an atomic bomb to destroy Berlin in one strike. Even as it was, some months would elapse before the destruction of Berlin was added to the tasks of Bomber Command.

The ordeal of Hamburg was not over after the Firestorm Raid of 27/28 July. The RAF returned on the 29/30 July, when 707 aircraft dropped another 2,000 tons of bombs on the ruins of the city, devastating more residential areas. Among the aircrew over Hamburg that night was Doug Curtis, a Canadian rear gunner in No. 9 Squadron RAF, whose account indicates that the *Luftwaffe* was already getting back in the game:

> We had dumped our load and were just turning for home when Bud, our mid-upper, spotted an Me 110 almost directly above us. He shouted, 'Dive starboard!', which Jimmy did, hoping the Jerry would not see us. But see us he did, and he peeled over to line us up. He must have been a 'sprog', as he should have known that it was not cricket to attack anyone in the target area. On the other hand it was probably our salvation, as with all the searchlights and the glare from the fires we saw him in time to take evasive action.
>
> It was in the split second before we started our dive that Mort, our navigator, stood up in the astrodome to take his one and only peek at the burning target. Because of our steep dive the gravity forced him to stay there, and he could not make it back to his cubby hole and had to hang on grimly, watching the tracer bullets zip past like fireflies. Seeing the fighter bearing down on us and the bullets coming our way with evil intent decided Mort then and there never to take another peek – and he never did. The fighter only made one pass after flying through our spray of return fire.

This raid caused little loss of life in the city, for most of the population – over a million people – had now fled and were sheltering in the surrounding countryside. Twenty-eight RAF bombers failed to return – a sign that the flak and *Luftwaffe* controllers were getting on top of *Window*.

The last raid on Hamburg, by 740 aircraft on the night of 2/3 August, was a total failure. The weather forecast was inaccurate, and the bombers ran into a large thunderstorm over Germany, a number of bombers being lost through icing; a total of 30 were lost to this cause, flak and fighters. And so the Battle of Hamburg ended.

Apart from providing one of the few examples of a European city shattered by bombing, the Hamburg raids added to the expertise of all the forces engaged in various ways: in the use of *Window* by the RAF, in a definite improvement in marking techniques with the use of H_2S on this coastal target, and, for the Germans, in the introduction of Major Hajo Herrmann's *Wilde Sau* technique, using day fighters over the target area. This last was perhaps the greatest tactical outcome of the these raids. *Wilde Sau* led to a break-up of the *Raum* 'box-fighting' system and more and more German night fighters – twin-engined ones equipped with the *Lichtenstein* as well as Me 109s – began to range at will among the bomber stream – a tactic which became known as *Zahme Sau* – 'Tame Boar'.

The devastation of Hamburg shook Germany to the core. It did not, however, nudge the German leaders in the direction of the conference table. Perhaps if Harris had been able to repeat the process and devastate another German city as completely as Hamburg within the next few days something decisive might have been achieved, but Harris did not have the force for that. His campaign continued while the USAAF mounted a different kind of operation – one which falls outside the main thrust of this book but must be included because it was the first major strike against a product vital to the German military machine: oil.

A number of books covering the end of the Second World War in Europe tend to give the impression that the importance of oil to the German war machine was a belated discovery, first chanced on in late 1944 by US target selectors, and that oil installations were attacked in the face of British opposition. That was not the case. As we have seen, oil was an RAF priority from the first days of the war but, as always, there was a problem. Germany has no natural sources of oil, and obtained the bulk of her supplies from Russia, from the occupied territories and above all from her satellite, Romania. Inside Germany, oil could only be produced synthetically, from coal, and the refineries which could do this were small and heavily defended – precision targets, hard to hit at night, impossible to reach in daylight.

Nevertheless, these synthetic plants were attacked, and oil targets remained an RAF priority, mentioned in all Directives, though, as Harris pointed out, knocking out the synthetic plants was of marginal importance while Germany got the bulk of her oil supplies from the occupied territories and, above all, from the vast, highly productive, oilfields at Ploesti in Romania – fields that supplied about a third of Germany's oil requirement and only needed half of their existing production capacity to do so. Even operating at half capacity, Ploesti could produce a million tons of refined oil products a month. Therefore just damaging the Ploesti oilfields would not be enough: they would have to be destroyed *totally*, and kept that way, to prevent a resumption of production.

Clearly, the Ploesti oilfields had to be attacked, and a small force of thirteen B-24s, known as the 'Halverson Detachment', had attacked them in June 1942; they reached Ploesti without loss, dumped 26 tons of bombs through the overcast, and eleven aircraft arrived back on airfields scattered from Iraq to Turkey. Damage to Ploesti was calculated as 'practically zero', and the raid had also alerted the Germans to the certainty of more and larger attacks.

By mid-1943 Ploesti was surrounded by a flak belt of 88 mm guns and a large quantity of lighter weapons, most of them dug in on the hills overlooking the oilfields to create an umbrella of flak over the target. As local air defence there were four *Gruppen* of Me 109s totalling some 120 aircraft, plus a further 200 Italian fighters, mostly Macchi 200s, ranged on airfields covering likely routes to the target.

In 1943 only the Consolidated B-24 Liberator had the range to reach Ploesti, and then only from bases in North Africa. The B-24 had a maximum range of 3,500 miles and the round trip from North Africa to Ploesti was 2,700 miles, but, allowing for the assembling of formations and other diversions, that range would only just be enough. Even so, during the late spring and early summer of 1943 a large force of B-24s – including the 44th, 93rd and 389th Bomb Groups detached from the Eighth Air Force in Britain – assembled in North Africa as part of General Lewis H. Brereton's Ninth Air Force. Though Ploesti was one vast oilfield, the aim was to attack ten of the main refineries, and the bomb load – a mixture of high explosives (many delayed-action bombs) and incendiaries – was supposed to shatter the oil tanks and start fires.

Early on the morning of 1 August 1943, 178 B-24 bombers of the Ninth Air Force's IX Bomber Command took off for Operation TIDAL WAVE, a low-level mission to destroy Ploesti. The various bomb groups, averaging between 30 and 46 aircraft, were organized in seven 'target forces', each tasked to attack a different refinery, but they were to fly out as one vast formation, before splitting up to attack their targets at very low level – 40 ft or even less (hence the use of delayed-action bombs).

Problems began on take-off at 0710 hrs, when one aircraft of the 98th Bomb Group crashed in flames, all the crew being killed; the B-24 had a tendency to catch fire. One had already been scratched from the mission, and another turned back and crashed soon after take-off, eight of the ten on board being killed. The force continued to lose aircraft as it flew across the Mediterranean, another eleven aircraft aborting the mission and turning back. Another aircraft of the 376th Bomb Group went down over

Corfu. These losses weakened the cohesion of the groups, and the formation was already breaking up when the aircraft crossed the Albanian border and ran into thick cloud. Some groups elected to fly over the cloud, some under it. As a result, the groups were well scattered when, at 1430 hrs, the first aircraft reached their IP and turned for the target, roaring in to the attack at *30 ft*.

Though the aircraft had reached Romania undetected, one group had then got lost and had flown over the capital, Bucharest – one bomber allegedly flew at low level up the main street. Since the Germans had no four-engined aircraft, these were quickly identified as Allied planes. As a result, the entire defence mechanism sprang into action: fighters took off, flak was alerted, and as the bombers went in at Ploesti they came under attack from everything from 88 mm guns and light flak to infantry machine-guns and rifles.

General John A. Brooks, then a major, flew on this mission with the 389th Bomb Group:

Our commander on this mission was Colonel, later General, Jack Wood. We had arrived in England in May, but were told not to unpack and we flew to Benghazi, in North Africa, in June and did a lot of low-level flying over the desert, though it was a while before we found out why.

I want to tell you that 29 aircraft from the 389th took off from Benghazi that day, and we even sent six spare crews to the 98th Bomb Group and they did real well; one of them, Lew Ellis, flew his crippled aircraft back to Africa – an aircraft that should not have been able to fly – with wounded and dead men on board. So 29 aircraft of the 389th took off, and 29 of us reached Ploesti and attacked the target. On the way we ran into cloud, and that split up the formations – some going over it, some under, some round. We followed Colonel Wood over the top and then down, and we went up a long valley, flying very low, towards the target. Then it did get confusing.

All the bombs had delayed-action fuses, so they did not go up under the following aircraft, but even inert bombs caused fires when they struck the oil tanks. There was a great deal of anti-aircraft fire, and we were flying at between 50 and 200 ft. We lost two aircraft over the target, and one of them, flown by Second Lieutenant Lloyd Hughes, was on fire and streaming gasoline even as he went in to bomb. We yelled at him to break off and climb, but he went on in, bombed, and then crashed in flames, only one man surviving. We got Hughes the Medal of Honor for that. I don't know what happened with the other groups, but the 389th hit its target. We lost six aircraft – about 20 per cent – two over the target, two nursed to Turkey and two that went down in Romania.

The details of what happened that day are hard to extract from the heat of combat, but chaos clearly reigned in the skies over Ploesti. Bombers attacked the refineries from all sides, criss-crossing the oilfields in an attempt to find their designated targets, but at low level, speeds of 200 m.p.h. and distracted by flak, navigation was extremely difficult. Some refineries were not bombed at all; others were bombed twice. Most of the bombers 'ranged over the general Ploesti target area and unloaded on anything that looked good'.[5]

Some bombers – up to six, at least – were blown out of the sky when delayed-action bombs dropped by previous aircraft went up underneath them. Others flew so low over burning refineries that the aircraft were coated with soot. Others were raked by machine-guns and light flak firing *down* on them from the surrounding hills. Major Potts, of the 93rd Bomb Group records, 'We went ahead and bombed what we thought was the right target, but probably not more than five planes in my formation actually hit the right target. They thought it was, but they were confused. As we went over – coming in from the south, the wrong direction – the planes on my right and left went down.'

Major Potts was 'deputy lead' of the 93rd Bomb Group and now in command: an 88 mm shell had hit the aircraft of the group commander, Colonel Baker, killing the co-pilot and wounding the Colonel. His aircraft on fire, Colonel Baker pressed home his attack and bombed before his aircraft fell out of the sky, all on board being killed. 'We expected to take losses', said Colonel John Kane of the 98th Bomb Group, who won the Congressional Medal of Honor at Ploesti, 'but I will never forget seeing those big Libs going down like flies.' Five US aircrew received the Medal of Honor for pressing home their attacks at Ploesti at great cost. Of the 38 aircraft of the 98th Bomb Group which reached Ploesti, no fewer than 21 were shot down over the target.

Losses over the target were due to ground fire; most of the enemy fighters had yet to appear, and those that arrived while the raid was in progress could not fly low enough to engage the bombers effectively. When the surviving bombers gained height to fly home, though, it was the turn of the *Luftwaffe*, who punished the surviving bombers all the way to the Albanian frontier and beyond.

The cost of the Ploesti raid makes grim reading. Of the 177 aircraft that took off, eleven turned back and 57 – 34 per cent – were lost on the raid, according to the official figure at the time; however, a later assessment, in 1945, put total losses at 73. Many of the aircraft that made it back were badly damaged, and some had to be written off.

As for the refineries, aerial reconnaissance suggested that the results had been uneven: some refineries had been hit and badly damaged and would be out of commission for about six months; others were completely unscathed. The conclusion was that less than half the refineries' capacity had been damaged; but a later report, coming from intelligence sources, said this conclusion was far too optimistic and little permanent damage had been done.

As happened in Germany, the Ploesti raid was not followed up and full production was soon resumed. Even had the raid achieved all its objectives, however, Germany's oil supplies would hardly have suffered, because the refineries were only operating at half-capacity; to achieve anything worthwhile it would have been necessary to destroy *all* the refineries and keep them out of commission. The USAAF would return to Ploesti, but not for another year and then with different tactics – and fighter cover.

There were tactical failures on this mission. Approaching the oilfields at low level was a mistake, both because the aircraft could not identify their targets and because attacking at low level made the aircraft extremely vulnerable to ground fire. There were also navigation errors, and the cohesion of the bomb groups broke up long before the target was reached, mostly because of cloud cover. The USAAF was finding out, again and again, that wartime flying in the cloudy European skies was a very different proposition to peacetime exercises in the blue skies over the USA – but it had its philosophy for the bombing war, and it was still determined to make it work.

Such losses, however, could not be sustained. If they continued at this level – 34 per cent – the USAAF would be shot out of the sky inside three missions. And they *were* to continue at this level: three weeks after the Ploesti raid, the USAAF took off on another deep-penetration raid, this time into Germany – an attack by two bombardment wings on the ball-bearing works at Schweinfurt and the aircraft factory at Regensburg. This raid, the Schweinfurt–Regensburg mission, was a turning point in the US bomber war.

Avro Lancaster 1

11

The Great Raids:
Schweinfurt–Regensburg to
Peenemunde
August 1943

When the planes came from behind the horizon, I counted them. 'I made a mistake,' I said to myself, and counted them again. I did not want them to be ours, we had sent out so many more.

James Good Brown, chaplain, 381st Bomb Group, 17 August 1943

The Eighth Air Force missions to Schweinfurt and Regensburg on 17 August 1943 formed part of a new offensive, directed from the highest level of command, the Combined Chiefs of Staff. In June 1943 the Allied bombing commanders – Spaatz and Harris – received a new set of instructions in a Directive codenamed *Pointblank*. This Directive, and an update on the war as it was being fought at the command level, will be fully described in the next chapter, but one requirement of the *Pointblank* Directive was a sustained attack on the *Luftwaffe*, with the aim of drastically reducing the strength of its flying arm, in the shape of operational aircraft, and its productive capacity, in the shape of aircraft factories – like the major plant at Regensburg.

The Directive also urged the commanders to strike at those factories producing items vital for a wide range of German war machines. One item singled out in this respect was ball-bearings, which were used in everything from submarines to aircraft, from artillery to tank tracking. Ball-bearing production inside Germany was concentrated in one place, the agreeable little town of Schweinfurt in Bavaria, so on the morning of

17 August 1943 a large force of American bombers took off from their bases in England to wipe the Schweinfurt and Regensburg factories off the industrial map.

By the summer of 1943 the commanders of the Eighth Air Force were fully aware that deep-penetration raids into Germany in daylight were high-risk affairs. They were, however, prepared to accept high losses, reaching 10 per cent or more, and believed that part of the problem was that they still did not have enough aircraft to make up a defensive bombing force – one capable of forcing its way into the heart of Germany, far beyond the range of fighter escort, and of fighting its way home again.

Then, in June 1943, close to the arrival of the *Pointblank* Directive, the magic figure of 300 USAAF bombers was reached. A plan was then prepared to send sixteen bomb groups from the 1st and 4th Bombardment Wings – a force totalling 288 B-17Fs – to attack the ball-bearing factory at Schweinfurt. This plan then expanded as more aircraft became available, and it was then decided to send another force out on the same day, to attack the aircraft plants at Regensburg. Ball-bearing plants and aircraft factories were 'choke points' in the USAAF's strategic bombing doctrine, vital targets which could be destroyed by daylight precision bombing and prove a great loss to the German military-industrial machine.

The plans for this joint mission were quite intricate, but were basically designed to disperse the German fighter strength. The final plan called for 230 aircraft of the 1st Bombardment Wing to attack the three ball-bearing plants at Schweinfurt and then return to the UK, while 146 aircraft of the 4th Wing, which had aircraft equipped with 'Tokyo tanks', would bomb the aircraft factory and airfield at Regensburg and then fly on to North Africa. There would be P-38 and P-47 fighter escorts to the frontiers of Germany and home again from that point, while a force of B-17s from the Fifteenth Air Force in North Africa would cause a useful diversion by bombing airfields at Istres near Marseilles in the south of France. Meanwhile, the RAF and other USAAF groups would fly diversion raids to other targets in northern France. The important element in the plan was that the two large missions should enter Germany *together*, to disperse and confuse the fighter controllers. If this could be achieved, the missions would probably succeed; if not, they could be costly.

The commanders of the USAAF recognized that this was a high-risk mission, and General Ira Eaker, for one, was dead set against it: 'There was always someone who wanted to do something facile to get a quick result. We were pushed into this before we were ready and I protested bitterly'.[1] Another person who had distinct reservations about attacking Schweinfurt and Regensburg was Air Chief Marshal Harris, who was being urged to follow up the USAAF daylight precision attacks with a night area attack. Harris regarded these piecemeal attacks on what others saw as the vital supply links in the German military machine as 'panaceas'

– attacks that looked good on paper, promised much, but achieved very little.

The Air Staff had been pressing Harris to have a go at Schweinfurt for some time. Harris had rejected this pressure on the grounds that, first, Schweinfurt was a precision target that needed a daylight strike and, rather more to the point, smiting Schweinfurt would do nothing to shorten the war, since, although ball-bearings were certainly important, the Germans would have other sources of supply from neutral countries like Sweden, and would maintain large stocks in some safe location. Harris wanted the Eighth to join him in an all-out attack on Berlin, arguing that if they did to Berlin what they had done to Hamburg the Germans would have to end the war. The USAAF commanders were unconvinced by this argument and pressed on with their efforts to get results with daylight precision bombing.

What happened over Schweinfurt and Regensburg was simply a larger and more horrific extension of what had happened over Ploesti. There were, in addition, a number of tactical errors, and these will be picked out as the story develops. But, as often happens when things go wrong in war, things began to go wrong at the start.

The joint mission should have begun at 0545 hrs on the morning of 17 August, but there was an immediate problem. Some of the airfields were 'socked in' by cloud, and no aircraft could take off. The first delay was official – a message from Brigadier-General Anderson at VIII Bomber Command, delaying take-off for one hour. There was then a round of telephone discussions between Anderson and his two commanders. General Robert B. Williams of the 1st Wing could afford to wait a while, as his aircraft were coming back to Britain. Curtis LeMay of the 4th Wing had no such latitude: his aircraft had to fly on to North Africa and needed every hour of daylight – and every gallon of fuel – they could get. Waiting or hanging about in flight was not an option for LeMay's wing.

The commanders agonized over what to do for some time; then Anderson made a decision. LeMay's 4th Wing, bound for Regensburg and North Africa, would take-off at once. The Schweinfurt force, which had more time to spare, would wait a little longer. The result was that the plan for a co-ordinated raid, designed to split the German fighter force, at once broke down: the *Luftwaffe* pilots were being handed a two-course feast.

Then there came another problem. The 4th Wing took off at 0620 hrs, but the cloud cover had thickened and the groups had a great deal of difficulty – and used a lot of precious fuel – in finding each other and getting into their 'lead', 'high' and 'low' group formations. Eventually, 139 B-17s of the 4th Wing, with a strong fighter escort of P-47 Thunderbolts and P-38 Lightnings, crossed the Belgian coast near Antwerp, with two hours and 425 miles of hostile air to go before they reached Regensburg. They were in three large formations, not tightly closed up, and, when the US fighters turned back, the bombers were immediately engaged by German fighters from II/JG 1 and III/JG 26. The bulk of the fighters, though warned by *Freya*, were still assembling or waiting for the US fighters to turn back, but from the moment the first FW 190s and Me 109s spotted the American *Pulks* crossing the Rhine the bombers were under constant attack – an attack augmented by a storm of flak rising from every town the bombers passed over.

Eventually, bombers began to go down, as this intelligence report of the 390th Bomb Group grimly records:

All attacks were persistent and vicious. Approximately 95 FW 190s, 25 Me 109s and 10 Ju 88s encountered. These attacks were in running relays from coast to Regensburg and definitely as far as rallying point. One series of attacks began at French coast and lasted for 30 minutes. Another combat began in the Regensburg area and lasted from 30–40 minutes. The attacking aircraft were very aggressive and attacked from three to nine o'clock (beam attacks) or from ten to two o'clock, continuing right through the formation. Others attacked out of the sun.

At 1110 hrs, one B-17 was seen going down. No chutes were seen. Another B-17 was seen descending north of Heidelburg; ten chutes seen. Twenty miles north of Nuremburg a B-17 was attacked by four FW 190s and disintegrated. Just before reaching Regensburg a B-17 of the 390th high squadron left formation with one engine out and was seen being attacked by fighters and losing altitude. No chutes seen. A/C No. 17 with two engines on fire and whole left wing burning exploded before reaching Regensburg at 1130 hrs; four or five chutes seen. A/C 313 observed going down just after Regensburg was reached at about 1150; no chutes seen. Two A/C high squadron left formation after leaving Regensburg. At 1157 one B-17 near Munich went down in a steep glide; no chutes were seen. A/C 305 at 1405 fell back slowly and headed for Spain, as per instructions from CO 390th Group. Another B-17 from 402nd Wing was seen afire and it crashed off the Italian coast, 50 miles from Bone. A/C No 333 was ditched; crew in dinghies, all safe. A/C 310 went down 25 miles from Bone, two dinghies seen. Within three miles of that location, three B-17s were ditched.[2]

This sad litany of loss comes from just one US bomb group.

When the first of the attacking fighters turned for their bases to refuel and rearm, other *Luftwaffe* fighters started to make their now classic frontal attacks, and as the big bombers droned steadily south and east a pattern developed. The German fighters, like children using a playground slide, came charging in from ahead, passed through the American formation with all guns firing, dived away, climbed, and flew back to the front of the American formations, where they turned to come in again. Three B-17s were shot down in quick succession and a large number received battle damage, but the US bomb groups held on. The bulk of the *Luftwaffe* fighters were running short of fuel and had to land. While they were refuelling, the 4th Wing's B-17s forged on into Germany.

Meanwhile, the 1st Bombardment Wing was still on the ground in England. Take-off was put back to 1118 hrs, and, after they had taken off, the nine regular 1st Wing bomb groups and the additional 'Composite' bomb group, made up of spare squadrons from various airfields, then had to get into their standard operational formation before crossing the Channel coast. This took time – almost two hours in the overcast – and it was not until 1313 hrs that the first aircraft of the 1st Bombardment Wing crossed the English coast by Shoeburyness. As they did so they were immediately picked up on German radar.

The German fighters were having a field day. Deep in Germany, a force of around 130 unescorted B-17s was being attacked by scores of German fighters; now a second US force was starting out, and every radar post, flak gun and fighter station between the Channel and the Rhine was on the alert and ready to give it a murderous reception. This Schweinfurt force was in for an especially hard time, for the Germans had no idea that the Regensburg force was to fly on to North Africa. The Germans anticipated that, after they had bombed, the 4th Wing survivors would turn back towards the UK, and so every available fighter, from Schipol in Holland to Brittany in France, was now mustering astride their route to ambush them on the way home.

The Schweinfurt aircraft were heading into this trap with every mile they covered. Estimates vary, but some 250 fighters, most of them Me 109s, took off to attack the American aircraft, most of them concentrating east of the Belgian town of Eppen, where a shortage of fuel would oblige the US escorts to turn back. There is no real need to cover what happened east of Eppen in detail – it is better imagined than described. But this account, from Eddie Deerfield of the 303rd Bomb Group, certainly sets the scene:

At the briefing we were told that the target was a complex of ball-bearing plants and the war would be shortened by six months if we pulverized it. P-47 Thunderbolts were to escort us to the German border, then the limit of their range, and when we got there they waggled their wings in salute and peeled away. Within minutes we were under attack by swarms of enemy fighters.

There were deadly 109s and FW 190s joined by the relatively cumbersome Me 110s and Ju 88s; the Germans were throwing everything they had at us. A 20 mm shell ploughed through our right wing, missing the gas tanks by inches, and the bombardier called out what looked like .30 mm holes in the cowling of the No. 2 engine – and we were still an hour from the target.

The box formations out on the far left and far right seemed to be getting most of the attention, and Fortresses were falling everywhere. As they dropped out of the protection of the formation, the enemy fighters roared in for the kill. Parachutes started peppering the sky as American airmen jumped from their burning B-17s; what sickened me to the point of tears was the Fortresses that exploded in mid-air, giving the crews no chance of escape.

We bombed the ball-bearing works at 1511 hrs and turned for home; from the fires and smoke it appeared the bombers had devastated the target. Then the Me 109s and FW 190s swooped in again. Our aircraft suffered no hits on the return journey, but B-17s in other formations were being pounded unmercifully. It was a bloody re-enactment of the inbound flight as American parachutes filled the air and more B-17s plunged to earth or became fireballs.

The surviving aircraft – many with wounded men aboard – landed at their bases about 1800 hrs. At the post-mission debriefing, it turned out that, of the 194 B-17s that crossed the enemy coast, 36 were shot down with the loss of 360 crew members. The Eighth's 'acceptable loss rate' at this time was 5 per cent. The Schweinfurt loss rate was 20 per cent.

Between Eppen and Schweinfurt the German fighters *chewed* into the US bombers, all the way there and all the way back. They came swarming in from 'twelve o'clock high' and from the beam, curving through the American formations, machine-gun and cannon flame glittering along their wings, showing their bellies as they broke off the attack and dived away.

Flak added its contribution, damaging aircraft and killing crewmen. Crippled aircraft falling behind or out of formation were hacked down by the German fighters, but still the bombers pressed on – every gun in action, every plane struggling to hold station. An RAF fighter pilot who saw the US bombers heading east into this slaughter wrote later that 'The disciplined flying of the remaining units was outstanding.'

Meanwhile the Regensburg force, now down to 122 aircraft, was nearing its target. Fourteen aircraft had been shot down and three had lost formation or jettisoned their bombs since crossing the Channel Coast. This represented about 10 per cent of the force – hardly 'acceptable losses' at this stage of the operation. When those remaining reached the IP the target was clear and they went in to bomb at heights between 16,000 and 20,000 ft, the pilots turning the control of the aircraft over to the lead bombardiers and the Norden bombsight; the first bombs fell on the Regensburg factory at 1146 hrs. All the bomb groups claimed to have bombed accurately, the 94th and 385th going round twice in order to do so. The 95th and 100th Groups were the last to bomb, using incendiaries, and the raid ended at 12.09 hrs, having lasted just 22 minutes.

Now the surviving aircraft had to reassemble and fly to North Africa, 1,000 miles and five hours' flying time away. Three crippled aircraft left the formation over the Alps and headed for Switzerland. Landing safely in neutral territory, the crews were eventually returned to Britain. There were no more fighter attacks as the rest flew south, but the battle damage already inflicted was having an effect: two B-17s went down over Italy, and two more went into the Mediterranean, all the crews being taken prisoner. This freedom from further attack was probably due to the German fighters south of the Alps having been drawn off by the bombers from North

Africa attacking the airfields near Marseilles. Even so, aircraft from the Regensburg force continued to fall into the sea, four more being lost before the North African coast came in sight, two because they ran out of fuel; all the crews were picked up by RAF rescue launches. Late that afternoon, at 1650 hrs UK time (1550 hrs local time), the Regensburg force started to land in North Africa; 122 aircraft had made it, 24 had been lost – 16 per cent of the force.

The Schweinfurt groups were still taking punishment, the German fighters using bombs and rockets as well as cannon and machine-guns to back up the usual storm of flak rising from the ground. Between crossing the Dutch coast and reaching the IP the Schweinfurt force lost 24 B-17s – ten more than the Regensburg force had lost up to this point. Around 198 bombers passed over the IP, and the lead group – made up of the 91st, 381st and 101st (Composite) Groups – bombed three minutes later. Not surprisingly, this was hardly a precision attack: the bombs fell over an area four miles in length and up to two miles from the factories.

The second formation – from the 351st, 384th and 306th (Composite) Groups – bombed too early and most of their effort was expended on open fields and on a small village a mile from the nearest ball-bearing factory. The third formation – from the 92nd, 305th and 306th Bomb Groups – was also unlucky. The Schweinfurt defenders had now ignited their smoke pots, and a great cloud of smoke obscured the target – leading many aircrew to assume that the factories were on fire. This third formation therefore elected to bomb the town centre, and the bombs from the lead group of this formation, the 306th Bomb Group, landed plumb in the heart of the town; the bombs of the other groups were released too soon and fell in open country. The final formation – from the 303rd, 379th and 103rd (Composite) Groups – stood no chance of finding an unobscured target and there are no reliable details on where its incendiaries fell. When the photographs were analysed later it seemed that only three of the twelve groups had bombed anywhere near the target and Schweinfurt's production of ball-bearings was unaffected.

The attackers incurred further loss. Schweinfurt was a heavily defended target, and the bomb groups running in from the IP were too big and too steady to miss. Many aircraft were hit and damaged by flak, a number of crewmen were killed, and three B-17s crashed within a few miles of the town. Twenty-nine bombers had now been lost from the Schweinfurt force – and they still had to get home. As they did so, the slaughter continued.

The final tally from the Schweinfurt–Regensburg mission is as follows. A total of 376 aircraft took off from the UK. After 'aborts', 361 aircraft crossed the Dutch coach and 301 returned to the UK or reached North Africa, so 60 aircraft were shot down on the mission; eleven aircraft were so badly damaged that they had to be written off later, and a further 162 aircraft received battle damage. The overall loss rate, including aircraft written off, was therefore 19 per cent. As for the casualties, 482 aircrew were lost, over 100 being killed.

The Eighth Air Force lost as many bombers on the Schweinfurt–Regensburg mission as it had lost in all its missions between August 1942 and March 1943. German losses were slight: the gunners claimed to have shot down 228 German fighters, a total which equals or perhaps exceeds the entire *Luftwaffe* contingent committed that day; actual German losses were 27.[3]

The USAAF was always willing to accept high losses in pursuit of victory. The USA wanted to finish the job and bring the boys home again, and was prepared to accept heavy losses in order to do so. The RAF frequently lost similar numbers of aircraft and pressed on with its attacks undaunted, but it was conceded that a *consistent* loss rate in excess of 4 per cent would soon bring RAF bomber operations to a halt. At a consistent 4 per cent loss rate, only thirteen out of every 100 aircrew members would survive their first tour of 30 missions. Having larger resources in men and machines – even if they were not available in the ETO in 1943 – the USAAF could contemplate higher losses, but the Eighth could not consistently take the current level of casualties. It was now obvious even to the most devoted advocate of daylight precision bombing that, until the Eighth found a way to cope with European weather and German fighters, daylight missions into Germany were just not on.

After Schweinfurt–Regensburg, the USAAF turned its attention to a number of the long-standing problems affecting its operations: the weather, navigation and target-finding. Here again it had the benefit of RAF experience and co-operation. The two air forces had always worked closely together, and this liaison now paid off. It was accepted that, since European weather was frequently poor, 'blind bombing' was inevitable, even in daylight, and the *Gee*-box and H_2S – known to the Eighth as H_2X or 'Mickey' – were introduced into US aircraft. Radar jamming, already in progress, was stepped up and, following on the growing success of the RAF Pathfinder Force and to cope with navigation and weather problems, the Eighth created the Scouting Force, a unit of which was attached to every US air force. Richard Atkins of the Scouting Force Association explains some of their duties:

> Aerial reconnaissance, in the usual sense, was not a Scout mission. Departing approximately twenty minutes ahead of the bomber stream, their primary duties in each of the three Scouting Forces, were (1) lead the bomber stream through en-route bad weather; (2) scout the primary target and inform the mission commander as to whether it could be bombed visually, advise him of alternative approaches to the target if the weather was marginal, (3) scout secondary and tertiary targets and be prepared to lead the stream if the commander chose to go to an alternate; (4) observe bombing results; (5) observe bomber formations and inform commanders, since tight formations were

one of the keys to survival; and (6), when the occasion demanded, defend the bomber stream.

While the basic concept was the same for each Scouting Force, there were a lot of variations within the three Forces. For example, it became standard procedure for the 3SF to assist in forming up the bomber stream over England using the three or four Scouts that did not fly that mission. A Scout formation was usually eight aircraft with one airborne spare, leaving the balance at home base. On occasion a single scout would be sent on a special mission, but two was generally the minimum number.

Each Scouting Force had its own and very distinct personality, formed by several factors: its commander, the bomb division it supported, the fighter group that supported it, and the particular period of the war. This is still reflected in the vets, when we meet at our reunions.

Scouting Force pilots, many of them tour-expired bomber pilots who knew what the bomb groups were up against, made a significant contribution to the success of the bomber war. One of them was Dave Mullen:

The B-17 was the most enjoyable aircraft I ever flew. I arrived in the UK an experienced B-17 pilot and used the B-17 on every kind of Scouting Force job: weather recon, photo recon, dropping lifeboats, air and sea rescue. At Wormingfold the P-51 Mustang pilots used to do 'peel ups' – great swoops over the runway – before landing, so we did the same in a B-17 until the CO put a stop to it, saying it would be his butt if some bigwheel saw us landing like that.

I flew 30 missions with the 833rd Bomb Squadron, 486th Bomb Group; in that time I lost all my officers to enemy action by the sixth mission. The squadron gave me a new co-pilot, navigator, and bombardier for thirteen missions before I was given a new crew that had lost its pilot. During this time Dick Grace was assigned to our group; you won't know him, but Dick was a famous Hollywood stunt pilot, who did the crashes in the movie *Wings* and wrote a book called *Squadron of Death* in which he mentions breaking 55 bones in his body. I had Dick for two missions and, frankly, he could not fly the B-17 and left our group to fly B-24s in combat.

The Germans were well aware of what the USAAF really needed – a long-range fighter. The *Luftwaffe* pilots, flying much-developed but old types of fighter, were already not keen to engage the more modern P-38s and P-47s and preferred to wait until these escorts had turned back before attacking the bombers; a fast, long-range Allied fighter would make this tactic impossible. But until the Eighth had a long-range escort fighter – and one that could take on the short-range fighter in combat – the far-flung targets in Germany were out of bounds. This lesson was learned on the Schweinfurt–Regensburg mission, but was quickly forgotten. In the following month, September 1943, 338 B-17s were sent against Stuttgart. The weather was again foul, German flak and fighters put up a stout defence, and 45 bombers were shot down, including the *entire* 563rd Bomb Squadron.

Then, on 14 October 1943, two months after the Schweinfurt–Regensburg mission, the Mighty Eighth flew to Schweinfurt again – and *again* 60 bombers were shot down. These losses achieved nothing. Clouds or smoke blinded the bombardiers, and very few bombs hit the target; attempting precision bombing in these conditions simply did not work – and, without a long-range fighter to assist the bombers, Germany remained a killing ground for the *Luftwaffe*.

On the night of the day when the USAAF flew the Schweinfurt–Regensburg mission, 17 August 1943, RAF Bomber Command launched an operation that was arguably one of the most important bombing raids of the war. After months of careful preparation it attacked the German V1 and V2 rocket factories at Peenemunde on the Baltic Coast. At Peenemunde the Germans were developing weapons which, had they been ready in time, would certainly have disrupted the invasion of Europe and could have had a decisive effect on the outcome of the entire war.

Peenemunde was an area target, but one with precision elements; the aim was to destroy the whole research and industrial complex, but blitzing certain parts of the facility – including the homes of the leading scientists – was especially important. Destroying Peenemunde was considered so important that the crews were told that if they failed to do the job on the first night they would have to return again and again, night after night, in the face of growing opposition, until the target was destroyed – whatever the cost. As to why this target was so important, the crews were told only that it was a plant developing radar aids for fighters; the word 'rocket' was never mentioned.

The rocket research station at Peenemunde had been set up in 1937 in conditions of great secrecy. Peenemunde lies about 100 miles north of Berlin and 70 miles from Stettin. Before the war it was a fishing village, but after 1939 the rocket laboratories and workshops steadily expanded and hordes of workers and scientific staff made their homes there. The chief scientist at Peenemunde was Dr Wernher von Braun, who in later years became a US citizen and the architect of the NASA space programme that put a man on the moon. In 1941 forced labour workers arrived from France and Holland, and in 1942 a small concentration camp was set up at Peenemunde to provide slave labour. This fact was well known to Wernher von Braun, who later became director of the Dora V2 production plant in the Hartz Mountains, where slave workers caught slacking on the production line were routinely hanged.

Secrecy remained a top priority at Peenemunde from the outset. There was strict Gestapo surveillance and censorship of letters and phone calls, false stories were planted in the press regarding the purpose of the site, and plenty of barbed wire and a blackout on news and restrictions on leave were deployed to keep the secret from the prying eyes and ears of Allied intelligence. Even so, the secret did leak out, partly in documents smuggled by some disenchanted German scientist to the British Embassy in Oslo shortly before the outbreak of war, partly from leaks coming from foreign workers, and partly from aerial reconnaissance and *Enigma*. Something as big and important as Germany's rocket programme could not be fully concealed, but it was not until 1943 that its full extent was known and Peenemunde was identified as the main research centre.

By that time the German rocket programme had already developed three types of weapon. The first was not a rocket at all but a flying bomb, the V1 – called a 'buzz bomb' by the British or a 'doodlebug' by those Americans serving in the UK who saw it in action in 1944. This flying bomb would be launched against Britain from sites on the Channel coast of France. The V1 was not a precision weapon and could not be precisely targeted, but when its fuel ran out the bomb would fall on whatever lay below. This fuel cut-off time could be calculated, and the V1s were intended to fall on London. The V2, on the other hand, was a proper rocket – the forerunner of the moon-mission space rocket. The V2 could reach the stratosphere and be targeted far more accurately than the V1, to consistently hit large city targets like London or Antwerp. It could also provide the perfect delivery system for an atomic bomb. The third device – less advanced than the other two in 1943 – was a form of long-range gun that would be sunk in the chalk on the French coast and subject London and the south-east of England to a constant rain of heavy shells. Once the existence of such weapons was known, Peenemunde had to be destroyed, and the task was passed to Air Chief Marshal Harris and RAF Bomber Command.

Harris disliked anything that diverted his attention from the 'Main Offensive' against the German cities, but he received a direct order from Portal to attack Peenemunde and saw at once that it was no 'panacea' target. The problem was how to hit it so hard that rocket research and production would cease or the rocket programme be at least delayed for many months. This would mean destroying Peenemunde and killing as many as possible of the people who worked there, especially the scientists. Having studied the aerial photographs that were now being taken – discreetly but on a regular basis by the RAF high-flying Spitfires – Harris and his staff identified three main areas for attack: the experimental station, the V2 production works, and the accommodation areas.

These would be the subject of specific attention and carefully marked with TIs. But the entire area was to be heavily bombed. Harris was in effect proposing a mixture of precision bombing and area bombing, and to achieve the best possible results he intended to employ the entire strength of Bomber Command.

Peenemunde lay 500 miles from the Bomber Command bases, and a return flight of 1,000 miles, most of it over enemy territory, to hit one small target on the Baltic coast was not something to be undertaken lightly. Harris did, however, have two assets: No. 617 Squadron and the crews of Air Vice-Marshal Cochrane's 5 Group – a group well used to striking specific targets – and the Pathfinder Force squadrons of Air Vice-Marshal Bennett's 8 (PFF) Group, which was now able to mark targets with considerable accuracy, especially if using *Oboe* and H_2S. Peenemunde was beyond *Oboe* range, but, being on the coast, was very suitable for H_2S.

In addition to bombing accuracy, when rehearsing for Peenemunde Air Vice-Marshal Cochrane made his 5 Group squadrons practise 'time and distance' bombing. In this the bombers fly over two known points close to the target, set their 'time' over that 'distance', and then, using this precise information, work out how long it will take from the second marker to the actual target, where their bombs can be released. In the absence of radar aids and at night or in cloud, 'time and distance' marking was fairly effective, *provided the two marker points could be seen and identified*. As an aid to this, and unlike most other Bomber Command targets, Peenemunde would be attacked in the full-moon period.

It has been claimed that Cochrane offered to attack Peenemunde with 5 Group alone; if so, this offer was rejected and 5 Group eventually provided the last wave of the attack, using 'time and distance' as well as observation of the fires started by earlier attacks as an aid to accuracy. The raid would involved the entire Command and, apart from PFF marking, would involve the use of a 'master bomber' over the target to direct the Main Force squadrons during the actual attack. This role went to Group Captain John Searby, the commander of No. 83 Squadron in 8 Group, formerly a colleague of Guy Gibson on No. 106 Squadron of 5 Group.

Thus directed, 596 heavy bombers – 324 Lancasters, 218 Halifaxes and 54 Stirlings – took off for Peenemunde. After losses and 'early returns', 560 aircraft attacked the target, dropping 1,800 tons of bombs. The aircraft composition is interesting: the twin-engined Wellingtons had gone from the RAF inventory and the Stirling force was clearly declining; from now on the weight of the RAF attack would be carried and steadily increased by Lancaster and Halifax bombers.

An account of the Peenemunde operation comes from Tommy Bishop of No. 12 Squadron, flying from Wickenby in East Anglia:

> The rendezvous was over Cromer, at a designated time depending on what wave you were in. We were in the second wave, and on leaving the English coast we went down to 200–300 ft until fifteen minutes from the Danish coast, then up to 8,000 ft. PFF dropped markers at the turning points, and bomb-aimers did a spot of map reading over the many identifiable pinpoints on the way. Sharp turn to starboard after bombing to avoid the flak defences of the Kiel Canal, and watch out for the heavy guns on Sylt. We had no H_2S.
>
> All went according to plan except for one brush with an Me 109, who

sheared off after our gunners gave him a burst. Bombing from 8,000 ft was a new experience for us, and we were credited with a direct hit from our photo-plot. As usual the navigator – me – worked like the clappers before we got out of *Gee* range 200–250 miles from the Danish coast, after which it was DR all the way there and back. Closeted in my 'office' most of the time, it was somewhat alarming to hear reports of aircraft being shot down, usually in flames, but once clear of the Danish coast it was a race to get back to base after a pretty monotonous tiring trip of seven hours.

Another account comes from Geoff Whitten, a navigator with No. 35 Squadron PFF:

We had just got back from an eight-hour round trip to Turin and the words 'Ops tonight' were especially pregnant for us, as this would be the last op of our tour – and a long one, to somewhere we could not find on the naviga-tor's chart: Peenemunde.

We were told that it was a place where radar aids were being developed against air raids, and if we did not eliminate it tonight we would have to go back the following night and again on subsequent nights if necessary. This attack was being made in full moonlight – a plus for enemy fighters – and visibility was exceptionally good too. I was able to announce that we would arrive over the target area just in time to perform our duty as final backers-up for the first phase of the raid, and drop our green markers on the best primary TI we could see. The target area was a kaleidoscope of colour, but one being rapidly submerged under a smokescreen. The master bomber was quickly in evidence, as some bomb loads were being wasted in the Baltic, and he began to broadcast, warning crews of this tendency.

Having dropped our own bombs and TIs we left the target area, losing height from 8,000 ft to 2,000 ft, Jimmy Davidson telling us that, in view of all the mayhem he could see developing, he proposed a low-level run as far as the North Sea, there being little risk of running into land over 600 ft. This quickly looked like a wise decision, because by now the *Luftwaffe* fighters were arriving and I saw enough in the next few minutes – bombers burning or falling, above or to either side – to realize that a high price was being paid for this operation. We made a very welcome landing at Graveley at 0415 hrs, almost exactly 24 stressful hours after our return from Turin.

The Peenemunde raid was successful, but it did not go entirely to plan. PFF marking was not accurate, and the first TIs fell on the labour camp and not on the rocket workshops. Fortunately this error was quickly detected by the master bomber, and the follow-up PFF crews then marked the right targets, which were soundly bombed. A later estimate held that the attack on Peenemunde put back the introduction of rockets into service by three vital months; the first V2 rocket fell on London on 8 September 1944, three months after Operation OVERLORD.

Losses were heavy: 40 aircraft were shot down, seventeen of them from

5 Group, which was rounding off the attack when the German night fighters arrived. The overall loss figure was nearly 7 per cent; 5 Group lost 14.5 per cent. One of the German fighter pilots in action that night was Peter Spoden, flying an Me 110 from out of Pachim:

> The first plane I shot down was on 18 August 1943, at Peenemunde. I shot down a Lancaster at about one in the morning, and I was so excited at the time. There were two of us in the Me 110, myself and the radar operator. Our group had the *Schrage Musik* cannon, and on the following morning, about five, I went to see the plane I had shot down. The crashed plane was still smoking and smouldering, and we saw the bodies – all youngsters like me, but terribly burnt. I told myself, 'That is what you have done', and after that I could not go again to any plane I had shot down. I asked the man who was guarding the plane, 'No survivors?' and he said there was a survivor in the fire station
>
> So I went over there and saw a young man in a white pullover and I spoke in English and asked him, 'Are you from this crew?' and he said he was and that his name was Sparkes. He asked if I was the night fighter, and I said yes and we shook hands – but not in a close or friendly way. Long after the war I got his address from Martin Middlebrook – William Sparkes of No. 44 Squadron – and wrote him a letter, but he never replied. Another flyer from another Lancaster I shot down did reply, and he became quite a close friend. I am very unhappy that I killed, among the 23 aircraft I shot down in the war, maybe 150 people.

Losses were also heavy on the ground at Peenemunde, especially among the civilians and the forced-labour workers, for a number of bombs fell on their camp at Tressenheide, where some 500 people were killed. About 170 civilians were killed in the bombing of the main facility.

Peenemunde marked a development in the defensive capability of the German night-fighter force. It was over Peenemunde that the German Me 110s first used their upward-firing '*Schrage Musik*' cannon – a highly effective device that was to take a heavy toll of British bombers during the rest of the war. It is estimated that Me 110s using *Schrage Musik* – German slang for jazz – shot down six RAF bombers at Peenemunde, and Peter Spoden explains how:

> We were the first to use *Schrage Musik*. We had two guns, 20 mm, and a reflex sight, and you flew in such a way that you kept your eyes on the sight as you flew under the bomber. The best point to attack was at the two engines, on the left or right side of the wing, because there were the fuel tanks. We stayed about 50 to 80 metres away – sometimes 100 metres. On some nights the visibility was pretty bad and the first indication that you were getting close was when you felt the prop wash, the turbulence from the bombers' propellers. Then you knew you were into something, and if you were lucky you were in the bomber stream.

The development of *Schrage Musik* is another example of how the German fighter pilots found and then attacked vulnerable areas on Allied bombers. British bombers used radar devices and carried heavy bomb loads; there was no space between the large bomb bay and the H_2S dome for a belly or 'ball' turret on the lines of the one used in the B-17. This meant that RAF bombers could be attacked in relative safely from their blind spot below, and from 1943 *Luftwaffe* pilots consistently attacked British bombers from this position – hence the 'banking search' flight pattern adopted by wiser and more experienced RAF pilots, to provide a view of that dangerous area under the aircraft.

The *Schrage Musik* gun was adapted for the Me 110 from an upward-firing gun used on German seaplanes, which usually flew low over the sea and therefore needed upward defence. The Me 110 stalked its prey using *Lichtenstein* radar, then flew up close from below, staying in the bomber's blind spot until it opened fire. To avoid a devastating explosion from the bomb bay, a *Schrage Musik*-equipped fighter usually concentrated its fire on the fuel tanks in the wings; once these were on fire the bomber was doomed. The RAF crews seem to have been unaware of *Schrage Musik*, perhaps because so few of the bombers attacked with it survived to bring the information home. At any event they took no special steps to counter it, apart from the 'banking search' flight pattern which the crews were warned to use at every operational briefing.

All the raids, operations and missions covered in the last two chapters have each been the subject of entire books. They are well known because they were important and were carried out with great skill and gallantry, but they are included here because they represent steps in the technical and tactical side of the bomber war and illustrate the way in which the air battle over Germany was still in a state of flux.

During 1943 new devices were introduced: *Window* and Wallis's bouncing bomb, and the *Schrage Musik* cannon. New tactics also came in: the use of the master bomber and 'time and distance' marking for the British, the use of *Wilde Sau* fighter tactics by the Germans. We see the US attacking area targets at low level by day – Ploesti – and the RAF attacking precision targets at low level by night – the Ruhr dams. We have also seen how bombers could devastate entire cities by night and the Eighth gallantly persisting in its attempts to make daylight precision bombing work, without radar aids to cope with European weather or a long-range fighter to beat off the German fighters.

None of these developments actually did a great deal by itself to win the bomber war. They were only steps to that end, providing tactics that might be useful or lessons that had yet to be learned. For a look at the wider picture during this time we must return to the broader battle and examine what was happening to RAF Bomber Command and the USAAF and not least to the actions of the High Command in the pivotal year of 1943.

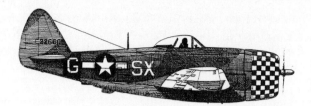

P-47D Thunderbolt

12

The *Pointblank* Directive
June 1943

The mission of the United States and British Bomber forces as prescribed by the Combined Chiefs of Staff at Casablanca . . . is to conduct a joint US–British air offensive to accomplish the progressive dislocation and disruption of the German military, industrial and economic system, and the undermining of the morale of the German people to a point where their capacity for armed resistance is fatally weakened.

Prelude to the *Pointblank* Directive, 14 May 1943

The Allied air force commanders, Portal and Harris, Spaatz and Eaker, did not fight a private war over Germany. They did not decide policy or have an entirely free hand in choosing targets. They were allowed a considerable degree of discretion in what they did, and rather more discretion in how they did it, but their overall aims and efforts were dictated by the Combined Chiefs of Staff Committee, which was composed of the US and British Chiefs of Staff. They also had to conform to decisions taken at national- or Allied-government level, while the air-force commanders were further controlled by their national Air Staffs. As we have seen, these decisions were sent to the bomber commanders in a series of 'Directives', covering bombing priorities and the types of target to attack.

These Directives had the aim of keeping strategic bombing qualities within the framework of overall Allied priorities, and they came out frequently. Bomber Command alone received about 47 Directives from the Air Staff between 1940 and 1945 – an average of one every four weeks.

The Combined Chiefs' Directives were often sent to the bomber commanders via one or other of the Chiefs of Staff. On 10 June 1943 one such Directive to Spaatz – for onward transmission to Harris and Eaker –

concerned the need for a *united* effort to destroy Germany's industrial base, in view of the upcoming Allied invasion of Europe – Operation OVERLORD – which was now moving to the head of the Allied agenda. To trace the origins of this new Directive we must go back to the Casablanca Conference.

At Casablanca in January 1943, the Allied Chiefs accepted that they would not be able to mount a successful invasion of Western Europe until some time in 1944. Before then, however, a great deal had to be done to weaken the enemy. One requirement was to end the submarine menace in the North Atlantic, and that task was in hand. So too was action to drive Italy out of the war. Another requirement was to reduce the strength of the *Luftwaffe* by attacking its plants on the ground and its fighters in the air. That latter task was the aim of the Directive of 10 June, a paper which came to be known as the *Pointblank* Directive.

Pointblank was an extension of the Directive issued after Casablanca which aimed to harness the united efforts of both US and RAF Bomber Commands to the destruction of the German industrial and military machine – a task which, though sharing many views and methods, they had hitherto been tackling in their own individual styles. *Pointblank* can in fact be traced back to the plan produced by Brigadier-General Eaker on 12 April 1943, proposing a 'Combined Bomber Offensive'. This plan, generally known as the 'Eaker Plan', pushed the point that 'it was better to cause a high degree of destruction in a few really essential industries than cause a small degree of destruction in many industries'. In short, 'precision' bombing would pay greater dividends than 'area' bombing.

This was true, up to a point, but the practical limitations were obvious. Setting the Dams Raid aside, it was currently *impossible*, in early 1943, to carry out precision bombing attacks in Germany, by day or by night, and none too easy to carry them out anywhere else in Occupied Europe. At night the RAF could not achieve sufficient accuracy, and by day the *Luftwaffe* was shooting the US VIII Bomber Command out of the sky. In any event, the only way to keep a German industrial plant inoperative was by *continuous* bombing – one raid simply would not do it – and the cost of this, in aircraft and lives, would be prohibitive.

That apart, the idea that attacking one industry, one industrial complex, or even a series of them, could seriously advance the prosecution of the war was itself debatable. The Germans had had years to diversify their industry, to move plants, and to duplicate facilities and ensure new sources of supply; they would have been foolish not to do all this. Bombing – precision or area – had to be seen as one element in the Allied military machine – one which concentrated on crushing German industrial capacity and carrying the war to the heart of the German homeland. If shattering the German cities could do that, their destruction would be a worthwhile task. This, however, was not a popular view: such action was too drastic, too barbaric even. Surely, in an industrial world, there must be an industrial way to defeat Nazi Germany – that at least was the American viewpoint.

In 1942 the USAAF had put forward a list of 76 specific targets drawn from *six* production areas: submarine construction, ball-bearings, the aircraft industry, oil, synthetic rubber and transport. All of these areas had already been targeted in the Casablanca Directive, and Eaker's force had already attempted to destroy some of them – often at considerable cost. Current US thinking attributed the previous failure of daylight precision bombing to a shortage of aircraft, arguing that the formations sent to attack the enemy were too small; it did not accept that the basic concept of the self-defending bomber formation was fatally flawed. To achieve the destruction of these 76 targets, Eaker calculated that he would need some 900 B-17 or B-24 bombers under command by the summer of 1943 and a steady increase in this force to 2,700 by the spring of 1944. While this build-up was going on, Eaker proposed that

> the most effective results from strategic bombing will be obtained by direct-ing the combined day and night effort of the US and British bomber forces against targets which are mutually complementary in undermining a limited number of selected objective systems. All-out attacks imply precision bombing of related targets by day and night where tactical conditions permit and area bombing by night against the cities associated with these targets.

This proposal met with general approval – which is hardly surprising since it codified the existing bombing philosophies of both Bomber Commands, did not conflict with strongly held opinions, and offered at least the possibility of a mighty and increasingly effective form of sus-tained attack against the German military-industrial machine – which was the prime purpose of bomber operations in the first place. Harris liked Eaker and he also liked the plan. Portal liked the plan. Arnold supported it, and when the plan went before the Combined Chiefs of Staff at their Washington Conference, in May 1943, it went through with acclamation – but not without some changes.

Eaker's original suggestion, that the best option was to concentrate on a few specific targets, had somehow disappeared from the document pre-sented at Washington. There the plan was regarded as one which *'recog-nizes the fact that where precision targets were bombed by the Eighth Airforce in daylight, the effort should be completed by RAF bombing attacks against the sur-rounding industrial area by night'*, and the Combined Chiefs acknowledged that the chief snag in executing the US part of this plan – daylight preci-sion bombing of selected targets – was the growth in the German fighter strength.

Since in May 1943 there was no Allied fighter capable of escorting day-light bombers all the way to Germany and back, Eaker proposed that a force of two bomb groups – say 50 bombers – escorted by fighters, should attempt to draw off the German fighter strength while the Main Force of 200–300 bombers would fly directly to its target, fighting off whatever opposition the *Luftwaffe* flak and fighters could put up along the way.

This seems to be the sort of matter that lies more within the realm of operational tactics than an issue that should concern the Combined Chiefs of Staff. However, this *tactical* plan – for that is what it was – was part of a *strategic* plan to help the Allied armies land on the Continent of Europe. First, beginning in May 1943, the USAAF would attack U-boat bases on the French coast. Then, in the second half of 1943, it would attack targets in Western Germany along the Rhine and in the Ruhr – areas just within the range of current fighter escorts – concentrating on fighter stations and aircraft factories. Even at this stage, though, there was scope for confusion over the plan's objectives – not least because phrases in it like '*the German fighter strength is designated as an intermediate objective second to none in priority*' were meaningless.

The broad thrust of the proposal was that, at every stage of this plan, efforts would be made to reduce the German fighter strength. Finally, in early 1944, the entire air-force effort would be switched to support for the coming invasion, by attacking any target which appeared to oppose the landing or which was requested by the Supreme Allied Commander, who had not yet been appointed but would almost certainly be an American. The Combined Chiefs were very concerned that the growth in German fighter strength would by mid-1944 provide enough aircraft to inhibit the successful execution of OVERLORD, so Eaker's proposal to write down that force came as a considerable relief.

As a result, the original Eaker Plan, duly modified and redrafted, was issued to the air force commanders in June 1943 as the *Pointblank* Directive, with the prime aim of weakening the German fighter force and destroying aircraft factories and fighter support facilities.

The *Pointblank* Directive had a confusing birth, so it might be as well to list its purpose in simple terms and then examine the thinking behind it. The main aim, following that of the Casablanca Directive, was to so weaken Germany's military and industrial might that an invasion of Europe was possible. To achieve that end, the strategic bombing of certain targets was an essential prerequisite. Unfortunately, the process of destroying these targets was proving too slow and too costly, largely because of the strong German air defences. Therefore a way had to be found to destroy or greatly reduce the German fighter force, because until that was done the main aim of the Casablanca Directive, as listed at the head of this chapter, could not be achieved.

Therefore the only aim of the *Pointblank* Directive should have been to destroy the German fighter strength. The question of whether the German fighter force would really have posed such a threat to the landings in 1944 will be covered later in this book, but the belief that it would do so was not disputed in the early months of 1943 when the *Luftwaffe* was still all-powerful in the skies over German-occupied Europe. In spite of *Pointblank*, however, the *Luftwaffe* remained formidable in those skies even a year later – a point illustrated by the next two accounts.

Art Livingston was a ball-turret gunner with the 446th Bomb Group:

I was just twenty when I arrived in England in November 1943, and when we arrived at our base at Flixton the training continued. I hated being a ball-turret gunner, as it was the most dangerous position in the ship. You could not get out in a hurry, and you had to leave your parachute outside. When hostiles were reported I got into my turret and ready for action, looking for the enemy and turning up, down and around until I saw them. When they approached I set the sight for the wingspan of the type recognized and fired at them, but most of the time they went past so fast I didn't score. The idea was to focus on the nose of the attacking ship, which was fine in the laboratory or wherever they work these things out, but it did not work when the fighter was coming in at 250 m.p.h. or better.

Of my 26 missions I would not say that fighters did us the most damage, because the P-51s were coming into service; we suffered more from flak. But there were times when the fighters concentrated on us. Thirty or forty fighters would turn up and make attacks from whatever quarter favoured them most – sometimes head-on or tail-on, but most time they hit the high groups first, passing down and through to the lower groups and then coming up to attack from below. This was when I had the best shot at them from the ball turret, as they turned away – I can still see them now, almost motionless at the top of their climb, exposing their bellies to me. I had 24 missions in when General Doolittle decided to increase the tour to 30 missions, but it was pro-rated, so if you had already done 24 you did one more and that was it. The rest of my crew had not done so many and got stuck to fly the 30, which caused distress as it gave five more chances to be killed.

My last mission was to Berlin – that would be in March 1944. It was a crystal-clear day, and as we flew over the city I could see the stadium where they held the 1936 Olympics. I hear there were 105 flak batteries around the city, and the flak was deadly – you could see ships going down all over the place, and they had our number and shot down three of our group. It is the sorriest thing to come back from a mission and find a quarter of the fellows had not made it back and later that evening the Graves Registration people came to pick up their possessions and send them home.

Melvin Larson of the 388th Bomb Group was also flying missions at this time:

I flew my first six missions and then got frostbite; my oxygen mask froze to my face and it tore away a lot of skin when the medics prised it off, so I had to be grounded for a week until it healed. My crew were all lost a week later on their tenth mission, over Bordeaux, and so I became a spare toggelier and flew the next 24 missions for a full 30 tour in this role. On the first Berlin mission our aircraft was singled out by two FW 190s and they shot out the left inboard engine on the first pass; then they got the right inboard, which started windmilling and we could not feather it. Our pilot then dived the Fortress from 25,000 ft to 10,000 ft and the FWs followed us down, attacking all the way, until we were rescued by a P-47 flown by one of the fighter aces, Major Francis Gabreski, who came up on the radio and said, 'Call me Gabby.' We lost seven of the 36 B-17s dispatched that day. Every aircraft suffered damage from flak or fighters, and many came back with dead or wounded crew on board.

There is therefore plenty of evidence that the *Luftwaffe* was still a formid-able force, even in 1944 – *over Germany*. Reducing that effectiveness was the prime aim of the *Pointblank* Directive, but it had a number of other aims. It involved two air forces with different ideas about what should be done and who should do it, and even after it was issued by the Combined Chiefs it was tinkered with by Harris and Eaker. The Directive first went to the British Air Ministry, where Air Vice-Marshal Norman Bottomley, was charged with redrafting it before sending it on to Harris and Eaker. Bottomley's draft, while stressing that writing down the German fighter strength by attacking airfields and factories was a 'first priority', also stated that the 'primary objectives' listed in the Casablanca Directive still stood. Including a 'first priority' and 'primary objectives' in the same doc-ument, which used these terms to describe different things, was a recipe for confusion, misinterpretation – and nit-picking.

Bottomley's interpretation then further fogged the issue by referring to the attack on the *Luftwaffe* as an 'intermediate objective' – something that had to be done not as an end in itself, but as a step towards the objectives in the Casablanca Directive, which, it will be recalled, told the Allied Bomber commanders that 'Your primary object will be the progressive destruction and dislocation of the German military, industrial and economic system and the undermining of the morale of the German people to a point where their capacity for armed resistance is fatally weakened' and then went on to list, in order of priority, the six industrial areas mentioned above.

Order and counter-order always lead to disorder, but the issue here was rather more complicated: what was the difference between a 'first priority' and a 'primary objective'? How could an attack on the *Luftwaffe* be both a 'first priority' and an 'intermediate objective'? If the Casablanca Directive of January still applied, as Bottomley said it did, then did that Directive override the more specific orders on targeting issued by the later *Pointblank* Directive?

Where confusion exists, the best way to clarify the situation is to lay out the problem in detail, demand an explanation, and obtain clear guidelines, but in this case Harris was not particularly interested in clarity from on high. The confusion suited him very well, for it gave him the opportunity to interpret *Pointblank* and the Casablanca Directive any way he liked, and to pick from the list of instructions whatever he needed as authority to fight the bomber war his own way. Bottomley showed his draft of *Pointblank* to both Eaker and Harris and, having heard their views, made some more changes.

The final version of *Pointblank* was issued to the Bomber Commanders on 10 June 1943. In it, as the main thrust of the Directive, an attack on the *Luftwaffe* fighter strength was stressed for both forces. However, while the USAAF was *specifically* charged (my italics) with reducing German fighter strength and attacking the six objectives listed in the Casablanca Directive, RAF Bomber Command was 'to be employed in accordance with the main aim in the general disorganisation of German industry'. What this boiled down to was that the USAAF was bound by the *Pointblank* Directive while Harris could obey it if he felt like it, or could carry on attacking the cities – in the final analysis, the choice was his.

The situation was compounded by the fact that if Harris and Spaatz were ever to prove that the bomber dream was realizable – that they could bomb Germany to the peace conference and make OVERLORD unnecessary – the time to do so was now, before the clock leading up to H-Hour on D-Day began to tick. Once that happened, the bomber dream was over and the land forces would, as in the First World War, dictate the outcome of the European war. It is from this point that the bomber dream starts to slip away and Harris's intentions become less easy to understand and rather harder to justify.

Ever since the outbreak of war in 1939, the experiences of both Allied bomber forces had forced the commanders to at least one definite conclusion: until the bombers were supported by a long-range fighter aircraft, daylight operations over Germany were simply not viable. The German fighters would shoot the day bombers – first British, then American – out of the sky, and no amount of on-board firepower seemed able to prevent this. The British therefore took up night bombing, which was notoriously inaccurate without a range of scientific aids, and the Americans restricted their raids to short-range operations, within the range of the existing fighter escorts, and had begun to adopt RAF equipment, like *Gee* and H_2S, in order to cope with the problems of navigation and target-finding. Given such limitations – and the need to prosecute the war – area bombing is understandable and was fully justified.

By the middle of 1943, though, a great deal had changed and other developments were in a very advanced stage. The RAF shattered Hamburg at the end of July. In spite of German jamming, *Gee, Oboe* and H_2S were making target-finding possible, more aids were on the way, and Pathfinder marking was making the task of hitting targets ever more possible, as would the post-Dams Raid introduction of the master bomber.

Bill Naylor, DFC*, a PFF bomb aimer, acted as master bomber on several operations, and explains how the system worked:

I am not sure whether I can be of much assistance, since I only did 24 trips with No. 405 PFF Squadron, but five of them were as master bomber, so here goes. The only special training I received was at Warboys, where the PFF course consisted of practice bombing, map reading and lots of technical data on procedures, *Paramatta, Wanganui,* and so on – the standard PFF routines. The training that really counted was the 'on-the-job' training with three different crews, to get experience. I started doing blind sky-marking, then visual supporter, then visual centerer and primary visual marker, and finally master bomber.

As I said, I did five trips as master bomber, and this is how we did it on No. 405 Squadron; perhaps other squadrons operated it differently. Pre-flight preparation was a big item, and we would spend a couple of hours or more studying blow-up photos of the target, large-scale maps and white silhouette pictures of the target area. The main purpose of this was to identify lakes, rivers, rail lines – anything that would help us find the aiming point. On the way out I used the front gun turret and lay in the nose, checking for flak positions and searchlights or fighters and calling for the appropriate evasive action.

On approaching the target the navigator or H_2S operator would help me by advising what he could see and advising that I should be able to see so-and-so or such-and-such on the ground. This would help me get oriented and hopefully identify some prominent landmark or marks to judge the position of the first target indicators. I would then decide which target markers to use as the AP and advise the skipper, and he would broadcast this instruction to the Main Force. As we continued to circle the target, back-up flares would be falling and I would have to ascertain which TIs to ignore and which ones to use, sometimes asking for undershoot or overshoot. Some of the time the indicators would be obscured by fog or smoke and you would have to use a fire as an aiming point. We would keep up the bombing instructions until the time for the raid had elapsed and then give the closing signature and scoot for home.

As for the USAAF, while it was persisting in its attempts to prove that daylight precision bombing could work, it was also realizing that it must have a long-range escort and needed to adopt or adapt some of the British navigation aids if it was to navigate its way to the target in the cloud-ridden skies of Europe. These aids were coming in fast: the *Gee*-box was installed in most Eighth Air Force bombers by October 1943; *Oboe* and H_2S were still in short supply but these too were being evaluated by the USAAF. Also, the P-51 Mustang, equipped now with the British Merlin engine, was in its final development stages. In August 1943 the 482nd (Pathfinder) Group, USAAF, was formed at Alconbury, equipped with B-17Gs and B-24s and charged with working up the deployment of H_2X and *Oboe* equipment as navigation and bombing aids on US missions. The necessary components of a successful bombing campaign were being moved into place.

The entire thrust of the Allied bomber war needed reappraisal in the late summer of 1943, not least because the factors that had driven the RAF to attack by night and the USAAF to persist in daylight precision bombing were being modified by new technology ranging from radar aids to the P-51 Mustang fighter. Another new development was the *Serrate*-equipped Mosquito, a night fighter that would fly with the RAF bomber stream to detect and attack German aircraft using *Lichtenstein* radar. These and other developments – and their potential effect on bomber operations – will be covered in future chapters, but with their advent and the experience gathered to date the whole question of Allied bombing strategy and tactics should have been reviewed.

That Allied bombing strategy did not get such an appraisal can be laid at the door of the bomber dream and its disciples. The USAAF kept on sending bombers into Germany by day and losing them in quantity, and Harris ignored the specifics of the *Pointblank* Directive and moved on to the next stage of his 'Main Offensive' – the Battle of Berlin.

Harris had intended to start the Battle of Berlin as soon as the Battle of the Ruhr ended. However, in the event he held back until the start of winter in 1943, partly to await the arrival of new target-identification aids, like the ground position indicator (GPI), and partly because it was a long way to Berlin and his crews needed the longer nights. He also wanted to build up the Lancaster and Halifax force, phase out the Wellington entirely, and reduce the Stirling content in the front-line squadrons. In terms of numbers, the strength of Bomber Command did not increase in the last months of 1943, but the proportion of Lancasters and Halifaxes rose considerably.

Another major step forward was the introduction of more radar aids to navigation, target-finding, night-fighter detection and radar jamming. Some of these were very technical, others quite simple but very effective. Among the latter was *Corona*, an attempt to confuse the German nightfighter pilots. Listening stations, manned by fluent German speakers, were set up in the UK and tuned into the German fighter control networks. These stations intervened by issuing false directions to the German aircrews, recalling them to their bases or giving non-existent targets and generally causing confusion. When the Germans realized what was going on and introduced female controllers, the British, as already related, had anticipated this move and brought their own women in to handle the broadcasts; it was all part of a long-running and wide-ranging war to limit the effectiveness of the German night fighter.

A supplement to *Corona* was ABC – *Airborne Cigar* – operated by No. 101 Squadron of 1 Group, which attempted to jam broadcasts by the fighter control stations; this device was first used in an attack on Stuttgart on 7/8 October 1943, and other devices to jam radar or confuse the fighters were introduced all the time. One such device was *Tinsel*, which sought to jam the radio frequencies used by the fighter controllers. All these devices became known as RCM – radio counter-measures – and the airborne element, including such later devices as the *Mandrel Screen* which masked the German radar emissions, became the particular task of a new RAF Group, 100 (Bomber Support) Group, commanded by Air Vice-Marshal E. B. Addison, which became operational in November 1943.

The bomber war went on relentlessly while all these new aids were coming into service and the Higher Command were debating strategy. Quite apart from the operations described in the previous chapter, the RAF operated on every night between the end of July and the start of the Battle of Berlin, and the USAAF was almost equally active, though its missions were, as ever, restricted by bad weather and fighter opposition.

The Mighty Eighth was growing yet mightier. At the end of July 1943 Eaker and Anderson had fifteen B-17 groups and could regularly put over 300 bombers in the air for any one mission. The last week in July 1943, following the USAAF's participation in the Hamburg raids, became known to the Eighth as 'Blitz Week', and in it the bombers struck at a wide range of targets in Germany, including the ports of Kiel and Wilhelmshaven and industrial centres like Hanover and Kassel, as well as a long-range strike at Trondheim and Bergen in Norway, which began the week. Results were good and many targets were comprehensively damaged, but losses were high. Over 100 US bombers – and 1,000 men – were lost during the seven days of Blitz Week, over one-third of the available force, and it was after this that the USAAF crews, still undaunted, set out for Schweinfurt and Regensburg – an example of professional tenacity, and sheer guts.

After Schweinfurt–Regensburg in August 1943, the USAAF had to rest and re-equip. The weather was poor, with weeks of ten-tenths cloud, and no more missions were flown into Germany until the middle of September. At the end of August some US groups began flying missions against flying-bomb sites on the coast of France, as follow-ups to the RAF raid on Peenemunde; the first of these '*Noball*' missions was flown on 27 August 1943, and these attacks were followed up by RAF bombers, especially Mosquito aircraft from 2 Group.

On 6 September, 338 B-17s went to Stuttgart – a mission which the Mighty Eighth's history calls 'the biggest fiasco of the year'. This is unkind, because the weather was foul and the Germans cunning. In thick cloud there was no chance of the bombardiers seeing the target, and the mission should have been aborted. The German fighters, as was now usual, stayed back until the bombers were well into Germany and then came swarming in. Twenty-one bombers were shot down before the IP and another ten over the target; another twelve came down in the Channel on the way home, from battle damage or lack of fuel, and five more landed in Switzerland. The total number lost was 48 aircraft – about 11 per cent – and most of the aircraft which got back to Britain had battle damage.

In September there was an organizational change to the Eighth, when a new level, the air division, was introduced between VIII Bomber Command and the combat or bombardment wings, though in effect the 'wings' simply became divisions; the 1st, 2nd and 4th Combat Wings became the 1st, 2nd and 4th Air Divisions, and the combat wings, controlling, say, two or three groups, became combat bombardment wings, which remained the term for a 'wing' of two or three 'group boxes'. Otherwise it was life as usual, with a string of missions to targets in France in the last days of September.

On 2 October 1943 a large force of B-17s attacked Emden, using H_2X for the first time. The device was installed in the two leading aircraft and was only partially successful, for one bomber dropped short and the other's smoke marker was carried away by high winds; nevertheless it was a start, a way of coping with the relentless European cloud cover, and the USAAF stayed with it and kept practising.

Five 'visual' missions were flown in October, but the *Luftwaffe* now had some 800 front-line day fighters on the Western Front and they took a terrible toll of the US bombers. These *Gruppen* – nineteen in all – were largely concentrated in Germany, to protect the cities there from 'round-the-clock' bombing, and their armament, radar equipment and ground control were now highly sophisticated. The bombers were picked up far out at sea, left alone until their fighter escorts were forced to turn back, and then savaged by large-scale attacks from single- and twin-engined fighters, using cannon and rockets as well as machine-guns. On 4 October, 361 bombers, B-17s and B-24s, were sent to Germany and sixteen were lost. On the 8th Bremen was the target for a three-division attack and another dozen aircraft went down, and most of the rest sustained heavy battle damage.

On the following day, 378 US aircraft set out for various targets in Germany and western Poland, the targets being well dispersed in an attempt to split the fighter force. Heavy losses were sustained, ranging up to and beyond the crucial 10 per cent level, but good bombing results were achieved, especially at Munster in western Germany, a major rail junction. Munster was the object of an area raid rather than a precision bombing mission, for the crews were directed to drop their bombs on the town centre in order to disrupt the working population. This instruction, says the Mighty Eighth's history, 'did not produce any moral qualms among the airmen; it is recorded that some cheered at this news – their own sufferings had bred bitterness'.

The Munster mission was another day-long battle, all the way there and all the way back. The *Luftwaffe* fighters arrived as the bombers crossed the German frontier, and 200 of them put in frontal attacks against the US aircraft for the best part of an hour. Six bombers went down in the first passes, and the 100th Bomb Group, which the *Luftwaffe* always seemed to single out, was broken up by these attacks and shot out of the sky. Legends have gathered about the 100th Bomb Group, alleging that one of its aircraft, unable to fly on or fight, had lowered its wheels as a sign of surrender. German fighters then came alongside and were promptly fired upon by the waist gunners, who had not been advised of the surrender – an action the *Luftwaffe* never forgave. From then on *Luftwaffe* pilots sought out bombers with the 'Square D' tail insignia of the 100th Bomb Group and attacked them with notable ferocity. Eight more aircraft went down before the bombers reached the IP, when flak added its contribution to their troubles. Then, once the bombers had passed their target and bombed, the fighters came back. The final total lost was 29 from the 3rd Division and the 'Bloody 100th' Bomb Group lost twelve aircraft out of thirteen dispatched – which seems to give some credence to the legend.

So it went on throughout October. The next mission, on 14 October, took the Eighth back to Schweinfurt of evil memory – and the result was another slaughter. When the results were totted up on the day after the mission, of some 300 aircraft dispatched – the exact count of aircraft which left the English coast is not known – 60 had been shot down over Germany. Another five, badly damaged, crashed in England, and no fewer than twelve crashed on landing at their home bases, through battle damage or crew exhaustion, and had to be written off. A total of 77 aircraft were lost at Second Schweinfurt – some 25 per cent of those dispatched – and a further 125 received battle damage. Six hundred airmen were missing, and a further 43 wounded and five dead were taken from the bombers that made it back. According to the Eighth Air Force's history, 'the Schweinfurt mission loss was more than double the 10 per cent loss of force figure the Eighth considered prohibitive to operations'.[1] The overall Eighth loss rate to mid-October was 11 per cent.

One of the aircraft lost was flown by B-17 pilot Roy Grady Davidson Jr, who flew on the second Schweinfurt mission with the 333rd Bomb Squadron, 94th Bomb Group:

We were woken at 0330 hrs on 14 October by a flashlight in the face and a ser-geant saying, 'Up and at 'em, you're flying today. Breakfast in the mess hall in 30 minutes.' Briefing began with the briefing officer reading out a telegram from General Eaker, stating that this mission was the most important mission of the war to date: we were to knock out a vital weak link in the German armaments industry, the ball-bearing works at Schweinfurt, and by doing so would shorten the war by many months. There were many moans in the back of the room, for many of the men had been to Schweinfurt in August, and that had been plenty rough.

This would be a long one. We would be in the air for nine hours, and were hitting them with all we had. There would be 200 B-17s and we would fly at 21,000 ft, followed by 200 B-24s and escorted by P-47 fighters as far as Paris, and we would be nice and safe in the middle . . . then we were issued with candy bars and taken to our aircraft, *Thunderbird*, a beautiful plane with three swastikas (for shot-down enemy fighters) and twelve bombs (for missions) painted on the nose. This would be its thirteenth mission, but the ground crew were not superstitious and wished us luck.

At precisely the same second, all 21 planes in our group started engines and taxied out. Being a typical fall morning in England, there was such a dense fog we could not see the end of the runway and we were at 2,000 ft before the visibility improved. Everywhere we looked we could see aircraft, but as we climbed to 21,000 ft we ran into our first problem – cloud cover. We could not fly in close formation until we reached 24,000 ft, and we were the last B-17 to get there – and where were the B-24s? They had been ordered back home, as they could not reach 24,000 ft, and this put us as the last aircraft in a long line of B-17s – a very vulnerable spot – instead of in the middle of 400 bombers. But we were young, and full of adventure and enthusiasm, so a little thing like that didn't bother us.

We picked up the P-47s and they stayed with us to Paris, where they had to turn for home. It seems they were barely out of sight when radio silence was broken by 'Fighters at six o'clock.' Our tail gunner, Richard Mungenast, then began firing his guns, as did Carl Gibson, our ball-turret gunner, who suddenly shouted, 'I got him I got him – look at him go down in smoke!' There was more excitement aboard our plane than there had ever been before. What fun, what a sport!

Suddenly it seemed that the whole German Air Force was coming at us and the air was full of radio chatter. We were miles from our target, and it seemed as if the more we shot down, the more they sent up. Of course we could see a bomber go down in smoke or explode occasionally, but it seemed that our fire was getting the better of the fighters. They had two cracks at us and then they had to land, rearm and refuel and be ready for us on the way back.

As we started our bomb run we were sitting ducks for the flak and we had to hold a steady straight course and maintain the same altitude in order to align the bombsights. Never have I seen such flak – the black bursts of shells formed a solid black cloud, and the shots were so numerous that it looked like an impossibility to fly a plane through it. However, very few bombers went down to the flak and we dropped our bombs quickly and turned for home. We were under heavy single-engined fighter attack from Me 109s and Focke-Wulf 190s for maybe another 45 minutes and then they had to land for more fuel. We felt good about having accomplished a most important mission and having shot down so many fighters. Kruger, our top-turret gunner, had shot off all his ammunition and had to go to the back for a refill, and Faudie, our navigator, had been so busy firing his nose gun he had no time to navigate so he did not know where we were. There seemed no need to navigate anyway – all we had to do was follow the leader.

We were in the vicinity of Mannheim when Mungenast reported an Me 110 twin-engine fighter approaching from the six o'clock level, but staying out of range. 'They are shooting something at us that leaves a black trail,' he reported. 'OK, it's burst 300 yards behind us . . . but here comes another. That has burst 100 yards back . . . but here comes another.' Before another word was heard, all hell broke loose. It seemed as if a bomb had exploded right under the plane, and it lifted us 200 ft above the formation; the flaps had been knocked down, as had the elevator trim tabs. We later found we had been hit by an air-to-air rocket – something we had never heard of and had no defence against. I firmly believe we were the first plane to be hit by a rocket in World War II.

Chichester, the co-pilot, and I had to press forward with all our might on the wheels to keep the plane on level flight, for the twin tab-cables had been severed. Then Mungenast called on the intercom, 'I'm hit, can somebody help me?' Then Koth called out that there was a fire in the radio room, and Chichester reported that two of the engines were gone and we could not feather the propeller on the No. 3 engine. Then we discovered that we had no oxygen. Mungenast reported that he had crawled up to the main door in the waist and it had gone, adding, 'Koth, Howell and Page have bailed out and Gibson is lying by the door with a 20 mm round in his knee. What do you want us to do?'

I looked around for our group and could not find them, but we saw two squadrons of another group and dropped down below them. We had to go down as we had no oxygen, and you cannot live without oxygen at 23,000 ft. We were in a fix, with no gunners and two lost engines, on one of which we could not feather the prop, which was creating drag, and the flaps would not come up. I still thought we could make it back to England, but that was not to be.

The raid had shattered the ball-bearing factories, and the subsequent photos caused the commanders, British and American, to regard Second Schweinfurt as a victory – not least in view of the number of German fighters allegedly destroyed. Up to a point this was true, but, as the US aircrew could attest, it seemed to make little difference to the number of fighters the Germans put into the air. The gunners put in the usual high claims – 288 fighters shot down – and even after downward revision it appeared that in these October missions the USAAF had actually destroyed some 700 German fighters and damaged or destroyed a further 300 – more than the entire *Luftwaffe* day-fighter force in Germany at that time. No one really believed these claims, but when a fighter dived through a bomber formation and every gunner fired at it, who should get the credit, when it was seen to go down? If only from the morale point of view, it was as well to credit everyone with a valid claim and adjust the totals later.

Since the Germans only had some 800 fighters on the Western Front – a figure obtained accurately from *Enigma* transcripts at Bletchley Park,[2] where the *Luftwaffe* code had been broken – it was hardly possible to shoot down or damage 1,000 in a single month, but the impression still got about that the USAAF aircrews were reducing the German fighter strength on every mission, though at some cost to themselves. The fact that the actual German losses were barely a tenth of this figure did not come out until much later.

The USAAF bomber crews were well aware that they were not making any significant impact on the German fighter force, which rose to meet them day after day, and pressed home its attacks with skill and courage – and was resisted in the same way. To suppress the enemy fighters, the USAAF bombers still needed a fighter that would come with them all the way to the target. Meanwhile, they fought on as best they could – and there were a few improvements to their armament and prospects. In September 1943 the first of the B-17Gs appeared, an improved version of the Flying Fortress, equipped with a 'chin turret' in the nose, firing two guns on movable mounts – a feature which added to the forward firepower and gave the bombers some means of replying to head-on attacks. So winter came, the weather worsened, and the war went on.

By November 1943 Harris was ready to start the Battle of Berlin. This was to be a major part of his offensive, a chance to prove that the bomber dream could become reality if every bomber in the UK was devoted to the same task, as he said explicitly in a minute to Churchill dated 3 November. This long letter began by listing the results of RAF operations since June, in the period covered by the *Pointblank* Directive, whose specific provisions Harris had largely ignored.

Harris's first claim was that some nineteen German cities – including Hamburg, Hanover, Cologne, Essen, most of the other Ruhr towns, and Rhine towns like Mannheim and Ludwigshafen – had been either totally destroyed or severely damaged by area bombing in recent months. His intention now was to take on Berlin. If Berlin could be destroyed, claimed Harris, then 'Germany must collapse.' His letter was a Last Testament of the bomber dream:

> I feel certain that Germany must collapse before this programme, which is more than half completed already, has proceeded much further. We have not got far to go. We must get the USAAF to wade in with greater force. If they will only get going according to plan and avoid such disastrous diversions as Ploesti . . . we can get through with it very quickly. We can wreck Berlin from end to end if the USAAF will come in on it. It will cost between us 400–500 aircraft. It will cost Germany the war.[3]

And there it is, the bomber dream as expressed by its most famous apostle. The RAF now had the aircraft and the aids and the long winter nights. The USAAF had a growing abundance of aircraft, and within a matter of weeks it would have the P-51D Mustang fighter – one that could escort the bombers all the way to Berlin and back and outfight any German fighter found en route. If all this force was turned on the German capital, all 500 square miles of it, and reduced it to rubble, how could Germany go on fighting the war?

Given the dramatic effects of bombing Hiroshima and Nagasaki less than two years later, it is hard to maintain the argument that Harris's idea was totally flawed. The essence of any attack – by land, sea or air – is weight and speed. The enemy must be hit hard and hit often, be given no chance to recover or recuperate, and be offered a choice of either death or surrender. Harris could not deploy the devastating force of the atomic bomb, which could destroy a city in a matter of minutes, but if RAF Bomber Command was combined with the bombers of the Eighth Air Force they certainly had the force to destroy Berlin in a matter of weeks.

Would the German people have stood for that? This was not simply a matter of morale: be the Germans ever so brave, what was the *point* of continuing a war which they were clearly going to lose, because the Allied bombers were shattering their cities one after another and could not be prevented from doing so? The case for Germany then surrendering is at least arguable, and had he been given full support Harris might have been able to prove his point. As it is, Harris never had the force and the proof is not available. There is, however, some evidence that the USAAF *did* contemplate joining in this attack, for on 23 November 1943 the Eighth was briefed for a mission to the 'Big B' – Berlin. However, this mission was 'scrubbed' – cancelled – and the USAAF did not make its first mission to Berlin until 3 March 1944, when Harris's Battle of Berlin was almost over.

The Battle of Berlin began on the night of 18/19 November 1943 and lasted until the night of 24/25 March 1944. The story of that battle occupies the next chapter, but, a week after the Battle of Berlin began, the moral argument against the entire area-bombing campaign resurfaced in Britain. The British people at large, and the bomber crews in particular, did not worry too much about the effects of area bombing; if they had been asked, they would have said then what the veterans say now: that the Germans had, to paraphrase Harris's words, 'sowed the wind and were reaping the whirlwind'.[4] After Warsaw, Rotterdam, Coventry, the Blitz and the Baedeker raids on Britain in 1940–1, what was happening to German cities and German civilians was of no great concern to their enemies. However, the point to note is that there were objections to the effects of the Allied bombing campaign long before the Dresden raid of 1945. Even while the war was being fought, a number of people in Parliament and in the public eye raised doubts on whether the bombing offensive was really effective or morally justified.

Some of the comments on the morality of bombing and means to improve it have a somewhat bizarre ring, including a proposal that RAF Bomber Command staff should include an art historian who could advise the commanders on any architectural gems in the cities they proposed attacking and be consulted over the matter of aiming points. This followed a note to the Air Minister, Sir Archibald Sinclair, from the chairman of the Society for the Preservation of Historic Buildings, asking for restraint in the bombing of certain historic towns and suggesting that some of them should be bombed only in daylight. This request was taken seriously, and Harris was told not to attack any of these towns without consulting the Air

Ministry first and obtaining specific permission. The acceptance of this proposal by the Allied bomber commanders probably saved the historic city centres of Rome, Florence and Paris – occupied cities. It did not, however, stop the tactical bombing of the famous Benedictine monastery at Cassino, Italy, in 1944, or the shattering of many ancient German cities.

Harris was also meeting opposition from within the ranks of his own staff. In July 1943 his chaplain, John Collins, protested strongly about the Hamburg firestorm raid, and Collins continued to protest at area bombing until the end of the war.[5] It is typical of Harris that he refused to sack Collins or send him away from his headquarters; free speech was one of the things that Harris and his aircrews were fighting for.

Another protest came from Lord Salisbury, who wrote to Sinclair in November 1943 declaring that he was unhappy about the area bombing campaign, which seemed to conflict with the government's repeated assertions that the RAF was concentrating on only military and industrial targets. There is, said Salisbury 'a great deal of evidence that this is not so, making some of us afraid that we are losing moral superiority to the Germans'.

Sinclair's reply was somewhat disingenuous. He quoted directly from the Casablanca Directive, telling Salisbury that 'our aim is the progressive dislocation and destruction of the German military, industrial and economic system', adding that, while he had never pretended that it was possible to pursue this policy without inflicting terrible casualties on the civilian population, 'neither I nor any responsible speaker on behalf of the Government has ever gloated over the destruction of German homes'.

This satisfied Salisbury, at least for a while, but rather misses the point – and, significantly, the quoted extract from the Casablanca Directive left out the passage on attacking German morale. Besides, no one was accusing Sinclair or anyone else of 'gloating': the allegation, as yet unformed but certainly forming, was that area bombing was morally wrong and was inflicting terrible and needless casualties on innocent civilians.

This argument was to come up again and again, with increasing force, for the rest of the war and in the decades since, in protests from such luminaries as the writer Vera Brittain, the historians A. J. P. Taylor and Basil Liddell Hart and, most frequently, the Bishop of Chichester, George Bell, who spoke out so often and so vehemently against the bombing of Germany that it is often alleged it cost him elevation to the See of Canterbury after the war.

Given that RAF aircrews were dying over Germany every night, these protests naturally aroused resentment, but, strangely enough, very little of this came from the aircrews themselves. Like Harris, they believed that the freedom to protest was one of the things they were fighting for – and they knew, as Bishop Bell and the Marquis of Salisbury did not, exactly what was happening to the German cities: they saw the post-raid photos, showing what they personally had done to Germany the night before; they saw the fires and the explosions, and flew through the multicoloured holocaust of flares and flak and tracer to reduce yet another German city to rubble. It is a point this book will return to, but now we must go to Berlin.

P-51D Mustang

13

The Battle of Berlin and Big Week
November 1943–March 1944

The last opportunity for decisive strategic air action before the direct preparations for, and launching of, Operation Overlord.

Sir Charles Webster and Noble Frankland,
The Strategic Air Offensive Against Germany, 1961

Early in November 1943, shortly before the opening of the Battle of Berlin, the RAF Air Intelligence Department and the Ministry of Economic Warfare reported that in Germany 'The maintenance of morale is the gravest problem confronting the home authorities. The full effects of air attack since the devastation of Hamburg have become known in all parts of the country . . . the general attitude is approaching one of peace at any price and the avoidance of wholesale destruction of further cities in Germany.'[1]

Well, perhaps. In view of the fact that the Germans continued to fight hard even after the Allied armies crossed the Rhine in March 1945, this report can now be seen as either extremely optimistic or wishful thinking. Even if it were accurate, the general attitude of the civilian population was not relevant to Germany's continued prosecution of the war. Nazi Germany was not a democracy, where the attitudes or opinions of the ordinary people had any real effect on the ruling party. Nazi Germany was a terrorist state, and anyone brave or foolish enough to speak out against the Nazi Party faced a hard time in the Gestapo cellars followed by a stay in a concentration camp – or worse.

There is also a shortage of evidence that the German people as a whole ever contemplated abandoning Hitler and suing for peace. This may have been due to a belief in what he told them, or fear of what would follow defeat, or a natural desire to fight on, but for whatever reason, and in spite of a few plots – only one of which was implemented – Hitler remained a hero to most of his people until the end of the war. Only when Allied troops were swarming all over Germany did this general enthusiasm abate. There is, however, some evidence that German enthusiasm for the war, or belief in a successful outcome, declined sharply towards the middle of 1943, when the Allied bombing offensive began to reveal its full awesome might.

Stephen Morz of Ludwigshafen: 'I recall my parents telling me that after 1943 they knew the war was lost, and what little enthusiasm there was locally for Hitler faded away. But life went on, of course.' Life went on, but not as before. The young men had gone, to the Army or the *Luftwaffe* or to serve in U-boats and now, as the bombing intensified, the children were evacuated from German cities. Richard Braun of Ludwigshafen, then four-teen, was sent to stay in Lorraine:

> I was put into a monastery in the town of Bitche, but the local people were very hostile and I decided to leave. I broke out at 0300 hrs in the morning, found my way to the station, and caught a train home, where my mother was very glad to see me.
>
> At fourteen you could join the *Hitlerjugend* – in fact you had to do so. There was not much interest in the swastika armband, but you also got a dagger and that was really something. There were more raids in 1943 and more bombs lying about the streets and more shot-down bombers in the country-side. Bombs are still being found: in 1998 an unexploded British bomb was found during building work in Ludwigshafen and 50,000 people had to be evacuated from their homes until it was made safe. By 1943 we had to go to the shelters more often and the bombers came over every night.
>
> We boys all collected shrapnel right from the early days, from the flak shells, but from now on I was mostly interested in collecting pieces from the shot-down bombers, some of which I still have. The adults tried to maintain what they could of a normal life. After a raid, if things were broken, you made a list and took it to the authorities and they gave you coupons to buy a replacement. You needed coupons for clothing, and there were no cars, no private transport – cars were only for the military, and a lot of the Army used horse transport, to save fuel. Food was now rationed, but plentiful; starva-tion came later, after the end of the war. Of course the prisoners and forced-labour people got less food than the Germans did.
>
> We even went on holidays, in the middle of the war, but schoolchildren also helped bring in the harvest – I remember there were leaflets about a pest called the Colorado beetle that ate the potato crop. I am sure the main burden of the war fell on the women. They had to look after the children, find the food, get a meal on the table, get the kids to school, and worry about their husbands, brothers or sons. There were not many young men about; they were all in the Army unless they were unfit or on essential work – over one-third of the workers at the I.G. Farben plant were foreigners, many being forced labour.

Some things were forbidden. Jazz was 'Negro music', so music by Louis Armstrong or Duke Ellington was not allowed, and music by Jewish composers – people like Mendelssohn and Mahler for example – was not played or permitted; there were lists of music that was not to be played. It was a terrible time, but – I must tell you this – it was the most interesting time. I was a young man, and to me and my friends it was terrible, yes, but utterly fascinating.

And so, slowly, the war squeezed normal life out of Nazi Germany. But the morale of the people generally remained intact.

In the end, Germany fell after a ground invasion from the East and West, but in November 1943, with the Normandy invasion at least six months away, Air Chief Marshal Harris still had everything to play for. If Berlin could indeed be destroyed, much might follow, so on the night of 18/19 November 1943 he sent 440 Lancaster and four Mosquito bombers to open the Battle of Berlin.

The Battle of Berlin lasted for four and a half months, right through the winter of 1943–4, and one immediate point of interest lies in the order of battle for the first operation, which involved only Lancaster bombers and Mosquitoes, the latter tasked to fly 'spoof', or diversion, operations.

The De Havilland Mosquito – the 'Wooden Wonder', a remarkable twin-engined aircraft – was now entering squadron service in quantity and would make a great contribution to the bomber war, as a night fighter, as an intruder, as an *Oboe* platform and, not least, as a bomber. This opening round of the Battle of Berlin, on the night of 18/19 November, was not a success; the city was covered in cloud, the 'blind' marking was poor, and the bombing was widely scattered. On the other hand the *Luftwaffe* and flak were not on form and only nine Lancasters were shot down.

The next Berlin raid, four nights later, on 22/23 November, was an altogether bigger affair, the heaviest attack on Berlin up to this point in the war. In a rare message to the crews before this operation, Harris told them that this raid against the enemy's capital would 'burn his black heart out', and they almost achieved that ambition. A total of 764 aircraft set out, including 50 Stirlings and eleven Mosquitoes, all the rest being Lancasters or Halifaxes. The target was again under ten-tenths clouds, and the bombs were dropped on blind markers. No photographs were obtained and the results were thought to be poor, but in fact this was the most devastating raid Berlin suffered during the entire war.

Berlin was the capital of Prussia before Germany was united in 1871, and it was – and is – a political and administrative centre rather than a major industrial city. Flat and sprawling, Berlin was hit hard, the bombs falling in a wide swath right across the centre of the city, from the central Tiergarten to the suburb of Spandau. More than 150,000 people were bombed out of their homes, a great many public buildings were destroyed, and a number of factories, including the Alkett tank works, were severely damaged. That was a bonus; the raid had been an 'area' attack and had brought the full horrors of the air war home to the capital of Germany. And losses were comparatively slight: 26 aircraft – less than 4 per cent of the force.

On the following night, 23/24 November, while the Berliners were still clearing up the rubble – a task that would continue until the end of 1947 – the RAF came back. This raid was half the size of the previous one, just 383 aircraft, none of which were Stirlings. The Stirlings carried a smaller bomb load but could not reach the altitude attained by the Halifax and Lancaster, and, as well as being more vulnerable to German flak and fighters, was liable to be hit by bombs dropped from higher-flying aircraft. Unable to stay with the bomber stream, the Stirlings also suffered heavier losses, so after this operation Harris removed them from the order of battle and they did not fly to Berlin again. This switched the area of weakness to the earlier versions of the Halifax, and these were also pulled out of the line as the battle against Berlin hotted up; this in turn reduced the force Harris was able to deploy against the 'Big City'.

On 23/24 November the cloud cover persisted, but the blind marking was accurate and the fires lit on the previous night glowed through the clouds and helped the bomb-aimers hit Berlin hard. Considerable damage was done, but losses were starting to mount: 30 Lancasters were lost – just over 5 per cent of the force.

By now PFF marking had become sophisticated, as a Canadian flyer, Russell Steer, of No. 405 Squadron, relates:

> The general idea was that the first two aircraft in the target area carried the master bomber and his deputy. They arrived before zero, to assess the situation and pass instructions to the 'primary markers', who arrived three minutes after the master bomber. The first to drop were the 'illuminators', to light up the target area. These were followed by the 'visual markers', who then placed red or green markers directly on the aiming points If this was well done, in came the Main Force to bomb on the markers, and following the 'primary markers' were the 'backers-up', who replaced the burnt out markers at regular intervals – say about every four minutes. The 'backers-up' were also guided to re-mark the target or mark fresh targets by the master bomber, who would be circling the target all this time, watching results; if he was shot down his place was taken by the deputy. All this assumes that the target was clear, and a different method – blind marking on flares – was used if the target was cloud-covered or obscured by smoke pots. There were other variations, but this is the way it usually worked.

The bombers were also assisted by '*Bull's-Eye*' operations or 'spoofs', when some of the Mosquitoes dropped flares and TIs north of the city to draw off the fighters, and the fighter pilots were further confused by *Corona* transmissions from the UK on the fighter radio network.

Three nights later, on 26/27 November, the RAF bombers returned to Berlin. As with his attack on the Ruhr, Harris had meanwhile been obliged to spread his attacks to other cities, in order to keep the flak and fighters well deployed; had he attacked Berlin night after night, the defenders would have seen his intention and the entire German fighter force and a great deal of flak would have been moved in to beat the bombers off – or cause such losses that the battle would have to be abandoned. Another approach would have been for Harris to have enough aircraft to attack Berlin in overwhelming force and still have enough aircraft available to mount heavy raids on other German cities. Harris did not have such a force, then or at any time. He was therefore obliged to disperse his effort and attack other cities, which had the effect of giving Berlin's citizens and defenders a chance to recover.

The 26/27 November raid had mixed results. The bombers attacked an area north-west of the city centre and hit a number of factories, most of them involved with war production, while the destruction of the city's residential areas also continued. The four raids mounted so far had killed some 4,000 Berliners and made some 400,000 homeless. As in many German cities, most of the population of Berlin lived in apartments, so, when a building was bombed or set on fire, more than one family lost their homes. This raid was mounted by 443 Lancasters, of which 28 were shot down and a further fourteen crashed on returning to base. The Halifax force was not engaged here, but put on a diversionary operation to Stuttgart.

During December the RAF attacked Berlin four times, and Canadian gunner Doug Curtis recalls one of these operations: 'There is no doubt that the one op that stands out in my mind was the trip we did with No. 97 Squadron to Berlin on the night of 16/17 December 1943. As a result of fog on our return to Bourn we lost a total of seven aircraft from the squadron in England, plus one lost over the target. That night, from our squadron alone, we had 28 aircrew killed within seven miles of the base.' A total of 583 bombers, ten of them Mosquitoes, took part in this raid, and 25 Lancasters were lost. A further 30 aircraft either crashed while attempting to land in fog or were abandoned by their crews, who parachuted to safety over England, unable to find an airfield.

Bombing results were mixed, and losses continued to mount. In all, 127 aircraft were lost during December, and bad weather made a significant contribution to this total. These raids took a steady toll of Berlin's scattered industrial sites but had a far greater effect on the civilian population, more than a quarter of whom were now homeless – and this in the middle of winter. Large parts of the city were being steadily reduced to rubble, yet there was no sign that the population were about to turn on the Nazi leadership.

These Berlin raids were being made by Lancasters and Mosquitoes, while the Stirlings and Halifaxes either made diversionary raids or added their weight to the mounting number of attacks being made against V2 launching sites along the Channel coast.

The December raids on Berlin also saw the introduction of the *Serrate*-equipped Mosquito to the defences of Bomber Command. *Serrate*-equipped night fighters flew with the bomber stream and sought out German fighters as they chased the bombers. This assistance was useful, for the German night-fighter pilots now had a new tactic to add to the *Wilde Sau* single-engined-fighter interception over Hamburg by Hajo Herrmann in July.

This new tactic was called *Zahme Sau*, or 'Tame Boar', and it proved very popular with the majority of the German fighter force – and employed more of them. Previously, the use of 'boxes' – *Räume* – in the Kammhuber Line meant that only the pick of the pilots had any chance of shooting a bomber down. Hajo Herrmann's *Wilde Sau* fighters, while effective over cities, were also limited, since the single-seat Me 109s used on *Wilde Sau* operations had no navigator or landing aids and losses were high. *Zahme Sau* was different: *Zahme Sau* aircraft were proper night fighters, Me 110s or Ju 88s, with two crew members and radar. They had the freedom to roam at will about the night skies, flying along with the bomber stream, using radar aids and ground control first to pick up the stream and then to find individual bombers. Once these fighters got into the bomber stream – and there were almost 400 of them in action by the end of the Battle of Berlin – they could hack down the bombers in quantity. Many of the *Zahme Sau* aircraft were fitted with *Schrage Musik* and crept up on the bombers totally undetected until they opened fire. Aids like *Monica* and the *Serrate* Mosquitoes were invaluable in reducing the threat from these skilled and relentless opponents, though they could not eliminate it.

Harris could not let the Lancasters concentrate on Berlin while the other types mounted diversions; he had to spread his effort about – even though this reduced its effect – so, in December, Main Force operations were also mounted against Frankfurt and Leipzig. The crews were getting very little rest, for thanks to the radar navigation and bombing aids the weather now had little effect on Bomber Command operations; they went out night after night, to the Big City or to one of the other targets, and by the start of the New Year the effort was beginning to tell. Even with such aids, this was still flying in winter, with all the hazards of ice in the air and fog at the home airfield. Devices like FIDO – fires lit along the runways to disperse the fog – were eventually introduced, but the strain did not go away. Bomber Command continued to attack – 'Press on regardless' remained the Command's unofficial motto – but the strain of constant operations in poor weather had an inevitable effect.

Harris, however, had his teeth set into Berlin, and was not about to relax his grip. The bombers flew to the Big City on the nights of 1/2 January 1944 and again on 2/3 January, losing 28 Lancasters on the first night – almost 7 per cent of the 421 dispatched – and 27 on the second night – exactly 7 per cent of the force dispatched, and a loss which included a large number of PFF aircraft. These two raids did not pay a dividend in damage caused: the bombing was scattered and the city was virtually untouched, bombs falling on the outskirts or on the existing rubble.

Apart from major operations to Stettin on 5/6 January and Brunswick on 14/15 January, the Command was restricted to small-scale sorties until the night of 20/21 January, when Harris's revitalized Command, with rested crews and many recently arrived replacements, again set out for Berlin. A total of 769 aircraft – a mixed force of Lancasters and Halifaxes, with ten Mosquitoes flying spoofs – attacked the city; 35 aircraft were lost and the raid was a failure. As on all the previous raids of this relentless battle, the city was covered by cloud – many of the crews flying frequently to Berlin at this time never saw the target at all. The Pathfinders used H_2S to find their aiming point and dropped sky-markers, but the city records no significant damage on this night; where the bombs went is a mystery. The German fighters, however, were up in force and followed the bomber stream to Berlin and back, hacking down bombers all the way to the North Sea.

A week later, on the night of 27/28 January, the bombers had another go, 515 Lancasters and fifteen Mosquitoes being dispatched to the Big City, their efforts assisted by an elaborate series of spoof operations that had the effect of drawing off some of the night fighters. Even so, 33 Lancasters were lost – more than 6 per cent – and the bombing was scattered over the southern sector of the city and on the towns and villages beyond. A lack of accuracy due to the relentless cloud cover was one thing; a rather more pressing concern was the loss rate: Bomber Command aircrew, flying 30 ops, could not, statistically, survive a tour if the loss rate regularly exceeded 4 per cent – and on these long Berlin operations 6 per cent and 7 per cent losses were almost the norm.

Nevertheless, 'pressing on regardless', back they went again on the night of 28/29 January, finding broken cloud which enabled the PFF to use ground markers and the Main Force of 677 aircraft, Lancasters and Halifaxes, to make an effective attack – though losing 46 aircraft, almost 7 per cent of the force. Two nights later, on 30/31 January, they went again, in 534 aircraft, mostly Lancasters but with 82 Halifaxes and twelve Mosquitoes. The city and the surrounding countryside were both bombed and considerable damage was done – most of it by fire, which would indicate that this raid hit an undamaged part of the city; 33 aircraft, 32 of them Lancasters, failed to return.

There is something wonderful and terrible about these constant, dogged attacks that went on throughout the winter, night after night. The routine was always the same: the warning order, the early call, the flight test and briefing, then out in the early afternoon as the winter day began to end, the crews climbing into their dank, chilly aircraft to go through the pre-flight checks, start the engines and taxi out. Then the green light flashed and one by one the bombers lumbered away down the runway, took off into the night sky, and turned east. When they had gone, the watchers at the end of the runway – that small group that always assembled to wave the crews goodbye – went back to the mess or their billets, to get what sleep they could before the aircraft returned. There was no glamour, no adventure, and very little excitement left in this war. It was just something that had to be done, so you went on and did it.

After the 30/31 January raid, Harris then rested his crews for two weeks; the weather was foul, and the men clearly needed a rest and a spot of leave. But some attacks continued – smaller or shorter operations, of which the most significant was an attack by moonlight on the Gnome-Rhône aero-engine works at Limoges in the centre of France, a precision attack by No. 617 Squadron under its newly appointed commander, Group Captain Leonard Cheshire, DSO**, DFC.

Leonard Cheshire – 'Chesh' to his crews – was a remarkable man and a superb leader, who went on to win the Victoria Cross when flying with Bomber Command, watch the atomic bomb drop on Japan, found the Cheshire Homes for the chronically sick and terminally ill after the war, and be widely regarded as a saint. Cheshire was also a superb bomber pilot, who flew 103 operations during the war, but he was always a very human hero. One Australian contributor to this book wrote to say that Cheshire had applied to join the PFF, only to be rejected by Bennett on the grounds that he was a 'pot-hunter' – someone far too interested in getting medals. Cheshire later admitted that at the time this was true. Douglas Mourton, who flew with Cheshire in No. 102 Squadron, records an occasion when Cheshire was still a junior officer:

> When Chesh got the DSO for bringing a burning Whitley back from an oper-
> ation over France – I saw it in the hangar and the entire side had been blown
> out – he went with several officers to celebrate at an hotel in Harrogate. A
> band was playing, but the music was interrupted for the band leader to
> announce 'Ladies and gentleman, I have great pleasure in letting you know
> that Flying Officer Leonard Cheshire is here tonight and he has just been
> awarded the DSO for an act of bravery.' Chesh stood up, apparently sur-
> prised, and acknowledged the ovation. One of the other officers then said, 'I
> wonder who told them?' and Chesh said, 'I did, you bloody fool.'

Mourton goes on to add that Cheshire was 'extremely efficient, completely fearless and had a wonderful sense of humour'.

Winston Churchill and the Air Staff were very reluctant to allow bombing raids on French targets for fear of causing heavy casualties among the French population, and the Limoges operation was permitted only on the understanding that no bombs were to fall outside the factory area. Leonard Cheshire went further than this, Like Air Vice-Marshal Cochrane he was dubious about the accuracy of high-level PFF marking and wanted to try another idea: marking at low level from a Lancaster. Since this was not yet a tried and tested method, Cheshire experimented with it over Limoges. To warn the workers and get them into the shelters, Cheshire flew across the factory at rooftop height. Then he returned and dropped his load of 30 lb incendiaries in the centre of the buildings from about 60 ft. The other eleven aircraft of No. 617 Squadron then moved in, using 12,000 lb bombs. Ten fell on the factory and the one that missed fell into the nearby river; there were no civilian casualties, and no aircraft were lost. Some weeks later a message from the factory workers, forwarded by the Maquis, arrived at No. 617's headquarters, thanking the pilot of the first aircraft for his warning.

Cheshire's initiative was to lead to an improvement in RAF bombing accuracy and the coming to a head of a long-standing dispute between 5 Group and Air Vice-Marshal Bennett and the PFF. Air Vice-Marshal Cochrane of 5 Group – which included No. 617 Squadron – was not happy with the accuracy of PFF marking. Since PFF markers were dropped from high level they not infrequently missed the target; Cochrane believed that low-level marking would be better, but the matter was debatable.

Bennett felt that low-level marking would lead to heavy losses among the PFF crews, whose losses were higher than Main Force crews already. Bennett also believed that low-level marking was impossible because (1) the pilot would be flying too low and too fast to see the target and (2) any marker so dropped would skid past the target and end up somewhere else.

Don Bennett was no fool and, although he was clearly peeved that someone was questioning the methods he and his men had spent so much time, effort and blood in perfecting, a lot of what he said was true: low-level marking was not without snags. Eventually, however, Leonard Cheshire found the answer. By flying in a small, fast Mosquito rather than a large, cumbersome Lancaster he could be over and past the target before the flak gunners could get on to him. However, he would not fly out at low level, which would cause all the navigation problems rightly predicted by Bennett. He would fly out at height, find the target, and then dive on it, which solved the marking problem at the same time. By diving down from several thousand feet and *aiming* the whole aircraft at the target like a dive-bomber, the markers could be placed accurately and did not bounce or skid away. This method of marking precision targets became common practice within 5 Group – or 'The Independent Air Force', as Don Bennett was inclined to call it – and they used it continually from then on.

Bomber Command resumed the attack on Berlin on the night of 15/16 February, when a large force – 891 aircraft: 561 Lancasters, 314 Halifaxes and sixteen Mosquitoes – was dispatched, dropping a total of 2,642 tons of bombs on the city. The damage was extensive and the death roll small: 320 people were killed that night – an indication that a large percentage of the population had left the city, probably because they had nowhere left to live. Bomber Command lost 43 aircraft – almost 5 per cent of the force. That concluded Bomber Command's Berlin campaign for February, and there was only one more raid before the battle ended in March.

Before that, on 19/20 February, the Command mounted a major operation against Leipzig – a disaster in which 823 aircraft set out and 78 were shot down, 9.5 per cent of the force dispatched. On 24/25 February Bomber Command put in an attack by 734 bombers on Schweinfurt, a follow-up to a daylight attack on the previous day by 266 B-17s, part of an 800-strong bomber force put up by the Eighth Air Force as part of its all-out 'Big Week' attacks on German strategic industries. Results were slight, and 33 RAF aircraft were lost.

The US aircraft attacking Schweinfurt on 24 February came from the 1st Air Division and, although they struck the ball-bearing plants, their bombs were widely scattered and also damaged 'a jam factory, a gelatine plant and a malt works', none of which, comments the Mighty Eighth's history, 'could be deemed to further the strategic bombing campaign'. The USAAF strength was still growing steadily: the Eighth now had three air divisions in Britain – a total of 40 bomb groups – and was able to put up 800-plus bombers any day the weather permitted, though this force was normally split between a number of targets to divide the German fighters. And these fighters were no longer so troublesome, for the P-51 Mustang was starting to appear and providing close escort on some of the missions.

This joint operation against Schweinfurt on 24/25 February was a rare example of the Combined Bomber Offensive in action: the Americans going in first, by day, when there was no smoke from fires to obscure the target; the RAF following up that night, using the fires lit by the US attack as an aid to finding the target. Harris also tried a new tactic, splitting his force into two groups which bombed two hours apart, in the hope that after the first attack the night-fighter force would land and leave clear skies for the second attack. Bombing operations were now cerebral affairs, a game of bluff and double-bluff played out with aircraft and men's lives.

On the following night, 25/26 February, the RAF was over Germany again when 594 aircraft attacked the ancient city of Augsburg, a target that might rival Dresden as a tragic victim of the bomber war. Augsburg was a beautiful medieval city, as yet virtually untouched by bombing and with only a token amount of flak for defence. It did contain military targets, including an aero-engine factory and another of the MAN plants which manufactured diesel engines for submarines; these lay in the suburbs and were hit by bombs. But the main weight of the attack fell on the Augsburg's medieval centre, which was totally destroyed in an extremely accurate attack. The German radio referred to this attack as a 'terror bombing', but there is no record of any subsequent protest in the UK nor any indication that the Air Ministry was consulted before this ancient city was bombed.

So it continued, night after night. Stuttgart and Frankfurt got particular attention, with two heavy raids each, until the night of 24/25 March, when the final attack of the Battle of Berlin went in against the Big City with another heavy loss of aircrew. Earlier chapters have emphasized the importance of wind-finding to navigation, and on this night a strong north wind had a dire effect on the bombers plugging east, carrying many of them well away to the south. As a result, the bomber stream broke up and the attack was scattered. Many aircraft came down to find out where they were and were picked off by flak, and the final account showed that 72 aircraft were missing, most of them to night fighters.

That was the last Main Force operation against Berlin, though attacks by Mosquito aircraft of Bennett's recently formed Light Night Striking Force continued until the end of the war. To end the Battle of Berlin with a failed operation that cost 72 aircraft might have caused critical comment, but these losses were overshadowed six nights later when Bomber Command set out for Nuremberg: 795 aircraft were dispatched and 95 were lost – 12 per cent of the force dispatched, the biggest single Bomber Command loss of the war.

Len Thompson of No. 550 Squadron flew on the Nuremberg operation:

> Nuremberg was a complete disaster for Bomber Command – one which even today the brass are not keen to discuss. The weather beat us as the skies cleared over Germany and we were flying in moonlight. The broadcast winds were also well out in miles per hour, but fortunately our navigator used his own. Then the track took us close to a night-fighter base and we were just sitting ducks for them. My navigator refused to log any further aircraft shot down as he said that what he was seeing could not be right; those of us in the crew could see these attacks taking place and aircraft on fire which had to be logged, and in the morning we were proved right. People were way off track due to wind speeds, and some bombed other places thinking they were at Nuremberg. We were sure we reached Nuremberg and bombed what we took to be the correct markers and staggered home with headwinds slowing us all the way. I can assure you we were all pleased to have made it back, especially after we heard the grim news on the BBC.

The arguments over the causes of the Nuremberg disaster were numerous and still rumble on. Accusations of bad management abound, but the real reason seems to be a combination of bad weather, bad luck and shrewd use of the night-fighter force by the German controllers. There was certainly an error over the meteorological report, for the data was presented as saying there would be cloud to conceal the bombers on the way out and no cloud over the target, whereas the reverse was true. But such errors were not uncommon. Once over Germany the weather was clear and cold and the RAF bombers created vapour trails in the moonlit sky that made them easy marks for German fighters. The German fighter controllers ignored all diversions or spoof operations and concentrated their aircraft on the main bomber stream, which the fighters found easily and attacked vigorously, shooting down 82 bombers before the target was even reached. Strong winds were another problem, spoiling accurate navigation; more than 100 aircraft bombed Schweinfurt, 50 miles north-west of Nuremberg, and the marking over Nuremberg itself was poor. The Nuremberg raid was a shambles, and many Bomber Command aircrew remain bitter about it.

The Battle of Berlin was a defeat for the RAF. In his memoirs Harris attempts to refute this, but it is hard to come to any other conclusion. Berlin was not destroyed, the Germans did not rise against Hitler, and, though the attacks mounted against Berlin were pressed home in the now traditional Bomber Command style, they seem to have gradually petered out, with only one in February and one in March. This was just at the time when the attacks should have been pushed with vigour to finish the city off – assuming that was possible – and when the USAAF, with its growing force, Mustang fighters, and longer hours of daylight, should have been expected to enter the fray.

The first USAAF mission to Berlin went in on 4 March 1944, when one combat wing of the 3rd Air Division, consisting of two squadrons from the 95th Bomb Group and one from the 100th Bomb Group, failing to hear the recall signal, pressed on to the city, accompanied by their fighter escorts. Five bombers were lost, but the US contribution to the destruction of Berlin had begun.

To trace the actions of the USAAF bombers during this period, though, we must go back to the autumn of 1943. The October mission to Schweinfurt was the last major mission flown without long-range fighter support, a belated admission that the concept of the self-defending bomber was fatally flawed. Once that fact was grasped it made good sense to hold off until the Mustang fighter was available in sufficient quantities to provide an adequate level of protection. Anyway, the winter skies over Europe were no place for the successful use of the Norden bombsight.

Flying time could be better employed practising escort tactics with the fighters and gaining experience with H_2X and *Oboe*, both of which were gradually being installed in American Pathfinder aircraft; the first US *Oboe* mission was flown at the end of October 1943, and the first US Pathfinder-led mission using H_2X – nicknamed '*Stinky*' or '*Mickey*' by the US crews – was a mission to Wilhelmshaven on 3 November. H_2X worked well on coastal targets and, although there was cloud cover over the target, Wilhelmshaven was soundly hit. US Pathfinder aircraft using *Oboe* or H_2X then led missions to Düren and to the synthetic-oil refineries at

Gelsenkirchen. Results were not impressive – mainly because of operator inexperience and equipment failures – but these initial flaws could be corrected and at least the US missions were no longer entirely dependent on the clear skies necessary for the use of the Norden bombsight.

In November the Eighth attacked targets in Norway and western Germany, including Bremen, and its attacks were growing heavier; 633 heavy bombers were sent to Bremen on 29 November, and the port was attacked three times in December. The end of the year saw a longer mission by 650 bombers to Ludwigshafen, on 30 December, when, in spite of the appearance of the P-51 Mustang, 23 bombers were shot down. Bad weather back at base also reduced the bomber strength: on New Year's Eve, eighteen bombers crashed on landing after a mission to attack German airfields on the Atlantic coast, in addition to 25 aircraft being lost to flak and fighters on the mission itself.

And so the Mighty Eighth moved on into 1944, when the year began with some organizational changes. Following the formation of the Fifteenth Air Force in North Africa and Italy, General Arnold had decided to create a new Command, the United States Strategic Air Force – USSTAF. Consisting of the Eighth and Fifteenth Air Forces, this was established on 1 January 1944, and commanded by Lieutenant-General Carl Spaatz, who would also exercise some authority over the US Ninth Air Force. The Eighth would be commanded by General Jimmy Doolittle, veteran of the carrier-launched bomber raid on Tokyo in 1942 in reprisal for Pearl Harbor, and the Fifteenth by General Nathan F. Twining, while General Ira Eaker – to his open regret – was sent to command in the Mediterranean.

One reason for this new arrangement – at least according to Spaatz's biographer – was 'to keep the bulk of American airpower from failing into British hands'.[2] This hardly accords with the statement in the US official history, that 'The American leaders had hoped for more than this . . . an inclusive organizational structure incorporating under one commander all operations against the Axis from the Atlantic and Mediterranean and combining in one air command all British and American strategic bomber forces.'[3] It is hard to believe that the head of this 'one air command' would have been British.

During January and early February 1944, the Eighth continued to attack targets using *Oboe* and H_2X – on only one occasion in six weeks were the skies clear enough for visual bombing. One feature of its attacks was the growing range of the fighter escort, which now consisted of two groups of P-38 Lightnings, equipped with drop tanks, and a single P-51 group of around 50 aircraft; these could fly with the bombers all the way to the target area. Claims for enemy fighters destroyed were still excessive – on 11 January the 1st Air Division gunners claimed to have shown down 210 German fighters and damaged a further 127, for a loss of 60 bombers, when the actual number of fighters shot down was just 39 – but as the US fighter pilots got the hang of air combat the number of German aircraft really destroyed would grow. With the arrival of the P-51 Mustang in early 1944, everything changed in the daylight skies over Europe.

The P-51 Mustang has an interesting history. It was developed in the United States to a British design and specification, but it used all-American components, including the Allison engine. The aircraft performed well enough in flight tests in the USA, but when it was put into squadron service by the RAF in Britain the Allison engine proved woefully under-powered and the aircraft was found to be totally inadequate in combat, with a low operational ceiling. There was a point at which the P-51 might have joined the long list of Second World War aircraft that had failed to live up to expectations, but then Ron Harker, the Rolls-Royce test pilot, suggested that it might do better if it was fitted with the latest Merlin engine – one of the type used to power the British Mark IX Spitfire. This suggestion was taken up, and the combination of an American airframe and a British engine created a new and highly effective fighter – the finest piston-engined fighter of the War.

Fitted with long-range tanks, the P-51 Merlin-powered Mustang was capable of escorting heavy bombers all the way to Germany and back, and when it met the *Luftwaffe* fighters in combat it outclassed them in every way: in speed, ceiling and rate of climb. The growing success of USAAF bomber operations over Germany after March 1944 was due *entirely* to the arrival of the P-51 Mustang.

With the arrival of the Mustang the Eighth Air Force was able to resume its attacks on the heart of the Reich and was soon sending huge fleets of bombers to batter away the foundations of German industry. There was still the problem of the weather, however, and USAAF attacks deeper into Germany were therefore delayed until the spring, when the bombers and long-range fighters began to take a heavy toll of German aircraft factories and the *Luftwaffe* fighters that came up to offer battle. From this time on US claims for shot-down enemy fighters began to have some basis in reality; it was now the turn of the *Luftwaffe* fighters to get shot out of the sky.

But these fighters could be replaced, and the attacks on German aircraft plants had little effect on fighter production, which was now well dispersed and could be increased by putting on more shifts. The significant effect was in the loss of experienced German fighter pilots, and this loss was cumulative. If an experienced pilot was lost, his replacement, being less experienced, was more likely to go down. Shoot down and kill enough pilots, and pilot training has to be shortened to keep up pilot strength in the front-line squadrons; but a pilot that has not been fully trained is even more vulnerable – and the German fighter aircraft, all of a pre-war design, were no real match for the P-51. So, imperceptibly at first, the cream of the *Luftwaffe* pilots gradually drained away.

This battle was not yet won for the Allies, however, for the German fighter force remained strong. The day-fighter *Geschwader* contained 25 *Gruppen* in the West and in Germany – approximately 750 aircraft, Me 109s and FW 190s – plus several *Gruppen* of twin-engined fighters which specialized in attacking the bomber formations with rockets. These aircraft were now pulled back into Germany and eastern Holland to form a bulwark against heavy raids now pounding the Reich by day and night. And there was always the flak – battering away at the bomber formations, knocking aircraft out of the sky.

Some idea of the effect of flak can be obtained from the following account by William Chapin, co-pilot of a B-24 Liberator which was struck by flak just at the end of its bomb run:

I barely felt the bombs leave the aircraft, just the finest of jolts, a slight lift of the aircraft, now unburdened. I did not hear Geiger call out 'Bombs away', or if I did what happened so rapidly after that has obscured the memory of it. Because right after that a piece of flak ripped noisily through the starboard windshield of the cockpit and smashed into the body of Major Clark, our pilot.

It is a strange thing. That flak entering the cockpit is like an explosion. It is a sensation of vibrating and shuddering and the pulsating of a cloud of dust. And I always think of a man lying down and shaking violently, as if in the throes of death. I can only see part of him and I don't know who he is. His legs are drumming the floor like those of an epileptic and I am suspended in time and space, motionless, waiting to be hurt myself. I cannot understand why it should be this way, why there should be an angry cloud of dust at 19,500 ft, and why I wait for something more? It is not at all pleasant.

Major Clark's body, and I believe it was nothing more than a body, bounced up and out of his seat, as if the flak had released a great steel spring within him. He shot straight up, turned in the air, dropped down between the seats, and was still. I could only see him obliquely, but I followed that harsh parabola described by his body and saw that he did not struggle. I believe that he was instantly dead.

I watched the lead airplane slip to the right, beneath my own plane and then, for the first time, realized that my own controls were shot away. The steering wheel turned easily; I turned it. The control column pushed back and forth, offering no resistance. I remember that I moaned a little when I fully sensed this. I pressed the throat mike hard into my throat and called into the interphone, 'Pilot to crew, stand by to bale out.'

I could not hear my own voice: the mike was obviously dead; I listened to the engines grinding on and on, at 2500 r.p.m., high-pitched, screaming. I felt desperately alone, isolated. I worked on the automatic pilot, but got no reaction from it. I twisted dials and snapped switched and tried the flabby, dead-weight controls. The entire system was gone, apparently all the cables were cut. Not a single member of the crew communicated with me over the interphone, even the electrical system was destroyed, and yet we were not on fire. I was sure we were not on fire. I noticed that the No. 3 engine manifold pressure gauge needle was fluttering behind the glass face of the gauge but I think I actually decided to bail out when I saw the air speed reading was 280 m.p.h.; at that altitude an indicated 280 m.p.h. meant that our ground speed was about 400 m.p.h. That was too much.

The ship, *Jenny*, did not seem to be going down rapidly but suddenly her left wing rose, flung itself up into the sky and the plane spiralled steeply towards the right. I yelled, 'Pilot to crew, bale out.' I yelled it three or four times and received no response. No answer, just silence. I started to climb out of the cockpit, tearing off my flak suit, and then crawled out of my seat and over the body of Major Clark, on to the flight deck. Clark was motionless. I could see what I took to be blood but I could not see where it was coming from. He was dead. Sergeant Brooks had left his top turret and when I first saw him he was kneeling by the open bomb bay, snapping his parachute on to his harness. He seemed to be fumbling, moving slowly, and it occurred to me that he might be hurt. I can't remember his face at all. We didn't speak; there was too much noise.

I motioned Brooks to go on out, waving toward the bomb bay. He shook his head. I took this to mean he wasn't ready and then he motioned to me to go first. I looked down into the open bomb bay and saw the horizon whirling round in a gigantic, sweeping curve. I could see more sky than ground and I thought that this was not the way it was supposed to be.

I dropped out head first. Standard procedure. There was a terrific *CRACK* in my ears and then I was falling, down, down, down . . . and out and it was quickly black. All black.[4]

Lieutenant William Chapin struck the tailplane of his B-24, shattering the bones in his right leg, which had to be amputated in a German hospital. He survived the war, returned to journalism, and now lives in California.

Aircraft could be lost from other causes, such as mid-air collisions, as Myron Loyet of the 385th Bomb Group can confirm:

The first hint of disaster was the bombardier rushing past and out of the escape hatch. Then there was a moment of darkness and the Fortress seemed to hesitate, shaking itself like a wet dog, the Plexiglass nose and side windows shattered, with an immediate jet-stream blast of air at minus 55° coming in through the nose section and out the escape hatch, causing all the dirt, maps and any accumulated paper to go with it.

My first impression was 'We're going down – all I need do is get one hook of my chest parachute on the harness, then if this ship blows I'll be OK.' Then I began unplugging my suit, throat mike and oxygen mask, ready to bale out. Fortunately the last item was the headset, for the pilot called me to salvo the bombs and give him a heading home. I hit the salvo switch and said, 'Take 270°' which was due west to somewhere in England.

With a lighter load the aircraft pulled out of the dive and now we were heading home. I hooked up to my walk-around air bottle and got out of that wind tunnel, but each time I tried to get out of the wreckage through the catwalk door I was drawn and pushed toward the open escape hatch. Finally the co-pilot came and caught me and hauled me up to the flight deck as the pilot went back to the waist.

Then I had the first glimpse of the damage. The two port-side engines were feathered, with badly bent props that had cut our low-echelon leader to bits; the front end of the nose section was missing, and the bombardier and flight engineer were no longer aboard. I looked at the co-pilot and saw that he was not going to be of much help, so I was happy that I had had some pilot training. He had already been shot-up once and ditched in the Channel and was said to be 'snake-bit'. Anyone can fly an airplane once airborne, so we were chugging merrily along except for one thing – the Ruhr. As we flew over the Ruhr – too low – the flak batteries opened up and began to shake us about.

The pilot had gone back to the waist to get the ball-turret gunner out of his jammed turret. He had lost his power and oxygen, and we had to go down to 15,000 ft or lower, to keep him alive until we could get him out. When the turret was manually cranked round and opened up, he was sitting in there, smoking, and he said, 'I thought all you SOBs had bailed out and left me here, so I was having a last cigarette.'

You may wonder how collisions like this happened. Most occurred over England during assembly, where there were a lot of bases within a few miles, all putting up aircraft and these were flown by 20- or 21-year-olds, flying a four-engined aircraft through cloud. The 'low lead' aircraft had flown too close underneath us and his tail had hit the ball turret, knocking him up into our props, which killed all in the forward section instantly; three baled out and became prisoners of war. We got in on two engines, and flew no more missions for three weeks, to calm our rattled nerves.

Many US bombers were lost to flak or in accidents, but, with ever greater strength and its fighter escorts growing in number and expertise, the USAAF fought on towards the spring of 1944. Losses remained high: 34 B-17s were lost from the 174 sent to attack the FW 190 plant at Oschersleben on 11 January – almost 20 per cent of the force committed and just over half the total number of US bombers lost that day on missions to Germany. These missions continued, as did *'Noball'* attacks on the flying-bomb launching sites along the Channel coast, where light flak also took a toll of the bombers. All this was a prelude to the major Eighth Air Force offensive, a concentrated week of attacks on the German aircraft industry – Big Week – in February 1944.

Spaatz and his commanders had been planning Big Week for some time. The targets were known, the orders were prepared and ready for dispatch to the air divisions and bomb groups; what was needed was a weather forecast offering several days of good weather and clear skies. This forecast finally landed on Doolittle's desk on Saturday 19 February 1944, and Big Week was launched next day.

The first day of Big Week was a memorable one for the Eighth. At last, 1,000 US four-engined bombers were setting out from Britain, escorted by hundreds of fighters and bound for twelve separate targets in Germany, most of them aircraft plants, like the Me 109 factory at Leipzig. And when the bombers were counted back at the end of the day, only 21 had been lost; the *Luftwaffe* had come swarming in, but the P-38s and P-51s were able to beat them off. One of those bombers was piloted by Lieutenant William R. Lawley, who, in 1999, was the last survivor of the Eighth Air Force's Medal of Honor winners:

> Our troubles began on 20 February, when were tasked to attack Leipzig. All went well until we were over the target and tried to bomb, but we had a hang-up and as we were trying to get the bombs free the *Luftwaffe* came in and really let us have it. A cannon shell exploded inside the cockpit and killed the co-pilot; his body fell across the controls and put us into a dive. It was just terrible, with his blood all over the windshield, and we had to tie his body back in the seat. Mason, the bombardier, still trying to get the bombs away, reported that we had an engine on fire, and about then I realized that I had been hit myself and I kept fading away as I hung on to the controls.
>
> It gets a bit vague after that, but I remember that I decided to get the crew out. The flight engineer had already baled out when it came to me that most of the crew were wounded like me and in no state to jump. So we had to stay with the ship and do what we could.
>
> Then it picked up some, because we put out the engine fire and Mason managed to get the bombs away, just before the *Luftwaffe* came back in, and set *another* engine on fire. They somehow failed to put us down, though, and thanks to Mason, who had done pilot training before switching to bombardier, we flew back to England. Mason could fly the plane but he could not land it, and I kept slipping in and out of consciousness, so it was a real effort to get the aircraft down on the first field we came to.
>
> Just as we were about to land we ran out of gas and one engine stopped, and something was wrong with the hydraulics so we could not get the gear down. Anyway, we made a belly landing at a fighter strip near Redhill, south of London – a field occupied by a Canadian squadron – and we got down fine. I'm happy to say that Mason and another crew member, who looked after the wounded when he was not manning a turret, both got Silver Stars – and all the crew came through.[5]

Next day – Monday – more than 900 US bombers set out for aircraft factories at Brunswick. The target was socked-in by cloud, but the US Pathfinders were able to mark the target and considerable damage was done by an area attack.

The Tuesday mission was less successful, mainly because the weather was poor. Curtis LeMay called back the 3rd Division, the 2nd Division got badly strung out in the clouds, and of the 1st Division's 289 aircraft only 99 found and bombed their targets. There were also a number of collisions, and one bomb group bombed the Dutch town of Nijmegen, killing 200 Dutch civilians. A total of 41 bombers were lost on this day, the majority from the 1st Air Division.

The bombers stayed on the ground on 23 February, to rest the crews and allow the crew chiefs and their teams to repair a large amount of battle damage, but on the following day they went out again. As already related, a large force attacked Schweinfurt as the advance guard for the RAF operation scheduled for that night. Over 800 bombers were dispatched, and other targets hit included the aircraft plant at Gotha, which was thoroughly blitzed by aircraft of the 2nd Division. Bomber losses were heavy: the 445th Bomb Group alone lost thirteen aircraft out of 25 dispatched, and the total loss for the day came to 49 aircraft – and nearly 500 men.

These losses might have been far worse but for the presence of the escort fighters, which denied the *Luftwaffe* the opportunity to concentrate on the bombers and did away with the German fighter pilots' ability to wait until the escorts had turned for home before wading into the bombers. The escorts now flew all the way to the target, and the German fighter pilots were forced either to take on the fighters or to let the bombers through. The aim of the *Pointblank* Directive, to write down the German fighter strength, was certainly being achieved – not least in the steady loss of experienced German pilots.

On the fifth and final day of Big Week, 830 bombers attacked Augsburg, Stuttgart and Regensburg, this last being the target for the Fifteenth Air Force coming up from Italy. The sky was clear, the bombing was accurate, and just 31 bombers were lost. The USAAF commanders ended *Big Week* justifiably satisfied with the results – both the success of their own tactics and the results achieved against the aircraft plants. For the next few weeks German fighter production fell, and it would not rise again until later in the spring, when the number of US escorts available would prove more than a match for anything the *Luftwaffe* could put up.

Big Week marked another turning point in the Bomber War: the USAAF had put up 1,000 bombers for the first time and had carried out long-range missions into Germany with high but acceptable losses. It also marked the moment when the strength of the Eighth Air Force first exceeded that of RAF Bomber Command. From then on, Bomber Command and the RAF in general would take a subordinate role in the Allied Order of Battle.

At this point, with Big Week concluded and RAF Bomber Command almost at the end of the Battle of Berlin, it is necessary to restate some of Harris's thinking, both on the bomber offensive and on ground operations on the Continent of Europe. Harris believed – he *really* believed – that if he was given a large enough force – about 4,000 heavy bombers was the force he had in mind, be they British or American or both – and a free hand to attack the industrial cities of Germany, an invasion and the consequent loss of life in ground fighting all the way to the heart of the Third Reich would be unnecessary.

Harris was not alone in this conviction: it was shared by his US colleague, Carl Spaatz. Here again, it is necessary to restate the bomber dream

– the concept that if the bomber was employed correctly, and in great force, ground warfare would certainly be unnecessary and war itself probably impossible. Harris had been able to demonstrate what strategic bombers could do at Hamburg, and if Bomber Command could do to the other cities of Germany what it had done to Hamburg, surely the people of Germany would not be able to stand it? They would come to see that resistance was impossible and rise up against their Nazi rulers, demanding peace.

That was what Harris *believed*. That was the thinking that underlined his concentration on area bombing. Smash the cities, carry the war to the people, crush the beast. Compared with that decisive task, attacking oil refineries or marshalling yards or any part of the Nazi military machine was simply, in Harris's words, a 'panacea'. The question that has to be asked is, Was he right? And that question has to be asked now, in the spring of 1944, because once the Allies land in Normandy the bomber dream is over and the land campaign begins. So, was Harris's dream feasible or not?

Air Chief Marshal Arthur Tedder, the Deputy Supreme Allied Commander under Eisenhower, certainly did not believe so, stating in 1944 that 'I do not myself believe that any modern war can be won either at sea, on the land alone or in the air alone . . . in other words, war has changed to three-dimensional, and very few people realise that.'[6]

Harris believed otherwise. But surely the true answer is that nobody knows. It is, however, possible to speculate and, although the speculation will depend on the point of view of the speculator, it may be that, had he been given all he asked for, Harris may have been right. The devastation wrought on German cities was truly awesome, but, as the number of aircraft put up in these constant sorties indicates, Harris could rarely put more than 700 bombers into the air over any one target – the 1,000-bomber raids were the exception until the last six months of the war, and his total force of heavy bombers never exceeded, 1,600 aircraft.

View the photos of the damage Harris's bombers caused and it is not hard to see what might have been achieved with 2,500 more – and with the USAAF bombers adding their weight as well the bomber dream might have become a reality. There is also the point that Harris was never able to achieve *sudden, total* devastation – though Hamburg came close – and only that kind of attack, to city after city, as at Hiroshima and Nagasaki – which did bring Japanese resistance to an end – offered any real possibility of victory. Would something similar to Hiroshima and Nagasaki, even if non-nuclear, have achieved the effect necessary to provoke a rising against Hitler's rule or to stun the German leadership into surrender? Nobody knows.

This point is not made to advocate the deployment of the atomic bomb in Europe, or indeed in Asia; it simply states that the tough and resolute people of Japan were battered into surrender by two such attacks and we have no reason to suppose that similar devastation on Germany, though achieved with 'conventional' weapons, would have been any less effective. The effect of dropping two atomic bombs – area-bombing weapons par excellence – on the Japanese cities of Hiroshima and Nagasaki in August 1945 was the destruction of two cities and of most of their civilian population; the result of this horror was that Japan surrendered. Had the Japanese elected to fight on, the Americans would have destroyed their country, city by city – and, unlike Air Chief Marshal Harris, they had the means to do it.

Perhaps that was the main flaw in Harris's plan: he did not have the weapon to devastate Germany in a way that would also destroy the German will to resist. He was also hindered throughout his campaign by a classic piece of military miscalculation, a failure by the Allied Combined Chiefs of Staffs to maintain the aim.

The aim of Bomber Command operations, from the time they began in 1939, was *to carry the war to the heart of the enemy homeland*. That was what the strategic bomber was *for*, and no one in authority disputed this. 'There is one thing that will bring him [Hitler] down, and that is an absolutely devastating, exterminating attack by heavy bombers on the Nazi homeland. We must be able to overwhelm him by these means, without which I do not see a way through'. Thus wrote Winston Churchill in 1940,[7] and throughout the war the Directives that landed on Harris's desk continued to press this point on him. Harris needed no such urging; what he needed was more aircraft and a free hand.

Instead there was a failure, at all levels, to maintain this intention and carry it through. The main failure lay in not providing Bomber Command with the wherewithal to carry out this declared intention; it was not the fault of Air Chief Marshal Harris. From the earliest days of the war there was a continual diversion of bomber strength, with aircraft and crews sent to North Africa and Italy, to Coastal Command and to the Far East. This steady drain prevented Harris from ever achieving the size of force he needed to carry out the instructions he was given. And then, in the spring of 1944, orders came that would divert Harris yet again from his chosen task – orders to apply his Command to the task of softening up the enemy before Operation OVERLORD.

Hawker Typhoon F

14

Overture to OVERLORD
January–June 1944

The comparatively brief period when the strategic bomber forces of both the RAF and the USAAF were placed under the control of Eisenhower ... was absolutely the only time during the whole of my command when I was able to proceed with a campaign without being harassed by confused and conflicting directives.

Sir Arthur Harris, Marshal of the Royal Air Force, *Bomber Offensive*, 1947

Operation OVERLORD, the Allied landing in Normandy in June 1944, was the crucial operation of the Second World War. Had OVERLORD failed, Western Europe would be very different today. While the war would have been won, eventually, by the Allied powers, it is probable that Russia would have overrun much of Western Europe in the process and the war would certainly have lasted a few more years. There is also the possibility that the use of V2 rockets by the Germans and any subsequent delay in OVERLORD would have provoked the use of the atomic bomb by the Allied powers. The success of OVERLORD prevented all that.

Since OVERLORD was crucial, and was seen to be crucial, it is not surprising that General Eisenhower, the Supreme Allied Commander, asked for and received all the military forces he felt necessary for the successful execution of the Allied invasion. These included control of the Allied strategic bomber forces – including Bomber Command – for the months before and after the landings on 6 June 1944.

The first draft of a plan for the invasion of Europe was drawn up in 1943 by a British General, Sir Frederick Morgan, and as Morgan was Chief of Staff to the Supreme Allied Commander his draft was known as the COSSAC Plan. In January 1944, General Eisenhower sent his designated land-forces commander – at least for the invasion phase of the operation – General Sir Bernard Montgomery, back to Britain from Italy to study the COSSAC Plan.

Montgomery did not like it. He thought the invasion front too narrow and the forces employed too weak. When Eisenhower arrived and saw the COSSAC Plan he did not like it either, and the plan was therefore changed and enlarged. The invasion beaches on the bay of the Seine were extended to include Utah beach on the Cotentin peninsula, more divisions were to be put ashore in the early phases of the landing – and the pre-invasion bombing programme was greatly increased.

The Supreme Allied Commander had already been given a *tactical* air force, consisting of the British Second Tactical Air Force (2nd TAF) based around the former 2 Group of Bomber Command. Composed of medium bombers plus two fighter groups, and two transport groups for the dropping of parachute troops, this force was activated in June 1943. In October 1943 the 2nd TAF was joined by the US Ninth Air Force, these being mustered for the invasion as the Allied Expeditionary Air Force (AEAF) under the command of Eisenhower's Air Commander-in-Chief, Air Chief Marshal Sir Trafford Leigh-Mallory.

By 1944 Britain had put all her forces and available strength, military and economic, into the struggle against Hitler. Britain had no more to give, but the US contribution to the struggle was steadily increasing and was already far in excess of Britain's. This was largely a matter of demography: the United States has far more people and can therefore produce far more soldiers than the United Kingdom. Numbers count, and by 1944 Britain had been eased into a subordinate position. That position was to sink still further as the US share of the war effort increased. This was inevitable and quite fair in the circumstances, but it did produce certain strains among the military men.

General Montgomery, for example, felt that his role as land-forces commander should be continued after the invasion phase; this proposal was anathema to the US generals – or most of them – for Montgomery, though an acknowledged master of the set-piece battle, was an exceedingly vain man with a great knack for rubbing his US colleagues up the wrong way. Besides, Eisenhower eventually intended to take direct command of the Allied armies himself, and since he was the Supreme Commander no one could object to that – though Montgomery certainly tried.

The position of Air Chief Marshal Trafford Leigh-Mallory as commander of the Allied Expeditionary Air Force was complicated by that of General Carl Spaatz who, as already related, on 24 December 1943 became commander of the United States Strategic Air Force – a force whose numbers far exceeded those of the Royal Air Force. Like Montgomery, Leigh-Mallory was none too popular with the Americans, but the real snag was that Spaatz had no intention of placing his large command under what he saw as British control. In this he had the support of Hap Arnold, who had already told Spaatz that he wanted him seen as 'the supreme air commander in Europe'.

This view was not *entirely* chauvinistic. Spaatz was well aware that the decision on who gave the orders rested with Eisenhower, and he would have followed the agreed chain of command had SHAEF insisted on it, but there was another, more cogent, reason for his refusal to recognize the authority of the AEAF commander. Spaatz thought that the AEAF set-up was one layer of command too many, which is arguable, but probably correct. The two tactical air forces, the US Ninth Air Force under Lieutenant-General Lewis H. Brereton and Air Marshal Alan Coningham's 2nd TAF, worked well together, and on the strategic level Spaatz and Harris were old comrades; when asked about the relations between the USAAF and Bomber Command, Harris is on record as saying that: 'I should say that we had no relations. The word is inapplicable to what actually happened; we and they were one force.'[1] If so, then why have an extra layer of command at SHAEF? As Air Marshal Coningham pointed out later, 'the establishment of an extra Headquarters in the Air Force chain of command caused constant difficulties'.[2]

Spaatz was probably right: there *were* too many links in the SHAEF air plan. Tedder was an airman, as well as being Deputy Commander, and then there were the Air Chiefs of Staff – Portal and Arnold – then Spaatz with two full air forces and a host of senior commanders, and Harris with Bomber Command. Why introduce another element into the air-force command structure, when the existing set-up worked perfectly well? It should be added that this argument related only to the strategic bombing forces – Spaatz had no objection to any arrangements SHAEF might have for the two tactical air forces.

At this point it might be as well to deal with another matter that came to a head about this time: the deep-seated American belief that the British, specifically the RAF, were trying – and indeed had always been trying – to take command of the USAAF in Britain. This is a well-established, American myth – and total nonsense.

It is nonsense because it was never going to happen, and everyone knew then – and certainly ought to know now – that it was never going to happen. If anyone got overall command of the Allied air forces in 1944, that someone would have been an American. And yet, in his biography of Spaatz,[3] David R. Mets refers constantly to this fear of a British takeover. In this biography Mets records Ira Eaker writing from England in 1942 to say that the RAF was 'showing signs of wanting to absorb American air units piecemeal as they arrived in the United Kingdom' (p. 120). Mets also reports Spaatz, on the day after he arrived in Britain, telling a group of reporters – 'some of whom were British' – that 'while he intended to cooperate closely with the British air arm, there would be no overall commander and American operations would be separate from those of the RAF' (p. 131).

For the period covered in this chapter, Mets says that Spaatz 'successfully resisted attempts by the Royal Air Force to gain control of the American Strategic Air Forces' (p. 175), but what these attempts consisted of remains unspecified. Lacking such evidence, one is forced to the conclusion that the bogeyman was Leigh-Mallory, who was certainly an RAF officer and British but who was at this time a member of Eisenhower's staff and one of the SHAEF commanders. It was in *this role*, as a SHAEF commander, and not on behalf of the RAF or Britain, that Leigh-Mallory was supposed to command the Allied Expeditionary Air Force during the invasion and for some weeks after it – as Eisenhower, the American commander, wanted.

The belief that the RAF nursed some long-held and deep-seated dream of getting command of the US air forces in the ETO is total rubbish. It so happens that the USAAF could not have functioned in 1942 without the wholehearted co-operation of the RAF, which supplied bases, logistical support, intelligence information, photoreconnaissance, fighter escorts and even aircraft. It was indeed suggested in 1942 that until the USAAF could provide such assets from its own resources it might integrate its offensive with that of the RAF. It was also proposed that US fighters should take a share in the air defence of the UK, if only to gain operational experience. Both suggestions were rejected by the US commanders, and the subject was not pursued.

Yes, when Harris proposed bombing Berlin in 1943–4, his memo to Churchill did indeed say, 'We can wreck Berlin from end to end if the USAAF will come in on it' – but that 'if' is significant. The choice was the USAAF's, but the USAAF did *not* come in on it and neither Harris nor Churchill had any authority to make it. To extrapolate from these few incidents some cunning British plot to take over the American air forces in Britain is not far short of paranoia.

Chauvinism is a waste of time, and British military historians have become used to this sort of selective reporting by their overseas colleagues, but it is necessary to put in an objection here, if only in the interests of truth and accuracy. By 1944 it was very clear that the Americans intended to take command of every aspect of the war and at every possible level – evidence for which appears in a significant memorandum produced by Spaatz's staff regarding the re-formation of the AEAF after Leigh-Mallory's original formation had been wound up, amid great American glee, in October 1944. 'Its chief must be an American with the rank of Lt-General. The Chief of Operations must be an American with the rank of Major General. Signals and Plans should be headed by American officers with the rank of Brigadier General. The Chief of Intelligence must be a Britisher with the rank of Air Commodore, but the Camp Commandant must be an

American with the rank of Colonel.'[4] The need for a British officer to serve as Chief of Intelligence is not to fit a 'Britisher' in somewhere, but because, even at the end of 1944 – three years after the United States entered the war – the bulk of intelligence information for the USAAF was still being supplied from British sources.

It therefore appears that in the early spring of 1944 a great deal of time and energy was wasted at SHAEF, wrangling over the question of who would command the strategic air forces just before, during, and immediately after the landings. Meanwhile the bombing offensive went on. Until March, Harris was busy with the Battle of Berlin, and from March the USAAF bombers, now happily endowed with a long-range fighter, were at last able to set about the destruction of Germany in daylight and in considerable force, as air gunner Virgil Marco describes:

On Monday 24 April 1944 our squadron, the 366th of the 305th Bomb Group, was part of an armada of 750 heavy bombers heading for a number of targets around Munich, deep into Germany. Our particular target was a twin-engine-aircraft repair yard at Oberpfaffenhopen, fifteen miles south of the city. We were to have an escort of British Mustang fighters, but were warned that we should not rely on fighter protection over the target. I was a gunner, and when were over the Channel we tested our guns and both my .50s fired, but later failed.

We were nearing the target after a very long flight when suddenly silver Messerschmitts flew past and down in front of my guns. I opened fire, but my right gun would not fire and I could not hold the left gun steady. Twenty or so Me 109s flew past and disappeared, and when I looked back I saw five or six B-17s peeling out of formation, engines smoking and parachutes appearing as the crews baled out; I learned later that the 41st Bomb Wing bore the brunt of this attack and lost fifteen bombers.

We had been hit and lost an engine and could not maintain formation and began to drift back and continued our flight to the target alone and dropped our bombs. Then we saw American fighters escorting our group back to England, and out pilot radioed the P-47s and asked for an escort home, only to be told that they had to stick with the main group and we were on our own. Someone suggested we should head for Switzerland, but Captain Lincoln, our pilot, said we were heading back for our base at Chelveston; we were unaware that fourteen damaged B-17 aircraft would make their way to Switzerland. And so we flew on falling further behind and getting lower, down to 5,000 ft.

Then we flew over Frankfurt, by mistake, and got hit by flak. We continued to lose height until we were down to 1,400 ft and passing over small villages, I assume in Belgium or northern France. Everything looked peaceful, and where were the enemy? Then, about 1700 hrs, I saw a small dot about the same altitude and coming up from the rear – an FW 190.

I called out a warning and began firing and the right gun again jammed, so I continued firing the left gun. I could see fire on both sides of the FW's wings and assumed I had hit him, but it was his guns firing at me; 20 mm shells began bursting above my head, ripping the skin off the plane.

When the firing stopped, small pieces of metal were embedded in my face and I was bleeding, and when I tried to communicate with the rest of the crew the intercom did not work. I crawled into the waist section and found that one of the waist gunners had already baled out; I saw the ball-turret gunner, Mayfield, standing in the radio room, pointing at the body of the radio operator, Denemy, on the floor. Gene Snodgrass left the plane and I waved at Mayfield to leave, and my last memory is of standing in the door, seeing Gene's parachute opening and deciding not to jump and the wing having a large number of holes in it, some the size of grapefruit. Then I was out, my chute opened with a terrific jerk, and suddenly I hit the ground. James Mayfield jumped after me and his chute failed to open.

Two of Virgil Marco's fellow crew members were killed. The rest were hidden by French civilians and passed on to the resistance, who sheltered them for some weeks; all the survivors eventually returned to England.

Omer Van Huylenbrouck recorded the details of one of his missions in February 1944:

Our target today was Schweinfurt. The last time we went there, in October last year, they lost 60 ships, and when the briefing officer told us our target, it was amazing how quiet the room got. They gave us a very good route to the target, with other groups going to targets nearby. Enemy fighters were plentiful; at one time about fifteen of them came in abreast of one another shooting their cannons into our formation, but they must have missed for no planes went down. Two B-17s from the low group went down when they tore through that formation, and I only saw two parachutes come out.

Also saw one B-24 go down, do a barrel roll and then catch on fire and only three chutes came out. Those B-24s sure got hell knocked out of them today, sure am glad that I am on B-17s, we were carrying 40×65 lb incendiaries and they went away at 1.27 p.m. and right smack on the target. Flak over the target was thick and pretty accurate; we had no enemy fighters to contend with on the way back, but there was some flak. Jerry throws it up before we get to it and then all we do is fly round it; sometimes it is too thick and widespread and then we have to fly right through it. We landed back at the field at 4.30 p.m. I thank God for bringing us all back safe once more; No. 13 is coming up.

The RAF was also deep in the fray, and the night of 24/25 March was a memorable one for Bomber Command – 'the night of the strong winds'. It is some indication of how unused the world's air forces were to high flying in 1944 that the existence of what is now called the 'jet stream' was virtually unknown; until the middle of the Second World War, aircraft did not fly high enough to encounter this phenomenon. But, as Australian rear gunner Max Ladyman of No. 35 PFF Squadron relates, they met it in force on this operation:

The winds that night were supposed to be about 30–40 knots. Instead they were about 120 knots, from the north. This scattered the planes all over Germany, and while we managed to bomb Berlin many didn't and were so far off course that some planes may have run out of fuel on the way home. There was also a lot of flak coming up as well, and as we started to slow down on the runway at base I came out of my turret and found a hole about two feet across right by the door. Another two feet and it would have gone right through the turret and myself.

Bomber Command put up 811 aircraft for this operation to Berlin and lost 72 – nearly 9 per cent of the force committed.

Steve Musolino of the 305th Bomb Group was flying missions at this time:

Of the 28 missions we flew over Germany in 1943–4, 24 were deep-penetration raids into the eastern end of Nazi Germany. This meant we were usually under constant flak or fighter attack. Most of our targets were of the industrial type, such as aircraft and aircraft-parts manufacturing plants, the Erkner ball-bearing plant at Schweinfurt, marshalling yards, the I.G. Farben chemical works, and so on.

On the subject of the Erkner plant, we were the replacements for the original group who went to that target previously, which was a disaster. Only one aircraft of the 305th returned to base; it seemed that the whole of the *Luftwaffe* was waiting for them that day. But when we went to Schweinfurt on 24 February, we blasted the place wide open. Next month, on one of the first runs to Berlin, the briefing officer told us that 'The aiming point will be the centre of Berlin, and I mean the (expletive) centre', apparently because Goering had boasted that the USAAF could never get to Berlin in daylight.

The raids on Germany by day and night continued, but D-Day was approaching and the strategic air forces – the USAAF Eighth and Fifteenth and RAF Bomber Command – were now required to lend direct support to the coming invasion, as the Allied commanders appear to have been deeply concerned over the likely *Luftwaffe* reaction to the landings. This provoked another argument with Harris – one which dated back to an exchange with Portal at the end of December 1943, though the matter had been brewing for some time.

At the end of October 1943 – four months after the issuing of the *Pointblank* Directive – Churchill had asked Portal to suggest what Bomber Command could do in support of OVERLORD. Portal proposed that Bomber Command might devote its entire strength to whatever tasks Eisenhower wanted in the fourteen days leading up to the landings, when 50 per cent of Bomber Command would be committed to SHAEF, rising to 100 per cent on D-Day itself, then declining steadily until D-Day plus 50, after which everyone would think again. Portal did not mention that this meant a disruption in the strategic campaign against the industrial and economic resources of the Reich.

Portal was aware that an American proposal was also being mooted under which the Supreme Allied Commander would take command of *all* the Allied air forces in Britain and the Mediterranean, when he wanted and for as long as he wanted. There was then a great deal of discussion – and not a little argument – until, at the Tehran Conference in December 1943, the Combined Chiefs of Staff agreed that 'in the preparatory phase, immediately preceding the invasion, the whole of the available airpower in the United Kingdom, tactical and strategic, will be employed in a concentrated effort to create the conditions essential to assault'.

Portal must have expected some resistance from Harris, who was by then deeply engaged in the Battle of Berlin, but when he put the matter to him he found Harris surprisingly amenable and declaring himself 'most ready to discuss the matter of co-operation with the AEAF commanders with the object of making the execution of Overlord as inexpensive as may be in lives which we can ill afford to lose'. The use of the word 'discuss' is interesting, and it soon appeared that Harris had a couple of points to make, on matters that needed to be clarified.

First, Harris wanted an assurance that the *Pointblank* Directive still pertained. Second, he insisted that the current bomber offensive must be maintained against Germany proper, since, he said, 'any failure of the Combined Bomber Offensive to restrict German fighter production would rule out Overlord altogether'.[5]

The letter in which he made these points was written on 27 December 1943, six months before D-Day, and, although it is a thinly veiled hint that Harris saw hitting the German industrial cities as his contribution to OVERLORD, it also reveals that something was wrong with Allied thinking at this stage in the planning for invasion.

Hindsight is a wonderful gift – historians would be lost without it – but the fixation of the Allied planners and commanders on the German fighter force and its possible effect on the D-Day operation made no sense even in December 1943. Command of the air over the D-Day beaches and the offshore shipping was clearly essential, but there could be no problem in providing it. The D-Day beaches lay barely 80 miles from Britain's south-coast airfields, but Allied fighters were already escorting Allied bombers as far as the Rhine, and fighter range was steadily increasing; in fact Allied fighters ranged 70 miles into France on D-Day. Also, Allied air forces had more than enough fighter aircraft to overwhelm any number the *Luftwaffe* could put up over the invasion beaches – in quantity and in quality.

Air power on D-Day was vital, but the Allies already had command of the air over Normandy. The fact that the Normandy beaches lay within fighter range of England was one of the reasons they had been chosen for the landings. Even Field Marshal Rommel, the German commander in

Normandy, knew that the Allied command of the air would be total. His decision to dig in his forces well forward and fight the battle on the beaches was taken in this knowledge: Rommel knew that Allied air power would prevent him from moving his forces about. If Rommel knew the battle for air supremacy had been won before the first Allied soldier stepped ashore, why were the Allied commanders still wittering on about it up to a few weeks before the landing?

On 1 April 1944, the German single-engined day-fighter force was deployed as follows:

Defence of the Reich	850
Northern France/Low Countries	135
Norway	30
Italy	145
Eastern Front	515
Total	1,675

These figures show that approximately 50 per cent of the German day-fighter force was deployed for the defence of Germany, and the way to keep it so deployed was to carrying on attacking strategic targets inside the Reich. There was little or no change in this strength or dispositions up to the time of the Normandy landings, and the notion that the *Luftwaffe* could deploy enough aircraft to disrupt the landings has no foundation whatsoever.

Besides, if the *Luftwaffe* fighters did appear over Sword or Omaha beaches, thousands of Allied fighters would fall upon them. On D-Day itself the *Luftwaffe* managed just *three* fighter sweeps along the 50 miles of D-Day coast and only about 300 sorties over the whole of Normandy. While this small reaction could not be known in December 1943, it is still hard to see why the OVERLORD planners and commanders were then so concerned about the effect of German fighters on the D-Day landings due six months later – by which time the P-51 Mustang, now entering service, would have come to dominate the skies of Europe. The situation over the Normandy beaches on D-day itself is emphasized in this account from USAAF ground-crew mechanic Donald Kabitzke:

> I was a member of the 88th Fighter Service Squadron, based at Lymington on the south coast of England in 1944. Our job was to service the aircraft of the 50th Fighter Group of the 9th Air Force, which was equipped with P-47s. We were so close to the English Channel we could throw rocks into it. One day in June we were told to stop what we were doing, grab a paint brush, and paint wide white stripes on the wings of every aircraft – any plane that went over Normandy without them would be shot down immediately.
>
> Before dawn on 6 June – D Day – we were up to watch the fighters taking off. When they were airborne we were told they would patrol the beaches at 9,000 ft and any German aircraft that came into their territory was fair game.

The pilots were to be disappointed. Later that day the Fighter Group Commander, Colonel Greenfield, invited us to hear what the pilots had to say. They had flown over the Normandy beaches all day and could not find a single German aircraft.

In his biography of Spaatz (p. 190), David Mets states that Spaatz was 'appalled' by Leigh-Mallory's assertion 'that it was not necessary to win air superiority before the invasion was launched but rather that the battle could be won over the beaches'. If Spaatz was indeed 'appalled' he was also wrong and – given the Allied air superiority over Normandy – Leigh-Mallory was absolutely right.

The German fighter force was, by any reasonable calculation, the least of the OVERLORD commanders' worries, and Harris was right to draw attention to the benefits of a continued air offensive against Germany. Portal was well aware of Harris's fixation about the cities, and he wrote back advising him that the continuation of bombing attacks on German targets during the invasion phase would depend on the extent to which they helped the execution of OVERLORD 'and not on the extent to which they weaken Germany's general power to make war' – a comment that left plenty of scope for debate.

This issue also brought Harris into conflict with Leigh-Mallory and the AEAF. The original AEAF proposal was that the heavy bombers should make all-out attacks on railway lines and marshalling yards all over northern and eastern France, with the aim of sealing off the Normandy bridgehead and reducing German ability to rush troops and tanks to the front. Harris protested at this idea, pointing out that his Command was designed for the destruction of industrial centres and was equipped for that task with highly specialized aircraft. The AEAF replied that, as far as they could judge, an industrial centre or marshalling yard in France was not very different from a similar target in Germany, so what, exactly, was Harris's problem?

They did agree that Harris's force was totally unsuited for daylight operations – which is again debatable – and Harris promptly pressed this advantage, pointing out the highly specialized nature of night bombing, the importance of target-marking and the function of the Pathfinder Force, all of which Bomber Command had carefully honed to attack Germany. Harris still believed that bombing alone could bring Germany to its knees, and he was therefore trying to stop Bomber Command being diverted from what he saw as its main task: the destruction of German cities.

The AEAF staff then pointed out that on short-range operations to northern and western France aids like *Oboe* would be even more effective and weather forecasting more accurate and spring was coming, promising better weather. As a counter to Harris's first point, it was added that Bomber Command would be aiding OVERLORD only for a matter of weeks, not months, and this diversion of efforts, apart from being essential, would not seriously infringe on Bomber Command operations against the heart of Germany. Harris was clearly trying to wriggle out of any long-term commitment to OVERLORD, but he was more than willing to help the landings, provided he could do so in his own way.

This exchange was followed up on 14 January 1944, when Air Vice-Marshal Bottomley – Deputy Director of Bomber Operations at the Air Ministry – wrote a letter to Harris in the form of a Directive, ordering him to adhere to the spirit of the 10 June 1943 Directive (*Pointblank*) and attack, 'as far as practical, those industrial centres associated with German fighter airframe factories and the ball-bearing industry' – i.e. Schweinfurt, as well as aircraft factories at Brunswick, Gotha, Augsburg and Leipzig.

Harris regarded all these as 'panacea' targets from which the main production lines would have long since been dispersed, but he duly mounted attacks – on Brunswick on the night of 14/15 January, on Leipzig early in February, on Schweinfurt on the night of 24/25 February, and on Augsburg on 25/26 February, interspersing these attacks with operations against Berlin, which was soon to come under attack from the Eighth as well. Mort Fega of the 305th Bomb Group flew on the USAAF's first Berlin missions:

> The defining date for the first daylight bombing raid on Berlin was 6 March, when a massive force of B-17s and B-24s attacked the city. The losses were the highest recorded by the Eighth Air Force, and 69 four-engined bombers were shot down. Truth to tell, though, a small cadre of bombers had dropped bombs on Berlin a few days earlier, on the 3rd, having gotten through to the target when the rest of the force was recalled. My group was operational that day but obeyed the order to abort the mission and return to the UK; I do recall that before we turned back I saw two Forts collide in the clouds.
>
> On the 6th we were called at 0315 hrs for a 0500 hrs briefing, took off at 0810 hrs, and this time we made it to Berlin. But we did not hit the primary target; we dropped in the north-east portion of the city. Fighters galore and heavy flak. By the time I got back to my room it was 2000 hrs and they got us up for another mission next day, but it was scrubbed.
>
> I remember that the primary target was a ball-bearing plant, south-east of Berlin. We were briefed to fly east of the target and bomb on an east-to-west heading – a tactic that would make us less vulnerable to Jerry fighters. Unfortunately the weather did not permit us to use that tactic and, as I said, we did not bomb the primary. I have a vivid memory of the flak, which came in all sizes – 88 mm and 105 mm I'm sure of, and probably 155 mm, judging from the size of the ominous black puffballs that were abundantly visible. There was a vast array of defending aircraft – small wonder that we lost 69 bombers.

Losses continued in both air forces and from all the usual causes, as this account from Jim Mallinson, an Australian air gunner with No. 186 Squadron, indicates:

My crew consisted of five Australians, a Pom and a Scot. It was the only pre-dominantly Australian crew on the squadron because two of the original crew, Charlie, our wireless operator, a happy and handsome young Pom, died when we ditched in the North Sea during OTU, and our original skipper failed to return from Stuttgart when flying as Second Dicky with another crew. He was Jim Houghton, a Kiwi and a good bloke. Incidentally, Jim lost his 'Tiki' good-luck charm coming back from the pub the night before the op; the entire crew hunted high and low for it, all along the road while Jim was being briefed, but we could not find it; he went without it and we never saw him again. Both were replaced by Australians, who just happened to be the only ones available at the time.

Our second skipper, Jeff Clarson, had lost his entire crew at 1651 HCU on a night when they were on an air test with another pilot – for some reason Jeff was not flying – and a German intruder aircraft on the circuit shot them down. In the meantime the rest of us had survived as spare 'bods' for a few weeks on XV Squadron. We fronted the CO, a one-armed wing commander who had the DSO, DFC and DFM and was seen to crash later when operating as master bomber over the Ruhr.

While these operations and missions went on, the commanders contin-ued to argue. The next development in the Allied bombing offensive came in a plan put forward by Professor Solly Zuckerman, scientific adviser to Leigh-Mallory and Tedder, who suggested that if the Allied air forces bombed railway communications – bridges, tunnels, marshalling yards and stations – in France during the weeks before the landings it would have a dramatic effect on Germany's ability to support and supply its front-line troops. This plan, the Transportation Plan, was swiftly adopted by AEAF, but met with equally swift opposition from Churchill, Spaatz and Harris.

Harris was against it because he had no wish to attack precision targets in France with a force equipped and trained to attack area targets in Germany. Churchill was against it because he believed it would cause heavy civilian casualties among the French. Spaatz did not like the Transportation Plan because he had settled on another way of ending the war – an attack on Germany's always limited and now shrinking oil supplies.

Now that the USAAF bombers could reach Germany in daylight and in large numbers, precision bombing attacks on Germany's synthetic-oil plants were certainly possible. However, Harris and the British Air Staff were against the Oil Plan, Harris inevitably regarding oil as another 'panacea' target, and the Air Staff pointing out that the destruction of oil refineries, even if successful, would take months to affect the operations of the German military machine in France in the immediate aftermath of the invasion, and something offering a more immediate benefit was needed.

These arguments rumbled on through February. In early March, Air Chief Marshal Portal, his patience now growing thin, persuaded Harris to make some experimental night precision attacks on twelve German aircraft component factories in France. Harris delegated the task to Cochrane at 5 Group, and Cochrane passed the job to No. 617 Squadron, commanded by Wing Commander Leonard Cheshire and equipped with Wallis's new 12,000 lb blast bombs. All twelve attacks were made at low level and were highly successful, so the experiment was extended to six railway marshalling yards. These too were swiftly obliterated, and even Harris expressed himself gratified with the results.

It was now three months before the invasion, and Eisenhower was becoming increasingly frustrated by the apparent inability of his air commanders to come up with a workable command system or decide on target priority for the invasion. On 22 March he declared that if some satisfactory answers were not obtained soon he would go to the Combined Chiefs of Staff and resign his command, but before taking that drastic step he called a meeting to discuss the whole matter yet again.

This meeting was held on 25 March.[6] Portal wisely took the chair, and all the main commanders – Spaatz, Harris, Leigh-Mallory, Tedder and Eisenhower – were there, accompanied by their senior staff officers and advisers. The declared aim of this meeting was 'to consider what target system ought to be attacked with the effort remaining after what had been necessary had been allocated to the attack on GAF [German Air Force – *Luftwaffe*] targets'. From this it appears that even now, just ten weeks before D-Day, the aims of *Pointblank* still had priority over targets in direct support of OVERLORD.

The current target systems were, in order of priority:

1. the *Luftwaffe*,
2. transportation,
3. oil,
4. the cities.

These targets needed evaluating. The attack on the *Luftwaffe* should clearly be maintained, but need not be stepped up – *Luftwaffe* strength was obviously declining, if not in terms of numbers, then certainly in terms of effectiveness. The transportation system was an obvious OVERLORD priority, and, if 617's success were anything to go by, it appeared that it could be attacked without heavy casualties among French civilians. Oil – yes, an excellent idea, but before concentrating everything on synthetic oil it would be necessary to destroy Ploesti, which was still in full production, and Portal, while agreeing on the importance of oil in the medium term, did not feel that attacking German refineries would do much to help the Allied armies land in Normandy. And finally the cities, which were the particular priority of Air Chief Marshal Sir Arthur Harris.

Tedder spoke first, putting forward the merits of the Transportation Plan, while stressing that keeping up the attacks on the *Luftwaffe*

(*Pointblank*) 'remained the highest priority'. Eisenhower gave this view his full support. Spaatz then took the floor and spoke up in favour of his Oil Plan, suggesting that the order of priority should be;

1. attacking *Luftwaffe* factories and airfields,
2. oil,
3. assistance to OVERLORD and the land battle.

Clearly the argument was going round in circles, because the senior commanders either had lost sight of their war aims or were confused over what they were doing at this stage in the war. There were, in fact, only two main aims, and somebody – preferably Eisenhower – needed to point them out and insist on concurrence. The first was to land an Allied force in Normandy. The second was to defeat Nazi Germany, a task in which everyone around the table wanted to play a part – there was no dispute on that point. Harris's views were well known and had not changed: strategic bombing, the shattering of Germany, could make a seaborne invasion unnecessary. Spaatz shared this view – provided the strategic offensive concentrated on oil. 'In the early months of 1944 . . . Spaatz on several occasions expressed his belief that full-scale use of the air forces – including the tactical air forces – would eliminate the need for the highly dangerous Overlord operation.'[7] The question that had to be resolved at this meeting was, Which aim had priority *now*? The answer, surely, was the Normandy landings, which were also seen by most of those round the table as a step towards the achievement of the second aim and not an unnecessary diversion. Apart from Harris and Spaatz, no one thought that bombing alone was going to win the war against Germany.

The wrangling went of for some time, but the meeting did finally reach some useful conclusions. OVERLORD took priority, and Transportation was seen as more crucial to its success than Oil. Harris then offered to use his force against the marshalling yards, using *Oboe* in the moon periods when operations over Germany were not normally mounted. Eisenhower accepted this, although he did not see that Harris's concession on this point involved any departure from what Harris was already doing. Spaatz confirmed that his aircraft would play their part in implementing the Transportation Plan. Finally, to resolve the command issue, Tedder took over control of air operations from Leigh-Mallory and it was tacitly agreed that Spaatz would report to him or directly to Eisenhower.

Eisenhower therefore withdrew his threat of resignation. The results of this meeting were the subject of a Supreme Commander's Directive that was issued on 17 April, less than two months before D-Day. *Pointblank* remained the priority, but 'with Overlord the supreme operation for 1944, all possible support must be provided to the Allied Armies to assist them in establishing themselves in the lodgement area'.

Further Directives would be issued covering air operations after the landings, but in the period before D-Day the air forces were to concentrate on *Luftwaffe* and transportation targets. These attacks proved highly effective. In the three months before D-Day, only four of the 80 main transportation targets in France escaped damage and rail traffic within France dropped by 70 per cent. That apart, and when circumstances permitted – or precision bombing missions were ruled out by weather – the RAF and the USAAF were to attack German cities, especially Berlin, the latter using 'blind' bombing techniques which Nathanial Glickman of the 44th Bomb Group recalls:

> I am not aware that my squadron was referred to specially as a pathfinder group, though that terminology was used in our midst. We did not drop coloured flares to point out a target as the RAF did, inasmuch as we bombed in daylight. Our bomb groups would unload their bombs after seeing us drop ours. The 44th Bomb Group was, to the best of my knowledge, the only group in the Second Air Division to have PFF equipment, other than the 389th at Hethel, where we trained to use our *Mickey* [H_2X] unit. We flew B-24s, and although it is possible that the B-17 division had a similar system within their groups I never saw a B-17 with a grey radar unit instead of a belly turret. I cannot confirm that the equipment was indeed H_2X since I was not the operator of that equipment; as bombardier, my sole piece of equipment was the Norden bombsight. I do recall that, as lead bombardier in the group, I often complained that the use of our bombsights and their accuracy was dependent on a clear view of the assigned target. When there was complete cloud cover or when the Germans lit smoke candles that obscured the primary target we had to switch to the secondary.
>
> The 23 PFF missions I flew with the 44th Bomb Group rarely needed the use of the radar equipment; we usually found broken cloud or clear weather, and I do recall that the PFF equipment would sometimes malfunction or be damaged by flak. I also recall one occasion when my plan moved up from 'deputy lead' to 'lead' on a mission to Munich and the primary, Riem airfield and the city of Munich, was completely covered by cloud. We then received a coded signal to leave the airport and bomb Munich. It was a max raid, with my aircraft leading 1,000 planes, and my aiming point was the Bahnhof Platz in the centre of the city. On the next day we went back and bombed it again; both flights took nine hours plus. When acting as a gunner I was also fortunate to shoot down an FW 190 that was attacking our formation; that resulted in the lead crew buying me drinks for a month.

So the Eighth also began bombing German cities, which were still being stoutly defended by the *Luftwaffe*, as this account from the 345th Bomb Squadron, 384th Bomb Group, on 13 April 1944 can testify:

> The Group learned today, at terrific and tragic expense, that the *Luftwaffe* despite its huge losses in the past still retains combat strength and is capable of inflicting damaging blows against our bombers. The target today was

Schweinfurt but of the nineteen planes that entered enemy territory, only ten attained their objective – nine of the original force were destroyed through enemy action.

Flak en-route to the target was reported ranging from meagre to moderate, over the target, intense and accurate. Destruction of the bombers was achieved through the tactic of drawing off our fighter escorts. Two attacks were then made, one lasting approximately 25 minutes, the other three minutes, but it was during the latter than seven of our bombers were knocked out of formation. As to the mission, photos disclosed that the bomb pattern was 400 yards off, extending out into the marshalling yards area. The leader of the group formation was First Lieutenant Joseph I. Bedsole, Jr. His pilot was First Lieutenant Clarence Stearns, who was flying his final mission. Lieutenant Bedsole's ship was shot down a few minutes before the IP; hits were scored by enemy fighters on the No. 3 engine and the gas tank and the wing broke into flames. Observations of chutes leaving the aircraft vary from four to nine.

The lead was then taken by First Lieutenant Philip N. Bennett, Jr., who flew his depleted formation to the target, bombing in ideal weather conditions; the specific target at Schweinfurt was the machine shops holding the ball bearing and piston ring industries. Sgt Kenneth Wyatt, nineteen, a left waist gunner, said that all he could see was 'a huge cauldron of flames with oily smoke pouring out', adding 'we were too busy to watch it long; during the big attack every gun was firing and the very atmosphere was vibrating from the concussions'.

The first attack on the Group was made by fifteen Me 109s, and lasted about 25 minutes, and destroyed one Fortress in the low squadron. Other enemy fighters were observed attacking another Wing to the rear of our formation and the P-47 escort veered away to assist. As soon as they were gone, fifteen FW 190s made a head-on attack, flying in between the lead and low squadrons; a second wave followed, using the same tactic. The low squadron, consisting of planes from the 545 Squadron sustained the brunt of this attack and six of the seven aircraft in it were shot down, the only survivor being the plane piloted by Second Lieutenant Dewayne Bennett. A P-51 escort then appeared and no further interceptions were made by the enemy.[8]

Describing the action, Lieutenant Philip N. Bennett stated:

Some 109s had attacked but caused no trouble. Then four enemy a/c came in and were chased off by our escort and it was then that the FWs hit us. The lead ship nosed down, the whole right wing on fire. The FWs went by so close we could see the pilots faces; we were giving them everything we had and the last one through was smoking badly as he left. The plane piloted by 1st Lt James R. Lavin received a direct hit from flak in the left wing tank and exploded in mid-air with two chutes seen to emerge. 2nd Lt Verlyn C. Tollisen's plane was lost in the first attack and as already mentioned we lost six in the second vicious attack; one of these six, the plane piloted by 1st Lt Edward A. Fieretti, exploded. Seven parachutes were seen emerging from this aircraft.

The 384th Bomb Group was in strife again eleven days later, on 24 April, when it took part in the mission to Oberpfaffenhofen, described here by Dewayne 'Ben' Bennett, sole survivor of the 'low' group on the Schweinfurt mission:

This was my sixth mission, and our target was the Dornier Werk Gmbh factory and airfield. The entire mission was plagued with problems. We were flying in the low squadron of the high group, almost but not quite 'Tail-End Charlie' but far enough back for any increase in speed by the combat wing leader to have a devastating effect. The aim was to maintain an air speed of 150 m.p.h. and stay together, but on this mission we had a lot of trouble staying in formation. There were five combat wings on this mission, each containing between 54 and 63 heavy bombers – our group put up 56 – and instead of flying in a bomber stream we would be going in two wings abreast or in echelon. Briefing was before dawn, taxi time 0830, and Lieutenant Boger was the first off at 0854. All thirty planes in our group got off by 0934, and we eventually formed our combat wing of 54 aircraft and crossed the English coast at 1100 hrs, flying at 15,300 ft.

On crossing the enemy coast at 1123, a 306th Group aircraft was hit by flak and pulled out of formation with flames coming from the No. 4 engine; parachutes started coming out, but only three or four had opened when the aircraft blew up. Cursing and shouting then started over the radio as exasperated pilots struggled to keep up and stay in formation, urging Smokestack Blue Leader to slow down. Forty miles east of Paris, Lieutenant Harvey received a direct hit from a burst of flak. For a few moments the plane flew on as if nothing had happened, and then fire and smoke were seen and four parachutes came out; only three were seen to open, and the plane went down. Changes of course and speed broke up the formation, and no sooner had we re-formed than we changed course again. The result was that there was an entire combat wing away from the main bomber stream, strung out, all alone, and ripe to be plucked. And that is what the German fighters did.

The first attack came in between 1215 hrs and 1230 hrs by Me 109s. This attack was driven off by our P-51 Mustang escorts; the Me 109s dived through the formation with the P-51s following, all firing. No bombers went down, but at 1319 hrs, east of Leiphelm, the roof fell in. We were hit by 50 Me 109s and 190s, coming in two, four and eight abreast from twelve o'clock high. Some flew straight through the groups only to return to the head of our flights and come in again. Alfred Humble, one of our pilots, reported that 'Over the target there was utter confusion because one group had turned on to the bomb run early, causing mid-air collisions.'

Before the target was reached, sixteen B-17s were shot out of our 56-strong wing – the total loss for the day, from 754 bombers dispatched to various targets, was 40 planes, so 40 per cent of the losses that day were from our wing. In our plane, 42-102430-JD-O, we were in plenty of trouble. The tail was shot full of holes, the batteries in the right wing root had been hit, and the hydraulic system behind the upper turret was on fire. Seeing the flames, I gave the order to bale out, but the only one who heard me was the ball-turret gunner. Fortunately things calmed down and my crew did not leave the plane; it would have been embarrassing to bring that aircraft back with no crew. The plane was all shot up; she had over 280 holes in the skin and several damaged systems. We landed without brakes, rolled to the end of the runway, and managed, with the aid of the outboard engines, to turn off on to the taxiway and cut the engines. As a crew we worked well together, and I take pride in them.

As for Bomber Command, Harris intended to carry out attacking German industry – in short, the cities – but would also carry out attacks in northern and eastern France co-ordinated with those of the USSTAF – attacks which aimed to 'reduce the strength of the GAF, destroying and disrupting enemy rail communications'. Harris took up this task at once, using the Halifax IIIs of 6 (RCAF) Group and 4 Group to attack marshalling yards in France. And so the build-up to OVERLORD gradually got under way. These attacks had to be spread out all over France; they could not be concentrated on the perimeter of Normandy or they would tip the Germans off about where the Allied armies would actually come ashore. A large number of attacks also went on down the Pas de Calais to help the OVERLORD deception plan. By the first week of June these Allied bombing raids had succeeded in paralysing most of the French transportation system. The bomber operations were coupled with low-level attacks by ground-attack aircraft, RAF Typhoons and US P-47 Thunderbolts, against trains and locomotives and attacks by heavy and medium bombers against flying-bomb (*Noball* or *Crossbow*) sites on the coast of the Pas de Calais.

Eisenhower's headquarters took command of the strategic bomber forces – including Bomber Command – on 14 April 1944, and retained control for five months, until 14 September. During that period the day-to-day control over the air campaign was delegated to Tedder. There is no need to follow the missions and operations of the bomber forces in any detail, for they were both engaged in carrying the war to the enemy by well-tried means. *Nickelling* and *Gardening* operations continued, arms drops to the French Maquis intensified as D-Day drew near, and the battering of German resources continued, inside and outside the frontiers of the Reich and around the perimeter of the invasion area in Normandy.

On 3 May, Bomber Command mounted a major attack on the German Army supply base at Mailly-le-Camp in France and suffered severe losses. The target was first marked by Cheshire and No. 617 Squadron, who had developed considerable skill in precision marking, and the Main Force were ordered in to bomb. Unfortunately, the master bomber of the Main Force was unable to transmit the order to his aircraft, as his radio had been accidentally jammed by a US Forces broadcast on the same wavelength. While this was being sorted out, the *Luftwaffe* arrived in strength and shot 42 Lancasters down – over 11 per cent of the force committed. Nevertheless, the raid was a great success: the deputy master bomber took over, 1,500 tons of bombs were dropped accurately on the *Wehrmacht* base, and a great deal of damage was done to the tanks and transport.

Harris had now made some changes to the structure of Bomber Command. Following the losses at Nuremberg, he had decided to split his force whenever possible and tackle at least two targets, or more if possible, on every night an operation was mounted. To this end, he took three PFF squadrons – Nos. 83 and 97 Lancaster Squadrons and No. 627 Mosquito Squadron – away from Bennett's 8 (PFF) Group and sent them to Cochrane's 5 Group, which was now to operate as an almost independent force, concentrating on precision attacks. Cochrane's group had been specializing in low-level marking and precision bombing since the middle of 1943, and was now very good at it.

This reduction in his strength did not please Don Bennett, who also saw it as a slight to the PFF, but Bennett too had not been idle: to the PFF activities he had now added the Light Night Striking Force of fast Mosquito bombers, which were now devoting their time to the bombing of Berlin, carrying 4,000 lb of bombs – as much as a Flying Fortress – on every sortie and sometimes making two sorties to Berlin in a night.

Nor was Harris totally wedded to area bombing. He now wanted to develop the precision side of Bomber Command's operations – a sensible move after the long-standing attempt to combine RAF area attacks with USAAF precision attacks had failed to work. A number of RAF squadrons – No. 617 and No. 9, flying Lancasters, and No. 106 in Mosquitoes – became, in effect, Bomber Command's precision bombing force, for use against small targets like the Antheor Viaduct, the Dortmund–Ems canal and the battleship *Tirpitz*, as well as for target-marking. Other groups, notably 1 Group, were developing their own target-marking techniques, but Main Force operations were still led and marked by PFF squadrons, who would continued to take the lead until the end of the war.

While supporting preparations for OVERLORD, Harris continued to batter the German cities, and Spaatz, while faithfully doing his share of work on the Transportation Plan, had not forgotten the Oil Plan. In April three massive strikes were made against the Ploesti oil fields by the Fifteenth Army Air Force, and on 12 May Spaatz mounted several attacks on synthetic-oil refineries in Germany, claiming that they would bring the *Luftwaffe* up to do battle. And so the war went on, as the time approached for the Normandy invasion.

On the morning of 6 June the skies over Britain, the Channel and the coast of France were full of Allied aircraft: heavy bombers, medium bombers, fighters, transport planes, even gliders – so many that, in an attempt to aid swift identification and avoid collision, each aircraft had been marked with broad stripes of white paint, the OVERLORD markings. Bomber Command played a significant part in this enterprise, and if the *Luftwaffe* was hardly seen on D-Day itself, it became active again that night, as Canadian rear gunner Warren Quigley of No. 61 Squadron can testify:

My last operational sortie – the thirteenth of our tour – was on the night of 6/7 June, my second trip on D-Day. The whole invasion was in progress below us as we crossed the English Channel: Dakota C-47s were towing Horsa and Waco gliders, the Navy was bombarding the coast, and the sea was a weaving mass of landing craft, taking the troops ashore. It was a clear night, and the sky at our level was filled with aircraft en route for targets behind the German lines. We bombed our target, Argentan, south of Falaise, and on our return were attacked by two FW 190s. On the first attack I was not hit, and as the attacking FW peeled away, slightly above and to the right, I engaged it with my guns, the tracer bullets hitting him. There was one tracer in every five rounds, the others being armour-piercing, explosive, incendiary and ball. Each gun fired at the rate of 1,150 round a minute, and I raked the FW along the fuselage and around the cockpit area. He went into a spin and I believe I shot him down, though there was never any official confirmation and I was never asked for a report.

We were now in corkscrew and I saw the second FW approaching from astern and above; I engaged him and kept firing until I was hit by his fire. I can recall a terrible smell of smoke in the turret, hot sparks flying everywhere, and felt a violent jerk in my left leg as it was slammed against the side of the turret. My turret and guns would no longer function and there was a strange feeling of calmness and quiet; I am not sure that I was not unconscious for a moment. My next feeling was of warmth as my flying boot was filling with blood, and this was followed by a terrible pain in my left leg.

The next sensation was of someone hitting me in the back. This turned out to be the wireless operator, hacking me out of the turret with an axe. He than dragged me out of the turret, and my next sensation was that of being choked – the wire from my earphones and microphone had become caught and was strangling me – and then Ken was able to drag me into the back of the aircraft and attend to my wounds.

There is no doubt that I owe my life to Ken. He cut off the flying clothes around my leg and applied a field dressing and a tourniquet; a bullet had gone right through the fleshy part of my calf, taking a part of the tibia with it. He did not realize that I had also been hit in the back of the thigh. This other wound was quite large – about the size of my fist – and the bullet had shot away a lot of muscle; the only thing that stopped me bleeding to death was that my suit was quite tight and I was lying on my back and the combination of my weight and the suit helped to stop the bleeding.

He gave me one shot of morphine – all that was allowed – and I was alternately conscious and unconscious until the Lancaster landed. The brakes were not operational, as our hydraulics had been shot out, and we careered beyond the end of the runway, through several fences, and ended up in a ploughed field. We were chased by an ambulance, and I was taken out and rushed to hospital.

One of the surgeons wanted to amputate my leg, but another thought it could be saved and he succeeded. I can recall waking up, and standing round the bed were the rest of my crew – Bert, Bryan, Terry, Mac, Ken and Jack. I cannot recall any conversation, and when I came round they had gone. That was the last time I saw them – they were all lost on operations a few weeks later.

D-Day, 6 June 1944, was a great day for the Allied air forces – proof that Giulio Douhet's theory that 'he who commands the air commands the bat-tlefield' was a working reality. The *Luftwaffe* stayed away, and at 0730 hrs, as the SHAEF communiqué states 'Allied forces, supported by strong air and naval forces, began to land this morning on the Northern Coast of France.' There was, however, another way to look at this event: now that a land campaign had been launched on the continent of Europe, the bomber dream was over.

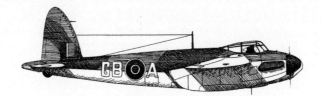

De Havilland Mosquito B

15

The Destruction of Germany
September 1944–February 1945

I am not satisfied that we are using our air power really effectively. The various types of operation should fit into a more comprehensive pattern, whereas I feel that at present they are more like a patchwork quilt.

Arthur Tedder to Portal, October 1944

On 14 September 1944 command of the strategic bombing forces reverted once again to Spaatz and Harris – but the return of their forces was accompanied by yet another Directive, issued jointly by Arnold and Portal but sent to Spaatz and Harris via Air Vice-Marshal Bottomley of the Air Staff. This Directive charged the commanders with 'the progressive destruction and dislocation of the German military, industrial and economic systems and the direct support of land and sea forces'.[1] This task was then broken down into the specific target areas. The *Luftwaffe*, severely reduced as a day-fighter force in the last six months, had now vanished from the list of prime targets, and of the other targets one in particular was now listed as a 'first priority' – oil.

Between 6 June and 14 September the Allied air forces – both tactical and strategic – had been involved in supporting the Allied armies in Normandy. The landing had been a success, but the Allied offensive soon stalled in the face of stout German opposition and an inability on the part of the Allied logistical organization to supply the Allied armies with sufficient fuel for an advance by their ever increasing mechanized forces.

The support of the strategic forces, if willingly given, was not always beneficial. The carpet bombing of Caen by the RAF, apart from destroying a beautiful city, did not materially help the advance of Canadian forces, since the streets were full of rubble and bulldozers had to clear a way for the tanks. On the American front, the first day of Operation COBRA, the 'Saint-Lô breakout', was marked by the bombing of the leading American units by a large force of American bombers. This was caused by a failure to identify the ground markers and the confusion caused by the drifting smoke from previous explosions, effectively creating 'creep-back.' News of the catastrophe did not get back to all units of the USAAF, as Manny Abrams, a B-24 navigator with the 392nd Bomb Group records:

> On 24 July a maximum effort was scheduled to drop a great tonnage of bombs on to that fairly confined area of German resistance [around Saint-Lô]. I remember that we did reach the peninsula but we were recalled due to a solid undercast. Although we frequently bombed through such a cloud cover, the possibility of a bombing error so close to the Allied line prohibited such a gamble. American soldiers were just too close to the target area. The risk was greater than the reward. All planes returned to bases without accomplishing the mission.

Not all, alas. Jack Capell, a radio wireman in the US 4th Infantry Division, was under the aircraft that bombed:

> The Saint-Lô breakout – Operation COBRA – began on 24 July 1944, when thousands of US bombers started to blast a path through the German defences. Visibility was bad that day and some bombs fell on our positions. My regiment, the 8th Infantry of the 4th Division, was spearhead for the attack and when 2,700 bombers came over we caught most of it. First there was this tremendous, gigantic, earth-shattering sound – the roar of thousands of engines. Some bombers hit the German defences to our front, right on time and on target, and I thought we were doing pretty well. Then came the B-17s . . .
>
> The first bombs again fell right on the German line. I was watching from my foxhole and I got out for a better view. The bombs were going off like machine-gun fire. Then a bomb fell in my field, knocking me off my feet and I got back in my hole, fast.
>
> From then on it was indescribable. The whole earth was shaking, the air was full of dust and smoke and bits of steel and earth, and the roar of engines overhead went on and on. We had about 600 casualties in the 4th Division from that 'short bombing', with over 100 killed, including Lieutenant-General McNair, the deputy commander, who is now buried in the US cemetery at Saint-Laurent near Omaha. The earth looked like the surface of the moon, but our 'B' Company advanced anyway and we all followed.

British and American strategic and tactical air forces bombed their own troops on several occasions, and before long the Allied troops were becoming as wary of their own air forces as they had been of the enemy's. However, close support of the armies also cost the Allied air forces a number of casualties, as Major Albert Hill of the 386th Bomb Group recalls:

> On 12 June the British Air Ministry received an urgent warning from the French resistance that the Germans were unloading tanks at the Bretigny marshalling yards, south of Paris. In a short time we had 36 B-26s on the way, each carrying eight 500 lb bombs. Our pilot, Ted Hankey, kept our box of eighteen aircraft in close formation and a little below the lead formation, and I was looking down at the ground, watching out for anti-aircraft fire. I saw what I was looking for – a battery of guns, all firing at once. It takes about seven seconds for an 88 mm shell to reach altitude, so I said just two words on the intercom: 'Turn left.' I should have said, 'Flak coming up – turn left', for, instead of turning, my friend and pilot, Ted, came back with a question 'Why?' Before I could answer, the B-26 just ahead of us exploded from a direct hit that broke the plane into two pieces. For the first time in my military career I called my superior officer by an unprintable name: 'That's why, you so and so!'

The *Luftwaffe* did put in some night raids on the Allied lines, but without great effect; its main contribution to the defence of Normandy was the dispatch of single aircraft to roam over the Allied lines at night, dropping flares and the occasional bomb to disrupt the sleep of the troops below, the aircraft responsible being known to the US infantry as 'Bedcheck Charlie' or 'Washing Machine Charlie'.

Allied ground forces – American, British, Canadian and Polish – had the constant support of two tactical air forces: the American Ninth and the British 2nd TAF. These two forces, equipped with medium bombers, fighter-bombers and rocket-firing aircraft – British Typhoons, US P-51 Mustangs and P-47 Thunderbolts, flying in 'cab ranks' over the battlefield, waiting for a call to assist the struggle below – were of inestimable help in easing the Allied armies forward, a task they completed with the savaging of the German Seventh Army in the 'Falaise Pocket'.

Tactical air power was not, however, restricted to direct army co-operation. When no attack was in progress, the fighter-bombers and rocket-firing fighters roamed at will across France, attacking trains, road transport, truck and tank parks, anything they could see, supporting the actions of the strategic bombers.

Tactical air forces had yet again demonstrated their value on the battlefield; the strategic air forces still had something to prove, and eliminating Germany's oil resources would be one of their major contributions to shortening the war.

The idea of concentrating on Germany's oil resources was not new. Oil had been listed as a prime RAF target as long ago as 1939, but all the usual difficulties – long range, small targets, stout defences – had inhibited any decisive moves to reduce Germany's oil stocks and supply, though everyone knew that oil was the Achilles heel of the German military-industrial complex. The first task was to knock out Ploesti, a concentrated target and the one which supplied the largest single proportion of German oil. Fortunately, this task was already in hand.

The USAAF Fifteenth Air Force had attacked Ploesti again in April 1944, and kept up the attacks relentlessly throughout the summer months. Losses among the US bombers were extremely high – one account refers to Ploesti, the third most heavily defended target in Europe after the Ruhr and Berlin, as 'the graveyard of the Fifteenth',[2] – but the Americans kept going back: on 5 April, on 15 April and on 24 April, then again on 5 May, and yet again on 26 May. Benedict Yedlin of the 449th Bomb Group flew to Ploesti on 6 June 1944:

> This was our crew's second mission to Ploesti – we had already been there on 5 May – and our plane, *The Buzzer*, was one of 39 B-24s from the group that took part in this raid. As far as I could tell from my position in the ball turret, the mission had been reasonably successful, as evidenced by the huge columns of black smoke that penetrated the defensive white smokescreen, though I had yet to see the city of Ploesti or track our bombs down to the target. This was the most heavily defended target in Europe, next to Berlin and the Ruhr, and we saw intense flak and some B-24s were seen to explode, others to head down with chutes coming out. Holding our collective breaths, we got through the flak and sustained very little damage – just some holes in the fuselage, tail and right wing.

These constant missions set large areas of Ploesti alight, and the oil fires burned for weeks, stoked up by other raids throughout the summer. The final missions – on 10, 17, 18 and 19 August, involving over 1,000 aircraft on every raid – finally stopped Ploesti's production.

The destruction of Ploesti took 24 separate raids and cost the Fifteenth Air Force 305 heavy bombers and over 3,000 men. This series of missions and the cost involved indicate that destroying the oil refineries supplying Germany would never have been easy and successful raids on Ploesti were only possible at this stage in the war, when the German fighter forces had been much reduced and the P-51 was available for escort.

The destruction of Ploesti made Germany's synthetic-oil plants the prime oil target, and even Harris, with his dislike of single-industry 'panaceas', now seemed more than willing to concentrate his attention on the German oil industry. Indeed, on the day before the 14 September Directive arrived, Harris sent 140 aircraft to attack the Nordstern oil plant at Gelsenkirchen, the second RAF oil raid of the week. Compared with city targets, oil refineries were small, so to pursue these attacks meant a return to precision bombing and where possible bombing by day, but this concentration on helping the land battle in Normandy did not prevent Harris diverting some of his strength to the continued attack on Germany.

Peter Weston of No. 186 Squadron recalls several daylight operations against oil targets:

> Our first operation was to Gelsenkirchen, Germany, our load consisting of fifteen 500 lb bombs and one 4000 lb 'Cookie' – a heavy load, so not so much fuel. Halfway to the target we had a runaway propeller so we had to shut down one engine and could not maintain the briefed height of 17,000 and had to go in at about 13,000, while those above were going faster. We were not too happy about this. We did hear the master bomber giving instructions but there was no doubt where the target was and we blitzed it. (By the way, though, we heard that it was up and running again a few weeks later and it had to be hit again.) This was a daylight op, as was our next one – to Dortmund; cloud cover was complete over the target, but even daylight raids were marked and I remember we dropped on purple flares while other aircraft were told to drop on red and green. Total effort this time meant 1,083 Lancasters and Halifaxes.
>
> We also did night ops. One to Kiel was to sink the battleship *Admiral Hipper* and render the port useless; both tasks were achieved. Fighter warnings were given on the way out, and when I was in the astrodome watching for fighters I saw a Heinkel zoom past us in the opposite direction, slightly above and to starboard, about 150 ft away. Another nerve-trembler was the raid to Potsdam in April, when many of the crews identified German jet aircraft shooting past at super high speed with flames shooting out the back. We did not hear of them shooting down any of our aircraft, and the radar-directed flak of Berlin was more of a worry at this time.

German night fighters were still taking a steady toll of RAF bombers and being increasingly crafty – a fact revealed by this account from William I. Davies, a Canadian navigator with No. 156 Squadron, PFF:

> Operation No. 24 of our 43 completed operations was to Politz, a suburb of Stettin on the Baltic, which contained an oil refinery. We were flying at 18,000 ft, pressing on with three engines, one having overheated, when Mike McCrory, our cat's-eyed Canadian mid-upper gunner, switched on his mike and said, 'There's a Ju 88 on the starboard beam, with its cockpit lights on – watch out for his friend, coming up behind blacked out.' I took a quick peek and clearly saw the German pilot; this was an old dodge, known to our crew, but scarcely had Mike called out corkscrew instructions to Wally, our pilot, than we experienced a tremendous raking from cannon and machine-gun fire, from an almost invisible Ju 88 behind the one with lights on. Mike and Jim, the rear gunner, engaged the fighters, while Wally threw the aircraft about and I saw dividers, computer, eraser and pencils fly into the air before me. We then became aware that our second engine had been hit and there were holes all over the aircraft, though amazingly no one had been hit. However the engine we had now lost provided the power to one of the

turrets and that was now out of operation as another tremendous burst of fire shook the aircraft and knocked out another engine, reducing our Lanc to one.

We headed down, diving for a bank of cloud, and Eddie Ogden, our flight engineer, swore that he and Wally only managed to restart the first engine, the one lost before the attack, when we were 50 ft above the chilly waters of the North Sea. We made it back to base, but when the sergeant in charge of our ground crew saw the holes he said he could not believe how any aircraft could stay in the air with that amount of damage.

Incidentally, we were then given a 48-hour-leave pass, and I was in civilian cloths in a café, eating Spam and chips, when a woman came up, asked me why I was not in the Army, and gave me a white feather. Everyone in the café stared at me as I collected my things and left. I never ordered Spam and chips again.

During July 1944 Bomber Command launched a series of attacks on the city of Stuttgart, and three devastating raids – on 24, 25 and 28 July – finally reduced the city to rubble. James Berry flew on all three operations with No. 7 Squadron, PFF:

We went back to the Reich at the end of July, starting with an attack on Kiel. Groans at briefing, for Kiel was *always* awful and I hated the place. We were primary blind marker, and as we were going in our cockpit glowed. I thought we were on fire, but when I turned my head for a look I saw that above us and to the right a Lancaster was on fire. If it fell to port we would have real problems, but it fell the other way.

On 24, 25 and 28 July to Stuttgart, as secondary blind marker. Each night the same route, the same height, the same time over target. The first two raids were OK, but the third one wasn't. The winds were not as forecast, and we soon realized our spare minutes had gone. The route was such that we had no corners to cut to get there on time, so we decided to go straight in, diverting from the given track, and that, plus a few extra knots, would get us to the target on time. No one wanted to be out of the stream, and it soon began to look not at all nice, with aircraft being shot down. Being off the given track and the events around us really affected me, to the extent that I literally began to shake a lot. The engineer had to speak to me about something, and having to reply brought me back to reality. We lost 39 aircraft that night; the tactics were not good and the Germans were not stupid. I was 22 at this time.

At this point, with the German day-fighter force so much reduced, it might be asked why Harris did not switch the bulk of his operations to daylight bombing. Granted, his force was trained and equipped for night operations, but, as the Americans had discovered, night navigation aids like *Gee*, *Oboe* and H_2S, as well as PFF marking, were also needed in daylight if targets were to be found and hit. Harris's force could and did operate by day – not least on ground-support operations – and with winter coming on it would find its expertise in night attacks equally useful in the short, gloomy days between October and March – if the war lasted that long.

Freddy Fish recalls one daylight operation which illustrates the effect of weather even at this stage in the war:

> On 6 November 1944 we made a daylight raid on a refinery in the Ruhr area; 256 Lancasters and 21 Mosquitoes from 1 and 8 Groups were supposed to form up behind a 'vic' of three aircraft which would lead the stream. Take-off time 0815 hrs; time over target 1036 hrs. All went well, and we got *Gee* fixes throughout so track-keeping was very good. However, as we neared the target we ran into cloud reaching up to 21,000 ft and the sky-markers dropped by the *Oboe* Mosquitoes just disappeared into the murk. Obviously dropping on markers was impossible, so the master bomber – code-named *Applesauce* – ordered the Main Force – codenamed *Grenville* – to bomb any built-up area.
>
> Although we were some miles from the target area, all the aircraft around us promptly opened their bomb doors, released their loads, turned around, and got the hell out of it. Our gunners were urging us to do the same, but I felt we had not come all this way to waste our effort on open fields so I persuaded the pilot to press on. The gunners were calling me all the names under the sun, but with one other aircraft we pressed on for a few more miles, while the flak was coming up, to reach the edge of the Ruhr, where I said, 'Let 'em go!'
>
> We had an uneventful return, and as it was a nice sunny day I took over flying the Lanc, after he had trimmed it to fly straight and level, while the bomb-aimer practised getting fixes on the *Gee* set; we did this now and then on daylights, when the pilot got a bit bored. Later on that day, back at base, we listened to the BBC News, where they announced that 'Today large forces of RAF bombers attacked targets in north Germany', roaring with laughter for we knew we had only killed a few cows. This was confirmed later when the town of Wanne-Eickel reported only two buildings destroyed and ten people killed.

Quite apart from the fact that daylight bombing was fundamentally more accurate unless the cloud cover was total, daylight bombing was now much safer. German day fighters were being shot down in quantity by the USAAF fighters, but the German night-fighter force was protected by the darkness and was still able to shoot down significant quantities of RAF bombers. In short, the boot was now on the other foot: the darkness that had once protected the British bombers was now protecting the German fighters. Careful questioning of the surviving bomber crews and examination of the RAF records fails to reveal why the RAF continued to press on with night bombing after September 1944, but there were probably a number of reasons.

First, with the USAAF ranging over Europe in ever increasing numbers and sending thousands of bombers and fighters to attack a shrinking amount of enemy territory every day, the skies over Germany, and North-West Europe in general, were getting very crowded. It made sense to let the USAAF use the daylight skies and for the RAF to take up the task at dusk. Second, Bomber Command was reaching the height of its technical and operational power: it had the aids, the aircraft, an abundance of trained crews and a great deal of experience *in night operations*. Finally, Bomber Command *was* mounting more and more daylight operations, and using a wider variety of marking and bombing methods as each group began to develop its own individual technique. This had begun before D-Day, when, as already related, Harris sent some Pathfinder squadrons back to Cochrane's 5 Group and this group began attacks on precision targets, using low-level marking techniques.

Although Bennett's 8 (PFF) Group continued to mark for the Main Force, with ever increasing precision, other groups, notably 1 Group, followed Cochrane's lead and by the autumn of 1944 the Pathfinder's hold on navigation and target-making was less secure than it had been in 1943. On 18 October 1944, 3 Group started making independent raids when it attacked the town of Bonn, using the newly developed *G-H* radio-pulse 'blind' bombing technique. This was not unlike the USAAF toggelier technique, in that the *G-H* bomber found the target under heavy cloud cover and when the *G-H* aircraft bombed, all the other aircraft did likewise. *G-H* remained a useful aid until the end of the war, and 3 Group in particular became highly proficient in its use. This did not concern Bennett, who had enough to do with marking for Main Force raids and organizing operations for the Light Night Striking Force – the LNSF – which by March 1945 contained eleven Mosquito Squadrons capable of putting up over 200 aircraft every night.

The LNSF had started life in 1943 with just one squadron of Mosquito bombers, No. 139 Squadron. Bennett employed this squadron on small-scale raids deep into Germany, and the speed, height and accuracy of the Mosquito led to more squadrons being added to the 8 Group bomber force. The LNSF was often used for diversion or 'spoof' raids, dropping a few bombs on some target well away from the main one, to distract the German fighter controllers, and often dropping large amounts of *Window* to create the illusion of a much larger force on the German radar screens. Bennett, with Harris's approval, began to build up the LNSF for bombing operations and during the pre-invasion phase, from March to June 1944, LNSF Mosquitoes dropped most of the RAF's bombs on Germany, becoming, as the 8 Group history says, 'a menace to the Germans, rather than a mere nuisance'.[3] The size of LNSF operations gradually increased from a couple of aircraft to a full squadron or more; in July 1944 27 LNSF Mosquitoes raided Berlin, and by the winter of 1944–5 LNSF aircraft were both marking and bombing. The most important feature of the Mosquito was not its bomb load but its speed. The German night fighters could not catch it, for it flew too high and too fast – though Mosquitoes could be shot down on occasion, as Paul Zorner relates:

> Normally we did not attack Mosquitoes; compared with the Me 110 they were much too fast. But there is always an exception to the rule, and on the night of 20/21 April 1944 the RAF flew in over the north of Holland to attack Cologne. The weather was not good, the visibility poor. I had been posted to III/NG 5 as commander, and we were only ordered off when bombs were actually falling on Cologne and then my take-off was delayed by a technical problem, so I did not get airborne until 0139 hrs and it was not until 0240 hrs that my *Funker* picked up a single target which appeared to be flying on a north-westerly course.
>
> He guided me on to it, but we remained in clouds and at 0250 hrs I saw a shadow in front of me. I got closer and saw it was a twin-engined aircraft like a Ju 88, peacefully flying in a westerly direction, which I could not understand. So I got even closer and realised that it was a Mosquito, flying on one engine, the propeller feathered. I closed in, aimed at the unfeathered engine, and opened fire. He immediately fell and plunged away in a steep right-hand dive and disappeared into the mist. We circled over the area for a while and saw something ignite and a fire on the ground; next morning the loss of a Mosquito from the air space south of Antwerp was confirmed.

Bomber Command lost two *Serrate* Mosquitoes on the night of 20/21 April 1994. One of these must have fallen to Paul Zorner, and it is curious that the *Serrate*-equipped Mosquito did not pick up the night fighter on its radar.

Serrate Mosquitoes shot down a considerable number of German night fighters – until the Germans woke up to the existence of this aid and brought in counter-measures, as David 'Taffy' Bellis of No. 239 Squadron relates:

> My pilot, Denis Welfare, and myself were posted to 239 in January 1944, to fly Mosquito IVs. Like the other crews, we had no experience of offensive night fighting. There was, of course, no fighter ground control over Germany, and that is where *Serrate* came in – a radio receiver in the Mossie picking up the *Lichtenstein* transmissions from the German night fighter (usually an Me 110 or a Ju 88). A *Serrate* receiver had two screens, one giving the vertical and the other the horizontal direction of the German transmission, and we tracked the fighters either near their radio beacons, where they waited for the bombers, or along the edges of the bomber stream when they were trying to attack.
>
> We had no luck on our first sorties, but on the night of 31 May we had a contact, converted it to a visual sighting, and shot down an Me 110. We shot down another near Aachen on the night of 5/6 June. Our squadron destroyed many night fighters at least until the end of July, but after that successes became few and far between as the Germans did not use their radio

beacons as before and our contacts dried up. We also experienced massive radio interference with our AI [air-interception system] and it was impossible to pick up a contact from more than a few hundred feet.

Mosquito bombers were not armed: they relied on their speed to elude attack. This factor led a number of people to suggest that the LNSF should be expanded and take over the bulk of the RAF's night bombing, which would reduce the current losses and allow the rest of Bomber Command to switch to daylight bombing. Other Mosquitoes, of 100 (Bomber Support) Group, equipped with *Serrate*, joined the bomber stream to hunt down German night fighters. Jack Furner was a navigator in 100 (Bomber Support) Group:

> I was in No. 215 Squadron as 'navigation leader', flying B-17s. My task was to monitor the efforts of all the other navigators and act as the squadron commander's navigator on his ops. 100 Group had been established for the purpose of creating confusion using radio counter-measures, and the B-17s were equipped with a long list of pieces of kit with intriguing names like *Jostle, Mandrel, Airborne Cigar, Airborne Grocer, Piperack* and *Carpet*, each designed to jam a specific piece of enemy radar or a specific part of the defensive radio transmission system. The main advantage of the B-17 in this role was that it could fly at say 25,000 ft – some 5,000 ft above the main bomber stream – and thus provide jamming on all frequencies.

100 (Bomber Support) Group had been formed in November 1943, to bring together under one command all the various radar and radio aids now available to support the Main Force on operations. The Group was commanded by Air Vice-Marshal Addison, who had been involved in this kind of warfare since the 'Battle of the Beams' in 1940. The devices at his disposal included *Tinsel*, to jam the frequencies used by German fighter controllers, and *Airborne Cigar*, which disrupted the night fighter's own radio communications. Another device which was increasingly used with great effect in 1944–5, was the *Mandrel Screen*, an electronic 'blanket' put up before the bomber stream to conceal its inward flight from the German radars; by the time the bombers emerged from the *Mandrel Screen* they were well inside Germany and the German fighter force had that much less time to assemble and attack.

It will be seen that the scientific war still went on. The Americans had now developed the '*Azon*' bomb, ancestor of the modern 'smart' bomb, as Robert W. Vincent reports:

> The '*Azon*' was basically a 1,000 lb bomb with a radio-steerable tail. The bombardier could guide the bomb using a joystick in the aircraft, and the bomb was designed for small, hard-to-hit precision targets, like bridges. It was not very successful in combat and only a few *Azon* missions were flown in the ETO, but it was a start on the road to modern missile weapons.

The latest German night-fighter aids were *Naxos*, a radar device which could home in on Allied aircraft using H_2S or H_2X, and *Flensburg*, which could track down a bomber using *Monica* and its improved follow-up, *Fishpond*, the device installed to enable an RAF bomber to detect a fighter closing from below. *Flensburg* had a range of 45 miles, and with these aids and the still unsuspected *Schrage Musik* the *Luftwaffe* continued to take a steady toll of British bombers.

In this it was aided by the flak, which was increasing in concentration as more guns were pulled back from defending factories in France and the Low Countries and were deployed around industrial centres inside the Reich. US bomber losses from fighter interdiction fell to around 1.5 per cent per mission – a rapid fall from the double-figure losses of the previous year – but the flak continued to take a toll. As the US bombers continued to increase in number, the flak guns had more targets. Frederick Gerritz's crew met heavy flak on a raid to Saarbrücken:

> The target was a marshalling yard. The trip out was uneventful, but over the target the flak was furiously heavy. I think the rectangular pattern we flew down was the target for all the flak guns. A piece of flak came though the top-turret Plexiglass, hit Piazza, the gunner, on the helmet, and went out again. Another piece came up through the floor and ripped its way through the upholstery, sending cotton flying around like a snowstorm. It also knocked out our hydraulic system, so we had to land without brakes. As we hit the runway, six of us ran to the back of the aircraft to get the tail skid on the deck and at the same time a parachute was attached to each waist window and thrown out to billow forth and help slow us down. We ran off the end of the runway and came to a halt in another 100 yards. The unofficial count was 42 flak holes in the aircraft – and no one was hit. The Lord was with us that day.

Fred Gerritz also bombed Munich:

> The three successive attacks we made to Munich were perhaps the most devastating ever inflicted on any German city. Each mission involved some 1,000 heavy bombers, and each aircraft was carrying 3 tons of bombs. First the 500 lb GP [general-purpose] bomb was released, to blow up the buildings. Next the two 500 lb clusters went down, scattering 500 incendiary bombs over the area to ignite the debris left by the GP bombs. In those three missions we dropped 3,000 tons of GP bombs and 6,000 tons of incendiary bombs amounting to 12 million incendiary devices. Munich must have burned for weeks.

The logbook of Robert Geisel, an RCAF rear gunner flying with No. 115 Squadron in 3 Group, confirms both that Bomber Command was flying more daylight sorties and that the German defences were by no means quelled:

Of the 26 operations flown by No. 115 Squadron between 29 December 1944 and 18 April 1945, 15 were flown in daylight. Among the night operations was one against Ludwigshafen. Our first night trip was to Nuremberg, on 2 January; this took us past Ludwigshafen. It was an awesome sight, as the target area was surrounded by searchlights which pointed straight up and looked like the bars of a lion cage at a circus. The flak was within the cage, and the bombers had to fly through this well-defended target area. It was obvious that the night fighters would be waiting in the darkness outside.

Three nights later it was our turn to attack Ludwigshafen and we too had to enter the cage, where we sustained a heavy encounter with the flak, returning with a cracked main spar, a number of perforations in the main frame, and minor holes in the tailplane, on either side of my rear-gunner turret.

Daylight operations brought the Bomber Command aircrews into closer contact with the *Luftwaffe* aircrews, as Bill Borrows of No. 433 Squadron recalls:

We were returning from a daylight raid over France, relaxing as we neared the Channel and listening to Glen Miller on the radio, when an FW 190 appeared alongside. The pilot was apparently out of ammo, for he flew along just out of range, grinning at us, giving the thumbs-up, and pointing at the painted nude straddling a bomb that Colin Clark had painted on the nose of our Halifax – *Q for Queenie*. As the gunners swivelled their turrets towards him, the German pilot waved, flipped over, exposing his armoured under-belly, and dived away.

Meanwhile, the Eighth was turning its ever increasing strength against Germany, each bomber element now able to put up twice the number of aircraft it had in 1942, as Howard 'Pete' Henry of the 44th Bomb Group relates:

By the summer of 1944 each division in the Eighth could put up about 700 aircraft, which averages about 50 planes per group, but in the 44th Bomb Group we had 70 aircraft and we were getting stronger all the time. We averaged 36 B-24s per mission – twelve per squadron, instead of the six in the manual. I flew my first mission on 11 June, just after D-Day, to a target in Normandy. My diary indicates that it was to the invasion coast, no fighters, no flak, no excitement and lasted six hours.

Pete Henry's crew flew another 31 missions, and they were not all that easy, as his bombardier, Albert Jones, confirms:

On 20 June we flew to Politz in Germany, a deep penetration beyond Berlin, so full tanks – 2,700 gallons of gasoline. We were to hit an oil refinery, and the 44th was leading the whole Eighth Air Force over the target.

We take off at 0500 hrs and head in over Denmark and then south-east to the target. The first squadron in does not get too much flak, but we catch hell! It seems like the sun is blotted out, and it is also accurate. They told us 85 guns would be turned on us, and there were all of that. The Germans also tried to cover the target using smoke pots, but the strong westerly winds blew it away. Our ship is hit as we cross the target, but our bombs do a really good job. Our top and tail turrets are hit and two ships in the 44th are hit and lose altitude; both are under control. But the 49th Bomb Group runs into a whole mess of fighters and loses fourteen aircraft out of 24.

After D-Day it was clear that Germany had lost the war, and on 20 July a plot to assassinate Hitler came close to succeeding. But Hitler survived, the plotters were hunted down and executed, and the failure of the July Plot meant that Germany would fight on to the end, however bitter that end might be. Germany's ability to do so was enhanced by the development of several new weapons.

At sea the arrival of snorkel-equipped U-boats was causing problems, especially for Coastal Command, since the U-boats could now make the dangerous passage to and from their bases fully submerged. Also, the U-boats were now equipped with anti-aircraft cannon, and when attacked on the surface they tended to stay up and fight it out, rather than dive and offer a target for depth charges. German V-weapons were pounding London and Antwerp and, although the *Crossbow/Noball* V1 sites along the Channel coast had been overrun by September, V2 rockets continued to fall and were now in full production in the Hartz Mountains, at the Dora–Nordhausen–Kleinbordungen factory, set deep underground and impervious to Allied bombers. This one factory employed 60,000 slave workers – 40,000 of whom died of ill-treatment or exhaustion by the end of the war. Hitler and his cronies placed great faith in these 'terror weapons', and assured the German people that victory was not impossible by this means. Like all the other parts of the German military machine, however, the rocket programme was vulnerable to a cut in fuel supplies. Meanwhile another promising development might bring the Allied bombing offensive to a halt – the jet fighter.

Britain and Germany had both been developing jet aircraft. Frank Whittle's prototype first flew in 1941, and the Gloster Meteor twin-engined jet fighter just made it into RAF squadron service by the end of the war. The Germans had two experimental types, which eventually became the Me 262 and the Arado(Ar) 234. The Me 262 first flew in 1942, but, in spite of strenuous objections from people like the fighter ace Adolf Galland, in 1943 Hitler insisted that it should be developed as a bomber and the first jet bomber squadron was formed in October 1944. But by then it was clear that some answer had to be found to the Allied bombers, and the Me 262 was rapidly converted to fighter use; by the end of the year some 50 Me 262s were in service over the Reich. (The Arado never made it into service.)

One basic rule of fighter warfare is that the faster fighter always wins in combat. The Me 262 was very fast – faster even than the P-51. It could elude or run away from Allied fighters, attack or retire at will, and run rings round the bombers and their escorts – at least in daylight. The Me 262 was too fast for use at night, when a slower aircraft is needed to stalk the enemy bomber.

If the Me 262 was virtually invulnerable in the air, it could be attacked on the ground; it needed long runways, and these were easily identified and, once located, heavily bombed. And the Me 262 *could* be shot down, as F. W. Walker of No. 428 Squadron RCAF, recalls:

> On 4 November we were flying an op against Bochum, an oil target, when an Me 262 was spotted by the wireless operator, off to one side and above at a range of about 1,200 yards. It looked like a blot trailing vapour and according to our rear gunner, Ben Rakus, was moving faster than anything he had ever seen. Ben gave me the word to corkscrew, and the jet shot over to our other side before closing in to 500 yards. We then took further evasive action, throwing the aircraft about, while Ben went to work with his guns, hitting the jet along the fuselage and wings, giving it another burst as it peeled over and dived towards the ground, where several crew members saw it explode. This was the first time a heavy bomber shot down one of these jets, so they were vulnerable.

These German jet aircraft also needed large amounts of fuel, and it was a shortage of fuel rather than combat losses that proved the downfall of the Me 262. Adolf Galland recounts that by early 1945 the shortage of fuel was so acute that these jet fighters were towed out to the runways.[4] Since no other method of haulage was available – also through a lack of fuel – the aircraft were towed out by cows.

In November the RAF finally put an end to one potential menace to Britain's supply lines, sinking the battleship *Tirpitz*. There is still some controversy in Bomber Command over which Squadron – No. 617 or No. 9 – actually delivered the fatal blow, but Bob Knights of No. 617 has no doubts:

> All three attacks on *Tirpitz* were led by Wing Commander J. B. (Willie) Tait, DSO, DFC, commanding 617; he was followed by his own squadron, and No. 9 followed as the back-up force.
>
> The ship was sunk on 12 November by *Tallboys* from the first wave of 617 – two direct hits and three very close to the ship's sides – and my aiming-point photo shows this. There is no evidence to show that any of the later bombing fell near the target, and in fact I have evidence to the contrary. No. 617 Squadron had the SABS bombsight; this allowed the squadron to bomb precision targets with devastating accuracy. No. 9 Squadron had the Mark XIV bombsight, the one in general use with Bomber Command and suitable only for area bombing; it was not accurate enough for precision bombing.
>
> We had a good straight bombing run, and both my bomb-aimer and my

flight engineer followed our *Tallboy* right down to the ship; they reported two direct hits and three near misses. After taking our aiming-point photo we circled the ship to observe the subsequent bombing and stayed in the vicinity for about fifteen minutes, and before we left the ship was beginning to capsize. When I read some of the accounts of this event I begin to wonder if I was really there.

Tirpitz had gone, but the Germans fought on. The war not over and the killing went on in eastern Germany and in Belgium and Holland; the transports continued to leave the occupied cities of Europe for concentration camps like Auschwitz. There was a lot of fighting and dying still to do before Germany surrendered. The Allied task was to induce that surrender as soon as possible – perhaps by a rapid advance across the Rhine, perhaps from the air. The war had gone on long enough; it was time to put an end to it.

Some people thought that the war could be ended by showing the Germans what was going to happen next. In early August 1944 the Air Ministry put up a proposal for a massive strike against Berlin – Operation THUNDERCLAP – in the hope that this would make Hitler's people see sense; this was shortly after the July bomb attempt on Hitler's life had revealed that support for the Führer was not as solid as many people supposed. The plan for THUNDERCLAP called for a precision strike against Berlin by the largest force possible of the USAAF, aiming to put some 5,000 tons of bombs into the city centre in a couple of hours. Then the RAF would follow this up with a night raid. One calculation estimated that this operation would cause some 275,000 casualties; if that did not concentrate Nazi minds, nothing would.

The USAAF commanders rejected THUNDERCLAP. Spaatz's objection was that 'The RAF were attempting to tar the US airforce with the morale bombing aftermath which we feel will be terrific'[5] – though he was willing to assist THUNDERCLAP with precision attacks on Berlin and a month later, on 8 September, he was telling the Eighth Air Force commander, General Doolittle, that 'we would no longer plan to hit definite military objectives but be ready to drop bombs indiscriminately on the town'. The THUNDERCLAP proposal was shelved, however, and Spaatz continued to direct the weight of his attacks against oil, leaving the cities to Harris. In fact both air forces were now area bombing – or 'blind bombing' as it came to be called in USAAF circles – and the USAAF official history records that:

Approximately 80 per cent of all Eighth Air Force and 70 per cent of all Fifteenth Air Force missions during the last quarter of 1944 were characterized by some employment of blind-bombing radar devices. Without these aids important targets would have enjoyed weeks or months of respite and on several occasions major task forces failed even with radar to reach their objectives because of adverse weather . . . In mid-November, 1944, operations analysts of the Eighth estimated that nearly half the blind missions were near failures, or worse.[6]

From September 1944 Harris could devote all his force to the attack on Germany, and whatever damage had been done in the years before D-Day was nothing to the destruction caused to the cities when the Allied bombers went back to Germany in the autumn of 1944. Bomber Command attacked Germany continuously from the end of September 1944 to the end of the war in May 1945, nine months later, and the weight of its attack can be gauged from just a few of its operations in September and October 1944.

On 6 September, 181 RAF bombers made a daylight raid on Emden. Emden was reduced to a bonfire, and only one Lancaster was lost. Four nights later, RAF bombers tore out the heart of Munchen-Gladbach. On the night of 11/12 September, Darmstadt, until then untouched, was shattered by RAF bombers; over 8,000 people were killed. On 12 September Harris attacked the oil refineries of Dortmund, Beur and Wanne-Eickel by day; the Dortmund refinery was badly damaged, but smoke pots and flak protected the other two from serious harm.

The RAF was certainly putting a good deal of effort into smashing oil refineries – a fact confirmed by the logbook of Canadian mid-upper gunner Ralph Mainprize, of No. 189 Squadron, RAF:

> 13.1.45. Target Politz – a synthetic oil plant. Saw some big fires but TIs were off so doubtful if we pranged the required thing. Weather was quite good. Flight time 10 hrs 30.
>
> 16.1.45. Target Brux – a synthetic oil plant. Ten-tenths cloud over target but able to bomb on red and green TIs glowing through. Flight time 9 hrs 15.
>
> 8.2.45. Target Politz – a synthetic oil plant. Our second visit. Saw a few fighters, but they did not bother us. There were many fires when we left the target, so the feeling is that we really got it this time. Bomb load was one 4,000 lb 'Cookie' and ten 1,000-pounders. No aircraft were lost from our squadron. 9 hrs 45.
>
> 19.2.45. Target Bohlen. The aim was to knock out a synthetic oil plant and an electrical works. *Gee* was u/s so we used *Loren* all the way, there was ten-tenths cloud over the target but a fire was distinguishable, which we bombed. Very little flak. Time 8 hrs 05.
>
> 7.3.45. Target Harburg – a synthetic oil plant. Our stiffest trip to date. Our route went over Denmark then south to the target, where we made three orbits to get on the correct heading for the run-up. Bags of night fighters were seen and our squadron lost four aircraft and 49 Squadron one, with another badly shot up. Bomb load was one 'Cookie' and 14×500-pounders. Time 7 hrs.

Ralph Mainprize's logbook shows that between January and April 1945 his squadron attacked eight oil refineries, some of them more than once, as well as troop concentrations, marshalling yards, submarine pens, a jet-aircraft factory and the Nordhausen V2 assembly point. It also supported the crossing of the Rhine at Wesel by the British Second and US Ninth Armies on 23 March. All of these attacks were on military or industrial targets, and all were hit with great force and accuracy in spite of the weather and the still active opposition from flak and fighters, which John Whiteley can confirm:

> In 5 Group we attacked oil *and* transportation targets. On 21 November 1944 our target for a night operation was the Mittelland Canal at Gravenhorst. During the Second World War the Germans were very reliant on their canals for transportation, but they were hard to hit. Our bomb load on this occasion was 12 × 1,000 lb bombs, and we dropped from 4,000 ft. The target indicators had been dropped very accurately on the banks of the canal, but as we started our run-up it became apparent that the canal was well defended by light flak. My bomb aimer asked me to open the bomb doors, and as I concentrated on the flying I had the momentary glimpse of a Lancaster ahead of me blowing up; it had been hit by light flak, and we were next in line.
>
> Towards the end of my tour we attacked an oil refinery near Leipzig. We had about two hours to go before the target when the gunners reported that both their turrets were unserviceable. I concluded that the hydraulics had failed, and this was serious for we were almost defenceless against fighter attack. Do we abandon the op or press on to the target? I decided to press on, and full marks to my crew, who did not demur.
>
> Then I had the dreaded report – one that all crews feared: that the rear gunner had seen a fighter which was about to start its curve of pursuit on the port upper side of the Lancaster. After some violent corkscrewing I managed to shake him off and we proceeded to the target and dropped our bombs. I hope you do not think I am 'shooting a line' here – this incident is mentioned in the citation for my DFC. At the subsequent debriefing the gunnery leader made the pointed comment that I obviously did not believe in gunners, but the CO was very complimentary and congratulated me for pressing on.

Clearly, while the USAAF had started to make area attacks, the RAF was now making precision ones, by day and night, to tick off specific industrial or military targets. On the night of 14/15 September, 490 RAF aircraft attacked the naval base at Kiel. On 18/19 September, 200 bombers destroyed the heart of Bremerhaven, another naval centre. On 23/24 September, 549 RAF aircraft struck Neuss and another 136 Lancasters of 5 Group breached the banks of the Dortmund–Ems Canal, again using *Tallboys*. On 27/28 September, 227 aircraft destroyed more than a third of Kaiserlautern, an oil target – only two aircraft were lost. These attacks on Germany were complemented with attacks on towns in France in support of the now advancing Allied armies; thousands of tons of bombs fell on the German garrisons under siege in Calais and Boulogne.

October began in the same way, when 260 RAF bombers attacked the sea defences on the island of Walcheren in the Schelde estuary in support of the amphibious landing by the 4th Commando Brigade, a successful attempt to open the Schelde estuary and the port of Antwerp. During the rest of the month, large forces of RAF bombers – 500-plus in most cases – attacked Saarbrücken, Dortmund, the Wanne-Eickel oil plant (with 137 aircraft) and Duisburg (with 1,013 aircraft).

This last raid – code-named *Hurricane I* – was one of a series of combined attacks, co-ordinated with the USAAF. It was made in daylight, the RAF attacking soon after dawn, followed later that day with an attack by 1,251 bombers from the Eighth Air Force, escorted by 749 fighters. Duisburg's flak was overwhelmed, no fighters appeared, and this attack – by 2,000 bombers in a single day – totally devastated the town. There was no pity: the RAF returned that night, 14/15 October, and struck the city again with a further 1,005 aircraft, of which 941 bombed. When the bombers finally flew away, hardly anything was left of Duisburg.

On the following night, 500 RAF aircraft attacked Wilhelmshaven; then 565 aircraft attacked Stuttgart and 1,055 aircraft attacked Essen, then 771 aircraft attacked Essen again and 773 attacked Cologne, then 905 aircraft attacked Cologne, then 493 aircraft attacked Cologne . . . and so Cologne joined Duisburg as a shattered city. And so it went on, night after night and day after day, for months. There is no need to continue this litany of destruction, for the pattern must be clear. The wind that the Germans had sown in the early years of the war – at Warsaw and Rotterdam and during the Blitz – was back as a whirlwind and destroying everything that stood in its path.

Nor was Germany suffering only by night. The history of the US Eighth Air Force records that 'operations continued at a prodigious rate and on a vast scale; in the area of the East Anglia bases it seemed the sky was never still'. Spared German fighter interference, the bombardiers of the Eighth were able to concentrate on precision targets, at least when the weather permitted a view of the ground. Their list of targets attacked includes oil plants, aircraft factories, marshalling yards and ordnance parks. These missions went on day after day for weeks on end, turning Germany into a sea of rubble, for these were not all 'precision' attacks, whatever their declared objectives.

On 3 February 1945, for example, 1,000 B-17s attacked the marshalling yards in Berlin. Spaatz's biographer, David Mets, records that 'the bombing was done visually, accuracy was good, with the bombs hitting the rail yards and administrative centers in the city . . . twenty-five thousand Berliners lost their lives'.[7] Such a casualty rate indicates that this was an area attack – and bombing 'visually' was a rare event during the winter months. If the accuracy was indeed 'good' and only precision targets were hit, as this statement claims, German civilian casualties on those US blind-bombing missions in 1944–5 can only be wondered at.

The USAAF commanders were still worried about the morality of area bombing. Eaker is on record as saying that the CLARION plan for an all-out attack on German transportation – railway yards and stations – must, as at Berlin, cause massive civilian casualties and 'we should never allow the history of this war to convict us of throwing the strategic bomber at the man in the street'. But the CLARION plan is an interesting example of how the US commanders attempted to 'square the circle' on this aspect of their strategic bombing operations. The roots of the CLARION plan go back to the THUNDERCLAP idea, mooted in Britain in July 1944, for an all-out, combined USAAF–RAF attack on Berlin, or, failing that, for widespread attacks on towns across Germany with the aim of convincing the German people at large that further resistance was futile. This proposal was sent to Washington, where it did the rounds and was rejected as not being in line with US policies and unlikely to succeed anyway. However, the idea did not go away, and in the autumn of 1944 Arnold directed the USSTAF – Spaatz – to prepare a plan for an all-out attack on Germany – 'widespread roving attacks so that all Germans could see the ease with which Allied air-power roamed at will through the airspace of the Reich'.[8]

Spaatz prepared two plans: one for attack in conjunction with the Army, another for an air operation in conjunction with the RAF. The implementation of this plan was disrupted by the German Ardennes offensive in December 1944, but by the end of January 1945 Spaatz was ready again; by now the all-out attack on transportation had been extended to include a smashing blow against Berlin. Eaker was still totally opposed to the entire scheme, but was assured that the USAAF was not proposing to attack *civilians*, but only transportation targets.

The old precision-bombing doctrine had gone the way of other doctrines, dented out of shape by the pressures of war. Blind bombing had had to come in, otherwise the USAAF in Europe would have spent most of its time on the ground – but 'blind' bombing through cloud by 1,000-plus bombers was no different from the RAF's 'area' bombing. It was also common practice, if the primary and secondary targets could not be found, to allow the bombers to attack 'targets of opportunity' – hopefully military or industrial, but in practice anything the crews could see below. The alternative was flying back through the flak to the North Sea bomb-jettison area with a cargo of live, primed bombs or landing with a full bomb load; neither prospect was attractive to the crews, and so their bomb loads went down on Germany – anywhere in Germany.

USAAF losses to fighter attack were now generally small. Most of the aircraft shot down were lost to flak, and though twelve B-17s were shot down by fighters on an 11 September mission to German oil targets this was now exceptional. During August 1944 the Eighth lost 131 bombers to flak as against 39 to fighters. As the attack on oil targets intensified, so the flak grew stronger, for the oil refineries were targets the Germans had to defend. The USAAF history estimates there were 1,000 flak guns of various calibre defending the Leipzig refineries alone, and 29 Fortresses were lost to flak over the Merseburg refinery on 30 November.

The concentration was on precision targets, notably oil, but the USAAF was also preparing to try out a new scheme, *Project Aphrodite*, the American version of a flying bomb. By now the Eighth had a large and growing number of 'war-weary' aircraft – those that were too battered for further front-line service or not worth repairing. *Project Aphrodite* was a scheme in which these 'old' aircraft would be filled with high explosives and flown east, towards Germany or the still occupied parts of Western Europe. Once they were over France and on course for their target – anywhere in German-held territory – the skeleton crew on board would engage the automatic pilot and bale out, leaving the bomber to fly on until it ran out of fuel and crashed. Clearly there was not much 'precision' involved in this method of attack.

The early experiments with *Aphrodite* aircraft were not too successful. One crashed in Suffolk in August 1944 and the 20,000 lb of explosive on board made a crater 100 ft across; another blew up in the air over the east coast of England, killing the crew. The brother of the later US President John F. Kennedy was killed on an *Aphrodite* mission. A few such missions were flown, but the project soon petered out – not least because the advance of the Allied armies made this experiment a waste of resources.

The Eighth had gone over largely to 'blind' bombing' using H_2X, and by the end of 1944 all the US bomb groups had at least two H_2X aircraft manned by trained crews. Missions now routinely employed 1,000-plus aircraft, escorted by several hundred fighters, but the war on the ground was going slowly and the New Year arrived with no sign that the Germans were in the mood to capitulate. Nor was the war entirely restricted to the conflict between the Allies and the Axis powers: plenty of conflict was taking place among the High Command.

By the New Year of 1945, relations were strained almost to breaking point between Arthur Harris and the Air Ministry. The problem was over Harris's well-practised reluctance to carry out the Directives he was given or, more frequency, his tendency to study them for a way in which, while paying lip-service to his instructions, he was able to go his own way and tick off items on his own agenda. During the early winter of 1944–5, however, the issues were too clear-cut for fudging: the Air Ministry wanted Harris to attack oil refineries; Harris wanted to go on blasting the cities.

By the end of October, six weeks after he had received the latest Directive specifying oil as a first priority, Portal and his team, but notably Air Marshal Bottomley, were beginning to suspect that, while Harris was indeed striking oil refineries, the weight of Bomber Command attacks was swinging back inexorably towards the cities. In part this was inevitable, for many of the oil refineries were in or on the outskirts of cities, but it was a question of priority – of which was the actual target and which was receiving the overspill.

Matters had started to come to a head at the end of September, when Harris sent Churchill a letter pointing out that the Germans were still fighting hard and would certainly fight a good deal harder when the Allied armies reached the Rhine and crossed the frontiers of the Reich. Therefore, said Harris, now was the time to smite the Germans hard and 'knock Germany flat' using the overwhelming Allied air superiority. The Germans had just destroyed the British 1st Airborne Division at Arnhem, halting Montgomery's MARKET GARDEN thrust to the Rhine. They were also putting up a stiff resistance against the US forces around Aachen, a battle that would develop into the costly struggle for the Hurtgen Forest. Clearly the Germans were not about to give up the struggle, and Harris's suggestion for an all-out attack by the heavy bombers received due consideration. But, as Churchill commented, 'I am sure he [Harris] is right in a great deal in what he says . . . but I do not rate the contribution of the air force as high as he does.'

Harris's letter reveals that, despite D-Day, he had not yet given up on the bomber dream. There may have been several Allied armies fighting their way to the Rhine, and Russian armies pressing across the Vistula and up to the Oder, but they were not yet in Germany. The possibility of defeating Germany from the air still – just – existed. While that window of opportunity was open Harris wished to exploit it, and his proposal had the advantage of simplicity.

Germany was going to lose the war, and quite soon – that much was clear. So what was the point of fighting on until Allied armies crossed the Rhine and the Russians forced their way across the Oder and carried the war into the heart of the Reich? Surely the sane and sensible thing for the Germans to do was to surrender now, before matters got worse – and, to concentrate German minds on this point, Harris intended to go on shattering their industrial cities.

It is easy now to see the flaw in this argument: Hitler, his Nazi Party cronies, the SS, the people who actually controlled Germany would – and did – hang anyone who even considered surrender. The German people had voted Hitler into power in 1933, but that was their last glimpse of democracy. They had no means of voting Hitler out again and coming to terms with the Allies. The July Plot of 1944 had killing Hitler as its first aim because that was the only way to get rid of him. That plot had failed, and the plotters were strangling to death on loops of piano wire in Gestapo prisons even as Harris wrote his note to Churchill. Nevertheless, Harris's proposal was perfectly sensible – but it never stood a chance of success.

The issue of RAF bombing priorities hotted up at the end of October, when Portal sent Harris a copy of a note from Tedder at SHAEF. This note stated that 'I do not believe that by concentrating our whole Air effort on the ground battle area we shall shorten the war. Nor do I believe that we would shorten the war by putting our whole Bomber effort against industrial and political targets in Germany.' This would seem to limit both facets of the bomber war – tactical and strategic. But Tedder did have some positive suggestions, and went on to urge further attacks on German communication targets – stations, tunnels and marshalling yards – as the Allied armies moved up to the German frontier. In other words, Tedder, urged on by his scientific adviser, Solly Zuckerman, was advocating that the bombers concentrate on the dismemberment of the German military-industrial complex, specifically *transportation* targets, rather than supporting the slow progress of the Allied armies – which would grind to a halt as winter came on – or smashing the German cities by constant raids. Taken as a whole this seems a sensible proposal, but the Allied air commanders were not at one on this: Spaatz was wedded to attacking oil targets, Tedder wanted transportation, and Harris was still set on the cities.

As we have seen, Spaatz eventually came round to the transportation plan because it was really an extension of his own belief that certain elements in German industry – like oil – were common factors: destroy or disrupt the supply of them and you destroyed or disrupted German industry as a whole. Therefore the weight of USSTAF attacks began to include transport targets as well as oil targets. But transport targets – the stations and the marshalling yards – were usually in cities.

Harris's reply to Portal was predictable, claiming that Tedder was suggesting a series of 'panacea' targets, ignoring the fact that Bomber Command had already destroyed 45 out of 60 German cities and should be allowed to get on and finish the job, without any further diversions. Harris's letter arrived at Portal's headquarters just after yet another a letter from Bottomley landed on Harris's desk on 14 November, instructing him that oil was the priority target, and that 'no opportunity of attacking oil plants must be lost . . . we must attack whenever opportunity serves . . . we must endeavour to inflict long term damage', and so on with several references to the oil refineries at Leuna, Politz and Harburg – especially Politiz, which, because of the shortening daylight hours, was now beyond the reach of the USAAF until the spring and needed the attention of the RAF.[9]

Harris was still digesting this missive when he received a reply to his letter from Portal: 'At the risk of you dubbing me another 'panacea merchant' I believe that the air offensive against oil gives us by far the best hope of complete victory in the next few months.'

Portal was quite right in this belief, and Harris was wrong. The best course at the time was to turn the full weight of Bomber Command against Germany's shrinking oil resources. This is not hindsight. The dependence of modern armies on oil had been clearly demonstrated earlier in 1944, not least by what happened to the Allied armies in the period after D-Day, when Eisenhower's broad-front offensive in August and September 1944 was stopped in its tracks by a shortage of fuel for the trucks and tanks. At one point the fuel shortage was so acute that American divisional commanders were sending out patrols to hijack oil tankers carrying fuel to other divisions in order to keep their own division advancing. In the autumn of 1944 RAF and USAAF bombers were even taken off bombing missions, loaded with petrol cans, and sent to deliver fuel to airfields in France and Belgium. James H. Lorenz of the 466th Bomb Group flew some of these missions:

> IN September 1944 our 466th Bomb Group and the 477th were stood down from combat to haul gas to Patton's advance area in France. Using war-weary B-24s, the gasoline was either in five-gallon jerrycans or in huge rubber tanks installed in the bomb bays, which could carry up to 2,500 gallons of gasoline. I made two of these missions and we got no mission credits, though we did lose several planes. We also got to see the war close up – and we were glad our job was flying missions.

If fuel shortages could demand such measures from the Allied forces, the effect of cutting off supplies of petrol and oil to Germany's beleaguered troops and airmen could be decisive. But Harris would not accept this point, and he responded to Portal's letter with all his well-honed arguments against 'panacea' targets and for area bombing. These need not be rehashed yet again, but as the latest round of correspondence flowed between the two men it gradually became acrimonious. Harris did increase the number of attacks Bomber Command made on oil targets and he continued to attack military targets ahead of the Allied armies now closing up to the Lower Rhine around Cleve and the Roer; but he also kept blasting the cities, and it is at least arguable that this part of the bombing campaign was by then a waste of time.

The German military machine was collapsing. Only the winter kept the Allied armies from surging into Germany, and even though a few shots remained in Hitler's locker – the Ardennes offensive for one – the outcome of the European war was no longer in doubt. The course of the war would not be altered by further attacks on German cities, but the war might be shortened perceptibly if the bombers smashed Germany's oil and transport resources and denied the German armies the means to fight. Shortening the war was a worthwhile aim: even if it brought victory only one day earlier that would be useful, for every day of fighting cost lives – and every day brought the Soviet armies closer to Berlin.

On 12 December, Harris wrote to Portal saying that Bomber Command's own Operational Research Unit had been examining the Oil Plan and estimated that it would take some 16,000 sorties every month, to destroy the 57 active synthetic-oil plants in Germany and keep them out of action thereafter – a task that was beyond Bomber Command's resources during the winter months, unless the Americans joined in.

Further comment on this issue was limited by the opening on 16 December of the German Ardennes offensive, the 'Battle of the Bulge'. The Battle of the Bulge gave the Allied commanders a good fright, for the American forces in the Ardennes were driven back some 50 miles by this German armoured thrust towards Antwerp. However, the Ardennes attack was one of the final efforts of a dying beast; the German panzers did not capture the Allied fuel and supply dumps on which the progress of their attacks depended, and their tanks and trunks eventually ran out of fuel. When the winter skies cleared at the end of December, the Allied tactical air forces came swarming in to take a heavy toll of the remaining tanks, and the final verdict on the Ardennes offensive is that it cost the German army in the west more than it could afford to lose.

There was therefore a delay in their correspondence, but just before Christmas Portal wrote back to Harris. He pointed out that the Americans were already bombing the oil refineries at every opportunity – something Harris was well aware of – and no one was suggesting that Bomber Command could or should be able to destroy the German oil industry unaided. But, Portal continued, 'over the winter months it is essential that no opportunity is lost, whether by day or night . . . I believe the task is within the capability of the three strategic air forces if they put their hearts into it. If they do and the job can be done this winter strategic bombing will go down in history as a decisive factor in winning this war.'

It was a good letter, and the point that 'strategic bombing will go down in history as a decisive factor in winning this war' was calculated to appeal to Harris's own beliefs in strategic bombing. It was a sound, even a persuasive, argument; but it did not work. On 28 December, Harris replied with a bitter letter in which he commented that 'the history of bombing throughout this war will, when it is summed up, show repeated lapses from that essential principle of war, maintenance of the aim'. This was a good point, but Harris then continued, 'Three years of bitter struggle have gone on in area blitzing . . . We know that on more than one occasion they have nearly collapsed under it. As the programme nears completion we chuck it all up . . . for a panacea.'

Harris stated that he had no faith in the Oil Plan but added that, even so, he had ordered his Command to carry out the various Directives sent to him on this subject and make attacks on oil targets. This is true, but only up to a point. In December 1944 over 30 per cent of Bomber Command's attacks were on cities and fewer than 8 per cent on oil. Given this difference in percentages, there is little doubt that Harris could have done more against oil had he really wanted to – especially by using the Light Night Striking Force and the precision-bombing skills of No. 617 and No. 9 Squadrons.

The argument went on into the New Year, and the various overlapping letters between the commanders make one wonder why the two men, who had known each other for years, served together in peace and war, and clearly liked and respected each other, did not get together over dinner or in the privacy of an office and thrash the matter out. As it was, the argument became increasingly strident, at least on the part of Air Chief Marshal Harris.

Portal remained relentlessly polite but held to his point of view in supporting the Oil Plan, which, he said, 'lies so well within our capabilities that it can be pressed to a point at which the operational effectiveness of the German armies and airforces on all fronts will be decisively restricted; but to do this it is essential to hold firmly to this aim'.

This point about needing to 'hold firmly to this aim' was another shrewd thrust, throwing another of Harris's arguments back at him – and Harris did not like it. He accused Portal of not consulting him about the use of Bomber Command in this role, and made bitter comments about Bufton and Bottomley, who, he said, were either junior in rank or had served under him in subordinate capacities, and were now giving him orders.

All the old arguments were taken out for an airing: 'panacea' targets, Germany's having abundant supplies of oil from a variety of sources – which was no longer true – the effect of area bombing on the cities, and the constant variation of his instructions. Harris also complained that he was being blamed for the lack of success of a policy which he had said at the start would not work, and his letter on this point concludes, 'That situation is simply one of heads I win, tails you lose, and is an intolerable situation. I therefore ask you to consider whether it is best for the prosecution of the war and the success of our arms, which alone matters, that I should remain in this situation.'[10]

Opinions vary, but the only reasonable interpretation of that last sentence is that Harris is either offering to resign or inviting Portal to sack him. The questions that then arise are, What caused the situation to get to this point, and what should Portal have done about it?

Any answers are speculation, and Portal did not rise to the bait and Harris remained in charge of Bomber Command until the end of the war. Even so, speculation is interesting and valid, because had Harris left Bomber Command in January 1944 his reputation might well stand higher in the public mind than it does today and the responsibility – and blame – for the notorious Dresden raid, which was even then being planned, would have been laid at some other door.

Harris was a driven man, but he was not a foolish one. Most of what he said regarding the overall conduct of the bomber offensive was perfectly true and will be analysed in the final chapter, but he was clearly wrong over the Oil Plan and stubborn to the point of obsession in his desire to keep on attacking the cities from September 1944. It is not too much to say that at this stage in the war his judgement was faulty. But, given that Harris was a most experienced bomber commander and a fine leader of men, why was his judgement so wrong at this time?

From that question, other questions flow. Why was he quarrelling with Peter Portal – someone who was his stout supporter, his respected superior, a great admirer and a personal friend? Why was Harris so blind to the benefits of the Oil Plan and so determined to concentrate on the cities? Why was he unable to see any views other than his own and not open to any argument that did not fit with his own deeply entrenched opinions?

It is purely speculation, but the most obvious answer is that Harris was tired. An answer may not be wrong simply because it is obvious, and tiredness is the explanation that makes sense, the one that fits, that accounts for the irrationality, the failures of judgement, the irascibility. Harris's tiredness was not the sort of tiredness that comes from lack of sleep or a few late nights, but the deep-seated mental and physical exhaustion that results from years of strain and heavy responsibility – not least for men's lives.

Harris had now been commanding Bomber Command for three long, hard years. He had a stomach ulcer when he took up his command, and rarely took a day off in all that time. He must have been tired. Indeed, there was no way he could not be tired. In his memoirs, published in 1947, he writes:

> I wonder if the frightful mental strain of commanding a large air force in war can ever be realized except by those who have experienced it. While a Naval commander may at the most be required to conduct a major action once or twice in the whole course of a war, and an Army commander fight a battle say once in six months or, in exceptional circumstances, once a month, the commander of a bomber force has to commit the whole of it every twenty-four hours.[11]

Harris had had to send his men, his 'old lags', out against Germany night after night for three years, and had seen them wither and die in great numbers – 51 per cent of Bomber Command aircrew died in the war – or be used for attacks whose benefits were now being called into question. That clearly hurt: Harris would have been less than human if he did not resent the implication that all those lives had been lost for nothing.

Decades after the war and many years after his death, most of the men of Bomber Command *adore* Arthur Harris – 'Butch' – and this affection was reciprocated. The aircrews of Bomber Command were not fools; they knew Harris cared about them and would do everything in his power for their safety and welfare. But what they may not have been able to judge was how much the conduct of the bombing offensive, the constant Directives and changes of focus, bore down on their revered commander, how much he minded being unable to provide them with the aircraft, equipment and direction they needed. Now the war was ending, Germany could not last more than a few months, and Harris wanted his men to be there at the end and get a full share of the credit they so richly deserved – and all he could hear from on high was a lot of talk about bombing oil plants. Perhaps it was time to go and let someone else try to make sense of it all. If that is what Harris was suggesting he was probably right and his offer should have been accepted.

To suggest that Portal should have removed Harris from Bomber Command will not be a popular thing to say, but, clutching the benefits of hindsight, perhaps Portal should have done so. It would hardly have affected the outcome of the war, but it would have been a kindness to Harris, who had already been in post far too long and would normally have been given a new appointment or promoted in the natural course of events. He needed a rest, and if he was reluctant to take a rest there were plenty of other appointments where his experience could have been useful – not least at SHAEF, where Britain's voice was fading. Harris liked and respected Eisenhower, and it is hard to imagine anyone ignoring Arthur Harris. Harris might also have been sent to the Far East, to prepare the way for Britain's eventual part in the air offensive against Japan, paving the path for the RAF's 'Tiger Force'.

Quite apart from the personal benefits to the health and future reputation of Air Chief Marshal Harris, a change of command would have given some of the other officers in Bomber Command a taste of high command and great responsibility before the war ended. Some critics have said that to lose Harris at this stage would have been a blow to the morale of Bomber Command, but that seems unlikely. Bomber Command was a service organization, not a family firm; in the services, when one commander goes, another is appointed to replace him and the organization continues to function. Suitable candidates for the post of AOC at Bomber Command range from Saundby to Bottomley or group commanders like Cochrane or Bennett. In 1945 the RAF was full of talent – and in February 1945 Ralph Cochrane of 5 Group was promoted to Air Marshal and sent to run Transport Command, so promotions of this kind were clearly not impossible.

The policy of relieving senior commanders so that their subordinates could gain experience of high command was adopted in the British Army during the last few months of the war and was seen as both useful and sensible. Being in overall command is much harder than being even a close subordinate, and command in war is very different from command in peace. Therefore war command experience, if it could be obtained without delaying the coming victory, was experience well worth having.

Portal could have taken Harris at his word, but his reply on 20 January was both measured and placatory. He had clearly given up attempting to convince Harris of the merits of the Oil Plan and was willing to settle for a reasonable amount of attention to the refineries, a task which, he pointed out, will ensure the successful execution of the policy laid down. I am very sorry you don't believe in it, but it is no use my craving for what is evidently unattainable. We must wait until after the end of the war to see who was right and I sincerely hope that until then you will continue in command of the force which has done so much towards defeating the enemy and has brought such credit and renown to yourself and the Air Force.

There was a further exchange of letters between the two men on 24 and 25 January, before Portal departed for Malta and then the next Allied summit at Yalta. Harris turned his attention to the bombing offensive, and clearly Portal's 'more in sorrow than in anger' approach had some effect, for the Bomber Command effort against the oil refineries was stepped up considerably from mid-January to mid-February. On the night of 14/15 January 573 Lancasters carried out major attacks on the important synthetic-oil plants at Leuna. On 15 January 82 Lancasters attacked the benzol plant at Recklinghausen and 63 Lancasters attacked the benzol plant at Bochum – both of these were daylight attacks, and no aircraft were lost. On the night of 16/17 January 328 Lancasters attacked the Braunkohle-Benzin plant at Zeitz while another 369 Lancasters made attacks on oil plants in Austria and Czechoslovakia; twelve Lancasters were lost from these three operations.

These strikes against oil targets large and small continued by day and night until the middle of February, when the USAAF and Bomber Command joined forces for one of the largest and by far the most controversial attack of the bomber war: the all-out assault on the capital of Saxony – Dresden.

Handley Page Halifax Mk II

16

Dresden
February 1945

We should use available effort in one big attack on Berlin and related attacks on Dresden, Leipzig, Chemnitz, or any other cities where a severe blitz will not only cause confusion in the evacuation from the East, but will also hamper the movement of troops from the West.

Air Marshal Sir Norman Bottomley, Deputy Chief of the Air Staff, to Sir Arthur Harris, 27 January 1945

The attacks on the city of Dresden by RAF Bomber Command and the US Eighth Air Force in 1945 have become the subject of great controversy since the end of the war and have also been the basis of a considerable number of myths. Indeed, in the public mind the Dresden raid has become the focus of all the arguments surrounding the strategic bombing campaign and the morality of area bombing as a whole.

That subject will be unravelled in the final chapter, but it is necessary here to analyse what happened at Dresden in some detail, if only to get that well-known issue in perspective. Examining the bombing of Dresden also illustrates how an action that is well known and regularly ventilated can still be the subject of deeply engrained popular myths. The best way to kill a myth is with a fact, but myths tend to get embedded in the public conscience. It might therefore be as well to air a few of them now, before going on to a full account of the Dresden operation and placing the responsibility for the raid where it properly belongs.

To begin with, let us refute the most popular public belief: that the raid on Dresden on the night of 13/14 February 1945 was conceived by Air Chief Marshal Sir Arthur Harris and entirely executed by RAF Bomber Command. As we shall see, the order to attack Dresden came from much higher up the chain of command, and the operation involved the USAAF as well as the RAF. Indeed, the fact that they involved both Allied air forces is conclusive evidence that the Dresden attacks were sanctioned at a much higher level than Bomber Command. The accusation that Harris decided to destroy Dresden from sheer bloodlust would be too stupid to merit a reply were it not so widely believed by the general public in Britain and several other countries. If the general public in Great Britain and elsewhere wish to blame someone for the destruction of Dresden, they will have to spread their net far wider than Air Chief Marshal Sir Arthur Harris and the men of RAF Bomber Command.

Nor was Dresden a 'virgin' target, a city as yet untouched by Allied bombers, in February 1945. It had been attacked on previous occasions. The USAAF first bombed it on 7 October 1944, when 30 B-17s bombed Dresden in lieu of their 'primary' target, the oil refinery at Ruhland; 435 people were killed. Dresden was also the target of a major USAAF attack on 16 January 1945. USAAF bombers were usually given a 'military or industrial' objective as their primary target, and on 16 January the designated target for 400 B-24s of the 2nd Air Division was the Dresden oil refinery and marshalling yards. The attack started at noon, when some 133 bombers bombed the city. Bombs fell on the marshalling yards and on the oil refinery, but bombs also fell in the city centre and in the grounds of the Friedrichstadt hospital; 376 civilians were killed. While Dresden had not been savaged like Mannheim or Ludwigshafen, it was certainly not a 'virgin' target in February 1945.

Nor was Dresden a 'non-military' target. The city contained the Zeiss-Ikon optical factory and the Siemens glass factory, and the immediate suburbs contained factories manufacturing radar and electronic components and fuses for anti-aircraft shells. Other factories in the suburbs of the city manufactured most of Germany's cigarettes – a vital product for maintaining wartime morale – as well as gas masks, engines for Junkers aircraft and cockpit parts for Messerschmitt fighters. These war factories employed somewhere in the region of 10,000 people – 1,500 of them in the shell-fuse factory alone – so it can hardly be maintained that Dresden made only a small contribution to the German war effort.

The German claim, made after the February raids, that Dresden's industry was only engaged in manufacturing talcum powder and toothpaste is simply not true. There were good reasons for attacking Dresden – certainly as good as those advanced for attacking many other German cities. Dresden's factories were in the suburbs; so too were the factories in most other European and American cities – which had not prevented the *Luftwaffe* destroying the City of London in 1940. Dresden had not been declared an 'open city', by the Germans – one which had no military significance and should be spared attack. Dresden was, in brief, an enemy city as liable to attack in wartime as any other German city.

The argument over Dresden has arisen partly because of the myths ventilated above, partly because of the loss of life – which, though certainly terrible, was no worse than the loss of life suffered in other German cities – but mainly because it seems pointless to have shattered Dresden at this stage in the war. This last is a valid point, but one that can be easily answered. The main reason for the attack in 1945 was that Dresden was a *transportation* target, and this type of target had been under attack for months by all the Allied air forces. Ross Spencer, who flew on the Dresden raid, has some answers to these points:

> During the post-war years I have read several accounts in which RAF crews destined for this attack expressed dissatisfaction on learning of Dresden's selection as a target. According to these accounts, it had been presumed by a few that Dresden had no military significance except for a few barracks which accommodated second-line or home-guard soldiers. Our orders, if memory serves me correctly, were to dislocate the transport and communications systems in and around Dresden. The Russian–German battle zone at this stage in the war lay about 80 miles to the east of Dresden, and if any of our squadron personnel had second thoughts regarding the Dresden assignment it was not apparent to me. Certainly we felt it regrettable that such a fine city had to be destroyed, but we needed no reminder that Rotterdam, Warsaw, London, Coventry and the rest had had their beauty shattered by the *Luftwaffe* bombs.

John Whiteley of No. 619 Squadron recalls his briefing for the Dresden operation:

> This took place at 1430 hrs. Briefing room contained large covered map of Europe. Cover withdrawn by station commander to reveal target DRESDEN. Route to and from target explained. Reason for attack: to assist Russians who were approaching Dresden from the east; 5 Group with 250 aircraft would attack first; 619 would put up thirteen Lancasters. Two hours later remainder of Bomber Command, approx, 750 aircraft, would attack, followed by American Eighth Air Force at first light. Route out: Reading, Beachy Head, France and Germany.
>
> Surprised by lack of fighter activity, a dark night, no moon, and thin layer of cloud. Remember being able to pick out the river Elbe. Bombed from 17,000 ft; little or no flak or searchlights. Dived out of target area in southerly direction, levelled out at 6,000 ft, and returned to base. Dresden burning fiercely as we left target area; consider we hit the jackpot. Fires visible when 150 miles away.

Charles P. Johnson flew to Dresden on 14 February with the Eighth's 303rd Bomb Group:

> On the 13th we were informed that the crew was scheduled to fly its first mission the following day. The target was Dresden, to help the Russians in

their efforts to capture Berlin. We were woken at about 3 a.m. and my first lesson was how dangerous it was to assemble the squadron through the clouds, with hundreds of other aircraft in the vicinity.

The second lesson was how dangerous combat could be. About halfway to the target we were flying close to a B-24 group which allegedly was to attack a ball-bearing plant – well, that is what we were told later. Black puffs of smoke suddenly appeared in the sky from anti-aircraft shells, and in a matter of a few minutes almost half the attacking B-24s fell out of formation; some appeared to regain control, but others either exploded or went into a steep spin. I was shaken, because I could see this happening as we got to Dresden. But fortune smiled on us, and after a successful bomb run in which only one plane was damaged we turned west for the run home. I later heard this mission described as the 'St Valentine's Day Massacre' because so many civilians were killed – somewhere around 30,000.

It would appear from these accounts that the crews were in no doubt why they were attacking Dresden, and it is hard to see why the fact that Dresden was an important military target – *specifically at this stage in the war* – has been so frequently dismissed as a reason for the attack.

Dresden is the capital of Saxony. In January and February 1945 it was a major transportation centre, and reinforcements and supplies for the Eastern Front and a large quantity of wounded men and refugees heading for the elusive safety of the West all flowed through it. A glance at the map confirms that Dresden was – and is – an important road and rail link, and those who regard the city's position as irrelevant to the bombing must explain why so many refugees, fleeing before the Russian advance, ended up there. At this stage in the war, with defeat staring the country in the face, Germany was more concerned with the defence of the Eastern Front than with the Western Front, for most Germans felt it would be better if their country fell to the Americans, British and Canadians, rather than to the vengeful Russians.

In February 1945, therefore, Dresden was jammed with soldiers heading east to bolster the defences of the Reich against the Red Army and with tens of thousands of people fleeing west before the rape and murder that had accompanied the advance of the Soviet armies into Silesia, the province to the east of Saxony. This advance had begun on 12 January 1945. A month later many of the refugees had made their way to Dresden and the situation on the Eastern Front was critical and it was the presence of so many refugees that added so much to the death roll.

Robert R. Geisel of the RCAF flew on the Dresden Raid with No. 115 Squadron:

This target was given to the crews as a main railhead supporting the German Eastern Front. Recent reports would indicate this was a target just to destroy, with no military value, but it was indicated to the crews that, with all the refugees jamming the roads and this being the closest railhead to the Eastern Front, the Russians had requested assistance and we complied with this request. It was to be many years before I heard of the destruction wrought on this raid, but I do recall that the fires were to be seen from a long distance after we left.

The RAF struck the first blow at Dresden on the night of 13/14 February with a force of 796 Lancasters and nine Mosquitoes. This was a two-part attack, the first being made by the bombers of 5 Group after low-level marking. The USAAF should have made the first attack earlier in the day, for the reasons already described – that smoke from the fires created by a previous RAF raid would otherwise obscure the target from the US bombardiers – but bad weather prevented the US attack so the RAF bombed first and the Eighth struck on the following day, sending in 311 B-17s, which as 'the bombing was done by radar . . . unloaded their bombs into the inferno'.[1] The Americans attacked the city again on 15 February and again on 2 March. After the bombers had attacked, USAAF fighters came down to strafe traffic on the roads leading out of the city, causing further loss of life and chaos among the refugees. The fact that the USAAF bombed Dresden *three times* in this period alone is a fact of which the man in the street is largely unaware – and about which the USA is surprisingly reticent.

Karin Hughes (née Reppe) was seven when the bombers flew to Dresden:

I was born in Dresden in 1938 and brought up by my mother as my father was in the *Luftwaffe*. Every time the sirens went off we went to the cellar of our block of flats, where every family had a cosy niche equipped with blankets and food; sometimes we spent an awful lot of time in the dark.

On that fateful night, as before, when the sirens went off my mother grabbed my baby sister and a bundle of essentials and we scrambled down six flights of stairs to the cellar. I do not know how long we stayed there, but we could hear the bombs dropping and suddenly the warden appeared and ordered us out as the flats in our road had been hit. Outside the house we were met by clouds of smoke and burning debris was all around. We only had one escape route, into a field for which we were heading. What followed was a long trek from the city centre to the outskirts of Dresden, and I had to clear branches or debris while my mother pushed the pram with my baby sister. Many times we had to stop and take shelter in the cellars as the sirens went off again or walk under balconies to shelter from the fire which was dripping from above. The only bridge still passable over the Elbe was the Blaue Wunder, and passing over that was what seemed to be an endless stream of people, young and old, carrying bundles or pushing carts. My baby sister was the one who suffered most, and it was months before she recovered from smoke poisoning. The new threat was the Russian soldiers, who were taking Dresden with a vengeance; pilfering, rape and murder were their daily routine, and I once overheard my mother pleading with an officer not to kill her children. It was 1948 before we finally left Dresden for good and joined my father in Bückeburg, in the British zone.[2]

Spaatz's biographer, David Mets, claims that the RAF bombed Dresden again on 15 February: 'on the fifteenth the RAF followed up with another attack on the hapless city'.[3] This is not correct: the only air force attacking Dresden on 15 February was that of the United States. On the night of 14/15 February the RAF bombed Chemnitz – as part of the THUNDERCLAP operation against the East German cities – and sent 244 bombers and eight Mosquitoes of 5 Group to attack the oil refinery at Rositz near Leipzig. A quantity of other aircraft was employed on diversion raids on a number of German cities and on *Gardening* sorties. Dresden was not included in any of this. Bomber Command flew only one operation on 15 February: an RCM sortie by a single Halifax of 100 Group.[4]

The biggest question of all, after five years of city bombing, is, Why has the Dresden raid been singled out as so uniquely terrible? Why, of all the cities shattered in the Second World War, is Dresden the one that people remember – a raid that has become a byword for aerial terror, the albatross offsetting the reputation of Arthur Harris and the men of RAF Bomber Command? Richard Braun of Ludwigshafen has some suggestions on this point:

> I feel that, with the end of the war in sight, it was certainly not necessary from the military point of view to carry out those raids on Dresden in February and March 1945. In other parts of our country too the continuation of the air bombing seemed pointless from a certain stage of the war. In Ludwigshafen, for example, we observed already in December 1944 that many bombs landed in craters caused by previous bombardments, or they produced new craters and filled up old ones. The only reason we could think of was that our enemies continued attacking us to empty their bomb stores in a relatively simple way, as long as it was possible. To some extent this opinion still prevails among the witnesses to the attacks.
>
> You dwell on the importance of Dresden, as a target, pointing out that there were factories in the suburbs of the town. I am sure this explanation cannot be questioned, but at the same time I am tortured by the question of why the RAF, and probably the US Eighth Air Force too, placed their aiming point in the centre of the town. I have often tried to find an answer to that, on my own and together with friends. The only motive for the bombardment I can think of as a plausible one is that the Western Allies wanted to demonstrate their air power to the Soviet Union, which already at that time was becoming a threat to them. I fully agree with the comment that the sanction for the Dresden raid came from a far higher level than Bomber Command HQ. It was a political decision, and I am sure that Winston Churchill was the man responsible for it. He can certainly be considered responsible for all the bombing of German cities, not Sir Arthur Harris, who was only his executive.

Ludwigshafen city archivist Stefan Morz also has some views on this subject:

> Reading your account as a German, one cannot help feeling that there may be some more clues as to why Dresden: why it was chosen, why it is still remembered. First of all Dresden was, and still is (what is left of it), part of the world's cultural heritage, something that could not be said of Mannheim or – goodness no – Ludwigshafen. Secondly, the cruelty with which the raids were carried out – sparing no parkland, sparing nobody in the streets, etc. And, thirdly, it was so late in the war, at a time when nobody in their senses could seriously expect the Germans to win, when the question was just, How many more weeks? Last but not least, the main reason to destroy the city was, I suppose, just revenge, a desire to destroy as many of 'their' beautiful buildings as possible and kill and maim as many as possible of those horribly perverted Germans who had brought such misery to Europe. There certainly were not a lot of people about who wanted to differentiate between guilty and innocent Germans, except for the bishop, Dr Bell, or John Betjeman with that lovely poem about a lady praying inside Westminster Abbey:
>
> > *Gracious Lord, oh bomb the Germans.*
> > *Spare their women for Thy Sake,*
> > *And if that is not too easy*
> > *We will pardon Thy Mistake.**
>
> That such resistance, such words were possible, that awkward words were asked about the bombing in the House of Commons, is more to Britain's credit than many other things I could think of.

Much of what Herr Braun and Dr Morz have to say is true, but the question remains: If any single raid has to be the one by which to judge the moral worth of the bomber war, why not that on Warsaw or Rotterdam or London or Coventry, those cities blasted by the *Luftwaffe*? The horrific casualty figures at Dresden are not the answer. The lower death roll in those other cities in 1940 merely indicates a shortfall in bomb load or technical ability, not a failure of intent. The *Luftwaffe* dropped bombs on Coventry for hours in 1940, until the city was blazing; if it could have started a firestorm and killed tens of thousands of people that night it would have done so. It is worth adding that the increasing efficiency and strength of Bomber Command and the Eighth Air Force in 1945 certainly contributed to the Dresden catastrophe – neither air force could have shattered a city so effectively earlier in the war.

If only RAF attacks on Germany are to be considered, again, why is Dresden the one that people remember? Why not Hamburg or Berlin?

---

* Stefan Morz omits the last two lines of this verse: *But, gracious Lord, whate'er shall be,/Don't let anyone bomb me.'*

Why not Cologne or Lübeck? Why not Mannheim or Ludwigshafen, which were bombed relentlessly throughout the war – 124 times according to Erwin Folz, the local air historian? Ludwigshafen was still being struck relentlessly in 1945, as the operations book of No. 153 Squadron confirms:

> 1.2.45. Scampton, Lincs. Take off 15.45 hrs. Target Ludwigshafen. Fifteen aircraft detailed to take part in this attack, taking off at 15.45 hrs in good visibility. Crews reported that the ground markers were plentiful and accurate and the bombing was concentrated round these markers. Ground defences consisted of moderate heavy flak in barrage form; fighter activity was moderate. F/O Bolton was engaged in combat with an enemy fighter no damage was sustained and the enemy a/c was claimed as destroyed. 'H' flown by F/O Freeborn was engaged by two enemy aircraft but no damage was sustained and no claims were made. Crews saw several large explosions in the target area and were of the opinion that the attack had been a success.

Dave Francis, of No. 460 Squadron, RAAF, reports that the particular target on this occasion was the railway yards.

Mannheim, just across the Rhine from Ludwigshafen, had been the object of the first 'area bombing' attack in December 1940 – an attack which destroyed the centre of this fine city in reprisal for the German attack on Coventry. Mannheim was also struck again and again throughout the war. Why not Mannheim?

If the Americans are brought into court for their part in the destruction of Dresden, again why Dresden? Why not the city of Tokyo, devastated in a conventional bombing raid by the USAAF on the night of 9/10 March 1945, when nearly 90,000 people died in the bombing and the subsequent firestorm? Surely no one can advance the argument that the Asian bombing raids were 'different', at least not without suggesting that the lives of European people have more intrinsic value than the lives of Asians. USAAF raids on Japan are on record as having killed some 400,000 Japanese civilians even before the atomic bombs fell on Hiroshima and Nagasaki, which were area bombings par excellence. The RAF never dropped a single bomb on Japan.[5] All this might be considered in examining why the arguments over the morality of Second World War bombing focus on Dresden and are *entirely* directed against Harris and RAF Bomber Command.

At this point, with some of the Dresden myths aired, let it be admitted that the destruction of Dresden and the resulting death toll were a terrible event and a great tragedy. The casualty figures cited vary and no finally agreed total now seems possible, but something over 30,000 dead seems to be the most generally accepted figure, though some estimates would add a hundred thousand to that. The actual total hardly matters: if Dresden was indeed a war crime, just one death would make it so.

However, a crime requires a criminal, and allocating the blame for

Dresden will not be easy. The first point to discuss is whether any 'blame' should be attached to the Dresden raids at all. Was Dresden not simply another tragedy in the six-year-long tragedy of the Second World War? Pursue the subject in the search to apportion blame and the argument returns to the same point: Why Dresden?

The most important of the myths surrounding Dresden is the myth that the destruction of Dresden was in some way uniquely horrific, a greater crime than any other. Not everyone would rate Dresden so high in the long calendar of Second World War atrocities. For example, Ben Halfgott, a Jewish prisoner, witnessed the bombing of Dresden from a nearby concentration camp – and rejoiced:

> After my mother and sister were shot, I was left behind with my father and elder sister. 1943 was a terrible time in our ghetto, at Piotrkow, near Łódź in Poland: people were being killed by the SS for no reason. My uncle and other relatives were taken out and shot, and then in April–May they decided to liquidate the ghetto of the 1,600 or so that were left, though my father and my elder sister and my three-year-old cousin Hania were left to work in the woodworking factory until November 1944. Then, with the Russians getting near, they decided to deport us to Buchenwald, and then to a camp at Schlieben, which is near Dresden. We were transported there by rail in cattle trucks, for five days during December. Soon after we got to Buchenwald my father was killed in a camp at Buchau and I was on my own.
>
> I do not hate the Germans, because there were decent Germans even in the camps; if that were not so, none of us would have survived. We saw the bombing of Dresden from the satellite camp at Schlieben, where we worked with German women making *Panzerfausts*, anti-tank rockets. The fires in the sky, a huge red glow – it was like heaven for us. We went out to watch and it was glorious, for we knew that the end of the war must be near and our salvation was at hand. I was fifteen years old when the Russians arrived and I weighted 50 kilos. You could see all my bones.[6]

The bombing of Dresden may in fact have saved some lives – Jewish lives. In February 1945 there were just 198 Jews left in Dresden, the last of the 1,265 listed by the Gestapo in 1941. All the rest had gone to their deaths in Auschwitz, Treblinka or Theresienstadt, and on the morning of 13 February the survivors were ordered to report for deportation three days later, on 16 February. After the bombing, the Gestapo in Dresden had other things to think about than the murder of two hundred starving Jews.[7]

The simple defence against the charge levelled against the aircrew who destroyed Dresden is that *there was a war on*. It was the *war* that killed the citizens of Dresden and the citizens of a thousand other cities, towns and villages in a score of countries spread around the world. That war killed millions of people. And who should be blamed for that?

That war was started by the elected leaders of Nazi Germany, and the deeds that took place in Germany and in the occupied countries during that war shocked the civilized world. During the research for this book, one RAF air gunner, Derek Jackson of No. 149 Squadron, remarked, 'We bombed Dresden in mid-February. It was not until six weeks later, in early April, that the papers were full of what the Army found at Belsen and Buchenwald and the other places. Had we know about Belsen at the time of Dresden, we would have been willing – anxious – to dish out exactly the same treatment to all the other German cities.'

That sort of comment may not sit well with the public at the start of the twenty-first century, but it reflects a common opinion in 1945. Dave Francis of No. 460 Squadron, RAAF, sums up the general attitude: 'Our feeling at this stage in the war was that the more damage and disruption we could inflict the sooner the war would end. We had no qualms about Dresden. To us it was another target to be attacked, a multiple rail and road target between the Eastern and Western Fronts.'

The previous pages may at least have dented the popular notion that what happened to Dresden can be blamed entirely on Bomber Command, though even refuting that notion opens the door to the argument that blame exists *somewhere*. It is therefore advisable to put the attack on Dresden in context and discuss how it came about. For that we must go back six weeks, to 1 January 1945.

When the year opened, the Battle of the Bulge was still going on in the Ardennes, but gradually improving weather enabled the Allied tactical air forces to fly sorties and savage the German panzers, which had been slowed by tenacious American resistance, most notably at Bastogne, and were now running out of fuel. However, the *Luftwaffe* could still strike savagely, and it opened the year with a major onslaught – *Der Grosse Schlag* – on Allied airfields in Belgium and northern France. Some 900 *Luftwaffe* fighters and bombers took part in this attack, and they caught a large part of the Allied air forces on the ground and quite unprepared.

Alfons Altmeier, a *Luftwaffe* officer, has some comments on *De Grosse Schlag*:

> In all the documents I have this operation is called Operation BODENPLATTE, but I believe that term '*Grosse Schlag*' covered all the air operations of the German fighter command in the Western theatre since November 1944 but very bad weather forced the fighters to stay on the ground for some weeks. The official description reads, 'This operation on 1 January 1945 brought the end to the German fighter weapon in the West because within a few hours 168 pilots were killed or lost in action, 67 ended their career as POW and eighteen returned wounded or heavily wounded. At least nineteen of the most experienced wing or squadron commanders were killed – the total loss for the day was 253.'

Der Grosse Schlag cost the Luftwaffe some 360 aircraft and aircrew it could ill afford to lose, and the effect on the Allied air forces was minimal.

The RAF lost 144 aircraft and 46 men on New Year's Day, but on the following day 521 RAF bombers attacked Nuremberg and another 389 aircraft, mostly Halifaxes, struck again at Ludwigshafen. On 3 January the USAAF sent 1,000 B-17 and B-24 bombers, escorted by no fewer than 650 Thunderbolt and P-51 fighters, to scour the Ardennes battlefields. *Der Grosse Schlag* did nothing to halt the Allied bombing offensive.

The Ardennes battle ended in mid-January 1945, and the next step on the road to Dresden took place on 27 January 1945, when Air Marshal Sir Norman Bottomley, Deputy Chief of the Air Staff, wrote to Harris, directing him to open a series of attacks on 'the industrial areas of Berlin, Dresden, Chemnitz and Leipzig . . . in particular with reference to the critical situation which confronts the enemy in the Eastern battle zone'. Bottomley added that the Chief of the Air Staff (Portal) was doubtful if a major attack, even on the THUNDERCLAP scale, would be decisive against Berlin, but

> subject to the overriding claims of oil and other approved target systems, we should use available effort in one big attack on Berlin and related attacks on Dresden, Leipzig, Chemnitz, or any other cities where a severe blitz will not only cause confusion in the evacuation from the East, but will also hamper the movement of troops from the West . . . I am therefore to request that, subject to the qualifications stated above, and as soon as the moon and weather conditions allow, you will under take such attacks.

This traces the origins of the Dresden raid back to Portal in January 1945. But the background to the Dresden raid is complicated, and the decision to attack the city may have an even earlier origin. The official history records that on 1 August 1944 Portal wrote a memo to the British Chiefs of Staff Committee suggesting that, instead of the major attack on Berlin which had been proposed at their July meeting, 'immense devastation could be caused if the entire attack was concentrated on a single big town other than Berlin, and the effect would be especially great if the town was one hitherto relatively undamaged'.

This proposal was code-named THUNDERCAP and, as described in a previous chapter, it went no further at the time. But January 1945 seemed a good time to resurrect the THUNDERCLAP plan, not least because, with the Western armies stalled on the Lower Rhine and the Russians pushing hard for Berlin from the Oder, it seemed likely that it would be Soviet Russia that would conquer Germany and gain all the political kudos that that feat would provide. If the Allied air forces could make a significant contribution to the final collapse of Germany, that would be some compensation and demonstrate Western commitment to the common cause. The Joint Intelligence Committee (JIC) therefore re-examined the THUNDERCLAP plan and, in a report to the Joint Chiefs on 25 January 1945 – a report which was the basis of Bottomley's letter to Harris written two days later –

recommended that, while the attack on oil and transportation should continue, there should also be some concentration on *communication* targets – specifically Berlin – in an attempt to stop the Germans moving reinforcements to the Eastern Front. On that same day, 25 January 1945, the Russian Armies crossed the Oder into Germany.

In a second report, the JIC stressed that an attack on communication targets in the East would help the Russians, demonstrate Allied solidarity to the Germans, and have political value, as it would show the Russians that the Western Allies were determined to assist them in their current offensive. With this much on the table, Bottomley wrote that 27 January letter to Harris and then met with Spaatz on 28 January to draw up a list of joint targets.

This urgency can be traced to Downing Street. On the evening of 25 January, the day the Russians crossed the Oder, Churchill telephoned the Secretary of the State for Air, Sir Archibald Sinclair, demanding to know what Bomber Command had in mind for 'basting the Germans in their retreat from Breslau'. With the Prime Minister involved, matters speeded up. On the following day Portal sent a minute to Bottomley saying that, subject to keeping up the pressure on oil and submarine targets etc., all available effort should be used 'in one big attack on Berlin and attacks on Dresden, Leipzig, Chemnitz, or other cities where a severe blitz will not only cause confusion in the evacuation from the East but will also hamper the movement of troops from the West'.

Clearly, this operation would have to be co-ordinated with attacks by the Eighth Air Force and, since the Allied bombers still had to assist the American and British Armies 'if required', this diversion to help the Russian armies had to be cleared with SHAEF, and specifically with Air Chief Marshal Tedder. There was then a further flurry of memoranda, during which Sir Archibald Sinclair suggested that the communication targets could be hammered by the tactical air forces while the bombers continued to attack oil and transport – in other words, Sinclair did not want yet another divergence from a clearly defined and effective task. This response did not meet with approval from Winston Churchill, who sent Sinclair a frosty memo: 'I did not ask you about plans for harrying the German retreat from Breslau. I asked whether Berlin and no doubt other large cities in East Germany should not now be considered especially attractive targets. I am glad that this is "under consideration". Pray report to me tomorrow on what is going to be done.'

Apart from the fact that Churchill *had* asked about plans for harrying ('basting') the Germans retreating from Breslau, this note was a clear instruction to press on with plans to attack the cities of eastern Germany and the upshot was that Bottomley wrote his 27 January letter to Harris. Therefore the roots of the Dresden raid clearly lie not with Arthur Harris but with the Prime Minister, Winston Churchill, and with 'Peter' Portal, the Chief of the Air Staff. News of the dispatch of Bottomley's letter was passed to the Prime Minister, and duly acknowledged.

However, on the day after this letter was sent, the trail broadens. On 28 January, Bottomley had a meeting with Spaatz. The meeting had been suggested by Churchill and the US Chief of the Combined Staff, General George Marshall, and at this meeting Bottomley and Spaatz drew up a new list of target priorities. Oil remained at the top of the list. Then came 'attacks on Berlin, Leipzig, Dresden and associated cities'. Third came 'communications' – actually transportation targets, railway stations, marshalling yards and so on, especially those which could be used to move troops to the Eastern Front. Finally 'jet aircraft and communications in Southern Germany' – the Allies were now concerned about *Werewolves*, behind-the-lines operations by remnants of the German Army, and had the notion that the Germans would establish a redoubt for a last stand in the mountains of Bavaria.

The drift of this agreement was that, when not engaged on precision attacks on oil, the USAAF would attack cities behind the retreating German Army. 'If possible they would hit industrial targets. But since the weather would prevent the Americans from bombing precisely, they would really be delivering area attacks.'[8] Spaatz's objection to THUNDERCLAP-type missions seems to have evaporated, and the first of these attacks was the devastating US mission to Berlin on 3 February. Dresden, for the moment, remained untouched.

The next step towards Dresden took place at *Argonaut*, the conference at Yalta in the Crimea in early February, between Roosevelt, Churchill, Stalin and their political and military advisers. This conference was preceded by a meeting of the British and American military leaders – the Combined Chiefs of Staff – in Malta, where they hoped to agree on a common strategy before meeting their Soviet opposite numbers in Yalta. The meeting in Malta convened on 30 January, and with the end of the war and Allied victory clearly in sight the discussions were largely concerned with strategy for the final advance into Germany, the expected meeting with the Russian armies advancing from the East, and the subsequent defeat and occupation of Germany. The British and US Chiefs were not seeing eye to eye at this time and there was a considerable amount of argument. Most of this lies outside the context of this book, but one of the subjects that came up concerned the operation of the bomber forces and bombing support for the Russian armies coming from the East.

The Combined Chiefs considered a Soviet request that, to aid the Russian advance into Germany, the Allied strategic bomber force – specifically the USAAF Eighth Air Force and RAF Bomber Command – should carry out major attacks on certain communications centres in eastern Germany – specifically Berlin, Chemnitz, Leipzig . . . and Dresden. The Combined Chiefs agreed to this request, and their decision was endorsed by the political leaders at Yalta a few days later. Therefore, the *sanction* for the Dresden raid can be traced directly to the highest reaches of the Allied Command – to the political leaders and the Combined Chiefs of Staff. It did not originate at Bomber Command HQ near High Wycombe.

There is no evidence that the attacks on Dresden and the other cities were discussed in any detail at Yalta. The subject of bombing appears in only one part of the agenda, where the matter of establishing 'bomb lines' marking the enemy-occupied area between the advancing armies was discussed and the Russians suggested that the Western bomb line should run through Berlin, Dresden, Vienna and Zagreb, which would allot the bombing of these places to the Western Allies. Otherwise there is no firm evidence that the raids formed any part of the discussions at the *Argonaut* conference, which ended on 11 February, two days before the RAF bombers took off for Dresden. However, on 12 February, the day after the conference ended – and the day before the raid – a signal was sent from Spaatz's HQ to Major-General Edmund W. Hill, the senior USAAF officer with the US Military Mission in Moscow, asking him to inform the Soviet General Staff that the Eighth Air Force would attack 'the marshalling yards' at Dresden 'on the following day'. This message tends to confirm that the Soviets knew about the proposed attacks on the eastern cities; the Western Allies did not normally keep the Soviets abreast of day-to-day bombing operations. The statement that the USAAF would attack Dresden 'on the following day' is also interesting, for it tends to confirm the view that the Russians knew of the combined attack, if not the precise date. Had all gone to plan the USAAF would indeed have attacked Dresden on 13 February, and been followed up that night by the RAF.

The declaration that only 'marshalling yards' would be attacked enabled the Russians to deny later that they knew the city was to be destroyed and to imply that, had they known, they would not have approved – and this from a country that was allowing its soldiers to rape and murder at will as the Red Army advanced into Germany.

Spaatz had requested that his agreement with Bottomley should be shown to General Lawrence Kuter, who was at Yalta in place of Hap Arnold, but Kuter did not receive his copy until 13 February. This was after the first heavy US raid on Berlin on 3 February and at a time when preparations for the US mission to Dresden on 14 February were well advanced. According to German reports, over 25,000 civilians were killed on the 3 February mission to Berlin, many of them refugees from the East, and this figure is not disputed in US official accounts. These transportation raids were designed to spread confusion and block communications, and achieving that would certainly involve massive destruction of city centres – a policy to which (whatever happened in practice) the USAAF was publicly opposed. Bombing 'blind' using radar, was known to be haphazard: on 26 January 1945 Doolittle received a note from his bombing advisers informing him that the average bombing error using instruments was still about two miles and that to hit the target 'involved drenching an area with bombs to achieve any results'.

As for the US aircrews, they simply, and understandably wanted to finish the war, as Harold Jones points out:

> I do have a list of the cities I bombed, but the details of these missions have faded, though some can be remembered. Munich was a long trip, the rail yards were covered with cloud and our radar was not good. The SOP [standard operating procedure] was that if we could not pinpoint our target, drive over the town and drop on it, *all* Germans were the enemy. I didn't care where the bombs fell, but I knew we could not carry them back home, because we had used up two-thirds of our fuel getting there.

It is more than likely that Spaatz wanted to obtain some backing from Washington for these transportation attacks and the resulting civilian casualties; he was certainly cautious later in the year, when it came to the bombing of Hiroshima. However, as already related, the US attacked Dresden on 14 February, again on the 15th, and yet again on 2 March – a day, two days and fifteen days after the RAF attack on the night of 13/14 February. If the USAAF commanders or politicians had really disapproved of the Dresden missions they had ample time to stop them.

The details of the Dresden raids have been endlessly presented and need only be summarized here. By mid-February 1945, Dresden's pre-war population of around 650,000 had been increased to well over a million – many of them refugees from the East, plus a not inconsiderable number of refugees from the West, who had fled from cities bombed by the RAF and USAAF. In truth, there was no place of shelter in Germany in 1945, and to these hapless civilians can be added a large quantity of soldiers, plus over 20,000 Allied prisoners of war, forced workers from the countries of Occupied Europe, and slave labour from nearby concentration camps.

Dresden was not well defended. Most of the flak, and all the vital 88 mm guns in the city had been dismantled and sent east towards the Oder to serve in the anti-tank role against the advancing Russians; other batteries were sent west to fight the Americans. Dresden had a certain amount of 20 mm and 30 mm light flak but was in most respects an undefended city. Nor was there much in the way of fighter support; by this time the *Luftwaffe*, if still active, was running very short of fuel and obliged to restrict its activities to mainly night sorties by aircraft other than the jet fighters which alone could outrun the P-51s.

Dresden lay within the defensive orbit of the 1st Fighter Division, which was controlled from a bunker near Berlin. One night-fighter *Gruppe*, V/NJG 5, flying Me 110s, was based at Dresden-Klotzsche airfield, and when the RAF bombers came through the *Mandrel Screen* on the night of

13/14 February and were seen to be heading for Dresden eight fighters took off to intercept them.

The German flak and fighters achieved very little. The force dispatched put in two separate attacks: one a precision, low-level marking attack by 244 aircraft of 5 Group – the *Platerack* force – which attacked at 2215 hrs on the 13th and bombed the area between the Neustadt, Wettin and Central stations, and the other a much larger attack by the rest of the Main Force – 529 aircraft – which attacked at 0130 hrs on the 14th and ravaged the centre of the city. A total of 2,660 tons of bombs was dropped – a mixture of high explosives and incendiaries which gradually created a massive firestorm. Six Lancasters were lost on the operation, and three more crashed on the way home.

On the following day 311 USAAF B-17s attacked the city, dropping 771 tons of bombs and using the railway yards just to the west of Wettin station as their aiming point. This raid added to the chaos below, and after the bombers had flown away their escorting Mustang fighters came down to machine-gun people in the streets and traffic on the roads around the city – attacking 'targets of opportunity' is the term employed for this activity – to spread the confusion still further. The USAAF attacks on 15 February and on 2 March were also followed by machine-gunning and strafing of the streets by American fighters, which had become a standard tactic of US fighters after their escort duties had been completed.

No one really knows how many people died in the destruction of Dresden. Estimates range from 35,000 to 135,000 but, when comparisons are made with other raids, including the 1943 firestorm raid on Hamburg and the USAAF daylight raid on refugee-crammed Berlin the previous month, something close to the lower figure – which is terrible enough – seems the most probable. Another ghastly sum had been added to the ever growing total of Second World War dead, and the war still had three months to run.

The controversy over the Dresden raid began almost at once, and has continued to rage ever since. Dresden has become the focus for all the accusations made about 'terror' bombing, area bombing and the destruction of cities, and the Dresden raids have provided those who think that area bombing is wrong with all the ammunition they need to condemn the entire bomber offensive. Their criticism began on the morning after the RAF raid on the night of 13/14 February 1945, has continued ever since, and is mainly directed at RAF Bomber Command and Air Chief Marshal Sir Arthur Harris. How justified such criticism has been, readers must now decide for themselves.

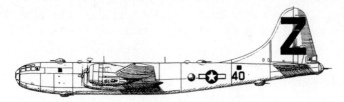

B-29 Superfortress

17

The Road to Hiroshima
February–August 1945

Our policy has never been to inflict terror bombing on civilian populations.

Henry L. Stimson, US Secretary of War, 22 February 1945

The RAF bulletin announcing the attacks on Dresden was issued by the Air Ministry at 0900 hrs on 14 February. Unlike previous bulletins, this one went into great detail about the target, stressing Dresden's contribution to the German military machine and emphasizing that it was a legitimate target and the centre of a railway network sending troops to the East. This emphasis, this tendency to protest too much, inevitably attracted attention. The raid was then covered in the BBC's popular nine o'clock news that night, in which Dresden was referred to as 'a great industrial city'.

By the following day Germany and neutral countries were starting to broadcast details of what had happened to Dresden, the German reports rebutting the British claims that Dresden was a transport centre and a military target and claiming that the main products of the city factories were toothpaste and talcum powder. The German claims could be disregarded as propaganda, but the protests coming from neutral radio stations in Switzerland and Sweden could not be so easily dismissed and were soon picked up by radio stations in the USA and Canada.

This rapidly growing clamour over Dresden obliged the USAAF to divert its planned mission of 15 February to oil targets, but poor weather forced a diversion to secondary targets and Dresden was struck again, this time by 461 tons of bombs. On the following day an intelligence officer at SHAEF outlined the new Allied bombing plan, which, according to the USAAF official history, was 'to bomb large population centres and then to attempt to prevent relief supplies from reaching them or refugees from leaving them – all part of a general programme to bring down the German economy'.[1]

In the question period that followed his statement, this officer, an RCAF air commodore, referred to German allegations of 'terror raids', and this term was picked up by the Associated Press correspondent in his subsequent dispatch to various newspapers in the USA: 'Allied air chiefs have made the long-awaited decision to adopt deliberate terror bombing of German population centres as a ruthless expedient of hastening Hitler's doom. More raids such as those recently carried out by heavy bombers of the Allied Air Forces on residential sectors of Berlin, Dresden, Chemnitz and Kottebus are in store for the Germans.'[2] This report received front-page coverage across the USA and caused outrage. That the British had been bombing German cities had been known for some time; now it appeared that the Americans were doing it as well, and intended to go on doing it. The American public picked up its collective pen and began to protest, and its protests soon reached the desks of General Arnold and General Eisenhower.

Before this part of the saga continues, a few more myths can be ventilated. First of all, the Germans had been referring to the Allied bomber crews and to those of the RAF in particular as 'terror bombers', *'Terrorflieger'*, long before the attack on Dresden. It was good propaganda, and the German minister in charge of propaganda, Dr Josef Goebbels, was an expert in this field. His broadcasts whipped up German resentment against the aircrews and, as previous accounts have indicated, Allied aircrews parachuting into Germany were often attacked, beaten and even lynched on landing, the fury of the attacks depending more on who seized them than on which air force they were flying for. In the immediate aftermath of Dresden, Goebbels suggested that several thousand Allied aircrew prisoners should be executed in reprisal for the attack – a suggestion welcomed by Hitler, Jodl, Keitel, and other members of the Nazi hierarchy, but totally opposed by Goering.

These actions had official, if secret, sanction under the *Kugel Erlass* – the 'Bullet Decree' – of 1944, which called for captured aircrew, especially those recaptured after attempting to escape, to be sent to the Austrian concentration camp at Maulthausen near Vienna, where they were either executed at once or worked to death hauling rocks up the Maulthausen quarry staircase. More than 40 American, British and Dutch officers were so treated within a few months – the latest in a long series of German actions against captured soldiers, ranging from the notorious Commando Order of 1942, which led to the murder of many British Commando soldiers, to the execution of 50 RAF officers captured after the 'Great Escape' from Stalag Luft III in March 1944.

Many other aircrew were also murdered by the Gestapo or by Nazi Party fanatics, either on capture or in the course of escaping from POW camps. It is worth repeating that Hermann Goering, head of the *Luftwaffe*, and many German soldiers and civilians were totally opposed to such actions. Goering offered Allied aircrew his personal protection, and the *Luftwaffe* and *Wehrmacht* soldiers generally took no part in reprisals against Allied flyers, frequently rescuing them from beatings or murder at the hands of Nazi Party members or the mob. This point is brought out accurately by Richard Braun of Ludwigshafen:

> I do not know of violence against short-down Allied aircrew taking place in our towns and cities. What I do know is that such outrages seemed to happen relatively often in the open countryside, committed by villagers and NSDAP [Nazi Party] officials. By contrast the shot-down crew were almost always safe when captured by soldiers, particularly by the *Luftwaffe*.

The USAAF had been bombing cities and striking residential areas for years, ever since it had started bombing operations in Europe, and everyone in the USAAF knew it. When the weather, navigation and bombing accuracy were taken into account it was *inevitable* that residential areas in cities would be hit, and hit severely, if the USAAF was to bomb German military targets at all. This was especially true of communications targets, like marshalling yards and railway stations, because these targets were *in cities* – and the Germans were not going to help America's moral dilemma on the matter of strategic bombing by moving their industrial assets out of the cities and on to greenfield sites.

Nor was Dresden the only occasion on which the USAAF had been involved in attacks which the Germans referred to as 'terror bombing'. That 3 February attack on Berlin, which caused heavy loss of life, produced what the USAAF history refers to as 'lurid accounts in Swedish newspapers'. The US response to those accounts was the claim that 'The Americans were not bombing cities indiscriminately, but attacking transportation facilities inside cities on missions which the Russians had requested and seemed to appreciate.'[3] So that was all right then.

If the USAAF aircrew and commanders found comfort in declaring that, no matter where the bombs *fell*, they were always *aimed* at marshalling yards and other military targets, that is one thing; to go further and imply that this intention somehow made American bombing more ethical than the British version is simply nonsense. But, however nonsensical, this line played very well at home. Many decent Americans, living at a comfortable distance from the daily realities of war, were therefore shocked to discover that their boys, instead of harassing the armed and dangerous enemy, were bombing civilians – just like the British . . . and the Gemans.

This is not the entire picture. Millions of Americans were fighting in Europe, and their families naturally wanted them back in one piece even if that meant bombing Germany flat. It is probably fair to say that the protests and outrage over the bombing of Dresden represented a minority view, and one that shrunk perceptibly in the next few weeks as the advancing British and American armies overran Belsen, Buchenwald and the other concentration camps and found out exactly what had been going on inside Nazi Germany. But, at the time, the voices of protest and moral outrage were sounding loud and clear and attracting a lot of attention.

The first official reaction to these protests was denial. The British government, hearing of the SHAEF press conference on 17 February, immediately imposed a total media ban in the hope that the statement would be forgotten, while Arnold and Eisenhower denied that the USAAF was going in for area bombing. Arnold then wrote to Spaatz, seeking an assurance that there *was* a distinct difference between the 'blind' bombing of the USAAF and the 'area' bombing of the RAF. Spaatz replied stating that the USAAF had not departed from its policy of only bombing military targets on either the Berlin mission of 3 February or the Dresden missions of 14 and 15 February. A more blunt and honest answer to the question posed would have been 'There is no difference.'

There was an interesting follow-up to this part of the affair. When the Associated Press dispatch reached London and the government proposed banning its publication, SHAEF – General Eisenhower's HQ – stated that it could not be banned, as the statement did indeed represent the official SHAEF policy of destroying large population centres and the communications networks supporting them. This was confirmed by another raid on 26 February, as Charles P. Johnson of the 303rd Bomb Group recalls:

> 26 February 1945, began with an early wake-up call and the briefing that day was for Berlin – the 'Big B' – which the briefing officer assured us was not the formidable target it had been earlier in the war. The real shock came when he told us we were to bomb from the east. We flew east, past Berlin, and then turned 180° in order to bomb into the wind, which, with the strong headwinds, took us over the city at around 35 knots, ground speed, which seemed like an eternity in range of the anti-aircraft guns but because of the cloud cover and the fact that we bombed from 25,000 ft we encountered only ineffective flak. The bomb drop was by means of radar and we were unable to observe the result, but since the target was the marshalling yards within the city we assumed that we accomplished some damage to the enemy.

Nevertheless, in spite of this continued attack on city centres, Spaatz's denial was the answer Arnold wanted, and he used it to pacify the US media and the critics at home. The bombing continued as before, but the blame for Dresden was laid on the British – where it has largely remained ever since. In this sustained campaign against the reputation of Bomber Command and Sir Arthur Harris, British politicians and public figures were right in the van of the attack.

The protests against the RAF's area-bombing campaign had been going on for much of the war, led by, among others, Dr George Bell, the Bishop of Chichester, who was totally against area bombing and repeatedly put the case against it in the press, from the pulpit and from his seat in the House of Lords. There is no need to go into detail about these protests: Bishop Bell had every right to make them, and it is some indication of Britain's generally moral attitude to the conduct of the war that he was allowed to do so and received many letters of support. Dr Bell's efforts were then taken up on the floor of the House of Commons by Mr Richard Stokes, a Labour MP.

Mr Stokes had been asking questions about the bombing offensive since the summer of 1942, and he was far from convinced by the answers he had been getting. Assurances from Sir Archibald Sinclair, the Secretary of State for Air, that the RAF attacks were precision attacks on military targets failed to convince him, and now, after Dresden, he had the ammunition for a telling attack on both RAF policy and the obfuscation he had received from the Air Ministry and its spokesmen over the last years.

Like many Labour MPs at this time, Mr Stokes was a Soviet sympathizer and drew comparisons between the 'tactical' bombing of the Russians and the area, 'blanket', bombing of the RAF. Was 'terror bombing' now the open policy of the government, asked Mr Stokes, and, since the whole world now knew what was going on, why did the government not admit it?

To ensure that the SHAEF statement *did* reach the ears of the British public, government ban or not, Mr Stokes then read out the Associated Press dispatch, so that it would be recorded in *Hansard*, the parliamentary record. Was this statement true, asked Stokes, and, given that this information had now been published everywhere else in the world, 'why were the British people the only ones not to be told what was being done in their names'? It was, said Stokes, 'complete hypocrisy to say one thing and do another' and one day 'the British Government would rue the day it had permitted these raids, which would stand for all time as a blot on our escutcheon'.

Mr Stokes clearly had the government on the ropes over this issue, and the subsequent reply from the Joint Under-Secretary for Air, Commander Brabner, speaking on behalf of Sir Archibald Sinclair, did little to mollify him. Having stated that the SHAEF report had been denied in London, Commander Brabner stated unequivocally, 'We are not wasting bombers or time on purely terror tactics. It does not do the Hon. Member [Mr Stokes] justice to come to this House and suggest that there are a lot of Air Marshals or pilots or anyone else sitting in a room trying to think how many German women or children they can kill.'

Richard Stokes, Dr Bell and many other people, like the writer Vera Brittain and the military historian Basil Liddell Hart, sincerely believed that area bombing was morally wrong and maintained that view at some personal cost. Coming in the middle of total war, their views were not popular; many people maintained that such protesters were stabbing the RAF in the back and decrying the efforts and sacrifices of the aircrew. Whether one agrees with them or not, the views of Bishop Bell and Richard Stokes were honestly held and fairly maintained, and it is possible to have respect for them. Others who became involved in the propaganda surrounding the Dresden raid come out of it less well. After trying denial, some people proceeded to distance themselves from the Dresden operation and area bombing in general, being more than happy to let the 'blame' (if blame there be) and all the resulting odium descend on Sir Arthur Harris and Bomber Command. Chief among these was the British Prime Minister, Winston Churchill.

A stream of newspaper articles from neutral countries was reproduced in the British press and this kept the debate alive until, on 28 March, Winston Churchill sent a memo to the Chiefs of Staff which seemed to endorse all the public criticisms of Bomber Command policy and distance the Prime Minister from any part in forming it:

> It seems to me that the moment has come when the question of bombing cities simply for the sake of increasing terror, though under other pretexts, should be reviewed. Otherwise we shall come into possession of an utterly ruined land . . . The destruction of Dresden remains a serious query against the conduct of Allied bombing. I am of the opinion that military objectives must henceforward be more strictly studied in our own interests rather than that of the enemy.
>
> The Foreign Secretary has spoken to me on this subject, and I feel the need for more precise concentration upon military objectives, such as oil and communications behind the immediate battle zone, rather than mere acts of terror and wanton destruction, however impressive.[4]

This minute went out on 28 March. The Prime Minister seems to have forgotten that just *three weeks previously*, on 6 March, a member of his Cabinet, the Secretary of State for Air, Sir Archibald Sinclair, had sat by while his deputy had stated categorically, in the House of Commons, that 'We are not wasting bombers or time on purely terror tactics' – a statement Sir Archibald had promptly endorsed.

The Prime Minister had also conveniently forgotten his various memos and telephone conversations with Sinclair in January, urging attacks on the eastern cities. Churchill was well aware that the RAF was going to attack Dresden and the other eastern cities; the decision to do so had originated in Cabinet and had his full spport. To deny it now did him no credit and was clearly an attempt to distance himself and his government from the political fallout among the neutral countries and in the USA – the comment that 'The Foreign Secretary has spoken to me on this subject' is a pointer in this direction.

History was repeating itself, as is history's habit. In the First World War the then Prime Minister, Lloyd George, distanced himself from his Commander-in-Chief, Sir Douglas Haig, over the conduct and direction of the war, then disparaged Haig in his memoirs at the end of the 1920s and so began the campaign of vilification that has followed Haig ever since. In this minute of 28 March, Winston Churchill dealt a similar blow to Sir Arthur Harris and Bomber Command, shifting the blame from his shoulders to theirs and providing their enemies, at the time and since, with invaluable ammunition. The minute implies that Churchill had been misled and that the air commanders were conducting a 'terror campaign' on their own initiative and without his knowledge, which was patently untrue.

Fortunately, the matter did not stop there. When Portal received his copy of the minute he flatly refused to accept it and requested that it be withdrawn. Portal's biographer makes no reference to this business, and a full account of this matter would be interesting, but Churchill, an essentially fair-minded man, immediately agreed to withdraw that minute and substitute another one, dated 1 April:

> It seems to me that the moment has come when the question of the so-called area bombing of German cities should be reviewed from the point of view of our own interests. If we come into control of an entirely ruined land there will be a great shortage of accommodation for ourselves and our allies . . . We must see to it that our attacks do not do more harm to ourselves in the long run than they do to the enemy's immediate war effort. Pray let me have your views.

This memorandum left out all reference to 'terror bombing', and the Chiefs of Staff accepted it without further comment. Nevertheless the damage had been done, and the effects of that original minute – which went into the official record – have been far-reaching.

In the USA the outcry over the Dresden missions quickly faded away. The military and political leaders had the answer they wanted, the American public accepted it, and Dresden was allowed to disappear from the headlines – which is curious, because the American bombers continued to attack Dresden. However, the condemnation for Dresden was now gathering about Bomber Command, and the USAAF, quite understandably in the circumstances, was more than happy to leave it that way.

Besides, the war continued. The USAAF and the RAF were now busy with the revived Operation CLARION, an all-out attack on the German railway system, and the USAAF was running into some controversy of its own. CLARION had had an uneasy birth and attracted a great deal of opposition, not least from Ira Eaker, who on 1 January 1945 had stated that 'The idea stems from the Zuckerman crowd who have gone nuts on transportation . . . and will give credence to German assertions that the Allies were barbarians, for 95% of the casualties are sure to be civilians' – a point that had been made against the Allied plan to destroy the French rail network in the period before D-Day.

The CLARION plan had therefore been shelved, at least for a while, but at the end of February 1945 it came out again and was implemented by all the air forces. CLARION required a clear day, during which all the air forces – tactical and strategic – would range at will over Germany, attacking whatever targets they could find, but concentrating on the railways. Clear skies finally appeared on 22 February, and in the aircraft went, Bomber Command tackling the Ruhr, the two tactical air forces savaging western and north-western Germany, the Fifteenth Air Force operating over Bavaria, and the Eighth attacking the centre of Germany, the B-17s and B-24s ignoring the flak to bomb from low level – 10,000 ft or less – with dramatic effect, as German fighter pilot Peter Spoden remembers:

> I saw some of the towns after they had been attacked and it was terrible, and after a few times I could not do it any more. One town I was in – we went down in daylight to help, because at night I was flying – and the American bomber force came. I saw – and I will never forget this – people lying under the debris of their houses and only their faces showing, crying 'Help, Help', and you could not do a thing for them.

There was little resistance. Only about 70 German fighters came up to offer themselves as a sacrifice to the P-51s, and only 87 of the 1,400 Eighth Air Force bombers sent out that day suffered flak damage. About 80 towns of varying size were hit, and this first CLARION operation was judged so successful that a repeat was ordered for 23 February, which, though on a smaller scale, was deemed equally successful.

One town attacked during the second CLARION attack was Pforzheim. 'Whisky' Wheaton, an Australian of No. 582 Squadron, PFF, took part in this attack, flying as Navigator II in a Lancaster, *M for Mike*, piloted by Captain Edwin Swales, DFC, of the South African Air Force. An account of what happened to *M for Mike* is given by Alan Bourne, the rear gunner:

> On 23 February 1945, we were briefed to be master bomber (master of ceremonies) in an attack on the marshalling yards at Pforzheim, a watchmaking centre which was said to be producing V2 warheads. The raid by about 600 aircraft was to take twenty minutes, with a deputy MC to orbit the target with us in case we got the chop. Met gave us a forecast of five-tenths to six-tenths cloud, meaning that bombing could be visual or blind, and while we were orbiting the target for the second time I noticed some movement on our starboard side, low. It could not be a Lanc, so I made a note to keep a watch, rotating the turret, but then the skipper started to broadcast to the Main Force and I was cut off from the aircraft intercom.
>
> At that moment an enemy aircraft appeared, dropped astern of us, and seemed to rise, coming in on our starboard quarter at a range of less than 400

yards. 'Fighter starboard, go!' I cried into the intercom, but the pilot could not hear my call when he was broadcasting, so I began flashing my starboard-fighter call light visually, to get Ted's attention, and opened fire with all four guns from the rear turret. At the same time I felt the aircraft shudder and go into a starboard corkscrew as the enemy aircraft opened fire with cannon.

As we levelled out, the enemy aircraft was still on our tail and his shells straddled the rear turret and registered hits on both rudders and the inboard engines, As the rudder control surfaces disintegrated, they looked like washing on a clothes line on a windy day. Also, with both engines hit, I realized that all power for the turrets and guns was gone (the inboard engines provided power for the turret hydraulics) – and still I heard nothing on the intercom but my own breathing. At this time Bryn Leach, our mid-upper gunner, let out a shout; only then did I realize that, as our attacker rose into view from the stern, Bryn too had opened fire, to good effect.

A call from the skipper confirmed that no one was injured, but with two engines gone we were losing height at an alarming rate. Ted decided to make one last broadcast to the Main Force, passing on the aiming point, and the decision was made to head for the Schaffhausen salient in Switzerland, the nearest friendly place, though it would mean internment for the rest of the war. However, after some discussion it was decided that we might just make it to base, and the unanimous decision was 'Let's head for home.'

The next hour was a nightmare, with *M for Mike* slithering violently from side to side as we lost more of that much needed height, the skipper fighting to keep control. Finally, by the time we were over the German border and into France, the skipper had his feet braced on the instrument panel and both arms wrapped around the control column and gave the order to prepare to abandon the aircraft. I left the rear turret, and by the time I got to the main door the urgent call came over the intercom 'Jump, jump, I can't hold her any longer.' We went out the main hatch . . . my chute opened and the sound of the aircraft receded, and there was a deafening explosion and a flash as the aircraft struck the ground somewhere below.

We must have been very low, for within a few seconds I was in the mud of a ploughed field, sinking in over my boot tops. Minutes later, by blowing on our aircrew whistles, the crew gathered, without Ted, at the fiercely burning remains of *M for Mike*. A quick check showed that we had all landed safely, except for 'Whisky' Wheaton, who had badly sprained ankles. Without Ted's determination to get us back, even at the cost of his own life, we would never have made it.

Two months later, on 24 April 1945, Captain Swales, 'who gave his life that his comrades might live', was awarded a posthumous Victoria Cross.

Twelve Lancaster bombers were lost that night over Pforzheim; the Lancaster force dropped 1,551 tons of bombs and wrecked 350 acres of the town's built-up area.

The German pilots' attitude at this time is summed up by Peter Spoden:

I think the worst times for me were when I was flying over Essen and saw the fires and not knowing where my family was or what might have happened to them. That is why we kept on fighting to the end, because we felt we could not give up. We could not win the war any more, but with every bomber you shot down you felt it was your duty; you just had to do it and maybe, just maybe, you were helping your family or your friends, you know?

Evidence that the Germans were still willing to fight on, in spite of this day and night pounding, comes in an account supplied by Canadian Ken Rosu-Myles, which recounts his father Sam's first – and last – mission, on 7 March 1945, as described to him by the tail gunner, Kitchener Seaman, a US volunteer from California:

The target was Dessau, about 70 miles north of Berlin. We were travelling at about 18,000 ft and feeling perfectly safe when Kitch heard the navigator say, 'Right on the tick for time and slightly off route but nothing to worry about.' Those were the last words Kitch heard from any of the boys. Then the plane was hit by flak underneath the starboard wing, which threw the Lancaster up for about 50 ft. The plane flew straight for a few seconds and then went into a steep dive. Only Kitch got out, after getting stuck halfway out of his turret and only getting his parachute open at about 1,000 ft, hitting the ground hard and breaking some bones in his foot.

He hid in the woods till morning, then walked down the road towards the sound of gunfire, only to be taken into custody by a German officer, who questioned him about his aircraft and other members of his crew. Then he said, 'I suppose you know that Cologne has fallen to the Americans and I suppose you think you will win this war? Well, in two weeks our new V-weapons will be ready and we will push your troops into the English Channel – and you will rot in jail for the rest of your life.' Kitch was then taken to a farmhouse where the bodies of five members of the crew were decently laid out. These included that of my father, Sam Rosu. The body of the missing man, Flying Officer T. S. Lawrence, was never found. Kitch was released by the Americans three weeks later and walked for 150 miles across Germany to reach the Canadian forces in Holland.

These massive CLARION attacks caused a considerable number of civilian casualties, as General Eaker had predicted, but the Germans still declined to surrender. The CLARION missions also created another, and rather more delicate, problem for General Spaatz. During these missions some USAAF bombers strayed across the Swiss frontier and bombed the Swiss town of Schaffhausen, which had already been bombed by the USAAF the year before. This was bad enough, but on 5 March fifteen US bombers attacked two major Swiss cities, Basle and Zurich, doing a small amount of damage, but killing a number of Swiss citizens. The Swiss were not pleased, and this time their complaints went all the way to the White

House. Spaatz was sent to Berne in early March, to offer apologies and compensation, and therefore had other things to think about than the destruction of Dresden, not least his impending departure for the Pacific theatre, where the war against Japan was being prosecuted with vigour – and area attacks.

One of the objects of the island-hopping campaign waged by the US Navy and the US Marine Corps in the Pacific had been to seize forward airfields and get US bombers within range of Japan. By the end of 1944 this project had been realized and Japan came under attack from US heavy bombers – especially the high-flying B-29 Superfortresses of the US Twentieth Air Force, with their long range and large bomb loads.

The target-planners for the Twentieth had a problem when they were called on to select targets in Japan. First of all, they had much less information on Japanese industry than was available on Germany's military-industrial complex. What information they had seemed to indicate that the Japanese cartels, like Mitsubishi, relied heavily on small-scale factory production and outworkers. It also became apparent that the Japanese cities had one common factor that made them particularly susceptible to aerial bombardment: the houses were close-packed, made of wood, and highly flammable. Fire was the weapon to deploy against Japan, and the most devastating fire raid took place on 9/10 March, on the capital city of Tokyo, barely a month after the destruction of Dresden.

For this and other attacks on Japanese cities the USAAF used its M-69 incendiary bomb, tons of which were sent cascading on the city, starting thousands of fires. The USAAF's intention, even in early 1944, was to drop some 1,690 tons of M-69 bombs on six Japanese cities – Tokyo, Yokohama, Kawasaki, Nagoya, Osaka and Kobe – as soon as the bombers had Japan in range. Since there was still plenty of time before that happened, experiments in fire bombing were conducted to estimate the problems and find solutions, and the committee in charge of the experiments concluded that fire bombing Japanese cities would produce 'tremendous casualties' among the civilian population.[5] So it proved.

The fire raids on Japan began with a few experimental sorties from bases in the Marianas. In August 1944, there was a small-scale raid against Nagasaki, but only 24 aircraft found the city. On 29/30 November the B-29s attacked Tokyo, and in December a small force attacked Nagoya, but the results on both occasions were inconclusive. By now the Twentieth Air Force's Bomber Command, XXI Bomber Command, had a new commander – a man with vast experience in air bombing, hard-won in the ETO – General Curtis LeMay, and he began to work up his crews for a major strategic attack.

LeMay was too experienced to let the crews go out without being entirely sure they could deliver the bombs in the right place and in quantity. Practice flights intensified, and there were more experimental raids –

on Kobe on 4 February and on Tokyo on 4 March. Ironically, the problems that necessitated these practice missions and trial raids were caused by the superb technical performance of the B-29. To avoid flak and fighters the B-29 flew very high and so entered the jet stream, an unknown quantity in 1945. The jet-stream winds blew at over 200 knots and could get a down-wind-flying bomber travelling at 600 knots – much too fast for accurate bombing. If, on the other hand, it flew upwind, the aircraft's speed could drop to little over 100 knots, making the slow-moving bomber an easy mark for defensive fire. LeMay ironed these difficulties out and then sent a heavy force against Tokyo.

The Tokyo raid on 9/10 March was carried out by B-29s of XXI Bomber Command, flying from bases in Guam, Saipan and Tinian. The first bombers fell just after midnight, Tokyo time, and the raid lasted until 0345 hrs. The fires started almost at once, the wind carried them about the streets and houses, and a huge pall of smoke soon hung over the city; as the last bombers flew away, it was noticed that their bellies were coated with soot. The fires in Tokyo were visible for 80 miles, and when the next day dawned USAAF reconnaissance flights recorded terrible destruction.

Sixteen square miles of the city had been destroyed – 18 per cent industrial, 63 per cent commercial, and the entire working-class residential zone, amounting to around 250,000 houses. The US Strategic Bombing Survey estimated that 87,792 people lost their lives, 40,918 suffered injuries, and over 1 million lost their homes on that one mission. And yet this raid on Tokyo is virtually unknown outside Japan. It is a fair assumption that every reader of this book will know about Dresden but that not one in a hundred – at a generous estimate – will know what happened to Tokyo on 10 March 1945, just three weeks later. And worse was to follow, after the war in Europe ended.

By mid-March 1945 Germany was in ruins. On 7 March the US First Army crossed the Rhine at Remagen. On 22 March Patton's Third Army crossed the Rhine at Oppenheim, and on the following day the British Second, the Canadian First and the US Ninth Armies crossed the Rhine at Wesel and pushed on to surround the Ruhr and head towards Hamburg and the north-German plain. The Russians broke through on the Oder on 16 April and sent two armies to Dresden and a third to advance on Berlin. By 20 April – Hitler's fifty-sixth birthday – the Russians had Berlin surrounded, and ten days later, on 30 April, Hitler and his mistress, Eva Braun, committed suicide in the Berlin bunker. The remaining garrison of Berlin surrendered two days later, on 2 May, and the European war ended on 8 May.

In the last weeks of the war the bombing campaign subsided. Bomber Command flew its last operation, against Kiel, on the night of 2/3 May: sixteen Mosquitoes were dispatched to bomb German troop transports, and 1 Mosquito was shot down. The Eighth Air Force flew its last

European mission on 25 April, when it launched a major attack on the city of Pilsen: six B-17s were lost and a further 180 were damaged by flak. Most of the operations and missions flown in the final weeks were humanitarian, either flying food to the starving citizens of Holland – Operation MANNA for the RAF or Operation CHOWHOUND for the Eight – or flying home thousands of prisoners of war from the recently liberated POW camps.

And then, finally, it was over – at least for a while, until the air forces now committed to the European Theatre of Operations were sent to add their weight to the bombing offensive against Japan, which would go on for another three months and culminate in the attacks on Hiroshima and Nagasaki. In the end, very few of the air-force flyers, RAF or USAAF, made their way to the Far East before the Second World War ended. They stood down, relaxed for the first time in years – and counted the cost.

The USAAF Eighth Air Force had lost 26,000 men, representing a loss rate of 12.4 per cent of the 210,000 US airmen who flew missions from England between 1942 and 1945, and one-eleventh of all Americans killed in the Second World War.[6] This was the highest casualty rate of any of the US armed forces in the Second World War. Another 18,000 were wounded and some 20,000 were shot down over enemy territory and became POWs, raising total aircrew losses in the Eighth to some 53,000. A total of 6,537 US bomber aircraft were lost in combat in the ETO. The Fifteenth and Ninth US Air Forces also lost heavily.

RAF Bomber Command lost a total of 55,564 men killed in the Second World War, representing a loss rate of 51 per cent of the 110,000 Bomber Command aircrew. The national totals break down as follows:

RAF	38,462
RCAF	9,910
RAAF	4,050
RNZAF	1,679
Polish	929
Other Allied*	473
Other Dominions	34
South Africa	27

* Americans, Czechs, Chileans, French, Danes, Norwegians.

This was the highest casualty rate of any of the British Empire armed forces in the Second World War. A total of 8,953 RAF bombers were lost on operations over Europe. During the Second World War, from September 1939 to May 1945, the RAF alone dropped 955,044 tons of bombs on Germany or on German-occupied territory. Over 600,000 Germans were killed by bombing.

The *Luftwaffe* was totally destroyed and the losses of the German fighter arm are approximately as follows. Between 1939 and 1945 the training schools produced about 30,000 fighter pilots for the *Luftwaffe* fighter arm. Of these, 18,000 were killed in action or in training, 750 became POWs, and approximately 2,000 were badly wounded and removed from flying duties. There were only around 5,500 *Luftwaffe* pilots left by the end of the war, and the loss rate among German fighter pilots was second only to that suffered by the U-boat crews.[7]

And so, while the air forces in Europe were counting their dead, we come to the last act in the bomber war – that savage month of August 1945, when the days of the great bomber fleets ended, 30 years after the first strategic bomber raids began.

The Tokyo raid on 9/10 March was only the start of the campaign against Japanese cities. During March and April the B-29s went back to Tokyo again and again; by the time they had finished, 56 square miles of the city was a charred and blackened ruin. XXI Bomber Command also attacked other cities on the original target list – Kobe, Nagoya, Osaka and Yokohama. These were all fire raids, and a major attack on Tokyo on the night of 25/26 May destroyed another half a million homes; the death rate was lower on this occasion, largely because so many Japanese had fled to the countryside.

After Germany surrendered, these attacks increased. The next major Allied task was the surrender of Japan and it was feared that this could be achieved only by an invasion. Unless the Japanese could be quelled, estimates of likely US casualties in this invasion ranged into the millions. General LeMay and his superior, General Lauris Norstad, the commander of the Twentieth Air Force, felt that if they continued pounding Japan from the air the Japanese must surrender in less than six months, without the need for an invasion, and the RAF was preparing to send 1,000 heavy bombers, the 'Tiger Force', to add its weight to the attacks on Japan. It all sounds very familiar.

Certainly the destruction in Japan in 1945 was massive. Up to half the habitable area of 66 of Japan's largest cities were destroyed. Over 8 million people – a quarter of the country's urban population – lost their homes. At least 300,000 Japanese civilians – some US estimates say 900,000 – were killed and upwards of a million were injured even before the atomic bombs fell.

The crushing of Japan went on throughout the summer of 1945 as the US air forces moved closer to the Japanese homeland and began to reduce it to ruin with – at least according to one Twentieth Air Force staff officer – 'the prime purpose of not leaving one stone standing on another'.[8] In July the USAAF tried the tactic of leafleting Japanese cities, telling the inhabitants that their city would be destroyed – and then destroying it. The Japanese still refused to surrender.

And so the days ticked away towards mid-August, when the aircraft of the 509th Composite Group – a bomb group in the Twentieth Air Force based on the island of Tinian – were modified to carry a new weapon. One of these modified bombers was the aircraft of the group commander, Colonel Paul Tibbets, and, on the day before the mission to Hiroshima, Tibbets named the aircraft after his mother – *Enola Gay*.

Tibbets had a new commander, General Carl Spaatz, who was taking a great interest in the 509th Composite Group. Spaatz had arrived from the ETO on 29 July and taken overall command of the US Strategic Air Force in the Pacific. Spaatz did not think it necessary to use the atomic bomb – which he knew all about – on Japan. He believed that conventional strategic bombing was enough to bring Japan to its knees; it might also be the case that, following the outcry over Dresden, he was wary about getting involved in what clearly – if 'The Bomb' worked – would be a massive slaughter of civilians.

When Spaatz received his instructions to prepare for and bomb the Japanese cities using atomic weapons, he declined to accept an oral order and demanded his instructions in writing. This written order arrived in the shape of a Directive from General George C. Marshall and Secretary of State Henry Stimson – an order later confirmed, again in writing, by no less a person than the new US President, Harry S. Truman. Thus convinced, on 6 August 1945 Carl Spaatz sent the *Enola Gay* to drop an atomic bomb on the city of Hiroshima. When the *Enola Gay* returned, Spaatz was waiting at dispersal to award Colonel Tibbets the Distinguished Service Cross as he stepped out of his aircraft.

When he heard about the results of the mission and what the crews had seen, Spaatz telephoned Washington and suggested that the next atomic bomb – only one more was available – should be dropped somewhere outside a town, so that the effect 'would not be so devastating to the city and the people'. This suggestion was rejected. Japan had still not surrendered by 9 August, three days after Hiroshima, when the USAAF sent another B-29 – one with the unromantic name of *Bock's Car* – to destroy the city of Nagasaki.

Six days after the ruin of Nagasaki the Japanese finally surrendered and the Second World War was over. So too was the bomber war. The day of the great air fleets ended on that bright, violent morning over Nagasaki, but a new age of terror – nuclear terror – promptly arrived to replace them.

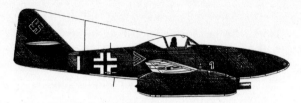

Messerschmitt Me 262A

18

Moral Issues and the Bomber War
1999–2000

The question, 'What sense does it make to think of applying moral ideas to war', is very abstract.

Barrie Paskins and Michael Dockrill, *The Ethics of War*, 1979

The previous chapters have covered the course of the bomber war, explaining what was done over Germany between 1939 and 1945, and why. The final question that has to be addressed is, Should that war have been waged at all? Was the bomber offensive a waste of resources and lives and, more to the present purpose, was it morally flawed? The first part of the question is the more easily answered and is posed today, at the start of the twentieth-first century, only to discuss the argument that the cost in lives – Allied and German – was far too high for the results achieved.

On the matter of effectiveness, looking at photographs of the devastation wrought in Germany by the Combined Bomber Offensive from 1943 to 1945, it is hard to see how anyone can seriously maintain that strategic bombing had only a marginal effect on German industry. Even if the production of tanks, guns and aircraft proceeded unabated, what heights that production would have reached *without* the bombing of Germany can only be wondered at. It is also arguable that the reason why bombing did not have a totally devastating effect on German industry was that, even in 1943–4, German industry was not fully stretched. There was plenty of spare industrial capacity to cover the damage caused by bombings and even to increase production – a point made by Albert Speer in his memoirs:

To state that despite the bombing German production increased is to ignore the fact that up until 1943 Germany industry only worked one ten-hour shift a day. In 1943, as a result of the losses they were sustaining, the factories changed to three shifts and twenty-four hour operation and introduced a new labour force of thousands of slave labourers.[1]

Bombing alone did not defeat the Axis powers. In spite of the beliefs held by Harris and Spaatz and many more in similar circles, there was never any real possibility that it would – at least not without the deployment of the atomic bomb or the use of an *overwhelming quantity of conventional bombs, suddenly delivered.* The reasons why such a force was not available for most of the war have been extensively aired in this book and need not be repeated, but bombing, *suddenly and forcefully delivered* at Hiroshima and Nagasaki, did end the war with Japan without the need for a costly invasion.

The belief that strategic bombing could end wars without a land campaign therefore has some basis in fact and, it could be argued, a moral dimension. If bombing could bring the war to an end without a land campaign and a great expenditure in lives, then the attempt to bomb Germany into surrender had a certain moral validity. Finally – and this point should be added to every other point mentioned above or below – *there was a war on.* Moral arguments which overlook, dismiss or devalue that point are fundamentally flawed.

Some estimates of the effect of the Allied bomber offensive were obtained immediately after the war by the US Strategic Bombing Survey (USSBS), an organization set up in 1944 to conduct a comprehensive study of the effect of the bombing offensive on Germany. To ensure objectivity, the US government appointed a civilian, Franklin D'Olier, president of the Prudential Insurance Company, to head the Survey, and by the winter of 1944–5 D'Olier had set up the Survey's headquarters in London, with a staff of 1,200 officers and men. As the Allied armies advanced into Germany, USSBS teams followed, visiting the shattered towns, assessing the damage and the way it was caused.

The British were rather less well organized. Churchill was not interested in the creation of a British Bombing Survey Unit (BBSU) or was talked out of creating one by his scientific advisers, probably Professor Lindemann. Although this opposition was eventually overcome, the BBSU was small, underfunded, and incapable of doing much work before it was disbanded. The BBSU report was classified as 'Confidential' until 1956, and was finally made available to the general reader only in 1998, when it was published with a critique written by Sebastian Cox of the Air Historical Branch. The broad conclusion of the BBSU was that the bombing of transportation targets was the greatest factor in the final defeat of Nazi Germany, with the bombing of oil targets and area bombing in general being subsidiary factors. In others words the BBSU report tended to support with the views that had been put forward by Solly Zuckerman, scientific adviser to Air Chief Marshal Tedder.

The bulk of the survey work was carried out by the USSBS, and its con-clusions, claiming the victory for the bombing of oil targets and precision bombing in general, have gained wider acceptance. Moreover, the USSBS verdict seems to justify the Allied bombing campaign as a whole:

> Allied air power was decisive in the war in western Europe . . . Its power and superiority made possible the success of the invasion. It brought the economy which sustained the enemy's armed forces to virtual collapse, although the full effects of this collapse had not reached the enemy's front lines when they were overrun by Allied forces. *It brought home to the German people the full impact of modern war, with all its horror and suffering. Its imprint on the German nation will be lasting.* [My italics]

The last two sentences make a point we shall return to, but for further confirmation that the bombing war had a decisive effect we need look no further than some authoritative Allied and German sources.

After the Normandy invasion in 1944, Field Marshal Erwin Rommel told the German Military High Command bluntly, 'Stop the Allied bombing or we cannot win.' During the Ardennes offensive in January 1945, General Sepp Dietrich, in reply to an order from Hitler to press on at all costs said, Go on? How can we go on? All our supply lines have been cut by air attacks . . . we have no fuel.' These comments relate to tactical bombing, but the strategic offensive also had a direct effect on the battlefield.

Alber Speer repeatedly asserted that 'the strategic bomber is the cause of all our setbacks', and referred to the strategic bombing of Germany as 'the greatest lost battle on the German side'. Speer was in a position to know: he was in total charge of every aspect of German military and indus-trial production from 1942 until the end of the war, and his views deserve attention:

> The real importance of the air war consisted in the fact that it opened a Second Front long before the invasion of Europe. That front was in the skies over Germany. The fleets of bombers might appear at any time over any large German city or important factory. This front was gigantic. Every square metre of our territory became a front line. Defence against air attacks required the production of thousands of anti-aircraft guns, the stockpiling of tremendous quantities of ammunition all over the country and the holding in readiness of hundreds of thousands of soldiers, who had to stay in posi-tion by their guns, totally inactive, often for months at a time.[2]

Germany had to devote vast resources to fending off the bombers. For the defence of the Reich, Goering had to deploy 8,876 of the formidable

88 mm flak guns, the most effective artillery piece of the war, and one which, when supplied with armour-piercing ammunition, was equally effective against tanks. The flak units also deployed some 25,000 pieces of 20 mm and 30 mm cannon. To put these figures in perspective, Rommel's Afrika Korps, about to attack the British in the Western Desert in the autumn of 1941, had just 35 of those useful 88 mm guns. To man these guns, the flak regiments in Germany required some 900,000 fit men; Rommel's army for the defence of Normandy in 1944 numbered around 500,000 men. Those men and guns tasked to flak units might have proved very useful indeed had they been deployed on the Western or Eastern Fronts in the anti-tank or artillery role, rather than for the air defence of the Reich – where another million men had to be constantly employed clearing up and repairing bomb damage. It is also a fact that the Allied bombing campaign forced the Germans to concentrate on the production of fighters – especially night fighters – and diverted their resources away from the development of a long-range bomber which might have carried the war to Britain and beyond after 1941.

There can be no doubt that tactical bombing was of inestimable help to the ground troops in many Second World War campaigns, and this help is easy to assess. An attack is held up, the bombers or ground-attack fighters arrive and blitz the enemy, resistance subsides, and the attack moves forward – simple.

The effects of strategic bombing are harder to gauge, because the results come more slowly. It is the *gradual degradation* of the enemy's military-industrial complex, the destruction of the means for normal life to continue, the need to divert resources in guns and aircraft to home defence that represent the true contribution of the strategic bomber to the overall conduct and outcome of a war.

Because such results are neither immediate nor clear-cut, the benefits of a strategic air campaign are less easy to verify, but that strategic bombing had a considerable effect on the outcome of the Second World War cannot be denied. By 1944, resisting the bombing offensive was costing Germany 30 per cent of all artillery produced, 20 per cent of heavy shells, 33 per cent of the output of the optical industry for sights and aiming devices, and 50 per cent of the country's total electro-technical output, all of which had to be diverted to the anti-aircraft role.

Towards the end of the war, the relentless heavy bomber attacks on oil and transportation were decisive indeed. Without fuel for the tanks and fighter aircraft or the means to take advantage of 'interior lines' to shuttle troops from front to front after the wrecking of the transportation system, German resistance finally collapsed.

Another contribution to the eventual outcome of the war was the part played by the air forces in carrying the reality of war to the heart of the Reich. That was a continuous process, starting with the first RAF raids in

1939 and 1940 – raids which made the point to the people of Germany and their hapless victims in other countries that, even with most of the Continent in his grasp, Hitler had yet to win the war. The reasons why the oil and transportation campaigns were decisive only towards the end of the war have already been covered, but that they made a considerable contribution to the rapid conclusion of the fighting is undoubted, though the extent of that contribution is still debated. A fair conclusion would be that the Allied bomber offensive played a major role in the defeat of Germany.

Attention now turns to the final and more enduring issue: Was the bombing campaign morally justified? That question, the moral question, is where the argument over strategic bombing has come to focus in the decades since the war. It is only possible to answer that question by placing the bombing campaign in the context of total war, and that at once leads to a rather wider question: Has morality any place in war at all?

Karl von Clausewitz (1780–1831), who is widely regarded as the greatest military thinker the Western world has yet produced, had no doubt that, in addition to the enemy's military force and territory, the enemy's will to resist is also a legitimate objective: 'the destruction of his capacity to resist, the killing of his courage rather than his men . . . warfare is an act of policy'. Clausewitz expressed those opinions in *On War* more than a hundred years before Bomber Command set out for Germany, so there is nothing new in the concept of attacking enemy morale: the strategic bomber simply gave the RAF the means to carry it out.

Many people would argue that to talk of morality in war is ridiculous – a poinit of view summed up by Lord Macaulay in 1831: 'The essence of war is violence; moderation in war is imbecility'.[3] This view holds that, once war has broken out, the important thing to do is to win it, at any cost, and especially if that cost can be met by the enemy.

This is a point that can be endlessly debated by moral philosophers, who tend to find so blunt a point of view unacceptable; but wars are not usually fought by moral philosophers. They are fought by ordinary people, who have no wish to be in the armed forces or to fight a war at all. They are in this situation because their governments failed to maintain the peace, and, once in it, they find moral questions largely academic: their main aim in war is to stay alive, and to win. To win, these people may be obliged to do dreadful things to their fellow men, often in the interests of personal survival, but most of these ordinary people would agree that even in war some actions are beyond the pale. The killing of prisoners or women and children is certainly among them. In short, there has to be morality in war; to suppose otherwise is to condone barbarism.

Moral restrictions are not absolute. Quite often, an atrocity in war is a matter of timing. For example, if prisoners are killed at the moment of surrender, or in the heat of battle immediately afterwards, that is generally regarded as the fortune of war; it should not happen, but it does. On the other hand, if prisoners are shot when passions have cooled somewhat – say a hour or a day later – that is murder. Similarly, if women and children, innocent civilians, are killed in the shelling of a village, that is a matter for regret; if they are killed wilfully, after the village has been taken, that is a matter for a court martial and a firing squad.

Timing does not always provide an excuse, for some actions are both morally flawed and criminal at any time and no excuse can justify them. To give an example illustrating this point, the German Army attacked Poland and conquered the country in a swift campaign during which the bombing of Warsaw might – though not by this author – be seen as a matter of military necessity. Then, when the fighting was over, the SS *Einsatzgruppen* moved in, shooting Jews and torching Jewish synagogues. Those were criminal acts, and would have been so even if the fighting had still been in progress.

These simple examples demonstrate that morality in war is not subject to absolute rules. Battles and wars are fought to be won, and the basic moral issue of the bomber war was well summed up by Dr Noble Frankland, one of the official historians and a former Bomber Command navigator, as follows: 'The great immorality open to us in 1940 and 1941 was to lose the war against Hitler's Germany. To have abandoned the only means of direct attack which we had at our disposal would have been a long step in that direction.'[4]

That seems to be absolutely true. Those who doubt it have only to consider what would have been the fate of Europe's people had Hitler completed his conquests. The prospects would not have been good. Considering the camps alone, Auschwitz killed at least 1 million Jews, and many thousands of other people; Treblinka took 700,000 lives, Belzec 600,000, Sobibor 250,000, Majdanek 200,000, Kulmhof 150,000 – and to these must be added those who died in Belsen, Buchenwald, Dachau and the *hundreds* of other concentration camps – for every main camp had a score of satellites – that were spread across Germany and all the other parts of Hitler's 'Thousand Year Reich'. The deaths caused by bombing should not be taken out of this context.

Germany had grievances before the Second World War; that cannot be denied. The origins of that conflict can be traced back to the Great War, which killed nearly 3 million German soldiers and a great many women and children, but did not, apparently, reduce the German propensity for settling disputes by military means. The big dispute in the inter-war years was over the terms of the 1919 Treaty of Versailles, which were indeed harsh and, apart from demanding reparations costing Germany 136 *billion* gold marks, deprived Germany of 13 per cent of her territory, 12 per cent of her population, 16 per cent of her coal, 48 per cent of her iron, and 10 per cent of her industrial capacity.[5] Paying reparations from this reduced industrial base destroyed the Weimar Republic and its democratic constitution and paved the way for Hitler and Nazi Germany. But all Europe suffered in the Great War, and in the war's aftermath many countries descended into dictatorships – sixteen out of 28 European nation states were ruled by dictators by 1939 – yet only one, Germany, adopted mass murder as part of its political philosophy.

This being so, another notion that has to be refuted is that the struggle between the Allies and Hitler during the Second World War was one between two opposing but equally valid ideologies. One can admire the courage and tenacity of the German fighter pilots, flak gunners, soldiers and private citizens in defending their homeland against terrible attacks, but that should not be allowed to obscure the fact that Nazi Germany was a vile and murderous tyranny, attempting to impose its will on the civilized world. In rooting out that tyranny, a great many harsh actions were necessary and can therefore be excused. The Dresden raid and Auschwitz are not the same thing.

To quote the Conservative MP Michael Howard, 'The defeat of Nazi Germany gave humanity a future. Almost everything we value about our life today – freedom, democracy, prosperity, let alone an existence without the constant fear of the firing squad, the death camp and the torture chamber – exists only because Hitler was crushed.'[6]

This is true, but there remains a problem, for the 'only means of direct attack' referred to by Dr Frankland was the bomber, and in 1940–1 the bomber simply did not work as a weapon of war. As a result, the British were forced to abandon their pre-war ideal of attacks on purely military targets, and to go over first to night attacks and then to area attacks on cities. It is these attacks which remain the nub of the moral argument against RAF Bomber Command and Air Chief Marshal Sir Arthur Harris.

One of the allegations advanced in support of that argument is that area bombing was unnecessary, because the USAAF was able to employ *precision* bombing and only attacked military or industrial targets. That allegation is one reason why the activities of the USAAF over Germany and Japan have been so extensively ventilated in this book – not to 'tar the USAAF with the morale-bombing brush', as the wartime USAAF commanders so frequently feared would happen, but because what the US bombers were said to be doing – and indeed claimed to be doing – *daylight precision bombing* – has been used to decry the actions and methods of RAF Bomber Command.

The USAAF's daylight-precision-bombing doctrine is often cited in an attempt to show that Harris's area bombing was unnecessary. But, as has been shown, daylight precision bombing did not work at all until the P-51 fighter came into squadron service in January 1944, and even in 1945 the USAAF was still finding accuracy a problem, as its official history confirms:

Weather conditions during the last days of January greatly restricted the air war. The air forces had made much progress in the last year toward overcoming their worst opponent, the weather, but radar bombing methods continued to prove disappointing. The Eighth Air Force had an average circular probable error of two miles on its blind missions which meant that many of its attacks depended for effectiveness on *drenching the area with bombs*. [my italics][7]

What the USAAF was *actually* doing throughout the war in the ETO, and later in Japan, has already been described. As with the RAF, its actions were not the result of some moral deficit among the USAAF commanders and crews; rather, because of technical and climatic factors in Europe and Japan – and pre-war misconceptions on what the bomber could actually achieve in combat – its precision-bombing doctrine was fundamentally flawed and had to be adjusted to wartime realities. The USAAF attacked civilian industrial targets by 'blind' bombing in Germany and by area attacks in Japan. The alternative was not to attack at all but to leave the enemy's homeland an intact arsenal of aggression.

Finally there is the point that bombing Germany gave great comfort to the beleaguered citizens of Britain, who warmly supported the efforts of the RAF and USAAF in shattering Nazi Germany – a point made by Canadian pilot Kenneth McDonald of No. 78 Squadron:

What many of today's revisionists ignore, or don't try to recapture, is the atmosphere in Britain at that time. When we finished our tour in 1943 we were sent as a crew on a morale-rising tour around factories making Halifaxes. My job was to describe a typical op and introduce the crew members. Each time I came to Tim McCoy, the rear gunner, and told them he could see the fires burning in Germany from 50 miles as we flew home they burst into cheers. These men and women had lived through the Blitz, had lost homes and close relatives, and were still at risk from German bombs. They felt, I am sure, that here in front of them was living proof not only that their work was worthwhile, but that there was some hope for an end to the war – and their privations.

The arguments, difficulties and solutions surrounding the bomber war have been extensively described in previous chapters, but the moral factor remains intact if we consider it as something separate from the political, technical and military issues of the time. To do so is to take the moral factor out of context, but to argue that point at all we must first return to the question of military technology and the way wars are actually fought.

Now and again, in the history of warfare, a weapon appears that renders all previous weapons and tactics obsolete, or poses a fundamental problem that has to be addressed. One simple example is the case of Captain Claude Minié and his famous bullet.

Captain Minié was a French officer who, in the middle decades of the nineteenth century, realized that something had to be done to improve the range and accuracy of infantry weapons. The chief weapon at the time was the musket, which had not changed a great deal in the last 150 years and could not be relied upon to hit the side of a barn at 200 yards. The problem was that, to get the ball down the barrel, the barrel had to be wider than the ball, with the result that, when the musket was fired, most of the charge was dissipated and the ball rattled down the barrel and went wild. The same was true with the early forms of rifled musket.

Captain Minié applied what would now be called 'lateral thinking' to the problem of improving accuracy. He could do nothing about the barrel, so he did something about the bullet. He invented a bullet with a thin lead skirt; when the rifle was fired, the heat of the charge caused the lead to expand, the expanded skirt gripped the rifling – and the range of the rifled musket leapt from 200 yards to 600 yards, with accuracy improved in proportion. The effect of Captain Minié's invention was to make the main contemporary infantry tactic, the advance in line to the point where a bayonet charge could be launched against the enemy position, completely impossible. Soldiers could now be killed in quantity at ranges up to half a mile, and a change in tactics seemed essential. It did not happen: infantry continued to put in frontal attacks against defended positions throughout the rest of the nineteenth century, up to the first years of the Great War, with disastrous consequences to the attacking troops.

Now consider the case of the strategic bomber. The invention of the Minié bullet enabled soldiers to kill more soldiers; the invention of the strategic bomber enabled commanders to kill civilians. The Minié bullet created a tactical problem; the bomber created a moral one. The Minié bullet, and what it could do to soldiers, did not change military tactics. The advent of the bomber, and what it could do to civilian populations, did not prevent its employment over cities far from the battlefield – quite the opposite. Like the Minié bullet, the bomber, once created, was going to be used.

It should be clear that the bomber always was a 'terror' weapon. It was the ability of the bomber to overfly defence lines and reach centres of population that made the bomber threat so effective. Claims that bombing could destroy the enemy's industrial base are always cited to justify the use of bomber forces, and to a certain extent this claim is true; but it was the effect of bombing *on civilians* that gave the bomber threat its greatest potency.

Inspiring terror, causing massive destruction and killing civilians, *was what the strategic bomber was for*. The same is true today of nuclear weapons, and the argument is essentially the same. It was because the bomber could kill *civilians* that its use could not be contemplated by civilized nations and why many attempts were made to get the strategic bomber banned in the 1920s. The present Nuclear Test Ban Treaty and the Nuclear Non-

Proliferation Treaty are extensions of the same idea. Both have proved as ineffective against the testing and spread of nuclear weapons as the 1920s Hague Rules were in attempting to ban the development and use of the strategic bomber.

There is, of course, one difference. The bomber could not do what it was supposed to do: destroy precision targets and prevent wars. Nuclear weapons can destroy the planet and have already destroyed cities – and have prevented major wars. The argument over the use of nuclear weapons has generated considerable heat, because their use surely cannot be contemplated by any civilized nation – which is not to say that at some time in the future some maniac will not use them. That misuse is an argument for their abolition – which, alas, will not happen either – so the peace of the world and the future of the planet now rests again on terror. That balance of terror – Mutually Assured Destruction – had the apt acronym 'MAD'.

There is however, another point about bombing that moralists consistently overlook: Why is it right to kill young men in uniform, but not young men in overalls? Why is it permissible to kill the man firing the weapon and not the one making it? There is a great deal of cant in the moral argument against bombing; the truth is that those who are prepared to see soldiers die in quantity, from the Minié bullet or the tactical-strike aircraft, become strangely concerned when the weapons switch their attention to the home front. Bombers were a step on the road to the terminal destruction now offered by nuclear weapons, but as the use of bomber aircraft was explored and expanded the military got used to them. Bombers were first seen as useful and then as essential tactical weapons in support of ground forces, and it was in their tactical role that the erosion of the arguments against their strategic use began.

People like Douhet, Trenchard and Mitchell – the apostles of the 'bomber dream' – saw bombers as decisive strategic tools and headed off the moral argument by declaring that bombers would either make wars impossible, as the notion of killing civilians (or, even worse, politicians) could not be contemplated, or, in the event that wars did break out, would rapidly bring them to an end and make land campaigns of the Somme/Passchendaele variety unnecessary. This belief was yet to be proven, but in the course of experimenting with bombers – in developing, testing and flying them – the revulsion against their use was gradually worn away. Unfortunately, the limitations of the bomber as a weapon of war were not revealed at the same time.

The first part of the moral erosion process was provided in the 1930s by the Germans at Guernica, the Italians in Ethiopia and the Japanese in China, but when the Second World War broke out, these countries made very little use of strategic bombing after the German Blitz on Britain and the strike at Pearl Harbor. Therefore the argument over strategic bombing and the accusations that the bombing offensive was a criminal campaign are now directed at the Allied air forces: partly at the USAAF over Hiroshima and Nagasaki – the Tokyo fire raids are apparently forgotten – but mainly at RAF Bomber Command over the area bombing of Germany – and Dresden.

This accusation carefully excludes the German Blitz of 1940–1, which killed over 40,000 British civilians. It has been argued that German city centres did not contain factories; few city centres do. The City of London had no factories, but that did not prevent the *Luftwaffe* destroying it so thoroughly in 1940–1 that this writer recalls practising street fighting in the ruins as a Royal Marine recruit in 1952. The London Blitz opened the way to the strategic bombing of German cities, partly through the need to show defiance of the Nazi war machine and partly as a reprisal for the German air raids. As Harris said in 1940, 'they are sowing the wind and they will reap the whirlwind' – and the bulk of the British people were solidly behind the relentless bombing of Germany at that time.

This tit-for-tat argument, however valid, is not a moral one. Two wrongs do not make a right, and the excuse that 'they did it first' is more suited to the playground than to a war. If the bombing of civilian targets is prima facie a war crime, then whoever does it, at any time, is a war criminal. And this raises the question of whether the strategic bomber is a legitimate weapon of war at all.

At this point the argument can be shifted to the Nuremberg war trials of 1947–8, when the indictment drawn up against the German defenders covered this point quite specifically. The Tribunal's Charter (Article 6B) stated that war crimes are:

> Violations of the laws or customs of war. Such violations shall include, but not be limited to, murder, ill-treatment or deportation to slave labour or for any other purpose of civilian population of or in occupied territories, murder or ill-treatment of prisoners of war or persons on the seas, killing of hostages, plunder of public or private property, *wanton destruction of cities, towns or villages, or devastation not justified by military necessity.* [my italics]

The last section would seem to relate to the bombing of city targets. The caveat 'not justified by military necessity' will be covered later, but at this point it should be mentioned that there appears to be no instance of any *Luftwaffe* officer being convicted for offences under this Article – not over the bombing of Guernica, Rotterdam, Warsaw, Coventry, London, in the Baedeker raids, or anywhere else.[8] This being so, it is hard to see why any Allied air-force officer should be judged culpable on these grounds. But, since the Nuremberg Rules are there, they can usefully serve as a yardstick.

It has been argued that the Nuremberg trials were 'victors' justice' and tried, judged, sentenced and executed Germans for actions that were not crimes in Germany at the time they were committed – though, given the nature of some of the crimes committed, one can only reflect on what that says about the state of Germany under Hitler's regime. However, the point about 'victors' justice' is valid; when he heard that a dozen leading Nazis had been sentenced to hang at Nuremberg, Winston Churchill remarked to General Hastings Ismay that 'It shows that when you start a war, it is essential to win it. Had we lost, we would have been in a pretty pickle.' This point has also drawn the comment that some Allied military commanders, notably Arthur Harris, would be found guilty if tried on the same basis. So let us see if that is true.

The one well-known and specific accusation, Harris's responsibility for the Dresden operation, has already been covered; if that issue came to trial, the dock would be very crowded indeed. The excuse that he was only obeying orders and that *'Befehl ist Befehl'*, 'an order is an order', so often invoked by German commanders on trial at Nuremberg, need not be employed and is anyway not valid. No soldier or airman is under any obligation to obey an 'illegal' order, and it is illegal to order a soldier to commit a crime. Disobeying an order may have serious consequences, but there is no legal requirement to obey and the claim of 'obeying orders' will not serve as an excuse. Nor is it possible to believe that Harris would have used that as a defence – or have needed to use it.

The order to attack Dresden was not illegal. There were cogent reasons for bombing Dresden and, though hindsight indicates that it probably was an unnecessary operation, that was not the opinion at the time. It is worth pointing out that the morality of bombing Dresden came into question only after the city was bombed. The moral argument should have come earlier, when the question of bombing Dresden was first discussed; wrangling about it afterwards, to spread blame and take the moral high ground, is being wise after the event, little short of cant – or at best ill-informed.

Speaking at a conference in 1996, Canadian historian Terry Copp pointed out that in February 1995 the many newspapers in Canada and Britain which commemorated the fiftieth anniversary of the Dresden raids referred to the 'fact' that the raids were cruel because the war was almost over. Copp then pointed out that the Dresden raids took place a full month before any German soldier was driven back across the Rhine, and three months before the European war ended.[9]

Regarding the policy of area bombing, the responsibility for initiating that policy cannot be traced to Harris. The decision to attack German industrial cities, as opposed to just armaments factories, was not taken by him, though he has been consistently blamed for it. As he says in his memoirs, written in 1946 and published in 1947:

There is a widespread impression that I not only invented the policy of area bombing but also insisted on carrying it out in the face of a natural reluctance to kill women and children that was felt by everyone else. The facts are otherwise. Such decisions on policy are not in any case made by Commanders-in-Chief in the field, but by the Ministries, the Chiefs-of-Staff Committee and by the War Cabinet. The decision to attack large industrial areas was taken long before I became Commander-in-Chief.[10]

This is as close as Harris gets to pointing out that the person who instigated area attacks was Portal, but the evidence is clear. In a Directive sent to Harris's predecessor, Air Marshal Sir Richard Peirse, AOC-in-C, Bomber Command, by the Deputy Chief of the Air Staff, Air Vice-Marshal Sholto Douglas, on 30 October 1940, shortly after Portal became Chief of the Air Staff, the 'second group of targets', after oil, is covered as follows:

> Secondly, I am to suggest that if bombing is to have its full moral effect it must on occasions produce heavy material destruction. Widespread light attacks are more likely to product contempt for bombing rather than fear of it. I am therefore to say that as an alternative to attacks designed for material destruction against our primary objectives, it is desired that regular concentrated attacks shall be made on objectives in large towns and centres of industry with the prime aim of causing heavy material destruction, which will demonstrate to the enemy the power and severity of air bombardment and the hardship and dislocation that will result from it.

This Directive went to Bomber Command more than a year before Harris became AOC-in-C. Pointing this out should not be taken to mean that the 'blame' is simply being shifted from one RAF officer to another. It is highly debatable if any 'blame' attaches to this decision at all.

The point at issue is whether the area bombing of Germany can be justified by military necessity. The short answer has to be 'Yes', again if one accepts the notion that Germany had to be bombed as a way of fighting the war – and, for the first three or four years of the Second World War, bombing was the *only way* the war could be brought to bear on the industrial capacity of Germany. Even if this involved striking at cities and endangering civilians the bombing of Germany was justified. The USAAF claims that it never set out to bomb civilians; it claims and feels good about the fact that US bomber missions were always sent against military or industrial targets. So too were those of Bomber Command, as RAF navigator Freddy Fish can confirm:

> I can assure you that at every briefing I attended – over thirty – we were *always* told that we were bombing a military target. My logbook shows references to 'Industrial centre' 'Armaments factory', 'Oil plant', 'Marshalling yards', 'Industries', etc. Only once, I recall, did the briefing include a remark by the intelligence officer that (or to the effect that) 'Tonight you are bombing the homes of the workers who work in the factories.' I remember he said this with a half-smile, so at the time we either did not believe him or thought it was a slip of the tongue. So, at all times, the aircrew I knew believed that we

were bombing genuine, selected, military targets only; so to make out that we were some kind of slaughterers, deliberately, of innocent civilians is utter nonsense. At the time we did not know how many people were being killed and could only go on PRU-[Photo-Reconnaissance Unit-] assessed damage. We certainly did not think of ourselves as 'terror flyers'. We all thought we were hitting vital enemy targets and assisting our armies to win the war.

Harris and his predecessors, Peirce and Portal, bombed the German cities because Bomber Command did not have the ability to bomb anything else at that time, but these were *industrial* cities, not spas, or holiday resorts, or dormitory towns. Even historic places like Rostock and Lübeck contained military installations. If Harris had been ordered to send Bomber Command to bomb schools or hospitals, he would have refused to do so, partly because he was not a monster and partly because he would have regarded it as pointless and a waste of aircraft and aircrew lives.

It must also be pointed out that the scientific side of the air war, detailed extensively in this book, consistently aimed at improving the accuracy of the bomber force in finding and hitting targets. *Gee*, *Oboe*, H_2S, *G-H* and the rest were invented to tighten up the bombing and stop the bombers scattering their bombs at random over Germany. That was why the RAF formed the Pathfinder Force and the USAAF adopted blind bombing using British navigation and target-finding equipment, set up the Striking Forces and developed the Mustang fighter – all to improve the efficiency and accuracy of bombing in the face of the weather, flak and fighters.

However, that argument though valid, evades the narrower question of 'city-centre' bombing, of whether it was right to pick aiming points in the centre of the cities, rather than in the industrial suburbs – or, to put it bluntly, was it right to target residential areas and by so doing directly endanger civilians. Can that be justified on the grounds of military necessity?

Without going into the details of every operation and mission, it has to be remembered that bombing was not an exact science during the Second World War. It is not an exact science today, if the NATO bombing of Kosovo is anything to go by, but to point out just one of the tactical problems affecting bombing accuracy in the Second World War we have only to look at 'creep-back'. This problem has been described in a previous chapter but, again, the basic problem was that the bombing tended to 'creep back' from the aiming point in the course of the raid, and many bombs missed the aiming point entirely.

This being the case, it was therefore sensible to put the aiming point in the heart of a city – the point queried by Richard Braun of Ludwigshafen – for the creep-back would then carry the bombing out over the industrial suburbs; in many raids a shelter under the aiming point was the safest place to be. Cologne Cathedral was frequently chosen as the AP for attacks on that city, but Cologne Cathedral survived the war. The AP was placed to take account of creep-back; if the AP had been in the industrial suburbs, creep-back would have carried the bombs either out into open country or back over the city. Therefore the fact that the AP was often placed in the city centre was not, in itself, evidence of an intent to deliberately target civilians. Other factors, like the wind direction and cloud cover, which affected the release point of target indicators, especially sky-markers, the amount and position of flak guns, and the position of the designated primary target all affected the decision on where to place the AP.

Harris certainly did not believe that attacking small, specific targets was worthwhile or profitable, except in certain cases like truck factories in France or submarine-engine plants, or the Ruhr dams, which called for the skills and talents of No. 617 Squadron; he believed that 'to be certain of destroying anything, it was necessary to destroy everything', and that meant the industrial city as a working, productive unit.

This is a perfectly sound argument. In a city, in a time of total war, every-thing is a valid target. The trains and buses, the power stations, the sewers, the markets and the entertainment areas, the bars, warehouses and restau-rants – and the private houses and apartment blocks – all contribute to the enemy's ability to fight on. Destroy these and problems are created. When Bomber Command hit a city, the aim was to leave behind a non-produc-tive ruin. That was a harsh policy, but a realistic one; there was a war on.

There is also an allegation that heavy bombing was increasingly unnec-essary as the war drew to a close, because Germany was already beaten and to continue shattering the cities was pointless brutality. This argument cuts both ways. If the war was drawing to a close, and would end with the defeat of Germany, then the sooner the war ended the better, for people were dying every day. When Germany surrendered, the bombing – and the deaths of civilian workers – would stop. The Allies could have stopped the bombing, but Germany could have surrendered. As it was, the bombing continued, in order to make Germany surrender and for no other reason – and Allied soldiers too were dying every day.

The fact is that Germany was still fighting in 1945, and fighting hard. Casualties in the ground fighting in North-West Europe reached Great War levels in the winter of 1944–5, and Allied bombers were still being shot down in quantity. Bomber Command lost 133 aircraft in January, 169 in February, 215 in March and 73 in April; that amounts to 590 aircraft from a front-line strength that never exceeded 1,600 – about a third. Canadian air gunner Al Hymers was in one of them:

> I was rear gunner, sergeant, RCAF, in a Lancaster of No. 12 Squadron, RAF, flying out of Wickenby. The date was 16 January 1945, and the target was Zeitz, a synthetic-oil refinery. We had bombed and turned for home; below us was a thin layer of cloud, which the fires and searchlights turned into a

field of light against which the bombers stood out, clearly visible from above – a night-fighter pilot's dream. Before taking off the whole crew had a premonition that something dreadful would happen; we even considered putting the kite u/s, but shrugged off the feeling and pressed on.

I could see several fighters below, but as I turned my turret astern I saw a fighter coming up, depressed my guns, opened fire, and yelled 'Corkscrew!' At that moment I saw his cannon blink and he dived away down. The whole action took maybe twenty seconds, and his cannon shells blew away one side of my turret and two of my guns. It also cut off my intercom and, although I could hear the pilot yelling 'Which way?', because I had been cut off after that one word, I could not answer. Then the intercom came on and I told the skipper what had happened and to dive down to the clouds as the fighter was still with us, underneath the aircraft. The skipper said he was afraid to do that as some of the controls had been shot away, but at that moment the fighter, an Me 410, tilted up and fired into us again, setting the fuel tanks on fire, and we began to burn.

The flame was roaring down the fuselage and out through my turret. The turret doors had been damaged by a cannon shell, but I managed to tear the door off and fall out. Luckily I was wearing a seat-type parachute and it opened as advertised . . . I was the only survivor of my crew.

Al Hymers can refute the idea that the air war was almost over by the early months of 1945. Ten Lancasters – and 70 men – were lost over Zeitz while attacking the Braunkohle-Benzin synthetic-oil plant, one of three oil refineries attacked by Bomber Command that night. Thirty RAF bombers were lost in air operations over Germany on the night of 16 January alone.

USAAF losses were also high, in spite of the P-51 Mustang and ever larger bomber formations. On 27–8 September 1944 the Eighth lost 64 aircraft in two days. On 7 October the Eighth lost 41 aircraft; on 2 November, 26. On 26 November 25 B-17s – and 250 young men – were lost over Hanover. A total of 174 bombers were lost in November, and a further 96 went down to flak or fighters in December. The *Grosse Schlage*/BODEN-PLATTE attack on 1 January 1945, cost the USAAF 36 aircraft. The notorious Berlin mission of 3 February cost 21 bombers . . . and so the losses continued.

These are just some of the larger daily totals: the USAAF and RAF lost aircraft and men every day they flew into Germany, and any suggestion that the Germans were already defeated but slow to surrender in 1945 can be refuted by these figures. Germany was still extracting a high cost in lives, and the only way to stop that grim total rising was to put an end to the war. To that end, almost any means could be justified.

There is also that previously mentioned point that the war had been going on for over five years, and those fighting it on the Allied side had certainly had enough of it. The idea that the air forces should have moderated their blows at this stage in the fighting is fine in post-war theory, but completely out of touch with opinion at the time. To quote John Terraine, 'When wars are over, people tend to forget how compelling was the desire to finish them.'[11] If the Germans could still not see that the war was lost, perhaps the bombers could draw that fact forcefully to their attention.

Melvin Larsen flew with the Eighth Air Force on bombing missions to Germany and is now an archbishop. This being so, his views on the bombing offensive are worth recording:

> We know that war is a horrifying situation, and yet the waging of war is often necessary – the only alternative that remains in guarding the path of justice and, strange as it may seem, finding a true peace.
>
> We realize that we are engaged in a grim situation, but our consciences are troubled about killing and we are concerned when we learn the art of killing our fellow human beings, for God has told us (Exodus 20:13) 'Thou shalt not kill.' But the Bible also says (Psalms 94:3) 'How long shall the wicked triumph?'
>
> What this boils down to is that war is an evil consequent on sin. It is one of the logical outcomes of sin. It is impossible for us to diagnose all the motives and violations that interact on one another and that bear the responsibility for the massive catastrophe of war, but how did I feel – and do feel – about bombing factories and civilian targets? I must confess that the thought of conducting these bombing missions never gave me any concern, or the thought that the bombs I would release would cause physical destruction. I knew that each time we dropped our bombs marked another day that helped to bring the ending of the war that much closer.

That may seem harsh today, but *there was a war on* between 1939 and 1945, and the earlier efforts of Bomber Command – dropping propaganda leaflets, or bringing back the bombs in case they might kill the wrong sort of enemy – were not the way to win it. At some time in war the gloves have to come off and the war has to be carried to the enemy with all and any means available. Harris was certainly ruthless, but ruthlessness was necessary in order to prosecute the war. Harris carried the war into Germany by the most effective means in his power, and to condemn him for doing so begs the question of what was the alternative – if Germany was to be fought at all?

If Harris is to be condemned on moral grounds, surely that condemnation should come from those who, while suffering under German rule, or actively engaged in fighting Hitler, still did not want Germany defeated at a high cost in civilian lives. Those fighting the war, those slave labourers in the German factories, those suffering in the concentration camps and in the V2 factory in the Hartz mountains, do they condemn Harris for bombing the cities? If they do, then the moral case against area bombing has some compelling adherents. Otherwise the case against Harris and Bomber Command is yet another of those attacks made on military leaders by people at some distance from the struggle – and obsessed with self-conscious virtue – who feel that moral issues are their particular prerogative and bolster their arguments by keeping them out of context. In the context of total war, Harris was right.

Joe Horn, once a concentration-camp prisoner and now a businessman in New Jersey, would certainly agree with that point: 'The first time I saw bombers in the sky I was a kid in Buchenwald, dressed in a striped suit and completely demoralized. The bombers – your bombers – gave us hope and led to the realization that this unrelenting nightmare could end sometime.' In a letter to an Eighth Air Force veteran he adds, 'The risks the air men took endeared you to us. No Allied action did more to demoralize the Germans, and with your bombing you guys really made a difference.'

Until the autumn of 1944 Harris has no case to answer whatsoever. The only way to prosecute the war against Germany was by bombing, which, given the difficulties in finding and hitting precision targets, meant area bombing. After September 1944 it could be said that Harris was mistaken in carrying on with his attacks on the cities, but he still believed that the German will to resist could be broken by area attacks. This view was shared by many people, including the senior air-force commanders, RAF and USAAF, who authorized the THUNDERCLAP and CLARION attacks in 1945.

Harris also pressed on, as directed, with attacks on oil and transportation targets, with support for ground operations, and with attacks on specific, precision, targets like viaducts and the battleship *Tirpitz*. Gradually, as the operations of Bomber Command in the last six or seven months of the war are examined, the case against Harris even then crumbles away. Yes, he could have gone after the oil targets with more enthusiasm, as Portal pointed out, but many of the cities did contain oil targets and the Bomber Command attacks on the German oil industry were devastating – and far more accurate than the US 'blind' bombing attacks during the winter of 1944–5, largely because Bomber Command crews had amassed far more experience in operating H_2S and *Oboe* equipment.

The harshest criticism that can be seriously maintained is that Harris could have done more to attack oil targets from September 1944. Not to do so was a mistake, but Harris is not accused of making mistakes: he is accused of being a monster, even in some circles a war criminal, but there is no basis for the charge. While he was not without faults, Harris was a fine and resolute commander, the right man in the right place to fight and win his corner of the war. He inspired Bomber Command with his own tenacity and will to win and, if he made a mistake or two in the process, few commanders have waged war without making mistakes.

There is a further point, raised by that comment in the US Strategic Bombing Survey, that the bombing offensive 'brought home to the German people the full impact of modern war, with all its horror and suffering. Its imprint on the German nation will be lasting.' One can only hope that this last comment is true. Peter Spoden, a German night fighter pilot says:

> I don't like the direction pressed by people today, the types who are still sur-
> facing in Germany. We had too many of those tough guys in the war, believe
> me. They argue that the war was all England's fault, and this is a big danger
> for it gives some of the youngsters now the idea that it was not Hitler's fault,
> it was England's – that Churchill was a bad man or Roosevelt was a bad
> man – and that is all too easy. I was a young man at that time and saw all
> these things.

The effect of the Second World War on Germany lasted until 1999, when, for the first time since 1945, German forces were employed in a role outside Germany, in KFOR, the NATO force occupying Kosovo after the retreat of the Serbs. German militarism seems to have been curbed, as the USSBS believed it would be, so perhaps the terrible destruction wrought in Germany by the Allied bombers has indeed had a lasting effect.

If so, it is not before time. All the wars started by Prussia and Germany from 1860 to 1939 – against Denmark and Austria in the 1860s, against France in 1870–1, and against France, Britain and Russia in 1914 – had been fought on foreign soil. Other countries were damaged or devastated; the German homeland remained intact. After their wars ended, in victory or defeat, the Germans marched home to their undamaged cities. Even after their crushing defeat in 1918, the military were able to tell themselves – and the more witless German citizens – that they had not been defeated on the battlefield but had been 'stabbed in the back' at home, by the Communists and the Jews – an accusation that was used by Hitler and his cronies to justify or initiate some of the Nazis' worst atrocities.

The bomber offensive of 1939–45 finally brought war home to Germany. Then the German people discovered that they had no more taste for war than any of the peaceful countries they had themselves so often occupied and despoiled. If the price of European peace and a final freedom from chronic German militarism was the physical destruction of Germany, many may argue that the price was well worth paying.

Not everyone supports that contention now, nor did so in 1945. As the war ended, Winston Churchill stopped being a war leader and went back to being a politician. The Soviet Union revealed its true nature at Yalta and stood revealed as an aggressive, expansionist power, and Germany was soon seen as a necessary bulwark against the westward spread of Communism. As a war leader, Churchill supported Arthur Harris, finding him a kindred spirit, a man who 'would not flag or fail', someone who would fight the war to a finish, however hard the road to victory, however high the cost. As a politician, Churchill found it advisable to distance himself from a man whose wartime actions, however justified and offi-cially approved at the time, were becoming contentious.

There is, however, no truth in the popular allegations that Harris and Bomber Command were denied any personal or official recognition. Churchill wrote personally to Harris in June 1945, praising the efforts and gallantry of Bomber Command:

> Now that Nazi Germany is defeated I wish to express to you, on behalf of His Majesty's Government, the deep sense of gratitude which is felt by all the nation for the glorious part which has been played by Bomber Command in forging the victory. For more than two years Bomber Command alone carried the war to the heart of Germany, bringing hope to the people of Occupied Europe and to the enemy a foretaste of the mighty power which was rising against him ... I believe that the massive achievements of Bomber Command will long be remembered as an example of duty nobly done.

Many Bomber Command veterans have complained that Harris was not offered a peerage – a seat in the House of Lords – but then neither were the heads of other RAF Commands, people like Sholto Douglas of Fighter Command or the commanders of Coastal or Transport Commands. Peerages in the rank of baron went to the High Command level at the Joint Chiefs of Staff, so Portal, who became Marshal of the Royal Air Force in January 1944, went to the House of Lords in August 1945, as Baron Portal of Hungerford – along with Admiral Sir Andrew Cunningham and Field Marshal Sir Alan Brooke, all of them honoured in Churchill's Resignation Honours List in 1945. Portal was raised to the dignity of viscount in the New Year's Honours List of 1946.

Like the former head of Fighter Command, Sholto Douglas, Harris was raised from a KCB – Knight Commander of the Bath – to a GCB – Knight Grand Cross of the Order of the Bath – as was Air Marshal Sir Keith Park, the RAF commander in the Middle East. The only RAF commander raised to the rank of baron immediately after the war, apart from Portal, was Tedder, in 1946 – but Tedder had also been the Deputy Supreme Allied Commander under Eisenhower for the last two years of the war, and that was worth some extra recognition.

Nor did Harris do badly when compared with some of the Army commanders. General Miles Dempsey, who commanded the Second Army in Europe from D-Day to the end of the war, was raised to KBE, and General Sir William Slim, who commanded the Fourteenth Army that beat the Japanese out of Burma, was rewarded in the post-war honours list with elevation from KBE to GBE – no barony for either of these distinguished commanders; it was only after many years and much more public service that Slim was summoned to the House of Lords.

Like Sholto Douglas, Harris was promoted to the rank of Marshal of the Royal Air Force in the New Year's Honours of 1946. He had already been awarded the US Legion of Merit in the rank of Chief Commander and the Soviet Order of Suverov, First Degree, and many other awards and distinctions would follow. He also received – on behalf of his Command – the personal thanks and congratulations of the Supreme Allied Commander in Europe, Dwight D. Eisenhower.

It is alleged that Prime Minister Clement Attlee, who came to power after the elections in July 1945, offered Harris a baronetcy – a very high honour and a hereditary title, just below the rank of baron – though it is also alleged that Attlee disliked him. It is said that Harris refused this offer on the grounds that he intended to retire from the RAF and return to Africa, where such honours were meaningless. He eventually accepted a baronetcy from Churchill in the New Year's Honours of 1953. Harris went back to South Africa in 1946, running a shipping company, the South African Marine Corporation, in Cape Town, until he retired and returned to England, living at Goring, Oxfordshire, until his death in April 1984, aged 91.

In several other areas, though, Harris clearly felt slighted and he appears to have some grounds for feeling aggrieved, not least in the matters of his Official Dispatch and the writing of the official history – *The Strategic Air Offensive against Germany, 1939–1945*. This was published in 1961 and was directly concerned with Bomber Command. Harris clearly did not see eye to eye with Sir Charles Webster, the senior of the two historians entrusted with its preparation, and he was not consulted by the historians about the work of his Command, which seems at best curious. In December 1958 Harris took exception to Webster's offer to show him a draft of the history 'unofficially', commenting that:

> As Commander-in-Chief for the major part of the war . . . I find it odd, to say the least of it, that I have received no *official* invitation to consult with the historians concerned in producing what purports to be a historical account of, *inter alia*, the period of my command. In such circumstances I could not accept the idea of playing any *unofficial* part in the production, beyond the chat we had in my flat in New York. There is nothing personal in this; but if this is the normal working method of the Historical Branch of the Government, then perhaps it is understandable that amongst others – I suspect – I would not wish to be associated with it.[12]

Harris's Official Dispatch was written in 1945, but not published. It was placed on a restricted list in 1948, when it was accompanied by a rebuttal from the Air Ministry, which objected to some of what Harris had said.[13] It was not finally available to the public until 1999. His autobiography, *Bomber Offensive*, was published in 1947, but the *Journal of the Royal United Services Institute* – Britain's most distinguished centre for military studies – declined to review it. From all this it is not hard to infer that the RAF and the political establishment were trying to distance themselves from Arthur Harris and the bomber offensive against Germany.

As for another allegation, that, because of the odium created by Dresden and the bomber offensive in general, Bomber Command was denied a campaign medal, this is at best debatable. Harris certainly wanted a special medal for his aircrews – and ground crews – and this was denied. However, RAF aircrews did earn and receive a large number of decorations for gallantry and two campaign medals, though very few survived long enough to earn both. Those serving 60 hours or more with an operational squadron between 3 September 1939 and 5 June 1944 got the Air Crew Europe Star. Those serving from D-Day, 6 June 1944, until VE Day, 8 May 1945, got the France and Germany Star, which was awarded to all forces – Army, Navy, or Air Force – serving in North-West Europe or coastal waters during that time.

The ones losing out in the medal stakes were the RAF ground crews, who got only the Defence Medal. They also got the enduring appreciation and respect of the aircrews – very few of the aircrew contributors to this book have failed to record their gratitude to the men who worked long hours in all weathers to give them aircraft fit to fly. Leonard Thompson, of No. 550 Squadron, is typical:

> The ground crews were just wonderful to us, and always ready to do whatever we asked. As the flight engineer, I had to liaise with them directly, and any problem with the aircraft was soon sorted out. People in all the different trades, including cooks and parachute-packers – I could go on and on – did their bit towards the end result of 550 Squadron getting as many aircraft into the air as possible. The war could not have been won without them.

This is perfectly true, and is equally true of the ground crews servicing the aircraft of 2nd TAF, Fighter Command and Coastal Command. If the Bomber Command ground crews were to get a medal, the men servicing these machines surely deserved one too.

Bob Smith, an RAAF navigator with No. XV Squadron, RAF, endorses this praise of the ground crews and gives his personal summing up of the bomber war:

> The safely of the aircrews was greatly enhanced by the dedication and expertise of the ground crews of all musterings who made sure that 'their' Lanc was in tip-top order for operations. Their industry did not go unnoticed, and we deeply appreciated it. Not only men were involved: the women of the WAAF also got their hands dirty – no wonder Bomber Command was a unique family. To put it in a nutshell, it was a wonderful experience to serve with so many honourable men and women, of all ranks, shapes and sizes, religions and political beliefs, social backgrounds and civilian occupations, and from so many Allied countries, who worked so diligently together in a common cause.

The attacks on Harris and Bomber Command over area bombing have continued, in Britain and abroad. On 19 January 1992 and again on 28

March 1992, the Canadian Broadcasting Corporation put out a three-part series on the Second World War, *The Valor and the Horror*. The second programme, 'Death by Moonlight: Bomber Command', about Harris and Canadian participation in the Combined Bomber Offensive, drew a storm of protest from Canadian Bomber Command veterans all over Canada, and similar protests in Britain when the programmes were shown here. The reasons for the veterans' fury are too numerous to list, but when the matter was referred to the Canadian ombudsman he found that the series was 'flawed as it stands and fails to measure up to CBC's demanding policies and standards'. Canadian veteran Ken Oakes puts it rather more forcefully:

> The message of the programme was clear and continuous: the Brit air marshals were manipulating our nice Canadian boys to do the dirty work and bomb nice German cities and kill nice German civilians, and to make that point the grossest manipulation was made. If the Germans did not like what they had started they could have followed the advice of Speer, Milch and Rundstedt and surrendered. However, they chose not to do so and they were eventually defeated. In the process I lost a brother from No. 640 Squadron and a cousin in No. 156 Squadron and many school colleagues and friends to provide these scumbag historians with this privilege – and privilege it is – to criticize the way the war was fought and won. If it had not been won they would not be here, so I say, 'Stop whining about how hard it all was.' I openly admit I contributed to winning the war and, though my contribution was minimal, I don't feel guilty about it.

While that matter was being pursued in Canada, the unveiling of a statue of Harris outside the RAF church of St Clement Danes in the Strand, London, was the scene of a noisy demonstration, with abuse being hurled at the assembled veterans and at HM The Queen Mother, who was performing the unveiling ceremony. That night the statue was drenched in red paint, and when that was removed the statue was attacked again on other occasions. In the course of writing this book I have met hundreds of Bomber Command veterans, and many report that they have encountered hostility from the public, especially over the matter of Dresden and the supposed 'brutality' of Arthur Harris.

The Second World War ended more than half a century ago, and most of the commanders are long since dead. 'Peter' Portal, Viscount Portal of Hungerford, died, loaded with honours, in April 1971. That much maligned air chief marshal Trafford Leigh-Mallory of the AEAF was killed in an air crash in the French Alps in November 1944. Hap Arnold survived four heart attacks during the war and retired as a five-star general in 1947 to farm in California. In May 1949 he was raised to the rank of General of the Air Force – the first such appointment ever made – dying at his home in 1950. Carl Spaatz went on to further glories after the end of the war, following Hap Arnold as Chief of the Air Force in 1946, and saw the Army Air Corps achieve separate service status as the United States Air Force in 1947. He retired in 1948 and died in Washington in 1974. Ira Eaker retired from the Air Force in 1947 and, after another successful career in industry, died in 1987. Harris managed to outlive most of them, but his name lives on, regrettably, as one irredeemably connected with the area bombing of Germany and the destruction of Dresden.

Whatever the public have been taught to think about Harris in the decades since the end of the Second World War, he remains popular with his veterans – the thinning ranks of his 'old lags' – though it has to be said that this popularity is not absolute. A small number of the letters from former Bomber Command aircrew voiced a different, more critical opinion, of Harris, largely over the losses on the Nuremberg operation and during the Battle of Berlin. The exercise of command is not a popularity contest.

A wise commander tries to be right rather than applauded, but if he is right in what he does, and professional in the way he does it, he will be popular. Because he was right in the way he fought the war, Harris was generally popular – and remains popular – with his aircrews. They should know the value of the man, for they were the ones who bore the brunt of his tactics, the ones he sent out, night after night, to serve at the sharp end of the bomber war. An account of a reunion of the Air Gunners Association long after the War says that 'after receiving a standing ovation, if Harris had asked the veterans "Will you fellows go back to Dresden or Nuremberg or Berlin tonight?" every man there would have stepped forward and said, "Yes, sir, we will go."'

Peter Firkins of No. 460 Squadron, RAAF, gives his opinion of Harris:

> I think Harris was a great commander. He gave the British and the rest of the free world something to shout about with the first 1,000-bomber raid on Cologne and the subsequent operations of Bomber Command. Towards the end of the war maybe he lost the plot with his reluctance to attack the transport systems in France and Germany. He was quite ruthless, with, I suspect, little regard for the casualties. But he remained popular with the crews, who admired his determination.

Ken Tweedie, a No. 460 Squadron navigator, adds:

> There was a story among the aircrew that Harris was driving back from London one night, going like a bat out of hell, when a policeman stopped him and said, 'If you drive like that you will kill someone', and Harris said, allegedly, 'Young man, I kill hundreds of people every night.' We all admired and respected 'Butch', in spite of our nickname for him. He seemed to be doing something positive about the war.

Unfortunately, the voices of the veterans are not often heard today. Before many more years have passed they will be silent for ever and their critics will have a clear field. That is why so many accounts from veterans have been included in this book – so that their stories may not be forgotten, so that something may be put down and remembered about the way it really was over Germany in the last, great, bomber war.

Notes

INTRODUCTION

1. Quoted by Harris in his *Bomber Offensive*, Collins, 1947, p. 118.

CHAPTER 1: THE ADVENT OF THE BOMBER, 1914–1939

1. Sir Charles Webster and Noble Frankland, *The Strategic Air Offensive against Germany, 1939–1945* (the official history), HMSO, 4 vols., 1961, vol. 1, p. 4.
2. Ibid., p. 7.
3. Trenchard, Official Dispatch, 1919.
4. Statement to the Parliamentary Committee on Air Power, 1923.
5. Webster and Frankland, *The Strategic Air Offensive against Germany, 1939–1945*, vol. 1.
6. Air Ministry Sub-Committee minutes, March 1938.
7. Webster and Frankland, *The Strategic Air Offensive against Germany, 1939–1945*, vol. 1, p. 129.
8. Quoted in General John Pershing, *My Experiences in the World War*, Da Capo, New York, 1995.
9. Statement issued in March 1954 on *Luftwaffe* policy, quoted in Cajus Becker, *The Luftwaffe War Diaries*, Macdonald, 1964, p. 478.
10. Willi Messerschmitt's first designs were manufactured at the Bayerisch Flugzeugwerke in Bavaria and therefore were designated as 'Bf' aircraft; Messerschmidt later created his own aircraft plant and the types were thereafter designated as 'Me'.
11. George Orwell, *Homage to Catalonia*, Penguin, 1986, p. 209.
12. Figures from Hugh Thomas, *The Spanish Civil War*, Penguin, 1990, pp. 624–5.
13. Richard Bessel, *Germany after the First World War*, Oxford University Press, Oxford, 1993; figures from *Krieg dem Kreig* by Renate Wurms.

CHAPTER 2: *BLITZKRIEG* AND THE BLITZ, 1939–1941

1. Becker, *The Luftwaffe War Diairies*, p. 59.
2. Ibid., p. 75.
3. Minute, Air Commodore N. H. Bottomley, SASO Air Ministry, to AOC-in-C, Bomber Command, 16 March 1940.
4. Becker, *The Luftwaffe War Diaries*, p. 145.
5. Webster and Frankland, *The Strategic Air Offensive against Germany, 1939–1945*, vol. 1, p. 144.
6. R. V. Jones, *Most Secret War*, Hamish Hamilton, 1978, p. 85.
7. See Jones, *Most Secret War*.
8. 'Maier', or 'Mayer', is a Jewish name.
9. Professor R. V. Jones in *The Secret War*, BBC Television, 1977.
10. Denis Richards, *Portal of Hungerford*, Heinemann, 1977, p. 77.
11. Memorandum to Prime Minister W. S. Churchill, 27 May 1941, quoted in Webster and Frankland, *The Strategic Air Offensive against Germany, 1939–1945*, vol. 1, p. 238.
12. Webster and Frankland, *The Strategic Air Offensive against Germany, 1939–1945*, vol. 1, p. 156.
13. Ibid., p. 157.
14. Ibid., vol. 4, p. 136.

CHAPTER 3: THE SCIENTIFIC AIR WAR, 1939–1942

1. Air Scientific Intelligence Report No. 6, 1940.
2. Webster and Frankland, *The Strategic Air Offensive against Germany, 1939–1945*, vol. 1, p. 156.
3. Air Intelligence Report, Public Records Office, 6963, submitted by Douglas Ross of St John's, Newfoundland; Douglas Ross Sr – his uncle, and the front gunner of the aircraft – was killed on this operation.
4. Historical notes on H_2S, TRE, 1944.
5. Webster and Frankland, *The Strategic Air Offensive against Germany, 1939–1945*, vol. 4, p. 37.

CHAPTER 5: HARRIS TAKES COMMAND, 1942

1. Charles Carrington, *Soldier at Bomber Command*, Leo Cooper, 1987.
2. Harris, *Bomber Offensive*, p. 73.
3. *Hansard*, quoted in Webster and Frankland, *The Strategic Air Offensive against Germany, 1939–1945*, vol. 1, pp. 328–9.
4. Webster and Frankland, *The Strategic Air Offensive against Germany, 1939–1945*, vol. 4, p. 148.
5. Letter, 16 April 1942, from Prime Minister's office, quoted in Webster and Frankland, *The Strategic Air Offensive against Germany, 1939–1945*, vol. 1, p. 337.
6. Singleton Report, quoted in Webster and Frankland, *The Strategic Air Offensive against Germany, 1939–1945*, vol. 1, p. 338.
7. Summary by Cologne city archivist Gerbhard Aders-Albert.
8. Webster and Frankland, *The Strategic Air Offensive against Germany, 1939–1945*, vol. 1, p. 421.
9. Letter from Portal to Harris, 12 June 1942, quoted in Webster and Frankland, *The Strategic Air Offensive against Germany, 1939–1945*, vol. 1, p. 431.
10. Air Vice-Marshal D. C. T. Bennett, *Pathfinder*, Frederick Muller, 1958.

CHAPTER 6: THE DEFENCES OF GERMANY, 1939–1942

1. Dr Stefan Morz, the city archivist, comments that 'The shelters were certainly not built by the municipality, which means that the mayor had very little to do with it. They were built by the Reich between 1940 and 1942.' This fact tends to indicate that the Germans were reacting nationally to the growing threat of Allied air attack certainly by 1940.
2. The actual target was Mannheim, on the other side of the Rhine, but RAF reports confirm that the bombing was scattered, and considerable damage was done to both towns: 269 people were killed and over 1,200 wounded.
3. Both towns were attacked on this occasion; 605 aircraft attacked and 34 were shot down – 5.6 per cent of the force. A considerable amount of damage was done and the I.G. Farben plant was hit. However, Richard Braun's comment on the increasing use of the shelters is borne out by the much lower casualty figures: 127 people were killed and 568 injured on this occasion – though a further 1,600 people suffered eye injuries from flying glass.
4. Summary by Gerbhard Aders-Albert, city archivist, 1999.
5. Bomber Command was operating to Schweinfurt that night and lost a total of 34 aircraft.
6. W. H. Tatum, and E. J. Hoffschmidt, eds., *The Rise and Fall of the German Air Force: A History of the* Luftwaffe *in WW2*, WE Inc., Old Greenwich, Conn., 1969, p. 289.

CHAPTER 7: ENTER THE MIGHTY EIGHTH, 1942

1. Curtis LeMay and McKinley Kantor, *Mission with LeMay*, Garden City Press, New York, 1965, p. 383.
2. Spaatz Papers on H_2S bombing, quoted in Ronald Schaffer, *Wings of Judgement: American Bombing in World War II*, Oxford University Press, New York, 1985, p. 68.
3. US Strategic Air Forces in Europe (Munitions Requirements); supplied by the Manuscript Division, the Library of Congress, Washington DC.
4. Richard D. Hughes's memoir quoted in Stephen Macfarland, *America's Pursuit of Precision Bombing, 1910–1945*, Smithsonian Institution, Washington DC, 1995, pp. 101–3.
5. From Top Sergeant Fifer's Second World War journal, kindly provided by his son, Scott Fifer.
6. Roger Freeman, *The Mighty Eighth: A History of the US 8th Army Air Force*, Macdonald & James, 1970.

CHAPTER 8: TOWARDS A COMBINED OFFENSIVE, AUGUST 1942–JANUARY 1943

1. H. H. Arnold and Ira C. Eaker, *Winged Warfare*, Harper, New York, 1941.
2. Wesley Frank Craven and James Lea Cate, *The Army Air Forces in World War II*, University of Chicago Press, Chicago, 4 vols., 1958, vol. 1, p. 655.
3. PRO AIR, 20/8146.
4. Note by the Chief of the Air Staff for the Chiefs of Staff, on an estimate of the effects of an Anglo-American Bomber offensive against Germany, 3 November, 1942, quoted in Webster and Frankland, *The Strategic Air Offensive against Germany, 1939–1945*, vol. 4, p. 258.
5. Gordon Musgrove, *Pathfinder Force: A History of 8 Group*, Crecy Books, 1992.
6. Interview with George Penfold in 1982.

7. Minutes of the Combined Chiefs of Staff meeting, 16 January 1943.
8. Extract – paragraph 28 – relating to the bomber offensive from a report by the Combined Chiefs of Staff on American–British strategy in 1943, 31 December 1942.
9. Harris, *Bomber Offensive*, p. 144.

CHAPTER 9: BOMBING ROUND THE CLOCK, 1943

1. Letter to the author, March 1999.
2. *Airpower 2000*, Ministry of Defence, Air, 1999.
3. Memo, Portal to Churchill, 27 May, 1941.
4. Jack Livesey of the Imperial War Museum Aircraft Collection at Duxford, Cambridgeshire, provided much of the information in this section.
5. Freeman, *The Mighty Eighth*, p. 54.

CHAPTER 10: THE GREAT RAIDS: THE DAMS TO PLOESTI, AUGUST 1943

1. Paul Brickhill, *The Dam Busters*, Pan, 1954, p. 27.
2. 5 Group operational order for CHASTISE, No. B 976, 1943.
3. Much of what follows, including the 5 Group operational order, No. B 976, comes from information provided by Freddy Fish.
4. Alfred Speer, *Inside the Third Reich*, Phoenix, 1995, p. 389.
5. Leon Wolff, *Low Level Mission – the Ploesti Raid*, Longmans, Green, 1958.

CHAPTER 11: THE GREAT RAIDS: SCHWEINFURT–REGENSBURG TO PEENEMUNDE, 1943

1. Martin Middlebrook, *The Schweinfurt–Regensburg Mission*, Penguin, 1985, p. 28.
2. Narrative report of Regensburg mission, to Commanding Officer, 4th Bombardment Wing, 26 August 1943.
3. Freeman, *The Mighty Eighth*, p. 68.

CHAPTER 12: THE *POINTBLANK* DIRECTIVE, JUNE 1943

1. Freeman, *The Mighty Eighth*, p. 79.
2. See also Tatum and Hoffschmidt, *The Rise and Fall of the German Air Force*, p. 290.
3. Harris, PRO 14/3507.
4. Harris, *Bomber Offensive*, p. 52.
5. After the war Collins became better known to the British public as Canon Collins, a leading figure in the Campaign for Nuclear Disarmament – the 'Ban the Bomb' campaign.

CHAPTER 13: THE BATTLE OF BERLIN AND BIG WEEK, NOVEMBER 1943–MARCH 1944

1. Joint Intelligence Reports, September and November 1943; PRO.
2. David R. Mets, *Master of Airpower: General Carl A. Spaatz*, Presidio Press, Novato, Cal., 1997, p. 178.

3. Craven and Cate, *The Army Air Forces in World War II*, vol. 3, p. 6.
4. From William Chapin, *Milk Run*, Wingate Press, Sausalito, Cal., 1992, pp. 35–6, by kind permission of the author.
5. Colonel William R. Lawley died in the summer of 1999, shortly after providing this account.
6. AHB-PRO, 11/117/1; press conference, October 1944.
7. Minute to Lord Beaverbrook, Minister of Aircraft Production, in July 1940.

CHAPTER 14: OVERTURE TO OVERLORD, JANUARY–JUNE 1944

1. Harris, *Bomber Offensive*, p. 246.
2. Coningham dispatch, PRO Air 37/286.
3. Mets, *Master of Airpower*.
4. Craven and Cate, *The Army Air Forces in World War II*, vol. 3, p. 622.
5. Harris to Portal, December 1943.
6. What follows comes from the minutes of the meeting of 25 March, quoted in Webster and Frankland, *The Strategic Air Offensive against Germany, 1939–1945*, vol. 3, p. 33.
7. Alfred Goldberg, 'General Carl A. Spaatz' in Michael Carver (Field Marshal Lord Carver), ed., *The War Lords: Military Commanders of the Twentieth Century*, Little, Brown, Boston, 1976, p. 577.
8. Daily record and diary, 345th Bomb Group, 13 April 1944.

CHAPTER 15: THE DESTRUCTION OF GERMANY, SEPTEMBER 1944–FEBRUARY 1945

1. Directive by Air Marshal Sir Norman Bottomley, Deputy Chief of the Air Staff, and General Carl Spaatz, Commanding General, USSTAF in Europe, for the control of Bomber Forces in Europe, 25 September 1944 (Directive No. 40).
2. Wolff, *Low Level Mission*, p. 211.
3. Musgrove, *Pathfinder Force*, p. 191.
4. Adolf Galland, *The First and the Last*, Fontana, 1970.
5. Letter to Arnold, August 1944.
6. Craven and Cate, *The Army Air Forces in World War II*, vol. 3, p. 667.
7. Mets, *Master of Airpower*, pp. 274–5.
8. Ibid., p. 269.
9. Letter from Air Marshal Bottomley, Deputy Chief of the Air Staff, to Air Chief Marshal Sir Arthur Harris, 13 November 1944, quoted in Webster and Frankland, *The Strategic Air Offensive against Germany, 1939–1945*, vol. 4, p. 298.
10. Harris to Portal, 18 January 1945, quoted in Webster and Frankland, *The Strategic Air Offensive against Germany, 1939–1945*, vol. 3, p. 93.
11. Harris, *Bomber Offensive*, p. 72.

CHAPTER 16: DRESDEN, FEBRUARY 1945

1. Mets, *Master of Airpower*, p. 275.
2. Personal account supplied by Mrs Hughes, née Reppe.
3. Mets, *Master of Airpower*, p. 275.
4. Martin Middlebrook and Chris Everitt, *The Bomber Command War Diaries*, Midland Publishing, East Shilton, Leics., 1985, pp. 664–5.
5. The RAF 'Tiger Force' of bombers, formed in 1945, was never deployed against Japan. However, Fleet Air Arm Corsair fighter-bombers, deployed from four

aircraft carriers of the British Pacific Fleet, then operating with Vice-Admiral William F. Halsey's 3rd US Fleet, did attack targets on the Japanese mainland, starting on 17 July 1945 and dropping 500 lb bombs on military targets, including airfields, at Matsushima, Sendai and Masuda.
6. Interview with the author, 1994.
7. See Victor Klemperer, *I Shall Bear Witness*, Weidenfeld & Nicholson, 1998, p. xi.
8. Schaffer, *Wings of Judgement*.

CHAPTER 17: THE ROAD TO HIROSHIMA, FEBRUARY–AUGUST 1945

1. Craven and Cate, *The Army Air Forces in World War II*, vol. 3, p. 727.
2. Associated Press report, 16 February 1945.
3. Craven and Cate, *The Army Air Forces in World War II*, vol. 3, p. 726.
4. Churchill to Portal, 28 March 1944.
5. Schaffer, *Wings of Judgement*, p. 153.
6. Figures from Gerald Astor, *The Mighty Eighth: The Air War in Europe, as told by the Men Who Fought It*, Dell Books, New York, 1997.
7. Figures from Gebhard Aders-Albert.
8. Target Committee and Manhattan Project archives, National Archives, Washington, quoted in Schaffer, *Wings of Judgement*, p. 140.

CHAPTER 18: MORAL ISSUES AND THE BOMBER WAR, 1999–2000

1. Alfred Speer, *Spandau: The Secret Diaries*, Macmillan, New York, 1976.
2. Ibid.
3. *On John Hampden*, 1831.
4. Talk to the members of the Royal United Institute for Defence Studies in 1961.
5. Figures from Stephen Lee, *The European Dictatorships, 1918–1945*, Routledge, 1988.
6. Article in the *Sunday Telegraph*, 5 September 1999.
7. Craven and Cate, *The Army Air Forces in World War II*, vol. 3, p. 723.
8. A small exception to this claim is the case of Luftwaffe General Hugo Sperrle, commander of the Condor Legion at the time of Guernica. Arrested by an American patrol in 1945, Sperrle was put on trial at Nuremberg in 1948, accused of war crimes over the *Blitzkreig* offensive in Poland. The former Basque Minister of Justice then applied to the court, requesting that Guernica should be added to this list, but this application was refused on the grounds that only Second World War crimes were relevant. In the event Sperrle was acquitted of all charges and died in Ludwigsburg, near Stuttgart, in 1953.
9. Terry Copp, paper at history conference, Portage la Prairie, Manitoba, Canada, 1996.
10. Harris, *Bomber Offensive*, p. 88.
11. John Terraine, *The Right of the Line*, Hodder & Stoughon, 1985, p. 792, note 28.
12. Dudley Saward, *Bomber Harris*, Cassell/Buchan & Enwright, 1984, p. 330.
13. PRO Air files, 14/1252.

Bibliography

(Place of publication London unless otherwise stated)

The primary sources for the Combined Bomber Offensive lie in the various record offices and air museums of the United Kingdom and the United States. The Public Records Office at Kew has the bulk of the RAF's Second World War records, and further help came from the Department of Defense in Washington DC, notably the US Strategic Bombing Survey. Great use was also made of squadron and group histories and aircrew-association magazines, especially those of the Bomber Command Association and the Eighth Air Force Historical Association. Many veterans sent in privately published books and detailed accounts originally prepared for family memoirs. The following titles proved particularly useful:

Aircrew Association, *Winged Chariots*, privately published, Manchester, 1997
Air Ministry, *Bomber Command*, HMSO, 1941
Arnold, General Hap, *Global Mission*, Hutchinson, 1951
Arnold, H. H., and Eaker, Ira C., *Winged Warfare*, Harper, New York, 1941
Astor, Gerald, *The Mighty Eighth: The Air War in Europe, as told by the Men Who Fought It*, Dell Books, New York, 1997
Atkins, E. Richard, *Fighting Scouts of the Eighth Air Force*, The Scouting Force Association, Arlington, Texas
Barker, Ralph, *The Thousand Plan*, Chatto & Windus, 1965
Becker, Cajus, *The Luftwaffe War Diaries*, Macdonald, 1964
Bennett, Air Vice-Marshal D. C. T., *Pathfinder*, Frederick Muller, 1958
Bishop, Edward, *Mosquito: Wooden Wonder*, Pan, Ballantine, 1971
Boiten, Theo, *Nachtjagd, 1939–1945*, Crowood Press, Marlborough, 1997
Bomber Harris Trust (Canada), *A Battle for Truth: Canadian Aircrews Sue the CBC over Death by Moonlight: Bomber Command*, Ramsay Business Systems, Agincourt Ontario, 1994
Bowman, Martin, *RAF Bomber Stories*, Patrick Stephens, 1998
Brickhill, Paul, *The Dam Busters*, Pan Books, 1954
Brookbank, Jim, *Before the Dawn*, Riverside Publishing, 1984

Brown, James Good, *The Mighty Men of the 381st – Heros All*, Publishers Press, Salt Lake City, Utah, 1989

Carrington, Charles, *Soldier at Bomber Command*, Leo Cooper, 1987

Carver, Michael (Field Marshal Lord Carver), ed., *The War Lords: Military Commanders of the Twentieth Century*, Little, Brown, Boston, 1976

Chapin, William, *Milk Run*, Windgate Press, Sausalito, Cal., 1992

Collier, Basil, *A History of Air Power*, Weidenfeld & Nicolson, 1974

Conway, Dan, *Trenches in the Sky*, Hesperian Press, Carlisle, Western Australia, 1995

Cooke, Ronald C., and Nesbit, Roy C., *Hitler's Oil*, William Kimber, 1985

Corum, James S., *The Luftwaffe, Creating the Operational Air War, 1918–1940*, University Press of Kansas, Lawrence, Kansas, 1997

Cox, Sebastian, ed., *The Strategic Air War against Germany 1939–1945* (report of the British Bombing Survey), Frank Cass, 1998

Cramer, Colonel William L., Jr, *Air Combat with the Mighty Eighth*, Eakin Press, Austin, Texas

Craven, Wesley Frank, and Cate, James Lea, *The Army Air Forces in the World War II*, University of Chicago Press, Chicago, 4 vols., 1958

Delve, Ken, and Jacobs, Peter, *The Six-Year Offensive*, Arms and Armour Press, 1992

Divine, David, *The Broken Wing*, Hutchinson, 1966

Douhet, Giulio, *The Command of the Air*, Coward-McCann, New York, 1942

Dunmore, Spencer, *Above and Beyond: The Canadians' War in the Air*, McClelland & Stewart, Toronto, 1996

Frankhouser, Frank, *World War II Odyssey*, Hamiltons, Bedford, Virginia, 1997

Frankland, Noble, *The Bombing Offensive against Germany*, Faber, 1965

——*History at War*, Giles de la Mare Publishers, 1998

Freeman, Roger, *The Mighty Eighth: A History of the US 8th Army Air Force*, Macdonald & Janes, 1970

Galland, Adolf, *The First and the Last*, Fontana, 1970

Gibson, Guy, VC, *Enemy Coast Ahead*, Pan Books, 1979

Goebbels, Josef, *The Goebbels Diaries*, Hamish Hamilton, 1948

Goulding, A. G., *Uncommon Valour: The Story of RAF Bomber Command, 1935–1945*, Goodall Publications, 1996

Greenhous, Brereton, Harris, Stephen J., Johnston, William C., and Rawling, William G. P., *The Crucible of War: The Official History of the RCAF*, University of Toronto Press, Toronto, 1994

Grierson, William, *We Band of Brothers*, J & KH Publishing, 1997

Harris, Sir Arthur T., *Bomber Offensive*, Collins, 1947; reprinted by Greenhill Books, 1998

——*Despatch on War Operations, February 1942–8th May 1945*, introduction by Sebastian Cox, Air Historical Branch, Frank Cass, 1998

Harvey, Maurice, *The Allied Bomber War, 1939–1945*, Spellmount, Staplehurst, 1992

Hastings, Max, *Bomber Command*, Michael Joseph, 1980

Herrington, John, *Air War against Germany and Italy: Australia in the 1939–1945 War*, Australian War Memorial, Canberra, 1954

Hewitt, Clement Barnes, *Swifter than Eagles*, privately published, Adelaide, Australia, 1987

Hudson, Lieutenant-Colonel Charles 'Combat', *Combat He Wrote . . .* , Airborne Publishing, Ventura, Cal., 1994

Jackson, Bill, and Bramall, Edwin, *The Chiefs – the UK Chiefs of Staff*, Brassey's, 1992

James, John, *The Paladins*, Futura, 1991

Jasper, Ronald, *George Bell, Bishop of Chichester*, Oxford University Press, 1967

Johnson, Brian, *The Secret War*, Arrow Books, 1979

Johnson, S. H. Syd, *It's Never Dark above the Clouds: Memoirs of an Australian Navigator*, privately published, Trigg, Western Australia, 1994

Jones, R. V., *Most Secret War*, Hamish Hamilton, 1978

Klemperer, Victor, *I Shall Bear Witness*, Weidenfeld & Nicolson, 1998

Lee, Stephen J., *The European Dictatorships, 1918–1945*, Routledge, 1988

Lee, Wright, *Not as Briefed*, Honoribus Press, Spartanburg, South Carolina, USA, 1995

LeMay, Curtis, and Kantor, McKinley, *Mission with LeMay*, Garden City Press, New York, 1965

Linenthal, Edward, and Engelhardt, Tom, eds., *History Wars: The 'Enola Gay', and Other Battles for the American Past*, Metropolitan Books, New York, 1996

Lovelace, James C., *The Flip Side of the Air War*, privately published, Sydney, Nova Scotia, 1996

Macfarland, Stephen, *America's Pursuit of Precision Bombing, 1910–1945*, Smithsonian Institution, Washington DC, 1995

McKee, Alexander, *Dresden, 1945*, Granada, 1983

Macksey, Kenneth, *The Encyclopedia of Weapons and Military Technology*, Penguin, 1995

——*Military Errors of World War Two*, Cassell, 1987

Mason, Francis K., *The Avro Lancaster*, Aston Publishing, 1989

Maynard, John, *Bennett and the Pathfinders*, Arms and Armour Press, 1996

Messenger, Charles, *Bomber Harris and the Strategic Bomber Offensive*, Arms and Armour Press, 1984

Mets, David R., *Master of Airpower: General Carl A. Spaatz*, Presidio Press, Novato, Cal., 1997

Middlebrook, Martin, *The Battle of Hamburg*, Viking, 1980

——*The Berlin Raids*, Viking, 1988

——*The Nuremberg Raid*, Collins, 1975

——*The Schweinfurt–Regensburg Mission*, Penguin, 1985

Middlebrook, Martin, and Everitt, Chris, *The Bomber Command War Diaries*, Midland Publishing, East Shilton, Leics., 1985

Millis, Walter, *Arms and Men: A Study of American Military History*, Mentor Books, New York, 1956

Moyes, Philip, *Bomber Squadrons of the RAF*, Purnell, 1964

Musgrove, Gordon, *Pathfinder Force: A History of 8 Group*, Crecy Books, 1992

Neillands, Robin, *The Conquest of the Reich, D-Day to VE Day: A Soldiers' History*, Weidenfeld & Nicolson, 1995

Neilsen, Robert S., *With the Stars Above*, The Jenn Company, Olympia, Washington, 1984

Overy, Richard, *Bomber Command, 1939–1945*, HarperCollins, 1997

Paskins, Barrie, and Dockrill, Michael, *The Ethics of War*, Duckworth, 1979

Pershing, General John, *My Experiences in the World War*, Da Capo, New York, 1995

Price, Alfred, *Instruments of Darkness*, William Kimber, 1967

Read, Squadron Leader Ron, DFC, *If You Can't Take a Joke . . .*, privately published, San Pedro, Alcántara, Spain, 1995

Richards, Denis, *The Hardest Victory*, Hodder & Stoughton, 1994

——*Portal of Hungerford*, Heinemann, 1977

Richards, Denis, and Saunders, Hilary ST G., *The Royal Air Force, 1939–45*, HMSO, 3 vols., 1975

Ross, Squadron Leader J. M. S., *The Royal New Zealand Air Force*, War History Branch, Wellington, New Zealand, 1955

Saundby, Air Marshal Sir Robert, *Air Bombardment: The Story of Its Development*, Chatto & Windus, 1961

Saward, Dudley, *Bomber Harris*, Cassell/Buchan & Enwright, 1984

——*The Bomber's Eye*, Cassell, 1959

Schaffer, Ronald, *Wings of Judgement: American Bombing in World War II*, Oxford University Press, New York, 1985

Speer, Alfred, *Inside the Third Reich*, Phoenix, 1995
——*Spandau: The Secret Diaries*, Macmillan, New York, 1976
Target Germany: The VIII Bomber Command's First Year over Europe, HMSO, 1944
Tatum, W. H., and Hoffschmidt, E. J., eds., *The Rise and Fall of the German Air Force: A History of the* Luftwaffe *in WW2*, WE Inc., Old Greenwich, Connecticut, 1969
Tedder, Marshal of the Royal Air Force Lord, GCB, *With Prejudice*, Cassell, 1966
Terraine, John, *The Right of the Line*, Hodder & Stoughton, 1985
Thomas Hugh, *The Spanish Civil War*, Penguin, 1990
Verrier, Anthony, *The Bomber Offensive*, Pan Books, 1974
Webster, Sir Charles, and Frankland, Noble, *The Strategic Air Offensive against Germany, 1939–1945* (the official history), HMSO, 4 vols., 1961
Wolff, Leon, *Low Level Mission – the Ploesti Raid*, Longmans, Green, 1958

Acknowledgements

A great many people helped me with this book, and I would like to acknowledge their kindness, generosity and assistance – in so far as words can do it. My request for information on the Combined Bomber Offensive went out all over the world and met with an overwhelming response, especially from the aircrew veterans.

Over a thousand assorted documents came in: letters, recorded tapes, closely typed personal accounts – many of 50 pages or more – family histories, memoirs, logbooks, diaries, photos, books, charts, intelligence reports – many marked 'Top Secret' – diagrams, citations, No. 617 Squadron's operational order for the Dams Raid of May 1943, damage assessments, plus a lot of privately published books, arrived by the sackful – a cornucopia of information from a score of countries, all of it fascinating, some of it very sad.

One American veteran sent me his medals, asking me to take care of them; a Canadian aircrew veteran sent me his photo collection, 'as my family are not interested'. To balance this bleak comment, a large number of accounts came in from the wives and children of the veterans, eager to make a contribution on behalf of a husband or a father. Oral history can be intrusive and has to be handled with care, but a pleasing number of veterans said how much they had enjoyed writing their accounts, that it had brought back a mixture of memories, some bad, some good, of those long-ago violent days.

I have attempted to get as many relevant personal accounts as possible into the book, but it will be appreciated that, given the number that arrived, I could not include them all. Nor could I quote in their entirety the accounts that have been included: there was simply not the space. I have had to be selective and to relate personal testimony to the overall story; the number of letters and documents I received alone filled three filing cabinets, and it would have taken several volumes, rather than one rather long book, to include them all. Even so, I am most grateful to all the contributors: every account was useful – not least in checking the accuracy of the other accounts.

I am sure that many contributors will recognize where their experiences have illuminated the text, and – unless the contributor has requested their return – their accounts will go to the various archive collections in the UK, Australia, Canada or the USA, so that future historians, many years or even generations from now, can hear the authentic voice of the Second World War aircrews.

As a practical acknowledgement of the veterans' assistance, a donation has been made on their behalf to St Dunstan's, the UK centre for war-blinded veterans, a splendid organization which receives no financial aid whatsoever from the British government.

For their particular help, I would like first to thank Douglas Radcliffe of the Bomber Command Association in the UK, both for tracking down veterans and for reading the book in draft, and Group Captain Peter Bird, formerly of 5 Group, Bomber Command, who offered much valued assistance, read and sorted out all the correspondence, checked my drafts, spotted the 'line shooters', and encouraged the work. Thanks also to Major-General Julian Thompson, Air Marshal Sir Ivor Broom and Air Chief Marshal Sir David Evans, who also read the manuscript and checked my views on the matter of High Command in war, to John J. Scott, once an air gunner with Coastal Command, for translating many German documents and reading the draft text, and to my tutor at Oxford University, Dr Tom Buchanan, for his help and suggestions.

In the USA, my particular thanks must go to Richard Atkins of the Scouting Force Association in Texas for reading the draft manuscript and correcting my errors, to my adopted 'cousin' Nick Knilans of No. 617 Squadron, 5 Group, RAF, and the US Army Air Force, and to my old 4th Division contact, Jack Capell of Portland, Oregon. In Australia, particular thanks go to Dereck French, DFC*, of No. 50 Squadron, RAF, for his advice, his assistance in reading and commenting on the drafts, and his informative and entertaining letters. My thanks for similar services go to Peter Weston and to my friend and professional colleague Don Graves, historian, of Ottawa, Canada.

In Germany my thanks go to Richard Braun and Stefan Morz of Ludwigshafen and to Gerbhard Aders-Albert of Cologne, for reading and commenting on the draft chapters and for particular help with the chapters on Germany. Thanks also to Paul Zorner for his accounts of *Luftwaffe* combat. In France my thanks go to Neville and Elisabeth Gay of Pressignac Vic for taping interviews with Wing Commander Ernest Millington, DFC, of Couze Saint-Front, and with Squadron Leader Ted Hicks. Thanks also go to Archie McIntosh of West Lothian for his accounts of his time in Bomber Command and as a POW, to Terry Brown, my old Royal Marine oppo, for his excellent map, and to Fred Aldworth of *Airforce Magazine* for his help in Canada. Also to Frau Jansen, Bundesarchiv Militarchiv, Freiburg, Germany, and William Spencer of the Public Records Office at Kew.

I am grateful to the following, who supplied information during my research:

Newspapers and Newsletters: F. N. Aldworth, *Airforce Magazine*, Ottawa; *American Legion* magazine; the *Bomber Command Association Newsletter*; the *Boston Globe*; *Briefing*, the North Texas Chapter, the Eighth Air Force Historical Society; the *Brisbane Courier*; the *Canberra Times*; the *Daily Gleaner*, Fredericton, Canada; *Eighth Air Force News*; the *IX Squadron RAF Newsletter*; the *Fighting 44th Logbook*; *Gaggle and Stream*, the journal of the Bomber Command Association of Canada; Bill Stevenson, *Glimlamp*, magazine of the No. 35/635 Squadron Association; *Intercom*, the journal of the Aircrew Association; *Jagerblatt*, the journal of the *Luftwaffe*, Cologne; the *Journal of the Second Air Division, Eighth Air Force*; *Leeming Lines, 1945*; *Legion*, the magazine of the Royal British Legion; the *London, Ontario, Free Press*; the *Mildenhall Register*; the *Mossie*, the magazine of the Mosquito Aircrew Association; the *Niagara Falls Review*; *Nostalgic Notes* of the 94th Bomb Group Memorial Association; the *Ottawa Citizen*; *Purple Heart* magazine, USA; the *San Francisco Chronicle*; the *Sentinel*, the journal of the Texas Military; *Short Bursts*, the journal of the Air Gunners Association of Canada; the *306th Bomb Group Newsletter*; the *385th Bomb Group Newsletter*; the *Turret*, the journal of the Air Gunners Association UK; the *Wickenby Register* (RAF); *Wings* magazine, Australia.

Associations and Institutions: This book could not have been written without the help of the Bomber Command Association, the various bomb-group associations of the United States Army Air Force, and other aircrew associations in Canada, Australia, New Zealand and Germany. Many of these associations are closing down from AD 2000. My thanks to them all, and especially to the following: the No. 44 (Rhodesia) Squadron Association; the 49th Squadron Association, the American Legion, New Providence, NJ; the 55th Fighter Group Association; the Nos. 57 and 630 Squadron Association, RAF; Clifford Hall, the 94th Bomb Group Association; the No 100 Squadron Association, RAF; the No. 150 Squadron Association; the No. 207 Squadron Association, RAF; the 303rd Bomb Group Association; Leon Mehring, the 305th Bombardment Group Memorial Association; Keith Busch of the 309th Bomb Group Memorial Museum Foundation, Tucson, Arizona, and the 97th Bomb Group Reunion Association; the No. 460 Squadron (RAAF) Association, Sydney, Australia; Bill Bridgeman, the No. 515 Squadron Association, Little Snoring; the No. 617 Squadron Aircrew Association.

Danny Boon of the Aircrew Association; Michael Allen; L'Amicale de l'escadrille, No. 425 (Alouette) Squadron Association, Quebec, Canada; Ron MacKay, Friends of the Eighth, Bishops Stortford, England; the Halifax Aircraft Association, Ontario, Canada; the Mosquito Aircrew Association; the Pathfinder Association of Australia; the Pilots and Observers Association, Canada; the RAF Bomber Command Association, New Zealand; the Returned Services League of Australia; the Royal Air Force Escaping Society; the Second Air Division Association, Eighth Air Force, USAAF; the Wartime Pilots and Observers Association, Canada.

Thanks also go to Dr Noble Frankland, CB, CBE, DFC, formerly an RAF Bomber Command navigator, a former director of the Imperial War Museum and co-author of the official history of the bomber offensive, *The Strategic Air Offensive Against Germany 1935–1945*, to Edward A. Kueppers Jr, Director of Information, the Eighth Air Force Historical Society, St Paul, Minnesota, to Rusty Bloxom, historian at the Mighty Eighth Air Force Heritage Museum, Savannah, Georgia, and to Terence A. Moody.

I am also grateful to Brad King and Jack Livesey, of the Imperial War Museum in London and at Duxford, who read the book in draft and made many helpful suggestions, to Sebastian Cox of the Air Historical Branch, London, to Katherine Williams of the Museum of Flight, Boeing Field, Seattle, Washington, USA, for her help with photographs during a visit to Seattle in 1999, and to Don Bowden of Alberta. Thanks too to the Mighty Eighth Air Force Heritage Museum, Savannah, Georgia, to the Canadian Dept of National Defence, Ottawa, to the Bomber Harris Trust, Canada, and Canadian historian Donald Graves and his wife, Diane, of Ottawa, for supplying a copy of the RCAF's official history, to the East Anglia Aviation Society, Bassingbourn, to Frank Phillips, Curator, the Legion Museum, Seaforth, Ontario, Canada, and to George A. Boyd, historian, the Bomber Command Association of Canada.

Thanks also to the RAF Aircrew Association and the Air Gunners Association in the UK and Canada, and to the Pathfinders Associations in Australia and New Zealand for their help in tracking down PFF veterans.

My special thanks naturally go to the veterans themselves or to the families of veterans who sent in accounts from their family archives. Wherever possible, the list that follows places their names in the context of their national air forces. This is not always accurate in the case of the RAF, for most RAF Bomber Command crews were 'mixed': RAAF and RCAF flyers flew in RAF squadrons, as did aircrew from the RNZAF and the South Africa Air Force and from many other nations – Poland, France, Czechoslovakia, the Caribbean, South America and the USA – while many British aircrew flew with Canadian or Australian squadrons. This can make the precise allocation difficult – where do you place an Englishman who flew with an Australian squadron and who now lives in Canada? I have therefore opted to place the contributors, whatever their nationality, with their old squadrons. All the contributors have, I hope, been included somewhere. These include:

RAF: W. Adams, Bomber Command Association; John Banfield, the RAF Ex-POW Association; Mrs L. Battle, WAAF, Bomber Command Association, Bickley, Kent; Harry Beardwell, No. 115 Squadron; David 'Taffy, Bellis, DFC*, No. 141 and No. 239 Squadrons; James H. Berry, No. 7 and No. 149 Squadrons; Tommy Bishop, No. 12 Squadron; Norman Bolt, DFC, No. 103 Squadron; Alan Bourne, No. 528 Squadron; Jim Brookbank, No. 9 Squadron; Air Marshal Sir Ivor Broom, KCB, CB, CBE, DSO, DFC; R. A. Brown, No. 61 Squadron; Jimmy Davidson, No. 35 Squadron, PFF; Squadron Leader Melvyn Davies, No. 57 and No. 630 Squadrons; Tom Edwards, DFM, No. 158 Squadron; Air Chief Marshal Sir David Evans, GCB, CBE; Frank Faulkner, No. 12 and No. 626 Squadrons; Freddie Fish, No. 153 Squadron, for his generous help with this and other books; Dave Francis, DFC, No. 460 Squadron RAAF; Air Vice-Marshal D. J. Furner, CBE, DFC, AFC, No. 214 Squadron; Mrs Betty Gardener, WAAF; Peter Gibby, No. 460 Squadron, RAAF; John Grimstone, No. 102 (Ceylon) Squadron; Dr W. Bill Grierson, No. 35 Squadron, PFF; Graham Hall, MBE, DFM, No. 102 (Ceylon) Squadron, for his accounts of early operations.

Desmond Harris, No. 49 Squadron and No. 97 Squadron, PFF; Ivor C. Heath, DFM, No. 406 Squadron; Squadron Leader Ted Hicks, CGM, DFC; Gilbert Howarth, DFC, DFM, for sharing his memoirs with me, a superb account of nearly 200 pages; Eric Howell, No. 44 (Rhodesia) Squadron, RAF; John Anderson Hurst, No. 102 Squadron; Derek Jackson, No. 149 Squadron and the Manchester Branch of the Air Gunners Association, for his tapes and photos; Squadron Leader W. Bill Jacobs, No. 102 (Ceylon) Squadron; John A. Johns, No. 153 Squadron, for permission to use extracts from the No. 153 Squadron History; Philip Keen, No. 150 Squadron; Bob Knights, DSO, DFC, No. 617 and No. 619 Squadrons, for reading draft chapters, telling me about his service time, and sinking the *Tirpitz*; my American 'cousin' Nick Knilans, DSO, DFC, No. 617 Squadron; Alastair Long, No. 156 Squadron, PFF; Archie McIntosh, No. 57 Squadron; Wing Commander Ernest Millington, DFC; Douglas Mourton, DFM, No. 102 (Ceylon) Squadron, for the loan of his memoirs, *Lucky Doug: Life in the RAF, 1937–1945*; Robert S. (Bob) Neilson, No. 156 Squadron, PFF, for a copy of his book *With the Stars Above*; L. E. Norris, No. 150 Squadron; W. J. Olley, DFC, No. 460 Squadron; Roy Pengilly, No. 582 Squadron; Edwin Perry, No. 139 (Jamaica) Squadron, LNSF; Ron Powell, No. 109 Squadron; Bryan Purser, No. 102 (Ceylon) Squadron.

Ron Read, No. 78 Squadron, for a copy of his book *If you can't take a joke . . .* (the line concludes, 'you shouldn't have joined'); Harry Reed, DFC, No. 169 Squadron; Stanley G. Reed, No. 78 Squadron; Lord Sandhurst, DFC, No. 419 Squadron, RCAF; Stan Smith, No. XV Squadron, for his account of *MacRobert's Reply*; Ross Spencer, for his account of the Dresden raid; Edward E. Stocker, No. 102 Squadron; Squadron Leader Eric Summers, MM, No. 142 and No. 150 Squadrons; Frank Tasker, No. 90 Squadron; Len Thompson, Croix de Guerre, No. 550 Squadron; Wing Commander John Tipton, No. 40 Squadron and No. 109 Squadron, PFF; Wing Commander A. R. Watkins, the Aircrew Association; Peter Weston, No. 186 Squadron; Ron Whinton, No. 207 Squadron; Roy Whipple, No. 102 Squadron; John Whiteley, DFC, No. 619 Squadron; Geoff Whitten, No. 35 Squadron, PFF; J. C. Whorton, No. 149 Squadron; Tom Wingham, DFC, No. 102 (Ceylon) Squadron; Geoffery Worley, No. 460 Squadron, RAAF.

RAAF: Phil Atwood; Keith Boyling, for his helpful suggestions on RAAF sources; R. W. 'Bill' Bullen, No. 102 Squadron and PFF; Don Conway, DFC, No. 467 Squadron, RAAF, for a copy of his book *Trenches in the Sky*; Peter Cornish, DFC*, No.

49 Squadron, RAF; Air Commodore Peter Cribb, CBE, DSO, DFC, No. 35 Squadron; C. N. R. Dodgson; Peter Firkins, No. 460 Squadron; special thanks to Dereck French, DFC*, No. 50 Squadron, for his valuable help and most enjoyable letters; Don Goudie, No. 460 Squadron; Squadron Leader Bill Grierson-Jackson, DFC, No. 35 Squadron; Dudley Hannaford, No. 463 Squadron, RAAF; Wing Commander Brian Hayes, DFM, of the PFF Association in Australia; Arthur Hoyle, DFC*, No. 460 Squadron, RAAF; Wing Commander Peter Isaacson, AM, DFC, AFC, DFM, No. 460 Squadron, RAAF, for permission to use his address at a recent RAAF reunion.

Syd Johnson, DFC*, No. 156 Squadron, PFF; Professor Alex Kerr, POW; Max Ladyman, No. 35 Squadron, for his excellent memoir, *My War*; Frank Lawrence, for his list of 'flak cities'; Jim Mallinson, No. 186 Squadron; Dr John Musgrove, No. 576 Squadron; Peter O'Connor, No. 83 Squadron, PFF, for his help in finding such a fine bunch of RAAF veterans; Richard Osborn, DSO, DFC, No. 9 and No. 460 Squadrons, RAAF; Air Marshal Sir James Roland, AC, KBE, DFC, AFC, No. 635 Squadron, RAAF; Eric Silbert, AM, DFC, the Pathfinder Association of Australia; R. W. (Bob) Smith, No. XV Squadron, RAF; Mervyn Stafford, No. 460 Squadron, RAAF; Ken Tweedie, No. 460 Squadron, RAAF; Alan J. Vial, DFC, No. 35 Squadron, RAF, and the PFF Association of Australia; John Watson, No. 460 Squadron; special thanks to Ross 'Whisky' Wheaton, DFC, No. 582 Squadron, PFF, another great supporter.

RCAF: J. L. Brown, No. 405 and No. 429 Squadrons; Lewis Bronson, No. 88 (Hong Kong) Squadron, RAF; Bill Borrows, No. 433 Squadron; George J. Bova, DFC, No. 432 Squadron; R. A. 'Bud' Brown, 6 (RCAF) Group; Paul Burden, No. 434 Squadron, 6 (RCAF) Group; Jack Calabrese, No. 433 Squadron, RCAF; Stan 'Nick' Carter, DFC, No. 207 Squadron RAF; Ed Carter-Edwards, No. 427 Squadron, RCAF, and Buchenwald Concentration Camp; Ron Cassels, No. 428 (Ghost) Squadron; Will Chabun, Canadian Aviation Historical Society; G. W. Clark, for the account of his brother, RCAF veteran Colin Clark of No. 433 Squadron; Sid Coles, RCAF; George Cullen, No. 424 Squadron; Doug Curtis, No. 9, No. 97 and No. 635 Squadrons, RAF; Robert Dale, 8 Group, PFF, Bomber Command; William I. Davies, DFC, No. 103 and No. 156 (PFF) Squadron; John Dunlop, 6 (RCAF) Group and 2nd TAF.

Robert Geisel, No. 115 Squadron, RCAF; Terry Goodwin, No. 61 Squadron; Jack C. Hall, No. 429 'Bison' Squadron, RCAF (a contribution from Jack's widow, now Margaret Grant); Fred Hammacott, No. 153 Squadron, RAF; John Harding, DFC, No. 550 Squadron, RAF; Sid Herbert, No. 109 Mosquito Squadron; Tom Hieland, No. 431 Squadron; Al Hymers, No. 12 Squadron; John Jarvis, No. 427 (Lion) Squadron, RCAF; William I. Jefferies, HCU; Mark Kearney, on behalf of his father, a navigator in No. 419 Squadron, RCAF; John B. Kennenley, 6 (RCAF) Group; John E. Lash, Air Force Association Toronto; Kathy Laushway, on behalf of her father, an RCAF veteran; Daivd Loomer, on behalf of his father; Squadron Leader James Lovelace, DFC, CD, MSM, No. 103 Squadron.

Helen McDonald, on behalf of her father, Lawrence McDonald, Bomber Command HQ; Kenneth McDonald, No. 78 Squadron; Norman McHolme, No. 420 (Snowy Owl) Squadron; Larry McKellar, for his account of his father's service with No. 410 Squadron; Alison Hope MacKenzie, 6 (RCAF) Group HQ, 1943–5; Ralph Mainprize, No. 189 Squadron, RAF; W. K. 'Bill' Naylor, DFC*; J. E. Poirier, 6 (RCAF) Group; Hugh Pollock, No. 420 (Snowy Owl) Squadron; Warren Quigley, RCAF, No. 61 Squadron, RAF; Ben Rakus, No. 428 Squadron; Linda Rivington, on behalf of her father, Garrett Rivington, 4 Group, RAF; Robbie Robson, Middleton St George; Doug Ross, on behalf of his uncle Douglas Ross, a rear gunner lost flying with 4 Group, RAF; Ken Rosu-Myles, on behalf of his father, Sam Rosu of No. 424 (Tiger) Squadron, RCAF, killed over Germany in 1945; Keith Rupert, No. 424 (Tiger) Squadron.

Frank Schofield, Pilots and Observers Association, Canada; Robert C. Skipper,

No. 424 Squadron; Ross Spencer and Douglas Spencer; A. H. Steen, No. 426 Squadron; Russell Steer, DFC, No. 405 Squadron, PFF; Peter Stevenson, on behalf of his father, John Stevenson, No. 153 Squadron, RAF; Doug Taylor, No. 12 and No. 626 Squadrons, RAF; F. W. Walker, No. 428 Squadron, RCAF; John Watters, No. 227 Squadron, RAF; Jim Weaver, DFC, Croix de Guerre, No. 102 Squadron, RAF, and 6 (RCAF) Group; Bob Westell, No. 428 Squadron, 6 (RCAF) Group; Mrs Blanche Williams, on behalf of her husband, George Williams, DFM, No. 61 Squadron; Mrs Rosalie B. Woodland, WAAF–WDs, 6 (RCAF) Group HQ; Wing Commander J. G. Wynne, DFC.

RNZAF: George Beca Jr, CBE, DFC; J. E. Fletcher, No. 75 (New Zealand) Squadron; Alan Gibson, No. 166 Squadron; Mrs Jeanette Hoffman, on behalf of her late husband, Rod Hoffman, No. 625 Squadron; Frank Jackson, No. 635 Squadron, PFF; Mrs D. K. Kelly, who wrote on behalf of her late husband, Squadron Leader C. W. S. Kelly, DSO, DFC, of No. 75 (New Zealand) and No. 156 (PFF) Squadrons – Mrs Kelly is one of a number of widows who sent in contributions to this book, and I am grateful to them all; Ron Mayhill of Auckland for his account of the raid on Kiel; Mrs Marygold Miller, on behalf of her husband, Wing Commander Hugh James Miller, OBE, DFC, AFC; W. J. (Bill) Simpson, RAF Bomber Command Association (New Zealand) and No. 109 (Oboe) Squadron, PFF, for his help and advice – ten of the 45 pilots in No. 109 Squadron came from New Zealand, including Frank Beswick, who now lives in Canada.

USAAF – Eighth and Fifteenth Air Forces: Maynard Abrahams, 728th Bomb Squadron; Emmanuel 'Manny' Abrams, 392nd Bomb Group; Harris Albright, 392nd Bomb Group; E. Richard Atkins of the Scouting Force Association, not least for reading draft chapters and his helpful comments on the text; Mrs Edith Ayres, on behalf of her late husband, Lloyd Ayres, 305th Bomb Group; John Bauer, 97th Bomb Group; special thanks to Dewayne 'Ben' Bennett of the 384th Bomb Group and his friends at the 390th Bomb Group Museum, Pima Air Force Base, Tucson, Arizona; Robert W. Bieber, 93rd Bomb Group; William 'Bill' Blaylock, 446th Bomb Group; Bill Brinn, 91st Bomb Group; General Allison C. Brooks, 401st Bomb Group and 1st Scouting Force; General John A. Brooks for his account of the Ploesti mission; Dave Brouchard, Second Air Division Association; Quintin V. Brown, 94th Bomb Group; Earnest W. Bruce, 446th Bomb Group; Marvin J. Byer, DFC, Eighth Air Force.

Bill Campbell, 94th Bomb Group; Bud Cannon, 351st Bomb Group; C. N. 'Bud' Chamberlin, 489th Bomb Group; special thanks to Bill Chapin, Fifteenth Air Force, for permission to use extracts from this wonderful book *Milk Run*; Forrest Clark, 44th Bomb Group; Luther E. Cloxton Jr, armaments officer with the 389th and 44th Bomb Groups; Colonel William L. Cramer, 351st Bomb Group, for his book *Air Combat with the Mighty Eighth*.

Roy Grady Davidson Jr, 333rd Bomb Group; Hal DeBolt, 91st Bomb Group; Eddie Deerfield, 303rd Bomb Group; Richard Denison, 386th Bomb Group; Robert Doherty, editor, *96th Bomb Group Newsletter*; Robert Elliott, 92nd Bomb Group; Mrs Dorothy M. Farrell, on behalf of her late husband, James Farrell, 322nd Bomb Group; Mort Fega, 305th Bomb Group; Lee Fegette, 303rd Bomb Group; Colonel Victor W. Ferguson, 385th Bomb Group; Scott Fifer, on behalf of his father, Walter Crane Fifer, 98th and 458th Bomb Groups; Bill Frankenhauser, 398th Bomb Group, especially for the copy of his memoir *World War II Odyssey*.

Mike Gallagher, 385th Bomb Group; Irving R. Garfinkle, 385th Bomb Group; Fred Gerritz Sr, 466th Bomb Group, for sending me his memoirs; Nathaniel Glickman, 93rd Bomb Group and 44th Bomb Group, Pathfinders; Harry D. Gobrecht, 303rd Bomb Group; Peter M. Gunnar, 2nd Air Division; Charles W. Halper, 385th Bomb Group, especially for his photographs; Milton Hamill, 303rd

Bomb Group; Clive Henning, 303rd Bomb Group; Howard 'Pete' Henry, 44th Bomb Group; Albert E. Hill, 386th Bomb Group, for sending me his combat diary; Malcolm H. Hinshaw, 392nd Bomb Group; Edwin Holmes, 384th Bomb Group; Theodore Homdrom, 381st Bomb Group; Raymond H. Hook, 450th Bomb Group; Edward Hooton, 467th Bomb Group; H. B. Howard, 100th Bomb Group; Lieutenant-Colonel Charles 'Combat' Hudson, 91st Bomb Group, for a copy of his book *Combat He Wrote . . .* , co-authored with Ross Olney; George C. Hunter, 385th Bomb Group.

Howard Jackson 454th Bomb Group; Charles P. Johnson 303rd Bomb Group; Artemon P. Johnston, 486th Bomb Group; Albert Jones, 44th Bomb Group; Harold L. Jones, 351st Bomb Group; Donald Kabitzke, 88th Service Squadron; Bruce Kilmer, 384th Bomb Group, for his account of the Antwerp and Schweinfurt missions; Del Kraske, 96th Bomb Group; Lloyd Krueger, 95th Bomb Group; Lieutenant-Colonel Ray Kubly, 34th Bomb Group; Kenneth J. Laffoon, 390th Bomb Group; the Most Reverend Melvin H. Larson, 388th Bomb Group – Melvin Larson, a 'toggelier' bombardier in 1944 is now an archbishop; Colonel William R. Lawley Jr, last surviving Eighth Air Force Medal of Honor winner – sadly, Colonel Lawley died in the summer of 1999; W. Wright Lee of Alabama and the 445th Bomb Group for information on the B-24 and a copy of his memoir *Not as Briefed*; George E. Letlow, 448th Bomb Group; Lieutenant-Colonel Robert M. Littlefield, 55th Fighter Group, Eighth Air Force; Art Livingston, 446th Bomb Group; James H. Lorenz, 466th Bomb Group, for his hospitality in Phoenix, Arizona; Ben F. Love 351st Bomb Group; Lieutenant-Colonel Myron M. 'Mike' Loyet, for his help with the photos and advice on navigation and US Pathfinder operations; Major-General Lewis Lyle, 303rd and 306th Bomb Groups; Milton E. Lytle, 95th Bomb Group.

Brigadier-General James McPartlin, 91st Bomb Group; Virgil Marco, 305th Bomb Group; Robert Mayer, 394th Bomb Group; Leon Mehring, 305th Bomb Group; Frederick Miller on behalf of his father; Harold L. Morris, 451st Bomb Group; Dave Mullen, 486th Bomb Group and 3rd Scouting Force; Patrick Muse and his twin brother, Peter, both of the 94th Bomb Group; Stephen Musolino, 305th Bomb Group, and his crew – pilot Harold 'Pop' Wiley, navigator Gerald Kreske and tail gunner Omer Van Huylenbrouck, who all sent in useful accounts; Tom Parry, 93rd Bomb Group; George Pederson, 306th Bomb Group; Clifford Peterson, 392nd Bomb Group; Al F. Pishioneri, 2nd Air Division; Irving R. Pliskin, 95th Bomb Group; Lieutenant-Colonel Hubert F. Radford, 93rd Bomb Group; Ralph Raines, 485th Bomb Group; Reggie Robinson, 306th Bomb Group; W. B. 'Bill' Rose, Eighth Air Force; Sam C. Ross, 384th Bomb Group; Charles C. Russell, Eighth Air Force.

Edwin J. Sealy; Doyle Shields, 447th Bomb Group; Charles Shinault, 388th Bomb Group, for his help with Aphrodite missions; Robert W. Shinnick, 463rd Bomb Group; Meyer 'Mike' Slott, 453rd Bomb Group; Ivan C. Stepnich, B-24 pilot; R. Stumpf, 97th Bomb Group; Jim Thomas, on behalf of his father and the 446th Bomb Group Association; K. W. Vanda, 92nd Bomb Group; Brigadier-General Robert W. Vincent, 458th Bomb Group and Second Air Division Association; Edgar Walsh; Robert Weinberg, 464th Bomb Group and Stalag Luft 3 veteran; Leroy C. Wilcox, 381st Bomb Group; Corbin Willis, B-17 pilot and POW; Dr Ralph Wilson, 390th Bomb Group; Bill Wray, 385th Bomb Group; Benedict Yedlin, 449th Bomb Group; Skip Young, 386th Bomb Group.

Poland: Michael Alfred Pezke, of Maryland, USA, on behalf of the four Polish squadrons which flew with Bomber Command.

Germany: Gebhard Aders-Albert, archivist of Cologne, for his comments and generous help in reading drafts; Alfons Altmeier of Faid, Cochem, Mosel, for his helpful comments on *Luftwaffe* operations and for translations; Alfred Ambs, Me 262 pilot; Gerhard Baeker, St Augustin; Claud Michel Becker, for his help with research; Heinz Benz; Cilly Bohmer, Ludwigshafen, for accounts of Allied raids; Dr Horst Boog, BA, Stengen; special thanks to Richard Braun of Ludwigshafen, for his constant support and shrewd comments on the text; Erbhard Burath, JG 1 and JG 2, Flensburg; Horst Diener, Nachtjagdzentrale.

Wolf Falck, fighter pilot; Erbhard Fanagdo, *Flakhelfer*, Ludwigshafen; Erwin Folz, private archivist of Ludwigshafen, for his help and hospitality during a visit to Germany; Oberst (a. D.) Willi Goebel, historian of the *Luftwaffe*, Lohmar, Bonn; Hauptmann (a. D.) Alfred Grislawki, 8/JG 1; Oberst (a. D.) Hajo Herrmann, Dusseldorf; General (a. D.) Walter Krupinski; Fritz Lamprecht, *Flakhelfer*; Dr Heinz Lange; Peter Menges, Ludwigshafen; Stefan Morz, archivist of Ludwigshafen, for his advice and support; Paul Mungersdorf, JG 2; Jorg Pottkamper; Generalleutnant (a. D.) Gunter Rall, Bad Reichenhall; Ernst Scheufeld, night-fighter pilot, JG 5, of Walldorf; night-fighter veterans Peter Spoden and Major Paul Zorner, II/NJG 3; Albert Stengel, Ludwigshafen; Generalleutnant (a. D.) Uwe Vogel; Dr Jurg Gunter Weiss, Kaiserslautern; Wilhelm Wirtz, Julich.

The names of other contributors are recorded in the index. My thanks to you all, and I hope that our joint efforts have produced a good, true story of the bomber war.

Index